NONVIOLENT ACTION

GARLAND REFERENCE LIBRARY OF SOCIAL SCIENCE
VOLUME 940

A Book

From the

Albert Einstein Institution

Nonviolent Action
A Research Guide

Ronald M. McCarthy
Gene Sharp

With the Assistance
of Brad Bennett

Garland Publishing, Inc.
New York and London
1997

QOp-8808

Library of Congress Cataloging-in-Publication Data

McCarthy, Ronald M.
    Nonviolent action : a research guide / by Ronald M. McCarthy and
Gene Sharp.
        p.   cm. — (Garland reference library of social science ; v. 940)
    Includes bibliographical references and indexes.
    ISBN 0-8153-1577-5 (alk. paper)
    1. Nonviolence—Bibliography.   2. Nonviolence—History—Case stud-
ies—Bibliography.   3. Protest movements—History—Case studies—
Bibliography.   I. Sharp, Gene.   II. Title.   III. Series.
Z7164.P19M33   1997
[HM278]
016.3036'1—dc21
                                          97-25316
                                                 CIP

Printed on acid-free, 250-year-life paper
Manufactured in the United States of America

Contents

Preface and Acknowledgments

The Twentieth Century has seen the discovery of nonviolent action and its significance as a means of struggle. This is true not only of the enormous growth in its use, but also of the scholarly effort to define, delineate, and understand this important alternative to violence, and to helplessness and passivity as well, for people engaged in acute and vital conflicts.

This research guide is our attempt to bring together a wide range of information on the worldwide experience of using nonviolent action, both historical and contemporary. It is intended to be useful for researchers at many levels of expertise—students, academics, journalists, and others—who want to draw on this experience. This research guide also stands as a demonstration, if one is needed, that the use of nonviolent action extends far back in history and is not limited to any nation, ethnic group, religion, or governmental form.

Gene Sharp began the work on this project in the late 1950s. At the time, he believed that all the significant existing knowledge about nonviolent action could be gathered by polling friends and colleagues in this field. As his conception of the field grew, he realized that there was a wealth of unexplored knowledge to be assembled and began to collect entries for what has become this volume. Ronald McCarthy took over the task in the late 1980s and saw it through to completion.

The authors could never have completed this study without the help and encouragement of many people. We have received research assistance from Jane Casey, Robert Cucci, William B. Vogele, Carl Etnier, Jon Klavens, Mark Haugen, and Jeff Welch. Robert Burroughs reviewed the section on Australia and suggested additions. William B. Vogele read and commented on the introduction. Roger Powers put the manuscript into shape, edited it, and offered many useful suggestions. Many thanks to Stephen Coady for his help while the manuscript was edited and printed. Sharon Fischer helped in the final stages of production. We owe a debt of gratitude to the reference and circulation staffs of the Harvard University libraries, especially Widener Library, where the majority of the work was done. Research was also conducted at the Boston Public Library, the Library of Congress, and the Hamilton Library, University of Hawaii. We thank the staffs at these institutions for their help.

This research was supported by grants from the United States Institute of Peace, which recognized the importance of studying nonviolent means of conflict at its inception. Research and writing were conducted primarily at the Program on Nonviolent Sanctions in the Center for International Affairs, Harvard University. The Albert Einstein Institution, established to advance the study and use of strategic nonviolent action in conflicts throughout the world, has been unstinting in its support of this project. Our sincere thanks to the institution's staff, executive director, and board for their faith in this project over the years.

Introduction

The Possibilities of Research on Nonviolent Action

Dr. Martin Luther King, Jr., was in the Birmingham, Alabama city jail in April 1963. He had been arrested for leading an illegal protest march in the city's streets as part of a campaign against racial segregation. He refused to pay bail and was waiting for his trial. After a few days in his cell, he read an article in the newspaper about a statement by an interfaith group of white clergymen who criticized Dr. King and his movement, especially the "unwise and untimely" demonstrations it held. Although "technically peaceful," they wrote, these protests led to "hatred and violence." They counseled that it would be better to abandon such protests, obey the law, and take any problems to court or settle them through negotiation (Branch 1988: ch. 18–20, pp. 737–38).

Co–workers recall that Dr. King began at once to draft his reply, which has become renowned as "Letter from Birmingham City Jail" (King, 1963 in Washington, ed. 1986: 298–302; Branch 1988: 738–44). Dr. King uses the occasion to issue a ringing justification of protest. He first tells his reasons for coming to Birmingham, both the specific reason that he was invited by local activists and a more general one: "I am in Birmingham because injustice is here."

In the following pages, Dr. King not only explains himself but he also challenges the clergymen to see that their views are not valid. He argues that the city's segregation laws are not only unjust but unjust for many reasons. Therefore, protesters have many reasons for opposing them. He challenges the complacency of "white moderates" who counsel the movement to avoid causing tensions that might lead to a violent response. He especially criticizes white church leaders who stand back when their help is needed and keep silent when the segregationists raise their voices.

But there is more than this in "Letter from Birmingham City Jail." Dr. King also explains the rationale for his strategy for challenging segregation. Separating this from the parts just on Birmingham and from Dr. King's dialogue with the white clergy, we find two kinds of statements. First, Dr. King describes how to prepare the ground for what he calls a "nonviolent campaign." Second, he describes the processes the campaign will set in motion that will encourage resolution of the grievances. Preparation has four steps, Dr. King writes, beginning with researching the facts that demonstrate that "injustices" exist, which is followed by negotiation with the adversary. The third step is "self–purification," which means personal preparation for the hardships to come and for maintaining group discipline. After these, and only if negotiation and other available avenues have failed, can nonviolent action begin.

Dr. King also explains how this action is expected to work. He shows that nonviolent action brings tensions and contradictions to the surface that already exist but are denied and covered up. The community then may see the need to resolve these tensions. Through "creative tension" or "constructive nonviolent tension," he argues, direct action creates such a crisis that people will want resolution, and negotiations will be held. Without this kind of pressure, people who benefit from existing conditions are unlikely to give in. Some of them will resort to violence against protesters to stop the campaign. These people must come to see that continued nonviolent pressure makes their own resistance toward change impossible to sustain.

Dr. King also sees a difference between evading or callously breaking a law and defying the law in full knowledge of its injustice, with a willingness to be subject to any penalties that result. He calls this "civil disobedience," and compares it to biblical and early Christian martyrs and to the refusal of Socrates to renounce his teachings. The clergymen misunderstand the true situation when they accuse the demonstrators of causing tension and violence, because the demonstrations actually serve the healthy purpose of bringing both tension and violence into the open. Once in the open and visible, they can be addressed.

Here, Dr. King expresses not only the moral and ethical purpose of nonviolent action, but also its practical political effects. He states several important propositions: (1) that a series of steps prepares the ground for nonviolent struggle, (2) that nonviolent disruption (by means of marches and economic "withdrawal" or boycotts) causes "creative tension" and forces adversaries to face the issues, (3) that this tension is already present in the situation and is exposed by direct action, (4) that tension and crisis bring about negotiations, (5) that only the maintenance of pressure convinces an adversary that resistance to change will not be successful, (6) that imprisonment or other punishment of sincere, but law–breaking activists touches the consciences of citizens and they see the injustice, and (7) that violence cannot be blamed on the nonviolent protesters but on those who actually undertake it trying to prevent resolution of the conflict.

Was Dr. King correct in his ideas about the political technique he had traveled to Birmingham to use? Were his assumptions and conclusions correct? Actually, he makes several assumptions and claims. Some relate to the reasons for adopting extra–legal methods—methods of political action that do not use courts, legislatures, and elections to settle a conflict—and to the justification for disturbing the domestic tranquillity of the white citizens of the city. Other ideas are directed toward the workings of his technique. In some ways, they have the "if–then" form of theoretical propositions. *If* nonviolent methods disrupt daily life, *then* they will create tension. *If* the tension reflects real but hidden underlying problems, *then* an incentive to reduce tension through negotiation will be created. *If* activists are jailed and accept the blows they receive unflinchingly, *then* the consciences of individual community members will be aroused. *If* protesters persist in disruption despite punishments, *then* their adversaries will see the futility of further violence. In short, Dr. King's beliefs and assumptions, developed during his education as a minister and in his experience as an activist since 1956, take on an almost logical or scientific cast when restated as formal propositions.

To decide if Dr. King's views are correct, researchers could look at evidence about the Birmingham conflict and the fact that protest did lead to a negotiated settlement (Branch 1988: 774–91). Researchers could also ask whether his views have wider significance. Do they teach anything about nonviolent action in conflicts far removed from the events in Birmingham in 1963? Can the propositions be tested comparatively to see if they are true elsewhere? Do the same factors operate in other contexts, other political systems, and in conflicts over essentially different issues? Likewise, could a strategy like Dr. King's work in societies where there are no constitutional guarantees? Does it work where morally–convinced leadership like his is lacking, or where the ethical high ground is less clearly held by one side or the other?

In short, ideas about nonviolent action might have significance beyond familiar personalities, actions, and ideas. Looked at this way, some question marks have to be added to the Dr. King's concepts. Studying nonviolent action with the methods of history, philosophy, and the social sciences will require a more skeptical and inquisitive point of view than is often brought to the study of great and morally significant events.

Understanding Nonviolent Action

There are still some questions to consider before beginning to think systematically about nonviolent action. They include how to define it, where to locate it, how rare or common it is, and whether it is usually associated with any particular philosophies or beliefs.

To define nonviolent action, the first thing to decide is where to look for it, in other words, what its context is likely to be. Is it usually an idea or an activity? Are there particular kinds of human relationships that cause it? These are difficult to decide, because the word "nonviolent" has several different meanings (the idea of nonviolent crime as opposed to nonviolent protest, for example). This is why the question of context needs to be decided first. The context of nonviolent action is some kind of serious disagreement—a conflict or dispute—in which two or more groups of people are adversaries. The facts of the conflict do not matter. They could be concerned with economics, rights, living space, identity, ownership, power, or any of a number of things. What does matter is that there is *contention*. Groups are attempting to influence the outcome of a dispute in ways that strengthen their position. Often they try to influence the behavior, ideas, or interests of others to achieve this. In Birmingham this active aspect of the dispute and the effort to get people to change their attitudes, actions, and practices is very evident.

The location of nonviolent action is in struggle rather than ideas and convictions themselves, and it is best understood as encompassing ways in which groups (or sometimes individuals) try to affect the course of a dispute. There are, of course, many ways of doing this that are not violent. These include public education, collecting and examining facts, holding discussions to work things out, bringing in a go–between to help, filing lawsuits, putting candidates up for election, and so on. These are not violent, but they are not the same thing as nonviolent action. Nonviolent action implies an active process of bringing pressure to bear (even if it is emotional or moral pressure) in wielding influence in a dispute–ridden and contentious relationship between groups. Therefore, to be consistent, activities such as educational campaigns and negotiation ought to be excluded from the idea of nonviolent action. Legal and political action, while usually free of violence, ought also to be excluded, as would other kinds of influence and problem–solving through institutional channels.

What does this winnowing process leave? It leaves what a pioneering social scientist of nonviolent action, Clarence Marsh Case, called "methods of social pressure." Case knew that nonviolent action (the term passive resistance was used then) was claimed as a special province by pacifists and conscientious objectors. They were against any form of coercion or pressure and therefore rejected a number of the actions that he thought should fit within the idea of nonviolent social pressure. He was interested in demonstrations, strikes, and economic boycotts as well as conscientious opposition to violence. He proposed, as a more consistent approach, studying "the exercise of social constraint by non–violent means" (Case 1923: 301). Case's lead, and that of others that followed, suggested the understanding of nonviolent action advocated by Gene Sharp (one of the compilers of this book) in *The Politics of Nonviolent Action* (1973). Sharp's idea is that researchers can best identify an example of nonviolent action by looking for the "methods" of social, political, and economic constraint that "collectively constitute the technique of nonviolent action" (Sharp 1973: 113). He divides these methods into three types: methods of nonviolent protest and persuasion, methods of noncooperation, and methods of nonviolent intervention.

"Methods," the actions used to accomplish social, political, or economic constraint, are the components of nonviolent action in conflicts. Sharp lists 198 of them in his book, but it is not the exhaustive listing that is key. What is more basic is the idea of discrete procedures for protesting, constraining, and pressuring an adversary in an acute and active conflict—methods that use sanctions other than those provided by violence, destruction, or the power of the government. These methods can be used to identify nonviolent action and make it possible to be studied. Examples of some methods found in the works in this guide include carrying banners in protest parades, singing protest songs, and resigning in protest. Some methods are old, such as walking off the job in a group in a dispute with an employer, in other words, a strike. Others are new, such as recording protest songs and statements on audio cassettes and distributing them. (Soviet Russian dissenters did this with protest songs and called it *magnitizdat*, while Chinese students of the 1980s recorded the words of protest "Big–Character" posters and sent them to activists in other cities.)

This research guide is based on the idea that people who want to do research about nonviolent action can most reliably recognize it or find it by looking for *methods of nonviolent action* used by groups or individuals involved in an acute conflict.

It might seem as if only certain historical periods or certain cultures, maybe peaceful ones, would ever use these methods with any consistency. Actually, research has found them in the distant past, including economic sanctions by ancient Athens against a smaller city in its empire. Walkouts of various kinds go far back in history, and strikes have been held since medieval Europe. The cultural argument does not stand up any better than the historical one. All sorts of cultures where violence is well established give rise to episodes of nonviolent action. One example is nineteenth–century New Zealand after the deadly Maori wars in which many Maoris, settlers, and European soldiers had died. There, an influential Maori leader named Te Whiti O Rongomai built a settlement on land that was never to be sold to *Pakeha* (whites) and defended it in a long campaign of nonviolent opposition to land–taking by the settlers. Called the Parihaka Rebellion by its opponents, the campaign included noncooperation and a kind of symbolic protest by plowing up enclosed land as a reassertion of native rights.

A counter–example comes from a culture sometimes considered not very violent, the India of Mohandas Gandhi's great nonviolent struggles. Gandhi is often considered an apostle of principled nonviolence like Dr. King, and he did express very strongly his view that Indian culture and the Hindu religion required *ahimsa* (non–harm) from its believers. Yet he struggled continually during his campaigns to prevent political and ethnic violence that broke out when people in their thousands and millions were mobilized in vast confrontations. Gandhi actually canceled his first major campaign of resistance or *satyagraha* against the British in India because of violence. Some historians maintain that Gandhi even came to accept a level of limited violence by supporters of his campaigns.

Not many people today think of India as a peaceful culture, but some people in earlier generations did because of Gandhi's example. In fact, they explained Gandhi by the peacefulness of the culture, an idea now much in doubt. Perhaps the question is instead *how* culture and beliefs function to bring about nonviolent action, remembering that it generally is not carried out by believers in some form of religiously principled rejection of violence.

For example, the history of strikes in the United States shows that many have been undertaken without any violence by strikers. Usually this was because strikers felt that violence would not help, and might harm, their cause, and that pressure for a settlement would come from withholding labor. Of course, the authorities, angry third parties, or industry may use violence in a strike, but one group's nonviolent action is not canceled out by the other's violence. Nonviolent action is likely to be chosen by just one party in a conflict. Therefore, it is not necessarily answered with "nonviolent" behavior by others. This *unilateral* aspect of choosing nonviolent action means that a conflict is not nonviolent or violent by nature, but by the choice of one of the parties. A conflict or campaign does not cease being nonviolent action when activists are subjected to violence. Often, nonviolent action is deliberately met with violence (or by legal or political suppression), and this "asymmetry" is a central feature of its workings. This issue brings up the broader question of how nonviolent action operates, the topic of the next section.

Factors in the Operation of Nonviolent Action

If the ideas just discussed make sense, then nonviolent action is not really rare, nor does it depend directly on principled or religious beliefs. This means that nonviolent action and its workings can be studied just like other political and social factors. For researchers, three questions are central: (1) where does nonviolent action originate? (2) what factors influence its course? and (3) what factors influence its outcome?

Causes and origins. Is a nonviolent challenge born (caused) or is it made (chosen)? Dr. King's answer in "Letter from Birmingham City Jail" was that it is chosen—he was invited and came to address injustice. He also writes that it is chosen within certain limits—there was injustice, and someone was responsible for its perpetuation. He writes that causes are also present—African–Americans in Birmingham suffered harm and loss that others were responsible for. Also, those others were not responsive to requests to change their ways. Of course, the causes of a conflict are broader than just assigning responsibility. Perhaps an economic, racial, or political system has become harsher and people cannot stand the suffering. Or perhaps changes that make a system less harsh provide opportunities for people to speak up against a regime that was previously too entrenched to oppose. Daniel Chirot, for example, argues that economic, political, and moral failure in the states of Eastern Europe led to the revolutions of 1989 (Chirot 1992). Change led to a thorough withdrawal of many people's willingness to accept the system. Also, several studies of the Civil Rights Movement find that economic and political changes assisted its rise (Piven and Cloward 1977, McAdam 1982). For example, migration to Northern cities created an African–American population that was not in the same kind of personal danger as Southerners when it supported desegregation in the South.

In other words, nonviolent action is usually not simply chosen with complete freedom because conscientious and concerned people recognize an injustice and prepare to address it. Causal factors create or intensify conflict between groups to the point of open dispute. Changes in a population or economic gains and losses provide both opportunity and interest in opposing a system. Factors that increase a government's ability to remain in power may simultaneously reduce the possibility of effective opposition—these may include the regime's capacity for violence, its electoral strength, the benefits it controls, or simply the unthinking support of the majority. Nothing prevents a few people from trying nonviolent action, but the real question is to understand how it gains the active support of a sufficiently large and crucial body of people to make a difference.

For example, the civil rights group CORE (Congress of Racial Equality) formed as an outgrowth of a war–resisters group (Fellowship of Reconciliation) in 1942. In its early years, CORE members tried to desegregate facilities and used several of the same methods as the Civil Rights Movement of twenty years later. These included sit–ins and freedom rides (Farmer 1985, Meier and Rudwick 1973). CORE also influenced the African–American labor leader A. Philip Randolph, who organized against segregation in Federal service and in the military in the 1940s. For some reason, CORE members' opposition to segregation at this time remained within bounds and no mass movement directly resulted. Was it because World War II was under way, because segregationists did not take them seriously, or because they did not make inroads into the South?

Even though nonviolent action did not proliferate then, there is something very interesting about CORE and its members, which is their choice to oppose racial separation when others tolerated it. Also interesting are their choices of means and methods. They turned to nonviolent action rather than the courts, politics, civic education, or some other method. This shows that there is a dimension besides causation in nonviolent action, the dimension of choice and action. McAdam presents a suggestive finding from a slightly later period when he compares the action choices of NAACP local chapters, church–affiliated groups, and students from 1955 through 1960 (McAdam 1982: 134). He finds that the highest proportion of court cases and political action was attributable to NAACP branches, while church affiliates sponsored the most economic boycotts, and students were the most avid initiators of sit–ins. Why did one group stick relatively to "the system," while another used economic pressure (not requiring direct confrontation), and yet another developed a very direct and confrontational approach? There is something here that goes beyond causes and leads toward thinking about choices and their implications.

To summarize, nonviolent action originates in the events and forces that come together to sharpen a conflict into open dispute (causes) and that make it possible for a people to undertake collective opposition (opportunities). Why they choose nonviolent action, how they go about it, and its contribution to the course of conflict (strategies) are the key questions when research is concerned with actions rather than causes alone.

Methods and dynamics. By putting the idea of nonviolent action into the realm of active struggles, it seems as if the methods of nonviolent action are comparable to "tactics" or "strategies" in a conflict. They appear to be the actions that people would take when they judged that they had a particular objective in a fight and considered what would be the most effective approach.

Methods are not precisely the same as tactics. Some methods of nonviolent action are found in cultural traditions, rather than being freely adopted with a goal in mind. One very old method is going on a fast to try to collect a debt. In India, some people used this as a very special means to redress their grievance against a debtor. The disappointed creditor would sit down in front of the debtor's house and refuse to eat until the debt was paid (Sharp 1973: 364). In a sense, people who were owed money would act out being "starved" by the one depriving them of their rightful due.

A similar method was used in old Ireland, but it operated differently. A person suffering loss because of an unpaid debt fasted at the other's door for a fixed term of three nights. By expectation, the fast should be honored by giving a pledge to pay the debt or to appear in a court. When this did not happen, the creditor was unable do more. The creditor's defense lay in the fact that the debtor risked suffering in turn, because judges refused to conduct further cases for people who did not pledge. Thus faithless people lost the ability to protect their own interests in court and collect their own debts (McCarthy 1975). The people compelled to fast in both cases obviously did not have the power to get their money back in some other way. We could only imagine how these methods originated, but they most likely became traditional because they offered the weak some chance of influence over the powerful.

Methods do not always come from tradition. Groups can innovate, spread, and develop methods by using them in unexpected ways. Two examples illustrate this. One comes from Hungary in the autumn of 1956. Before then, the Communist government had ignored the deeds of non–Communist anti–Nazi underground fighters. In 1956, the government hoped to benefit from the respect felt for these martyrs, and held a funeral ceremony to reinter the dead heroes with honors. Instead of going along with the government's plan, students and intellectuals demonstrated in anger at the funeral and seized the solemn moment for themselves. Demonstrations spread and soon students and others took up arms against the government, in what was the beginning of the Hungarian Revolution of 1956 (Kecskemeti 1961).

A government–sponsored funeral ceremony was also the occasion for demonstrations in China during the early days of the student Democracy Movement in 1989. As Esherick and Wasserstrom show, Chinese political funerals are very structured events that underscore in solemn rituals the strength and stability of the regime, even at a moment of change. In April 1989, the government held a memorial procession for deceased Party executive Hu Yaobang. Although Hu had not been a primary supporter of democracy, Beijing students thought that he had lost high office for his opposition to their great enemy Deng Xiaoping. Students joined actively in the funeral of Hu Yaobang, not only to show their mourning for the loss of a potential reformer but to exaggerate their grief and display their enmity and contempt for Deng Xiaoping.

Esherick and Wasserstrom stress the symbolism and political theater found in this kind of event. They write, "The particular danger in the case of political funerals arises from the possibility that unauthorized people will usurp the ritual and rewrite the script into political theater of their own." Put more simply, disaffected people might take over an event and turn it to their own purposes—in both of the cases here, by condemning the very regime that had hoped to solidify its support (Han 1990; Esherick and Wasserstrom 1992).

For all their similarities, these two funeral protests are quite different in their implications. The Hungarian demonstrations led directly to a paramilitary uprising and revolution and Soviet intervention to crush the revolution. In China, there were several weeks of mass nonviolent demonstrations, hunger strikes, and the occupation by demonstrators of Beijing's central Tiananmen Square before the government of Deng Xiaoping suppressed them. One protest triggered violent resistance; the other, the further development of nonviolent action.

These illustrations seem to imply that methods of nonviolent action are primarily symbolic, but that would be mistaken. Like so many human actions, many or most methods do have an expressive character or can be employed for their symbol–laden content. As the names of the classes of methods imply, however, there is more to it than that. Methods of noncooperation involve the withholding of some benefit that another person or group ordinarily receives from another's participation, acceptance, and cooperation. This withholding can obviously be partly symbolic. However, a blacklist is also a method of noncooperation. A register of people who will not be hired for a certain job, the blacklist might be kept completely secret. In being secret, it gives up its expressive content but prevents prying eyes from finding out about the list, adding to the fears of its victims.

Methods of nonviolent intervention also can have a dramatic side. The autoworkers union sit–ins in the Detroit plants of the 1930s, for example, were certainly theatrical. But the sit–ins also prevented corporations from using their property as they saw fit until they either expelled the workers (which was difficult) or settled with them (the usual outcome). With this in mind, it is possible to see the classification of methods as *additive*. Methods of protest and persuasion are primarily expressive and symbolic, methods of noncooperation add to it the withdrawal of expected cooperation and participation, and methods of nonviolent intervention add the further feature of direct psychological or physical presence to the expressive and noncooperative dimensions.

Sociologists John Lofland and Michael Fink have written a study that helps us to think about the concept of methods and their relationship to tactics. They observed sit–ins at the California state capital building. Basically, a sit–in involved more than just showing up in a group, because the protesters refused to leave the premises and insisted on staying put overnight, and sometimes for a fairly long period. In the classic version of sit–ins in the 1930s, the objective was literally a blockade. Lofland and Fink noticed in the California case that people thought up different forms of sit–in, which Lofland and Fink classified by names like pack–ins, lone–ins, and long–term vigils. They also found that these sit–ins, despite the fact that they involved the physical occupation of a place, were usually pursued to send a message (for symbolic expression) rather than trying to effect a change by physical blockage of business. For this reason, Lofland and Fink titled their book *Symbolic Sit–Ins* (1982). This study shows two things. First, a method of nonviolent intervention (or noncooperation) depends for its effects on how it is used—symbolically, as a sanction, or as a direct effort to prevent others from acting as they want to. Second, the way in which a method is used (its tactical performance) does not correlate directly with whatever outcome it has, but there is also a "how to" or tactical aspect to its effects.

To summarize, methods of nonviolent action can be part of tradition, innovated on the spot, a creative reuse of older ways of doing things, or the result of careful consideration of the needs of the moment. In any case, we see that they are not the same as thought–out strategy or tactics and may have differing effects in different situations.

It is for this reason that theoreticians of nonviolent action have introduced the idea of *dynamics* of nonviolent action. Recall Dr. King's ideas about the operating principles of mass nonviolent action as he introduced it into the struggle in Birmingham. His propositions rested on the idea that there was unresolved conflict in the city ("tension") and that nonviolent action could bring it to the surface. Once on the surface, this tension was likely to create two responses. Some people on the other side, who were not fully committed to the survival of segregation, would want to negotiate. Others, probably more committed to segregation, would use violence to stop the protests and defend the status quo. Once this happens, he writes, the violence done to brave and unflinching demonstrators would strengthen the negotiation–prone and at the same time shake the resolve of the users of violence.

In other words, Dr. King sees a nonviolent confrontation as a dynamic process in which certain factors increase the likelihood that challengers will prevail. In his view, careful preparation of the groundwork and the participants, a clear vision of what to expect, meeting violence without giving up or responding in kind, and remaining open to talk at any time increase the likelihood of success by reducing overall support for a regime that rests on injustice and violence.

But what if it does not work this way? Indeed, Dr. King himself had withdrawn from one fight before complete success—in Albany, Georgia—and would later pull out of another—in St. Augustine, Florida—where the technique did not work quite as he imagined (Branch 1988: ch. 16; Garrow, ed. 1989). In one case, there was less segregationist violence than anticipated, and in the other, there was more. In other words, the factors he identified are variable ones, and it is this variation that makes the study of nonviolent action interesting. If the principles Dr. King developed were absolutes and needed only to be applied a certain way, there would be very little more to study.

Scholars do find that many of Dr. King's proposed factors are important. Sharp, for example, also focuses on preparing the action group, strategy, and expected repression and violence, as well as the capacity to withstand it. His thinking differs somewhat from Dr. King's in suggesting that "third parties" often hold the balance of power. In other words, other groups may be drawn into the conflict by their reaction to the adversary's violence, whereas Dr. King stresses splitting the adversary's own ranks.

Sharp differs with Dr. King even more by suggesting three paths toward settlement or three "mechanisms" of change, rather than one. In the first, conversion, the adversary adopts the viewpoint of the challenger. The second mechanism, accommodation, is settlement through some form of negotiated or *de facto* agreement, including one that may not be considered a complete success. The third is coercion, by which Sharp means that an adversary loses so much of its power that it no longer can influence the outcome (Sharp 1973: ch. 9–14; Sharp 1990).

From the researcher's point of view, the factors that shape the course, conduct, and outcome of a campaign of nonviolent action are "variables," but from the activist's point of view, they represent an enormous puzzle that has to be solved successfully. The activist's problem is one of strategy, the task of understanding their technique and using it to increase the chance of success. Ackerman and Kruegler have explored the problem of strategy in nonviolent struggle by assessing several historical examples (or cases) according to a group of principles. Several of these cases were extensive and lengthy conflicts, and some adversaries had actually been at war with each other or would be later, so it is not surprising that many strategic principles in nonviolent struggle are similar to those used in war (Ackerman and Kruegler 1993).

To summarize, researchers can profitably do research on nonviolent action precisely because it happens in different ways in different times and places. No single factor determines whether people will use it, how they will use it, or how it will come out. The factors that lead to the end result are themselves variable. Some, such as large numbers and concentration of forces, are fairly evident. Others appear almost to go against what people might consider obvious, such as deciding when and where to accept violence and repression while maintaining the discipline of nonviolent conduct. Nonviolent action is a field in which the answers are not cut–and–dried and in which human inventiveness can enjoy free rein.

Doing Research on Nonviolent Action

The classic questions that any newspaper reader wants answered are who, what, where, when, why, and how. It is not so different for someone doing research on nonviolent action. Most studies of nonviolent action have been case studies, and users of this book will generally also be doing case studies. For these studies, identification of who, what, when, and where of course must be done carefully, but usually this will not be the greatest problem. Instead, establishing why, how, and what happened will present the chief difficulties.

For one thing, participants do not always use the term "nonviolent action" when they conduct protest and noncooperation. An example from American history can help explain. In the summer and autumn of 1774, the thirteen British colonies in North America faced the same kind of problem as some of the groups discussed earlier. They were nine years into a recurring conflict with England which had rapidly become very acute. After the Boston Tea Party in December 1773, Parliament passed laws to punish the Massachusetts colony and to make sure it could not be the source of radical action again.

The details of what happened next are not important here, but the colonists' thinking is. Massachusetts activists held a series of meetings to consult with each other about how to defend their rights. A September meeting of delegates in Suffolk County counseled refusal to obey any of the new laws or to recognize judges and other officers serving under them, as well as refusal to pay taxes and a boycott of British goods. The meeting cautioned specifically against violence and in favor of perseverance. Another meeting drew this boundary very precisely. It counseled a "mode of conduct" against injustice that was neither "submissive to tyranny" nor "degenerating into rage, passion, and confusion" (Conser, McCarthy, and Toscano 1986: 6; "Suffolk Resolves," 1986 [1774]).

Nowhere did the writers of these words use the term "nonviolent action," and indeed within eight months they would go to war with Britain. But clearly they were advising their fellow citizens to use methods of nonviolent action, as the term is used here, in their struggle. Economic boycotts, tax refusal, and refusal to obey officials they considered illegally appointed *are* nonviolent action so long as they are not just words, rather than deeds, and so long as they are not just a disguise or cover for violence. Why did the leaders of the colonies recommend these means? First, they avoided, or at least delayed, the resort to civil violence or war. Second, they prevented their adversary, Britain, from carrying out mandated changes in the Massachusetts government. Third, they put pressure, especially economic pressure, on the British to compel them to change their policies.

This example shows how the question of *why* nonviolent action is used in a particular case can be answered based on evidence. What did the protesters think they were doing? What methods did they choose and how did they choose them? What effects did they think their methods would have and what would the process be?

The next question to consider is how nonviolent action operates in a conflict. This also can be subdivided into further questions. How did the action group go about doing what it did? How was it organized and how did it actually deploy the methods it chose? How did it get started? How did successive action follow the first actions, either because the participants wanted to try something new, because of the response they received from their opponent, or because they believed that their approach was not effective? In other words, what kind of strategic judgments did the conflict group make and how were they carried out? One of the classic studies of nonviolent action, *Conquest of Violence* by Joan Bondurant, contains a way of organizing material on these questions. Bondurant actually developed this model to assess the fit between Gandhi's concept of *satyagraha* and the workings of a specific case, but it could be used without the Gandhian assumptions to describe other kinds of cases also (Bondurant 1958).

Looking at the case studies in Ackerman and Kruegler's book on strategy in nonviolent conflict, one thing that stands out very clearly is that nonviolent struggle is active, dynamic, and interactive. The fortunes of groups rise and fall, the intensity of conflict ebbs and flows, and much depends on the decisions and actions of leaders and followers (Ackerman and Kruegler 1993: ch. 3–8). Research should try to capture this sense of the back and forth of collective action and relate it to the outcomes.

The final question that must be answered is, what difference did it make that people used nonviolent action to settle their differences with another group? What has changed in a situation where nonviolent action is used, and how can its significance be determined? It is well worth being clear about this and somewhat skeptical of the answers that different sources will give. Some will stress the emotional and psychological changes that activists experience, while others emphasize building organizations and institutions that persist even beyond a losing cause. Not all outcomes are readily quantified, as are the increased wages of a successful striker, but it is important to be clear about the significance of changes that are achieved. This means in part to avoid the easy answer that all struggles are worthwhile because they contribute to future successes even by present–day losses, but also to avoid the cynicism that says that no change is real unless it is absolute.

Making a Contribution

The size of this research guide might give the impression that it has all been done and that there is nothing more to say about nonviolent action. In fact, the opposite is true. The majority of the sources cited here were written by people who did not intend to write about nonviolent action and may never have heard the term. This field is open to many new contributions and is growing through and with them. The authors of this book welcome anyone who wants to look into what there is to say about nonviolent action and assure new researchers that their contributions are basic and vital.

Ronald M. McCarthy
Cambridge, Massachusetts

References

Ackerman, Peter and Christopher Kruegler. 1993. *Strategic Nonviolent Conflict: The Dynamics of People Power in the Twentieth Century*. Westport, CT: Praeger.

Bondurant, Joan V. 1958. *Conquest of Violence: The Gandhian Philosophy of Conflict*. Princeton, NJ: Princeton University Press.

Branch, Taylor. 1988. *Parting the Waters: America in the King Years, 1954–1963*. New York: Simon & Schuster.

Case, Clarence Marsh. 1923. *Non–Violent Coercion: A Study in Methods of Social Pressure*. New York: Century (reprinted New York: Garland, 1972).

Chirot, Daniel. 1992. "What Happened in Eastern Europe in 1989?" Pp. 215–243 in Jeffrey N. Wasserstrom and Elizabeth J. Perry, eds. *Popular Protest and Political Culture in Modern China: Learning from 1989*. Boulder, CO: Westview.

Conser, Walter H., Jr., Ronald M. McCarthy, and David J. Toscano. 1986. "The American Independence Movement, 1765–1775: A Decade of Nonviolent Struggles. " Pp. 3–21 in Conser, Walter H., Jr., Ronald M. McCarthy, David J. Toscano, and Gene Sharp, eds. *Resistance, Politics, and the American Struggle for Independence, 1765–1775*. Boulder, CO: Lynne Rienner.

Esherick, Joseph W. and Jeffrey N. Wasserstrom. 1992. "Acting Out Democracy: Political Theater in Modern China." Ch. 2 in Jeffrey N. Wasserstrom and Elizabeth J. Perry, eds. *Popular Protest and Political Culture in Modern China: Learning from 1989*. Boulder, CO: Westview.

Farmer, James. 1985. *Lay Bare the Heart: An Autobiography of the Civil Rights Movement*. New York: Arbor House.

Garrow, David, ed. 1989. *St. Augustine, Florida, 1963–1964: Mass Protest and Racial Violence*. Brooklyn, NY: Carlson.

Han Minzhu, ed. 1990. *Cries for Democracy: Writings and Speeches from the 1989 Chinese Democracy Movement.* Princeton, NJ: Princeton University Press.

Kecskemeti, Paul. 1961. *The Unexpected Revolution: Social Forces in the Hungarian Uprising.* Stanford, CA: Stanford University Press.

King, Martin Luther, Jr. 1986 [1963]. "Letter from Birmingham City Jail." Pp. 289–302 in James Melvin Washington, ed. *A Testament of Hope: The Essential Writings of Martin Luther King, Jr.* San Francisco: Harper & Row.

Lofland, John and Michael Fink. 1982. *Symbolic Sit–Ins: Protest Occupations at the California Capital.* Washington, DC: University Press of America.

McAdam, Doug. 1982. *Political Process and the Development of Black Insurgency, 1930–1970.* Chicago: University of Chicago Press.

McCarthy, Ronald M. 1975. "The Coercive Fast in Ancient Irish Law: A Magical Sanction?" Seminar paper, Brandeis University.

Meier, August and Elliott Rudwick. 1973. *CORE: A Study in the Civil Rights Movements, 1942–1968.* New York: Oxford University Press.

Piven, Frances Fox and Richard Cloward. 1977. *Poor People's Movements: Why They Succeed, How They Fail.* New York: Pantheon.

Sharp, Gene. 1973. *The Politics of Nonviolent Action.* Boston: Porter Sargent.

———. 1990. "The Role of Power in Nonviolent Struggle." Albert Einstein Institution Monograph Series, No. 3. Cambridge, MA: Albert Einstein Institution.

"Suffolk Resolves." 1986 [1774]. Appendix E in Conser, Walter H., Jr., Ronald M. McCarthy, David J. Toscano, and Gene Sharp, eds. *Resistance, Politics, and the American Struggle for Independence, 1765–1775.* Boulder, CO: Lynne Rienner.

Washington, James Melvin, ed. 1986. *A Testament of Hope: The Essential Writings of Martin Luther King, Jr.* San Francisco: Harper & Row.

Wasserstrom, Jeffrey N. and Elizabeth J. Perry, eds. 1992. *Popular Protest and Political Culture in Modern China: Learning from 1989.* Boulder, CO: Westview.

How to Use This Book

This book is divided into two parts, one somewhat longer than the other. Chapters one through four compile references from history, sociology, political science, journalism, personal experience and observation, policy statements, official reports, and other fact-oriented sources. These are arranged by country. Many of these are case studies of conflicts in which nonviolent action was used. Many entries are not on single cases, in the sense of lengthy and focused campaigns of nonviolent struggle, but instead describe or assess aspects of the experience that people of a country or region have had in the uses of nonviolent action. This section is arranged first by geographical regions (chapters), then alphabetically by country within each chapter. In each national section, three principles of organization are used: (1) by history, from earlier to more recent times, (2) by topics, and (3) by cases.

Some of the issues that have arisen again and again in nations' experience of nonviolent action include labor conflicts, environmental issues, anti–colonial struggles, war, conscription and conscientious objection, and military preparations. You will find these topics listed under separate subject headings where appropriate, while in other instances they will be integrated into the case studies. In a few chapters and sections, these topic areas will be further subdivided if there is a great deal of material. One example of this is the section on South Africa, where entries on the struggle against apartheid are subdivided both chronologically and by topic. Similarly, entries on the Indian Independence Movement are subdivided by period corresponding to important campaigns, and the labor movements of the United States and Great Britain are listed chronologically under the general topic heading of labor. Most sections do not require this degree of subdivision and we hope that you will find the organization to be reasonably straightforward. Where you see that there is a good deal of subdivision in an area of interest, the table of contents can give you a sense of the progression of topics covered.

The second part of this book compiles references on the nature of nonviolent action itself and on related theories and perspectives that we feel make a contribution to an understanding of its workings. As the introduction discusses, we take the view that nonviolent action is composed of methods employed in prosecuting conflicts. That is, *methods* of nonviolent action are used in attempts to influence the course of a conflict through nonviolent protest and persuasion, noncooperation, and nonviolent intervention. Bearing this in mind, you will find that Chapter Five contains entries on individual methods of nonviolent action; such as *protest voyages, boycotts,* and *hunger strikes;* and on their nature and uses. Although there are nearly two hundred identifiable methods of nonviolent action, our entries cannot be grouped neatly by individual method in most cases. You will find them grouped so that reasonably similar methods fall together in the list. Chapter Five also compiles references on the technique of nonviolent action (in other words, texts focused upon the question of what it is and how it operates). Chapter Six includes entries on some significant related areas, such as principled nonviolence, collective violence, political and social power, conflict, and social movements. Generally, wherever there is a choice between placing an entry in the country–by–country list or in one of the chapters on methods and theories, we choose to enter it by country except where the theoretical content appears to be the more significant.

Finding Entries

We provide a table of contents, cross–references, a subject index, an author index, section introductions, and annotations to help you select the entries of greatest interest for your own work.

Table of contents. Based on the principles of organization just explained, the table of contents lists each section and subsection within this book. If you are searching for information about a specific country, period, or theoretical topic, the table of contents can help you to locate it readily.

Cross–references. Each section introduction includes a list of cross–references which identify other subjects that have information on the section's topic. This is helpful since each entry is printed only once, and in many cases anthologies or comparative studies cover several countries or topics. Cross–references correspond to the headings found in the table of contents, and are listed in the order they appear in the table of contents.

Subject index. We suggest relying heavily on and being creative in using the subject index. Consult the subject index not only as another source of the same information found in the table of contents and cross–references but also for works elsewhere in the volume on your topic and on similar themes. For example, while there is no separate topic section on gender and women's issues or the environment, the subject index may help you to construct lists relevant to either of these. As noted above, anthologies or multi–case studies may also have information on your topic.

Author index. Consult this index to locate authors of interest to you who may be represented here or to find other works by the authors whose names you find here.

Annotations. We use a style of annotation called commentary annotation. In other words, these annotations point out the parts of a book or article that are most important for understanding nonviolent action, whether as a concept or as an element of a case. Consequently, the notes do not assess the value or trustworthiness of the facts or the interpretation offered in a work. Likewise, there is often far more background information in a book than is indicated here.

The goal of the annotation is to alert you to the presence, nature, and effects of nonviolent action in a conflict or social movement as well as to point out critical views of nonviolent action when they are part of the book's argument. In a typical annotation you will find some of the following items: guidance on where to look for information on nonviolent action, pointers on the methods of nonviolent action used, suggestions on where to look for evidence of violence and repression or success and failure, and occasionally a brief outline of the author's argument about the role of nonviolent struggle.

At the end of each annotation, there is also information about some of the auxiliary sources of information that an author might have included. These are arranged in rough order of their usefulness to the researcher, with the most useful (indexes and bibliographies) coming last. Generally, selective reference lists or suggestions for further reading have not been identified as bibliographies, while authors' full reference lists have been noted as bibliographies. Nor have highly selective indexes been noted. Some of the other features listed include chronologies, photos, and documents, although not maps and tables.

    Section introductions. Introductions to each section outline the important points in the following works. Country names in capital letters indicate similar topics elsewhere in the guide. Note that reference works generally follow directly after the section introduction.

    The critical eye. The primary tool of research is a discriminating and critical eye. This is nowhere more true than in the study of nonviolent action, where, as the introduction stresses, incautious thinking and unexamined assumptions reign. Readers should approach the evidence assembled here in this spirit. Simply put, most of the human experiences identified here as "nonviolent action" were never thought of in those terms by the people who undertook them. The idea of nonviolent action is a way of understanding what people have done. We believe that it is a perspective that offers new insights into an entirely common human activity—that of being unruly, uncooperative, and obstreperous in patterned ways in order to influence the behavior and thinking of one's opponents. It is the authors' goal in this work to offer evidence of the shape and significance of the often misconceived phenomenon of nonviolent action in conflict. We hope that each user of this book will make an addition to our knowledge of this subject and will bring a critical eye to its understanding.

Authors' Note

The work begun here cannot stop with the publication of one bibliography in one language. The authors trust that other researchers will take up the task of compiling the literature available in their own languages and in their own countries.

The authors encourage users of this book to offer their comments and suggestions on our work, either critical or supportive. Especially, we would accept suggestions for material to appear in later versions of this work. Please contact us at:

The Research Guide Project
Albert Einstein Institution
50 Church Street
Cambridge MA 02138
USA

NONVIOLENT ACTION

PART I

CASES OF NONVIOLENT STRUGGLE

Chapter 1
Africa and the Middle East

Section I
Africa South of the Sahara

Africa's history of nonviolent struggle disproves the idea that nonviolent action was invented in India or the West. Research on Africa shows an extensive pre–colonial repertoire of traditional methods of protest, noncooperation, and ridicule that continued to influence protest in the colonial period. During and after the colonial period, African societies introduced labor strikes and boycotts, student protests, noncooperation by officials, and many other methods in their struggles with colonial and indigenous powers. The level of political innovation of methods is high, for example in NIGERIA, where market women conducted a campaign of tax refusal against the British and especially in SOUTH AFRICA's century–long struggle against the racial system in that country. It was also in SOUTH AFRICA that Mohandas K. Gandhi, the leader of the twentieth–century independence movement in India, began his experiments in nonviolent politics. Gandhi's example and ideas continued to influence African independence movements into the 1960s, sometimes under the concept of "positive action."

African countries have also been the target of international political and economic sanctions. One example of this is RHODESIA (ZIMBABWE), where the European minority government was the object of relatively unsuccessful sanctions, and another is SOUTH AFRICA. Likewise, nonviolent action has been used in Africa in struggles that relied largely on violence and guerrilla forces, such as in MOZAMBIQUE.

1.   Friedland, William H., *Unions, Labor, and Industrial Relations in Africa: An Annotated Bibliography.* 159 pp. Ithaca NY: Center for International Studies, Cornell Univ., 1965. (Partially annotated

bibliography of journal articles on labor issues. See subject index under *disputes and strikes*. Index.)

2.   Schlachter, Gail A., ed., *Africa since 1914: A Historical Bibliography*. 402 pp. Santa Barbara CA, Denver CO, and Oxford: ABC–Clio Information Services, 1985. (Consult index under *boycotts, demonstrations, general strikes, independence movements, political protest, strikes, students,* and names of countries. Index.)

STUDIES

3.   Beshir, Mohamed Omer, *Revolution and Nationalism in the Sudan*. 2nd ed. 327 pp. London: Rex Collings, 1977. Orig. publ. 1974. (Limited discussion of nonviolent action in connection with a revolt in 1924 in ch. 4, 5. See also a student strike, pp. 115–117, and labor conflict, for example, pp. 190–92, 212–16. Illustrations. Index. Bibliography.)

4.   de Braganca, Aquino, and Immanuel Wallerstein, eds., *The African Liberation Reader*. Vol. 2, *The National Liberation Movements*. 196 pp. London: Zed Press, 1982. (Although most chapters examine the armed struggle, ch. 2 contains statements on the role of nonviolent action, pp. 34–36, 40–42, and on its rejection by the movements, pp. 43–47, 53–65.)

5.   Bunker, Stephen G., *Peasants Against the State: The Politics of Market Control in Bugisu, Uganda, 1900–1983*. 284 pp. Urbana and Chicago: Univ. of Illinois Press, 1987. (Case study of state control and coercion and how coffee–growers of the Bugisu district reacted. Shows the role of indigenous elites ["ascendant groups"] in mobilizing the peasantry and their opportunism in exploiting the privilege they gained. The coffee–growers tried various means to retain control over the market, supported by threats to hold crops off the market or even to abandon their plantations in retaliation against state intervention, a threat partly implemented during the Amin regime. Summary of the politics and economics of bargaining

through threat appears in pp. 227–40 and the conclusion. Appendixes. Index. Bibliography.)

6. Cronje, Gillian, and Suzanne Cronje, *The Workers of Namibia.* 135 pp. London: International Defence and Aid Fund for Southern Africa, 1979. (See ch. 7, 8 on a major strike in 1971–72 suppressed by South Africa and efforts to cause inter–ethnic conflict. Photos. Index.)

7. Crummey, Donald, ed., *Banditry, Rebellion, and Social Protest in Africa.* 404 pp. London: James Currey; Portsmouth NH: Heinemann, 1986. (Writings in the "primitive rebels" tradition and related approaches. See Leroy Vail and Landig White, "Forms of Resistance: Songs and Perceptions of Power in Colonial Mozambique," ch. 9 on protest and organizing songs; Julia Wells, "The War of Degradation: Black Women's Struggle Against Orange Free State Pass Laws, 1913," ch. 11 on women's "unprecedented passive resistance campaign"; and Stephen G. Bunker, "Property, Protest, and Politics in Bugisu, Uganda," ch. 12. Illustrations. Index.)

8. Fawzi, Saad Ed Din, *The Labour Movement in the Sudan 1946–1955.* 189 pp. London, New York, and Toronto: Oxford Univ. Press, 1957. (History of Sudanese labor movement from 1946 to 1955 with accounts of marches and strikes. Index.)

9. Friedland, William H., *Vuta Kamba: The Development of Trade Unions in Tanganyika.* 293 pp. Stanford CA: Hoover Institution Press, Stanford Univ., 1969. (Study of militant trade unions and their motto *vuta Kamba* [strike]. Several strikes and boycotts discussed. See esp. pp. 101–9 on protest and representation and index under *boycotts* and *strikes.* Photos. Index. Bibliography.)

10. Gray, Richard, *The Two Nations: Aspects of the Development of Race Relations in the Rhodesias and Nyasaland.* 373 pp. London, New York, and Toronto: Oxford Univ. Press, 1960. (Background and developments, 1918–53. See part 2, ch. 5; esp. pp. 290–94, 316–36; on strikes in Southern Rhodesia [Zimbabwe] and pp. 342–55 on political organization in Nyasaland [Malawi]. Bibliography.)

11.   Grillo, R.D., *Race, Class, and Militancy: An African Trade Union,*
        1939–1965. 159 pp. New York and London: Chandler, 1974.
        (Ethnography of African railroad union and its "militancy."
        See discussion of links among militancy, confrontation, and
        strikes throughout, esp. ch. 3, 5. Index. Bibliography.)

12.   Gutkind, Peter C.W., Robin Cohen, and Jean Copan, eds.,
        African Labor History. 280 pp. Beverly Hills CA: Sage
        Publications, 1978. (Essays by various authors on strikes, labor
        unions, and decolonization in different African contexts. See
        esp. Gerard Althaber, "Strikes, Urban Mass Action and
        Political Change, Tananarive 1972," ch. 8.)

13.   Hanna, William John, *University Students and African Politics.*
        296 pp. New York and London: Africana, 1975. (See esp.
        William John Hanna, "Students, Universities and Political
        Outcomes," ch. 1; William John Hanna, Judith Lynne Hanna,
        and Vivian Zeitz Sauer, "The Active Minority," ch. 4; and
        William John Hanna, "Systematic Constraints and Individual
        Activism," ch. 10. Index.)

14.   Isaacman, Allen, and Barbara Isaacman, *Mozambique: From*
        Colonialism to Revolution, 1900–1982. 235 pp. Boulder CO:
        Westview Press; Hampshire, England: Gower, 1983. (Brief
        references to a variety of nonviolent actions in resistance to
        colonial rule and liberation, pp. 61–84. Illustrations. Photos.
        Index. Bibliography.)

15.   Jones, Griff, *Britain and Nyasaland.* 315 pp. London: Allen &
        Unwin, 1964. (See pp. 149–50, 177–89, 203, 218, 221 on African
        noncooperation and resistance to Federation, and pp. 231–65
        on "The Emergency" and its aftermath.)

16.   Liebenow, J. Gus, *Liberia: The Quest for Democracy.* 336 pp.
        Bloomington and Indianapolis: Indiana Univ. Press, 1987.
        (Political history of modern Liberia. See esp. pp. 171–78 for
        demonstrations that erupted into the Rice Riots of 1979, and
        the subsequent founding of MOJA [Movement for Justice in
        Africa], a political organization devoted to direct action.
        Index.)

17.   Maguire, G. Andrew, *Toward "Uhuru" in Tanzania: The Politics of Participation*. 432 pp. London: Cambridge Univ. Press, 1969. (Study of the development of support for independence in one region; examples of protest and noncooperation in parts 2, 3. Consult index under *civil disobedience* and *Geita crisis* as well as names of organizations. Index. Bibliography.)

18.   Mazrui, Ali A., ed., *The Warrior Tradition in Modern Africa*. 260 pp. Leiden, Netherlands: E.J. Brill, 1977. (See Ali A. Mazrui, "Gandhi, Marx, and the Warrior Tradition in African Resistance: Towards Androgynous Liberation," pp. 179–96.)

19.   Middlemas, Keith, *Cabora Bassa: Engineering and Politics in Southern Africa*. 367 pp. London: Weidenfeld & Nicholson, 1975. (See pp. 167–69 for brief account of anti–colonial protest boycott in Germany against participation in building of a hydroelectric dam in Portuguese Mozambique. Consult index on evasion of Rhodesia economic sanctions. Photos. Index. Bibliography.)

20.   Ohaegbulam, Festus Ugboaja, *Nationalism in Colonial and Post–Colonial Africa*. 176 pp. Washington DC: University Press of America, 1977. (See ch. 4 on resistance to colonialism.)

21.   Pieterse, Cosmo, and Donald Munro, *Protest & Conflict in African Literature*. 127 pp. London, Ibadan, and Nairobi: Heinemann, 1969. (See esp. Dennis Brutus, "Protest Against Apartheid," pp. 93–100 and Louis James, "The Protest Tradition," pp. 109–24.)

22.   Rotberg, Robert I., and Ali A. Mazrui, eds., *Protest and Power in Black Africa*. 1274 pp. New York: Oxford Univ. Press, 1970. (Chapters on resistance, rebellion, protest, and coups from 1879 to 1969. See esp. Dharam P. Ghai, "The Bugandan Trade Boycott: A Study in Tribal, Political, and Economic Nationalism," pp. 755–70; Robert Melson, "Nigerian Politics and the General Strike of 1964," pp. 771–87; and an assessment of nonviolent struggle in South Africa by Leo Kuper, "Nonviolence Revisited," pp. 788–804. Index. Bibliography.)

23.   Sandbrook, Richard, and Robin Cohen, eds., *The Development of an African Working Class: Studies in Class Formation and Action.* 336 pp. Toronto and Buffalo: Univ. of Toronto Press, 1975. (Brief coverage of strikes and labor action in several African nations, including Kenya, pp. 31–44; Tanganyika [Tanzania], pp. 57–69; Rhodesia [Zimbabwe], pp. 74–77; Guinea, pp. 101–9; Nigeria, pp. 153–58, 173–76; South Africa and Namibia, pp. 215–32; and Ghana, pp. 262–65. Index. Bibliography.)

24.   Scott, Roger, *The Development of Trade Unions in Uganda.* 207 pp. Nairobi: East Africa Publishing House, 1966. (History of organizing and action by Ugandan trade unions, with accounts throughout of strikes and other actions. Illustrations. Bibliography.)

25.   Sithole, Ndabaningi, *African Nationalism.* 2d ed. 196 pp. London, New York, Nairobi, Ibadan: Oxford Univ. Press, 1968 [orig. publ. 1959]. (See ch. 11, 16 on the actions of nationalists and white responses. Photos.)

26.   "Sudan's Revolutionary Spring." *MERIP Reports* 15 (1985): 2–28. (Articles on Sudanese 1985 rebellion, which included both violent and nonviolent actions. See, e.g., pp. 4–6 on demonstrations and general strike and article by Abbas Abdelkarim, Abdallah el–Hassan, and David Seddon, "The Generals Step In," pp. 19–24 on relationship between mass protest and governmental change. Photos.)

27.   Taryor, Nya Kwiawan, Sr., ed., *Justice, Justice: A Cry of My People.* 319 pp. Chicago: Strugglers' Community Press, 1985. (Partisan essays and manifestoes on history and agenda of MOJA [Movement for Justice in Africa] and its role in the Liberian political scene. See pp. xx, 18, 64–65 for examples of MOJA's tactics, including mass actions and worker organization. Ch. 7 describes student organizing and the state's reprisals, and ch. 8 looks at organizing rubber tappers. Bibliography. Appendix.)

28.   Warmington, W.A., *A West African Trade Union: A Case Study of the Cameroons Development Corp. Workers' Union and Its Relations with the Employers.* 150 pp. London: Oxford Univ. Press, 1960.

(See ch. 4 for history of strikes in relation to labor–management system, 1945–55. Illustrations. Index.)

29.   Winter, Colin O'Brien, *Namibia*. 234 pp. Guildford and London: Lutterworth Press, 1977. (Memoirs of author, the Bishop of Damaraland, who was active in the protest movement and a 1971–72 strike, and was eventually forced to leave Namibia. See ch. 1, 2, 9, 12–14, 16, 17.)

GHANA

Ghana's independence movement, which ended successfully in 1960, was strongly influenced by the idea of "positive action" advocated by leader Kwame Nkrumah. Nkrumah's concept of positive action adopted many of Gandhi's views on protest and noncooperation in anti–colonial politics but was also concerned with economic development and the nature of the post–colonial state. (Positive action ideas also developed in other countries, such as ZAMBIA.)

30.   Agbodeka, Francis, *African Politics and British Policy in the Gold Coast, 1868–1960: A Study in the Forms and Force of Protest*. 206 pp. Evanston IL: Northwestern Univ. Press; London: Longman, 1971. (On anti–colonial protest broadly defined, including several insurrections. See ch. 6 for protests against taxation and political change. Illustrations. Index. Bibliography.)

31.   Carter, Gwendolen M., ed., *Politics in Africa: Seven Cases*. 283 pp. New York, Chicago, and Burlingame: Harcourt, Brace & World, 1966. (See St. Clair Drake and Leslie Alexander Lacy, "Government versus the Unions: The Sekondi–Takoradi Strike, 1961," ch. 3. Illustrations).

32.   Cowan, E.A., *Evolution of Trade Unionism in Ghana*. 203 pp. Ghana: Trades Union Congress, [n.d.]. (Report on trade unions; see ch. 3 on the history of strikes and ch. 5 on positive action and the 1949 general strike.)

33.   James, C.L.R., *Nkrumah and the Ghana Revolution.* 227 pp. London: Allison & Busby, 1977. (Personalistic history of Ghana's revolution with references to general strikes as nonviolent positive action throughout. See esp. "Positive Action," ch. 7. Index.)

34.   Nkrumah, Kwame, *Ghana: The Autobiography of Kwame Nkrumah.* 302 pp. New York, Edinburgh, and Toronto: Thomas Nelson, 1957. (Account of the independence movement after 1947 by the founder of the Convention People's Party and later president of Ghana. See esp. pp. xiv–xv, 69–146, 163. Photos. Appendixes.)

35.   ————, *Revolutionary Path.* 532 pp. New York: International Publishers, 1973. (Ch. 5 contains short articles on positive action and protest. Ch. 6 contains a 1949 speech, "What I Mean by Positive Action." Index.)

36.   Timothy, Bankole, *Kwame Nkrumah: His Rise to Power.* 198 pp. London: George Allen & Unwin, 1955. (See ch. 4–11 on the independence campaign, esp. ch. 9 on positive action. Photos. Index.)

KENYA

While positive action (see GHANA) was somewhat influential in the Kenyan anticolonial struggle, England's methods of rule there also led to many labor conflicts in the period before independence. Strikes were often strongly political and several "general strikes" made their contribution to anticolonialism.

37.   Clayton, Anthony, and Donald C. Savage, *Government and Labour in Kenya, 1895–1963.* 481 pp. London: Frank Cass, 1974. (In addition to discussion of strikes and protest throughout, see descriptions of general strikes in Mombasa, pp. 222–25, 276–83; and Nairobi, pp. 328–33. Index. Bibliography.)

38.   Mboya, Tom, *Freedom and After.* 288 pp. Boston and Toronto: Little, Brown, 1963. (Personal memoirs of leader of Kenya

union organizing and Minister for Labor on nationalism and independence. See ch. 2–4, 6, including comments on pp. 43–46 on debate between proponents of violence and proponents of Gandhian positive action. Photos. Index.)

39. Singh, Makhan, *History of Kenya's Trade Union Movement to 1952.* 332 pp. Nairobi: East African Publishing House, 1969. (Thorough, detailed account of trade union activity until 1952. See ch. 3, 10, 14, 18 on local general strikes during colonial period. Photos. Index.)

40. Wipper, Audrey, *Rural Rebels: A Study of Two Protest Movements in Kenya.* 363 pp. Nairobi, London, and New York: Oxford Univ. Press, 1977. (Two case studies of politico–religious protest as anti–colonial resistance. Index. Bibliography.)

NIGERIA

Women's War of 1929 and Other Women's Protests

Rumors of a coming tax on the property of market women in colonial Nigeria prompted a demonstration in 1929 against the colonial authorities and local African functionaries. Women gathered outside local administrative offices to demand resignations and public apologies for the mistreatment of demonstrators. This public display of solidarity escalated into a mass movement of thousands of women in various parts of the countryside. Tax protests in the town of Abeokuta continued for some time, while in Aba rioting destroyed government buildings. Women were fired upon to quell the rioting and many were killed. The casualties, as well as inept administration that caused misunderstandings which first sparked the riots, led to a full Commission of Inquiry investigation and report.

41. Hafkin, Nancy J., and Edna G. Bay, eds., *Women in Africa: Studies in Social and Economic Change.* 306 pp. Stanford CA: Stanford Univ. Press, 1976. (See Judith Van Allen, "'Aba Riots' or Igbo 'Women's War'? Ideology, Stratification, and the Invisibility of Women," pp. 59–85 for reconstruction of

women's use of traditional protest methods in the colonial context. Index. Bibliography.)

42.   Leith–Ross, Sylvia, *African Women: A Study of the Ibo of Nigeria.* 367 pp. New York and Washington: Praeger, 1965 [orig. publ. 1938]. (Anthropological study of the daily routine of Ibo women and how it has been affected by Western contact. Events of the "women's war" are described on pp. 23–39. Their influence on the development of Nigerian women's self–image vis–á–vis the European encroachment is mentioned throughout. Photos. Index.)

43.   Mba, Nina Emma, *Nigerian Women Mobilized: Women's Political Activity in Southern Nigeria, 1900–1965.* 344 pp. Berkeley: Univ. of California Institute of International Studies, 1982. (Study of women's collective action, with description of protests, tax resistance, letters, petitions, and demonstrations. See ch. 3 on the "women's war" of 1929, ch. 4 on mass protest in the eastern region, ch. 5 for a case study of tax protest in Abeokuta over several years, and ch. 6 for analysis of women's organizations. Illustrations. Index. Bibliography.)

44.   Soyinka, Wole, *Aké: The Years of Childhood.* 230 pp. London: Rex Collings, 1981. New York: Vintage Books, 1982. (Autobiography containing a memoir of tax protest in Abeokuta, in which author's mother was a leader. See pp. 180–224.)

Labor

Nigerian labor history has been marked by both pre–independence (1945) and post–independence (1964) general strikes, as well as others not documented here. They have been aimed largely at the incumbent governments.

45.   Ananaba, Wogu, *The Trade Union Movement in Nigeria.* 336 pp. London: C. Hurst, 1969. (History of organization, strikes, and protest. See ch. 4 on personal disobedience to racial system, ch. 7 on 1945 general strike, and ch. 11–13, 20 on the 1964 general strike. Illustrations. Photos. Documents. Index.)

46.   Cohen, Robin, *Labour and Politics in Nigeria, 1945–71*. 302 pp.
        New York: Africana, 1974. (See esp. ch. 5, 6 and index under
        strikes, general strike [1945], and *general strike [1964]*.
        Illustrations. Index. Bibliography.)

SOUTH AFRICA

Struggles Against the Racial System

*Actions by Africans, Indians, and others to oppose the spread of racial
separation and deprivation of rights date to the late nineteenth century. In
1948, the Afrikaners' National Party enacted legislation that extended and
enforced South Africa's system of racial segregation. The most tangible goal of
the South African liberation movement became to resist and dismantle this
system of "apartheid," which was based upon an elaborate classification and
separation of racial groups. After 1948 the "homelands" policy set up
nominally–independent African republics as satellites to the Afrikaner regime.
Opposition groups of the early period, from 1948 to 1960, focused primarily
on nonviolent means of resisting apartheid and limiting its effects on the
African majority. In 1961, the African National Congress officially abandoned
nonviolent action as a program. Nevertheless, nonviolent methods including
strikes, bus boycotts, rent boycotts, school strikes, and economic boycotts
emerged as part of the African repertoire in subsequent years. Entry 71 is a
virtual encyclopedia of these means.*

*See also: Methods of Nonviolent Action: Sports Boycotts; New Zealand:
Protest Against Sports with South African Teams.*

47.   Ansari, S., *Liberation Struggle in Southern Africa: A Bibliography
        of Source Material*. 148 pp. Gurgaon, Haryana, India: Indian
        Documentation Service, 1972. (Includes references to petitions
        as well as other source material. Index.)

48.   Dag Hammarskjöld Library, *Apartheid: A Selective Bibliography
        on the Racial Policies of the Government of the Republic of South
        Africa, 1970–1978*. New York: United Nations, 1979. (See part 1,
        section 8 on sanctions and part 2, section 7.)

49.   Karis, Thomas, and Gwendolen M. Carter, eds., *From Protest to Challenge: A Documentary History of African Politics in South Africa*. 4 vols. Stanford CA: Hoover Institution Press, 1972–77. (Selected documents arranged chronologically and topically, concerned with organizations, statements of grievances, and some petitions. Biographical sketches of prominent figures of the period covered by document collections are in vol. 4. Editors' introductions. Index of names and organizations. Bibliographical notes.)

Vol. 1. Johns, Sheridan, III, ed., *Protest and Hope, 1882–1934*. 378 pp. 1972. (Documents. Index.)

Vol. 2. Karis, Thomas, ed., *Hope and Challenge, 1935–1952*. 536 pp. 1973. (Documents. Index.)

Vol. 3. Karis, Thomas, and Gail M. Gerhart, eds., *Challenge and Violence, 1953–1964*. 825 pp. 1977. (Documents. Index.)

Vol. 4. Gerhart, Gail M. and Thomas Karis, eds., *Political Profiles, 1882–1964*. 178 pp. 1977. (Photos. Index.)

50.   Potgieter, P.J.J.S., *Index to Literature on Race Relations in South Africa, 1910–1975*. 555 pp. Boston: G.K. Hall, 1979. (Compilation of books and periodical articles arranged by subject and author. Subject headings list, pp. 1–28.)

51.   Seekings, Jeremy, *South Africa's Townships 1980–1991: An Annotated Bibliography*. 236 pp. University of Stellenbosch (South Africa), Department of Sociology, Occasional Paper No. 16. February 1992. (Compiles references to papers, articles, books, and dissertations concerned with township conflicts and related questions. Many of the references are concerned with protests, rent and school boycotts, and aspects of violent and nonviolent struggles in the localities. See introduction for references to specific years and issues, including pp. 41–42 on protests. Indexes.)

STUDIES

52.   Adam, Heribert, and Kogila Moodley, *South Africa without Apartheid: Dismantling Racial Domination*. 315 pp. Berkeley, Los Angeles, and London: Univ. of California Press, 1986. (Analysis of apartheid and possibilities of dismantling it. See pp. 103–17 on political violence and consult index under *boycotts, extra–institutional protest, resistance, squatters camps/squatters,* and *strikes.* Chronology. Index. Bibliography.)

53.   African National Congress, *Unity in Action: A Photographic History of the African National Congress South Africa, 1912–1982.* 156 pp. London: African National Congress, 1982. (Photo essay of South African struggle focusing on organized resistance to apartheid and the emergence of the ANC. Includes many photos of strikes, demonstrations, and related topics, as well as texts of the "Freedom Charter," the ANC's "Programme of Action," and the "Umkhonto We Sizwe Manifesto." Photos. Documents.)

54.   American Friends Service Committee, *South Africa: Challenge and Hope.* Ed. Lyle Tatum. Rev. ed. [New York?]: Hill and Wang, 1987 [orig. publ. 1982]. (Report and policy statement on South Africa conflict. Ch. 3, 4 discuss resistance within South Africa to extension of racial system; ch. 7 identifies opportunities for economic pressure; ch. 8 examines feasibility of nonviolent action; and ch. 9 details compilers' proposals. Bibliography.)

55.   Bot, Monika, *School Boycotts 1984: The Crisis in African Education.* 54 pp. Durban, South Africa: Indicator Project South Africa, Centre for Applied Social Sciences, Univ. of Natal, 1985. (Study of 1984 South Africa school boycotts. See ch. 2 for case study of boycotts in Atteridgeville/Saulsville, May 1984. Ch. 3 presents a history of student movements in South Africa. See esp. appendix A, "A Chronology of Events, 1984." Illustrations. Documents. Bibliography.)

56.   Bozzoli, Belinda, ed., *Town and Countryside in the Transvaal: Capitalist Penetration and Popular Response.* 446 pp. Johannesburg: Ravan Press, 1983. (See part 3, "Urban

Organisation and Resistance," esp. Maureen Tayal, "Indian Passive Resistance in the Transvaal, 1906–08," pp. 240–68; Julia Wells, "The Day the Town Stood Still: Women in Resistance in Potchefstroom, 1912–1930," pp. 269–307; and Tom Lodge, "The Parents' School Boycott, 1955," pp. 365–95. Photos. Index.)

57.   Brink, Andre, *Writing in a State of Siege: Essays on Politics and Literature*. 256 pp. New York: Summit Books, 1986. Originally published as *Mapmakers: Writing in a State of Siege*. London: Faber & Faber, 1983. (Essays by Afrikaaner writer. See "Introduction: A Background to Dissidence," pp. 13–40, on Afrikaans dissident writers and "Mahatma Gandhi Today," pp. 54–70, for story of Bram Fischer and discussion of relevance of Gandhi in South Africa.)

58.   Davis, Stephen M., *Apartheid's Rebels: Inside South Africa's Hidden War*. 238 pp. New Haven CT and London: Yale Univ. Press, 1987. (Primarily on the ANC's armed struggle as conducted from exile and its politics. Ch. 1, pp. 1–14 discuss the era of ANC's policy of nonviolent struggle as reassessed at the time of the Treason Trial and Sharpeville killings of 1960. Ch. 3 is on "linking protest to revolt," or the ANC presence in violent and nonviolent protest within South Africa in the 1980s; see pp. 86–96 on the UDF and other groups and pp. 98–106 on COSATU and labor. Index.)

59.   Finnegan, William, *Crossing the Line: A Year in the Land of Apartheid*. 418 pp. New York: Harper & Row, 1986. (Memoirs of American teacher in Capetown. See part 2 on student boycott of 1980 and index under *Alexandra Bus Boycott, boycotts, civil rights movement, American, Committee of 81, guerrilla theater, pamphlets, shopping center protests*, and *student boycott*. Index.)

60.   Gann, L.H., and Peter Duignan, *Why South Africa Will Survive: A Historical Analysis*. 312 pp. New York: St. Martin's Press, 1981. (See pp. 229–34 for brief discussion of why authors believe that nonviolent means will not bring change to South Africa).

61.   Katz, Elaine N., *A Trade Union Aristocracy: A History of White Workers in the Transvaal and the General Strike of 1913*. 601 pp.

ASI Communication no. 3. Johannesburg: African Studies Institute, Univ. of the Witwatersrand, 1976. (See discussion of the general strike concept, pp. 255–259; 1911 Industrial Workers of the World Johannesburg tram strike, pp. 297–314; and 1913 general strike and its aftermath, pp. 381–429, 459–471. Illustrations. Photos. Appendixes. Index. Bibliography.)

62. Kobach, Kris William, *Political Capital: The Motives, Tactics, and Goals of Politicized Businesses in South Africa*. 171 pp. Lanham MD, New York, London: University Press of America, 1990. (Study of the "politicization" of the South African business community and the dynamics of its location between the government and resistance groups. Ch. 2 is a history of business and politics from the late 1940s to the end of the 1980s. See esp. pp. 61–70, which describe businesses' noncooperation with apartheid requirements as "low–intensity civil disobedience.")

63. Magubane, Peter, *Magubane's South Africa*. 116 pp. New York: Alfred A. Knopf, 1978. (Photo essay on South African society and politics by veteran black journalist. Photos of demonstrations, demonstrative funerals, and acts of repression from 1958 to the Soweto uprising on pp. 5, 6, 11, 12, 17–31, 52–53, 86–87, 90–113.)

64. Mbeki, Govan, *South Africa: The Peasants' Revolt*. 158 pp. Harmondsworth, England; Ringwood, Australia; and Baltimore MD: Penguin Books, 1964. (See ch. 9 on peasant resistance, especially in Pondoland, including the burning of passes by women, illegal meetings, tax refusal, boycotts, independent courts, and other actions. Appendixes.)

65. Moorhouse, Fred, *Politics, Nonviolence, and Social Justice: An African Perspective*. 20 pp. Surrey, England: Fellowship of Reconciliation, 1977. (Seeks to demythologize violent revolution and suggests that nonviolence has not yet been tried in South Africa.)

66. Moroney, Sean, and Linda Ensor, *The Silenced: Bannings in South Africa*. 56 pp. Johannesburg: S A Institute of Race Relations, 1979. Mimeo. (Pp. 3–5 describe the legal nature of a

banning order, followed by discussions of the relevant legislation, pp. 6–9, and statistics, pp. 14–15. Bulk of volume is a list of those banned as of 1978, with some information about the majority of those listed.)

67.   Naidoo, Indres, as told to Albie Sachs, *Island in Chains: Ten Years on Robben Island*. 278 pp. New York: Penguin Books, 1982. (Prison memoir with accounts of protest and noncooperation. See esp. ch. 33, 40, 48 on hunger strikes organized by ANC prisoners.)

68.   Neame, L.E., *The History of Apartheid: The Story of the Colour War in South Africa*. 200 pp. London: Pall Mall Press, with Barrie and Rockliff, 1962. (See pp. 43–45, 100–104, 148–49 on noncooperation.)

69.   Ngubane, Jordan K., *An African Explains Apartheid*. 243 pp. New York: Praeger, 1963. (See parts 2, 3 for brief accounts of the politics of African resistance, including the role of Communists.)

70.   Roux, Edward, *Time Longer than Rope: A History of the Black Man's Struggle for Freedom in South Africa*. 2d ed. 469 pp. Madison WI: Univ. of Wisconsin Press, 1964. (History of conflict between black Africans and South African racial system by veteran Communist activist. See ch. 25 on the Alexandra bus boycott, ch. 31 on the Defiance Campaign, ch. 32 on the Treason Trial, and ch. 33 on Sharpeville. Chronology. Index.)

71.   Smuts, Dene, and Shauna Westcott, eds., *The Purple Shall Govern: A South African A to Z of Nonviolent Action*. 165 pp. Cape Town: Oxford Univ. Press and Centre for Intergroup Studies, 1991. (An encyclopedia of nonviolent action for the use of S.A. audiences, most of whose entries are on methods of nonviolent action as illustrated by examples from the S.A. press. Among the many entries with a particularly South African flavor are *advertisement, alternative structures, boycott, clothes, defiance, exposé, funerals, hunger strike, ignoring authority, jogging and jolling, journeys, keening, marches, naming, overloading, quitting, resisting removal, stayaway, symbolic action,*

taking over, toyi–toyi, unmasking, wading–in, x–factor, and *Zabazala*. [*clothing* refers to wearing symbolic colors or clothing, *keening* refers to women's mourning cries, *stayaways* are a sort of strike, *toyi–toyi* is dancing, the *x–factor* is the unexpected, and *Zabazala* is struggle.] Photos.)

72. Steward, Alexander, *The World, the West, and Pretoria*. 308 pp. New York: David McKay, 1977. (South African government official presents the pro–apartheid view. See ch. 9, 10, and esp. pp. 147–55 on the sports boycott, pp. 176–85 on Sharpeville, and pp. 185–90 on the banning of the Pan–African Congress and African National Congress as justified by movement violence. Index.)

73. Wilson, William J., *Power, Racism, and Privilege: Race Relations in Theoretical and Sociohistorical Perspectives*. 221 pp. New York: Free Press, 1973. (Comparative study of race relations in U.S. and South Africa. See ch. 7, 8 for violent and nonviolent struggle in both countries.)

GANDHI–LED STRUGGLES, 1906–1914

Mohandas K. Gandhi (see INDIA) went to South Africa as a lawyer for an Indian firm in 1894. He soon began to work for protection of Indians' civil rights in the colony, including the right to travel freely and to conduct business and family life without interference. Gandhi developed many methods of mass nonviolent action, part of his approach called satyagraha, *and at the same time worked out the ideas about communal living, a simplified economy, and asceticism that are identified with his life and philosophy.*

See also: Mohandas K. Gandhi: Biography and Works

74. Gandhi, Mohandas K., *Satyagraha in South Africa*. Trans. Valji G. Desai. 351 pp. Ahmedabad: Navajivan, 1950 [orig. publ. 1928]. (Gandhi's own story of his first attempt to apply the principle of *satyagraha* to politics on a large scale in the South African Indians' struggle for defense of rights against the developing racial system, dating from 1906 to 1914.)

75.   Hancock, William K., *Smuts: The Sanguine Years, 1870–1919*. 619
        pp. London and New York: Cambridge Univ. Press, 1962. (See
        pp. 321–48 on Smuts and Gandhi and the Indian question.)

76.   Huttenback, Robert A., *Gandhi in South Africa: British
        Imperialism and the Indian Question, 1860–1914*. 368 pp. Ithaca
        NY and London: Cornell Univ. Press, 1971. (History of Indians'
        civil rights campaigns, 1893–1914, including the 1907–10
        Transvaal *Satyagraha* and the development of Gandhian
        methods. Photos. Appendix. Bibliography.)

77.   Pillay, Bala, *British Indians in the Transvaal: Trade, Politics and
        Imperial Relations, 1885–1906*. 259 pp. London: Longman, 1976.
        (Study of policy toward Indians and their response in colonial
        South Africa. See ch. 6–8 on Gandhi and Indian protests, esp.
        ch. 6 and pp. 212–20. Photos. Documents in appendix. Index.
        Bibliography.)

78.   Swan, Maureen, *Gandhi: The South African Experience*. 310 pp.
        Johannesburg: Ravan Press, 1985. (Study of Indian commercial
        communities in South Africa and Gandhi's role in their
        politics, 1894–1914. Includes material on political activity by
        "elite" leaders other than Gandhi and Gandhi's role as a "full–
        time organizer." See esp. ch. 2–6 for studies of two "passive
        resistance" campaigns, including an account in ch. 5 of the
        Market Boycott Movement of 1909. Photos. Index.
        Bibliography.)

MASS ACTION AND DEFIANCE, 1948–1960

*As apartheid became more entrenched in law, the preeminent opposition
group, the African National Congress (ANC), pursued a policy of
noncooperation as a demonstration of the power of the majority. Strikes, civil
disobedience, and noncooperation replaced an earlier emphasis on working
within constitutional bounds. The Defiance Campaign of 1952 was the first
organized large–scale protest against the Afrikaner state. Despite organizers'
denunciation of violence, riots occurred that resulted in more severe state
action against organized opposition and public protests. Later, the ANC
adopted the Freedom Charter as its political blueprint for a post–apartheid
South Africa. In response, the government arrested leaders of the congress*

that had drafted the charter under a charge of treason—forcing them to spend several years contesting the charges in court. The ANC's increasing belief that nonviolent action was unsuccessful in combating apartheid was strengthened when demonstrators were shot down at Sharpeville in 1960. In the next year, armed struggle was added into official policy by the ANC and other organizations.

79. Benson, Mary, *The African Patriots: The Story of the African National Congress of South Africa.* 310 pp. London: Faber and Faber; Chicago: Encyclopedia Britannica Press, 1964. Reprinted as *South Africa: The Struggle for a Birth Right.* 314 pp. New York: Funk & Wagnalls, 1966. (History of the ANC into the early 1960s. See ch. 3 on early "passive resistance," ch. 12 on a post–WWII miners' strike, ch. 15–17 on the Defiance Campaign of 1952, and ch. 20 on the Treason Trial and its effects. See also pp. 42–53, 117–20 on the intransigence of government and increasing opinion in ANC circa 1960 that nonviolent methods were futile. Index.)

80. ———, *Chief Albert Lutuli of South Africa.* 68 pp. London: Oxford Univ. Press, 1963. (Political biography. See esp. ch. 4–8 on activities from 1952 to 1961. Photos.)

81. ———, *Nelson Mandela: The Man and the Movement.* 269 pp. New York and London: W.W. Norton, 1986. (See pp. 32–34 on a 1946 miners' strike, pp. 40–43 and ch. 4 on Defiance Campaign in early 1950s, ch. 6 on campaigns in late 1950s. Ch. 7–9 are on the issue of violent versus nonviolent struggle in the ANC, 1960–61. Index.)

82. Feit, Edward, *African Opposition in South Africa: The Failure of Passive Resistance.* 223 pp. Stanford CA: Hoover Institution on War, Revolution, and Peace, 1967. (Critical study of ANC performance in two 1954–55 campaigns, one against forced removals and one against the Bantu Education Act. See esp. pp. 117–38, 156–89 on strategic and tactical problems in these struggles. Index.)

83. ———, *South Africa: The Dynamics of the African National Congress.* 73 pp. London and New York: Oxford Univ. Press, 1962. (A brief analysis of why the ANC "did not become an

effective movement" during the 1950s. See ch. 5, 6, 7 on the Defiance Campaign. Appendixes.)

84.   Harsch, Ernest, *South Africa: White Rule, Black Revolt*. 352 pp. New York: Monad Press, 1980. (Ch. 14–20 contain accounts of nonviolent action in mass movements since late nineteenth century, stressing activities of Marxist organizations. Bibliography.)

85.   Heimler, Eugene, ed., *Resistance against Tyranny*. 168 pp. London: Routledge & Kegan Paul, 1966. (See André Unger, "South Africa," pp. 25–62 for personal reflections on resistance and protest in the 1950s.)

86.   Joshi, P.S., *Unrest in South Africa*. 303 pp. Bombay: Hind Kitabs, 1958. (History of European domination. On nonviolent demonstrations, see especially pp. 179–201, 242, 244, 249–50. Appendixes.)

87.   Kuper, Leo, *Passive Resistance in South Africa*. 256 pp. London: Jonathan Cape, 1956. New Haven CT: Yale Univ. Press, 1957. (Sociologist's study of the 1952 Defiance Campaign. See ch. 3 for analysis of the phenomenon of "passive resistance," leaning heavily on Gandhian categories, and part 2 for chronicle of the 1952 struggle. Photos. Appendixes.)

88.   Lodge, Tom, *Black Politics in South Africa since 1945*. 389 pp. London and New York: Longman, 1983. (History of black resistance movements in South Africa from WWII to 1983. See esp. ch. 2 on the Defiance Campaign, ch. 5–7 on protests and boycotts in mid–1950s, and ch. 9 on the anti–pass campaign at the time of the Sharpeville killings, as well as pp. 328–36 on Soweto and student revolts. Index. Bibliography.)

89.   Luthuli, Albert, *Let My People Go*. 255 pp. New York: McGraw–Hill; London: Collins, 1962. Reprint, New York: Meridian, World, 1969. (Memoir by a leader of the ANC. See ch. 10–14 on the 1952 Defiance Campaign, its origins and aftermath, and ch. 16–18 on the Treason Trial and after. Photos. Appendix. Index.)

90.   Magubane, Bernard Makhosezwe, *The Political Economy of Race and Class in South Africa*. 364 pp. New York and London: Monthly Review Press, 1979. (Ch. 10, 11 are largely on the ANC from its founding to the 1970s. See pp. 299–317 on "extra–parliamentary campaigns" of the ANC until its reassessment of its resistance policy in 1961. Index.)

91.   Peterson, Robert W., ed., *South Africa and Apartheid*. Rev. ed. 244 pp. New York: Facts on File, 1975 [orig. publ. 1971]. (Succinct account of the development of apartheid and opposition to it, 1944–70, including many cases of internal and international nonviolent action. Index.)

92.   Sonkosi, Zola, "African Opposition in South Africa from 1948–1969: An Analysis of the African National Congress of South Africa's Non–Violent and Violent Campaigns." 273 pp. Ph.D. diss., Free Univ. of Berlin, 1975. (Ch. 2–4 discuss campaigns of the 1950s; ch. 7 analyzes tactical problems of nonviolent action as used by ANC; and ch. 9 discusses the transition to violence. See esp. pp. 220–37, where author presents his view of greater effectiveness of violent struggle).

FROM SHARPEVILLE TO SOWETO AND AFTER, 1960–1990

The ANC national protest of 1960 aimed at pass laws limiting the movement and residence of Africans, Indians, and others. Pass refusers surrendered in great numbers at police stations around the country, confounding the system and slowing down the economy. In Sharpeville, police fired on a crowd, killing sixty–seven and injuring hundreds. Subsequent demonstrations were responded to by a state of emergency in which the ANC and Pan–Africanist Congress (PAC) were declared illegal and more leaders imprisoned. The apparent failure of nonviolent action prompted the formation of Umkhonto we Sizwe (Spear of the Nation) as a military offshoot of the ANC. In 1962, shortly after the founding of Umkhonto we Sizwe, Nelson Mandela was arrested, tried, and imprisoned. Demolitions and sabotage increased as mass protest fell temporarily into abeyance.

In 1976, Soweto township protests challenged the state mandate to teach African school pupils in Afrikaans. Police killing of a student protester spurred nationwide protests and subsequent state violence resulted in hundreds more shot and killed, many of them schoolchildren. Shortly after the uprisings, Steve Biko of the South African Students Organization (SASO) and leader of the growing Black Consciousness Movement died in police custody, evidently by mistreatment at the hands of the authorities.

93.   Benson, Mary, *The Sun Will Rise: Statements from the Dock by South African Political Prisoners.* 50 pp. London: International Defence and Aid Fund for Southern Africa, 1974. Rev. ed., 80 pp. London: International Defence and Aid Fund for Southern Africa, 1981. (Brief excerpts of statements made at trials from the Rivonia trial of 1964 to 1978. See esp. Nelson Mandela, Robert Sobukwe, and Wilton Mkawyi on violence, nonviolence, and noncooperation.)

94.   Biko, Steve, *Black Consciousness in South Africa.* Ed. Millard Arnold. 298 pp. New York: Random House, 1978. British ed., *The Testimony of Steve Biko.* 298 pp. [London?]: Maurice Temple Smith, 1978. (Transcript of Steve Biko's May 1978 trial testimony about the Black People's Convention [BPC] and the South African Students Organization [SASO]. See scattered references on p. 73 and following on student strikes, 1972–73; pp. 82–87 on BPC and trade unions; pp. 115–17 on sports and politics; pp. 208–17 on overseas investment; and pp. 265–66 for distinction between protest and confrontation.)

95.   Bunting, Brian, *Moses Kotane: South African Revolutionary.* 309 pp. London: Inkululeko Publications, 1975. (Biography of the general secretary of the South African Communist Party. See ch. 17 for discussion of the shift to emphasis on armed struggle after Sharpeville. Illustrations. Index. Bibliography.)

96.   Callinicos, Alex, *Southern Africa after Zimbabwe.* 178 pp. London: Pluto Press, 1981. (Ch. 6 examines 1979–80 nonviolent actions in South Africa, including the 1979 Ford plant strike against government's relocation efforts and 1980 school and consumer boycotts. Ch. 7 proposes reasons that guerrilla war would be unsuccessful.)

97.   Callinicos, Alex, and John Rogers, *Southern Africa after Soweto.* 2d ed. 246 pp. London: Pluto Press, 1978. (Marxist–informed view of political and economic struggles in Southern Africa, particularly South Africa. See pp. 47–50 for discussion of

economic struggles in 1930s; pp. 54–64 for analysis of stay–at–homes and passive resistance of the early 1960s and failure to involve the masses; pp. 79–87, 168–73 on labor struggles and tactics of the 1970s. Bibliography.)

98.   Cobbett, William, and Robin Cohen, eds., *Popular Struggles in South Africa*. 234 pp. Review of African Political Economy 1988. Trenton NJ: Africa World Press; London: James Curry, 1988. (Articles on the politics of conflict and protest in South Africa focusing on issues, organizations, and specific conflicts. Of the several articles of interest, noteworthy are Mark Swilling, "The United Democratic Front and Township Revolt," ch. 5 and Jonathan Hyslop, "School Student Movements and State Education Policy, 1972–87," ch. 10. Index.)

99.   Counter Information Services, *Black South Africa Explodes*. 63 pp. London: The Transnational Institute, 1977. (Brief chronicle of the Soweto events, depicting a spiral from demonstrations and boycotts to violence. Photos. Bibliography.)

100.   Davis, John A., and James K. Baker, eds., *Southern Africa in Transition*. 455 pp. London: Pall Mall Press, 1966. (See section 6 for two papers on aspects of nonviolent struggle in South Africa before 1963, and section 7 on violence.)

101.   Feit, Edward, *Urban Revolt in South Africa, 1960–1964*. Evanston IL: Northwestern Univ. Press, 1971. (Introduction and ch. 1–4 analyze the theoretical framework of protest, violent and nonviolent struggle, organization of the ANC, and attempts to mobilize mass support. Ch. 5–6 discuss the shift to armed struggle. Bibliography.)

102.   Gerhart, Gail M., *Black Power in South Africa: The Evolution of an Ideology*. 364 pp. Berkeley, Los Angeles, and London: Univ. of California Press, 1978. (Includes pass law defiance. See ch. 7, 9 and esp. pp. 42, 220, 309 for violent versus nonviolent means; pp. 77, 89, 301 on strikes; and pp. 212–56 on "Sharpeville and Quiescence.")

103.   Gibson, Richard, *African Liberation Movements: Contemporary Struggles against White Minority Rule*. 363 pp. New York and

London: Oxford Univ. Press, 1972. (See part 2 for discussions of the role of nonviolent action in the South African struggle and the shift to armed struggle as a strategy. Illustrations. Index. Bibliography.)

104.   Hirson, Baruch, *Year of Fire, Year of Ash: The Soweto Revolt: Roots of a Revolution?* 348 pp. London: Zed Press, 1979. (Analysis of the Soweto revolt. Includes a brief account of nonviolent action. See ch. 3, 4, 7–14 on boycotts, strikes, stay–at–home, and other actions. Bibliography.)

105.   Horrell, Muriel, *Action, Reaction and Counter–Action: A Brief Review of Non–White Political Movements in South Africa.* 156 pp. Johannesburg: South African Institute of Race Relations, 1971. (On the 1900–70 period. See esp. pp. 19–25 on the Defiance Campaign and pp. 27–39, 48–57 on demonstrations in 1950s and early 1960s. Discussion of the structure of apartheid throughout. Index.)

106.   ———, ed., *A Survey of Race Relations in South Africa, 1959– 1960.* 304 pp. Johannesburg: South African Institute of Race Relations, 1961. (Report on events that include boycotts and pass resistance. See pp. 49, 54–68 on Sharpeville and its aftermath, pp. 100–101 on church actions, and pp. 193–95 on strikes by black workers. See also pp. 274–76 on international boycotts and pp. 277–89 on international relations.)

107.   ———, *A Survey of Race Relations in South Africa, 1961.* 309 pp. Johannesburg: South African Institute of Race Relations, 1962. (Report on events that include demonstrations in May 1961, pp. 31–39; church activities, pp. 63–73; and international action, pp. 284–96.)

108.   Johnson, R.W., *How Long Will South Africa Survive?* 328 pp. London and Basingstoke: Macmillan Press, 1977. (South African political history. See ch. 1–3 on Sharpeville, the later recovery, and the role of nonviolent sanctions. Glossary in appendix.)

109.   Kane–Berman, John, *Soweto: Black Revolt, White Reaction.* 268 pp. Johannesburg: Ravan Press, 1978. Reprinted as *South*

Africa: The Method in the Madness. London: Pluto Press, 1979. (Account of the student revolt in Soweto, its causes and effects. See ch. 1, 2, 7–11, 13, 15 [esp. 9 and 10] on nonviolent action, including economic boycotts and protests; pp. 209–15 on parallel government in Soweto; and pp. 218–19 on decline of the nonviolent movement.)

110.   Mandela, Nelson, *No Easy Walk to Freedom*. 189 pp. Reprint, London: Heinemann, 1986 [orig. publ. 1965, 1973]. (Memoirs of imprisoned ANC leader. See pp. 20–31 on the Defiance Campaign of 1952; ch. 7, "Our Struggle Needs Many Tactics," pp. 61–66 on the boycott tactic and the relevance of alternatives; ch. 11 on a general strike in 1961, pp. 94–106; and ch. 13, an apology for violence and argument against nonviolence, pp. 110–21. Photos.)

111.   ———, *The Struggle Is My Life*. Ed. Mary Benson. 208 pp. London: International Defence and Aid Fund for South Africa, 1978. 2d ed. 249 pp. 1986. (Collected speeches and writings the South Africa black leader, former president of ANC, and co–founder of Umkonto We Sizwe [Spear of the Nation]. See pp. 31–42 for actions in the early 1950s, including an address on the 1952 Defiance Campaign; pp. 67–71 for a 1958 address on boycotts and representation; pp. 89–92 for trial testimony on the ANC position on nonviolence; pp. 95–112 on resistance to formation of the republic; pp. 153–65 for 1964 Rivonia trial testimony on the history of African campaigns and nonviolent and violent means; pp. 187–92 on Robben Island prisoners' actions; and pp. 198–210 for prison reflections on violent and nonviolent means. Revised edition adds material on 1961 stay–at–home, pp. 107–18. Photos. Documents. Bibliography.)

112.   Phillips, Norman, *The Tragedy of Apartheid: A Journalist's Experiences in the South African Riots*. 217 pp. New York: David McKay, 1960. (An account of the 1960 resistance, including the Pan Africanist Campaign and the Sharpeville massacre.)

113.   Reeves, Ambrose, *Shooting at Sharpeville: The Agony of South Africa*. 141 pp. London: Victor Gollancz, 1960; Boston: Houghton Mifflin, 1961. (Account of the 1960 demonstration

against passes and police shootings. Chief Luthuli's handbill urging a stay–at–home included. Photos. Documents.)

CHURCHES

Church leaders in South Africa, including (Afrikaner) Dutch Reformed and Anglican and Catholic leaders, have been among apartheid's opponents. A "Message to South Africa," which identified apartheid as immoral, was published in 1968 by the South African Council of Churches. The World Council of Churches also defied the government and provided moral and financial support to the ANC in exile. In addition, South Africa's churches explored the possibility of conscientious objection and draft refusal by white youths unwilling to join in enforcement of the racial system and government policies.

114.   Catholic Institute for International Relations and Pax Christi, *War and Conscience in South Africa: The Churches and Conscientious Objection.* 112 pp. London: Catholic Institute for International Relations and Pax Christi, 1982. (Examination of church–advocated conscientious objection on the part of white South Africans. See ch. 2 on war resistance and ch. 3 on conscientious objection. Documents. Index.)

115.   Center for Intergroup Studies, *Conscientious Objection.* 78 pp. Occasional Paper no. 8. Capetown: The Center for Intergroup Studies, Univ. of Capetown, 1984. (Review of conscientious objection arguments in the context of South African conscription and resistance to it. See pp. 8–11, 63–66 for biographical sketches of convictees; pp. 13–14 on nonviolent action.)

116.   De Gruchy, John W., *The Church Struggle in South Africa.* 267 pp. Grand Rapids MI: William B. Eerdmans, 1979. (Accounts of Cottlesloe, ch. 2; Christian Institute, ch. 3; and Pass Law defiance, Soweto, and conscientious objection, esp. pp. 138–47.)

117.   Hope, Marjorie, and James Young, *The South African Churches in a Revolutionary Situation.* 268 pp. New York: Orbis Books, 1981. (Examines churches' role in South Africa. Includes accounts and discussion of nonviolent action. See esp. ch. 19

and consult index under *boycotts, civil disobedience, labor disputes, noncooperation, nonviolence,* and *nonviolent action.* Index.)

118.   Kirby, Alexander, ed., *The World Council of Churches and Bank Loans to Apartheid.* 90 pp. Geneva: Programme to Combat Racism, World Council of Churches, 1977. (WCC's effort to stop financial cooperation with the South African government by the European–American Banking Corporation. Documents.)

119.   Regehr, Ernie, *Perceptions of Apartheid: The Churches and Political Change in South Africa.* 295 pp. Scottsdale PA: Herald Press, 1979. (Focuses on repression of society and churches, ch. 2, 3; and choice of violent or nonviolent means, ch. 12. Brief accounts of resignations, protests, and noncooperation.)

120.   Sjollema, Baldwin, *Isolating Apartheid: Western Collaboration with South Africa: Policy Decisions by the World Council of Churches and Church Responses.* 112 pp. Geneva: World Council of Churches, 1982. (See ch. 4, 10, 11 and pp. 28–31 on war resisters; and pp. 57–107 on disinvestment actions. Documents.)

121.   Villa–Vicencio, Charles, *Civil Disobedience and Beyond: Law, Resistance, and Religion in South Africa.* 165 pp. Cape Town, S.A.: David Philip; Grand Rapids MI: Wm. B. Eerdmans, 1990. (Religious and theological inquiry into the history and present status of resistance, focusing esp. on civil disobedience, armed struggle, and denunciation of illegitimate government. Ch. 1, 2 trace resistance to white rule from first contact until 1985. Ch. 3 discusses several views of civil disobedience, including "civil disobedience as revolutionary action," pp. 83–85. Index.)

INTERNATIONAL RELATIONS

Apartheid eventually made South Africa the target of international condemnation, partly because of grass–roots action in countries like the United States and within the United Nations. The UN consistently condemned apartheid and the methods employed to perpetuate it. Some of South Africa's trading partners withdrew from the country and institutions divested their shares in the South African economy. Likewise, many governments and firms declined to participate in sanctions and sought opportunities to end them or to profit. Entries in this section are on the feasibility of sanctions and possibilities they might offer for substantial and long–term change. In addition to the more direct forms of political and economic sanctions, anti–apartheid activists have encouraged visibly ostracizing and condemning the regime in the international community by boycotting sports competitions with South African teams and the exclusion of South Africa from organized international sport.

See also: Methods of Nonviolent Action: Sports Boycotts; New Zealand: Protest Against Sports with South African Teams.

122.   Bethlehem, Ronald William, *Economics in a Revolutionary Society: Sanctions and the Transformation of South Africa*. 367 pp. Craighall, S.A.: A.D. Donker, 1988. (Account of the economic crisis of the 1980s and sanctions, supporting the thesis that neither armed force nor sanctions could effectively support the transformation of S.A. to democracy. See ch. 4 on financial sanctions in 1985–86, ch. 5 on wider economic sanctions in 1986–88, and ch. 6 on the "adjustments" in the S.A. economy and their costs to the black population. See also pp. 195–203 for a contrast between "violent confrontation" and "constructive confrontation," which draws in part on Polish Solidarity for a comparison. Postscript is on the crisis of the late 1980s and sanctions. Chronology. Index.)

123.   Bissell, Richard E., *Apartheid and International Organizations*. 231 pp. Boulder CO: Westview Press, 1977. (Examines sanctions by international organizations, including ILO, ECA, WHO, OAU, FAO, and others. See ch. 2–6.)

124.   Clarke, D.G., *Economic Sanctions on South Africa: Past Evidence and Future Potential*. 35 pp. London: Africa Bureau, 1981. (Report on past economic sanctions and their effects on South Africa. See esp. pp. 7–20.)

125.   ———, *Policy Issues and Economic Sanctions on South Africa*. 56 pp. London: Africa Bureau, 1981. (Report surveying materials for debate on sanctions against South Africa.)

126. Crocker, Chester A., *South Africa's Defense Posture: Coping with Vulnerability.* 99 pp. The Washington Papers, no. 84. Beverly Hills and London: Sage Publications, 1981. (See ch. 5 and 6. Ch. 5, sections 2 and 4, describes the South African government's vulnerability to international arms and energy embargo and assesses the effects of the arms sales ban.)

127. Dag Hammarskjöld Library, *Sanctions against South Africa: A Selective Bibliography.* 28 pp. Bibliographical Series, no. 32. New York: United Nations, 1981. (Selective annotated bibliography of sources from 1962–80. In French and English. See section A on sanctions.)

128. De Lint, George J., *The United Nations: The Abhorrent Misapplication of the Charter in Respect of South Africa.* 121 pp. Zwolle, Netherlands: W.E. Tjeenk Willink, 1976. (Examines the "inappropriateness" of U.N. attempts to apply sanctions to South Africa. See ch. 8, 11–13, 18. Appendixes.)

129. Hanlon, Joseph, ed., *South Africa — The Sanctions Report: Documents and Statistics.* 342 pp. London: James Curry; Portsmouth NH: Heinemann, 1990. (Volume of reports and statistics compiled for the foreign ministers of the Commonwealth states. Ch. 1, 2 survey the status of sanctions and related trade statistics. Ch. 3–5 survey the international and domestic contexts of sanctions, while ch. 6 discusses the tightening of sanctions. Index of tables, p. vi.)

130. Hanlon, Joseph, and Roger Omond, *The Sanctions Handbook.* 399 pp. New York: Penguin Books, 1987. (Appraises sanctions policy from British and U.S. perspectives. See "Sanctions Do Work," ch. 22, which offers Rhodesia as a successful example of the power of sanctions. See also "Directory of Sanctions," pp. 300–365 for categorical listing of sanctions with brief summaries of each one's method and degree of effectiveness. Index. Bibliography.)

131. *International Conference on Sanctions against South Africa: UNESCO House, Paris (May 20–27, 1981).* Vol. 1. 73 pp. New York: United Nations Centre against Apartheid, 1981.

(Discusses recommendations for a sanctions program. See esp. pp. 44–48. Documents.)

132.   Khan, Haider Ali, *The Political Economy of Sanctions Against Apartheid*. 115 pp. Boulder CO and London: Lynne Rienner Publishers, 1989. (Ch. 2 discusses the "logic" or presumed effects of sanctions and use of the Social Accounting Matrix to model actual effects. Ch. 4, 5 discuss trade sanctions and disinvestment. Data set in appendix. Index. Bibliography.)

133.   Koenderman, Tony, *Sanctions: The Threat to South Africa*. 278 pp. Johannesburg: Jonathan Ball, 1982. (Assessment of efficacy of sanctions against South Africa, with a review of the general debate on sanctions. Ch. 11 is on sports boycotts and ch. 13 is on counter–sanctions. Bibliography.)

134.   Legum, Colin, and Margaret Legum, *South Africa: Crisis for the West*. 333 pp. London: Pall Mall Press, 1964. (See part 1 on the political situation in South Africa as of 1964. See part 2, esp. ch. 5–10 on economic sanctions against South Africa.)

135.   Leiss, Amelia C., ed., *Apartheid and the United Nations Collective Measures*. 170 pp. New York: Carnegie Endowment for International Peace, 1965. (See esp. William A. Hance, "Efforts to Alter the Future: Economic Action," ch. 6 for a review of potential trade sanctions. Appendix.)

136.   Litvak, Lawrence, Robert DeGrasse, and Kathleen McTigue, *South Africa: Foreign Investment and Apartheid*. 100 pp. Washington DC: Institute for Policy Studies, 1978. (Examines extent and importance of U.S. business for S.A., including a brief discussion of the history and effects of disinvestment; see parts 2, 3.)

137.   Minty, Abdul S., *South Africa's Defence Strategy*. 31 pp. London: Anti–Apartheid Movement, 1970. (Concise examination of foreign involvement in the militarization of South Africa, 1960–69.)

138.   Mogoba, Stanley, John Kane–Berman, and Ronald Bethlehem, *Sanctions and the Alternatives*. 49 pp. Johannesburg, S.A.: South

African Institute of Race Relations, 1988. (Opinion on the outcomes of economic sanctions against South Africa. The first section is on sanctions and economic growth policies, and the second is on the significance of collective action in eroding apartheid.)

139. Moorsom, Richard, *The Scope for Sanctions: Economic Measures against South Africa*. 102 pp. London: Catholic Institute for International Relations, 1986. (Assesses the feasibility of sanctions with respect to South Africa's "external exposure," short and long term effects, and costs to the black population of South Africa and the United Kingdom economy.)

140. Myers, Desaix, III, *Business and Labor in South Africa*. 147 pp. Washington DC: Investor Responsibility Research Service, 1979. (See ch. 6 for brief discussion of international sanctions. Appendixes.)

141. ———, *U.S. Business in South Africa: The Economic, Political, and Moral Issues*. 375 pp. Bloomington IN and London: Indiana Univ. Press, 1980. (Analysis of U.S. business involvement and the use of economic sanctions. See part 1, ch. 3–6; part 3. Appendixes.)

142. *Oil Tankers to South Africa 1980–1981*. 99 pp. Amsterdam: Shipping Research Bureau, 1982. (Report by a bureau set up to support the oil embargo against South Africa, with proposals for action, ch. 5. Illustrations. Documents. Index. Bibliography.)

143. Orkin, Mark, ed., *Sanctions Against Apartheid*. 328 pp. New York: St. Martin's Press, 1989. (Reader on a wide variety of issues associated with sanctions, their effects, and disputes in various countries over joining them. Index.)

144. Scheuttinger, Robert C., ed., *South Africa: The Vital Link*. 120 pp. Washington DC: Council on American Affairs, 1976. (Collected essays by U.S. notables advocating against strategic, economic, or political sanctions.)

145.   Segal, Ronald, ed., *Sanctions Against South Africa*. 272 pp. Middlesex, England; Baltimore MD; and Ringwood, Victoria, Australia: Penguin, 1964. (Papers presented at the International Conference on Economic Sanctions against South Africa.)

146.   Sethi, S. Prakash, ed., *The South African Quagmire: In Search of a Peaceful Path to Democratic Pluralism*. 481 pp. Cambridge MA: Ballinger Publishing, 1987. (Articles, reprints, and commentary by scholars, activists, and officials. See esp. part 3, "The Debate on Economic Sanctions"; part 5, "U.S. Pressure for Sanctions"; and part 6, "European Pressure for Sanctions." Also includes "Bibliography of Publications on South Africa," by Eric Neubauer, pp. 413–44. Index. Bibliography.)

147.   Shepherd, George W., Jr., *Anti–Apartheid: Transnational Conflict and Western Policy in the Liberation of South Africa*. 246 pp. Westport CT and London: Greenwood Press, 1977. (See ch. 3 for the background of international organizations' involvement in anti–apartheid action, ch. 5 on the early phases of the arms embargo, and ch. 7, 9 for the mix of sanctions available to states and organizations, and their effects. Among the sanctions discussed are financial and energy embargoes and the sports boycott of South Africa. See pp. 36–46 for contrast of nonviolent and violent methods, discussed as "pacific" versus "liberation tactics." Index.)

148.   Shepherd, George W., ed., *Effective Sanctions on South Africa*. 148 pp. New York, Westport CT, and London: Greenwood Press, 1991. (Collection of technically–oriented papers on the use and effects of sanctions. See esp. Stephen P. Davis, "Economic Pressure on South Africa: Does It Work?", ch. 4 for overview and assessment. Appendixes include chronologies of arms and economic embargoes, "sanctions–bursting strategies," and a bibliography, each prepared by Timothy U. Mozia. Appendixes. Index. Bibliography.)

149.   Spandau, Arnt, *Economic Boycott against South Africa: Normative and Factual Issues*. 200 pp. Kenwyn, South Africa: Juta & Co., 1977. (Examines the nature and potential effects of various economic and resource boycotts usable against the South

African government and alternative ways to influence change. See ch. 4 on a hypothetical boycott and consequences.)

150.   Turner, Terisa, *Trade Union Action to Stop Oil to South Africa*. 35 pp. Port Harcourt, Nigeria: Univ. of Port Harcourt, 1985. (Description of U.N. oil embargo against S.A. and role of oil–worker involvement in halting flow of oil. See esp. pp. 8–18 on "Direct Action by Trade Unions and Workers to Enforce the Oil Embargo." Section C discusses targeting companies that break the embargo. Appendixes contain various official documents outlining terms and proposed duration of embargo.)

151.   Venter, D.J., *South Africa Sanctions and the Multinationals*. 234 pp. Chichester, Eng.: Carden Pubs., 1989. (Comparison of "punitive" and "confrontational" with "non–confrontational strategies" toward challenging apartheid by means of sanctions. Concludes that the limitations of sanctions offer no evidence that they will "unseat the South African government" and therefore advocates other approaches to modify apartheid. Appendix. Index.)

WOMEN'S STRUGGLES

Certain aspects of the struggle for a nonracial South Africa have been particularly the province of women. Although the majority of women's resistance activities have not been documented, entries below offer some examples. They include protests and noncooperation by African women as well as accounts of the Black Sash organization, a liberal constitutionalist movement of white women.

152.   Bernstein, Hilda, *For Their Triumphs and for Their Tears: Conditions and Resistance of Women in Apartheid South Africa*. 65 pp. [London?]: International Defence and Aid Fund, 1975. (Introduction to women in South Africa. See photos following p. 32. Pp. 40–49, 55, and ch. 8 are on women's involvement in boycotts, protests, strikes, and other action. Photos.)

153.   Lapchick, Richard E., and Stephanie Urdang, *Oppression and Resistance: The Struggle of Women in Southern Africa*. 197 pp.

Westport CT and London: Greenwood Press, 1982. (See pp. 121–37 on women in the labor movement, pp. 137–48 on nonviolent and violent resistance actions by women, and pp. 151–56 on struggles in the townships, including resistance against removals. Photos. Bibliography.)

154.   Michelson, Cherry, *The Black Sash of South Africa: A Case Study in Liberalism*. 204 pp. London, New York, and Capetown: Oxford Univ. Press, 1975. (History of the women's political organization devoted to calling attention to racial injustice in South Africa. See ch. 2, 4 on Black Sash nonviolent protest; pp. 78–80, 189 on a theory of protest.)

155.   Rogers, Mirabel, *The Black Sash: The Story of the South African Women's Defence of the Constitution League*. 256 pp. Johannesburg: Rotonews, 1965. (History of the first years of Black Sash and its growth in opposition to Nationalist Party's circumvention of South Africa's constitution. Illustrations. Documents.)

156.   Strangwayes–Booth, Joanna, *A Cricket in the Thorn Tree: Helen Suzman and the Progressive Party*. 282 pp. (Institutional history, with some discussion of protest movements. See pp. 177–83 on the Anti–Pass Campaign from parliament's viewpoint. See also *protest movements* in index. Bibliography.)

157.   Van Vuuren, Nancy, *Women against Apartheid: The Fight for Freedom in South Africa, 1920–1975*. 133 pp. Palo Alto CA: R and E Research Associates, 1979. (Focuses on political action and repression of women activists. See ch. 7 for brief accounts of nonviolent action since 1960. Appendixes. Bibliography.)

158.   *Women under Apartheid: In Photos and Text*. 119 pp. London: International Defence and Aid Fund for Southern Africa, in co-operation with the U.N. Centre against Apartheid, 1981. (See ch. 5 for photographs of squatter camps and ch. 6, 7 for protests and collective action. Photos.)

LABOR UNDER APARTHEID

During the years when direct political protest and noncooperation were in abeyance, both before and after the Soweto uprising, African labor organizations were a de facto opposition to apartheid. Entries below discuss many of the strikes in which African labor was involved as well as labor–oriented political actions such as bus boycotts and stay–at–homes. Stay–at–homes are a form of mass protest strike conducted just as the name implies, by staying out of work. They have been employed in various causes, including protests against forced removal of Africans from their homes or to pressure for political change.

159. *The Durban Strikes, 1973*. 195 pp. Durban and Johannesburg: Institute for Industrial Education and Ravan Press, 1974; reprint 1976, 1977. (Study of a wave of spontaneous strikes by African workers, the conditions that created them, and their connection with the broader political and social situation in South Africa. See ch. 1 on the course of the strikes; ch. 2, 3, 6 on participants and publics; and ch. 4 on the political setting. Bibliography.)

160. Du Toit, D., *Capital and Labour in South Africa: Class Struggle in the 1970s*. 495 pp. London and Boston: Kegan Paul International, 1981. (See ch. 3, pp. 226–34, for history of African strikes and trade union movement; part 3, esp. pp. 239–324, 396–99, for detailed accounts of 1970s strikes, including Durban, Nautilus, Conac, Heinemann, Armourplate, and Soweto. Bibliography.)

161. Haarlov, Jens, *Labour Regulation and Black Workers' Struggles in South Africa*. 80 pp. Research Report no. 68. Uppsala: Scandinavian Institution of African Studies, 1983. (Ch. 2 describes "mass strikes" in Durban, 1973; Soweto, 1976; and countrywide, 1981. Bibliography.)

162. Luckhardt, Ken, and Brenda Wall, *Organize or Starve! The History of the South African Congress of Trade Unions*. 485 pp. New York: International Publishers, 1980. (Accounts and analysis of general strikes, boycotts, the role of women, and international support. See ch. 5–10, 13–15.)

163.   MacShane, Denis, Martin Plant, and David Ward, *Power! Black Workers, Their Unions and the Struggle for Freedom in South Africa.* 196 pp. Boston: South End Press, 1984. (Begins with a brief chapter on transport strikes in Durban in 1973 and 1984. See ch. 2–4 on the history and recent status of unions and organizing and ch. 7 on women workers. Appendix.)

164.   Murray, Martin J., ed., *South African Capitalism and Black Political Opposition.* 773 pp. Cambridge MA: Schenkman, 1982. (Essays on trade unionism and strikes. See pp. 709–34 on Durban, Heinemann, and Armourplate strikes and pp. 741–50 on Soweto. Bibliography.)

165.   Sachs, E.S. [Solly], *Rebels Daughters.* 238 pp. London: MacGibbon and Kee, 1957. (Personal history by a union leader of white trade unions. References to strikes and strike threats throughout, but see esp. ch. 10–13, 29. Ch. 12, 13 are on "general strikes" in the early 1930s.)

166.   Saul, John S., and Stephen Gelb, *The Crisis in South Africa.* 2nd ed. 245 pp. London: Zed, 1986. Originally published as *The Crisis in South Africa: Class Defense, Class Revolution.* New York: Monthly Review Press, 1981. (See esp. pp. 156–74 focusing on the "mass strike" as a tool of revolution in South Africa and postscript by John S. Saul, "The Crisis Deepens.")

167.   Seidman, Judy, *Facelift Apartheid: South Africa after Soweto.* 83 pp. London: International Defence and Aid Fund for South Africa, 1980. (Brief accounts of 1979 bus boycotts and strikes at Pebco–Ford, General Tire, Adams Paper Mill, and Pebco stay–at–home against relocation, pp. 73–77, 81.)

168.   Shane, S., and J. Farnham, *Strikes in South Africa, 1960–1984.* 76 pp. Pretoria: Human Sciences Research Council, 1985. (Statistical survey of strike activity; in addition to overall view, figures 7–14 and 18–25 report statistics by race. Bibliography.)

169.   Simons, Jack, and Ray Simons, *Class and Colour in South Africa, 1850–1950.* 702 pp. London: International Defence and Aid Fund for Southern Africa, 1983. (History of industrial and racial conflict from 1850 to 1950. See ch. 4, 6, 10, 13, 14, and pp.

156–64. Indexes of "Legislative Measures," "Organizations and Newspapers," and "Selected Names." Bibliography.)

ZAMBIA

Kenneth Kaunda, first head of state of Zambia, was one of several African independence activists influenced by Gandhi and the concept of "positive action." While the ideology of positive action was not the only impetus for nonviolent methods in Zambia's independence campaign, it gained particular attention there as a result of Kaunda's theory of positive action and its limits as a policy of state. Zambia was also in the front lines when sanctions were declared against neighboring Rhodesia.

170. Bates, Robert H., *Unions, Parties, and Political Development: A Study.* 291 pp. New Haven, London: Yale Univ. Press, 1971. (Study of the relationship of the Zambian Mineworkers' Union to development policy, and therefore to governing–party efforts to control strikes. See pp. 32–36 on "discipline" and strikes; pp. 128–34, 214–15 and index on strikes. Appendix 1 comments on strike data. Index. Bibliography.)

171. Berger, Elena L., *Labour, Race, and Colonial Rule: The Copperbelt from 1924 to Independence.* 271 pp. Oxford: Clarendon Press, 1974. (Ch. 8, pp. 137–58, discusses strikes and "rolling strikes" in the copperbelt, 1955–56. See also index under *African Mineworkers Union* and *Strikes, African and European.* Chronology in Appendix C. Illustrations. Index. Bibliography.)

172. Hall, Richard, *Zambia.* 357 pp. London: Pall Mall Press, 1968. (See esp. pp. 157–234 on boycotts, sit–ins, strikes, political noncooperation, demonstrations, and political mobilization from 1953 to Zambia's independence in 1964. Also contains historical background and post–independence analysis. Appendixes.)

173. Kaunda, Kenneth David, *Kaunda on Violence.* Ed. Colin M. Morris. 184 pp. London: Collins, 1980. U.S. title, *The Riddle of Violence.* San Francisco: Harper & Row, 1980. (Informed personal essay in which author struggles with ethical or

absolutist justifications of nonviolent conduct and their opposition to the realities of struggle; explains why he supports liberation struggles.)

174.   ———, *Zambia Shall Be Free: An Autobiography*. 202 pp. London, Ibadan, and Nairobi: Heinemann Educational Books, 1962. (See pp. 45–160; especially pp. 73–80, 84–92, 139–45, 157–59; for accounts of noncooperation against the British. Photos. Appendixes.)

175.   Macpherson, Fergus, *Kenneth Kaunda of Zambia: The Times and the Man*. 496 pp. Lusaka, Nairobi, London, and New York: Oxford Univ. Press, 1974. (Biography and appreciation of Kaunda. See ch. 11 "Non–violence on Trial" and consult index under *non–violent positive action, non–cooperation, Gandhi*, and *political weapons*. Illustrations. Photos. Index. Bibliography.)

176.   Mason, Philip, *Year of Decision: Rhodesia and Nyasaland in 1960*. 282 pp. London, New York, and Cape Town: Oxford Univ. Press, 1960. (See pp. 107–21 on strikes and economic boycotts in Northern Rhodesia in 1955–57 and pp. 203–36 on "the Emergency.")

177.   Mulford, David C., *Zambia: The Politics of Independence, 1957–1964*. 362 pp. London: Oxford Univ. Press, 1967. (For accounts of boycotts, demonstrations, and noncooperation against the Federation, see pp. 26, 36–48, 61–69, 86, 93–103, 111–14, 148–49, 160, 167–69, 198–200. Bibliography.)

178.   Rotberg, Robert I., *The Rise of Nationalism in Central Africa: The Making of Malawi and Zambia, 1873–1964*. 362 pp. Cambridge: Harvard Univ. Press, 1965. (Study of nationalism and independence struggles in British colonial Nyasaland [Malawi] and Northern Rhodesia [Zambia]. See ch. 3, 5–11 on early protests, African associations, and religious agitation. See pp. 161–78 on miners' strikes in the 1940s. The national political movements are discussed in ch. 8, 11. Bibliography.)

179.   Tordoff, William, ed., *Politics in Zambia*. 452 pp. Manchester, England: Manchester Univ. Press, 1974. (Thomas Rasmussen, "The Popular Basis of Anti–Colonial Protest," ch. 2 discusses

local issues in strikes, boycotts, and violence, before and after independence. Richard Sklar, "Zambia's Response to the Rhodesian Unilateral Declaration of Independence," ch. 9 is a detailed political and economic analysis of Zambia's choices during the Rhodesia sanctions episode, including offering havens to guerrillas while also keeping the Rhodesia rail link to S.A. open. Index. Bibliography.)

ZIMBABWE (SOUTHERN RHODESIA)

After the unilateral declaration of independence by Rhodesia's white minority on November 11, 1965, nationalist struggle largely relied on guerrilla forces concentrated in the country's hinterlands. Internationally, however, a serious effort was made to inflict economic sanctions to force the government to capitulate or negotiate. These sanctions appear, both at the time and in subsequent accounts, to have been remarkably ineffective. This lack of effect has been traced to "sanctions busting" and evasion, in continued trade with Rhodesia, and to the limitations of sanctions in reducing the well–being of white Rhodesians.

See also: Methods of Nonviolent Action: International Economic Sanctions.

180.   Doro, Marion E., ed., *Rhodesia/Zimbabwe: A Bibliographic Guide to the Nationalist Period.* 263 pp. Boston: G.K. Hall, 1984. (See sections on "Protest" literature, pp. 50–51; economic sanctions, pp. 121–28; and nationalist movement, pp. 135–46. Index.)

181.   Muzorewa, Bishop Abel Tendekai, *Rise Up and Walk: An Autobiography.* Ed. Norman E. Thomas. 301 pp. London and Ibadan, Nigeria: Evans Brothers, 1978. (Scattered references to protest and civil disobedience, e.g., pp. 58–60, 78–82, 85–86, 119–20, 212–13, and thoughts on nature and role of nonviolent struggle, pp. 82, 104, 174–77, 184–87. Photos. Index.)

Economic Sanctions

182.   Arnold, Guy, *The Last Bunker: A Report on White South Africa Today.* 270 pp. London: Quartet Books, 1976. (Ch. 11, pp. 156–

67, reviews the history of economic sanctions against Rhodesia and ch. 16, pp. 258–69, argues the wisdom and efficacy of both violent and nonviolent actions on the part of black Africans. Bibliography.)

183.   Bell, Ralph Graham, *Rhodesia: Outline of a Nonviolent Strategy to Resolve the Crisis.* 34 pp. London: Housmans, 1968. (Attempt at a plan for "nonviolent intervention" in Rhodesia crisis as it then stood. Introduction and outline of plan are in pp. 9–14 and a "note on the use of nonviolent action" is on pp. 15–16. Subsequent sections discuss logistics, willingness to accept casualties, and training. Bibliography.)

184.   Curtin, Timothy, and David Murray, *Economic Sanctions and Rhodesia.* 56 pp. London: Institute of Economic Affairs, 1967. IEA Research Monograph no. 12. (Study in theory and applied economics of sanctions against Rhodesia. See introduction, pp. 11–12, for brief history and overview and ch. 4 on predicting impact of sanctions.)

185.   Jardim, Jorge, *Sanctions Double Cross: Oil to Rhodesia.* 154 pp. Lisbon: Intervencao, 1978. Originally published as *Rodesia–O Escandalo Das Sancoes.* (Personal view of U.K. oil embargo and sanctions busting written by former envoy of Portuguese Prime Minister Salazar. See pp. 51–62, 140–47 on Rhodesian counter–sanctions against Zambia. Photos.)

186.   Kapungu, Leonard T., *The United Nations and Economic Sanctions Against Rhodesia.* 155 pp. Lexington MA, Toronto, and London: D.C. Heath, 1973. (Discusses background to the Rhodesian crisis, implementation of economic sanctions, Rhodesian responses, and the future of U.N. economic sanctions.)

187.   Kuyper, Pieter Jan, *The Implementation of International Sanctions: The Netherlands and Rhodesia.* 358 pp. The Hague: T.M.C. Asser Institute, Sijhoff & Noordhoff International, 1978. (Case study examining the role of the Netherlands in the U.N. regarding sanctions against Rhodesia and the constraints on imposing sanctions. See ch. 4–6. Index. Bibliography.)

188. Strack, Harry R., *Sanctions: The Case of Rhodesia*. 296 pp. Syracuse: Syracuse Univ. Press, 1978. (Analysis of effectiveness of sanctions against Rhodesia, 1965–77. See ch. 2 on nature and purposes of Rhodesian sanctions and following chapters for evaluation of sanctions in selected areas of activity. Index. Bibliography.)

189. Zacklin, Ralph, "Challenge of Rhodesia: Toward an International Public Policy." *International Conciliation* 575 (1969):1–72. New York: Carnegie Endowment for International Peace; Division of Intercourse and Education. (Part 1 argues for the implementation of an international public policy; part 2 outlines the U.N.'s "homeopathic" approach to sanctions against Rhodesia as an example; and part 3 assesses the reasons for its failure.)

190. ———, *The United Nations and Rhodesia: A Study of International Law*. 188 pp. New York, Washington, and London: Praeger, 1974. (Part 2 describes the origins of the sanctions approach from the viewpoint of U.N. law and politics and part 3 analyzes the implementation of sanctions through U.N. agencies. Appendixes.)

Section II
North Africa and the Middle East

Continued Western fascination with the Middle East took on a political and imperial dimension in the nineteenth century when several European countries competed for positions of influence. After World War I, Britain alone retained its influence, based partly on its control of Palestine. This period also saw the rise of nationalism (as in EGYPT and IRAN early in the century) as well as the internationalism of the Arab identity. In addition, the emigration of Jews to PALESTINE supported the creation of new institutions there, from the kibbutzim to growing Jewish towns. Nearly every entry below is concerned with this mix of colonialism, nationalism, competition for resources, and the conflicts arising out of it. Also, disputes in the Middle East often have an international aspect to them. An example is the Arab League boycott of Israel, in which Arab countries have combined to bring economic sanctions against Israel and its international supporters.

191.   Crow, Ralph E., Philip Grant, and Saad E. Ibrahim, eds., *Arab Nonviolent Struggle in the Middle East*. 128 pp. Boulder CO: Lynne Rienner Publishers, 1990. (Essays on ideological, historical, and strategic aspects of nonviolent struggle in the Middle East, several of which focus on the question of whether "nonviolence" has a place in Islam or in the contemporary struggle. Of interest are Khalid Kishtainy, "Violent and Nonviolent Struggle in Arab History," ch. 2; Chaiwat Satha-Anand [Qader Muheideen], "The Nonviolent Crescent: Eight Theses on Muslim Nonviolent Action," ch. 3 which explores justifications in Islamic thought for nonviolent action; Brad Bennett, "Arab–Muslim Cases of Nonviolent Struggle," ch. 4 containing brief sketches of eight examples of nonviolent action by and on behalf of Muslims; and Philip Grant, "Nonviolent Political Struggle in the Occupied Territories," ch. 5 which traces the origins and early phases of the Palestinian *intifadah*. Brief appendixes on the technique of nonviolent action are Gene Sharp, "The Role of Power in Nonviolent Struggle," pp. 91–106 and Ronald M. McCarthy, "The Techniques of Nonviolent Action: Some Principles of Its Nature, Use, and Effects," pp. 107–20. Appendixes. Index. Bibliography.)

ARAB LEAGUE BOYCOTT OF ISRAEL

Hostilities between the Arab states and Israel continued after the 1948 war between them and resulted in several other wars. The Arab League also pursued hostilities through an ongoing international commercial boycott of Israel. To enforce the boycott, the League declared that no business firm that had economic relations with Israel would be permitted to do business with Arab League states. Consequently, in addition to the direct boycott of Israel (primary boycott), there was also a boycott of firms that traded with Israel (secondary boycott), and at times a further boycott of firms doing business with blacklisted companies (tertiary boycott). Even though it was illegal in the U.S. and other countries to honor the boycott, many firms apparently did so, and a bureaucracy was created (both by the League and by those countries that declared the boycott illegal) in order to track compliance.

192.   Chill, Dan S., *The Arab Boycott of Israel: Economic Aggression and World Reaction*. 121 pp. New York: Praeger, 1976. (Study of operation, structure, and effects of the Arab boycott of Israel from the 1945 Arab League declaration. Documents. Index. Bibliography.)

193.   Hotaling, Edward, *The Arab Blacklist Unveiled*. 288 pp. N.P.: Landia, 1977. ("Research report" on Arab boycott of Israel and other nations. Includes brief introduction and description, pp. 1–26. List of companies and ships targeted by the boycott. Documents.)

194.   Joyner, Nelson T., Jr., *Arab Boycott/Anti–Boycott: The Effect on U.S. Business*. 160 pp. McLean VA: Rockville Consulting Group, 1976. (Report on Arab boycott and its effect on U.S. businesses. See p. 1 for brief discussion of "shadow boycott," pp. 3–4 on "explicit boycott," and pp. 5–7, 61–91 on anti–boycott activities. Appendix B lists "boycotts through history.")

195.   Mersky, Roy M., ed., *Conference on Transnational Economic Boycotts and Coercion: Feb. 19–20, 1976, Univ. of Texas Law School*. 2 vols. 819 pp. Dobbs Ferry NY: Oceana Publications, 1978. (Papers presented at conference on Arab boycott of Israel. Vol. 1 includes introductory papers and papers on the

legal and civil rights issues of the Arab boycott. Vol. 2 includes Arab and U.S. documents, brief bibliography, and legal materials.)

196.   Nelson, Walter Henry, and Terence C.F. Prittie, *The Economic War against the Jews.* 269 pp. New York: Random House, 1977. (Study of various economic sanctions employed by Arab nations against Israel. See ch. 2 on boycotts. See also index under *boycotts, Central Office for the Boycott, international boycotts, oil: embargo of, primary and secondary boycotts,* and *tertiary boycotts.* Index.)

197.   Sarna, Aaron J., *Boycott and Blacklist: A History of Arab Economic Warfare against Israel.* 270 pp. Totowa NJ: Rowman & Littlefield, 1986. (History of Arab economic sanctions against Israel. Part 1 is on history and current practice, and part 2 covers anti–boycott policies. Documents in appendixes. Index.)

198.   Sharif, Amer A., "A Statistical Study on the Arab Boycott of Israel," 19 pp. Beirut, Lebanon: Institute for Palestine Studies, 1970. (Effort to assess condition of Arab states' boycott of Israel statistically.)

199.   Teslik, Kennan Lee, *Congress, The Executive Branch, and Special Interests: The American Response to the Arab Boycott of Israel.* 280 pp. Westport CT and London: Greenwood Press, 1982. (Examination of the expansion of the Arab boycott of Israel circa 1974 and the tensions it created between support for Israel and U.S. oil interests. See ch. 5 on the influence of interest groups over enactment of anti–boycott legislation. Appendix. Index. Bibliography.)

200.   U.S. Congress. House. Committee on Interstate and Foreign Affairs. Subcommittee on Oversight and Investigation. *The Arab Boycott and American Business.* 94th Cong., 2d sess., 1976. H502-37. 115 pp. (Congressional investigation into boycott of Israel by Arab states. Explores relevance of U.S. civil rights laws and antitrust laws to foreign boycotts. See ch. 2 on history of Arab boycott and pp. 29–46 on its conduct. Documents. Appendixes. Bibliography, pp. 57–58.)

OPEC OIL BOYCOTT (EMBARGO), 1973

The Organization of Petroleum Exporting Countries (OPEC), a cartel for control of international commerce in oil, consisted mostly of Arab states at the time of the 1973 war between Israel and its Arab neighbors. Many North American, European, and other industrialized states supported Israel in this war. OPEC then tried to sanction these countries based upon their economic dependence on petroleum by conducting an embargo on oil shipments lasting several months. Some countries, such as The Netherlands, were singled out for particularly harsh punishment, perhaps as an object lesson to the others. In the wake of the embargo, international oil prices rose, at least for a time. However, the long–term prospects of OPEC proved to be a weakening, not an increase, of its powers, and a reduction of its political influence in favor of economic interests.

201.   Ahrari, Mohammed E., *The Dynamics of Oil Diplomacy: Conflict and Consensus.* 439 pp. New York: Arno Press, 1980. (Analytical examination of relations between oil–producing countries and oil–consuming countries. Ch. 6 on Arab Oil Embargo 1973 and its success. Bibliography.)

202.   Ali, Sheikh Rustum, *Saudi Arabia and Oil Diplomacy.* 197 pp. New York and London: Praeger, 1976. (See ch. 5–7 on oil embargoes. Appendix. Bibliography.)

203.   ———, *OPEC: The Failing Giant.* 256 pp. Lexington: University Press of Kentucky, 1986. (Ch. 5 analyzes the embargo and its effects. See also index under *oil embargo, Arab.* Chronology. Index.)

204.   Allen, Loring, *OPEC Oil.* 287 pp. Cambridge MA: Oelgeschlager, Gunn & Hain, 1979. (See pp. 6–21, 84–85 on war, the use of the "oil weapon" in 1973, and its effects on prices. Pp. 13–14 are on factors weakening the effects of embargo. Also discusses economic problems of cartels, e.g., ch. 11. Index. Bibliography.)

205.   Doran, Charles F., *Myth, Oil, and Politics: Introduction to the Political Economy of Petroleum.* 226 pp. New York: Free Press; London: Collier Macmillan, 1977. (Pp. 104–8 contain

observations on the possibility of "deterrence" of future embargoes. See also index under *boycott, embargo*. Index.)

206.   Paust, Jordan J., and Albert P. Blaustein, with Adele Higgins, *The Arab Oil Weapon*. 370 pp. Dobbs Ferry NY: Oceana Publications; Leyden: A.W. Sijthoff, 1977. (Part 1 contains documents and commentary on the 1973 embargo, emphasizing legal questions. See also pp. 255–62 for data and analysis on possible U.S. food embargo as response to oil boycott. Documents.)

207.   Rustow, Dankwart A., *Oil and Turmoil: America Faces OPEC and the Middle East*. 320 pp. New York and London: W.W. Norton, 1982. (Pp. 152–79 discuss the "oil weapon." See also index under *oil embargo, Iranian Revolution*, and *strikes, oil*. Index.)

208.   Schneider, Steven A., *The Oil Price Revolution*. 630 pp. Baltimore MD and London: Johns Hopkins Univ. Press, 1983. (See ch. 8 on the politics of the oil embargo and associated price rise. Index.)

209.   Terzian, Pierre, *OPEC: The Inside Story*. Trans. Michael Pallis. 325 pp. London: Zed Books, 1985. (See ch. 8, 9 on the politics and diplomacy of the 1973 embargo and related events. Index.)

210.   Vernon, Raymond, ed., *The Oil Crisis*. 301 pp. New York: W.W. Norton, 1976. (See Klaus Knorr, "The Limits of Economic and Military Power," pp. 229–43 for an interpretation of the embargo from the viewpoint of its power potential. Other chapters review economic sources and state and corporate actors in oil markets. Appendixes. Index.)

211.   Weisberg, Richard Chadbourn, *The Politics of Crude Oil Pricing in the Middle East, 1970–1975: A Study in International Bargaining*. 170 pp. Berkeley: Institute of International Studies, Univ. of California, 1977. (See pp. 41–50 on strategy and economic sanctions in 1970, and ch. 6, "The 1973–1974 Arab Oil Embargo." Bibliography.)

EGYPT

The British presence in Egypt (1882–1922) was met by Egyptians with increased nationalist activity at the time of World War I. In addition to violence and attacks, nationalists used various forms of "passive resistance," such as demonstrations and strikes. This was especially true in the aftermath of an uprising that was suppressed by Britain in 1919. The result ultimately was independence for Egypt in 1922.

212.   Chirol, Sir Valentine, *The Egyptian Problem*. 331 pp. London: Macmillan, 1920. (See ch. 11 on "passive rebellion," which concludes that the April 1919 strikes and demonstrations "had more enduring results" than earlier violence, p. 204. Index.)

213.   Harris, Christina Phelps, *Nationalism and Revolution in Egypt: The Role of the Muslim Brotherhood*. 276 pp. The Hague, London, and Paris: Mouton, in association with the Hoover Institution on War, Revolution, and Peace, Stanford CA, 1964. (See esp. ch. 2, pp. 91–97, and background on British rule. Index. Bibliography.)

214.   Young, George, *Egypt*. 352 pp. New York: Charles Scribner's Sons; London: Ernest Benn, 1927. (Ch. 8, esp. pp. 238–54, discusses 1919 riots, which were followed by "passive resistance," strikes, and noncooperation. Index.)

215.   Zayid, Mahmud Y., *Egypt's Struggle for Independence*. 258 pp. Beirut: Khayats, 1965. (Ch. 3, 4 present a political history of the 1919–23 period against a background of protest resignations, officials' boycotts, and the strikes and demonstrations of the revolt. Appendix. Index. Bibliography.)

IRAN

Iranians have conducted resistance and protest movements against several forces, from British moves to dominate the country in the late nineteenth century to the revolution of 1979. Themes to look for in each case are those of Iran's religious heritage of Shi'a Islam, actions against foreign domination, and opposition to the governments of the Shahs..

Tobacco Boycott and Revolution, 1891–1909

European penetration of Iran in the late nineteenth century included demands for trade concessions. Political and religious resistance to these included an organized boycott of the British–monopolized tobacco trade in the 1890s. In later years, religious and civic sectors demanded constitutional reforms from the British–supported shah, a movement that lead to a new constitution following demonstrations, protests, and the organized withdrawal of the religious sector into the mosques and religious schools.

216.   Browne, Edward G., *The Persian Revolution of 1905–1909*. 470 pp. Cambridge: Cambridge Univ. Press, 1910. (See ch. 2, "The Tobacco Concession and Its Consequences" for summary of events that led to boycott. Pp. 52–57 describes the boycott itself and the instrumental role that the religious establishment played in rallying the Persian people. Photos. Index.)

217.   Keddie, Nikki R., *Religion and Rebellion in Iran: The Tobacco Protest of 1891–1892*. 163 pp. London: Frank Cass, 1966. (On the causes and conduct of protests centering on the British tobacco concession in Iran, see esp. ch. 3. Appendixes. Index. Bibliography.)

218.   Nirumand, Bahman, *Iran: The New Imperialism in Action*. Trans. Leonard Mins. 192 pp. New York and London: Monthly Review Press, 1969. (Critical study of both Western policy toward Iran and its support for the brutality of the then–ruling Shah's regime. For examples of demonstrations by Iranian civilians, see pp. 22, 37, 90, 119, 154–157. See also "The Oil Boycott," pp. 68–73, for details of British plan to boycott Iran in order to defeat Mossadeq's plan to nationalize Iran's oil industry. Chronology.)

219.   Shuster, W. Morgan, *The Strangling of Persia*. 423 pp. New York: Century, 1912. (Western financial expert's report on the then–present state of political and economic affairs of Iran. See introduction, pp. xvii–xxi on the revolution of 1905–1906 and the role of commercial boycotts in earlier conflicts. Text of the constitution of December 30, 1906, on pp. 337–55.)

Revolution Against the Shah, 1979–1980

Disputes over religion and the authority of religious teachings and leaders were very significant in creating the opposition to the regime of Shah Reza Pahlavi, beginning in the 1970s. These included demonstrations in mid–decade in the holy city of Qum, the site of important religious schools. In later years, both leftist and religious rebels came to believe that the Shah's forces could be overwhelmed by street demonstrations, actions in which they were joined by students and the disenchanted commercial classes. Despite the post–revolutionary violence of the new regime and its foes, this approach of mass protest was significant as a political strategy of the anti–Shah forces.

220.   Abrahamian, Ervand, *Iran between Two Revolutions.* 537 pp. Princeton NJ: Princeton Univ. Press, 1982. (See pp. 496–537 for a summary of the events which led to the overthrow of the Shah, including more vocal emergence of opposition groups and subsequent strikes and public demonstrations. Index. Bibliography.)

221.   Albert, David H., ed., *Tell the American People: Perspectives on the Iranian Revolution.* 2d ed. 212 pp. Philadelphia PA: Movement for a New Society, 1980. (See chronology and Lynne Shivers, "Inside the Iranian Revolution." Photos.)

222.   Bashiriyeh, Hossein, *The State and Revolution in Iran, 1962–1982.* 203 pp. London and Canberra: Croom Helm; New York: St. Martin's Press, 1984. (Analysis of Iranian revolution, emphasizing causes of revolution and phases. Ch. 5–7 cover revolutionary years. See index under *demonstrations, mobilisation, strikes,* and *students.* Index. Bibliography.)

223.   Fischer, Michael M.J., *Iran: From Religious Dispute to Revolution.* 244 pp. (Discusses Qum demonstrations of 1975 and revolutionary movement, 1979–80, in context of growing religious disputes. See pp. 123–24, 181–231. Illustrations. Photos. Index. Bibliography.)

224.   Green, Jerrold D., *Revolution in Iran: The Politics of Countermobilization.* 150 pp. New York: Praeger Publishers, 1982. (Contends on p. xi that the revolution was "for the most part nonviolent." Analyzes revolution in terms of theory of

causes of revolution and participation. Chronology. Index. Bibliography.)

225.   Keddie, Nikki R., *Roots of Revolution: An Interpretive History of Modern Iran*. 321 pp. New Haven and London: Yale Univ. Press, 1981. (See ch. 9, pp. 231–58, for account of the revolution, including violent and nonviolent actions. Photos. Bibliography.)

226.   Saikal, Amin, *The Rise and Fall of the Shah*. 279 pp. Princeton NJ: Princeton Univ. Press, 1980. (See pp. 193–97 for protests, strikes, and Shah's response. Photos. Bibliography.)

227.   Stempel, John D., *Inside the Iranian Revolution*. 324 pp. Bloomington: Indiana Univ. Press, 1981. (Chronological account by U.S. Foreign Service officer. Stresses the role of Marxism and "militant opposition" as well as the "weakness" of the Shah. See ch. 5–9.)

228.   Sullivan, William H., *Mission to Iran*. 287 pp. New York and London: W.W. Norton; Toronto: George J. McLeod, 1981. (U.S. ambassador's account of political resistance to Shah, his responses, and U.S. policy. See ch. 15–25. Photos. Index.)

ISRAEL

Studies of the role of protest within Israeli political life are generally of two kinds, one concerned with protest by citizens who see themselves without a voice in normal political life and the other concerned with resistance to war and militarization. Most references here are on the first kind, especially the protests of those who see themselves as affected by policy yet unable to influence it as they wish.

See also: Arab League Boycott of Israel; Palestinians and the Intifadah, 1967–1972.

229.   Blatt, Martin, Uri Davis, and Paul Kleinbaum, eds., *Dissent and Ideology in Israel: Resistance to the Draft, 1948–1973*. 211 pp. London: Ithaca Press, 1975. (Interviews with war resisters in

of war resistance in Israel; also glossary, which includes descriptions of major leaders and organizations of war resistance in Israel.)

230. Cohen, Stuart A., and Eliezer Don–Yehiya, eds., *Conflict and Consensus in Jewish Political Life*. 218 pp. Comparative Jewish Politics, vol. 2. Israel: Bar–Ilan Univ. Press, 1986. (Sam Lehman–Wilzig, "Conflict as Communication: Public Protest in Israel, 1950–1982," pp. 128–45 explores the hypothesis that internal protest in Israel undertakes citizenry–government communication in a situation characterized by "lack of formal opportunities for political communication" [p. 141].)

231. Weisburd, David, *Jewish Settler Violence: Deviance as Social Reaction*. 164 pp. University Park PA and London: Pennsylvania State Univ. Press, 1989. (Research on vigilante violence by members of Gush Emunim–sponsored West Bank settlements, in which such violence is viewed as a question of social deviance and social control; consequently without detail on the violence itself. See, however, ch. 4, 5 on vigilantism toward Arabs as an effort at social control and pp. 26–49 on settlements, social control, and changing governmental policy. Index. Bibliography.)

232. Wolfsfeld, Gadi, *The Politics of Provocation: Participation and Protest in Israel*. 210 pp. Albany: State Univ. of New York Press, 1988. (Traces increased use of protest as a political tool in Israel to citizens' "sense of blocked opportunities" for influence in politics. See history in pp. 11–19 and research approach in ch. 2. Ch. 3, 4 view protest readiness from the standpoint of individual attitudes. Ch. 5, 6 discuss the mobilization and forms of collective action, including case studies in ch. 6 of a protest against the Israeli ceding of the town of Yamit as part of the Camp David Sinai agreement with Egypt, protests against the invasion of Lebanon in 1982, community protest in a Tel Aviv suburb, and a religious protest group. Ch. 7 discusses the correlates of protest and ch. 8 attempts to integrate findings into a theory of political activity. Index. Bibliography.)

PALESTINE

Palestine, a region on the shores of the eastern Mediterranean Sea extending to what is now Jordan, was for centuries a part of the Ottoman Empire and consequently was ruled from Turkey. During the late nineteenth century, Jews from Europe and some other places migrated to Palestine to live. For some years, there was relatively little strife between resident Palestinians and Jews. Economic competition led to some disagreements, but the end of World War I introduced a major change because Great Britain became the new power in the region when the victorious European countries divided the old Ottoman regions into new states and areas of influence. Britain, governing with a mandate from the League of Nations, appeared to some Jewish groups to be a power that could help them, partly because a declaration named for Foreign Secretary Arthur Balfour gave support, at least in name, for a Jewish state. Struggle among the three parties occurred notably in four periods. The first was a general strike and uprising by Palestinians starting in 1936, while the second involved Jewish efforts to bring immigrants into Palestine during World War II, at a time when Britain forbade immigration. In 1948, the formation of the state of Israel initiated the third stage, a semi–permanent state of war between Israel and the Arab states. In 1967, Israel took over territory on the West Bank of the Jordan River during one of these wars and consequently now ruled over Palestinians residing there. This led to the fourth phase of conflict, ranging from low–level Palestinian resistance to the extension of Israel powers to the intifadah of 1989–1992.

General Strike, 1936

Of the two forces struggling with Britain over the shape of post–World War I Palestine (local Palestinian Arabs and Jewish immigrants), the Palestinians were the first to turn to militant opposition. Perceiving that the British Mandate and Jewish economic gains lessened their own opportunities, Palestinian nationalists conducted a lengthy general strike and uprising starting in 1936. Some students of the period maintain that the general strike had the paradoxical effect of strengthening Jewish economic institutions, since it compelled them to become more self–sufficient and reduced their economic ties to Palestinians.

233.   Abu–Lughod, Ibrahim, ed., *The Transformation of Palestine: Essays on the Origin and Development of the Arab–Israeli Conflict.*

522 pp. Evanston IL: Northwestern Univ. Press, 1971. (Barbara Kalkas, "The Revolt of 1936: A Chronicle of Events," pp. 237–74 discusses the general strike of 1936 and the "triangle" of Palestinian, British, and Jewish involvement. Index. Bibliography.)

234. Hurewitz, J.C., *The Struggle for Palestine*. 404 pp. New York: Schocken Books, 1976 [orig. publ. 1950.] (Ch. 5, 6 discuss violent and nonviolent action within the Palestinian nationalist movement, esp. pp. 68–72 on general strike. Index. Bibliography.)

235. Kayyali, A.W., *Palestine: A Modern History*. 243 pp. London: Croom Helm, [1978?]. (See ch. 7 on political aspects of general strike and other nationalist nonviolent and violent actions. Index. Bibliography.)

236. Lesch, Ann Mosely, *Arab Politics in Palestine, 1917–1939: The Frustration of a Nationalist Movement*. 257 pp. Ithaca and London: Cornell Univ. Press, 1979. (History of Palestinian nationalism from 1917 to 1939. See ch. 4, 5 on mobilization, and ch. 9, "The Political Use of Violence," esp. pp. 217–21 on general strike. Index. Bibliography.)

237. Marlowe, John, *Rebellion in Palestine*. 279 pp. London: Cresset Press, 1946. (See ch. 10, "The Rebellion: First Phase," esp. pp. 150–72, for origins of general strike and its objectives. Appendixes. Index.)

238. Quandt, William B., Fuad Jabber, and Ann Mosely Lesch, *The Politics of Palestinian Nationalism*. 234 pp. Berkeley, Los Angeles, and London: Univ. of California Press, 1973. (History of Palestinian nationalism from 1917. See Ann Mosely Lesch, "The Palestinian Arab Nationalist Movement under the Mandate," part 1, esp. pp. 25–29 on "peaceful resistance" of the mid-1920s, and pp. 34–40 on general strike of 1936. Index. Bibliography.)

Illegal Immigration of Jews During British Mandate, 1944–1948

Jewish immigration into Palestine became an issue of survival in the period just before and during World War II, as Jewish organizations conducted Jews compelled to leave their European homes into the routes that led to the Middle East. Britain's response was to declare an halt to immigration as a sort of moratorium to allow breathing room while policies were reviewed. The Jewish emigration organizations countered by "illegally" bringing people to Palestine by any means they could find, especially through secret voyages, mass landings, and flooding internment camps on Cyprus where the British housed people stopped from going into Palestine. In addition to accounts of the struggle over immigration, entries below contain information on assistance to escaping Jews and, very commonly, refusal by governments to assist Jewish refugees from war, Holocaust, and the chaos of post–war Europe.

See also: Europe: Jewish Resistance; Hiding and Rescue of Jews.

239. Auriel, Ehud, *Open the Gates! A Personal Story of "Illegal" Immigration to Israel.* 369 pp. New York: Atheneum, 1975. (Memoir by participant in rescue work organized by Haganah underground, or "Mossad," from 1938 to 1948. See index under *"illegal" immigration to Palestine.* Index.)

240. Bethell, Nicholas, *The Palestine Triangle: The Struggle for the Holy Land, 1935–48.* 384 pp. New York: G.P. Putnam's Sons, 1979. (See ch. 3, 10 on illegal immigration, also pp. 113–17, 272–77, 313–15, and photos between p. 96 and p. 97. Illustrations. Index. Bibliography.)

241. Cohen, Michael J., ed., *The Holocaust and Illegal Immigration, 1939–1947.* 365 pp. New York and London: Garland Publishing, 1987. (Part of a documentary series on the origins of Israel, containing documents on Britain's maintenance and enforcement of its anti–immigration policy during the years of war and Holocaust.)

242. Dekel, Ephraim, *B'riha: Flight to the Homeland.* 352 pp. Trans. Dina Ettinger; ed. Gertrude Hirschler. New York: Herzl Press, [n.d.]. (History and analysis of B'riha, illegal immigration of

Jews from Europe to Palestine with country–by–country studies. See "What Was B'riha?", pp. 29–43. Photos include DP camp demonstration, travel, arrival in Palestine. Chronology, pp. 7–13. Index.)

243. Eliav, Arie L., *The Voyage of the Ulua.* 191 pp. Trans. Israel I. Taslit. New York: Funk and Wagnalls, 1969. (Personal account of sailing of illegal immigrant vessel *Ulua* by commander of operation. See pp. 107–8 for official noncooperation in Denmark and pp. 110–15 for Swedish assistance.)

244. Gefen, Aba, *Unholy Alliance.* 277 pp. New York: Yuval Tal, 1973. (Story of the author's experiences in hiding during the WWII years, his flight from Poland, and work with *Brichah* from a base in Salzburg, Austria in 1945–47, along with the extraordinary political barriers endured by the rescue work. Photos.)

245. Holly, David C., *Exodus 1947.* 306 pp. Boston and Toronto: Little, Brown, 1969. ("Biography" of ship that became *Exodus 1947.* See parts 5, 6 for details of operation and voyage. Photos. Index. Bibliography.)

246. Kimche, Jon, and David Kimche, *The Secret Roads: The "Illegal" Migration of a People 1938–1948.* 223 pp. New York: Farrar, Straus & Cudahy, 1955. (History of Jewish mass emigration from Europe to Palestine; including breaking of British immigration ban. See esp. ch. 10 on 1946 Spezia camp hunger strike, including photo facing p. 128; ch. 11 on question of violent response and discovery of an alternative; ch. 12 on the *Exodus* affair; and ch. 13 on aftermath, including pp. 208–9 on "flooding" the Cyprus internment camps. Illustrations. Photos. Index.)

247. Mardor, Munya, *Haganah.* 295 pp. Trans. H.A.G. Schmuckler; ed. D.R. Elston. New York: New American Library, 1964. First Hebrew edition, 1957. (Personal story of Haganah, underground "illegal" Jewish resistance organization. See part 2 on illegal immigration as tactic. Index.)

248.   Ofer, Dalia, *Escaping the Holocaust: Illegal Immigration to the Land of Israel, 1939–1944.* 408 pp. New York and Oxford: Oxford Univ. Press, 1990. (Political history of illegal immigration of Jews from WWII–era Europe into British Palestine. Divided into three sections; the pre–war period, the first years of WWII, and the period beginning with the inception of the German final–solution policy in 1942. See ch. 1, 2, 4, 7, and 11 especially for political and policy aspects, including debates in Zionist circles. Other chapters focus on organizations and their actions. Photos. Index. Bibliography.)

249.   Perl, William R., *Operation Action: Rescue from the Holocaust.* 414 pp. New York: Frederick Ungar Publishing, 1983. Rev. ed. of *The Four–Front War: From the Holocaust to the Promised Land.* 376 pp. New York: Crown Publishers, 1978. (Detailed account of networks undertaking the transport of Jewish refugees to Palestine even before WWII began. Largely from the personal knowledge of the author, who was a member of the Viennese rescue group *Die Aktion.* Appendix, pp. 405–9, contains a list of 62 voyages from 1937–44, their organizers, and their results. Photos. Index.)

250.   Sachar, Abram L., *The Redemption of the Unwanted: From the Liberation of the Death Camps to the Founding of Israel.* 334 pp. New York: St. Martin's/Marek, 1983. (Ch. 6 on B'richa, the illegal Jewish rescue organization, and ch. 7 on illegal immigration. Index. Bibliography.)

Palestinians and the Intifadah, 1967–1992

The war of 1967 ended with Israel holding new territory, especially parts of Jerusalem, the West Bank of the Jordan River (formerly under Jordan), and a Palestinian–settled area in Gaza. Asserting its national security needs and other justifications, the Israeli government determined to control and rule these areas. Israel responded with severity to opposition to their administration and its methods as well as to the taking of land. Palestinian opposition, protest, and resistance culminated in the "intifidah" that began in 1987. Palestinian writers describe the attitude of resistance before 1987, which they called "sumud," or standing fast, as a kind of defensive posture against Israel's policies in the West Bank. In the intifidah, Palestinian activists turned to a great variety of methods of opposition, both nonviolent and violent, to shake Israeli control over the region and its life, as did Israel in turn in its methods of suppression and control of the uprising.

251.   Al–Haq, Law in the Service of Man, *Punishing a Nation: Human Rights Violations during the Palestinian Uprising, December 1987– December 1988.* 299 pp. Boston: South End Press, 1990. (Report prepared by the legal group *Al–Haq*, documenting methods of suppression, control, and punishment, both individual and collective, as determined by the organization's representatives. Ch. 1 is on the methods of the Israeli military, focusing on the use of violence, ch. 2 is on the withholding of medical treatment to the injured and more broadly of health care to the populace, and ch. 3 is on the role played by settlers. In the second part, administrative and legal sanctions are detailed, including non–judicial expulsion, detention, demolition of houses, and curfews. Ch. 6 discusses the legal system and conditions under detention. The third part covers Palestinian economic and social structures as objects of repression; including the local economy in ch. 7, the educational system in ch. 8, and labor, political, and social organizations in ch. 9.)

252.   Aronson, Geoffrey, *Creating Facts: Israel, Palestinians, and the West Bank.* 334 pp. Washington DC: Institute of Palestine Studies, 1987. (A political history of Israel's occupation of the West Bank and other areas from 1967 to the invasion of Lebanon, with attention to policies of control and integration as well as Palestinian opposition. Ch. 3, on the years 1967–77, chronicles the alternation of "protest and repression" and "depression" among Palestinians. Ch. 9 picks up the story of efforts at political control of the Palestinians and their opposition, followed by ch. 10 on the repressive "crackdown" that underlay Israeli rule and increasing direct confrontations after ca. 1979. In the following chapters, see pp. 257–66 on "escalation" of conflict in late 1981 and pp. 278–94 on the removal of West Bank mayors and "war on the Palestinians" in 1982. Index.)

253.   Dajani, Souad Rashed, *The Intifadah.* 124 pp. Amman, Jordan: Centre for Hebraic Studies, 1990. (Monograph on occupation methods and resistance, subdivided into sections on Israeli

policy and Palestinian resistance before 1988 and on the *intifadah* viewed as "civilian resistance" against occupation. The first section of part 1 details Israel's occupation policies and methods of punishment and repression. Section B of part 1 divides Palestinian resistance into three areas, "popular resistance," "organized resistance," and "alternative institutions." In part 2, section A presents a model for understanding nonviolent civilian resistance in the *intifadah*, followed in part B by an analysis of the *intifadah* into categories of organization, unity, fearlessness, solidarity, determination, and nonviolent discipline. Index.)

254.   Hudson, Michael C., *The Palestinians: New Directions*. 268 pp. Washington DC: Center for Contemporary Arab Studies, Georgetown Univ., 1990. (Of interest are Salim Tamari, "Revolt of the Petite Bourgeoisie: Urban Merchants and the Palestinian Uprising," ch. 2; Joost R. Hiltermann, "Mass Mobilization and the Uprising: The Labor Movement," ch. 3, as well as articles on Palestinian women, the U.S., the U.S.S.R., Israel, and Jordan as affected by the *intifadah*. Appendix. Index.)

255.   Hunter, F. Robert, *The Palestinian Uprising: A War By Other Means*. 356 pp. 2nd ed. Berkeley and Los Angeles: Univ. of California Press, 1993. (Account rewritten after the *intifadah* was "effectively over." Ch. 3 is on the methods, motives, and organization of the early part of the uprising, ch. 4 is on the Israeli response and Palestinian counteraction, and ch. 5 is on the organization of the later struggle. Ch. 7–9 are on the decline of the *intifadah*. Chronology. Index. Bibliography.)

256.   Peretz, Don, *Intifada: The Palestinian Uprising*. 246 pp. Boulder CO, San Francisco, and London: Westview Press, 1990. (An "overview" of the *intifadah* with attention to its origins, Israel's policies and methods in controlling the uprising, and effects in the Palestinian areas, in Israel, and internationally. Historical background is in ch. 1. Ch. 2 opens with a look at the beginning of the *intifadah* and Israel's "iron fist measures," followed by discussion of "nonviolent civil resistance" on pp. 52–58 and some detail on Israeli methods of repression. The creation of political culture around the uprising is discussed on pp. 83–94, 113–16; effects on Israeli society and soldiers on pp.

119–34; Israeli anti–war groups on pp. 139–43; and effects on U.S. governmental policies and Jewish opinion on pp. 167–81. Appendixes include political documents of the *intifadah*. Photos. Index.)

257.   Shehadeh, Raja, *The Third Way: A Journal of Life in the West Bank*. 143 pp. London, Melbourne, and New York: Quartet Books, 1982. (Stories of life under occupation in 1979–80 intended in part to reveal the nature of *sumud*, or standing fast, in the face of efforts to separate the Palestinians from the land.)

Chapter 2
The Americas

Section I
Latin America and the Caribbean

POLITICAL AND SOCIAL CONFLICT AND REPRESSION

Entries here are concerned largely with the role of nonviolent action in resistance to government and transitions toward democracy from various forms of authoritarian rule. Latin American forms of authoritarianism have often been "patrimonialist" or traditional, meaning the traditionally-oriented personal rule of an individual or sometimes of a clique or family. They have also been "bureaucratic," which suggests that they are situated in institutions, such as the military and military–dominated state sectors. Also in Latin America, ideologies of state security and anti–communism have been turned inward on the society during authoritarian and military regimes, in the sense that the state see itself as surrounded by subversion and radicalism. In such a climate, power–holders see themselves justified in resorting to, and even normalizing, the most extreme means to combat the internal threat. Because of this, extra–judicial punishments and killings, torture, and causing persons to "disappear" have been part of several of the struggles discussed in the entries here. Some material is also included here about conflicts over the condition of the peasantry, industrial labor, and indigenous peoples. The role of the United States and U.S.–based industries in either creating or preventing change is also a significant theme. More recently, issues of unchecked exploitation and environmental destruction have gained significance.

258.   Arias, Esther, and Mortimer Arias, *The Cry of My People: Out of Captivity in Latin America.* 146 pp. New York: Friendship Press, 1980. (Religiously oriented. Much material on repression, as well as fasts in Chile, pp. 61–63, and Bolivia, pp. 90–92; women's strike in Chile, pp. 87–90; and Christian action groups, pp. 104–09. Illustrations. Bibliography.)

259.   Debray, Regis, *A Critique of Arms.* Vol. 1. 315 pp. Middlesex, England; New York; Ontario; Victoria, Australia: Penguin Books, 1977. (Advocacy of author's particular view of revolutionary warfare. See esp. ch. 2, 3 on strategy.)

260.   Duff, Ernest A., John F. McCamant, and Waltraud Q. Morales, *Violence and Repression in Latin America: A Quantitative and Historical Analysis.* 322 pp. New York, London: Free Press, 1976. (Relates the conditions conducive to political violence either by the state or opposition to the conditions conducive to political stability. See ch. 3 for quantification of repression, pp. 24–42, and of violence, pp. 42–52. Note inclusion of apparently nonviolent collective action in definition of violence, pp. 44–47. Index. Bibliography.)

261.   Eckstein, Susan, ed., *Power and Popular Protest: Latin American Social Movements.* 342 pp. Berkeley, Los Angeles, and London: Univ. of California Press, 1989. (Collected case studies of protest and its causes and effects in Latin America. The editor's introduction notes, p. 8, that the focus is on "coordinated and overt nonviolent forms of defiance" and adds that the groups studied here "combine overt with more subtle forms of resistance and defiance, and a few have combined violent with nonviolent protest." In addition to discussion of forms of protest in the introduction, see esp. June Nash, "Cultural Resistance and Class Consciousness in Bolivian Tin–Mining Communities," ch. 5; Marysa Navarro, "The Personal Is Political: Las Madres de Plaza de Mayo," ch. 7; Manuel Antonio Garretón M., "Popular Mobilization and the Military Regime in Chile: The Complexities of the

Invisible Transition," ch. 8; Maria Helena Moreira Alves, "Interclass Alliances in the Opposition to the Military in Brazil: Consequences for the Transition Period," ch. 9; and John Walton, "Debt, Protest, and the State in Latin America," ch. 10. Index.)

262. Goff, James, and Margaret Goff, *In Every Person Who Hopes . . . The Lord Is Born Every Day*. 120 pp. New York: Friendship Press, 1980. (Includes some documents, anecdotes, and memories, often from Catholic journalism sources, plus a vignette of the 1977–78 Bolivian women's group fast, pp. 21–24; and "expressions of protest and hope," such as poems, songs, and prayers, on pp. 76–118. Illustrations.)

263. Horowitz, Irving Louis, Josué de Castro, and John Gerassi, eds., *Latin American Radicalism: A Documentary Report on Left and Nationalist Movements*. 653 pp. New York: Vintage Books, 1969. (See essays on revolutionary violence in part 3, introduced by John Gerassi, "Violence, Revolution, and Structural Change in Latin America," pp. 471–95; esp. criticism of "nonviolent" or "peaceful" revolution, pp. 486–90. Index.)

264. Jerman, William, ed. and trans., *Repression in Latin America: A Report on the First Session of the Second Russell Tribunal, Rome, April 1974*. 163 pp. Nottingham: Spokesman Books, 1975. (Comments and testimony on protest, protest organizations, and repression on pp. 29–32, 34–49, 53–61. Documents.)

265. Johnson, John J., Peter J. Bakewell, and Meredith D. Dodge, eds., *Readings in Latin American History*. Vol. 2, *The Modern Experience*. 464 pp. Durham NC: Duke Univ. Press, 1985. (On Peru, see Steve Stein, "Populism in Peru: APRA, The Formative Years," pp. 80–100, on growth of APRA from strikes of 1923. On Brazil, see Alfred Stepan, "Political Leadership and Regime Breakdown," pp. 125–52, on Joao Goulart's efforts to use mass mobilization in his favor and his response to a naval mutiny in the origins of the 1964 coup.)

266.   Kohl, James, and John Litt, *Urban Guerrilla Warfare in Latin America*. 425 pp. Cambridge and London: MIT Press, 1974. (Essays and documents on urban guerrilla warfare in Latin America, esp. Brazil, Uruguay, and Argentina. Index. Bibliography.)

267.   *Latin America 1972* through *Latin America 1978*. 7 vols. New York: Facts on File, 1973–78. (Data on opposition and revelations of torture by authorities in Brazil and other countries may be found in these yearly compendia. Index.)

268.   Leacock, Eleanor B., et al., *Women in Latin America*. 164 pp. Riverside CA: Latin American Perspectives, 1979. (Marxist analyses of the situation of women, mostly in a Latin American context. Anthologized from the journal *Latin American Perspectives*. See esp. Maria Amalia Irias de Rivera and Irma Violeta Alfaro de Carpio, "Guatemalan Working Women in the Labor Movement," pp. 156–64.)

269.   Lernoux, Penny, *Cry of the People: United States Involvement in the Rise of Fascism, Torture, and Murder, and the Persecution of the Catholic Church in Latin America*. 535 pp. Garden City NY: Doubleday, 1980. (Engaged overview of church activities for social change and violent response in many Latin American countries. See, e.g., pp. 69–80 on El Salvador, pp. 107–19 on Honduras, pp. 244–47 on the Dominican Republic, pp. 327–30 on Brazil, and pp. 336–37 on Argentina. Also ch. 6 on the national security doctrine and accounts of institutionalized terror throughout. Index.)

270.   McManus, Philip, and Gerald Schlabach, eds., *Relentless Persistence: Nonviolent Action in Latin America*. 312 pp. Philadelphia PA, Santa Cruz CA, and Gabriola Island BC: New Society Publishers, 1991. (Editors place these brief selections on historical and contemporary nonviolent action within a context of "active nonviolence," a Christian pacifist approach. Many readings, however, are essentially on the technique of nonviolent action as employed in Latin America in a variety of conflicts. Of interest are Pablo Stanfield, "Guatemala: When Spring Turned to Winter," ch. 1 on the civic strike and revolution of 1944 and its political

aftermath; Wilson T. Boots, "Miracle in Bolivia: Four Women Confront a Nation," ch. 3 on the 1977–78 hunger strike by women in a Bolivian tin–mining community; Gerald Schlabach, "The Nonviolence of Desperation: Peasant Land Action in Honduras," ch. 4 on land takeovers; Philip McManus, "Argentina's Mothers of Courage," ch. 5 on the Mothers of the Plaza; and Blanca Yáñez Berrios and Omar Williams, "Cultural Action for Liberation in Chile," ch. 7 which is partly on women's "lightning" protests against the Pinochet government. Appendix B, "Preparing for Nonviolence," contains excerpts from a document on nonviolent struggle prepared by a Brazilian branch of Servicio Paz y Justicia [SERPAJ]. Photos. Appendixes. Index.)

271.   O'Donnell, Guillermo, Phillipe C. Schmitter, and Laurence Whitehead, eds., *Transitions from Authoritarian Rule: Prospects for Democracy.* 748 pp. Baltimore MD and London: Johns Hopkins Univ. Press, 1986. (These essays, based on a theory of reform from above, contain limited direct reference to popular action from below. See the studies of Bolivia, esp. pp. 55, 59, 60–67; Brazil, esp. p. 82 on the effects of regime violence on support; Chile, pp. 113–15 on "national protests" and response; Mexico, esp. pp. 126–27 on effects of repression in 1968 and pp. 141–42 on PRI response to implicit electoral boycotts; Peru, esp. discussion of efforts to coopt popular movements and the National Strike of 1977, pp. 153–72 *passim*; Uruguay, on rallies and strikes, pp. 175–76, 187–90, 195; and Venezuela, on role of civil action in Sallon Perez Jimenez, p. 209.)

272.   Perez Esquivel, Adolfo, *Christ in a Poncho: Testimonials of the Nonviolent Struggles in Latin America.* 139 pp. Maryknoll NY: Orbis Books, 1983. First published as *Le Christ au Poncho, Suivi de Témoignages de Luttes Nonviolentes en Amérique.* Paris: Editions du Centurion, 1981. (Written by recipient of 1980 Nobel Peace Prize and director of the Service of Peace and Justice. Part 1 discusses his views on nonviolent action. Part 2 contains documents on specific struggles, including the Mothers of the Plaza de Mayo, Argentina, ch. 1; Brazilian strikers at the Peres Cement Company, ch. 2; and Indian and peasant questions in several

countries, ch. 3, 4. Appendix A contains statement of Latin American bishops on nonviolence and nonviolent action. Documents.)

273.   Ropp, Steve C., and James A. Morris, eds., *Central America: Crisis and Adaptation*. 311 pp. Albuquerque: Univ. of New Mexico Press, 1984. (Chapter on El Salvador details strikes and protests since 1930s, pp. 85–90, 94, 106; and protest resignations, pp. 99–100. See also description of "demand-making" in Costa Rica, pp. 173–76 ff. Index. Bibliography.)

274.   Simpson, John and Jana Bennett, *The Disappeared and the Mothers of the Plaza*. 416 pp. New York: St. Martin's Press, 1985. (Political history of Argentina from the *coup d'état* of 1976 until the elections of 1983, focusing on the military regime's methods and motives in repressing all dissent and its sources, especially by "disappearing" and murdering some eleven thousand people. Ch. 5–8 are on repression and torture; ch. 9, 10 on the "Mothers of the Plaza" who marched in the central square to demand an accounting for their disappeared loved ones. Ch. 5 is on the U.S. role in reopening Argentina and ch. 20 is on the aftermath of the Falklands War. Photos. Appendix. Index.)

275.   Valentine, Lee Benson, "A Comparative Study of Successful Revolutions in Latin America, 1941–1950." 297 pp. Ph.D. diss., Stanford Univ., 1952. (See pp. 58–66 for discussion of civic strike and coup in Guatemala, 1944; pp. 72–79 for civic action in El Salvador's 1944 change of government and subsequent events; and pp. 180–88 on demonstrations related to Bolivia revolution of 1946. Also references to demonstrations and strikes in other countries, pp. 123–29, 153. Bibliography.)

LABOR AND PEASANT MOVEMENTS

The distinction between peasant–labor and political movements and suppression of them is not absolute by any means. Entries here are concerned with the movements themselves or with politicized peasant–labor struggles that used the typical methods of labor, such as unions, strikes, and the like.

276. Angell, Alan, *Peruvian Labor and the Military Government since 1968*. 38 pp. London: Univ. of London Institute of Latin American Studies [n.d.]. (History of the Peruvian labor movement from 1968 through 1977 and an effective national general strike. Examines role of organized labor, popular protest, and social movements under a military regime.)

277. Baptiste, Owen, ed., *Crisis*. 417 pp. St. James, Trinidad: Inprint, 1976. (Journalist's inquiry into oil and sugar strike in Trinidad in 1975. See pp. 9–38 and "Bloody Tuesday," pp. 65–93, on union actions and police treatment of procession on March 18, 1975. Photos. Documents.)

278. Bergquist, Charles, *Labor in Latin America: Comparative Essays on Chile, Argentina, Venezuela, and Colombia*. 397 pp. Stanford CA: Stanford Univ. Press, 1986. (On Argentina, see pp. 118–33, 171–73 on industrial expansion and strikes; pp. 160–62, 164–67 on Peronist manipulation of labor's collective action; and pp. 169–70 on mass demonstration of October 1945 to free Peron from coup plotters. On Venezuela, see pp. 230–40 on oil strike of 1936. On Colombia, see pp. 351–54 on women coffee workers' strike and pp. 359–68 on La Violencia. Illustrations. Photos. Index. Bibliography.)

279. Blanchard, Peter, *The Origins of the Peruvian Labor Movement, 1883–1919*. 214 pp. Pittsburgh: Univ. of Pittsburgh Press, 1982. (Consult index under *strikes* and *strikes: general* for references to numerous strikes attendant upon the growth of labor organization. Index. Bibliography.)

280. Burns, E. Bradford, and Thomas E. Skidmore, *Elites, Masses, and Modernization in Latin America, 1850–1930*. Ed. Virginia Bernhard. 156 pp. Austin TX and London: Univ. of Texas Press, 1979. (Thomas Skidmore, "Workers and Soldiers: Urban Labor Movements and Elite Responses in Twentieth–Century Latin America," identifies strikes, lockouts, and rent strikes in several countries after WWI, pp. 97–98, 100–01, 103–8, but notes difficulty of specifying details, p. 151, n. 44.)

281.   Burrowes, Reynold A., *The Wild Coast: An Account of Politics in Guyana*. 348 pp. Cambridge MA: Schenkman, 1984. (Political history of Guyana chronicling the emergence of a multiracial and multicultural nationalism. References to the role of organized labor and its effect on political change throughout. See esp. index under *strikes* and *unions*. Appendixes. Index. Bibliography.)

282.   Dunkerley, James, and Chris Whitehouse, *Unity Is Strength: Trade Unions in Latin America: A Case for Solidarity*. 132 pp. London: Latin America Bureau, 1980. (Heavily illustrated journalism on labor activities from left perspective. See pp. 29, 33–34, 36–59 on labor strikes and protests; country–by–country accounts in part 2. Photos.)

283.   Kepner, Charles David, Jr., and Jay Henry Soothill, *The Banana Empire: A Case Study of Economic Imperialism*. 392 pp. New York: Russell & Russell, 1967. (Economic history of banana companies in Latin America. See ch. 12 for labor struggles, esp. pp. 323–30 on Colombian strike of 1928 and pp. 330–35 on Costa Rican strike of 1934. Index. Bibliography.)

284.   Landsberger, Henry A., ed., *Latin American Peasant Movements*. 476 pp. Ithaca and London: Cornell Univ. Press, 1969. (Essays on various peasant movements. See ch. 1 for an overview of such movements, ch. 5 on a 1953 strike in Chile, and chapters on Venezuela, Mexico, Bolivia, Peru, Guatemala, and Brazil. Index. Bibliography.)

285.   MacCameron, Robert, *Bananas, Labor, and Politics in Honduras, 1954–1963*. 166 pp. Syracuse Univ., Maxwell School of Citizenship and Public Affairs, Foreign and Comparative Studies/Latin America Series, no. 5. Syracuse NY: Maxwell School of Citizenship and Public Affairs, 1983. (A 66–day general strike, characterized by "almost total absence of violence," achieved Honduras's first collective bargaining agreements. See ch. 2, 5 and pp. 27, 28, 33, 43, 45, 49 on the control of violence and nonviolent conduct of strikers. Documents in appendixes. Bibliography.)

286. McClintock, Cynthia, *Peasant Cooperatives and Political Change in Peru.* 418 pp. Princeton NJ: Princeton Univ. Press, 1981. (An examination of the civilian structures conceived and implemented in Peru under the Velasco government, 1968–1975, with an analysis of their effectiveness in light of the stated goals, namely to create a new peasant consciousness. See index under *cooperatives, strikes,* and *unions.* Photos. Appendixes. Index. Bibliography.)

287. Rodney, Walter, *A History of the Guyanese Working People, 1881–1905.* 282 pp. Baltimore: Johns Hopkins Univ. Press, 1981. (Class–based discussion of non–European workers in colonial Guyana. See esp. "Resistance and Accommodation," ch. 6 for a record of resistance methods, both violent and nonviolent. Ch. 8 chronicles riots that ensued after workers organized and held demonstrations in 1905. Photos. Appendixes. Index. Bibliography.)

288. Rotberg, Robert I., with Christopher K. Clague, *Haiti: The Politics of Squalor.* 456 pp. Boston: Houghton Mifflin, 1971. (Interesting in large part for its discussion of the factors restraining collective action, e.g., pp. 17, 244, 366–67. See pp. 140–41, 186–88, 192–94 on protests, general strikes, and "passive resistance" before the elder Duvalier. Index. Bibliography.)

289. Spalding, Hobart A., Jr., *Organized Labor in Latin America: Historical Case Studies of Workers in Dependent Societies.* 297 pp. New York: New York Univ. Press, 1977. (Detailed history of organized labor in Latin America, with many references to workers' actions; chapter case studies of Mexico, Argentina, Brazil, Bolivia, and Cuba. Consult index heading *strikes* for numerous page references. Index.)

290. Stavenhagen, Rodolfo, ed., *Agrarian Problems and Peasant Movements in Latin America.* 583 pp. Garden City NY: Anchor Books, Doubleday, 1970. (In addition to several essays on the conditions of land reform, ch. 3–5, counter–mobilization by elites, ch. 7, and analysis of peasant campaigns, ch. 10, see pieces on Colombia, ch. 12, Brazil, ch. 13, and Peru, ch. 15.)

291.   Urrutia, Miguel, *The Development of the Colombian Labor Movement*. 297 pp. New Haven and London: Yale Univ. Press, 1969. (Explores the role of the state in emergence of a labor movement in Colombia. See esp. ch. 9, "The Tactics of Structural Violence," for a study of the conditions that transformed nonviolent forms of resistance into violent ones. Appendix. Index. Bibliography.)

BOLIVIA

Bolivia's 1952 revolution and civilian rule were followed by an authoritarian government starting in 1964, which caused the fragmentation of the groups that had democratized politics. Toward the end of the 1970s, mass–based protests and politicization began again, especially when tin–miners grew more vocal and organized. Methods such as hunger strikes for the release of political prisoners gained a wider audience and fostered support for civilian opposition groups. Political tensions grew within Bolivia and fear of leftists became more acute, leading to a military coup in 1980 shortly after a hotly contested election. Bolivian politics has become somewhat less polarized recently.

292.   Barrios de Chungara, Domitila, with Moema Viezzer, *Let Me Speak! Testimony of Domitila, a Woman of the Bolivian Mines*. Trans. Victoria Ortiz. 235 pp. London: Stage 1, 1978. Originally published as *"Si me permiten hablar . . ." Testimonio de Domitila, una Mujer de las Minas de Bolivia.* Mexico City: Siglo Editores, 1978. (Interviews with a woman involved in organized workers' movement and conflicts with the government. Mention of protest demonstrations and strikes throughout. See section entitled "1976" on the strike of June–July 1976. Photos.)

293.   Booth, John A., and Mitchell A. Seligson, eds., *Political Participation in Latin America*. Vol. 2, *Politics and the Poor*. 262 pp. New York and London: Holmes & Meier, 1979. (See Thomas Greaves and Javier Allso, "An Anatomy of Dependence: A Bolivian Tin Miners' Strike," ch. 13 for an

analysis of the impact of dependence on labor's ability to sustain a strike. Index. Bibliography.)

294. Lora, Guillermo, *A History of the Bolivian Labor Movement, 1848–1971.* Trans. Christine Whitehead; ed. Laurence Whitehead. 380 pp. Cambridge, London, New York, and Melbourne: Cambridge Univ. Press, 1977. (History of labor organization and labor's relations with government, military, and other elites, written by a veteran unionist. See ch. 11, 15–20; esp. pp. 175–77, 216–30, 310–20. Bibliography.)

295. Nash, June, *We Eat the Mines and the Mines Eat Us: Dependency and Exploitation in Bolivian Tin Mines.* 363 pp. New York: Columbia Univ. Press, 1979. (Study of tin miners' labor movement in Bolivia. See ch. 8 on labor conflict and p. xiii and following for discussion of price rises and highway blockade in 1974 and other protests. See also index under *Cochabamba, collective action, hunger strikes,* and *strikes.* Index. Bibliography.)

296. Rohrlich–Leavitt, Ruby, ed., *Women Cross–Culturally: Change and Challenge.* 669 pp. The Hague and Paris: Mouton Publishers, 1975. (See June Nash, "Resistance as Protest: Women in the Struggle of Bolivian Tin–Mining Communities," pp. 261–71. Index.)

BRAZIL

Anti–Slavery Movement

The first African slaves were brought into Brazil in 1550, following "unsuccessful" attempts to enslave indigenous populations. Although the slave trade was outlawed in 1852, slavery continued within Brazil until formal abolition occurred in 1888.

297. Conrad, Robert, *The Destruction of Brazilian Slavery, 1850–1888.* 344 pp. Berkeley, Los Angeles, and London: Univ. of California Press, 1972. (Account of the abolitionist movement, including mass demonstrations and the abandonment of

plantations, combining nonviolent and violent action. See ch.
9–17, esp. pp. 137–40, 235, 239–57, 261, 265–68. Illustrations.
Appendixes. Index. Bibliography.)

Political Conflicts Before 1964

*Brazil's republican government came under military influence with
the installation of Getúlio Vargas as president in 1930. A popular and
individualistic ruler, Vargas committed suicide after the military's
demand for his resignation in 1954. Several presidents followed and
tensions within the society grew. In the early 1960s, demonstrations
demanding change increased along with growing opposition
organizations (including church, labor and student groups). Vargas
protégé Joao Goulart attempted to use popular demonstrations to
support his presidency but was deposed in a military coup in 1964
that installed a military government.*

298.   Chilcote, Ronald H., ed., *Brazil and Its Radical Left: An
        Annotated Bibliography on the Communist Movement and
        the Rise of Marxism, 1922–1972.* 455 pp. Millwood NY: Kraus
        International Publications, 1980. (Consult general index under
        *peaceful   change, peaceful   revolution, strikes, student
        movements,* and similar topics. Index.)

299.   Levine, Robert M., *Brazil since 1930: An Annotated
        Bibliography for Social Historians.* 336 pp. New York and
        London: Garland, 1980. (See pp. 88–106 for entries in several
        languages on the state and military since 1964. Index.)

STUDIES

300.   Dulles, John W.F., *Unrest in Brazil: Political–Military
        Crises, 1955–1964.* 449 pp. Austin and London: Univ. of Texas
        Press, 1970. (See book 7, ch. 1, 2, on demonstrations organized
        by Goulart in 1964 and counterdemonstrations against him.
        Photos. Index. Bibliography.)

301.   Juliao, Francisco, *Cambao—The Yoke: The Hidden Face of
        Brazil.* Trans. John Butt. Baltimore MD; Middlesex, England;
        and Victoria, Australia: Penguin Books, 1972. (Personal

account of work as organizer of the Peasant League before 1964. See esp. part 3, pp. 113–69. Index.)

302.   Landsberger, Henry A., ed., *Latin American Peasant Movements*. 476 pp. Ithaca and London: Cornell Univ. Press. (Cynthia N. Hewett, "Brazil: The Peasant Movement in Pernambuco, 1961–1964," ch. 9 describes attempts to organize peasants in the Northeast. Index. Bibliography.)

Military Rule, 1964–1985

The 1964 coup began an era of increased political repression and consolidation of authoritarian rule. While governments differed as to whether they took a "hard line" or "soft line" with opposition, repression was often very severe in these years. Most entries here cover the period of military rule, when the incidence of torture and persecution of political dissidents became more frequently documented. The military ruled until 1985, when José Sarney, a civilian, became president.

303.   Alves, Marcio Moreira, *A Grain of Mustard Seed: The Awakening of the Brazilian Revolution*. 194 pp. Garden City NY: Doubleday Anchor Press, 1973. (Written by an exiled regime opponent. Comments on repression by torture in ch. 6, on revolutionary organizations in ch. 8, and on violent and nonviolent resistance on pp. 149–52, 182–88. Index.)

304.   Alves, Maria Helena Moreira, *State and Opposition in Military Brazil*. 352 pp. Austin TX: Univ. of Texas Press, 1985. (Sophisticated study of the development of military controls within the Brazilian national security state, ch. 1–5, and the nature of violent and nonviolent opposition, esp. ch. 6–8. On movements of opposition and the reaction to state violence, see pp. 37–38, 44–45, 56–57, 73, 81–94, 99–100, 119, 126–27. On Catholic grass roots groups, see pp. 153–60, 177–82. On labor strikes, including the general strike of 1983, see pp. 182–210, 240–44, 247–48, and tables A–9, A–10, and A–11. Index.).

305.   Amnesty International, *Report on Allegations of Torture in Brazil: An Amnesty International Report*. 97 pp. London: Amnesty International Publications, 1972. (Documentation of methods and extent of torture of political prisoners.)

306.   Antoine, Charles, *Church and Power in Brazil*. Trans. Peter Nelson. 275 pp. London: Sheed & Ward, 1973. (On dilemmas of reformist action by church, labor, and students in face of extensive repression, see pp. 64–65, 78–84, 107–14, 124–30, 138–41, 158–79, 187–94, 211–14, and esp. part 2, ch. 4, on counter-mobilization against the church's "active wing.").

307.   Arraes, Miguel, *Brazil: The People and the Power*. Trans. Lancelot Sheppard. 232 pp. Middlesex, England; Baltimore MD; and Victoria, Australia: Penguin Books, 1969. (Written by exiled former governor of a Brazilian state. See ch. 4 for an overview of movements in Brazil's history and ch. 8 on the 1964–68 struggle. Index.)

308.   Bruneau, Thomas C., *The Political Transformation of the Brazilian Catholic Church*. 270 pp. London and New York: Cambridge Univ. Press, 1974. (Ch. 7 reviews church–state clashes from 1964 on, with a section on restraining effects of Fifth Institutional Act of 1967 in pp. 209–16. See also a brief note on conservative women's marches of 1963–64, pp. 119–20. Index. Bibliography.).

309.   Bruneau, Thomas C., and Phillipe Faucher, eds., *Authoritarian Capitalism: Brazil's Contemporary Economic and Political Development*. 272 pp. Boulder CO: Westview Press, 1981. (See Thomas G. Sanders, "Brazil in 1980: The Emerging Political Model," ch. 9 and Ronaldo Munck, "The Labor Movement and the Crisis of the Dictatorship in Brazil," ch. 10. Bibliography.)

310.   Camara, Helder, *Spiral of Violence*. Trans. Della Couling. 83 pp. London and Sydney: Sheed & Ward, 1971. (The archbishop's personal manifesto on motives for nonviolent resistance. See pp. 30–37 on opposition violence and government repression and section 2 on the Gandhian approach.).

311. Erickson, Kenneth Paul, *The Brazilian Corporative State and Working–Class Politics*. 225 pp. Berkeley, Los Angeles, and London: Univ. of California Press, 1977. (See ch. 6 on "political strikes" in years before the coup and pp. 169–74 on labor and repression. Index. Bibliography.)

312. Fernandes, Florestan, *Reflections on the Brazilian Counter–Revolution*. 185 pp. Armonk NY: M.E. Sharpe, 1981. (See pp. 126–42, "Revolution or Counter–Revolution," esp. pp. 135–36 on pressures from below and pp. 140–42 on national struggle by means of "firm and continued civil disobedience." Bibliography.)

313. Flynn, Peter, *Brazil: A Political Analysis*. 564 pp. Boulder CO: Westview Press; London: Ernest Benn, 1978. (See ch. 9–11 on the alternation of protest and repression since 1964. Index. Bibliography.)

314. Hewlett, Sylvia Ann, and Richard S. Weinert, eds., *Brazil and Mexico: Patterns in Late Development*. 349 pp. (See Kenneth Paul Erickson and Kevin J. Middlebrooks, "The State and Organized Labor in Brazil and Mexico," esp. pp. 239–41, 246–54. Index.)

315. Marighela, Carlos, *For the Liberation of Brazil*. Trans. John Butt and Rosemary Sheed. 191 pp. Baltimore: Penguin Books, 1971. (Pieces on the advocacy of guerrilla struggle by author of the *Handbook of Urban Guerrilla Warfare*, which is included here.)

316. Mendes, Candido, *Beyond Populism*. Trans. L. Gray Cowan. 112 pp. Albany: Graduate School of Public Affairs, State Univ. of New York at Albany, 1977. (Effort to develop an interpretation of civil–military relations and the role of "dissent." See esp. pp. 27–31, 37, 42–56 for concepts and typology of "confrontation.")

317. Raine, Philip, *Brazil: Awakening Giant*. 268 pp. Washington DC: Public Affairs Press, 1974. (Ch. 5 contains brief reviews of political and demographic groups active in politics, including action by church, labor, and student groups. Index.).

318.   Roett, Riordan, *Brazil: Politics in a Patrimonial Society.* 218
        pp. New York: Praeger, 1984. (See pp. 35–39 on
        Patrimonialism and the resulting attitudes toward
        autonomous interest–group activity and pp. 98–113, 133–45,
        148–53 on labor, church, and other opposition. Index.)

319.   Skidmore, Thomas E., *The Politics of Military Rule in Brazil,
        1964–1985.* 420 pp. New York: Oxford Univ. Press, 1988.
        (History of Brazilian leadership after the 1964 coup. Pp. 73–
        82 detail student unrest and demonstrations in 1968, as well as
        several labor strikes. Brazilian "direct collective action" as a
        means for effecting political change is described on p. 262.
        Index.)

320.   Stepan, Alfred, ed., *Democratizing Brazil.* 404 pp. New York
        and Oxford: Oxford Univ. Press, 1989. (Scott Mainwaring,
        "Grassroots Popular Movements and the Struggle for
        Democracy: Nova Iguaçu," ch. 6 maintains that local social
        movements influenced the loosening of authoritarian control
        within the elite sponsored transition to electoral democracy
        and Margaret E. Keck, "The New Unionism in the Brazilian
        Transition," ch. 8 discusses, among other points, the role of
        metal workers' strikes in focusing labor and popular
        discontent. Other articles review economic and institutional
        aspects, the church, and the mobilization of women. Index.)

321.   ———, *The Military in Politics: Changing Patterns in Brazil.*
        313 pp. Princeton NJ: Princeton Univ. Press, 1971. (Study of
        military structure and the nature of military involvement in
        politics since 1945. Of greatest use is ch. 12, which traces
        repressive responses to civilian opposition by "hard–liners";
        see also part 2 and 3 on military ideology and coups. Index.
        Bibliography.)

322.   *Torture in Brazil: A Report by the Archdiocese of Saõ Paulo.*
        Trans. Jaime Wright; Ed. Joan Dassin. 238 pp. New York:
        Vintage Books, 1986. Originally published in Brazil as
        Brasil: Nunca Mais. Petrópolis: Editora Vozes, 1985. (Report
        on torture and repression in the first fifteen years of military
        government, compiled from official court records of over 700
        cases. Documentation project is explained in introduction to

the Brazilian edition, pp. 3–9. Parts 1, 5 describe torture itself and part 2 describes the growth, ideology, and methods of the repressive system. In part 3, ch. 9 presents a statistical profile of repression and its victims, ch. 10 discusses leftist organizations that were an object of repression, ch. 11 details the sectors of society of particular interest to the security organs, and ch. 12 discusses the acts considered subversive under the military–authoritarian state. In part 4, judicial procedure and typical cases are examined. Hints of the role of nonviolent collective action in Brazil, in opposition to the military and as activity viewed as subversive, may be found in pp. 45–48, 51–52 and sections of ch. 9 on union leaders, students, and political figures. Appendixes.)

323.　Weil, Jean–Louis, "Brazil 1976: Political Prisoners and the State of Exception," pp. 1–34 in Jean–Louis Weil, Joseph Comblin, and Judge Senese, *The Repressive State: The Brazilian "National Security Doctrine" and Latin America. Brazilian Studies* (Canada) Collection "Documents" 3, 2 (1976). (Discusses the criminalization of dissent, methods of dissent, and the treatment of arrestees and political prisoners.)

CHILE

Opposition to the Allende Government, 1972–1973

Chile's long history of uninterrupted democratic government ended in 1973 with the overthrow by the military of Salvador Allende. The Allende government had experienced opposition and organized pressure not only from its right—conservative parties, the military, and private enterprise—but also from its left—mobilized revolutionary groups that organized strikes and violent demonstrations. Opposition on Allende's right centered on the military, and the privileged classes allied with it and on small entrepreneurs. This opposition tried to humiliate Allende and his government with "empty pots" demonstrations. More telling on his power were two work stoppages or strikes by the independent truckers who hauled most of the country's goods. These independent entrepreneurs had it in their power to paralyze traffic throughout the country and did so on two occasions, in 1972 and 1973.

324.   Alexander, Robert J., *The Tragedy of Chile*. 509 pp. Westport CT and London: Greenwood Press, 1978. (See ch. 20 for a debunking view of accusations of U.S. economic action against the Allende government and CIA participation in transport strikes. Ch. 25 is on the truckers' strike of 1972 and pp. 321–22 are on the truckers' strike of 1973. Brief description of church-related protests and organizations after the coup, pp. 367–70. Documents. Index. Bibliography.).

325.   Bitar, Sergio, *Chile: Experiment in Democracy*. Trans. Sam Sherman. 243 pp. Philadelphia: Institute for the Study of Human Issues, 1986. (Political–economic analysis by former Allende cabinet member. See esp. pp. 96–97, 108–16 on middle class and October 1972 stoppages; pp. 126–27 on the "financial blockade"; pp. 159–62 on the El Teniente Strike of 1973; and pp. 203–12 for analysis of the middle–class opposition sector. Index.)

326.   Boorstein, Edward, *Allende's Chile*. 277 pp. New York: International Publishers, 1977. (On collective action in opposition to, and sometimes in support of, Allende, 1972–73, see pp. 174–75, 177, 183, 192–95, 203–4, 207–8, 222, 234. See also discussions of violence in these and adjacent pages. Index.)

327.   *Chile and Allende*. Ed. Lester A. Sobel. 190 pp. New York: Facts on File, 1974. (For role of demonstrations and strikes, both nonviolent and violent, in opposition to Allende, see pp. 48–49, 73, 80–83, 86–87, 94–96, 123, 125–29, 133–40. Index.)

328.   Cusach, David F., *Revolution and Reaction: The Internal and International Dynamics of Conflict and Confrontation in Chile*. 147 pp. Monographs Series in World Affairs, Univ. of Denver, Graduate School of International studies, vol. 14, book 3, 1977. (Analysis of confrontation politics in Allende's Chile. See pp. 6–10 on the nature of confrontation politics, pp. 38–39, 42–43, 51–76 on the role of the opposition in conflicts, and pp. 110–12, 115–18 on U.S. involvement.)

329. Davis, Nathaniel, *The Last Two Years of Salvador Allende.* 480 pp. Ithaca NY and London: Cornell Univ. Press, 1985. (Memoirs, narrative, and analysis by U.S. ambassador to Chile, claiming little direct knowledge of U.S. government intervention with which he is associated in many publications. See pp. 47–48 on the "march of the empty pots" of December 1971, pp. 109–13 on the first truckers' strike of October 1972, and pp. 182–83, 188–90, 192–96, 202, 206 on the second truckers' strike of July–September 1973, actions by other economic groups, and their impact on the Allende government. Ch. 9 describes the role of strikes, merchants' boycotts, and conservative women's direct action in the coming of the *coup d'etat.* Pp. 123–29 discuss Chilean accusations of a U.S. financial blockade, which the author finds groundless. Index.).

330. De Vylder, Stefan, *Allende's Chile: The Political Economy of the Rise and Fall of the Unidad Popular.* 251 pp. Cambridge: Cambridge Univ. Press, 1976. (For economically–oriented interpretations of transport strikes and resistance by middle sectors, see pp. 96–98, 139, 159–62, and notes. For description of the "invisible blockade" of finance, see pp. 104–6, 128–30. Bibliography.)

331. Kaufman, Edy, *Crisis in Allende's Chile: New Perspectives.* 376 pp. New York, Westport CT, and London: Praeger, 1988. (Employs a structural analysis method to identify systems relationships and crises during the Allende era. See pp. 9–13, 24–25 on the U.S. financial blockade, pp. 65–69 on conservative women and their demonstrations, pp. 74–82, 155–57 on the *gremios*, or guild–like organizations, the middle class, and right wing politics, and pp. 266–68 on crisis behavior in response to the strikes of 1973. Index. Bibliography.).

332. Israel Z. [Zipper], Ricardo, *Politics and Ideology in Allende's Chile.* 306 pp. Tempe AZ: Center for Latin American Studies, 1989. (Strategies of opposition to the Allende government are discussed in pp. 40–48, 60–61, and ch. 6, 7. On the opposition's use of mass mobilization see, in ch. 6, pp. 190–95, 215–16, 219–26 and, in ch. 7, pp. 258–59, 265. Chile–U.S. economic and

political relations are discussed in ch. 5, esp. pp. 160–67 on "instruments of North American pressure" and the financial blockade. Glossary of abbreviations. Chronology. Index. Bibliography.)

333.   Loveman, Brian, *Chile: The Legacy of Hispanic Capitalism.* 427 pp. New York: Oxford Univ. Press, 1979. (See pp. 339–45 for comments on the inability of the socialist government to cope with "passive resistance" by property owners and the role of strike movements in 1972–73. Chronology. Index. Bibliography.)

334.   Moss, Robert, *Chile's Marxist Experiment.* 225 pp. Newton Abbot, Devon, England: David & Charles, 1973. (Pp. 143–54 offer some detail on the transport strike of October 1972, including comment on the absence of violence, p. 153. P. 198 describes the officers' wives' demonstration against General Carlos Prats. Index. Bibliography.)

335.   Nunn, Frederick M., *The Military in Chilean History: Essays on Civil–Military Relations, 1810–1973.* 343 pp. Albuquerque: Univ. of New Mexico Press, 1976. (Ch. 12, "Marxism and the Military, 1970–73," comments on strikes and demonstrations, particularly the decision of Interior Minister General Carlos Prats to avoid repressive violence during the truckers' strikes and his own loss of power in the face of a humiliating demonstration against him. Index.)

336.   Petras, James F., and Morris A. Morley, *How Allende Fell: A Study in U.S.–Chilean Relations.* 125 pp. Nottingham, England: Spokesman Books, 1974. (See pp. 32–35 and ch. 5, 6 on the credit boycott, informal copper embargo, and disruption of Chilean economy.)

337.   ———, *The United States and Chile: Imperialism and the Overthrow of the Allende Government.* 217 pp. New York and London: Monthly Review Press, 1975. (Ch. 5 builds a case for the existence of credit–blockade sanctions by the U.S. against Chile and copper embargo after nationalization.)

338. Roxborough, Ian, Philip O'Brien, and Jackie Roddick, assisted by Michael Gonzalez, *Chile: The State and Revolution*. 304 pp. New York: Holmes & Meier, 1977. (Critique of Allende from the Left, discussing the role of demonstrations, strikes, and boycotts by the political Right, pp. 114–17, 128, 133–34, 172–76, 194–95; reaction by the Left, pp. 170–76, 208–10; and "informal blockade" of Chilean economy by U.S. and international business, pp. 151–58. Chronology. Index. Bibliography.)

339. Sigmond, Paul E., *The Overthrow of Allende and the Politics of Chile, 1964–1976*. 326 pp. Pittsburgh: Univ. of Pittsburgh Press, 1977. (For references to demonstrations, strikes, and the "invisible blockade" of capital, see pp. 163–64, 174–75, 184–89, 194–95, 209–12, 216, 221–22, 227–29, 231, 234, 237–39. See also index under *violence*. Photos. Index.)

340. Stallings, Barbara, *Class Conflict and Economic Development in Chile, 1958–1973*. 294 pp. Stanford CA: Stanford Univ. Press, 1978. (On opposition by economic organizations, including 1972 truckers' strike, see pp. 137–44, 149–51. Index.)

341. Valenzuela, Arturo, *The Breakdown of Democratic Regimes: Chile*. 140 pp. Baltimore MD and London: Johns Hopkins Univ. Press, 1978. (See ch. 3, 4 on opposition and the coming of the 1973 coup. Includes comments on the role of violence, pp. 62–63, 68–72, and nonviolent opposition, pp. 58, 61–63, 74, 77–80, from the Right and Left. Index.)

342. Valenzuela, Arturo, and J. Samuel Valenzuela, eds., *Chile: Politics and Society*. New Brunswick NJ: Transaction Books, 1976. (See Elizabeth Farnsworth, Richard Feinberg, and Eric Leenson, "The Invisible Blockade: The United States Reacts," pp. 338–73, for analysis of the *bloqueo invisible* consisting of credit cuts. Index. Selected bibliography.)

Opposition to the Military Regime After 1973

The coup of 1973 prevented open dissent in Chile and punished many of Allende's supporters, as well as activists to his left, with imprisonment, exile, or death. Protest against the regime of General Augusto Pinochet was sporadic until a surge of open opposition circa 1983. Women were notable as activists in this surge. Protest declined after a period, but networks forged in it were significant in the later campaign for "the no," which occurred when the Pinochet government held a referendum in 1988 that could be answered only yes or no by the voter. The referendum was defeated, leading later to the return to civilian government with the election of Patricio Aylwin.

343.   Americas Watch Committee, *Chile Since the Coup: Ten Years of Repression.* Ed. C.G. Brown. 137 pp. An Americas Watch Report. New York: Americas Watch Committee, 1983. (Focuses on repressive political–legal system. Also contains scattered information on acts of protest and their suppression. See pp. 30–32, 33, 35–36, 52 for descriptions of protests; pp. 80–81, 95 on commemoration of disappeared persons; pp. 60, 81 for evidence of hunger strikes; and pp. 33–34, 63–64 on suppression of protest. Chronology.)

344.   Arriagada, Genaro, *Pinochet: The Politics of Power.* Trans. Nancy Morris with Vincent Ercolano and Kristen A. Whitney. 196 pp. Boston: Unwin Hyman, 1988. (See ch. 7, "The Protests: Rise and Fall of the Popular Struggle [1983–1986]," on the course of public protest in those years and ch. 8 on their effects on traditional party politics. Index.)

345.   Chavkin, Samuel, *Storm Over Chile: The Junta Under Siege.* 303 pp. Westport CT: Lawrence Hill, 1985. (Ch. 5, reprinted from an earlier edition, describes Swedish ambassador's efforts to protect political opponents of the coup and those sought for arrest. Ch. 9 discusses demonstrations and noncooperation in 1983–84. Index. Bibliography.)

346.   Drake, Paul W., and Iván Jaksic, eds., *The Struggle for Democracy in Chile, 1982–1990.* 321 pp. Lincoln and London: University of Nebraska Press, 1991. (Papers on the Chilean regime and its opposition from the renewal of protest against the Pinochet government until the election of Patricio Aylwin. See Arturo Valenzuela, "The Military in Power: The Consolidation of One–Man Rule," pp. 21–72 is on the character of the regime and methods of repression; María

Elena Valenzuela, "The Evolving Roles of Women under Military Rule," pp. 161–87 is partly on women in protest; and Manuel Antonio Garretón, "The Public Opposition and the Party System under the Military Regime," pp. 211–50 is partly on protest and the political parties. Index. Bibliography.)

347. Isaksson, Eva, ed., *Women and the Military System.* 455 pp. New York: Harvester–Wheatsheaf, 1988. (See Ximena Bunster, "The Mobilization and Demobilization of Women in Militarized Chile," for an outline of various women's organizations' efforts to combat the Pinochet dictatorship and restore civilian democracy. Draws comparisons with pro–Pinochet women's organizations. Index. Bibliography.)

348. Valenzuela, J. Samuel, and Arturo Valenzuela, eds., *Military Rule in Chile: Dictatorship and Oppositions.* 331 pp. Baltimore MD and London: Johns Hopkins Univ. Press, 1986. (Mostly written before the 1983 resurgence of opposition. See Manuel Banera and J. Samuel Valenzuela, "The Development of Labor Opposition to the Military Regime," ch. 7, esp. pp. 249–53, 260–62. Index.)

EL SALVADOR

General Maximiliano Hernández Martínez seized power in 1931 and remained as dictator for the next thirteen years, ruling as a traditional caudillo. Martínez was brought down in 1944 by a civilian–led, nonviolent civil insurrection that combined strikes and demonstrations to undercut support for the regime and compel him to retire. The Salvadoran model of a coalition of students, various social groups, and important citizens united in protest and noncooperation was an example for movements in other Latin American states.

349. Parkman, Patricia, *Nonviolent Insurrection in El Salvador: The Fall of Maximiliano Hernández Martínez.* 168 pp. Tucson AZ: Univ. of Arizona Press, 1988. (Detailed study of the 1944 "civic strike" in San Salvador which includes much information on the development of these events as a

nonviolent civil insurrection, the reasoning used by supporters, and the role of repression. Ch. 1, 2 study the background and behavior of the Martínez dictatorship and ch. 3 describes the structure of opposition. Ch. 4–6 are on the origin and events of the strike, focusing on the actions of groups opposed to Martínez and the process that forced him to withdraw. Ch. 7 studies the role of the U.S. in this outcome.

GUATEMALA

Civic Strike, 1944

This country's 1944 revolution took a similar course to that to El Salvador's, in the same year. Despite the threat of severe government repression, civilian forces brought about the fall of dictator General Jorge Ubico through protest and noncooperation. After the destruction ten years later of the system that emerged from this, Guatemalan governments have usually been quite repressive toward protest and opposition.

350.   Rosenthal, Mario, *Guatemala: The Story of an Emergent Latin–American Democracy.* 327 pp. New York: Twayne, 1962. (Ch. 12 discusses the "liberal dictatorships." See esp. pp. 199–214 on the fall of Ubico in the face of "civil acts of repudiation." Photos. Index. Bibliography.)

351.   Schneider, Ronald M., *Communism in Guatemala, 1944–1954.* 350 pp. New York: Praeger, 1958. (See ch. 1 for a brief description of the 1944 revolution, including pp. 10–13 on the role of students and the *huelga de brazos caidos.* Glossary. Index. Bibliography.)

352.   Silvert, Kalman H., *A Study in Government: Guatemala.* 239 pp. New Orleans: Tulane Univ., Middle American Research Institute, 1954. (See pp. 1–18 on the revolution of 1944 and its effects. Remainder is on the Arbenz government. Photos. Documents.)

Other Conflicts

353. Jonas, Susanne, Ed McCaughan, and Elizabeth Sutherland Martínez, eds. and trans., *Guatemala: Tyranny on Trial: Testimony of the Permanent People's Tribunal.* 301 pp. San Francisco: Synthesis Publications, 1984. (Firsthand accounts of social action and government repression in Guatemala. See esp. pp. 43–57 for the text of presentations by labor leaders which describe their participation in various organized actions and demonstrations and subsequent government clampdowns. See also index under *demonstrations.* Appendixes. Index.)

MEXICO

In the political system of Mexico, the coordination of all governmental activities, political life, and the representation of important constituencies has essentially been in the hands of one political party, the Institutional Revolutionary Party (PRI). This system has been intolerant of protests that it was unable to coopt, including the university students' protests at the time of the 1968 Mexico City Olympic Games, which were violently suppressed. More recently, the PRI has been challenged on issues of voting fraud by other mobilized parties.

354. Fagen, Richard R., and Wayne A. Cornelius, Jr., eds., *Political Power in Latin America: Seven Confrontations.* 419 pp. Englewood Cliffs NJ: Prentice–Hall, 1970. (Collected materials on several crises involving confrontation and, often, the transfer of power, both legitimately and illegitimately. Case 6, pp. 217–340, is on the student strike at UNAM, the University of Mexico, in 1966. Documents.)

355. Hellman, Judith Adler, *Mexico in Crisis.* 229 pp. New York: Holmes & Meier; London: Heinemann, 1978. (Ch. 5 is a case study of the student movement of 1968 and its repression. See also ch. 4, entitled "Opposition, Co–Optation, and Repression," and ch. 6 on implications for change of the Mexican political structure. Index. Bibliography.)

356.   Ladd, Doris M., *The Making of a Strike: Mexican Silver Workers' Struggles in Real del Monte, 1766–1775*. 200 pp. Lincoln and London: Univ. of Nebraska Press, 1988. (Historical reconstruction and interpretation of mine labor, protests, and a strike in the colonial Mexico of 1766–67. Grievance statements are in appendixes 1, 2. Glossary. Index. Bibliography.)

357.   Stevens, Evelyn P., *Protest and Response in Mexico*. 372 pp. Cambridge: MIT Press, 1974. (Concerned with politics and intra–cultural communication, this study describes railroad strikes of 1958–59, physicians' strikes of 1964–65, and student strikes and protests of 1968. Ch. 6 charts fate of movements of protest and ch. 9 offers some reasons for planning–oriented development approaches being intolerant of protest. Index. Bibliography.)

Section II
Canada and the United States

CANADA

Canada, as is true of most other countries, has seen the conflicts that mark its history divided into those that could be addressed and contained within the political system and those that resulted in direct action of various kinds. As students of the country will realize, even the Quebec separatism issue has been contained largely within political and constitutional boundaries. However, other conflicts relating to religion, race, ethnicity, and economics have been the source of open struggle. Relations among labor, management, and the state have marked several of the conflicts cited here. These include one of the few general strikes on the North American continent, the Winnipeg General Strike of 1919, and other "big strikes." Other conflicts involve Canada's "mosaic" of identities, including religion, race, and ethnicity. An example unique to Canada is the revolt of the Sons of Freedom Doukhobors and their unusual repertoire of direct action.

Labor

Labor conflicts have often involved the repertoire of strikes, slow-downs, and boycotts common in other countries. Strike "waves" have also occurred, notably during the 1930s. Canada's great spaces have also encouraged discontented workers to mount at least one mass trek, the "On to Ottawa" trek of 1935 by Western workers attempting to state their case at the capital. Many of the works cited here comment on the causes and dynamics of strikes, strike suppression, and labor organization also.

358.   Hann, Russell G., Gregory S. Kealey, Linda Kealey, and Peter Warrian, comps., *Primary Sources in Canadian Working-Class History, 1860–1930.* 186 pp. Kitchener, Ontario: Dumont Press, 1973. (List of manuscripts, newspapers, pamphlets, and

government sources, with locations. Consult index under names of organizations and actions, as well as under categories such as strikes and lockouts, names of industries, and names of particular actions. Strong on the Winnipeg General Strike of 1919. Index.)

359.   Vaisey, C. Douglas, with the assistance of John Battye, Marie DeYoung, and Gregory S. Kealey, comps., *The Labour Companion: A Bibliography of Canadian Labour History Based on Materials Printed from 1950 to 1975*. 126 pp. Halifax, Nova Scotia: Committee on Canadian Labour History, 1980. (Bibliography of secondary sources. Arranged alphabetically by author. Photos. Index.)

STUDIES

360.   Abella, Irving, ed., *On Strike: Six Key Labour Struggles in Canada, 1919–1949*. 196 pp. Toronto: James Lewis & Samuel, 1974. (Collection of essays on major strikes from the 1919 Winnipeg General Strike to the 1949 Asbestos strike. Included are comments on causes of violence by strikers and police in ch. 1, 2, 6; the deployment of militia in ch. 3; and nonviolent strikes in ch. 4, 5.)

361.   Badgley, Robin F., and Samuel Wolfe, *Doctors' Strike: Medical Care and Conflict in Saskatchewan*. 201 pp. Toronto: Macmillan of Canada, 1967. (Policy–oriented study of a doctors' job action in Saskatchewan, 1962, in face of the socialization of medical care, written by opponents of the strike. See esp. ch. 3–5. Index.)

362.   Cameron, Silver Donald, *The Education of Everett Richardson: The Nova Scotia Fishermen's Strike, 1970–71*. 239 pp. Toronto: McClelland & Stewart, 1977. (Story of a long strike and its effects. See esp. pp. 55–76 on conduct of strike.)

363.   Caragata, Warren, *Alberta Labour: A Heritage Untold*. 162 pp. Toronto: James Lorimer, 1979. (General account of unionism and union action, 1880s–1950s. In addition to scattered material on strikes, see pp. 54–60 on labor opposition to WWI;

pp. 70–81 on post–war general strikes and "One Big Union" actions; and pp. 105–10 on Depression–era protest, including the On to Ottawa Trek and the Regina, Saskatchewan, confrontation of 1935. Photos. Index.)

364. Dumas, Evelyn, *The Bitter Thirties in Quebec*. 145 pp. Montreal: Black Rose Books, 1975. (Study of strikes in Quebec, 1934–44, and their relationship to socioeconomic change; see ch. 2–6 for cases. Methodological note in appendix. Index. Bibliography.)

365. Forsey, Eugene, *Trade Unions in Canada, 1812–1902*. 600 pp. Toronto, Buffalo and London: Univ. of Toronto Press, 1982. (Descriptive chronological study concentrating on labor organizations, with scattered mention of strikes, ch. 1–14. Index. Bibliography.)

366. Freeman, Bill, *1005: Political Life in a Union Local*. 278 pp. Toronto: James Lorimer, 1982. (See pp. 48–69, 79–81, 99–107, 120–24, 152–60, 182–85, 199–200 on the changing relationship between labor organization and strike activity in an industrial union local. Photos. Index. Bibliography.)

367. Hogan, Brian, *Cobalt: Year of the Strike, 1919*. 185 pp. Cobalt, Ontario: Highway Book Shop, 1981. (Description of strike in the silver mines of Cobalt, Ontario, 1919. See esp. pp. 102–15 and pp. 133–36 on third–party interventions. Bibliography.)

368. Jamieson, Stuart Marshall, *Times of Trouble: Labour Unrest and Industrial Conflict in Canada*. 542 pp. Ottawa: Task Force on Labour Relations, Study no. 22, 1968. (Chronological account of strikes and labor conflict, 1900–1966, both major and minor. Appendixes contain first–hand accounts of conflicts of the 1930s.)

369. Johnson, Walter, *Trade Unions and the State*. 172 pp. Montreal: Black Rose Books, 1978. (Accounts of five strikes in the 1970s, stressing wildcat strikes and factory occupations.)

370.   Laxer, Robert, *Canada's Unions*. 341 pp. Toronto: James
        Lorimer, 1976. (See esp. parts 2, 4, 5 on labor conflict in the
        1920s. Index.)

371.   ———, ed., *Union Organization and Strikes*. 103 pp. Toronto:
        Ontario Institute for Studies in Education, 1978. (Case studies
        of four strikes, primarily in the post–WWII "strike wave,"
        and their relation to union organizing. Photos.
        Bibliography.)

372.   Lipton, Charles, *The Trade Union Movement of Canada,
        1827–1959*. 3d ed. 384 pp. Toronto: NC Press, 1973. (Historical
        account of the relationship between organizing and strike
        activity, with information on many strikes. Photos. Index.)

373.   Liversedge, Ronald, *Recollections of the On to Ottawa Trek:
        With Documents Related to the Vancouver Strike and the On
        to Ottawa Trek*. 330 pp. Toronto: Carlton Library, McClelland
        & Stewart, 1973. (Memoirs of participant in 1935 Vancouver
        relief camp workers' strike, ch. 4; and the subsequent On to
        Ottawa Trek, ch. 5. Chronology. Documents.)

374.   MacDowell, Laurel Sefton, *"Remember Kirkland Lake": The
        History and Effects of the Kirkland Lake Gold Miners'
        Strike, 1941–42*. 292 pp. Toronto, Buffalo, and London: Univ.
        of Toronto Press, 1983. (Careful account of an unsuccessful
        1941–42 strike. Stresses the interaction of parties within the
        strike, including the question of whether pickets were
        violent, thus justifying greater police involvement, pp. 160–
        72. Documents. Index. Bibliography.)

375.   MacEwan, Paul, *Miners and Steelworkers*. 400 pp. Toronto:
        Samuel Stevens Hakkert, 1976. (Discusses many strikes and
        slow–downs during twentieth century in ch. 3, 7–8, 11, 17, 19.
        Photos. Index. Bibliography.)

376.   Montero, Gloria, *We Stood Together: First–hand Accounts of
        Dramatic Events in Canada's Labour Past*. 261 pp. Toronto:
        James Lorimer, 1979. (Oral history told by several labor
        leaders discussing various strikes and other actions, including
        the On to Ottawa Trek of 1935. Photos. Index. Bibliography.)

377. Palmer, Bryan D., *Working–Class Experience: The Rise and Reconstruction of Canadian Labour, 1800–1980*. 347 pp. Toronto and Vancouver: Butterworth, 1983. (Brief descriptions of many strikes in ch. 3, 4, 6. See also appendixes 1, 2 for listing of strikes and riots before 1850. Index. Bibliography.)

378. Penney, Jennifer, *Hard–Earned Wages: Women Fighting for Better Work*. 241 pp. Toronto: Women's Press, 1983. (Personal narratives of women's labor actions and strikes. See pp. 50–59, 147–51, 191–98.)

379. Radecki, Henry, and Susan Evans, *The Teachers' Strike Study: Sudbury, Ontario, 1980*. 189 pp. Toronto: Minister of Education, Ontario, 1982. (Study of 56–day public secondary school teachers' strike in Sudbury, Ontario, 1980. Chronology. Bibliography.)

380. Salutin, Rick, *Kent Rowley: The Organizer: A Canadian Union Life*. 163 pp. Toronto: James Lorimer, 1980. (Biography of a life–long unionist and his activities, including student, union, and anti–conscription politics. Index.)

381. Seymour, Edward E., *An Illustrated History of Canadian Labour, 1800–1974*. 91 pp. Ottawa: Canadian Labour Congress, 1976. (Many actions recounted. Illustrated with photos of demonstrations, mass meetings, strikes, and strikebreaking. See esp. pp. 2–3, 16–29, 33–36, 41–50, 56–63, 69–83. Photos. Bibliography.)

382. Stewart, Walter, *Strike!* 224 pp. Toronto: McClelland & Stewart, 1977. (Journalist's popularly written inquiry into strikes and unionism. See esp. ch. 4, which contends that "strikes are violent because violence works." Index.)

383. Trudeau, Pierre Elliot, *The Asbestos Strike*. Trans. James Boake. 382 pp. Toronto: James Lewis & Samuel, 1956. Reprint, 1974. (Articles on 1949 strike in Quebec asbestos industry. See ch. 3–5, 8, esp. pp. 144–75, on conduct of strike and pp. 272–73 on press response to violence in strike. Documents in appendixes. Bibliography.)

384.   Williams, Jack, *The Story of Unions in Canada*. 252 pp. Don
        Mills, Ontario: J.M. Dent & Sons, 1975. (Chronological
        history with scattered references to strikes. Index.)

WINNIPEG GENERAL STRIKE, 1919

*Winnipeg's strike of May and June 1919 was one of two general strikes
in North America in that year, the other being in Seattle,
Washington. Originating in the economic turmoil of the post–World
War I years, the strike was also encouraged by a "one big union"
ideology among working people. As the confrontation of labor and
employers escalated, a workers committee took on the task of
organizing and running the general strike. The committee's capacity
to organize and hold together the workers added strength to the
strike and permitted it to start controlling much of the economic life
of the city (including issuing passes for the transportation of goods).
In response, the employers, professionals, and middle class organized
the "citizens' committee of one thousand" to unite those opposed to
the workers in order to maintain services and encourage police
intervention. Several strikers were injured in a Mounted Police charge
along the city's streets, after which control of the streets and
commerce passed from the strikers' hands. With the exception of the
Mounted Police assault, there was little violence in the strike,
although several leaders were severely punished afterwards.*

385.   Bercuson, David Jay, *Confrontation at Winnipeg: Labour,
        Industrial Relations, and the General Strike*. 227 pp.
        Montreal and London: McGill–Queen's Univ. Press, 1974.
        (Detailed history of the general strike and the groups who
        fought it. See ch. 1, 5–8 on earlier strikes and the coming of
        the 1919 strike and ch. 9–12 on the strike itself. Index.
        Bibliography.)

386.   Citizens' Committee of One Thousand, *The Activities and
        Organization of the Citizens' Committee of One Thousand in
        Connection with the Winnipeg General Strike, May–June
        1919*. 56 pp. Winnipeg: Citizens' Committee of One Thousand
        [1919?]. (Statement by an anti–strike group engaged in
        maintaining services during the strike. Of particular interest
        are the group's self–justification and description of its

activities, pp. 3–16; discussion of its organization by "department," pp. 20–28; and a detailed memorandum maintaining the right of the citizen to intervene in event of "riot," pp. 29–40. Documentary material includes sample permits to carry on trade, issued by strikers' committee, pp. 8–9, and resolutions of citizens' committee.)

387. MacInnis, Grace, *J.S. Woodsworth: A Man to Remember.* 336 pp. Toronto: Macmillan of Canada, 1953. (Biography of one of the leaders of the general strike and lifelong advocate of nonviolence. See ch. 11 on role in the general strike. Photos. Index.)

388. Magder, Beatrice, *"Canadian Issues": The Winnipeg General Strike: Management–Labour Relations.* 49 pp. Toronto: McLean–Hunter, 1969. (Edited for student use; includes memoirs and eyewitness accounts. Photos.)

389. Masters, D.C., *The Winnipeg General Strike.* 159 pp. Toronto: Univ. of Toronto Press, 1950. (Detailed history of the general strike. See ch. 2, 3 on the strike itself. Photos. Index.)

390. McNaught, Kenneth, *A Prophet In Politics: A Biography of J.S. Woodsworth.* 339 pp. Toronto: Univ. of Toronto Press, 1959. (Biography of participant in the Winnipeg General Strike and later member of Canadian Parliament. See ch. 8 on the general strike. Index.)

391. McNaught, Kenneth, and David J. Bercuson, *The Winnipeg Strike: 1919.* 126 pp. Ontario: Longman Canada, 1974. (See ch. 3–5 on strike, with scattered references in pp. 47–90 to strikers' "policy of non–violence" and the question of whether it was correct, e.g., pp. 57–58; and ch. 6 for essay on changing interpretations of strike. Photos. Index.)

392. Penner, Norman, ed., *Winnipeg 1919: The Strikers' Own History of the Winnipeg General Strike.* 294 pp. Toronto: James Lewis & Samuel, 1973. (Reprint of entry 396 and two other publications from the post–strike period. Many photos, including a series on the Mounted Police charge, pp. 185–204. Index. Bibliography.)

393.   Rea, J. E., *The Winnipeg General Strike.* Canadian History through the Press Series. 121 pp. Toronto and Montreal: Holt, Rinehart & Winston of Canada, 1973. (Selected period newspaper accounts, primarily opinion. See section II–2 for alignments in strike and section III–3 on "Causes and Consequences of Violence." Photos. Bibliography.)

394.   Robin, Martin, *Radical Politics and Canadian Labour: 1880–1930.* 321 pp. Kingston, Ontario: Industrial Relations Center, Queen's Univ., 1968. (See pp. 119, 133, 151, 176, 180–85 on the development of labor concepts of the general strike. See 120–21, 127 on conscription protests. Index. Bibliography.)

395.   Sloane, D. Louise, Janette M. Rosenender, and Marilyn J. Hernandez, eds., *Winnipeg: A Centennial Bibliography.* 140 pp. Winnipeg: Armstrong Printers, 1974. (Helpful for background on social and economic development of Winnipeg.)

396.   [Winnipeg] Defense Committee, *"Saving the World from Democracy": The Winnipeg General Sympathetic Strike, May–June 1919.* 276 pp. Winnipeg: Winnipeg Defense Committee, [1920?]. (Description written after the strike by its supporters. Includes some transcripts from trials of arrested strike leaders.)

Other Conflicts

As noted above, many of Canada's social conflicts have to do with ethnic, racial, gender, and religious differences. Some of theses that have been sources of direct action in other societies have been relatively contained in Canada. An example is women's rights issues, where a preference has been shown for constitutional challenges and limited, non–disruptive protest and noncooperation.

397.   Smith, Dwight L., ed., *The History of Canada: An Annotated Bibliography.* 327 pp. Santa Barbara CA and Oxford: ABC–Clio Information Series, 1983. (Recent periodical literature catalogued by historical period and region. Subject and author indexes.)

398.   Weinrich, Peter, *Social Protest from the Left in Canada, 1870–1970*. 627 pp. Toronto, Buffalo, and London: Univ. of Toronto Press, 1982. (Select bibliography on "protest from the Left," containing chronological references to monographs, annual reports, and serials. List of bibliographies consulted. Indexes.)

STUDIES

399.   Cleverdon, Catherine L., *The Woman Suffrage Movement in Canada*. 2d ed. 324 pp. Toronto: Univ. of Toronto Press, 1974 [orig. publ. 1950]. (History of generally non–disruptive suffrage campaigns, whose actions included petitions, mock legislatures, and group lobbying. See also the influence of a court case on the question of the status of women as "persons" under the constitution, pp. 141–54. Photos. Index. Bibliography.)

400.   Epp, Frank H., *Mennonites in Canada, 1786–1920: The History of a Separate People*. 480 pp. Toronto: Macmillan of Canada, 1974. (Effects of religiously based nonresistance and refusal to participate in war discussed in ch. 4, on the early nineteenth century, and ch. 15–16, pp. 395–97, on WWI. Index. Bibliography.)

401.   Forsythe, Dennis, ed., *Let the Niggers Burn!: The Sir George Williams University Affair and Its Caribbean Aftermath*. 209 pp. Montreal: Black Rose Books, 1971. (On university sit-in culminating in arrests and destruction of a mainframe computer. See Leroy Butcher, "The Anderson Affair," pp. 76–110, for an engaged account of black students' position.)

402.   Giangrande, Carol, *The Nuclear North: The People, the Regions, and the Arms Race*. 231 pp. Toronto, Buffalo, London, and Sydney: Anansi, 1983. (Journalist's description of nuclear armaments issue in Canada, including protest and organizing activities, esp. pp. 11–17, 74–77. Brief but pointed description of effects of car bomb at Litton plant, which led to condemnation of the unconnected leafletting and protest

campaign as "indirectly responsible" for sabotage and injuries, pp. 29–33. Index.)

403.   Horn, Michiel, and Ronald Sabourin, eds., *Studies in Canadian Social History*. 480 pp. Toronto: McClelland & Stewart, 1974. (In part 4, see Kenneth McNaught, "Violence in Canadian History"; Desmond Morton, "Aid to the Civil Power: The Canadian Militia in Support of Social Order, 1867–1914"; and David J. Bercuson, "The Winnipeg General Strike, Collective Bargaining, and the One Big Union Issue.")

404.   Klinck, Carl F., general ed., *Literary History of Canada: Canadian Literature in English*. 944 pp. Toronto: Univ. of Toronto Press, 1965. (F.W. Watt, "Literature of Protest," ch. 25 reviews themes in the "spirit of protest and dissent" in Canadian writing from the 1860s to the 1930s. Index.)

405.   Kome, Penney, *The Taking of Twenty Eight: Women Challenge the Constitution*. 125 pp. Toronto: The Women's Press, 1983. (Journalist's account of women's lobby for a statement of rights in the Canadian Constitution, which included good deal of symbolic protest as well as standard lobbying methods. See pp. 15–18 on techniques used; pp. 39–41 on group resignation from women's status panel; and pp. 48, 77, 90–91 on symbolic actions.)

406.   Matheson, Gwen, ed., *Women in the Canadian Mosaic*. 353 pp. Toronto: Peter Martin Associates, 1976. (Gwen Matheson and V.E. Lang, "Nellie McClung: *Not a Nice Woman*," discusses McClung and the mock "women's parliament" in 1914, pp. 11–14; Deborah Gorham, "The Canadian Suffragists," esp. pp. 31–45, describes the movement's general avoidance of confrontation; and Kay Macpherson and Meg Sears, "The Voice of Women: A History," pp. 71–89, is on the anti–war group of the same name. Bibliography.)

407.   Robertson, Heather, *Reservations Are for Indians*. 303 pp. Toronto: James Lewis & Samuel, 1970. (See ch. 2 on a protest march in 1963 and ch. 11 on a "drink–in" protest in Alberta in 1967.)

DOUKHOBORS

The Doukhobors were a dissident religious sect that emigrated to Canada and took up residence in the country's far West. Pacifist in their beliefs, many were also fierce in the protection of their identity. In resisting both conscription, which they opposed on religious grounds, and what they perceived as government encroachment on their Western settlements, some Doukhobors burned their own homes, buildings, and property in protest. Others undertook hunger strikes and group or individual nude protests to underscore their non–attachment to worldly things. A subgroup, the Sons of Freedom, included some who stained the name of Doukhobor in the eyes of many Canadians by blowing up bridges and murdering Mounted Police officers.

408. Hawthorn, Harry B., ed., *The Doukhobors of British Columbia*. 288 pp. Vancouver: Univ. of British Columbia and J.M. Dent & Sons [Canada], 1955. (Revised report of British Columbia government research committee, 1952. References to protest and resistance found throughout, but see esp. pp. 16–17, 23–24, 30–31, 131–32, 190–91, 213–17, 259–63, 284–86. Also contains photos between pp. 148–49 of home burnings, nude protest parades, and sabotage. Ch. 5 provides a psychological analysis of Doukhobor "passivity." Photos. Index.)

409. Holt, Simma, *Terror in the Name of God: The Story of the Sons of Freedom Doukhobors*. 312 pp. Toronto and Montreal: McClelland & Stewart, 1964. (In the context of a thoroughgoing denunciation of the violence and way of life of the Sons of Freedom, the author discusses hunger strikes, pp. 33–34, 50–51, 97–102, 275–87; refusal to register, pp. 29–30, 273, 276; and protest nudity, pp. 41–44, 46, 50–51, 70–72; as well as protests at prisons, the burning of Doukhobors' own goods and homes, and various acts of noncooperation. Photos of marches and protests. Index. Bibliography.)

410. Tarasoff, Koozma J., *A Pictorial History of the Doukhobors*. 280 pp. Saskatoon, Saskatchewan: Prairie Books Department, The Western Press, 1969. (Extensive history of the Doukhobors, well illustrated with photographs and

drawings. For photos of Doukhobor protest and resistance activities, see pp. 8, 108–9, and "Aftermath.")

411.   Woodcock, George, and Ivan Avakumovic, *The Doukhobors*. 382 pp. Oxford: Oxford Univ. Press, 1968. (Account of communalist Doukhobors' resistance to assimilation and conscription. Nonviolent means included nude protest marches and burning of their own property. The Sons of Freedom subgroup also dynamited bridges. Index. Bibliography.)

412.   Zubek, John P., and Patricia Anne Solberg, *Doukhobors at War*. 250 pp. Toronto: Ryerson Press, 1952. (History of the Doukhobors, with special attention to the Sons of Freedom sect. See pp. 4, 25–26, 64–68, 117, 124, 129, 206 and ch. 6, 9, 14 on protests, esp. Doukhobor nude parades and mass exodus to British Columbia. Index.)

UNITED STATES OF AMERICA

As a society that has been turbulent, literate, and generally able to escape completely centralized control, the U.S. has produced enormous amounts of written evidence of the struggles of many of its peoples over a period dating from the seventeenth century. Many of these conflicts have been violent and many have been characterized as violent. This history offers researchers on nonviolent action an opportunity to determine for themselves to what extent the conflicts of the U.S. past have been typified by the use of nonviolent methods and to what extent violence has been used. It is possible that many movements that are characterized as violent have actually not been violent or not particularly violent. Instead, they may have largely employed nonviolent means but ones that were disorderly and disruptive. Likewise, researchers on nonviolent action will always ask which actors in a given conflict were violent, since it is known that the record often characterizes as "violent" those groups that received violence but may not have responded in the same way.

Researchers on U.S. history will note several recurring issues. One of these is race and its connection to slavery, domination of one race over others, and the conditions of citizenship. Contained within this are the struggles over slavery, native people's lands and rights, and the reach of the Constitution and laws with respect to race and ethnicity. A second recurring issue is labor and the power of labor versus owners, managers, and the state in a system characterized by few limits on the rights of private property. U.S. labor history has included several "great" strikes and boycotts that spilled across wide expanses of the country and drew in federal troops (see below on the Great Strike of 1877 and Pullman Strike and Rail Boycotts of 1894). There also have been several city–wide strikes (Lawrence, Mass., 1912, for example) and some "general strikes" (such as San Francisco, 1934).

Third, gender and women's rights, emerging with the Seneca Falls Convention of 1848, have been associated with protest in the U.S. for over a century. While aspects of women's rights and suffrage campaigns have been contained within the political and legal systems, protest as a strategy has likewise been a part of the women's struggle. This was especially true in the years before the suffrage amendment to the Constitution was passed and ratified and again during and after the 1970s. A fourth theme in U.S. protest and resistance movements has been religion, including the first campaign reflected in the pages following (Quaker opposition to the Massachusetts Puritan theocracy). One question has involved the rights and duties of religious believers to oppose perceived social or political injustices, war, conscription, and expansionism. Thus a fifth theme is that of war and national self–assertion. U.S. wars have generally been answered by opposition of some kind. The interplay of religious convictions, political ideologies, and the sense of national purpose make these movements significant for understanding the influence of protest in U.S. life.

A sixth theme found here is the individual versus collective expectations. An idea imbedded in the individualism of U.S. institutions, including the Constitution and law, it is also found in movements of protest and noncooperation. The seventh theme is order versus the rights and liberties of the people. One of the major justifications for the control of protests, strikes, and social movements in the U.S. has been the need for order and its superiority to arguments for change through conflict. Thus many significant nonviolent challenges have coped with the claim that they represent and promote disorder or disrespect for the law, even though they argue that they work for the recognition of essential rights and liberties.

History and Interpretation

These sections on reference materials and general interpretations contain both information and perspectives on the history and nature of U.S. protest movements.

See also: Vietnam: Prison Camp Resistance in North Vietnam; Methods of Nonviolent Action: Symbols and Statements; Methods of Nonviolent Action: International Economic Sanctions; Methods of Nonviolent Action: Strikes; Methods of Nonviolent Action: Political Noncooperation; Legal Aspects of Nonviolent Action; Dynamics of Nonviolent Action: Organizing and Community Organizations; Dynamics of Nonviolent Action: Legal Aspects of Nonviolent Action; Historic Peace Churches.

413.   Hoerder, Dirk, *Protest, Direct Action, Repression: Dissent in American Society from Colonial Times to the Present—A Bibliography.* 434 pp. Munich: Verlag Dokumentation, 1977. (Very thorough classified bibliography on civil conflict in the U.S., focusing largely on "riots and rebellions." In part 1, see sections 2, 3 on the colonial period, section 5 on labor conflict, section 6 on post–WWII conflicts, section 7.2 on war resistance and dissent during war, and section 9.1 on political power and protest. In part 3, see section 3 on the black struggle from the colonial period to the present, including the Civil War. Author index.)

414.   Manheim, Jarol B., and Melanie Wallace, *Political Violence in the United States 1875–1974: A Bibliography.* 116 pp. New York and London: Garland, 1975. (Contains sections on violence related to the labor movement, urban conflicts and race, "responses" to violence, and interpretations of American violence. Index.)

415.   Schlachter, Gail, and Pamela Byrne, eds., *Social Reform and Reaction in America: An Annotated Bibliography.* 375 pp. Santa Barbara CA and Oxford: ABC–Clio Information Services, 1984. (Bibliography of journal articles published between 1973 and 1982 concerned with social reform in the U.S. and Canada. Arranged according to major chronological

periods. Includes examples of both violent and nonviolent efforts at changing social and political structures and their outcomes. Index.)

416. Skidmore, Gail, and Theodore Jurgen Spalen, *From Radical Right to Extreme Left*. 3rd ed. 491 pp. Metuchen NJ and London: Scarecrow Press, 1987. (Annotated bibliography of newspapers, newsletters, magazines, and similar periodicals representing "protest, controversy, advocacy, or dissent." Categorized in general by the cause or issue involved. Indexes.)

STUDIES

417. Adamson, Madeline, and Seth Borgos, *This Mighty Dream: Social Protest Movements in the United States*. 143 pp. Boston and London: Routledge and Kegan Paul, 1984. (Pictorial essay and brief history on some of the larger protest movements of twentieth century U.S. life. Included are agrarian protest, labor struggles, civil rights, and community reform. Illustrations. Photos. Chronology. Documents.)

418. Barbrook, Alec, and Christine Bolt, *Power and Protest in American Life*. 375 pp. Oxford: Martin Robertson, 1980. (History of American "pressure groups," broadly conceived, esp. ethnic and economic groups. See ch. 2–5, 8. Index.)

419. Bright, Charles, and Susan Harding, eds., *State Making and Social Movements: Essays in History and Theory*. 404 pp. Ann Arbor: University of Michigan Press, 1984. (See Daniel R. Fusfield, "Government and Suppression of Radical Labor, 1877–1918," pp. 344–77 and Susan Harding, "Reconstructing Order through Action: Jim Crow and the Southern Civil Rights Movement," pp. 378–402.)

420. Cantarow, Ellen, with Susan Gushee O'Malley and Sharon Hartman Strom, *Moving the Mountain: Women Working for Social Change*. 207 pp. Old Westbury NY: Feminist Press, 1980. (Oral histories by Florence Luscomb, active in suffrage, peace, and labor causes; Ella Baker of SNCC; and Jessie Lopez

De La Cruz of the farmworkers' organization. Photos. Index. Bibliography.)

421.   Cooney, Robert, and Helen Michalowski, eds., *The Power of the People: Active Nonviolence in the United States.* From an original text by Marty Jezer. 240 pp. Philadelphia: New Society Publishers, 1987. Orig. publ. Culver City CA: Peace Press, 1977. (Introductory history of nonviolent social change movements in the U.S. from 1650 to the present. Focuses on "radical pacifists as the clearest exponents of nonviolence" but includes religious, suffrage, labor, and other movements. See pp. 9–11 for an effort to make the distinction between nonviolent action and pacifism. Updated version includes ch. 11, "Making Connections: Disarmament, Equality and a Healthy Environment." Illustrations. Photos. Documents. Index. Bibliography.)

422.   Deming, Barbara, *Revolution and Equilibrium.* 269 pp. New York: Grossman Publishers, 1971. (Essays on nonviolent action in the civil rights movement and movements against nuclear weapons and the Vietnam War. See esp. "On Revolution and Equilibrium," pp. 194–221 and "Nonviolence and Radical Social Change," pp. 226–30 which discusses church sanctuary for two draft resisters. Photos.)

423.   Goldstein, Robert Justin, *Political Repression in Modern America: From 1870 to the Present.* 682 pp. Boston: G.K. Hall; Cambridge MA: Schenkman, 1978. (Identifies political repression as responsible for the failure of left political movements. See pp. xvi–xxi for a definition and characteristics of political repression. Historical sections discuss anti–labor and anti–radical activities to ca. 1975. Index. Bibliography.)

424.   Jeffreys–Jones, Rhodri, *Violence and Reform in American History.* 242 pp. New York and London: New Viewpoints, 1978. (On the problem of industrial violence in the Progressive period. Ch. 1, 2 examine myths pertaining to violence. Subsequent chapters are on labor's and employers' violence from the 1880s to WWI. Ch. 11 examines the issue of violence and its relationship to reform. Index.)

425. Kessler, Lauren, *The Dissident Press: Alternative Journalism in American History.* 160 pp. Beverly Hills, London, and New Delhi: Sage Publications, 1984. (History of non–mainstream dissident groups which organized alternative media. Includes the journalistic activities of black Americans, utopians, feminists, non–English–speaking immigrants, populists, anarchists and communists, pacifists, noninterventionists, and war resisters.)

426. Lane, Roger, and John J. Turner, Jr., *Riot, Rout, and Tumult: Readings in American Social and Political Violence.* 399 pp. Westport CT: Greenwood Press, 1978. (Anthology, primarily of case studies in American history. See Michael Wallace, "The Uses of Violence in American History," pp. 10–27 and essays by Pauline Maier on colonial crowds, Richard Maxwell Brown on vigilantism, Clement Eaton on anti–abolitionist crowds, Philip Tufts and Philip Ross on labor violence, and Richard Wade on urban violence. Index. Bibliography.)

427. Rosen, David M., *Protest Songs in America.* 159 pp. Westlake Village CA: Aware Press, 1972. (Study of the history and evolution of protest songs in America from 1765 to the 1970s with descriptive text and lyrics. Bibliography.)

428. Rubinstein, Richard E., *Rebels in Eden: Mass Political Violence in the United States.* 201 pp. Boston and Toronto: Little, Brown, 1970. (History and evaluation of the use of group violence in the U.S., challenging the myths of "peaceful progress" as well as of the American character as a "violent people." See ch. 5 on American responses to collective violence.)

429. Shuman, Samuel I., ed., *Law and Disorder: The Legitimation of Direct Action as an Instrument of Social Policy.* 236 pp. Detroit: Wayne State Univ. Press, 1971. Franklin Memorial Lectures, vol. 20. (Essays on direct action, nonviolent and violent, in a "law and order context." See Tom C. Clark, "Some Historical Antecedents for the Use of Direct Action," ch. 1 for brief history of U.S. cases. Ch. 3, 5 are on student protest and direct action and ch. 4 is on direct action in the civil rights movement. Index.)

430.   Simon, Rita James, ed., *As We Saw the Thirties: Essays on
        the Social and Political Movements of a Decade.* 253 pp.
        Urbana, Chicago, and London: Univ. of Illinois Press, 1967.
        (Collected addresses by participants in the movements of the
        Thirties. See esp. A.J. Muste, "My Experiences in the Labor
        and Radical Struggles of the Thirties," pp. 123–50, and Hal
        Draper, "The Student Movements of the Thirties: A Political
        History," pp. 157–89.

431.   Zinn, Howard, *A People's History of the United States.* 614
        pp. New York: Harper & Row, 1980. (History of
        subordination and domination in the U.S. from colonial
        period to the 1970s, with accounts of nonviolent and violent
        conflict throughout. Index. Bibliography.)

Quaker "Invasion" of Massachusetts

*The seventeenth–century Puritan leadership of Massachusetts Bay
Colony had the right to banish unorthodox believers in order to
preserve uniformity and order. (A religious dissident named Anne
Hutchinson had been sent away from Boston early in the Puritan
period.) Banished members of the Society of Friends (Quakers)
refused to accept being expelled, partly because they had come to
Massachusetts to bear witness to their own truth. Several of them
came back to the colony to teach and witness. They also disrupted
church services and refused to show expected deference to the
magistrates. Quakers were beaten, imprisoned, subjected to corporal
punishment, and finally four of them were hanged before
Massachusetts abandoned its persecutions.*

432.   Bishop, George, *New England Judged by the Spirit of the
        Lord.* Rev. ed. 582 pp. Philadelphia: Thomas William
        Stuckey, 1885 [orig. publ. 1702–03]. (Extended and detailed
        chronicle of the lengthy confrontation between Quakers and
        the government of Massachusetts Bay Colony, 1656–65.
        Appendix contains statements by Quaker victims. Index.)

433.   Chu, Jonathan M., *Neighbors, Friends, or Madmen: The
        Puritan Adjustment to Quakerism in Seventeenth–Century
        Massachusetts Bay.* 205 pp. Westport CT and London:

Greenwood Press, 1985. (See esp. ch. 3, 4 on Massachusetts Bay politics and the Quaker visitors, including the punishment and hanging of Quakers who refused to stay out of the colony. Index. Bibliography.)

434. Ellis, George E., *The Puritan Age and Rule in the Colony of Massachusetts Bay, 1629–1685.* 576 pp. Boston: Houghton Mifflin, 1888. (The Quaker "intrusion" is recounted in ch. 12, esp. pp. 420–91, with some detail on Quakers who returned from banishment, the colonists' reactions, and Quaker protest methods, pp. 488–90.)

435. Evans, Charles, *Friends in the Seventeenth Century.* 666 pp. Philadelphia: W.H. Pile, 1875. (See pp. 155–63 on Puritan reactions to Quaker "heresy," including their fears of witchcraft and the influence of the Antinomian Anne Hutchinson. Ch. 11, 14 are on the persecution and executions of witnessing Quakers in Massachusetts. Betrays some confusion about the nature of Puritanism in New England and motives of magistrates in Massachusetts. Index.)

436. Hallowell, Richard P., *The Quaker Invasion of Massachusetts.* 2d ed. 227 pp. Boston: Houghton Mifflin, 1887. (Account of the sufferings of Quaker martyrs, although lacking in detail on their activities. Documents in appendixes.)

437. *Narrative of the Martyrdom, at Boston, of William Robinson, Marmaduke Stevenson, Mary Dyer, and William Leddra, in the Year 1659.* 40 pp. Manchester: John Harrison, 1841. (Justification of the Quaker martyrs in their confrontation with the Puritan "priests." Extracts from letters and statements.)

438. Selleck, George A., *Quakers in Boston, 1656–1964: Three Centuries of Friends in Boston and Cambridge.* 349 pp. Cambridge: Friends Meeting at Cambridge, 1976. (Ch. 1, 2 describe the Quaker evangelical challenge to the Puritan ascendancy in early Boston, downplaying its more unusual protest elements but demonstrating its persistence. Index. Bibliography.).

American Colonial Resistance and the Independence Movement, 1765–1775

During a period of ten years before the War of Independence, American colonists actively resisted perceived encroachments on their liberties by the British government. The chief events of this period included the Stamp Act resistance (1765–66), protests and economic boycotts against the Townshend Acts of 1767 (1768–70), and the organization of a broad intercolonial front (Continental Association) against the Coercive Acts (1774–75). Entries included here discuss all or some of these events. Readers will notice that the British American colonists developed many forms of protest over the decade. They combined these with economic and political noncooperation, such as refusal to buy or use British goods (nonimportation) or to serve on juries. Likewise, these colonists developed new kinds of political organization and nonviolent intervention in the form of committees and conventions that competed with the legal government for authority.

439.   Ammerman, David, *In the Common Cause: American Response to the Coercive Acts of 1774*. 170 pp. Charlottesville: University Press of Virginia, 1974. (History of the origin and conduct of resistance before and during the Continental Association, May 1774 to April 1775. See ch. 2, 3 on events before the First Continental Congress; ch. 6, "Resistance Short of War: The Continental Association"; and ch. 8, "Government by Committee." Note comment on pp. 122–24 on committees' restraint of violence. Index.)

440.   Becker, Carl L., *The History of Political Parties in the Province of New York, 1760–1776*. 319 pp. Madison: Univ. of Wisconsin Press, 1960 [orig. publ. 1909]. (See ch. 2 on the Stamp Act, ch. 3 on the Townshend Acts nonimportation agreements, ch. 4 on the 1773 Tea Act confrontation, ch. 5, 6 on the Continental Congress, and the following chapters on the reconstruction of politics within New York in 1774–75. Index. Bibliography.)

441. Brown, Richard D., *Revolutionary Politics in Massachusetts: The Boston Committee of Correspondence and the Towns, 1772–1774*. 282 pp. Cambridge: Harvard Univ. Press, 1970. (History of the colony's committees of correspondence and their role in mobilizing and shaping protest and resistance. See esp. ch. 7–10 on noncooperation and parallel government. Appendix. Bibliography.)

442. Christie, Ian R., and Benjamin W. Labaree, *Empire or Independence, 1760–1776*. 332 pp. New York: W.W. Norton, 1976. (History of the period as seen through the growing antagonism between Parliament and the colonies. Ch. 3 is on the Stamp Act, ch. 5, 6 on the Townshend Acts, and ch. 9–11 on 1774. Index. Bibliography.)

443. Conser, Walter H., Jr., Ronald M. McCarthy, David J. Toscano, and Gene Sharp, eds., *Resistance, Politics, and the Struggle for Independence, 1765–1775*. 332 pp. Boulder CO: Lynne Rienner Publishers, 1986. (Essays on the ten years of the independence movement giving both a general history and offering an interpretation based upon the idea that nonviolent action was a significant component of the strategy used by the colonists against Britain. Appendixes. Index.)

444. Gipson, Lawrence Henry, *The British Empire before the American Revolution*. 14 vols. New York: Alfred A. Knopf, 1936–69.

Vol. 10, *The Triumphant Empire: Thunder–Clouds Gather in the West, 1763–1766*. 414 pp. 1961. (See pp. 208–15 on the northern colonies' petitions against renewal of the Molasses Act of 1733 and pp. 220–21, 231–38 on legislative protests against the Sugar [American] Act of 1764. Ch. 13–18 describe the Stamp Act resistance in detail; note esp. the Stamp Act Congress of October 1765, pp. 329–35, and discussion of nullification of the act and of commercial resistance in ch. 15. Index.)

Vol. 11, *The Triumphant Empire: The Rumbling of the Coming Storm, 1766–1770*. 579 pp. 1965. (Pp. 54–66 discuss New York's protests against the Quartering Act of 1764, the colony's refusal to comply with it, and the resulting parliamentary sanctions. Ch. 5, 6, 8 are on colonial opposition to the Townshend Acts of 1767 and the government's responses. Pp. 181–90, 266–73 follow the course of the colonial nonimportation campaign of 1768–70. Index.)

Vol. 12, *The Triumphant Empire: Britain Sails into the Storm, 1770–1776.* 372 pp. 1965. (See pp. 47–50 on the origins of the committees of correspondence in Massachusetts and pp. 14–18 and ch. 3 on the Tea Act of 1773, the Boston Tea Party, and resistance to the Tea Act in other cities. Ch. 4 describes Parliament's reaction to the Tea Party, the Coercive Acts of 1774, and; in pp. 313–23, the growing confrontation in Massachusetts to April 1775. Index.)

Vol. 14, *A Bibliographic Guide to the History of the British Empire, 1748–1776.* 478 pp. 1969. (Ch. 4, 5 contain colony–by–colony references to bibliographic aids, published primary sources, and secondary works. Ch. 2, on Great Britain proper, contains references to sources on the workings of Parliament and the empire's constitutional structure. Index.)

445.   Hutchinson, Thomas, *The History of the Colony and Province of Massachusetts–Bay.* Vol. 3. Ed. Lawrence Shaw Mayo. 453 pp. Cambridge: Harvard Univ. Press, 1936. (Written after the events of the Independence Movement by the next–to–last governor of Massachusetts Bay Province. See esp. pp. 84–121 on resistance to the Stamp Act, pp. 121–24 on resistance to the quartering of British troops, and pp. 130–209, 221–98, 303–30 on other protest and resistance, esp. pp. 233–35. Appendixes.)

446.   Jensen, Merrill, *The Founding of a Nation: A History of the American Revolution, 1763–1776.* 735 pp. New York: Oxford Univ. Press, 1968. (Ch. 3–6 describe resistance to and "nullification" of the Stamp Act, ch. 9–14 discuss the Townshend Acts resistance and the politics of nonimportation, and ch. 17–20 discuss the months from the Boston Tea Party to early 1775. Index.)

447.   Labaree, Benjamin Woods, *The Boston Tea Party.* 347 pp. London, Oxford, and New York: Oxford Univ. Press, 1966.

Reprint, Boston: Northeastern Univ. Press, 1986. (The coming of the revolution as seen through the tea trade and conflicts associated with it. See ch. 2 on the Townshend Acts tea tax and the politics and economics of nonimportation, ch. 5–7 on the effects of the Tea Act of 1773, and ch. 9–12 on the Coercive Acts and resistance to them. Appendix. Index. Bibliography.)

448. Maier, Pauline, *From Resistance to Revolution: Colonial Radicals and the Development of American Opposition to Britain, 1765–1776*. 344 pp. New York: Alfred A. Knopf, 1972. (Ch. 1, 2 discuss the historical and ideological background to civil conflict in the colonies and Whig theories of the forms and methods of resistance. Other chapters discuss the nature and progress of "ordered resistance," stressing the role of the Sons of Liberty in the early stages of the conflict. Appendix on Sons of Liberty.)

449. Morgan, Edmund S., and Helen M. Morgan, *The Stamp Act Crisis*. 310 pp. Chapel Hill NC: Univ. of North Carolina Press, 1953. Rev. ed., *The Stamp Act Crisis: Prologue to Revolution*. 384 pp. New York: Collier Books, 1963. (Study of politics and personalities in the American protests of the mid–1760s. See ch. 3 on the Sugar [American] Act of 1764 and ch. 5 on the Stamp Act. Ch. 6–11 study the growth of the Stamp Act resistance, part 3 presents sketches of three of its opponents, and ch. 25 discusses its repeal. Index.)

450. Patterson, Stephen E., *Political Parties in Revolutionary Massachusetts*. 299 pp. Madison: Univ. of Wisconsin Press, 1973. (Focuses on the development of conflict groups into political parties, 1769 to 1780. Ch. 3 discusses the basis of protest and commercial resistance in Boston until after the Tea Party. In ch. 4, on the growing revolutionary coalition of 1774, see esp. pp. 95–100 on extralegal conventions and noncooperation to prevent the functioning of courts and pp. 109–13 on the First Provincial Congress. Appendixes. Index.)

451. Schlesinger, Arthur M., *The Colonial Merchants and the American Revolution, 1763–1776*. 647 pp. New York: Columbia Univ. Press, 1918. Reprint, New York: Frederick Ungar, 1966; New York: Atheneum, 1968. (Pioneering study of

merchants and commercial resistance. See ch. 2 on the Stamp Act resistance, ch. 3–5 on the Townshend Acts, ch. 7 on opposition to the Tea Act, ch. 8, 9 on factors determining the course of resistance in 1774, ch. 10, 11 on the making of the Continental Association, and ch. 12, 13 on its operation before the outbreak of war. Text of Continental Association in appendix. Index. Bibliography.)

452.   Walsh, Richard, *Charleston's Sons of Liberty: A Study of the Artisans, 1763–1789.* 166 pp. Columbia: Univ. of South Carolina Press, 1959. (See ch. 2, 3, pp. 56–70, on the role of artisans in the independence movement. Illustrations. Appendix. Index. Bibliography.)

453.   Warden, G.B., *Boston, 1689–1776.* 404 pp. Boston: Little, Brown, 1970. (On Boston's political transformation. See ch. 8 on the Stamp Act resistance, ch. 9, 11, 12 on the Townshend Acts resistance and after, ch. 13 on the Boston Tea Party, and ch. 14 on the events of 1774. Of particular interest is ch. 10, "Protest and Reform: Goals and Methods." Illustrations. Index. Bibliography.)

Embargo and Nonintercourse, 1807–1812

Perhaps remembering the "nonimportation" campaigns of 1765–1775, Presidents Thomas Jefferson and James Madison attempted to use commercial pressure on Britain. Britain was then using its naval power to stop trade with France, its enemy, even to the point of seizing U.S. flag vessels and sailors. Embargo and non–intercourse laws, basically stopping U.S. international trade for a time, were perhaps more unpopular in the northeastern U.S. than in Britain and did not stop the coming of the War of 1812.

454.   Adams, Henry, *History of the United States of America During the Administration of Thomas Jefferson.* Vol. 2, containing book 3, 471 pp., and book 4, 474 pp. New York: Albert and Charles Boni, 1930. Originally published New York: Charles Scribner's Sons, 1890. Reprint, New York: Antiquarian Press, 1962. (Contains Congressional debates regarding merits of trade restrictions with Britain, drafting

of Non–Importation Bill, and subsequent embargo. See esp.
book 3, pp. 147–55, 175, 394–401, 430–37 for events during
Jefferson's first administration. For the second
administration, see book 4, esp. ch. 7, 9, 11, 12, 15, 19, and pp.
33–35, 87–101, 144–45, 186–88, 198–205, 218–23, 245–47.)

455. Jennings, Walter Wilson, *The American Embargo, 1807–1809:
With Particular Reference to Its Effect on Industry.* 242 pp.
Iowa City: Iowa Univ. Press, 1921. (History of U.S. embargo
of 1807–1809, a result of the "non–intercourse" policy. Ch. 3
covers the passage of the Embargo Act and its effect on trade
with other nations and ch. 7–9 explore its effects on the U.S.
Index. Bibliography.)

456. Spivak, Burton, *Jefferson's English Crisis: Commerce,
Embargo, and the Republican Revolution.* 250 pp.
Charlottesville: University Press of Virginia, 1979.
(Examination of Thomas Jefferson's response to the threat of
Great Britain, its naval power, and increasing influence on
American economic, social, and political life. See pp. 67–70 on
the embargo concept in "Republican" political thought and
ch. 4 on the embargo of 1807–9. See also index under
*Chesapeake Affair, customs collectors, economic coercion,
embargo, embargoes, impressments, manageable war strategy,
market, American, nonimportation,* and *peaceable coercion.*
Index.)

Cherokee Resistance to Removal, 1827–1841

*The Cherokees of the southeastern United States adapted to
European settlement and to a point assimilated culturally also. They
possessed rich lands coveted by their white neighbors, all the more so
when some gold was found there. After years of debate and Cherokee
opposition, the administration of President Andrew Jackson passed
the Indian Removal Act in 1830, which authorized the relocation of
Indians to a newly–created Indian Territory in present–day
Oklahoma. A group of Cherokee leaders conducted elite–based
protest and petition campaigns but were opposed by another faction
that believed that the people must give in. White missionaries from
the North also became involved in the campaign, for which some*

were expelled and punished by the states despite being U.S. citizens engaged in a legal activity. In 1838, after the campaign of appeals and passive resistance, the remaining Cherokees were forced to travel along the "Trail of Tears" to the new territory.

457.   Carter, Samuel, III, *Cherokee Sunset: A Nation Betrayed: A Narrative of Travail and Triumph, Persecution and Exile.* 318 pp. Garden City NY: Doubleday, 1976. (History of the Cherokee expulsion from eastern U.S. lands. See esp. ch. 7–15 on the campaign of protest and resistance by the Ross party and missionaries to the Cherokees who defied Georgia's attempts to exclude them from the state. Illustrations. Index. Bibliography.)

458.   Eaton, Rachel Caroline, *John Ross and the Cherokee Indians.* 153 pp. Chicago: Univ. of Chicago Libraries, 1921. (Ross's career during the removal era is discussed in ch. 8–14. Ch. 8 looks at protests and petitions against the removal bill. Ch. 10 is on the Washington lobby and ch. 12 is on the opposition to the Schermerhorn treaty. See pp. 75–76 for a proto–hunger strike by Cherokees boycotting government rations.)

459.   Evarts, Jeremiah, *Cherokee Removal: The "William Penn" Essays and Other Writings.* Ed. Francis Paul Prucha. 314 pp. Knoxville: Univ. of Tennessee Press, 1981. (Essays by a leader of the campaign to prevent involuntary removal of the Cherokees. See pp. 11–38 for an account of the protest movement from 1829–31, including the petition campaign and protest meetings. See also ch. 5, "Protest Against the Indian Removal Bill." Documents. Index.)

460.   Finger, John R., *The Eastern Band of Cherokees, 1819–1900.* 253 pp. Knoxville: Univ. of Tennessee Press, 1984. (See ch. 2 on the resistance mounted by those Cherokees who managed to prevent their removal, thus becoming the surviving Eastern Band of Cherokees. Illustrations. Photos. Index. Bibliography.)

461.   Foreman, Grant, *Indian Removal: The Emigration of the Five Civilized Tribes of Indians.* 415 pp. Norman: Univ. of Oklahoma Press, 1932. (See ch. 18–24 on the Cherokees. Ch.

19 is on Cherokee defense of land and nation, including brief discussions of lobbying Congress, calls for noncooperation against removal plans, and petitions. Brief mention of these follows in later chapters. Illustrations. Photos. Bibliography.)

462. Lumpkin, Wilson, *The Removal of the Cherokee Indians from Georgia.* 328 pp. New York: Arno Press and the New York Times, 1969 [orig. publ. New York: Dodd, Mead, 1907]. (Biographical material, speeches, and correspondence of this U.S. senator and Georgia governor, 1827–41, much of which relates to his views and activities regarding the Cherokees. Illustrations. Index.)

463. McLoughlin, William G., *Cherokees and Missionaries, 1789–1839.* 375 pp. New Haven and London: Yale Univ. Press, 1984. (Although a sidelight to the Cherokee resistance as such, the ambivalent support of white Christian missionaries for the Cherokees' aspirations is described and assessed in ch. 10–12. See esp. the account of Georgia's effort to reign in the missionaries through a loyalty oath which was answered by "civil disobedience" and legal challenges by Samuel Worcester and Elizur Butler, both of whom were imprisoned, pp. 257–66, 297–99. Index.)

464. Moulton, Gary E., *The Papers of Chief John Ross.* 2 vols. 765 pp. Norman: Univ. of Oklahoma Press, 1985. (Correspondence and addresses of Ross and associates. See esp. the letters and public papers of the years 1828 to May 1838 for his steady opposition to removal. Index.)

465. Pessen, Edward, *Jacksonian America: Society, Personality, and Politics.* 408 pp. Homewood IL: Dorsey Press, 1969. (See pp. 317–22 for a brief account of President Jackson's Indian removal policy. Bibliographical essay.)

466. Prucha, Francis Paul, *American Indian Policy in the Formative Years: The Indian Trade and Intercourse Acts, 1790–1834.* 303 pp. Cambridge: Harvard Univ. Press, 1962. (See pp. 174–78, 202–03, 227–49, for U.S. Government reactions to the Cherokees' resistance. Index.)

467. Reid, John Phillip, *A Law of Blood: The Primitive Law and the Cherokee Nation*. 340 pp. New York: New York Univ. Press, 1970. (Explains Cherokees' traditions of law and peace; see esp. ch. 22, 23.)

468. Starkey, Marion L., *The Cherokee Nation*. 362 pp. New York: Russell & Russell, 1946. Reprint, 1972. (See ch. 6–19; esp. pp. 107, 112–13, 154–58, 260, 266, 269–74, 283 on protests and resistance against Cherokee removal from Georgia. Bibliography.)

469. Van Every, Dale, *Disinherited: The Lost Birthright of the American Indian*. 279 pp. New York: William & Morrow, 1966. (Describes, on p. 130, the Cherokee nation as "committed of necessity to an altogether nonviolent resistance." See ch. 11, 12, 15–18, esp. pp. 146–51 on U.S. and Georgia officials' refusal to heed Supreme Court decisions and pp. 198–202, 223–31 on John Ross's policy. Index. Bibliography.)

470. Wardell, Morris L., *A Political History of the Cherokee Nation, 1838–1907*. 383 pp. Norman: Univ. of Oklahoma Press, 1938. (Brief discussion of the internal politics of removal appears in ch. 1. Appendix A contains a summary of a John Ross petition to the House of Representatives. Photos. Appendixes. Index. Bibliography.)

Antislavery Movements and Abolitionism Before 1861

Decades of anti–slavery agitation before the Civil War represent one of the most concentrated efforts in U.S. history to develop nonviolent means of struggle. Strongly influenced by "nonresistance" views, abolitionists such as William Lloyd Garrison looked toward methods of protest and noncooperation to end slavery. Notable were the abolitionists' noncooperation with the Fugitive Slave Law, hunting of slave catchers, and participation in the Underground Railroad. Many of the dilemmas of combining effectiveness and principle, of the potential role of violence, and of confronting a determined opponent that were to be prominent in twentieth–century conflicts were equally present for the abolitionists.

471. Carter, George E., and C. Peter Ripley, eds., *Black Abolitionist Papers, 1860–1865: A Guide to the Microfilm Edition*. 571 pp. New York: Microfilming Corporation of America, 1981. (Listing of approximately 14,000 entries by approximately 300 black American authors who were involved in the movement to abolish slavery in the U.S. from 1830 to 1865.)

472. Dumond, Dwight Lowell, *A Bibliography of Antislavery in America*. 119 pp. Ann Arbor: Univ. of Michigan Press, 1961. (Bibliography of printed antislavery literature from the period, including British as well as U.S. sources.)

473. Irwin, Leonard B., comp., *Black Studies: A Bibliography*. 122 pp. Brooklawn NJ: McKinley, 1973. (Includes sources beginning with resistance to slavery and continuing to events in 1970. Index.)

STUDIES

474. Aptheker, Herbert, *American Negro Slave Revolts*. 409 pp. New York: International Publishers, 1952. (Brief mention of numerous acts of resistance, including violence, destruction of property, and nonviolent actions. See esp. pp. 140–49. Index. Bibliography.)

475. ———, *Essays in the History of the American Negro*. 216 pp. New York: International Publishers, 1964 [orig. publ. 1945]. (Documents on organized and spontaneous protest against the American slavery system. Emphasizes the active role that many slaves took in securing their freedom. See pp. 1–70 on the history of slave revolts and pp. 11–160 on blacks in the abolitionist movement. Chronology. Appendixes. Bibliography.)

476. Barnes, Gilbert H., *The Antislavery Impulse, 1830–1844*. 298 pp. New York: Harcourt, Brace & World, 1964 [orig. publ. 1933]. (See pp. 109–49, 179–80, 195–97 on the petition campaign of 1836–37. Index.)

477.   Bell, Howard Holman, *A Survey of the Negro Convention Movement 1830–1861.* 298 pp. New York: Arno Press and The New York Times, 1969. (Chronicles Northern blacks holding local, state, and national conventions as a method to advance their objectives. Appendixes. Bibliography.)

478.   Blackett, R.J.M., *Building an Antislavery Wall: Black Abolitionists in the Atlantic Abolitionist Movement, 1830– 1860.* 237 pp. Baton Rouge and London: Louisiana State Univ. Press, 1983. (History of efforts to internationalize abolitionism, esp. to the U.K. See ch. 1 on the methods used to construct a "moral cordon." Index. Bibliography.)

479.   Bracey, John H., Jr., August Meier, and Elliott Rudwick, eds., *American Slavery: The Question of Resistance.* 206 pp. Belmont CA: Wadsworth, 1971. (Collected articles on the general question of obedience and disobedience to slavery. See esp. pp. 37–71, 179–92 on slave resistance by noncooperation.)

480.   Bruns, Roger, ed., *Am I Not A Man and a Brother: The Antislavery Crusade of Revolutionary America, 1688–1788.* 551 pp. New York: Chelsea House Publishers, 1977. (Chronological documentary history of the early American abolitionist movement. Includes original selections by Phillis Wheatley, Thomas Paine, Alexander Hamilton, and others, interspersed with brief explanatory texts. Illustrations. Index. Bibliography.)

481.   Burritt, Elihu, *Thoughts and Things at Home and Abroad.* 364 pp. Boston: Phillips, Sampson; New York: J.C. Derby, 1854. (Essays by the nineteenth–century pacifist and abolitionist. See pp. 269–89 for short pieces on "passive resistance" with contemporary examples.)

482.   Cockrum, William M., *History of the Underground Railroad: As It Was Conducted by the Anti–Slavery League.* 328 pp. Oakland City IN: J.W. Cockrum, 1915. (Naive history of the Underground Railroad in Indiana based on recollections of the Anti–Slavery League's activities. Photos.)

483. Conrad, Earl, *Harriet Tubman*. 248 pp. Washington DC: Associated Publishers, 1943. (Biography of the leader of the Underground Railroad and later fighter in the Civil War. Part 2 is on Harriet Tubman's activities in guiding escaping slaves to the North and Canada. Index.)

484. Crosby, Ernest, *Garrison the Non–Resistant*. 141 pp. Chicago: Public Publishing, 1905. (A treatment of Garrison's politics with comments on his nonresistance, by an author influenced by Tolstoy. See ch. 2–3 for the biography and ch. 8, 9 for discussion of nonresistance.)

485. Degler, Carl N., *The Other South: Southern Dissenters in the Nineteenth Century*. 392 pp. New York, Evanston IL, San Francisco, and London: Harper & Row, 1974. (History of Southern dissent from the 1830s to 1900. See ch. 2, 3 on Southerners against slavery. Index.)

486. Demos, John, "The Antislavery Movement and the Problem of Violent 'Means'." *New England Quarterly* 37 (1964): 501–26. (On the religious derivation of "non–resistance" and efforts by abolitionists based on the religious theory of nonresistance to propose alternatives to revolt and war in the abolition of slavery.)

487. Dick, Robert C., *Black Protest: Issues and Tactics*. 338 pp. Westport CT and London: Greenwood Press, 1974. (A study of "ideas expressed in the rhetoric of northern black spokesmen" from 1827 to the Civil War, with biographical sketches of key individuals. See esp. ch. 4 on the issue of violent versus nonviolent tactics. Illustrations. Index. Bibliography.)

488. Dillon, Merton L., *The Abolitionists: Growth of a Dissenting Minority*. 298 pp. De Kalb: Northern Illinois Univ. Press, 1974. (A general history of the abolitionist movement. See ch. 3, 4 on Garrison, ch. 5 on anti–abolitionist sentiment and action, ch. 8 on noncooperation with the Fugitive Slave Law, and ch. 10 on the shift from nonresistance principles to acceptance of violence. Illustrations. Index.)

489.   Douglass, Frederick, *Autobiographies*. Henry Louis Gates, Jr.,
        ed. 1126 pp. New York: Library of America, 1994. (Frederick
        Douglass was born and grew to adulthood under slavery.
        After removing to the North and establishing himself there,
        he became involved in the cause of abolition. Considered a
        speaker and publicist of the first order, Douglass also wrote
        three autobiographies, each of which is published in an
        authoritative edition here. They are entitled *Narrative of
        the Life of Frederick Douglass, An American Slave; My
        Bondage and My Freedom;* and *Life and Times of Frederick
        Douglass.* Chronology.)

490.   Duberman, Martin, ed., *The Antislavery Vanguard: New
        Essays on the Abolitionists.* 507 pp. Princeton NJ: Princeton
        Univ. Press, 1965. (Part 2 includes studies of Wendell Phillips
        and Frederick Douglass. Silvan S. Tompkins, "The
        Psychology of Commitment: The Constructive Role of
        Violence and Suffering for the Individual and for His
        Society," ch. 12 discusses views of violence and reactions to it.
        Howard Zinn, "Abolitionists, Freedom–Riders, and the
        Tactics of Abolitionism," ch. 17 includes discussion of tactics
        and a comparison between abolitionism and early 1960s civil
        rights activism. Index.)

491.   Filler, Louis, *The Crusade against Slavery, 1830–1860.* 318
        pp. New York: Harper & Brothers, 1960. (Ch. 4, on the
        "antislavery concert," discusses the Lane Seminary case, the
        founding of Oberlin College as a counter–institution, and
        Garrison. See ch. 5–8 on the problems of abolitionism and
        consult index under *Garrison, pacifism, petitions,* and
        underground railroad. Illustrations. Index. Bibliography.)

492.   Filler, Louis, ed., *Abolition and Social Justice in the Era of
        Reform.* 367 pp. New York, Evanston, San Francisco, and
        London: Harper & Row, 1972. (Collection of documents
        written by abolitionists and reformers. See part 2, "The
        Antislavery Concert," and selection 46, Elihu Burritt's
        "Passive Resistance." Index.)

493.   Gara, Larry, *The Liberty Line: The Legend of the
        Underground Railroad.* 201 pp. Lexington: Univ. of Kentucky

Press, 1961. (Designed in part to reveal and correct the legend. See ch. 3–5 on methods and organization and ch. 6 on fugitives and the Fugitive Slave Law. Index.)

494. Garrison, William Lloyd, *The Letters of William Lloyd Garrison*. Cambridge: Belknap Press of Harvard Univ. Press, 1971–1981. Vol. 1, *I Will Be Heard! 1822–1835*. Ed. Walter M. Merrill, 616 pp. 1971. (See pp. xxvi–xxx for a chronology of Garrison's life.) Vol. 2, *A House Dividing against Itself, 1836–1840*. Ed. Louis Ruchames, 770 pp. 1971. (See pp. xxii–xxxi for short biographies of abolitionists.) Vol. 3, *No Union with Slave–Holders, 1841–1849*. Ed. Walter M. Merrill, 719 pp. 1973. Vol. 4, *From Disunionism to the Brink of War, 1850–1860*. Ed. Louis Ruchames, 637 pp. 1975. Vol. 5, *Let the Oppressed Go Free, 1861–1867*. Ed. Walter M. Merrill, 597 pp. 1979. Vol. 6, *To Rouse the Slumbering Land, 1868–1879*. Ed. Walter M. Merrill and Louis Ruchames, 637 pp. 1981. Illustrations. Photos. Index.)

495. Harding, Vincent, *There Is a River: The Black Struggle for Freedom in America*. 442 pp. New York and London: Harcourt Brace Jovanovich, 1981. (Personal view of African–American resistance to slavery and against laws supporting it from the seventeenth century to 1865. See esp. ch. 4–10. Illustrations. Photos. Index. Bibliography.)

496. Hersh, Blanche Glassman, *The Slavery of Sex: Feminist–Abolitionists in America*. 280 pp. Urbana, Chicago, and London: Univ. of Illinois Press, 1978. (History of the confluence of feminism and abolitionism in the mid–nineteenth century. Index. Bibliography.)

497. Huggins, Nathan I., *Slave and Citizen: The Life of Frederick Douglass*. 194 pp. Boston and Toronto: Little, Brown, 1980. (Biography of Douglass with emphasis on his political and reform activities. Index.)

498. Lader, Lawrence, *The Bold Brahmins: New England's War Against Slavery: 1831–1863*. 318 pp. New York: E.P. Dutton, 1961. (Study of issues, actions, and personalities in Boston's

abolition movement and its response to the fugitive slave laws. See esp. ch. 1, 4–9, 12. Photos. Index. Bibliography.)

499.   Lesick, Lawrence Thomas, *The Lane Rebels: Evangelicalism and Antislavery in Antebellum America*. 278 pp. Metuchen NJ and London: Scarecrow Press, 1980. (Case study of students' collective withdrawal from Lane Seminary in Ohio protesting a ban on antislavery activities, 1834. See ch. 4 on the rebellion. Index. Bibliography.)

500.   Lovejoy, Joseph C., and Owen Lovejoy, *Memoir of the Rev. Elijah P. Lovejoy: Who Was Murdered in Defence of the Liberty of the Press, at Alton, Illinois, Nov. 7, 1837*. 382 pp. New York: John S. Taylor, 1838. (An account of the 1835–37 defiant anti–slavery campaign of the editor of the St. Louis *Observer* in the face of threats, crowd actions against him, and arson. Lovejoy defended his print shop, pistol in hand, and was murdered by the crowd, his case becoming a focus for the discussion of the place of violence in abolitionism.)

501.   Lutz, Alma, *Crusade for Freedom: Women of the Antislavery Movement*. 338 pp. Boston: Beacon Press, 1968. (History of women active in the abolitionist movement. Protest and petitions mentioned throughout. See index under specific names, esp. *Chapman, Maria Weston; Garrison, William Lloyd; Mott, Lucretia*; and *Weld, Angelina Grimke*. Illustrations. Photos. Index. Bibliography.)

502.   Mabee, Carleton, *Black Freedom: The Nonviolent Abolitionists from 1830 through the Civil War*. 435 pp. New York: Macmillan; London: Collier–Macmillan, 1970. (History of abolitionists who chose nonviolent means in their struggle. Part 1 is on the issue of violence and the decision to choose nonviolent means. Part 2 is on methods of direct action against discriminatory laws, including railroad ride–ins, pray–ins, and school boycotts. Part 3 is on methods of action against slavery itself, including economic boycotts, speak–ins, noncooperation, the Underground Railroad, and resistance to the Fugitive Slave Law. Index.)

503.   McFeely, William S., *Frederick Douglass*. 465 pp. New York and London: W.W. Norton, 1990. (Detailed and thorough biography of abolitionist Frederick Douglass. The years from Douglass's first anti–slavery speech on the island of Nantucket, Massachusetts until the Civil War are discussed in ch. 8–16. Illustrations. Photos. Index. Bibliography.)

504.   Nuermberger, Ruth K., *The Free Produce Movement: A Quaker Protest against Slavery*. 147 pp. Durham NC: Duke Univ. Press, 1942. *Historical Papers of the Trinity College Historical Society*, series 25. (Account of an organized effort to boycott goods produced by slave labor. Appendix. Index. Bibliography.)

505.   Nye, Russell B., *Fettered Freedom: Civil Liberties and the Slavery Controversy, 1830–1860*. 273 pp. East Lansing: Michigan State College Press, 1949. (See pp. 41–85 on petition campaigns and antislavery mailings and pp. 174–218 on crowd actions against abolitionists. Index. Bibliography.)

506.   Ofari, Earle, *"Let Your Motto Be Resistance": The Life and Thought of Henry Highland Garnet*. 221 pp. Boston: Beacon Press, 1972. (Political biography of the African–American abolitionist Garnet, seen by the author as a revolutionary black nationalist. Appendix contains speeches by Garnet from 1840–1865. Index.)

507.   Olmstead, Frederick Law, *A Journey in the Seaboard Slave States in the Years 1853–1854: With Remarks on Their Economy*. Vol. 1, 418 pp. New York: Knickerbocker Press, 1904. (See esp. pp. 111–13, 208–27 for first–hand accounts of slave slow–downs, feigning sickness, and other methods of noncooperation.)

508.   Perry, Lewis, *Radical Abolitionism: Anarchy and the Government of God in Antislavery Thought*. 328 pp. Ithaca and London: Cornell Univ. Press, 1973. (Analytical essay on themes of nonresistance, anarchy, and the problem of authority in the radical antislavery movement. See ch. 3 on the origins and ideology of the New England Non–Resistance Society and the theme of nonresistance; ch. 4 on "come–

outerism"; ch. 5 on Adin Ballou, the conservative nonresistant, and his ideas of building nonviolent community; and ch. 8 on the issue of violence and the accommodation of nonresistants to violence. Index.)

509.   Perry, Lewis, and Michael Fellman, eds., *Antislavery Reconsidered: New Perspectives on the Abolitionists.* 348 pp. Baton Rouge and London: Louisiana State Univ. Press, 1979. (Essays on the abolitionist movement. See the introduction and Ronald G. Walters, "The Boundaries of Abolitionism," pp. 3–23 for historiographical discussions; Carol U.R. George, "Widening the Circle: The Black Church and the Abolitionist Crusade, 1830–1860," pp. 75–95 on the black clergy and black churches' participation in the abolition movement; William M. Wiecek, "Latimer: Lawyers, Abolitionists, and the Problem of Unjust Laws," pp. 219–37 on abolition and civil disobedience; and Ellen DuBois, "Women's Rights and Abolition: The Nature of the Connection," pp. 238–51. Index.)

510.   Quarles, Benjamin, *Black Abolitionists.* 310 pp. London, Oxford and New York: Oxford Univ. Press, 1969. (Ch. 7 discusses aid to escapees from slavery and ch. 9 describes black protest and defiance of the Fugitive Slave Law. Index.)

511.   Rather, Lorman, *Powder Keg: Northern Opposition to the Antislavery Movement, 1831–1840.* 172 pp. New York and London: Basic Books, 1968. (History of anti–abolitionist activity in New England and the Middle Atlantic states, 1831–40. See ch. 4 for the anti–abolitionists' charges that violence was instigated by abolitionists. Index. Bibliography.)

512.   Richards, Leonard L., *"Gentlemen of Property and Standing": Anti–Abolition Mobs in Jacksonian America.* 196 pp. New York: Oxford Univ. Press, 1970. (Study of the origins, organization, and conduct of anti–abolitionist violence of the 1830s. Index. Bibliography.)

513.   Richardson, Marilyn, ed., *Maria W. Stewart: America's First Black Woman Political Writer.* 136 pp. Bloomington and

Indianapolis: Indiana Univ. Press, 1987. (Series of essays and speeches by early abolitionist. Contains works from 1831–33 and post–Civil War memoirs. Illustrations. Index. Appendixes.)

514.   Ross, Alexander M., *Recollections and Experiences of an Abolitionist: From 1855–1865*. 224 pp. Toronto: Rowsell & Hutchinson, 1875. Reprint, Northbrook IL: Metro Books, 1972. (Memoirs of a man who trained and equipped slaves for escape to the North. See ch. 1–4.)

515.   Siebert, Wilbur Henry, *The Mysteries of Ohio's Underground Railroads*. 330 pp. Columbus OH: Long's College Book Co., 1951. (Overview of routes, conductors, and methods in several regions of the state. Photos. Index.)

516.   ———, *The Underground Railroad from Slavery To Freedom*. 478 pp. New York and London: Macmillan, 1898. (Detailed history based in part on interviews Siebert conducted in the 1890s. Ch. 2–4 discuss the origins of the Underground Railroad, ch. 5 plots its extent, and ch. 9, 10 detail the legal and political issues involved. Appendixes include federal legislation on fugitive slaves, significant legal cases, and a list of names of persons involved. Photos. Index. Bibliography in appendix.)

517.   ———, *The Underground Railroad in Massachusetts*. 78 pp. Worcester MA: American Antiquarian Society, 1936. Originally published in *Proceedings of the American Antiquarian Society*, new series, 45 (1935): 25–100. (Connects the Underground Railroad to the wider antislavery movement. See pp. 38–68 on the Boston Vigilance Committee and noncooperation with the Fugitive Slave Law. Photos.)

518.   ———, *Vermont's Anti–Slavery and Underground Railroad Record*. 113 pp. Columbus OH: Spahr & Glenn, 1937. (See ch. 7, 8 on the operation of Vermont escape routes to Canada. Illustrations.)

519.   Sillen, Samuel, *Women against Slavery*. 102 pp. New York: Masses & Mainstream, 1955. (Profiles of women who took

leading roles in the antislavery struggles. Illustrations. Bibliography.)

520.   Simms, Henry H., *Emotion at High Tide: Abolition as a Controversial Factor, 1830–1845.* 243 pp. Baltimore: Moore, 1960. (See ch. 6–8 on antislavery petitions, 1835–45. Index.)

521.   Smedley, R.C., *History of the Underground Railroad.* 407 pp. Lancaster PA: The *Journal*, 1883. Reprint, New York: Arno Press and The New York Times, 1969. (Early study of the Underground Railroad in Chester County, Pennsylvania, emphasizing the role of religious whites. Illustrations. Index.)

522.   Sorin, Gerald, *Abolitionism: A New Perspective.* 187 pp. New York, Washington, and London: Praeger Publishers, 1972. (Analysis of abolitionism as phase of the U.S. tradition of radical reform. See ch. 4 on the technique of "moral suasion" and ch. 5 on the issue of nonviolent versus violent approaches. Consult index under *noncoercion, noncooperation, nonresistance,* and *nonviolence.* Index. Bibliography.)

523.   Stewart, James Brewer, *William Lloyd Garrison and the Challenge of Emancipation.* 213 pp. Arlington Heights IL: Harlan Davidson, 1992. (Political and intellectual biographer of the abolitionist publicist and organizer, with attention to actions taken by Garrison and others to advance their cause. See ch. 6, "Martyrdom," for accounts of anti-abolitionist crowd violence and its effects on opinion leaders. Index.)

524.   Strother, Horatio T., *The Underground Railroad in Connecticut.* 262 pp. Middletown CT: Wesleyan Univ. Press, 1962. (See pp. 30–36 on violence to prevent the education of blacks and ch. 3 on the shaping of the Underground Railroad. Ch. 6 focuses on noncooperation with the Fugitive Slave Law and ch. 7–13 on Connecticut's assistance to blacks escaping slavery. Illustrations. Appendixes. Index. Bibliography.)

525.   Walters, Ronald G., *The Antislavery Appeal: American Abolitionism after 1830.* 196 pp. Baltimore and London: Johns

Hopkins Univ. Press, 1976. (History of the antislavery movement from 1831 to the Civil War. See ch. 1 on the organization of the movement and its factions and ch. 2 on means used in abolitionism and issue of violence. Illustrations. Index.)

Dorr Rebellion, 1841–1842

The state of Rhode Island did not adopt a written constitution but kept its old colonial charter intact, which included restrictions on suffrage. The Dorr Rebellion, or "war," as it is sometimes called, grew from a movement of the disenfranchised in Rhode Island to enlarge the suffrage. Landless and propertied Rhode Islanders separately held meetings to press for the vote, followed by the widespread acceptance of a "people's constitution" to replace the charter. Leader Thomas Wilson Dorr was elected governor of the state under the people's constitution and attempted to create a parallel government. In 1842, Dorr responded to a threat of arrest for treason by a military attack on the state armory. Its failure led to the collapse of the campaign.

526. Coleman, Peter J., *The Transformation of Rhode Island, 1790–1860.* 314 pp. Providence RI: Brown Univ. Press, 1963. (Pp. 254–73 are on the Rhode Island charter and the failure of franchise reform, pp. 274–82 discuss the People's Convention and Dorr's promotion of a parallel government, and pp. 283–94 are on Dorrite politics after the failed rebellion of 1842. Index.)

527. *Facts Involved in the Rhode Island Controversy with Some Views upon the Rights of Both Parties.* 43 pp. Boston: B.B. Mussey, 1842. (History of the Rhode Island charter dispute and arguments in favor of the suffrage party. See esp. pp. 12–29 for the founding of the Free Suffrage Party and the positions it took.)

528. Field, Edward, ed., *State of Rhode Island and Providence Plantations at the End of the Century: A History.* Vol. 1., 673 pp. Boston: Mason Pub., 1902. (See ch. 20 on the suffrage campaign.)

529.   Gettleman, Marvin E., *The Dorr Rebellion: A Study in American Radicalism, 1833–1849.* 257 pp. New York: Random House, 1973. (Historical study of the Dorr Rebellion as an example of a native radical movement. Description of petitions, parades, mass meetings, and other forms of nonviolent action throughout. Appendix A reprints "The People's Constitution." Illustrations. Documents. Index. Bibliography.)

530.   King, Dan, *The Life and Times of Thomas Wilson Dorr, with Outlines of the Political History of Rhode Island.* 368 pp. Boston: Dan King, 1859. (See, in general, ch. 3–10 for a narrative of the period from the writing of the people's constitution to Dorr's return to the state after his rebellion collapsed. See esp. ch. 5, 6 on the formation of a Dorr–led parallel government. Appendix.)

531.   Mowry, Arthur M., *The Dorr War or the Constitutional Struggle in Rhode Island.* 420 pp. Providence RI: Preston & Rounds, 1901. (Depicts the Dorr Rebellion as having failed because of its resort to violent means. Explores "the power of strong, moderately phrased and continuous public protest, and its superiority to forcible revolution," p. xv. Ch. 15 describes the Dorrite military attack and its failure. Illustrations. Appendix. Index. Bibliography.)

532.   A Rhode Islander [Catherine R. Williams], *Might and Right.* 324 pp. Providence: A.H. Stillwell, 1844. (Contemporary account of the suffrage movement by a supporter. See ch. 4–13 for the course of the campaign. Index. Bibliography.)

533.   Richman, Irving B., *Rhode Island: A Study in Separatism.* 395 pp. New York: Houghton Mifflin, 1905. (See ch. 14. Bibliography.)

Mormon Flight From Homes, 1858

After sending militia units to burn wagon trains and supplies being shipped to U.S. troops marching to subdue them in the "Utah War," Mormon settlers under Brigham Young gave up their military policy in July 1858. In its place, Mormons to the north of Salt Lake City took flight from their homes en masse, declaring that they would prefer to abandon and destroy their property rather than submit. Despite the earlier violence, federal authorities chose to settle with the Latter-Day Saints, who then returned to their homes.

534.   Alter, J. Cecil, *Utah, The Storied Domain.* Vol. 1, 509 pp. Chicago and New York: American Historical Society, 1932. (Ch. 21, 22 contain documents and news reports on the Utah War, including items on Mormon flight, pp. 270–80. Photos. Index.)

535.   Arrington, Leonard J., *Brigham Young: American Moses.* 522 pp. New York: Alfred A. Knopf, 1985. (See ch. 15–16 on the Utah War and its settlement, with pp. 264–67 discussing the "Move South" flight from Mormon settlements. Appendixes. Index.)

536.   ———, *Charles C. Rich: Mormon General and Western Frontiersman.* 386 pp. Provo UT: Brigham Young Univ. Press, 1974. (Biography of an early Mormon settler. Ch. 15, "General Rich and the Utah War," contains an account of the migration. See esp. pp. 217–18 on Mormon tactics. Bibliography.)

537.   ———, *Great Basin Kingdom: An Economic History of the Latter-Day Saints, 1830–1900.* 534 pp. Cambridge: Harvard Univ. Press, 1958. (Study of the Mormon economic development program, with an emphasis on the role of the religious authority in determining policy. Ch. 6, "Mobilization," contains accounts of the Utah War, including the planning, execution, and financing of the move, pp. 182–88. Bibliography.)

538.   Bailey, Paul, *The Armies of God.* 300 pp. Garden City NY: Doubleday, 1968. (See "The Utah War," pp. 185–255, esp. pp. 208–9 for Brigham Young's official statement regarding exile as preferable to occupation. Illustrations. Photos. Index. Bibliography.)

539.   Neff, Andrew L., *History of Utah: 1847 to 1869*. 955 pp. Salt
        Lake City UT: Deseret News Press, 1940. (Ch. 20–22, esp. pp.
        494–512, detail the Utah War and Mormon flight, plans for
        destruction of their property, and reconciliation.
        Bibliography.)

540.   Roberts, B.H., *A Comprehensive History of the Church of
        Jesus Christ of Latter–Day Saints: Century I*. Vol. 4, 557 pp.
        Salt Lake City UT: Deseret News Press, 1930. (Ch. 102–15
        discuss the era of the Utah War. See esp. pp. 360, 380–81,
        397–98, 416–18, 447–48 on the cessation of military resistance
        and the Mormon flight from their homes. Photos.)

541.   Schindler, Harold, *Orrin Porter Rockwell: Man of God, Son of
        Thunder*. 399 pp. Salt Lake City UT: Univ. of Utah Press,
        1966. (See pp. 287–91 on the Mormon "exodus from Zion."
        Photos. Index. Bibliography.)

542.   Whitney, Orson F., *History of Utah*. Vol. 1, 736 pp. Salt Lake
        City UT: George Q. Cannon, 1892. (See pp. 678–88 for an
        account of the exodus, public reaction to it, and the Peace
        Commission's eventual resolutions. Pp. 679–80 contain
        editorials from the *New York Times* and the *London Times*.
        Illustrations. Index.)

Women's Suffrage Movement, 1848–1920

*Campaigns for women's rights, which came to focus primarily on
winning the vote, were the task of a generation and more. Beginning
with a period of conventions and meetings following the Seneca Falls
Convention of 1848, women and their allies used various means to gain
the vote. Although, after the Civil War, women step aside because
the 1860s were "the Negro's hour," feminist suffrage campaigns
persisted. Susan B. Anthony presented a women's declaration of
independence at the 1876 centennial celebration and was later
prosecuted for attempting to register and vote in Rochester, New
York. In subsequent years, some states were convinced to enfranchise
women. During the final years of the campaign for the federal vote,
the Woman's Party under the leadership of Alice Paul held marches
and processions in several cities and picketed the White House.*

Arguing that President Woodrow Wilson was preaching democracy to the Europeans while denying it at home, suffragists "burned the president's words" in a cauldron on Pennsylvania Avenue. They were attacked by patriotic crowds, arrested, and jailed (see entry 562). English–influenced "militant methods" persisted until the federal amendment was ratified, although such methods were opposed by the mainline National American Woman Suffrage Association.

543. Buhle, Mary Jo, and Paul Buhle, eds., *The Concise History of Woman Suffrage: Selections from the Classic Work of Stanton, Anthony, Gage, and Harper.* 468 pp. Urbana, Chicago, and London: Univ. of Illinois Press, 1978. (Documents from the six–volume *History of Woman Suffrage* [entry no. 562] with prefatory remarks. See editor's introduction placing the suffrage struggle among U.S. movements of reform. Indexes.)

544. Krichmar, Albert, assisted by Barbara Case, Barbara Silver, and Ann E. Wiederrecht, *The Women's Rights Movement in the United States, 1848–1970: A Bibliography and Sourcebook.* 436 pp. Metuchen NJ: Scarecrow Press, 1972. (Partly annotated bibliography of works on the "women's rights movement," 1848–1970. See pp. 78–120 on the suffrage movement. Index.)

STUDIES

545. Adams, Mildred, *The Right to Be People.* 248 pp. Philadelphia and New York: J.B. Lippincott, 1967. (Ch. 1 describes the intellectual background of suffrage ideas and ch. 4, 6, 7 are on the suffrage campaigns. See esp. ch. 5 on suffrage parades and support for the labor movement. Documents in Appendix. Index.)

546. Anthony, Katharine, *Susan B. Anthony: Her Personal History and Her Era.* 521 pp. Garden City NY: Doubleday, 1954. (Biography of the movement leader. Bibliography.)

547. Blackwell, Alice Stone, *Lucy Stone: Pioneer of Woman's Rights.* 313 pp. Boston: Little, Brown, 1930. (Biography of a

leader in the early part of the women's rights movement and abolition movement, written by her daughter. See index under *marriage protest*. Photos. Index.)

548.   Blatch, Harriot Stanton, and Alma Lutz, *Challenging Years: The Memoirs of Harriot Stanton Blatch.* 347 pp. New York: G.P. Putnam's Sons, 1940. (Part 3 is on the New York State suffrage movement. See also index under *parades; woman suffrage; Pankhurst, Emmeline; Paul, Alice; "Silent Sentinels"; suffrage picketing; suffrage tent; suffrage van;* and *Women's Political Union.* Photos. Index.)

549.   Catt, Carrie Chapman, and Nettie R. Shuler, *Woman Suffrage and Politics: The Inner Story of the Suffrage Movement.* 504 pp. Reprint, Seattle and London: Univ. of Washington Press, 1969 [orig. publ. 1923]. (Political history based largely on National American Woman Suffrage Association archives. Of interest are pp. 234–36 on the renewal of petitions and demonstrations for federal suffrage after that method had lapsed for some time, pp. 241–46 on the appearance of English "militant" methods in Alice Paul's approach, and ch. 17–21 on divergent views among activists in the final years. Appendix.)

550.   Dorr, Rheta Childe, *Susan B. Anthony: The Woman Who Changed the Mind of a Nation.* 367 pp. New York: Frederick A. Stokes, 1928. (Political biography. See esp. ch. 5 on the Seneca Falls Convention, ch. 7–11 on early political activities, pp. 254–55 and ch. 20 on Anthony's trial for registering to vote illegally in Rochester, New York, and ch. 26 for the final phase of the suffrage campaign. Photos. Index.)

551.   Evans, Richard J., *The Feminists: Women's Emancipation Movements in Europe, America, and Australasia, 1840–1920.* 266 pp. London: Croom Helm; New York: Barnes & Noble, 1977. (Comparative analysis of women's movements, with many references to nonviolent action used as strategy and tactics in various movements. See index under *demonstrations, women's; elections, mock; militancy, feminist; pacifism; the*

Pankhursts; petitions; Alice Paul; taxation; and *trade unions.* Index.)

552. Flexner, Eleanor, *Century of Struggle: The Woman's Rights Movement in the United States.* 384 pp. Cambridge: Belknap Press of Harvard Univ. Press, 1959. (Social history of the suffrage movement, focusing on its later years, and especially on the lack of lasting social change following the passage of the Nineteenth Amendment. Illustrations. Index.)

553. Gluck, Sherna, ed., *From Parlor to Prison: Five American Suffragists Talk about Their Lives.* 280 pp. New York: Vintage Books, 1976. (Memoirs, oral history, and press reports on the suffrage movement. See pp. 136–40, 190–210, 235–50. Chronology. Bibliography.)

554. Harper, Ida Husted, *The Life and Work of Susan B. Anthony.* 3 vols., 1633 pp. Indianapolis: Hollenbeck Press, 1898 [vols. 1, 2] and 1908 [vol. 3]. (In vol. 1, ch. 5–13 describes Anthony's activities before the Civil War in temperance, abolition, and women's rights causes; ch. 15, 16 discuss "the Negro's hour"; and remaining chapters are on Anthony's organizational and publicity work in the 1870s. In vol. 2, ch. 30, 31, 35, 38, 39, 42–45, 47 describe state suffrage campaigns and ch. 33, 34, 35, 40, 41 discuss federal–level and organizational activities. In vol. 3, ch. 53, 55, 59, 60, 62, 64–65, 68 describe Anthony's activities in political fields after 1898. Photos. Appendixes. Documents. Index.)

555. Irwin, Inez Haynes, *The Story of the Woman's Party.* 486 pp. New York: Harcourt, Brace, 1921. (History of Alice Paul's Woman's Party, 1913–20. See part 3, ch. 1 on the "perpetual delegation" and picketing in front of the White House in 1917, with accounts of attacks by crowds, jailing of pickets, and maltreatment in Occoquan Prison. Part 4, ch. 6, 8, 11–13, discuss "burning the President's words," demonstrations, and pressure for ratification of a federal amendment. Illustrations. Index.)

556. Kraditor, Aileen S., *The Ideas of the Woman Suffrage Movement, 1890–1920.* 313 pp. New York and London:

Columbia Univ. Press, 1965. Reprint Garden City NY: Doubleday, 1971. 262 pp. (Traces the movement's progression from idealism to pragmatism as its goal changed from universal equality to obtaining the right to vote for women. See esp. ch. 8 on suffragist tactics. Appendix. Index. Bibliography.)

557.   Lutz, Alma, *Created Equal: A Biography of Elizabeth Cady Stanton, 1815–1902.* 345 pp. New York: John Day, 1940. (See ch. 20 and p. 317 on militancy. Index. Bibliography.)

558.   ———, *Susan B. Anthony: Rebel, Crusader, Humanitarian.* 340 pp. Boston: Beacon Press, 1959. (See pp. 108–37 on the clash of claims between blacks and women after the Civil War, pp. 180–216 on Anthony's efforts to claim voting rights for women under the post–war constitutional amendments intended to support the citizenship rights of freed slaves, and later chapters on Anthony's activities in state suffrage campaigns. Photos. Index. Bibliography.)

559.   National American Woman Suffrage Association, *Victory: How Women Won It: A Centennial Symposium, 1840–1940.* 174 pp. New York: H.W. Wilson, 1940. (Brief articles on the history of women's suffrage campaigns. See ch. 2, 3, 5, 6 on the nineteenth–century state campaigns, ch. 8–9 on the final years of the movement, and ch. 10 on "the winning plan." Photos. Appendixes. Bibliography.)

560.   Peck, Mary G., *Carrie Chapman Catt: A Biography.* 495 pp. New York: H.W. Wilson, 1944. (Biography of the president of the National American Woman Suffrage Association. See part 1, ch. 7, and parts 2, 3, 5 on her suffrage work in the U.S.; parts 4, 6 on activities in other countries; and part 7, esp. ch. 2, on her concern with peace and war. Brief comments on Alice Paul, the Women's Party, and mainstream objection to their methods on pp. 238–40, 270–71, 295, 305. Photos. Index.)

561.   Robinson, Harriet B., *Massachusetts in the Woman Suffrage Movement: A General, Political, Legal and Legislative History from 1774 to 1881.* 2nd ed. 279 pp. Boston: Roberts Brothers, 1883 [orig. publ. 1881]. (History of the women's

suffrage movement in its early phases with an emphasis on contributions of Massachusetts to the movement. Ch. 2, 3 discuss the convention phase of the movement and its relation to abolitionism; ch. 4 is on "political agitation"; and the appendix contains several documents on these issues. Index.)

562. Stanton, Elizabeth Cady, et al., eds., *History of Woman Suffrage*. 6 vols. (Detailed descriptive history of suffrage activities from 1840 to the end of the struggle. Much material on state campaigns. Somewhat partisan in later volumes as a history of the National American Woman Suffrage Association. See comments on each volume below.)

Vol. 1, 1848–1861. Ed. Elizabeth Cady Stanton, Susan B. Anthony, and Matilda Joslyn Gage. 878 pp. New York: Fowler & Wells, 1881. Reprint, New York: Arno Press and The New York Times, 1969. (History of the convention phase of the suffrage movement. Appendixes.)

Vol. 2, 1861–1876. Ed. Elizabeth Cady Stanton, Susan B. Anthony, and Matilda Joslyn Gage. 952 pp. New York: Fowler & Wells, 1882. Reprint, New York: Arno Press and The New York Times, 1969. (See pp. 90–97 for petitions to Congress and pp. 586–755 on women who registered and voted illegally and on their trials. Appendixes.)

Vol. 3, 1876–1885. Ed. Elizabeth Cady Stanton, Susan B. Anthony, and Matilda Joslyn Gage. 1013 pp. Rochester NY: Susan B. Anthony, 1886. Reprint, New York: Arno Press and The New York Times, 1969. (The suffrage movement in the centennial era. See pp. 17, 27–34, 54–56 for women's actions at the Philadelphia Centennial Exposition, pp. 506–9 for Ohio women's boycott of the national commemoration, and ch. 34 on illegal voting. Appendixes. Index.)

Vol. 4, 1883–1900. Ed. Elizabeth Cady Stanton and Ida Husted Harper. 1144 pp. Rochester NY: Susan B. Anthony, 1902. Reprint, New York: Arno Press and The New York Times, 1969. (See ch. 1 on Susan B. Anthony's trial and the Virginia L. Minor lawsuit. Appendixes. Index.)

Vol. 5, 1900–1920. Ed. Ida Husted Harper. 817 pp. Washington DC: National American Woman Suffrage Association, 1922. Reprint, New York: Arno Press and The New York Times, 1969. (See pp. 280–82 for Alice Paul's response to the British movement and pp. 675–79 for a characterization of the National Women's Party picketing and hunger strikes of 1917 as violence. Appendixes. Index.)

Vol. 6, 1900–1920. Ed. Ida Husted Harper. 899 pp. Washington D.C.: National American Woman Suffrage Association, 1922. Reprint, New York: Arno Press and The New York Times, 1969. (Covers the same time period as vol. 5, chronicling the efforts in individual states to secure suffrage amendments to their constitutions, in addition to work in other countries to gain the right to vote for women following the passage of the federal amendment in the U.S. Appendixes. Index.)

563.   Stevens, Doris, *Jailed for Freedom*. 388 pp. New York: Liveright, 1920. (Focusing on the Women's Party actions during 1913–19, this book presents a detailed account of demonstrations at the White House, the jailing of women picketers at the federal prison in Occoquan, Maryland, and their experiences in jail, including a description of the young Dorothy Day as a suffragist prisoner. Photos. Appendixes.)

564.   Strauss, Silvia, *"Traitors to the Masculine Cause": The Men's Campaigns for Women's Rights*. 290 pp. Westport CT and London: Greenwood Press, 1982. (History of men in the women's movements in the 1800s and early 1900s. See ch. 6, 7, esp. pp. 195–202, on Richard Pankhurst as a shaper of Emmeline Pankhurst's activism. Illustrations. Index.)

Opposition to War and Expansionism

The first U.S. foreign war to spark opposition was the War of 1812. Some wars have been the object of widespread and often violent opposition, either to the war itself or to conscription for war. An example would be the Civil War. By the 1890s, opposition to war has been likely to coincide with objections to the use of military power to expand the territories dominated by the country or its influence and powers abroad. Users of this guide will note that opposition to war has historically combined issues of politics, religion, opposition to service in war, individual rights, and the question of how far opposition may go and what means it may use.

See also: Pacifism and Principled Nonviolence.

565.   Chambers, John Whiteclay, II, *Draftees or Volunteers: A Documentary History of the Debate Over Military Conscription in the U.S., 1787–1973*. 656 pp. New York and London: Garland Publishing, 1975. (Documents on conscription and military service, including material on evasion, resistance, and conscientious objection. See pp. 182–95 on the Civil War era; A.J. Muste, "Conscription and Conscience" [1944], no. 32; and part 8, esp. nos. 49–64 on the draft in the Vietnam War years.)

566.   Green, Marguerite, ed., *Peace Archives: A Guide to Library Collections of the Papers of American Peace Organizations and of Leaders in the Public Effort for Peace*. 66 pp. Berkeley CA: World Without War Council, 1986. (Descriptions of major archival collections and individual peace collections.)

567.   Howlett, Charles F., and Glen Zeitzer, *The American Peace Movement: History and Historiography*. 64 pp. Washington DC: American Historical Association Pamphlet no. 261, 1985. (See pp. 3–41 for history of the American peace movement from the colonial period, pp. 43–47 for list of "noted peace advocates," and glossary of peace terminology in pp. 53–54. "Peace historiography" appears in pp. 55–64.)

STUDIES

568.   Brock, Peter, *Pioneers of the Peaceable Kingdom*. 382 pp. Princeton NJ: Princeton Univ. Press, 1968. (History of Quaker pacifism from colonial period to 1914. See index under *conscientious objectors, Mennonites*, and *Quakers*. Index. Bibliography.)

569.   ———, *Radical Pacifists in Antebellum America.* 298 pp.
        Princeton NJ: Princeton Univ. Press, 1968. (History of pacifism
        and its radical, abolitionist wing from 1812 to the Civil War,
        a major theme of which is the development of ideas of
        nonresistance and conscience. See ch. 1, 2 on precursors of
        abolitionism, ch. 3–6 on Garrisonian nonresistance and its
        pacifist alternatives, and ch. 7 on ebbing of pacifism.
        Appendix, pp. 268–79, discusses "Quakers and the Antebellum
        Peace Movement." Index. Bibliography.)

570.   Chatfield, Charles, *For Peace and Justice: Pacifism in
        America, 1914–1941.* 447 pp. Knoxville: Univ. of Tennessee
        Press, 1971. (History of pacifism broadly conceived with an
        emphasis on activists and thinkers, organizations, and
        actions. See ch. 3 on WWI–era conscientious objectors in
        prison; pp. 202–12 on Richard Gregg's expansions upon
        Gandhi's thought; pp. 212–20 on the Fellowship of
        Reconciliation and its explorations of nonviolent action in
        peace and civil rights causes; ch. 9, in part about debates on
        economic pressure and sanctions in the 1930s; and pp. 337–41 of
        the conclusion on pacifists and the problem of the meaning of
        nonviolence. Index.)

571.   Coakley, Robert W., Paul J. Scheips, and Emma J. Portunodo,
        *Antiwar and Antimilitary Activities in the United States,
        1846–1954.* [Washington DC?]: Office of the Chief of
        Military History, Department of the Army, 1970. (Study
        conducted by OCMH historians on nature of opposition to U.S.
        military policy from the Mexican War to the end of the
        Korean War, its effects on prosecution of wars, and responses
        of federal government and military services to dissent.
        Bibliography.)

572.   Curti, Merle, *Peace or War: The American Struggle, 1636–
        1936.* 374 pp. New York: W.W. Norton, 1936. (History of
        opposition to war and war service. Index.)

573.   Eagan, Eileen, *Class, Culture, and the Classroom: The
        Student Peace Movement of the 1930s.* 319 pp. Philadelphia:
        Temple Univ. Press, 1981. (See ch. 2 on protests of athletic

policies, ch. 3 on the "Oxford Oath," and ch. 5 on "Students Strike Against War." Photos. Index. Bibliography.)

574.   Gara, Larry, *War Resistance in Historical Perspective.* 24 pp. Wallingford PA: Pendle Hill, 1970. (Essay on war resistance in the U.S. from Quakers to the Vietnam War, including conscientious objection and opposition to conscription. Bibliography.)

575.   Isserman, Maurice, *If I Had a Hammer . . . : The Death of the Old Left and the Birth of the New.* 259 pp. New York: Basic Books, 1987. (Primarily a study of personal and organizational factors in the loss of influence on the part of the "old left" and the growth of leftist alternatives. Ch. 4, "Radical Pacifism: The Americanization of Gandhi," explores the influence of the pacifism of the 1930s and pacifists as anti–war and anti–weapons protesters until the late 1950s. Photos. Index.)

576.   Kohn, Stephen M., *Jailed for Peace: The History of American Draft Law Violators, 1658–1985.* 169 pp. Westport CT and London: Greenwood Press, 1986. (History of resistance to conscription and conscientious objection from colonial times. See pp. 17–19 on abolitionism and "passive resistance"; ch. 2, 3 on the world wars; ch. 6, 7 on the Vietnam era and after; and ch. 9, "The Draft and Social Change." Index. Bibliography.)

577.   Morison, Samuel Eliot, Frederick Merk, and Frank Freidel, *Dissent in Three American Wars.* 164 pp. Cambridge: Harvard Univ. Press, 1970. (Essays on dissent and protest, but not necessarily resistance, during the War of 1812 [Morison], Mexican War [Merk], and Spanish–American War and Philippine Insurrection [Freidel]. See pp. 5–12, 30 on individual and community acts of opposition to the War of 1812 and pp. 84–92 on statements against Philippine expedition. Illustrations. Index.)

578.   Robinson, Jo Ann Ooiman, *Abraham Went Out: A Biography of A.J. Muste.* 341 pp. Philadelphia: Temple Univ. Press, 1981. (Biography of the pacifist war–resister and advocate of nonviolent action. Part 2 examines Muste's participation in

movements for civil rights and anti–war action. See pp. 27–30 on 1919 Lawrence textile strike, ch. 3, 4 for other strikes, ch. 6 on war–resistance during WWII, ch. 8 on the civil rights movement, ch. 10 on protest of and resistance to nuclear weapons, and ch. 11 on resistance to the Vietnam War. See index under *Committee for Nonviolent Action*. Index. Bibliography.)

579.   Wright, Edward Needles, *Conscientious Objectors in the Civil War*. 274 pp. Philadelphia PA: Univ. of Pennsylvania Press; London: Humphrey Milford; Oxford Univ. Press, 1931. (History of conscientious objectors in the North and South, 1861–65, emphasizing the Society of Friends. See index under *Amana Society, Cristadelphians, commutation, conscientious objectors, Dunkers, Friends, Mennonites, Schwenkfelders*, and *Shakers*. Ch. 7 compares Civil War and WWI experiences and discusses factors which enable individuals to resist authority. Index. Bibliography.)

PHILIPPINES WAR AND IMPERIALISM, 1898–1900

The Philippines expedition began during the war with Spain and continued until it established U.S. dominion over the islands after crushing resistance led by Emilio Aguinaldo. It was thus the first expeditionary war conducted far beyond the country's borders. The relatively few political leaders who opposed it were dismayed by U.S. willingness to acquire the Hawaiian Islands (despite the illegality of the overthrow of Queen Lili'uokalani) and also by moves to establish U.S. power over Samoa. Opposition to seizure of the Philippines was led by members of the New England elite, including Edward Atkinson who raised the banner of "anti-imperialism" and publicized the cruelties inflicted on the Filipino people.

580.   Beisner, Robert L., *Twelve against Empire: The Anti-imperialists, 1898–1900*. 310 pp. New York, Toronto, London, and Sydney: McGraw–Hill, 1968. (History of U.S. anti-imperialist protest during the Philippine War in 1898–1900, focusing on Mugwumps and Republican dissenters. See ch. 5 on Atkinson's Anti–Imperialist League, ch. 6 on George F. Hoon,

and ch. 9 on "the impotent protest." Photos. Index. Bibliography.)

581.   Schirmer, Daniel B., *Republic or Empire: American Resistance to the Philippine War.* 298 pp. Cambridge MA: Schenkman, 1972. (History of anti–imperialist organizations and actions in Massachusetts, 1898–1903, and the Yankee reformers who led them. Author discusses class background and issues of racism in the war against Aguinaldo and Philippine resistance throughout. Index.)

582.   Tompkins, E. Berkeley, *Anti–Imperialism in the United States: The Great Debate, 1890–1920.* 344 pp. Philadelphia: University of Pennsylvania Press, 1970. (History of anti–imperialist thought and politics that places the movement of the 1890s in broader context. See index under *Hawaii* and *Samoa* for the annexation of the Hawaiian Islands and imperialist politics in Samoa. Ch. 4–9 are on the Anti–Imperialist League from its founding in 1898 to 1900, followed by discussion of the less–organized movement thereafter. Illustrations. Index. Bibliography.)

CONSCIENTIOUS OBJECTION AND OPPOSITION TO WORLD WAR I

The modern form of war resistance arose during the lead–up to U.S. involvement in World War I when a federal conscription law was passed. Perceived by adversaries as an imposition both on individual rights and religious freedom, the draft fostered two sorts of objections. One was the civil liberties position, giving rise to the American Civil Liberties Union. The other was the conscientious objector position, based on the view that religious and conscientious refusal to take part in war must be honored by the state. As hostilities began, conscientious objectors (c.o.'s) and leftists including Eugene V. Debs were arrested and imprisoned, with c.o.'s being isolated in labor camps.

583.   Chambers, John Whiteclay, II, *To Raise an Army: The Draft Comes to Modern America.* 386 pp. New York and London: Free Press, 1987. (Documents the evolution of the draft in the

U.S., primarily during WWI, with a view to understanding modern debates on how armies should be raised. Ch. 4 is on protests before the draft law was adopted and ch. 8 is on protest and resistance after its 1917 ratification. See index under *conscientious objectors, A U A M , antidraft, antimilitarists, compulsory military service, conscription, pacifism, selective service,* and *nonviolence.* Illustrations. Photos. Index. Bibliography.)

584.   Johnson, Donald, *The Challenge to American Freedoms: World War I and the Rise of the American Civil Liberties Union.* 243 pp. Lexington KY: Univ. of Kentucky Press, 1963. (History of American Civil Liberties Union and its origins during and after WWI. See esp. ch. 1, 2, 4, 7 on opposition to war by various groups, Roger Nash Baldwin and conscientious objection, and political prisoners. Index. Bibliography.)

585.   Moore, Howard W., *Plowing My Own Furrow.* 225 pp. New York and London: W.W. Norton, 1985. (Memoirs of a WWI conscientious objector. See ch. 15–19 for experiences in c.o. encampments, including details of military treatment of conscientious objectors and hunger strikes. Illustrations. Photos. Documents. Index. Bibliography.)

586.   Peterson, H.C., and Gilbert C. Fite, *Opponents of War, 1917–1918.* 399 pp. Madison WI: Univ. of Wisconsin Press, 1957. (History of individuals and groups opposed to United States involvement in WWI. See esp. ch. 3 on opposition to conscription in 1917 and ch. 12 on "the conscientious objector." See index under *conscientious objectors.* Other chapters are on the prosecution of radicals, legal status of the war, and the imprisonment of Eugene V. Debs. Illustrations. Index. Bibliography.)

587.   Thomas, Norman, *The Conscientious Objector in America.* 299 pp. New York: B.W. Huebsch, 1923. (History of conscientious objection during WWI. See esp. ch. 8–11 on treatment of objectors in prison camps and prisons, and ch. 12 on the 1919 prison strikes at Leavenworth. Index.)

INTERWAR CONSCIENTIOUS OBJECTION AND OPPOSITION TO WORLD WAR II

Peace and anti–conscription actions from the 1930s to the end of World War II were influenced by native traditions of radicalism and pacifism and by the European development of a rejectionist position toward participation in war. When war came, many c.o.'s were again imprisoned, often in camps. The case of Corbett Bishop, a c.o. who practiced total personal noncooperation with his imprisonment, attracted a good deal of attention.

See also: Great Britain: Conscientious Objection and the Inter–war Peace Movement.

588. Peck, Jim, *We Who Would Not Kill.* 208 pp. New York: Lyle Stuart, 1958. (Memoirs of conscientious objector imprisoned during WWII. Ch. 6 is on war resistance activity before the war and ch. 10–14 on work refusals and hunger strikes to protest segregation in prisons.)

589. Sibley, Mulford Q., and Philip E. Jacob, *Conscription of Conscience: The American State and the Conscientious Objector, 1940–1947.* 580 pp. Ithaca NY: Cornell Univ. Press, 1952. (Ch. 1, 2 discuss the history and types of conscientious objectors. Part 3, ch. 8–14, look at protest and other activities of c.o.'s and part 4 discusses the c.o. as lawbreaker.)

590. Wittner, Lawrence S., *Rebels Against War: The American Peace Movement, 1933–1983.* 364 pp. Philadelphia: Temple Univ. Press, 1984. Rev. ed. of *Rebels Against War: The American Peace Movement, 1941–1960.* New York: Columbia Univ. Press, 1969. (Thorough history of peace organizations and their thought and action in post–WWI era. Most chapters discuss actions, but see esp. ch. 3, 9, 10, and epilogue. See pp. 77–84 on Corbett Bishop; pp. 89, 92–94, 177, 247 on protests and noncooperation in prison and other contexts, and pp. 265–66 on refusal to take part in civil defense drills. On concepts of nonviolent action, as opposed to pacifism, see pp. 30–32, ch. 3, and pp. 153–58. Index. Bibliography.)

OPPOSITION TO WAR, 1945–1960

After the beginning of the Cold War, U.S. opponents of war were also faced with the problem of nuclear weapons. A small number of protesters raised objections against weapons testing and civil defense, on the grounds of their being preparation for war, while others worked within channels for the expanded legal recognition of conscientious objection.

591.   American Friends Service Committee, *The Draft? A Report Prepared for the Peace Education Division of the American Friends Service Committee.* 111 pp. New York: Hill & Wang, 1968. (Report by Working Party on Conscription, AFSC, on conscription and conscientious objection. See ch. 1 for brief history of conscription and ch. 3 on conscientious objection. Documents. Bibliography.)

592.   Miller, William D., *A Harsh and Dreadful Love: Dorothy Day and the Catholic Worker Movement.* 370 pp. New York: Liveright, 1973. (History of the Catholic Worker and life of Dorothy Day. See ch. 10 for pacifist arguments and actions during WWII and ch. 18 on Ammon Hennacy and the Catholic Worker protests against civil defense drills and nuclear weapons. Illustrations. Photos. Index.)

593.   Roberts, Nancy L., *Dorothy Day and the Catholic Worker.* 226 pp. Albany NY: State Univ. of New York Press, 1984. (See ch. 6 for discussion of Catholic Worker pacifism and support for conscientious objection, and ch. 7 on civil disobedience and opposition to nuclear weapons. Illustrations. Photos. Index.)

MOVEMENT AGAINST THE VIETNAM WAR, 1963–1971

The largest and lengthiest organized U.S. movement against a specific war began in the early 1960s, continuing in various forms for over ten years. Researchers identify several phases. From approximately 1963 to 1965, protest was promoted largely by leftists and radical pacifists, some with campus connections. By 1965, in addition to organizing the first demonstrations against the war, anti-war forces were concentrating on universities, where the first teach–

ins were held at mid–decade. Until 1968, steady increases in the size, number, spread, and intensity of anti–war demonstrations occurred. This was also the time of most intense resistance to the draft (see below). With a growing sense that neither draft resistance nor demonstrations were achieving an end to the war (and particularly after the violent suppression of a mobilization at the Democratic Party Convention in Chicago in the summer of 1968), the movement fractured. One wing opted to push for revolution and introduced property destruction and violence into the campaign. A more politically moderate wing returned to the concept of mass demonstrations in 1969. Both trends marked the next years, until the spring 1970 killing of students during on–campus turmoil at Kent State University in Ohio led to an extensive, but brief, student strike movement. Relative decline of the movement in following years is attributed by some to the Nixon administration policy of reducing U.S. combat presence, therefore reducing combat deaths of U.S. troops, and by the short–lived peace treaty between the two Vietnams.

See also: Methods of Nonviolent Action: Civil Disobedience; Legal Aspects of Nonviolent Action; Pacifism and Principled Nonviolence: Conscientious Objection.

594.   Bannan, John F., and Rosemary Bannan, *Law, Morality and Vietnam: The Peace Militants and the Courts.* 241 pp. Bloomington and London: Indiana Univ. Press, 1974. (An inquiry into justice and law enforcement in cases of persons tried for actions taken against the War in Vietnam. Includes case studies of a draft refuser, a draft–card burner, soldiers who refused to serve in Vietnam, two major conspiracy trials, and the trial of people who destroyed draft records. Observations on the concept of civil disobedience are on pp. 6–9, while ch. 8, "The Career of Civil Disobedience," has arguments for law–breaking in resistance to war and ch. 9 has judges' replies to these views. Index.)

595.   Baskir, Lawrence M., and William A. Strauss, *Chance and Circumstance: The Draft, the War, and the Vietnam Generation.* 312 pp. New York: Alfred A. Knopf, 1978. (Categorizes the draft–eligible generation as avoidees,

evaders, deserters, and exiles. See ch. 3 and chart on p. 69. Index.)

596.   Bloom, Lynn Z., *Doctor Spock: Biography of a Conservative Radical*. 366 pp. Indianapolis and New York: Bobbs–Merrill, 1972. (See ch. 11–15 on Spock's anti–war and anti–nuclear weapons activities, esp. ch. 13–15 on indictment and trial of Spock and four others, "The Boston Five," for conspiring to resist the draft. Index.)

597.   The Catonsville Nine–Milwaukee Fourteen Defense Committee, *Delivered into Resistance*. 78 pp. New Haven CT: Advocate Press, 1969. (Essays from "resistance community" against the draft. See James H. Forest, "In Time of War," pp. 1–10 on history of U.S. draft resistance; Staughton Lynd, "Letter from Jail: Telling Right From Wrong," pp. 11–17 includes discussion of justification of property destruction as form of "disruptive resistance"; and Barbara Deming, "On Revolution and Equilibrium," pp. 18–49 has a philosophical discussion of nonviolent action. See also pp. 65–67 for Catonsville Statement and pp. 71–74 for Milwaukee Statement. Photos. Documents.)

598.   Chomsky, Noam, *American Power and the New Mandarins*. 404 pp. New York: Pantheon, 1969. (Essay "On Resistance" and its supplement, pp. 367–400, present reflections on demonstrations, 1967. See also pp. 159–220, "The Revolutionary Pacifism of A.J. Muste.")

599.   Cortright, David, *Soldiers in Revolt: The American Military Today*. 317 pp. Garden City NY: Anchor Press/Doubleday, 1975. (Analysis of disaffection of U.S. troops in Vietnam era and its conversion to protest, noncooperation, and other manifestations. See ch. 2–7. Index. Research guide in appendix A.)

600.   Crowell, Joan, *Fort Dix Stockade: Our Prison Camp Next Door*. 169 pp. New York: Links Books, 1974. (Account based largely on interviews and personal experiences of civilian demonstration at Fort Dix, New Jersey, October 1969, in support of imprisoned soldiers involved in an earlier

disturbance. See esp. ch. 3, pp. 37–39, 40–41 on the role of the Weatherman faction and postponing of the demonstration to exclude them, also pp. 42–46 on the demonstration. Photos.)

601.   Dellinger, Dave, *More Power Than We Know: The People's Movement Toward Democracy*. 326 pp. Garden City NY: Anchor Press/Doubleday, 1975. (Primarily about anti–Vietnam War movement. Much on violence and nonviolent action as strategy in "the movement." Index.)

602.   Dougan, Clark, et al., *The Vietnam Experience: Nineteen Sixty–Eight*. 192 pp. Boston: Boston Publishing, 1983. (Journalistic and photo history of U.S. participation in War in Vietnam, 1968. See pp. 84–113, 162–75 on demonstrators and counter–demonstrators. Index. Bibliography.)

603.   Dumbrell, John, ed., *Vietnam and the Antiwar Movement: An International Perspective*. 182 pp. Aldershot UK, Brookfield VT, Hong Kong, Singapore, and Sydney: Avebury, 1989. (Of interest are John Dumbrell, "Congress and the Antiwar Movement, ch. 7; Adam Fairclough, "The War in Vietnam and the Decline of the Civil Rights Movement," ch. 8; Kenneth Maddock, "Opposing the War in Vietnam in Australia," ch. 10; and John Minnion, "Anger and After: Britain's CND and the Vietnam War," ch. 12.)

604.   Ferber, Michael, and Staughton Lynd, *The Resistance*. 300 pp. Boston: Beacon Press, 1971. (Contains material about nonviolent resistance to the Vietnam draft, such as burning and returning draft cards and offering sanctuary to resisters. Photos.)

605.   The Fifth Avenue Vietnam Peace Parade Committee, *In the Teeth of War: Photographic Documentary of the March 26th, 1966, New York City Demonstration Against the War in Vietnam*. 64 pp. New York: The Fifth Avenue Vietnam Peace Parade Committee and Oak Publications, 1967. (Text and photos documenting an anti–war parade.)

606.   Foner, Philip S., *American Labor and the Indochina War: The Growth of Union Opposition*. 126 pp. New York:

International Publishers, 1971. (Argues against the assumption that organized labor supported the war effort and opposed the peace movement. Illustrated with examples of labor protest advertisements and placards.)

607.   Gaylin, Willard, *In the Service of Their Country: War Resisters in Prison.* 344 pp. New York: Viking Press, 1970. (Psychiatric study of war resister populations in two institutions. Personal cases in ch. 3–8. Ch. 9 is on confrontation and ch. 10–12 present the analysis.)

608.   Gitlin, Todd, *The Whole World Is Watching: Mass Media in the Making and Unmaking of the New Left.* 327 pp. Berkeley CA: Univ. of California Press, 1980. (Focuses on Students for a Democratic Society, describing the "struggle over images" and its effect upon student dissent from 1965 and the effects of media coverage upon shaping action and organization. Index. Bibliography.)

609.   Gray, Francine du Plessix, *Divine Disobedience: Profile in Catholic Radicalism.* 329 pp. New York: Alfred A. Knopf, 1970. (Journalist's account of radical Catholic draft resistance in late 1960s, with emphasis on the Catonsville Nine and the Berrigan brothers. See pp. 45–58 on Catonsville and pp. 109–23 on blood–pouring in Baltimore 1968. See also index under *Baltimore war protest, Boston Five, Catonsville Nine, draft card burning, draft resistance, Milwaukee Fourteen,* and *pacifism.* Index.)

610.   Halstead, Fred, *Out Now!: A Participant's Account of the American Movement Against the Vietnam War.* 759 pp. New York: Monad Press, 1978. (History and recollections by 1968 Socialist Workers' Party presidential candidate, strong on the first marches and teach–ins and on organizational issues. Photos. Index.)

611.   Heath, G. Louis, ed., *Mutiny Does Not Happen Lightly: The Literature of the American Resistance to the Vietnam War.* 597 pp. Metuchen NJ: Scarecrow Press, 1976. (Document source containing pamphlets, letters, speeches, manuals, and other writings, 1964–74. Several selections contain references to

action choices, including nos. 18, 32, 35, 52, 108. Note that order of selections is not chronological. Chronology. Index. Bibliography.)

612.   Helmer, John, *Bringing the War Home*. 346 pp. New York: Free Press, 1974. (Characterizes Vietnam veterans opposed to the war as "radicals," as drug users, and as opposed to veteran supporters of the war. See pp. 88–99 for short account of Vietnam Veterans Against the War, esp. p. 95 for statement on nonviolent action. Index.)

613.   Hurwitz, Ken, *Marching Nowhere*. 216 pp. New York: W.W. Norton, 1971. (Memoirs of a student organizer and participant in the moratorium campaign, 1969. See pp. 16–17 on the moratorium idea.)

614.   Kail, F.M., *What Washington Said: Administration Rhetoric and the Vietnam War: 1949–1969*. 248 pp. New York: Harper & Row, 1973. (See "The Government's Line on Dissent," pp. 211–19, based on analysis of government statements reported in press.)

615.   Kerry, John, and Vietnam Veterans Against the War, *The New Soldier*. 174 pp. New York: Macmillan, 1971. (Photo–based account of protests and other actions by VVAW.)

616.   Lynd, Alice, ed., *We Won't Go: Personal Accounts of War Objectors*. 331 pp. Boston: Beacon Press, 1968. (Experiences and ideas of draft noncooperators and conscientious objectors, ca. 1963–67. Accounts of beliefs, organizing methods, and related protest activity.)

617.   Lyttle, Bradford, *The Chicago Anti–Vietnam War Movement*. 173 pp. Chicago: Midwest Pacifist Center, 1988. (Activist's history of the Chicago anti–war movement from its roots in existing peace organizations of the 1950s until its end. Ch. 4 is on draft resistance and draft counseling; ch. 6, 7 are on the march–and–rally of 1967; ch. 8 is on student politics; ch. 11–14 are on the Chicago Democratic Convention turmoil and resulting trials; ch. 15 is on the subsequent reorganization of protest; and ch. 17 is on the last phase of

activism. Ch. 10 discusses "nonviolent and violent tendencies" of the movement and ch. 16 is on war tax resistance. Appendix. Index. Bibliography.)

618.   Mantell, David Mark, *True Americanism: Green Berets and War Resisters: A Study of Commitment.* 285 pp. New York: Teachers College Press, 1974. (Psychological study of two small comparative samples of war participants and resisters. Bibliography.)

619.   Meconis, Charles A., *With Clumsy Grace: The American Catholic Left, 1961–1975.* 204 pp. New York: Seabury Press, 1979. (Discusses origins and problems of draft board raids and blood pouring as perceived resistance to war in Vietnam. For discussion of nonviolent action, see pp. 7–9, 17–20. On the conviction that property destruction was nonviolent because it was "not violent," see pp. 16–30, 36–38, 52, 65, and author's comment on this point, pp. 144–45. Index. Bibliography.)

620.   Menashe, Louis, and Ronald Radosh, eds., *Teach–Ins, USA: Reports, Opinions, Documents.* 349 pp. New York, Washington, and London: Frederick A. Praeger, 1967. (Collection of documents and opinions on origin, development, and impact of American teach–in movement, 1965–67. See ch. 1 for description of early teach–ins; ch. 3 on responses to teach–ins; ch. 4, parts 4 and 5, on the "national teach–in," May 1965; ch. 7 on the meaning of the teach–ins; and ch. 8 on escalation of teach–ins. Documents.)

621.   Powers, Thomas, *The War at Home: Vietnam and the American People, 1964–1968.* 348 pp. New York: Grossman, 1973. (Detailed account of opposition to U.S. presence in Vietnam up to the departure of Lyndon Johnson. See esp. preface, ch. 4, 5, 7, 9–11, and epilogue. Photos. Index.)

622.   Presidential Clemency Board, *Report to the President.* 409 pp. Washington, DC: U.S. Government Printing Office, 1973. (Report to President Ford on clemency program; includes some information on nature of civilian and military draft and service–related offenses, pp. 31–79, and historical perspective, pp. 345–89.)

623. Radine, Lawrence B., *The Taming of the Troops: Social Control in the United States Army.* 276 pp. Westport CT: Greenwood Press, 1977. (General study of social control in the U.S. Army, with research on army techniques for stifling anti–military political dissent. Partly a how–to–do–it manual, including advice for resisters. Index.)

624. Rosenberg, Milton J., Sidney Verba, and Philip E. Converse, *Vietnam and the Silent Majority: The Dove's Guide.* 162 pp. New York: Harper & Row, 1970. (A "partisan" period document by public opinion specialists counseling against protest and in favor of persuasion in efforts to change U.S. public views. See pp. 44–46 on public antipathy to protest, p. 67 on broadening of campus involvement from "elite" universities to others, p. 142 for disassociation of "persuader" from "peace demonstrator", and postscript, pp. 133–55, giving advice to persuaders. Bibliography.)

625. Sale, Kirkpatrick, *SDS.* 752 pp. New York: Random House, 1973. (Chronicle of Students for a Democratic Society, 1960–72, and its role in the anti–Vietnam War movement and other conflicts. Index.)

626. Schevitz, Jeffrey M., *The Weaponsmakers: Personal and Professional Crisis During the Vietnam War.* 191 pp. Cambridge MA: Schenkman, 1979. (On the personal adaptations of California workers in arms industry, categorized as "rationalizers," "drop–outs," and "political organizers." Some assessment of impact of protest and anti–war sentiment. Includes discussion of factors conducive to creating critical attitudes and behaviors. Bibliography.)

627. Small, Melvin, *Johnson, Nixon, and the Doves.* 319 pp. New Brunswick NJ and London: Rutgers Univ. Press, 1988. (The body of this work is a periodization of the anti–war movement from 1964 to 1975 combined with an assessment of Johnson and Nixon administration responses to it. See ch. 8 for summary and conclusions. Index. Bibliography.)

628. Taylor, Clyde, ed., *Vietnam and Black America: An Anthology of Protest and Resistance.* 335 pp. Garden City NY:

Anchor Books, 1973. (Compilation of essays, speeches, and literary pieces concerning black opinion and opposition to the war in Vietnam. See Robert S. Browne, "The Freedom Movement and the War in Vietnam"; Martin Luther King, Jr., "Bringing the War Home"; and Student Non–Violent Coordinating Committee statement. Documents. Index.)

629.   *Trials of the Resistance.* 246 pp. New York: Random House, 1970. (Essays from the *New York Review of Books* on actions and trials of several anti–Vietnam War resisters. See Andrew Kopkind, "Captain Levy I: Doctor's Plot" and "The Trial of Captain Levy: II," pp. 14–42; Ronald Dworkin, "On Not Prosecuting Civil Disobedience," pp. 50–73; and other articles on trials of activists.)

630.   Useem, Michael, *Conscription, Protest, and Social Conflict: The Life and Death of a Draft Resistance Movement.* 329 pp. New York: John Wiley & Sons, 1973. (A sociological study of the Resistance, a campaign of noncooperation with the draft, during its activity from 1967–69. See ch. 1, 2, 4, 7, esp. pp. 54–55, on early individual resistance and pp. 169–71 on "collective security" and "snowballing." Index. Bibliography.)

631.   Westmoreland, General William C., *A Soldier Reports.* 446 pp. Garden City NY: Doubleday, 1976. (Experiences of U.S. Army Chief of Staff during the Vietnam War. See pp. 225–26, 231, 364–66, 413–14 for observations on domestic anti–war protest. Index.)

632.   Zaroulis, Nancy, and Gerald Sullivan, *Who Spoke Up? American Protest Against the War in Vietnam, 1963–1975.* 460 pp. Garden City NY: Doubleday, 1984. (Chronological history of anti–Vietnam War movement, 1963–75, with discussion of actions throughout. See index under names and places, *civil disobedience*, and *nonviolence*. Index. Bibliography.)

Labor

The first labor boycott in American history may have been in 1774 when Boston–area workers withheld their labor from the British regiments fortifying the city. Since then, the confrontation of claims pitting labor against business owners, managers, and the government has shaped much of U.S. history. How these conflicts have been transmitted to the present in the work of scholars, journalists, publicists, and partisans is as much of that history as the events themselves. Users of this guide preparing to study labor conflicts will want to keep several points in mind. First, for the student of nonviolent action, it is important to verify for oneself whether a certain conflict was violent or nonviolent, rather than accepting contemporary opinion. The term "violent" can mean many things and accusations of violence, as well as justifications for it, are part of the politics of many conflicts. Likewise, reports do not always clarify which actors in a dispute use violence. Second, the circumstances of labor disputes change greatly over time as relationships between owner and worker or between worker and supervisor change and as technology and the uses of capital change. One example of this is found in the "great strikes" of 1877 and 1894, which were intimately connected to the extension of the railroads and the ways in which railroad labor was utilized and disciplined. Of course, ideology also affects the ways conflicts develop. Even though there is not sufficient published work on it yet, gender is also a significant factor to consider as women are drawn increasingly into the labor force and often restricted to certain kinds of work. Third, along with the worker, the supervisor, the manager, the corporation, and the owner or investor, the state has been a central participant in labor conflicts. Law shapes these conflicts by defining, and sometimes changing, the recognized rights on either side. State policy, and even military policy, are involved when the government must determine if it will define a conflict as a civil disorder and if it will employ the means of public force against it.

633. Stein, Emmanuel, ed., *The Labor Boycott: A Bibliography.* 89 pp. Reprint, Newton MA: Crofton Pub. Corp., [1973?]. New York: U.S. Works Progress Administration, 1936. 2d ed., 1938. (Bibliography of the labor boycott in the U.S. from its beginnings to 1935, with entries from book and periodical sources, statutes, and court cases.)

STUDIES

634.   Adamic, Louis, *Dynamite: The Story of Class Violence in America*. 495 pp. New York: Viking Press, 1934 [orig. publ. 1931]. (According to preface of revised edition, the author considers this "the story of the evolution of class violence in America" by describing labor and anti–labor violence in the eighteenth and nineteenth centuries. See ch. 27 on the 1919 steel strike, concluding that "non–violence was a poor method of winning demands," p. 291, and Samuel Gompers' belief in "moral suasion," p. 187. Ch. 32 discusses slow–downs as "sabotage" in Industrial Workers of the World parlance. Illustrations. Photos. Index. Bibliography.)

635.   Ambrose, Stephen E., and James A. Barber, eds., *The Military and American Society: Essays and Readings*. 322 pp. New York: Free Press, 1972. (See Stephen E. Ambrose, "The Armed Forces and Civil Disorder," pp. 241–48 and Martin Blumenson, "On the Function of the Military in Civil Disorders," pp. 249–56 on role of U.S. military organizations in quelling civil conflict and strikes. Index.)

636.   Auerbach, Jerold S., *Labor and Liberty: The La Follette Committee and the New Deal*. 246 pp. Indianapolis: Bobbs–Merrill, 1966. (History of civil liberties issues in labor conflicts, the Wagner Act, and the La Follette Committee investigations of violence against workers and violations of their rights in agriculture and industry. Ch. 1 studies the suppression of strikes and organizing before 1935, ch. 2 is on agricultural labor in that period, and ch. 3, pp. 49–51, discusses the effects of Edward Levinson's *I Break Strikes* [entry 706]. Of particular interest is ch. 5, "The Instruments of Industrial Warfare," on industrial espionage and strikebreaking during the 1930s, including a discussion of *agents provocateurs*. Ch. 8 follows the course of industrial conflict in the "farm factories" in the 1930s. Index. Bibliography.)

637.   Bernstein, Irving, *The Lean Years: A History of the American Worker, 1920–1933*. 577 pp. Boston: Houghton Mifflin, 1970 [orig. publ. 1960]. (History of labor conditions in America,

using the individual worker as unit of analysis. Covers through the early Depression years, emphasizing social effects of labor policy and the rise and fall of an organized, politically salient labor movement. Photos. Index.)

638.   ————, *Turbulent Years: A History of the American Worker, 1933–1941*. 873 pp. Boston: Houghton Mifflin, 1970. (Concerned with American labor conditions from the inception of the New Deal to the beginning of U.S. involvement in WWII, especially the effects of organized labor on the direction of public policy. Photos. Index.)

639.   Beshoar, Barron B., *Out of the Depths: The Story of John L. Lawson, a Labor Leader*. 372 pp. Denver: Colorado Labor Historical Committee of the Denver Trades and Labor Assembly, 1942. (Biography of United Mine Workers leader in Colorado, known for his activities in the 1913–14 coal strike that included the "Ludlow Massacre" of April 1914 and other violence. See ch. 4–17. Photos. Bibliography.)

640.   Boyle, O. [Ohio] D., *History of Railroad Strikes*. 110 pp. Washington DC: Brotherhood, 1935. (Brief histories of the great strike of 1877, the Pullman Strike of 1894, and rail strikes in 1916 and 1920, written for the education of rail union members.)

641.   Brecher, Jeremy, *Strike!* 329 pp. San Francisco: Straight Arrow Books, 1972. (History of six peak periods in the occurrence of "mass strikes" in U.S. history, with analysis of their significance and the factors that limited them. Photos.)

642.   Commons, John R., et al., *History of Labor in the United States*. 4 vols.

Vol. 1, 623 pp. New York: Macmillan, 1926. (Contains a series of monographs by various authors. Covers the period from colonial times to 1860. Indexed in Vol. 2.)

Vol. 2, 620 pp. New York: Macmillan, 1926. (Covers from colonial times to the depression of the 1890s. See John B. Andrews, "Nationalisation [1869–1877]" and Selig Perlman,

"Upheaval and Reorganization [since 1870]" on the relationship between early labor organizations and conflicts. Index. Bibliography.)

Vol. 3, 778 pp. New York: Macmillan, 1935. (Contains Don D. Lescohier, "Working Conditions," and Elizabeth Brandeis, "Labor Legislation." Covers the early twentieth century up to the period of the New Deal. Analyzes the changes in the American economic system and its impact on individual workers and the organized labor movement as a whole. Index. Bibliography.)

Vol. 4, 683 pp. New York: Macmillan, 1935. (Contains Selig Perlman and Philip Taft, "Labor Movements." Emphasizes the pragmatic aspect of the American labor movement. Index. Bibliography.)

643.   Cooper, Jerry M., *The Army and Civil Disorders: Federal Military Intervention, 1877–1900*. 299 pp. Westport CT and London: Greenwood Press, 1980. (Study of army participation in great strikes of 1877 and 1894 and the Idaho miners' disturbances. Suggestive observations on causes of violence in rail strikes as it occurred in striker confrontations with strikebreakers, the militia, and military units protecting rights of employers. See esp. ch. 3–6, 8, 9. Index. Bibliography.)

644.   Eggert, Gerald G., *Railroad Labor Disputes: The Beginnings of Federal Strike Policy*. 313 pp. Ann Arbor MI: Univ. of Michigan Press, 1967. (History of interrelations among labor conflicts, business, the courts, and federal authority in the growth of policies to restrict or halt strikes. See ch. 2 for great strike of 1877, ch. 3 for Knights of Labor strikes in 1885, ch. 5 on Coxey's Army "petition–in–boots" and strikes of 1893, and ch. 7 on the great rail strike and boycott of 1894. Index. Bibliography.)

645.   Foner, Philip S., *History of the Labor Movement in the United States*. 4 vols. New York: International Publishers, 1947–1965.

Vol. 1, *From Colonial Times to the Founding of the American Federation of Labor.* 576 pp. (Ch. 7 discusses the earliest strikes. Ch. 11 is on the Ten–Hour Movement before the Civil War, ch. 16 is on labor's relationship to the anti–Civil War Copperheads and wartime strikes, and ch. 22, 23 are on the depression of the 1870s that culminated in the great strike of 1877. Index.)

Vol. 2, *From the Founding of the American Federation of Labor to the Emergence of American Imperialism.* 480 pp. (This volume contains much information on the legal counterattack by capital after the Civil War. Ch. 14–17 discuss strikes of the 1880s and early 1890s, ch. 18 is on the Pullman Strike and boycotts of 1894, and ch. 27 looks at the connection between labor and the Anti–Imperialist League during the Philippine War. Index.)

Vol. 3, *The Policies and Practices of the American Federation of Labor, 1900–1909.* 477 pp. (See ch. 2 on attempts to ban closed–shop organizing and boycotts, ch. 4 on strikes in the early twentieth century, and ch. 16 on labor conflict in the mines. Index.)

Vol. 4, *The Industrial Workers of the World, 1905–1917.* 608 pp. (See ch. 5, 6 on methods, ch. 7–8 on Free Speech Fights, and ch. 13, 14, 15, 22, 23 on some of the famous IWW strikes, including Lawrence in 1912 and Paterson in 1913. Index.)

646.   ———, *Women and the American Labor Movement: From Colonial Times to the Eve of World War I.* 621 pp. New York: Free Press; London: Collier Macmillan, 1979. (See ch. 18 on the "waistmakers' revolt" in New York, 1909; ch. 19 on subsequent strikes in other trades; ch. 22 on women in the IWW Free Speech Fights; and ch. 23, 24 on the pre–war IWW textile strikes. Consult index under boycotts, strikes, and the names of labor leaders and labor organizations. Photos. Index. Bibliography.)

647.   Foster, William Z., *American Trade Unionism: Principles and Organization, Strategy and Tactics.* 383 pp. New York:

International Publishers, 1947. (Series of essays that chronicle the development of the labor movement and the author's involvement in it during the first half of the twentieth century. Emphasizes role of political parties [esp. the CPUSA] in the articulation and achievement of the labor movement's objectives. See esp. ch. 26, "Steel Strike Strategy," for Foster's opinions on the nature of union leadership and a proposed program of action. Index.)

648.   Ginger, Ray, *Eugene V. Debs: A Biography*. 543 pp. New York: Collier Books, 1962 [orig. publ. 1949]. Originally entitled *The Bending Cross: A Biography of Eugene Victor Debs*. (See pp. 131–67 on the Pullman Strike and boycott of 1894. Brief accounts of many other strikes and Debs's political activities. Bibliography.)

649.   Gould, Jean, and Lonena Hickok, *Walter Reuther: Labor's Rugged Individualist*. 399 pp. New York: Dodd, Mead, 1972. (Brief accounts of strikes, including the 1937 "sit–down strikes," pp. 117–32, 144–45. Bibliography.)

650.   Harris, Herbert, *American Labor*. 459 pp. New Haven: Yale Univ. Press; London: Humphrey Milford, Oxford Univ. Press, 1939. (Story of intellectual and personal elements in the growth of U.S. labor organizations in several industries. See accounts of the 1912 Lawrence strike, pp. 314–15, 319–25, and the sit–downs of 1936, pp. 286–303. Consult index under *boycott, injunction*, and *strike*. Illustrations. Index. Bibliography.)

651.   Howe, Irving, *The UAW and Walter Reuther*. 309 pp. New York: Random House, 1949. (See ch. 2 on early "sit–downs" or stay–in strikes.)

652.   [Jones, Mary Harris], *The Autobiography of Mother Jones*. Ed. Mary Field Parton. 242 pp. Chicago: Charles H. Kerr, 1925. Reprint, New York: Arno Press, 1969. (Memoirs of irrepressible labor leader, with accounts of strikes and related actions from Haymarket to the Steel Strike of 1919. Photos.)

653. ———, *Mother Jones Speaks: Collected Writings and Speeches.* Ed. Philip S. Foner. 724 pp. New York: Monad Press, 1983. (Collection of speeches, testimony, articles, interviews, and letters of the labor organizer from 1897 to 1930. See "Mother Jones: Dynamic Champion of Oppressed Multitudes," by Philip S. Foner for biographical sketch and pp. 51–59 for chronology. Documents. Index. Bibliography.)

654. Myers, James, and Harry W. Laidler, *What Do You Know about Labor?* 301 pp. New York: John Day, 1956. (History and analysis of labor relations in U.S., written shortly after the AFL and CIO merged. See esp. ch. 5, "Strikes and How to Prevent Them," on the reasons for strikes and their nature. See esp. pp. 74–80 on "peaceable" strikes and causes of violence. Index. Bibliography.)

655. Pinkerton, Allan, *Strikers, Communists, Tramps, and Detectives.* 412 pp. New York: G.W. Carleton; London: S. Low, 1882. (Written by the head of a famous strike–breaking organization. See chapters on various conflicts, esp. the "great strikes" of 1877.)

656. Powderly, Terence V., *Thirty Years of Labor, 1859–1889.* 372 pp. New York: Augustus M. Kelly, 1967 [orig. publ. 1890]. (Written by former Grand Master of the Order of the Knights of Labor. History of labor in U.S. in the era of industrial concentration. "The Storm Breaks," pp. 99–116 covers the great strike of 1877. Appendixes.)

657. Preis, Art, *Labor's Giant Step: Twenty Years of the CIO.* 538 pp. New York: Pioneer, 1964. (History of the CIO focusing on class conflict and political issues. See esp. ch. 4 on strikes of the early 1930s and ch. 7, 8 on the sit–down strikes and steel strikes of 1937. Author maintains that "the very non–violence of the sit–downs infuriated the employers and their government agents," p. 63.)

658. Rayback, Joseph G., *The History of American Labor.* 459 pp. New York: Macmillan, 1964 [orig. publ. 1959]. (Labor history from the colonial period to the 1950s, with attention to the legal environment of labor conflict. Consult index under

boycotts, court cases, injunctions, strikes, and the names of leaders, organizations, and movements. Index. Bibliography.)

659.   Salvatore, Nick, *Eugene V. Debs: Citizen and Socialist.* 437 pp. Urbana, Chicago, and London: Univ. of Illinois Press, 1982. (Biography of Eugene V. Debs [1855–1926] with emphasis on his role as labor organizer and leader and socialist advocate. See pp. 73–81 on the Burlington Railroad Strike of 1888–89 and labor disunity, pp. 119–25 on the American Railway Union's victory in the Great Northern Strike of 1894, and pp. 127–38 on the Pullman Strike and Boycott later in 1894. Debs's arrest and imprisonment under the WWI Sedition Action for demanding free speech for radicals is discussed in pp. 291–302, 308–28. Photos. Index. Bibliography.)

660.   Swinton, John, *Striking for Life: Labor's Side of the Labor Question.* 498 pp. [New York?]: American Manufacturing and Publishing, 1894. (See ch. 8, 10–12 on the Pullman Strike of 1894 and ch. 15 on the factors that cause violence in otherwise nonviolent strikes. Photos. Appendixes. Index.)

661.   Taft, Philip, *The A.F. of L. in the Time of Gompers.* 508 pp. New York: Harper, 1957. (Brief accounts of strikes and boycotts.)

662.   Tax, Meredith, *The Rising of the Women: Feminist Solidarity and Class Conflict, 1880–1917.* 332 pp. New York and London: Monthly Review Press, 1980. (Studies of women as workers, organizers, and activists in labor and feminist causes. See accounts of several conflicts in Illinois in part 2, studies of New York shirtwaist–makers strike, 1909–10, in ch. 8, and women in the 1912 Lawrence, Massachusetts strike in ch. 9. Index.)

663.   Ware, Norman J., *The Labor Movement in the United States, 1860–1895: A Study in Democracy.* 409 pp. New York and London: D. Appleton, 1929. (History of the Knights of Labor in the post–Civil War years. See ch. 7 on strikes in Knights of

Labor thinking and ch. 15 on boycotts as the Knights' "most successful form of union activity.")

664.   Yellen, Samuel, *American Labor Struggles, 1877–1934*. 398 pp. New York: Harcourt, Brace, 1936. Reprint, New York: Monad Press, 1974. (History of several strikes and labor conflicts. See introduction for views on the "weapons" of labor and capital. Ch. 1 is on the great strike of 1877, ch. 4 is on the Pullman Strike of 1894, ch. 6 is on the Lawrence strike of 1912, ch. 8 is on the 1919 steel strike, and ch. 10 is on the San Francisco waterfront strikes and general strike of 1934. Illustrations. Index.)

NINETEENTH CENTURY

This century is marked by the beginnings of labor organizations, such as the Knights of Labor and early craft "brotherhoods" in the railroads. Rapid technological change affected industrial labor, while agricultural labor had little opportunity for acting collectively. Post Civil War law and policy favoring the relatively unfettered uses of capital also led to strife in the mines, factories, and railroads. In addition to the two great strikes cited below, important events included the series mass strikes identified by Brecher (entry 641), movements to limit the hours of labor and gain the right to organize and bargain collectively, the Burlington rail strike of 1888, and the violent Homestead Strike of 1892. Note also the development of "weapons" of collective action including strikes, sympathy strikes, boycotts, and slow–downs by labor and strikebreaking and surveillance by management (see entries 655, 704, 706).

Studies

665.   Bensman, David, *The Practice of Solidarity: American Hat Finishers in the Nineteenth Century*. 240 pp. Urbana and Chicago: Univ. of Illinois Press, 1985. (Labor history of hat finishers from 1854 to 1915. See pp. 117–20, 123–24 on the "new weapon" of the consumer boycott; ch. 8 on the Orange Boycott of 1885. See also index under *boycotts, strikes*. Illustrations. Photos. Index. Bibliography.)

666.   Blewett, Mary H., *Men, Women, and Work: Class, Gender, and Protest in the New England Shoe Industry, 1780–1910.* 445 pp. Urbana and Chicago: Univ. of Illinois Press, 1988. (Within the context of a study of work, gender, and change in the Massachusetts shoe industry, the author discusses strikes and protests in ch. 5–9; see index under *labor protest, parades,* and *strikes.* Illustrations. Appendixes. Index.)

667.   Dawley, Alan, *Class and Community: The Industrial Revolution in Lynn.* 301 pp. Cambridge: Harvard Univ. Press, 1976. (In the context of a study of changes in work, social class, and urban life in this Massachusetts shoe–producing city, the author discusses the Great Strike of 1860 in pp. 78–89, 102–3 and other strikes in ch. 7, "Militants." Illustrations. Photos. Index. Bibliography.)

668.   Faler, Paul G., *Mechanics and Manufacturers in the Early Industrial Revolution: Lynn, Massachusetts, 1780–1860.* 267 pp. Albany: State Univ. of New York Press, 1981. (History of the shoe industry between Independence and the Civil War. See esp. ch. 11, "The Great Shoemakers' Strike," on the strike of 1860 that involved many of the industries of Eastern and Central Massachusetts. Index. Bibliography.)

669.   George, J.E., "The Coal Miners' Strike of 1897." *Quarterly Journal of Economics* 12 (1898): 186–208. Reprint. 25 pp. Boston: George H. Ellis, 1898. (Analysis of events causing a three–month strike in the Eastern coal fields. See pp. 199–208 on the strike, with comments on strikers' efforts to avoid violence.)

670.   Harriman, Job, "The Class War in Idaho." 32 pp. New York: Volks–Zeitung Library, vol. 2, no. 4 (July 1, 1900). (Account of the violence in the Coeur d'Alene region, 1892–1899. See esp. pp. 18–30 on 1899.)

671.   Laurie, Bruce, *Working People of Philadelphia, 1800–1850.* 273 pp. Philadelphia: Temple Univ. Press, 1980. (Labor history of antebellum Philadelphia. See index under *strikes.* Index. Bibliography.)

672.   McLaurin, Melton Alonza, *The Knights of Labor in the South.* 232 pp. Westport CT and London: Greenwood Press, 1978. (See ch. 4, "Strikes and Boycotts," on the use and misuse of strikes by the Knights of Labor and their effects on the organization. Index. Bibliography.)

673.   McMurry, Donald L., The *Great Burlington Strike of 1888: A Case History in Labor Relations.* 377 pp. New York: Russell & Russell, 1973 [orig. publ. 1956]. (History of rail strike and its impact. Of particular interest are ch. 7, 8 on labor boycott of Burlington cars by workers on other lines and injunctions against it. See also ch. 10 on public opinion and ch. 11, 12 on causes of violence. Appendixes. Index. Bibliography.)

675.   Slamons, C.H., *The Burlington Strike: Its Motives and Methods.* 480 pp. Aurora IL: Press of Bunnel and Ward, 1889. (Sympathetic account of the strike written shortly after actual events. Criticizes "ruthlessness of capitalism" and sees labor movement as wellspring of "the strong writers, thinkers and statesmen of the future." Ends with a first–person account of the strike by a former railroad worker. Illustrations.)

676.   Stromquist, Sheldon, *A Generation of Boomers: The Pattern of Railroad Labor Conflict in Nineteenth–Century America.* 353 pp. Chicago and Urbana: Univ. of Illinois Press, 1987. (Ch. 1 is on the "pattern" of railroad strikes, defining the various ends and issues to which they were put, and ch. 6 describes the system of labor management and control. Photo section following p. 63 includes several documents related to strikes. Illustrations. Photos. Appendixes. Index. Bibliography.)

677.   Twentieth Century Club, "The Strike of the Shoe Workers in Marlboro, Mass., November 14, 1898 – May 5, 1899." 23 pp. Boston: Twentieth Century Club, [1899?]. (Inquiry by civic-minded group into lockout and strike. See pp. 7–9 on causes in an anti–union lockout and pp. 9–13 for mediation and arbitration attempts. Appendix.)

678.   Ward, Robert David, and William Warren Rogers, *Labor Revolt in Alabama: The Great Strike of 1894.* 172 pp. University AL: Univ. of Alabama Press, 1965. (History of

April 1894 mining strike in north–central Alabama. See ch. 3–8 on strike itself, which includes discussion of using black workers to break strike by whites and the factors leading to violence despite leaders' desire to avoid it, ch. 3, 4. Index. Bibliography.)

679.   Watts, Theodore F., *The First Labor Day Parade, Tuesday, September 5, 1882: Media Mirrors to Labor's Icons*. 53 pp. Silver Spring MD: Phoenix Rising, 1983. (History of "first" Labor Day parade as a protest sponsored by New York City Central Labor Union. Illustrations. Bibliography.)

680.   Wolff, Leon, *Lockout: The Story of the Homestead Strike of 1892: A Study of Violence, Unionism, and the Carnegie Steel Empire*. 297 pp. New York, Evanston, and London: Harper & Row, 1965. (Ch. 4–10 discuss the bitter and violent conflict, which began with refusal to continue recognition of union organization, pp. 80–92. See ch. 5 on the origins of violence and the battle between strikers and Pinkerton guards. Illustrations. Photos. Index. Bibliography.)

Great Strike of 1877

This strike originated on the railroads and spread broadly throughout the Midwest and parts of the South. Labor organizations soon lost any ability to direct the strike and citizens in cities such as St. Louis feared being taken over by strikers. Despite threats being used to prevent trains from moving, violence was slight until the government sent troops out against the strikers, after which there was great destruction and loss of life.

681.   Burbank, David T., *Reign of the Rabble: The St. Louis General Strike of 1877*. 208 pp. New York: Augustus M. Kelley, 1966. (Day–by–day history of "general strike" that accompanied the great strike of 1877 in St. Louis. Frontispiece illustration is "Workingman's Party" proclamation in English and German against violence. General strike call discussed on pp. 55–57; strike's mass marches on pp. 70–76, 80; "moderating" effect of socialists on p. 122; and lack of violence on p. 173.)

682. Foner, Philip S., *The Great Labor Uprising of 1877*. 288 pp. New York: Monad Press, 1977. (Circumstantial account of extensive series of strikes beginning in railroads. Strikes characterized by much violence and destruction when troops were employed. Chronology in appendix. Index. Bibliography.)

683. Heywood, E.H., "The Great Strike: Its Relation to Labor, Property, and Government." 24 pp. Princeton MA: Cooperative Publishing, 1878. (Period comment on the strike of 1877, comparing it to the abolitionism of an earlier day. Pp. 13, 20–21 contain author's effort to apply nonresistance principles to labor conflicts.)

Pullman Strike and Rail Boycotts of 1894

The great strikes of 1894 began when production workers at the Pullman, Illinois, works of the Pullman Palace Car Company went on strike after wage reductions. With the participation of Eugene V. Debs's railroad union, sympathetic "boycotts" followed, in which rail workers throughout the West refused to handle Pullman cars. Transportation was disrupted over much of the nation until the railroad General Managers Association and allies in government succeeded in overcoming the boycotts with troops and arrests. A curious feature of the strike is that the town of Pullman had been founded as a model community with special amenities for the working people.

684. Buder, Stanley, *Pullman: An Experiment in Industrial Order and Community Planning, 1880–1930*. 263 pp. New York: Oxford Univ. Press, 1967. (Study of the Pullman community as an attempt at social reform. See ch. 3 on the reform impulse that motivated Pullman's origins, ch. 11 on business innovation and its effects, and ch. 12–15 on the strike. Photos. Index.)

685. Burns, W.F., *The Pullman Boycott: A Complete History of the Great Railroad Strike*. 318 pp. St. Paul MN: McGill Printing, 1894. (An extended account of the Pullman Strike of 1894, supportive of the American Railway Union and Eugene V.

Debs and hostile to the General Managers Association and
the railroad brotherhoods. Quotations from speeches,
discussions, and documents are interspersed, but without
attribution to sources.)

686.   Carwardine, William H., *The Pullman Strike*. 126 pp.
       Chicago: Charles H. Kerr, 1894. 4th ed. Reprint 1971. (Pro–
       labor account of the strike, written by pastor of a church in
       the town of Pullman. See ch. 3–5 on the strike itself.)

687.   Lindsey, A.P., *The Pullman Strike*. 385 pp. Chicago: Univ. of
       Chicago Press, 1964 [orig. publ. 1942]. (Depicts strike as
       inevitable conclusion of the growing tensions between labor
       and capital in late nineteenth–century U.S. Analyzes
       outcomes of strike on undeveloped national labor movement.
       See esp. pp. 130–35 for consideration of a national boycott of
       Pullman cars as a means of aiding labor's cause. Illustrations.
       Photos. Index. Bibliography.)

688.   [United States Strike Commission], *Report on the Chicago
       Strike of June–July 1894*. 725 pp. Washington DC: Government
       Printing Office, 1895. Reprint, Clifton NJ: Augustus M. Kelley
       Publishers, 1972. (Report of commission to investigate the
       Pullman Strike and associated labor boycotts and
       disturbances. Lengthy appendix contains transcripts of oral
       testimony by union leaders, strikers, and employers.
       Documents.)

689.   Stead, W.T., *Chicago To–Day; or, The Labour War in
       America*. 287 pp. London: Review of Reviews Office, 1894.
       Reprint, New York: Arno Press and The New York Times,
       1969. (Journalistic account of several phases of the conflicts of
       1894. See ch. 2 on Coxey's Army and the "petition in boots,"
       and parts 3, 4 on the Pullman Strike and conflict on the
       railroads.)

690.   Stein, Leon, ed., *The Pullman Strike*. Various pagings. New
       York: Arno Press and The New York Times, 1969. (Reprints
       pieces on the strike, including W.H. Carwardine, *The
       Pullman Strike*; Grover Cleveland, *The Government in the*

Chicago Strike of 1894; Statements of George H. Pullman and T.H. Wickes; and "Liberty," a speech by Eugene V. Debs.)

691.   Warne, Coulston E., ed., *The Pullman Boycott of 1894: The Problem of Federal Intervention*. 113 pp. Boston: D.C. Heath, 1955. (Anthology of texts on the Pullman strike and boycott edited for classroom use. Part 1 contains summary views of its effects, part 2 contains evidence on its origins as collected by the U.S. strike commission, part 3 briefly describes the events, and part 5 contains selections on the question of federal involvement, as taken from the strike commission report, Eugene V. Debs's Supreme Court challenge to his arrest, and the opinions of Governor Altgeld, President Cleveland, Debs, and others. Illustrations.)

TWENTIETH CENTURY

If there is a single theme to twentieth–century labor history it is undoubtedly the gradual regularization of relations between labor organizations, the corporations, and government. This transition occurred only through bitter struggle in many industries, and perhaps remains incomplete in coal mining. It has implied the decline of radicalism from early in the century, when the influences of socialists, communists, and the Industrial Workers of the World (IWW) were significant. A significant part of this transition has occurred as a result of the state's intervention in defying by law the rights and limits of labor organization and action. It might be said that organizing in steel and automobile industries led the way in much of this, a trend represented here by the section below on 1930s sit–downs. Lastly, there is evidence that the regularization referred to above, and increasingly bureaucratic structure of unions, is itself being resisted by some workers (see entries 701, 702).

692.   Bernstein, Irving, *Turbulent Years: A History of the American Worker, Vol. 2: 1933–1941*. 873 pp. Boston: Houghton Mifflin, 1970. (On the transformation of the labor movement in the U.S. and the effects of Roosevelt's presidency and policies upon labor. Includes extensive information on strikes, both violent and nonviolent, in various industrial sectors and the labor unions involved in them. Photos. Index.)

693.   Best, Harry, "The Men's Garment Industry of New York and
        the Strike of 1913." 25 pp. New York: Univ. Settlement
        Studies, University Settlement Society, [1913?].
        (Contemporary study of conditions in the industry and the
        two–month strike by garment workers, concluding that the
        strike won little and commending the role of arbitration.)

694.   Blankenhorn, Heber, *The Strike for Union: A Study of the
        Non–Union Question in Coal and the Problems of a
        Democratic Movement.* 263 pp. New York: H.W. Wilson;
        London: Grafton, 1924. (Detailed account of a lengthy strike
        in the Somerset, Pennsylvania coal fields in 1922, which was
        devoted in part to gaining union recognition. Ch. 6,
        "Maintaining a Strike," considers how strike organizations
        address the problems of wage losses, provocation, legal
        mistreatment, scab workers, and the like. Illustrations.
        Appendix. Index.)

695.   Cahn, William, *Lawrence, 1912: The Bread and Roses Strike.*
        246 pp. New York: Pilgrim Press, 1980. (Illustrated popular
        account, with many photographs of strike and personalities
        involved as well as associated documents, pp. 96–221.)

696.   Cornell, Robert H., *The Anthracite Coal Strike of 1902.* 279
        pp. Reprint, New York: Russell & Russell, 1971. Originally
        published by Catholic Univ. of America Press, 1957.
        (Chronicle of extensive strike in mining. See esp. ch. 6, "The
        Public Takes Sides," which discusses union leaders' attempts
        to convince strikers to avoid violence and any nonviolent
        actions that could be seen by the populace as threatening.
        Later chapters discuss federal intervention in ending the
        strike. Index. Bibliography.)

697.   David, Henry, *The History of the Haymarket Affair: A
        Study in the American Social–Revolutionary and Labor
        Movements.* 579 pp. New York: Farrar & Rinehart, 1936. (See
        esp. ch. 8 on the relationship between Haymarket and the
        eight–hour movement. Ch. 9, 10 discuss the bomb and its
        immediate effects and pp. 514–17 discuss the "agent
        provocateur thesis." Index. Bibliography.)

698. Durand, E. Dana, "The Anthracite Coal Strike and Its Settlement," *Political Science Quarterly* 18 (1903): 385–414. (Review of factors in strike and the role of labor and industry organization.)

699. Goldberg, David J., *A Tale of Three Cities: Labor Organization and Protest in Paterson, Passaic, and Lawrence, 1916–1921*. 276 pp. New Brunswick NJ and London: Rutgers Univ. Press, 1989. (Study of unionism and strikes in three industrial cities, with particular attention to strikes in 1919 and their effects on organizing by the .Amalgamated Textile Workers of America;. Index. Bibliography.)

700. Gooden, Orville Thrasher, *The Missouri and North Arkansas Railroad Strike*. 274 pp. New York: Columbia Univ. Press, 1926. Columbia Univ. Studies in History, Economics, and Public Law, no. 275. (Analysis of rail strike, 1921–23, that involved suspension of all service during nine months of that time. Contends on p. 7 that this strike was "unique" because those who suffered from loss of service drove out the strikers. See ch. 2–5, 14 on the strike itself, ch. 6, 7 on "citizens committees" opposed to strike, and ch. 8–11 on trials for bridge burning. Index. Bibliography.)

701. Green, Hardy, *On Strike at Hormel: The Struggle for a Democratic Labor Movement*. 368 pp. Philadelphia: Temple Univ. Press, 1990. ("Insider's" story of 1985–86 strike, lockout, and picketing at the Hormel meat–packing plant in Austin, Minnesota. Ch. 1, 2 describe the setting, participants, and issues of the strike. Subsequent chapters present a detailed chronicle of the strike, its conduct, and related issues for the community and strike organization. Strike strategy and methods and strike support measures discussed throughout. See pp. 195–98, 211–14, and ch. 8 on "civil disobedience" and demonstrations at the plant. Ch. 10 evaluates tactics, the decision to maintain large scale nonviolent action, and the possible introduction of violence. Photos. Index.)

702. Hage, Dave, and Paul Klauda, *No Retreat, No Surrender: Labor's War at Hormel*. 398 pp. New York: William Morrow, 1989. (Journalists' detailed account of a lengthy strike in the

Minnesota meat–packing industry in the 1980s and the personalities involved in it. Photos. Index.)

703.   Hoerder, Dirk, ed., *"Struggle a Hard Battle": Essays on Working Class Immigrants*. 375 pp. DeKalb: Northern Illinois Univ. Press, 1986. (Maxine Schwartz Seller, "The Uprising of the Twenty Thousand: Sex, Class, and Ethnicity in the Shirtwaist Makers' Strike of 1909," pp. 254–79 is on women garment workers on strike, conduct of the strike, and its impact. Strikes and other collective action are also discussed in other pieces collected here, see index under *boycotts, lockouts, strikes*, and the names of cities, labor organizations, and ethnic groups. Photos. Index.)

704.   Howard, Sidney, *The Labor Spy: A Survey of Industrial Espionage*. 72 pp. New York: Republic Publishing, 1921. (Reprinted from *The New Republic*. Condemns employers' use of spies to locate radicals within a company in order to remove them and silence industrial unrest. Describes methods of spying with several cases.)

705.   Langdon, Emma F., *The Cripple Creek Strike: A History of Industrial Wars in Colorado*. 595 pp. Denver CO: Great Western, 1904–05. Reprint, New York: Arno Press and The New York Times, 1969. (Firsthand account of bitter mining strike in Colorado, 1903. See part 1. Illustrations. Photos. Appendixes.)

706.   Levinson, Edward, *I Break Strikes! The Technique of Pearl L. Berghoff*. 314 pp. New York: Robert M. McBride, 1935. (Biography and exposé of professional strikebreaker Pearl L. Berghoff and his notoriously violent methods. The second chapter contains a history of strikebreaking before Berghoff's time, which itself began about 1907. Extensive information on employing *agents provocateurs*, development of strikebreaking techniques of violence, and the effects of violence either in breaking or strengthening strikes. Photos. Index. Bibliography.)

707.   McGovern, George S., and Leonard F. Guttridge, *The Great Coalfield War*. 383 pp. Boston: Houghton Mifflin, 1972.

(History of the Colorado strikes of 1913–14 and the "Ludlow Massacre," focusing on the violence and counterviolence of strikers and militia. Authors conclude that the "message" of Ludlow "is forever blurred by the bloodstains," p. 341. Photos. Index. Bibliography.)

708. Milkman, Ruth, ed., *Women, Work, and Protest: A Century of U.S. Women's Labor History.* 333 pp. Boston, London, Melbourne, and Henley: Routledge & Kegan Paul, 1985. (Essays emphasizing relationship among "gender, consciousness, and working–class activism." See ch. 2 on Chicago Women's Trade Union League, 1904–24, ch. 3 on the Lawrence strike of 1912, ch. 4 on Colorado Fuel and Iron Strike of 1913–14, and ch. 9 on 1934 Minneapolis Teamsters' Strike. See also index under *strikes.* Index.)

709. Murphy, Paul L., with David Klaassen and Kermit Hall, *The Passaic Textile Strike of 1926.* 185 pp. Belmont CA: Wadsworth, 1974. (A "source reader" of extracts from press reports and documents on the conduct of the Passaic, New Jersey textile strike. Narrative is in ch. 1 and a selection of "contemporary perceptions" is in ch. 3. Appendixes.)

710. Petro, Sylvester, *The Kohler Strike: Union Violence and Administrative Law.* 118 pp. Chicago: Henry Regnery, 1961. (Legalistic account of 1954 strike and boycott. See part 1 on strike itself and accusations of violence and intimidating mass action by pickets. Appendixes.)

711. Suggs, George G., Jr., *Union Busting in the Tri–State: The Oklahoma, Kansas, and Missouri Metal Workers' Strike of 1935.* 282 pp. Norman and London: Univ. of Oklahoma Press, 1986. (On the clash of CIO–sponsored and employer-sponsored labor unions in the Depression–era mining and metals industry along the Oklahoma–Kansas–Missouri border. Ch. 1–3 explore a 1935 strike in which a brief episode of violence by strikers energized an incipient back–to–work campaign to employ superior violence in breaking the strike. Following chapters discuss violence in a subsequent 1937 strike and legal entanglements. Photos. Index.)

712.   U.S. Congress. House. *Report on Strike of Textile Workers in
        Lawrence, Mass., in 1912.* Ed. Chas. P. Neill. 511 pp. 62d
        Cong., 2d sess., 1912. H. Doc. 870. (See ch. 1 for description of
        strike and appendix 2 for strike committee documents. Bulk of
        study consists of statistics on population, wages, and prices.
        Documents in appendix. Index.)

713.   Walker, Charles Rumford, *American City: A Rank–and–File
        History.* 278 pp. New York and Toronto: Farrar and Rinehart,
        1937. (A journalistic account of the two Minneapolis,
        Minnesota truckers' strikes of 1934, the "citizens' army" that
        battled them, and resulting violence is in ch. 6–8, 10–12.
        Photos. Bibliography.)

Industrial Workers of the World

*The Wobblies of the IWW, in addition to their romantic image, are
significant in two ways. First, the IWW's ideological insistence on
"one big union," rather than distinct trade or industrial unions,
underlay its successful mobilization of mass city–wide strikes at
Lawrence, Mass. in 1912 and Paterson, N.J. in 1913. Second, the IWW
was an active innovator of methods of industrial "direct action."
These included "free speech fights" held when IWW organizers were
jailed for speaking in public in the West. These fights flooded a
community with organizers and street speakers until the government
was forced to relent. Other IWW weapons were their inventive
protest songs, "folded arms" slow–downs, nonviolent "sabotage"
(which essentially means slow and inaccurate work and was a
favorite of the IWW). The union did not survive intact after World
War I, which it opposed, largely because of the continued legal and
extra–legal repression it met.*

714.   Bird, Stewart, Dan Georgakas, and Deborah Shaffer,
        Solidarity Forever: An Oral History of the IWW. 247 pp.
        Chicago: Lake View Press, 1985. (Recollections of the IWW
        and its struggles in various eras and various trades. In pp. 25–
        28, singer Bruce "Utah" Phillips explains the role of IWW
        songs. Accounts of work and the strike in Paterson, N.J. are in
        pp. 55–76. Illustrations. Photos. Index.)

715. Conlin, Joseph R., ed., *At the Point of Production: The Local History of the I.W.W.* 329 pp. Westport CT and London: Greenwood Press, 1981. (Anthology of studies of the IWW and its activities, including strikes, "direct action," and repression. See also bibliography, Dione Mills, "Sources for the Local History of the I.W.W.," pp. 237–318. Index.)

716. Dubofsky, Melvin, *We Shall Be All: A History of the Industrial Workers of the World.* 557 pp. Chicago: Quadrangle Books, 1969. (Part 3 focuses on the IWW in its years of most effective collective action. See ch. 8 on Free Speech Fights, ca. 1909–12; ch. 10 on the Lawrence, Mass. strike of 1912; and ch. 11 on the later strike in Paterson, N.J. Part 4 provides a good deal of detail on the suppression of the IWW in the factory and courtroom. Consult index under *Debs, Eugene; DeLeon, Daniel; Ettor, Joseph; Flynn, Elizabeth Gurley; Foster, William Z., Haywood, William D.; general strike; labor spies; St. John, Vincent; strikes; strikebreakers; vigilantes; violence;* and *Williams, Ben H.,* as well as the names of labor organizations and departments of the U.S. government. Photos. Index.)

717. Foner, Philip S., ed., *Fellow Workers and Friends: The I.W.W. Free Speech Fights as Told by Participants.* 242 pp. Westport CT and London: Greenwood Press, 1981. (Documents and accounts related to ten free–speech fights, 1909–16. See editor's introduction on the IWW, street speaking, free speech fights, and their effects. Index.)

718. Gambs, John S., *The Decline of the Industrial Workers of the World.* 268 pp. New York: Columbia Univ. Press; London: P.S. King & Son, 1932. (A study of the IWW from 1917 until the early years of the Depression. Ch. 1, 2 contain observations on IWW strikes in the early post–war years, while ch. 5 focuses more generally on strikes, slow–downs, and boycotts in the 1920s and early 1930s. Appendixes. Index. Bibliography.)

719. Kornbluh, Joyce, ed., *Rebel Voices: An IWW Anthology.* 419 pp. Ann Arbor: Univ. of Michigan Press, 1964. (Documents of many kinds on the IWW, its ideas, methods, and conflicts. Includes manifestoes, poems, songs, and cartoons. In ch. 1, see

no. 11, William Trautman, "How Strikes Are Lost," pp. 17–24. Ch. 2, entitled "With Folded Arms: The Tactics of Direct Action," includes selections on strikes and general strikes as well as several on sabotage [which, in IWW usage, included slow–downs and "passive resistance"]. Ch. 4 contains material from the Free Speech Fights of 1908–16, ch. 6 is on the Lawrence, Mass. strike of 1912, and ch. 7 is on the Paterson, N.J. strike of 1913, including material on the "pageant" held to support the strike. Ch. 5 is on Joe Hill, his protest and organizing songs, and his execution. Ch. 11 includes IWW opposition to WWI and conscription and the prosecution and imprisonment of militants. Illustrations. Photos. Glossary. Bibliography.)

720.   Mills, Dione, *Something in Common: An IWW Bibliography.* 560 pp. Detroit: Wayne State Univ. Press, 1986. (Annotated bibliography of materials by and about the IWW, classified into sections on books, articles, dissertations and theses, pamphlets, IWW periodicals, government documents, and miscellany including poetry and fiction. Illustrations. Index of authors and subjects. Separate index of journals in which the articles compiled appear, pp. 341–60.)

721.   Renshaw, Patrick, *The Wobblies: The Story of Syndicalism in the United States.* 312 pp. Garden City NY: Doubleday, 1967. (History of the Industrial Workers of the World from its origins to its decline at the end of WWI. See esp. pp. 116–28 on Free Speech Fights in the West and ch. 6 on IWW–led strikes of the textile workers of Lawrence, Mass. and Paterson, N.J. Photos. Index.)

722.   Tripp, Anne Huber, *The IWW and the Paterson Silk Strike of 1913.* 317 pp. Urbana and Chicago: Univ. of Illinois Press, 1987. (Ch. 2 is on the Lawrence strike of 1912 and ch. 4–7 on the Paterson "general strike," including an account of the Paterson Pageant. Ch. 9 assesses the strike and pp. 23–26, 228–35 discuss the role of the IWW's nonviolent conduct of the two strikes. Photos. Chronology in appendix. Index. Bibliography.)

Steel Strike of 1919

The Pennsylvania Steel Strike of 1919 is perhaps less significant in itself than in the documentation of its origins and workings. The strike itself began almost spontaneously, pulling the union along with it. During the strike, evidence of a good deal of strike breaking and police violence came to light, as well as attempts by management to brand the leaders as radicals. Readers will note the participation of William Zebulon Foster, later an important figure in the U.S. Communist Party, and attempted mediation by a group called the Interchurch World Movement.

723. Brody, David, *Labor in Crisis: The Steel Strike of 1919.* 208 pp. Philadelphia: Lippincott, 1965. Reprint, Westport CT: Greenwood Press, 1982. (History of 1919 strike in the context of steel–industry unionism. See pp. 89–95 on industry's effort to prevent mass meetings before the strike; ch. 4 on the national scene, including pp. 128–44 on the Red scare and William Z. Foster; and ch. 5 on strike process, including pp. 149–55 on police suppression and its effects. Index.)

724. Foster, William Z., *The Great Steel Strike and Its Lessons.* 265 pp. New York: B.W. Huebsch, 1920. (Partisan account of 1919 Pennsylvania steel strike by organizer. Ch. 5 describes preliminary "free speech fight" to hold unobstructed meetings, pp. 90–95 are on organizers' decision to lead strike likely to occur anyway, and ch. 6–10 are on the strike itself, focusing on firms' efforts to brand the strike as revolutionary, banning of meetings, and police violence.)

725. Interchurch World Movement, Commission of Inquiry, *Report on the Steel Strike of 1919.* 277 pp. New York: Harcourt, Brace & Howe, 1920. (Having failed to mediate the strike, this group investigated its causes. See introduction for methods; ch. 2 for response to charges of revolutionary intent among strikers; and ch. 7, esp. pp. 210–42, on industry's methods of control of strikers. Index.)

726. ———, *Public Opinion and the Steel Strike: Supplementary Reports of the Investigators.* 346 pp. New York: Harcourt, Brace, 1921. (Second volume of report. See ch. 1, "Under–

Cover Men," by Robert Little, on the use of agents to monitor the strike; ch. 3, "Civil Rights in Western Pennsylvania," by George Soule, on police–striker clashes and restriction or prevention of meetings in the strike region; plus report on Interchurch group as mediator, pp. 331–41. Index. Bibliography.)

727. Olds, Marshall, *Analysis of the Interchurch World Movement Report on the Steel Strike*. 475 pp. New York and London: G.P. Putnam's Sons, 1923. (Refutation of Interchurch World Movement inquiry. See pp. 3–14 on the relation of the strike to collective bargaining, ch. 15–17 on organizing and radicalism, and ch. 24 debunking nonpartisan claims of the Interchurch group. Ch. 22 challenges the Interchurch report and William Z. Foster's claim that strikers were not violent, and ch. 23 brands tales of police violence as "atrocity stories.")

Sit–Down Strikes, 1930s

These dramatic events hinged on the invention by the United Auto Workers union of a new form of action, the mass sit–down or occupation of a premises. General Motors was the first major object of these strikes, followed in 1937 by Ford. In each case the concentration of work and workers at massive plants permitted unionists simply to stay in the work place as a strike began, also making it difficult for management and police to dislodge them. While there were assaults on the sit–downers and, at Ford's River Rouge plant, beatings of organizers, the violence did not end the strikes. Researchers interested in biographies of activists may wish to consult the works on organizer Walter Reuther and his brothers.

728. Fine, Sidney, *Sit–down: The General Motors Strike of 1936– 1937*. 448 pp. Ann Arbor: Univ. of Michigan Press, 1969. (History of four–month long sit–down strike with extensive analyses of both GM's and UAW's positions. See esp. pp. 121– 31 for a brief history of sit–down strikes and analysis of their development. Index. Bibliography.)

729. Kraus, Henry, *The Many and the Few: A Chronicle of the Dynamic Auto Workers*. 308 pp. Los Angeles: Plantin Press, 1947. (Labor journalist's story of Flint, Michigan sit–downs of 1937. See ch. 2 on earlier sit–down, ch. 4–12 on conduct of strike, and ch. 7, 9 on the role of violence in efforts to halt strike.)

730. Levinson, Edward, *Labor on the March*. 325 pp. New York: Univ. Books, 1956 [orig. publ. 1938]. (See ch. 7, 8 for CIO–oriented account of the origin and progress of the sit–down strike, 1935–36, pp. 207–9 on violent suppression of steel strikes in 1936, and pp. 216–20 on anti–union organizations. Index.)

731. Reuther, Victor, *The Brothers Reuther and the Story of the UAW*. 537 pp. Boston: Houghton Mifflin, 1976. (Memoir of a family of labor organizers involved in the sit–down strikes of the 1930s. See pp. 134–42 and ch. 13 on sit–downs, including pp. 149–50 on their origins and goals. Discusses role and nature of violence in labor struggles, esp. police–striker fighting during GM sit–down, pp. 154–57; vigilantism, ch. 14; and beatings and terror dealt out by presumed company agents in River Rouge plant campaign, 1937–38, ch. 16. Photos. Index.)

Professionals' Strikes

These entries are generally on specific strikes involving teachers and other professionals. In the mix of issues that cause such strikes are often racial and community tension, changes in the professionals' status, and salary and working conditions.

See also: Methods of Nonviolent Action: Noncooperation in the Government and Military.

732. Begin, James P., Theodore Settle, and Paula Alexander, *Academics on Strike*. 134 pp. New Brunswick NJ: Institute of Management and Labor Relations, Univ. Extension Division, Rutgers Univ., in cooperation with Academic Collective Bargaining Information Service, Washington DC, 1975. (Case studies of two faculty strikes, October 1974 at Rider College

and November 1974 at eight New Jersey state colleges. Research framework described in pp. 3–5. Bibliography.)

733.   Berube, Maurice R., and Marilyn Gittell, *Confrontation at Ocean Hill–Brownsville: The New York School Strikes of 1968.* 352 pp. New York: Frederick A. Praeger, 1969. (Collection of documents, essays, and articles on strike of predominantly white teachers in predominantly black school district. Contains important viewpoints on reasons for strike and role of prejudice in parts 2, 3, 4. Chronology.)

734.   Gaswirth, Marc, William M. Weinberg, and Barbara E. Kemmerer, *Teachers' Strikes in New Jersey.* 165 pp. Studies in Industrial Relations and Human Resources, no. 1. Metuchen NJ and London: Scarecrow Press, 1982. (Study with statistical analysis of 127 public school teachers' strikes in New Jersey from 1946 to 1981. Extensive statistical tables on incidence, size, and issues of strikes.)

735.   Mayer, Martin, *The Teachers Strike: New York, 1968.* 122 pp. New York, Evanston, and London: Harper & Row, 1969. (Journalistic account of 1968 teachers' strikes in the Ocean Hill–Brownsville area of New York and associated community conflict.)

736.   Shostak, Arthur B., and David Skocik, *The Air Controllers' Controversy: Lessons from the PATCO Strike.* 274 pp. New York: Human Sciences Press, 1986. (Part 3 details the strike, its causes, and consequences. Ch. 15 discusses whether the strike was won or lost and the epilogue looks at "lessons." Illustrations. Documents. Index.)

737.   Urofsky, Melvin I., ed., *Why Teachers Strike: Teachers' Rights and Community Control.* 349 pp. Garden City NY: Doubleday, 1970. (Transcripts of seminar on 1968 Ocean Hill–Brownsville teachers' strike, with comments from leading participants. See "Reflections on Ocean Hill," pp. 2–33 for description of strike and pp. 35–47 for chronology.)

Agricultural Labor to 1960

The fields have been a difficult place to organize labor into unions, in part because farm labor has often been isolated, migratory, or non–wage sharecroppers. In Hawai'i, labor was not even completely free because of the plantation and indenture systems (entry 747). States on the Mainland also found that race and ethnicity were factors not only in causing strikes, but in the local reaction to strikes. Several of the entries compiled here show that rural communities regularly gave a free hand to growers or vigilantes willing to suppress strikes, often when the strikers were migrants to the area (as readers of John Steinbeck's Grapes of Wrath will remember).

738.   Cantor, Louis, *A Prologue to the Protest Movement: The Missouri Sharecropper Roadside Demonstration of 1939.* 204 pp. Durham NC: Duke Univ. Press, 1969. (History of 1939 roadside protest encampment held by evicted tenant farm labor. See preface, ch. 5–7, 13. Index.)

739.   Daniel, Cletus E., *Bitter Harvest: A History of the California Farmworkers, 1870–1941.* 348 pp. Ithaca and London: Cornell Univ. Press, 1981. (Views labor action and police–grower violence in the context of power relations in California agriculture. See ch. 5, 6 on a series of strikes in 1933 and consult index under *strikes* for other periods. Note esp. analysis of police and vigilante violence, pp. 144–45, 150–51, 162–64, 182–85, 195–201, and effects of nonviolent behavior by strikers, pp. 159–60. Photos include strike meetings, strike technique, and vigilantism, pp. 188–200, 207–11. Index.)

740.   Galarza, Ernesto, *Farm Workers and Agri–Business in California, 1947–1960.* 405 pp. Notre Dame IN: Univ. of Notre Dame Press, 1977. (Ch. 3 discusses several strikes, confrontations, and organizing campaigns, 1947–53. Index.)

741.   Jamieson, Stuart M., *Labor Unionism in American Agriculture.* 457 pp. U.S. Department of Labor Bulletin no. 836. Washington DC: U.S. Government Printing Office, 1945. Reprint, New York: Arno Press, 1975. (Thorough history of unionism and strikes in agriculture and related industries

nationwide, ca. 1914–40. Contains material on effects of region, ethnicity, radical versus status quo politics, and status of workers. Description of many strikes and their violent suppression. See ch. 4 for statistical view and ch. 23 for summary. Documents. Bibliography includes entries on government publications and periodicals printed by labor and growers.)

742.   Majka, Linda C., and Theo J. Majka, *Farm Workers, Agribusiness, and the State*. 357 pp. Philadelphia: Temple Univ. Press, 1982. (See pp. 61–91 for analysis of protests and strikes; ch. 9 on farm labor unions' methods, esp. pp. 172–78, 186–197; and ch. 10–12 on unions and their opposition. Index. Bibliography.)

743.   McWilliams, Carey, *Factories in the Field: The Story of Migratory Farm Labor in California*. 334 pp. Boston: Little, Brown, 1939. (An account of the years 1860–1937. See ch. 13–15 on farm strikes, their repression, and the drive for unionization in 1937.)

744.   ———, *Ill Fares the Land: Migrants and Migratory Labor in the United States*. 419 pp. Boston: Little, Brown, 1942. (See ch. 14, "A Kick from the Boot Heel," on 1939 sharecroppers' "roadside demonstration" and its consequences, esp. pp. 287–91. Index. Bibliography.)

745.   Reccow, Louis, "The Orange County Citrus Strikes of 1935–1936: The 'Forgotten People' in Revolt." 281 pp. Ph.D. diss., Univ. of Southern California, 1972. (See ch. 6–7 for 1937 strike, focusing largely on "classic anti–strike tactics," including pp. 173–76 on role of violence by strikers and pp. 184–87 on vigilantes. Bibliography.)

746.   Schwartz, Michael, *Radical Protest and Social Structure: The Southern Farmers' Alliance and Cotton Tenancy, 1880–1890*. 302 pp. New York, San Francisco, and London: Academic Press, 1976. (Social–movement study of Southern Farmers' Alliance, a key organization in U.S. populism. See ch. 10–12 on organized protest, ch. 13–14 on building counter-

institutions, and ch. 15 and pp. 262–65 on the "Great Jute Boycott" of 1888–89. Index.)

747.   Takaki, Ronald, *Pau Hana: Plantation Life and Labor in Hawaii, 1835–1920*. 213 pp. Honolulu: Univ. of Hawaii Press, 1983. (A study of immigrant field labor in Hawaii's burgeoning agricultural industries. See ch. 5 on resistance to imposed work systems and domination by overseers, including discussion of methods of "recalcitrance," *ha'alele hana* or flight from indenture, and group exodus. Ch. 6 is on strikes conducted by Japanese labor in 1919 and 1920. Glossary. Index. Bibliography.)

748.   White, Roland A., *Milo Reno: Farmers Union Pioneer*. 207 pp. Reprint, New York: Arno Press, 1975. Originally published, Iowa City: Iowa Farmers Union, 1941. ("The Farmer Takes a Holiday," pp. 65–80 discusses the farm strike idea of the 1920s and early 1930s, including actions taken under the slogan "stay at home—buy nothing—sell nothing." Reports of other farm protests throughout. Photos.)

749.   Witt, Howard D., *Violence in the Fields: California Filipino Farm Labor Unionization during the Great Depression*. 139 pp. Saratoga CA: Century Twenty One, 1980. (Ch. 4 contains a history of the Salinas lettuce strike, 1934. Index.)

Cesar Chavez and the United Farm Workers

This farm workers' movement arose in the early 1960s primarily under the charismatic leadership of Cesar Chavez, who was devoted to principles of nonviolent action in the tradition of King and Gandhi. In 1965, Chavez and the UFW declared a strike in Delano, a rural grape–growing town in Southern California. The strike lasted for years and led to the first collective bargaining agreement ever in the grape industry, resulting in health care plans for workers, more careful monitoring of pesticides, higher wages, and greater job security. Inter–union competition reduced the influence of the UFW later, as did the inherent difficulties of organizing migrant workers. The strikes themselves were supported locally by hunger strikes, protest theater, and mass processions and nationally by a boycott on California table grapes and the endorsements of celebrities and politicians.

750. Fodell, Beverly, *Cesar Chavez and the United Farm Workers: A Selective Bibliography.* 103 pp. Detroit: Wayne State Univ., 1974. (Revision and expansion of 1970 privately printed version, partially annotated.)

Studies

751. Brown, Jerald Barry, "The United Farm Workers Grape Strike and Boycott, 1965–1970: An Evaluation of the Culture of Poverty Theory." 348 pp. Latin American Studies Program Dissertation Series, Cornell Univ., No. 39 (1972). Ph.D. dissertation, Cornell Univ., 1972. (Detailed study of the UFWOC grape strikes and organizing, in part aimed at disputing predictions of the "culture of poverty" thesis holding that collective action among the poor is unlikely, and in part offering a more strategically–oriented critique of the shortcomings of strike and boycott strategies. Bibliography.)

752. Day, Mark, *Forty Acres: Cesar Chavez and the Farm Workers.* 222 pp. New York and London: Praeger, 1971. (Written by priest who helped to counsel and organize farm workers. For dynamics of boycott itself, see pp. 88–97. On

nonviolence, see pp. 65, 97, and ch. 10, "Cesar Chavez on Nonviolence." Illustrations. Photos. Appendix.)

753. Dunne, John Gregory, *Delano: The Story of the California Grape Strike*. 202 pp. New York: Farrar, Straus & Giroux, 1971 [orig. publ. 1967]. (Narrative of farm workers' strike. Photos.)

754. Hammerback, John C., Richard J. Jensen, and Jose Angel Gutierrez, *A War of Words: Chicano Protest in the 1960s and 1970s*. 187 pp. Westport CT and London: Greenwood Press, 1985. (See Ch. 3, "Teaching the 'Truth': The Righteous Rhetoric of Cesar Chavez." Index. Bibliography.)

755. Hoffman, Pat, *Ministry of the Dispossessed: Learning from the Farm Worker Movement*. 154 pp. Los Angeles: Wallace Press, 1987. (History of church's involvement with the farm workers' union in California. See index under *boycotts, Chavez, fasting, huelga, nonviolence, nonviolent movement, rent strike*, and *UFW*. Photos. Index. Bibliography.)

756. Horwitz, George D., and Paul Fusco, *La Causa: The California Grape Strike*. 159 pp. New York: Macmillan; Toronto: Collier–Macmillan Canada, 1970. (Primarily photographs, with text focusing on individual participants.)

757. Jenkins, J. Craig, *The Politics of Insurgency: The Farm Worker Movement in the 1960s*. 261 pp. New York: Columbia Univ. Press, 1985. (Study of California's farm labor organizing within context of developing theory of "insurgency" defined as "organized attempts to bring the interests of previously . . . excluded groups into centers of economic and political power." See ch. 2–7 on the movements and ch. 1, 8 on the theory of "turmoil" as a facilitating factor in success. Index. Bibliography.)

758. Kushner, Sam, *Long Road to Delano*. 224 pp. New York: International, 1975. (History of California farm labor written by a *People's World* reporter. Covers Delano strike and 90 years of struggle which preceded it. See ch. 9 for biographical sketch of Chavez. See also p. 165 for

explanation of the pragmatic aspect of Chavez's nonviolent stance.)

759. Levy, Jacques E., *Cesar Chavez: Autobiography of La Causa*. 546 pp. New York: W.W. Norton, 1975. (Story of Chavez's life, based largely on interviews with Chavez and his associates.)

760. London, Joan, and Henry Anderson, *So Shall Ye Reap*. 208 pp. New York: Thomas Y. Crowell, 1970. (Social history of California agricultural workers and their efforts to organize, from the outset of Californian agribusiness up until the Delano strike. See esp. pp. 182–85 on Chavez and nonviolence. Photos. Index.)

761. Matthiessen, Peter, *Sal Si Puedes: Cesar Chavez and the New American Revolution*. 372 pp. New York: Random House, 1969. (Narrative biography of Chavez, focusing on his efforts to organize farm workers. See esp. pp. 84, 88–9, 178–79 for Chavez's nonviolence. Appendix.)

762. Nelson, Eugene, *Huelga: The First Hundred Days of the Great Delano Grape Strike*. 122 pp. Delano CA: Farm Worker Press, 1966. (Covers early phases of strike. See esp. ch. 4 on Cesar Chavez and ch. 1, 3, 5–12 for insider's description of strikers' and growers' methods. Photos.)

763. Steiner, Stan, *La Raza: The Mexican Americans*. 418 pp. New York, Evanston, and London: Harper & Row, 1970. (See esp. pp. 310–323 on Cesar Chavez.)

764. Taylor, Ronald B., *Chavez and the Farm Workers*. 342 pp. Boston: Beacon Press, 1975. (Covers the effects of the Delano strike on other industries and on the immigrant labor movement in general. See esp. pp. 137–40 for role of nonviolent action in the movement. Photos. Index. Bibliography.)

765. United Farm Workers of America, *Why We Boycott*. 31 pp. Keene CA: UFW, [1973]. (Photos and text of violence on picket lines, 1973. Illustrations. Chronology.)

766.   Yinger, Winthrop, *Cesar Chavez: The Rhetoric of Nonviolence.* 143 pp. Hicksville NY: Exposition Press, 1975. (Contains a brief biography of Chavez as well as the background to and rhetorical analysis of his March 10, 1968 speech. Appendixes. Bibliography.)

767.   Young, Jan, *The Migrant Workers and Cesar Chavez.* 191 pp. New York: Julian Messner, 1974. (See ch. 7 on Cesar Chavez, ch. 12 on his 1968 fast, and ch. 8–14 on the grape strikes and boycotts of 1965–70. Photos. Index.)

General Strikes

Few strikes, not matter how large, have been defined as general strikes in U.S. history. The identifying signs of a general strike are the involvement of labor from several industries, encompassing a significant region, attempts to close as many as possible of the industries affected, and central organization.

See also: Methods of Nonviolent Action: General Strikes.

Seattle, 1919

768.   Friedheim, Robert K., *The Seattle General Strike.* 224 pp. Seattle WA: Univ. of Washington Press, 1964. (History of a brief sympathetic general strike, its conduct, and political issues surrounding it. See ch. 4–7. Index.)

769.   Hanson, Ole, *Americanism versus Bolshevism.* 299 pp. Garden City NY: Doubleday, 1920. (Partisan account of the strike and the author's role in it as mayor of Seattle. See ch. 2 on the IWW and waterfront strike and ch. 4, 5 on the general strike. Index. Bibliography.)

770.   History Committee of the General Strike Committee, *The Seattle General Strike.* 63 pp. Seattle WA: Seattle Union Record, 1919. (Account of strike written by a committee of worker participants. For tactical and strategic issues of the strike itself and how they were addressed, see pp. 15–23, "Organizing for the Strike." Pp. 40–45 describe how vital

community functions were maintained without compromising the strike's integrity. See also pp. 45–52, "Preserving the Peace," for an account of the general order and peacefulness of the strike.)

771.   Morgan, Murray, *Skid Road: An Informal Portrait of Seattle.* 282 pp. Rev. ed. New York: Viking Press, 1960 [orig. publ. 1951]. (Pp. 199–219 cover the 1919 general strike. Index.)

San Francisco, 1934

The maritime and dockyard general strike in San Francisco is an example of such an event in which, apparently, strikers deliberately confronted police and employers with violence.

772.   Eliel, Paul, *The Waterfront and General Strikes: San Francisco, 1934.* 256 pp. San Francisco: [Industrial Association of San Francisco?], 1934. (Account of maritime strikes and general strike of 1934 by researcher for employers' group. See ch. 2–5 on maritime strike and associated transport embargo, pp. 136–44 on coming of the general strike, and ch. 6 on the course of the strike. Activities of labor and owners' unions, charges of leftist influence, and episodes of violence discussed throughout. See pp. 108–14 on the "Battle of Rincon Hill" and pp. 127–28 on later funeral parade. Documents. Index. Bibliography.)

773.   Nelson, Bruce, *Workers on the Waterfront: Seamen, Longshoremen, and Unionism in the 1930s.* 352 pp. Urbana and Chicago: Univ. of Illinois Press, 1988. (Ch. 5 is on the "Big Strike" of 1934 and its relationship to unionism among the waterfront workers. Index. Bibliography.)

774.   Quin, Mike [Paul William Ryan], *The Big Strike.* 259 pp. Olema CA: Olema Publishing, 1949. Reprint, New York: International Publishers, 1979. (Journalistic account of San Francisco's violent 1934 dock strike, which became a short-lived "general strike" before its end. Description of the strike and police–striker clashes in ch. 6–13 and of the general strike in ch. 14–18. Documents in appendix.)

Terre Haute, 1935

This strike mostly involved the transportation industry.

775. Bailey, Gary L., "The Terre Haute, Indiana, General Strike, 1935." *Indiana Magazine of History* 53 (1984): 193–226. (History of Depression–era general strike, its causes, and its organization. Photos. Bibliography.)

Other Conflicts Before 1960

ANTI–NAZI BOYCOTT

As early as 1933, Samuel Untermeyer recognized the threat of Nazism to Germany's Jews and called for a boycott of German goods in order to pressure the German government into relaxing its anti–Jewish policies. The resulting boycott movement, supported by rallies and demonstrations, lasted until U.S. participation in World War II began.

776. Feingold, Henry L., *The Politics of Rescue: The Roosevelt Administration and the Holocaust, 1938–1945.* 394 pp. New Brunswick NJ: Rutgers Univ. Press, 1970. (See discussions of protest demonstrations and boycotts, Madison Square Garden rally, and references to "illegal immigration." Index. Bibliography.)

777. Gottlieb, Moshe R., *American Anti–Nazi Resistance, 1933–1941: An Historical Analysis.* 426 pp. New York: KTAV Publishing House, 1982. (Detailed and thorough study of the politics of the boycott of German products sponsored by Jewish and nonsectarian organization. See esp. ch. 4–6 on move from protest to boycott; ch. 12–15, 18–21, 29–31 on politics of boycott; ch. 25 on boycott enforcement; and ch. 32–36 on the impact of war, as well as the concluding chapter, pp. 341–49. See also ch. 2, 3 on the internal German boycott of Jews. Documents. Index. Bibliography.)

778.   *Nazis against the World: The Counter–Boycott Is the Only Defensive Weapon against Hitlerism's World–Threat to Civilization.* 134 pp. New York: Non–Sectarian Anti–Nazi League to Champion Human Rights, [1935]. (Pamphlet containing speeches and other documents advocating boycott of trade with Germany as a sanction against internal repression.)

779.   Untermyer, Samuel, *The Boycott Is Our Only Weapon Against Nazi Germany.* 43 pp. New York: American League for the Defense of Jewish Rights, 1933. (Text of speeches calling for a boycott by Americans of the products of German industry. Appendix.)

BLACKLISTING IN ENTERTAINMENT

A "blacklist" is a collection of names of people that will not be hired by members of some group. People in the film and entertainment industries who were considered Communists were blacklisted for their sympathies. Screenwriters, playwrights, actors, and others were investigated and banned from working, sometimes after being "named" by others. The "Hollywood Ten" were people, not otherwise members of any single group, who were called to testify about their affiliations and to "name names." While these ten refused to do so, others did offer names and expanded the blacklist's reach.

780.   Cogley, John, *Report on Blacklisting.* Vol. 2, *Radio–Television.* 287 pp. Fund for the Republic, 1956. (1954 study of blacklisting, its history, and effects in the named industries. See esp. pp. 49–70 on institutionalization of blacklisting and brief case study of a moral entrepreneur in promoting blacklisters, pp. 100–9. Documents. Index.)

781.   Kahn, Gordon, *Hollywood on Trial: The Story of the Ten Who Were Indicted.* 229 pp. New York: Arno Press and The New York Times, 1972. Reprint, New York: Boni & Gaer, 1948. (The hearings on the "Hollywood Ten." Statements on pp. 215–26. Documents.)

782. Kanfer, Stefan, *A Journal of the Plague Years*. 306 pp. New York: Atheneum, 1973. (Journalistic account of blacklisting in Hollywood from 1930s to 1950s. See pp. 7–8 for definition of blacklist. See index under *blacklisting*. Photos. Index. Bibliography.)

Struggle for Desegregation and Civil Rights

African–American movements of the twentieth century take their point of departure largely from one issue, which was that denial of rights was constitutionally legal under the separate–but–equal doctrine stated by the U.S. Supreme Court in the case of Plessy v. Ferguson. *Consequently, practices of segregation and discrimination in all areas needed little or no further justification. The struggle against this doctrine took various phases, from anti–lynching campaigns (not covered here) to the 1942 March on Washington. A different channel was taken in the legal field, notably by the NAACP Legal Defense Fund. After several suits successfully challenging segregation based upon state action where there was no "equal" alternative accommodation for African–Americans, attorneys demonstrated to the satisfaction of the Supreme Court in 1954's* Brown v. Board of Education *suit that no form of segregation in public education could achieve equality of treatment. One result of* Brown v. Board of Education *was that the federal government required a certain level of desegregation of public schools. It did not readily extend this policy to other aspects of segregation, even though they were formally illegal. Interstate transportation is an example of this. Likewise, activists soon discovered that segregationists would disobey or evade the law in order to maintain segregated institutions and, as the 1960s progressed, to prevent exercise of citizenship rights (voting) or economic inclusion (hiring). As many entries in the following sections show, segregationists also employed violence in their opposition to the Civil Rights Movement, 1954–1968.*

783. Miller, Elizabeth W., and Mary L. Fisher, comps., *The Negro in America: A Bibliography*. 190 pp. Cambridge: Harvard Univ. Press, 1966. 2d ed., 351 pp. Cambridge: Harvard Univ. Press, 1970. (Annotated. Name index. Suggested reading list following essays.)

784.   Porter, Dorothy B., comp., *The Negro in the United States: A Working Bibliography*. 202 pp. Ann Arbor: University Microfilms, 1969. (See esp. pp. 149–62. Annotated. Index.)

785.   Tuskegee Institute Department of Records and Research, *A Bibliography of the Student Movement Protesting Segregation and Discrimination, 1960*. 10 pp. Tuskegee AL: Tuskegee Institute Department of Records and Research, 1961. Pamphlet no. 9. Reprint, Ann Arbor MI: University Microfilms. (Bibliography of pamphlets and magazine articles on the student sit–in movement of 1960. Index.)

786.   Williams, Daniel T., *Eight Negro Bibliographies*. Various pagings. New York: Kraus Reprint, 1970. (Separately paginated bibliographies. See esp. sections on the Freedom Riders of 1961, Southern student protests, and Martin Luther King, Jr.)

STUDIES

787.   Brisbane, Robert H., *Black Activism: Racial Revolution in the United States, 1954–1970*. 332 pp. Valley Forge PA: Judson Press, 1974. (See esp. ch. 3, "Martin Luther King, Jr., and the High Tide of Nonviolence," for a chronicle of King's rise to preeminence and the centrality of nonviolent struggle. Index. Bibliography.)

788.   Broderick, Francis L., and August Meier, eds., *Negro Protest Thought in the Twentieth Century*. 487 pp. Indianapolis, New York, and Kansas City: Bobbs–Merrill, 1965. (Anthology containing selected protest and political writings. See esp. a 1904 street car boycott on p. 24; 1942 statement by A. Philip Randolph on pp. 201–10; wartime experiences of CORE on pp. 210–24; and various selections from the 1958–65 period, including John Lewis on "aggressive nonviolent action," pp. 313–21. Index.)

789.   Giddings, Paula, *When and Where I Enter: The Impact of Black Women on Race and Sex in America*. 408 pp. Toronto, New York, London, Sydney, and Auckland: Bantam Books,

1984. (On participation of black women in women's, civil rights, and labor movements. See ch. 3, 7, 15–16. Index. Bibliography.)

790. Grant, Joanne, ed., *Black Protest: History, Documents, and Analyses: 1619 to the Present*. 512 pp. New York: St. Martin's Press, 1968. (Collection of period documents and historical description of protest and resistance by and on behalf of black Americans. See part 1, pp. 26–35, for early protest against slavery and pp. 45–53 for include from Bauer and Bauer, "Day–to–Day Resistance to Slavery." Part 2 contains documents on abolitionism. Part 5, pp. 223–26, 240–50, covers the 1940s. Parts 6, 7 extract pieces from 1954–67. See esp. pp. 268–89 on the late 1950s; pp. 289–303, 375–77 on the early 1960s; Howard Zinn, "The Limits of Nonviolence," pp. 312–17; and pp. 318–65 on white and black violence. Index. Bibliography.)

791. Harding, Vincent, *The Other American Revolution*. 261 pp. Los Angeles: Center for Afro–American Studies, Univ. of California; Atlanta: Institute of the Black World, 1980. (Chronology of black protest and resistance in U.S., ca. 1700–1968. Index. Bibliography.)

792. Meier, August, ed., *Black Experience: The Transformation of Activism*. 2d ed. 193 pp. New Brunswick NJ: Transaction Books, 1973 [orig. publ. 1970]. (Essays on decline and change in civil rights nonviolent activism; see esp. Charlayne A. Hunter, "On the Case in Resurrection City" and Michael Lipsky, "Rent Strikes: Poor Man's Weapon.")

793. Meier, August and Elliott Rudwick, *Along the Color Line: Explorations in the Black Experience*. 404 pp. Urbana, Chicago, and London: Univ. of Illinois Press, 1976. (Collected papers, largely on historical aspects of African–American political action. Part 1 is on several leaders, including Frederick Douglass, W.E.B. Du Bois, the legal staff of the NAACP, and Dr. King. See also "The Boycott Movement against Jim Crow Streetcars in the South, 1900–1906," ch. 12; "Early Boycotts of Segregated Schools: The Case of Springfield, Ohio, 1922–23," ch. 13, and "The Origins of

Nonviolent Direct Action in the Afro–American Protest: A Note on Historical Discontinuities," ch. 14.)

794.   Meier, August, and Elliott Rudwick, eds., *The Making of Black America: Essays in Negro Life and History*. Vol. 1, *The Origins of Black Americans*. 378 pp. Vol. 2, *The Black Community in Modern America*. 507 pp. New York: Atheneum, 1969. (In vol. 1, see essays by Harding, Billington, Bell, and Gara. In vol. 2, see essays by Meier and Rudwick, Powdermaker, Howe and Widick, Pettigrew, Killian and Smith, Walker, Meier, and Marx.)

795.   Meier, August, Elliott Rudwick, and Francis L. Broderick, eds., *Black Protest Thought in the Twentieth Century*. 648 pp. Indianapolis: Bobbs–Merrill Educational Publishing, 1971. (Second edition of entry 788. See esp. pp. xxxvi–xliv, ch. 4, 19, 29–32, 38, 40–50. Index. Bibliography.)

796.   Powell, Adam Clayton, *Marching Blacks*. 216 pp. New York: Dial Press, 1973 [orig. publ. 1945]. (Narrative history of the black presence in America, with emphasis throughout on success in confrontation. Covers from colonial period until the March on Washington movement. Second edition contains additional chapter on then–present status of American race relations. See esp. pp. 69–79 for analyses of 1935 Harlem riots and the founding of the Citizens' League for Fair Play, which mounted boycotts, rent strikes, and other forms of noncooperation and direct action. Part 2, ch. 7, "On Our Way" chronicles the growth of organized nonviolent campaigns. Part 3, ch. 5, "Till the End of This War" describes central role of nonviolent action as part of a strategy to combat segregation and racism in postwar America.)

MARCH ON WASHINGTON MOVEMENT, 1941–1942

Philip Randolph, leader of a major African–American labor union, set his sights on garnering some of the jobs generated by war in Europe for African–Americans. He also saw the chance to challenge the segregated military and employed the credible threat of bringing thousands of marchers to Washington to support these demands to prompt President Franklin D. Roosevelt to issue orders against discrimination in the armed forces and promoting job opportunities for Randolph's constituency. When these demands were met, the march itself was subsequently called off, but it established the potential of similar future endeavors.

797.   Anderson, Jervis, *A. Philip Randolph: A Biographical Portrait*. 398 pp. New York: Harcourt Brace Jovanovich, 1973. (Biography of black unionist and civil rights leader. See esp. ch. 16–18 on the March on Washington movement of the 1940s and struggle to desegregate the military and ch. 21 on Randolph's role in the Washington march of 1963. Illustrations. Photos. Index.)

798.   Davis, Daniel S., *Mr. Black Labor: The Story of A. Philip Randolph, Father of the Civil Rights Movement*. 173 pp. New York: E.P. Dutton, 1972. (Political biography. Discusses WWI–era anti–racism march on pp. 20–21; 1941–42 March on Washington movement in ch. 9, 10; threatened "civil disobedience" campaign against segregation in military in 1948 on pp. 125–31; and the 1963 March on Washington in ch. 13. Photos. Index.)

799.   Garfinkel, Herbert, *When Negroes March: The March on Washington Movement in the Organizational Politics for FEPC*. 224 pp. Glencoe IL: Free Press, 1959. Reprint, New York: Atheneum, 1969. (Study of 1941–42 March on Washington Movement using a "natural history" approach. Defends thesis that the movement forced Roosevelt to create the Fair Employment Practices Commission. See ch. 2 on 1941 March campaign and FEPC; ch. 3 on rallies in 1942; and pp. 135–38, 143–46 on 1943 effort to introduce Gandhian methods. Chronology. Index.)

800.   Pffeffer, Paula, *A. Philip Randolph, Pioneer of the Civil Rights Movement*. 336 pp. Baton Rouge and London: Louisiana State Univ. Press, 1990. (Biography of labor leader Randolph focusing on his activities as a civil rights leader. See ch. 2 for the mass march on Washington idea, 1941–43, and the role of Bayard Rustin and CORE, pp. 62–65. Later chapters discuss opposition to the segregated military services, Randolph's

influence on protests in the 1950s, and the 1963 March on Washington. Index. Bibliography.)

CIVIL RIGHTS MOVEMENT

Even though direct action against segregation pre–dated Brown, as for example in lunch–counter sit–ins in the North and proto–Freedom Rides in the 1940s, this decision opened opportunities to challenge other forms of discrimination. It raised the possibility of engaging the federal government through the courts as part of lawsuits that might stem from direct action, as well as involving it politically in enforcement, peacekeeping, or intervention to settle a conflict.

As users of the resources compiled below will see, post–Brown direct action was composed of several phases. First, there was the period of challenges to specific features of segregation, including the Montgomery Bus Boycott, Freedom Rides, and sit–ins that stretched from 1954 until 1962. A second phase encompassed challenges to segregation in a locality, but with two differing strategies. The Student Nonviolent Coordinating Committee (SNCC) favored detailed and focused local actions, while Dr. Martin Luther King, Jr.'s, Southern Christian Leadership Conference (SCLC) relied on mass action. King's campaigns took him to Albany, Georgia in 1962 and Birmingham, Alabama and Washington, D.C. in 1963. Both groups then turned their attention to voting rights, the SCLC continuing its mass marches (for example, in Selma, Alabama in 1965). SNCC organized a house–to–house voter registration campaign during the Mississippi Freedom Summer of 1964, supported by volunteers from the North who worked on voting rights and Freedom Schools projects. After 1965, progress stalled as the mass approach dissipated against the unresponsiveness of northern cities and SNCC's grass–roots approach exposed it to segregationist violence.

See also: Martin Luther King, Jr.

801.   Adams, Frank, with Myles Horton, *Unearthing Seeds of Fire: The Idea of Highlander.* 255 pp. Winston–Salem NC: John F. Blair, 1975. (Journalist's biography of the Highlander Folk School and its involvement in labor and desegregation movements. Index.)

802. Agbayani, Amefil, "A Field Approach to the Study of Civil Rights Protest Participation of Southern Negro Students." 125 pp. Ph.D. diss., Univ. of Hawaii, 1969. (Relates personality and sociocultural environment factors to protest participation, finding that social supports explain much of the variance. Bibliography.)

803. Anderson, Alan B., and George W. Pickering, *Confronting the Color Line: The Broken Promise of the Civil Rights Movement in Chicago*. 515 pp. Athens and London: Univ. of Georgia Press, 1986. (History of the civil rights movement in Chicago, with analysis of collapse of the national movement. See ch. 4–6 on direct action and school boycotts, ch. 7 on differences between SCLC and CCCO and 1966 actions, ch. 8 on clash between violent and nonviolent strategies, ch. 9–12 on collapse of movement. See also pp. 331–33 on "tent-in" and pp. 419–24, "Nonviolence and Integration: Constructive Possibilities." Photos. Index.)

804. Bailey, Harry A., Jr., ed., *Negro Politics in America*. 455 pp. Columbus OH: Charles E. Merrill, 1967. (Collects important articles, several from early years of the struggle, including James Q. Wilson, "The Strategy of Protest, Problems of Negro Civic Action"; Jack L. Walker, "Protest and Negotiation: A Case Study of Negro Leadership in Atlanta, Georgia"; and Lewis M. Killian and Charles U. Smith, "Negro Protest Leaders in a Southern Community." Illustrations. Index.)

805. Barnes, Catherine A., *Journey from Jim Crow: The Desegregation of Southern Transportation*. 313 pp. New York: Columbia Univ. Press, 1983. (Examines the interplay of legal challenges, protest, and U.S. government involvement in ending segregated transportation. Ch. 3–6 detail the legal approach of the NAACP and ch. 7, 9 discuss the relationship between "nonviolent resistance" and legal strategies in the Montgomery, Alabama bus boycott and the Freedom Rides. Ch. 11 looks at the overall relation among protest, law, and federal action. Index. Bibliography.)

806.   Beardslee, William R., M.D., *The Way Out Must Lead In: Life Histories in the Civil Rights Movement.* 2d. ed. 193 pp. Westport CT: Lawrence Hill, 1983. (Personal accounts of participation in the civil rights movement; includes observations on the nature of protest and personal choice.)

807.   Bell, Inge P., *CORE and the Strategy of Nonviolence.* 214 pp. New York: Random House, 1968. (A study of the Congress of Racial Equality during 1961–63, its last two years as a nonviolent direct action movement. Appendixes. Index.)

808.   Bennett, Lerone, Jr., *Confrontation: Black and White.* 321 pp. Chicago: Johnson Publishing, 1965. (See ch. 3, 5, and epilogue, esp. ch. 3 on A. Philip Randolph and the influence of Gandhi in the 1940s. Index. Bibliography.)

809.   Blasi, Anthony J., *Segregationist Violence and Civil Rights Movements in Tuscaloosa.* 168 pp. Washington DC: University Press of America, 1980. (Sociological account of civil rights and white resistance movements in Tuscaloosa in the late 1950s and early 1960s. See esp. ch. 3, 4 on opposition to desegregation of the Univ. of Alabama and ch. 5 on black activism and boycotts. Illustrations. Bibliography.)

810.   Bloom, Jack M., *Class, Race, and the Civil Rights Movement.* 267 pp. Bloomington and Indianapolis: Indiana Univ. Press, 1987. (Class analysis of historical and social roots of the civil rights movement. Part 2 focuses on the movement itself. See pp. 137–50 on M.L. King, Jr., nonviolent direct action, and the Montgomery bus boycott. Ch. 6 is on "the second wave" of black movement in the early 1960s. Pp. 221–24 are on the effects of the civil rights movement. Index. Bibliography.)

811.   Blumberg, Rhoda Lois, *Civil Rights: The 1960s Freedom Struggle.* 209 pp. Boston: Twayne, 1984. (Study of movement rise, activity, and decline, 1957–70s. Stresses litigation, nonviolent protest and noncooperation, and self–defensive and urban violence as competing choices of action, as well as the interactions between the movement and its opponents. See esp. ch. 3–7. Photos. Chronology. Index. Bibliography.)

812. Bosmajian, Haig A., and Hamida Bosmajian, *The Rhetoric of the Civil Rights Movement.* 142 pp. New York: Random House, 1969. (See introduction for a view of dissent and nonviolent action as rhetorical and persuasive behavior. Contains excerpts from speeches, debates, and M.L. King, Jr.'s "Letter from Birmingham Jail.")

813. Bowen, Harry W., "The Persuasive Efficacy of Negro Non-Violent Resistance." 110 pp. Ph.D. diss., Univ. of Pittsburgh, 1962. (Tests four hypotheses on the conditions under which nonviolent action "converts" opponents and third parties based on the definition of nonviolent action as understood at that time. Appendixes. Bibliography.)

814. Bracey, John H., August Meier, and Elliott Rudwick, eds., *Conflict and Competition: Studies in the Recent Black Protest Movement.* 239 pp. Belmont CA: Wadsworth, 1971. (Part 1 contains several studies of conflict and leadership in nonviolent action. Part 2 reprints Donald von Eschen, Jerome Kirk, and Maurice Pinard, "The Disintegration of the Negro Non-Violent Movement.")

815. Brauer, Carl M., *John F. Kennedy and the Second Reconstruction.* 396 pp. New York: Columbia Univ. Press, 1977. (Study of national policy and law during the conflict over desegregation in the South. See esp. ch. 4, 6 on the issue of federal protection of activists and ch. 6, 9 on Albany, Georgia and Birmingham, Alabama; including pp. 242–45 on a personal confrontation between Robert Kennedy and black spokespersons. Index. Bibliography.)

816. Brooks, Thomas R., *Walls Come Tumbling Down: A History of the Civil Rights Movement, 1940–1970.* 309 pp. Englewood Cliffs NJ: Prentice Hall, 1974. (Traces the civil rights movement from a 1940 meeting between A. Philip Randolph and Franklin Delano Roosevelt on integration of the armed forces through the March on Washington and the murder of Martin Luther King, Jr. See esp. pp. 40–42 for A. Philip Randolph's advocacy of nonviolence as the movement gained momentum, pp. 48–51 on the Gandhian influence on the philosophical orientation of the movement, and p. 103 for

King's personal philosophy on the role of nonviolent struggle. Photos. Index. Bibliography.)

817.   Burns, W. Haywood, *The Voices of Negro Protest in America*. 84 pp. New York and London: Oxford Univ. Press, 1966 [orig. publ. 1963]. (Overview of civil rights movement actions, including the role of boycotts, ch. 3.)

818.   Carson, Clayborne, *In Struggle: SNCC and the Black Awakening of the 1960s*. 359 pp. Cambridge MA and London: Harvard Univ. Press, 1981. (Part 1 follows the Student Nonviolent Coordinating Committee from its sit–in movement origins in 1960 to Mississippi voting rights campaigns in 1964. Ch. 11 describes the 1965 Selma march and subsequent SNCC presence in Lowndes County, Alabama. Photos. Index.)

819.   Carson, Clayborne, David J. Garrow, Vincent Harding, and Darlene Clark Hine, eds., *Eyes on the Prize: America's Civil Rights Years. A Reader and Guide*. 355 pp. New York, Middlesex, Victoria, Ontario, and Auckland: Penguin Books, 1987. (Collection of guidelines and readings for television course on the civil rights movement, based on video series of same title. See ch. 2, 4–7 for readings pertinent to nonviolent action. See index under *nonviolence*. Chronology. Index.)

820.   Chafe, William H., *Civilities and Civil Rights: Greensboro, North Carolina, and the Black Struggle for Freedom*. 436 pp. New York and Oxford: Oxford Univ. Press, 1980. (On civil rights activities from 1940s to 1970s. See esp. the origins of protest activities ca. 1955, pp. 82–87; the pioneer sit–ins of 1960, ch. 3; and subsequent demonstrations and protests, ch. 4–6. Photos. Index.)

821.   Clarke, Jacquelyne Johnson, *These Rights They Seek: A Comparison of the Goals and Techniques of Local Civil Rights Organizations*. 85 pp. Washington DC: Public Affairs Press, 1962. (Comparative study of three early civil rights movement organizations in Alabama, including Martin Luther King, Jr.'s Montgomery Improvement Association. Discusses immediate precursors, pp. 18–23, and the nature and

goals of the organizations, ch. 2, 3. Ch. 4 analyzes data on groups' techniques and the commitment to nonviolent means.)

822.   Fager, Charles, *Uncertain Resurrection: The Poor People's Washington Campaign*. 142 pp. Grand Rapids MI: William B. Eerdmans, 1969. (Participant–reporter's account of 1968 campaign, with emphasis upon tactics and organization. See esp. discussions of strategy on pp. 16–19, efforts to run the encampment smoothly in ch. 2–3, and demonstrations followed by violence as the campaign disintegrates in ch. 5, 6.)

823.   Farmer, James, *Freedom—When?* 197 pp. New York: Random House, 1965. (Personal account of civil rights movement experiences and reflections on them. See pp. 54–82 on origins and growth of CORE.)

824.   ———, *Lay Bare the Heart: An Autobiography of the Civil Rights Movement*. 370 pp. New York: Arbor House, 1985. (In addition to extensive reminiscences on the movement in the 1960s, see ch. 9, 10, 19 on the origins of CORE and its later activities. Index.)

825.   Forman, James, *The Making of Black Revolutionaries*. 2d. ed. 568 pp. Washington DC: Open Hand Publishing, 1985 [orig. publ. 1972]. (Political autobiography. See discussions of tactical versus principled nonviolence and violence, pp. 104–7, 148–50 and ch. 19, 22. Index.)

826.   Garrow, David, ed., *Chicago 1966: Open Housing Marches, Summit Negotiations, and Operation Breadbasket*. (Collected essays and documents on the Chicago Freedom Movement of 1966, which was focused in large part on issues of economic and social equity, and how its failure affected the strategy of the struggle of the 1960s. See Mary Lou Finley, "The Open Housing Marches: Chicago Summer '66," pp. 1–47, esp. pp. 10–12 on the theory behind the use of nonviolent action in these marches. Index.)

827.   ———, ed., *We Shall Overcome: The Civil Rights Movement in the United States in the 1950s and 1960s*. 3 vols. 1201 pp.

Brooklyn NY: Carlson Publishing, 1989. (Collected articles from journals and reviews on aspects of the civil rights movement from ca. 1957 to 1968, many with a focus on nonviolent action, strategy and tactics, and legal aspects of the civil rights challenge. On nonviolent action, see in vol. 1, James W. Ely, "Negro Demonstrations and the Law: Danville as a Test Case," ch. 5 and Carl R. Graves, "The Right to Be Served: Oklahoma City's Lunch Counter Sit–ins, 1958–1964," ch. 10. In vol. 2, see Jan Howard, "The Provocation of Violence: A Civil Rights Tactic?," ch. 17; Doug McAdam, "Tactical Innovation and the Pace of Insurgency," ch. 27; August Meier, "The Successful Sit–Ins in a Border City: A Study in Social Causation," ch. 32; August Meier, Thomas S. Plaut, and Curtis Smothers, "Case Study of Nonviolent Direct Action," ch. 37; and August Meier, "Dilemmas of Negro Protest Strategy," ch. 39. Vol. 3 contains several selections directly concerning boycotts and sit–ins, as well as August Meier and Elliott Rudwick, "The Origins of Nonviolent Direct Action in Afro–American Protest: A Note on Historical Discontinuities," ch. 41. Photos. Documents. Index. Bibliography.)

828.   Geschwender, James A., ed., *The Black Revolt: The Civil Rights Movement, Ghetto Uprisings, and Separation*. 483 pp. Englewood Cliffs NJ: Prentice–Hall, 1971. (Sections 2–5 compile short selections on the civil rights movement. Section 4, on "tactics," contains pieces by Harry A. Bailey, Jr. on the choice of normal politics or nonviolent action, James W. Vander Zanden on nonviolent resistance, Martin Oppenheimer on sit–ins, and William M. Phillips, Jr. on a boycott campaign. Index.)

829.   Goldwin, Robert A., ed., *One Hundred Years of Emancipation*. 217 pp. Chicago: Rand McNally, 1964. (See James Farmer, "The New Jacobins and Full Emancipation," pp. 89–102, on movement strategy.)

830.   Graham, Hugh Davis, *Crisis in Print: Desegregation and the Press in Tennessee*. 338 pp. Nashville TN: Vanderbilt Univ. Press, 1967. (A study in public opinion through the editorial responses of the Tennessee press to desegregation in the

decade between the *Brown* decision and the Civil Rights Act of 1964. Includes discussion of several school desegregation conflicts. Ch. 7, "From the Courts to the Streets," is on direct action starting with the 1960 sit–ins and ch. 8 carries this story to 1964. Illustrations. Photos. Appendix. Index. Bibliography.)

831.   Graves, Carl R., "The Right to Be Served: Oklahoma City's Lunch Counter Sit–Ins, 1958–1964." *The Chronicles of Oklahoma* 59 (1981): 152–66. (Thorough account of civil rights action in Oklahoma City, 1958–64. Photos.)

832.   Guzman, Jessie Parkhurst, *Crusade for Civic Democracy: The Story of the Tuskegee Civic Association, 1941–1970.* 226 pp. New York: Vantage Press, 1989. (Historical study of the methods and issues of this Alabama organization, largely from its files and records. See "activities pertaining to race relations," pp. 110–15 and ch. 7 on the group's economic education program. This included a boycott of white–owned businesses resulting from political maneuvering and a particular insult to black voters—not using Mr. or Mrs. before their names in the published voter list. See appendixes for documents, including two from the boycott.)

833.   Hamburger, Robert, *Our Portion of Hell: Fayette County Tennessee: An Oral History of the Struggle for Civil Rights.* 255 pp. New York: Links Books, 1973. (Series of oral accounts by residents of a predominantly black rural southern community who describe their struggles for self–determination and the right to vote. Points out how localized, grassroots action preceded the rise of the major civil rights organizations, and bemoans lack of substantive change despite legislative gains. Photos.)

834.   Hansberry, Lorraine, *The Movement: Documentary of a Struggle for Equality.* 127 pp. New York: Simon & Schuster, 1964. (Photographic documentary of desegregation movement by renowned playwright and advocate.)

835.   Hawley, Earle, ed., *Civil Rights and Civil Wrongs.* 98 pp. Hollywood CA: Front Page Publications, 1964. (Press photos

of the movement up to 1964, with coverage of counter-
demonstrations.)

836.   Heacock, Roland T., *Understanding the Negro Protest*. 138 pp.
       New York: Pageant Press, 1965. (Advocate's description of
       the nonviolent civil rights campaign. See ch. 2 on motives for
       nonviolent action, with an effort to categorize methods, pp.
       20–32, and ch. 4 on potential causes of violence in movement
       actions. Chronology of demonstrations in appendix A.)

837.   Hentoff, Nat, *The New Equality*. 243 pp. New York: Viking
       Press, 1964. (See ch. 12, "Organizing for Action," for argument
       that direct action is the best method for effecting change.
       Illustrates argument with examples such as rent strikes and
       school boycotts. See esp. pp. 208–10 for analysis of nonviolent
       action as a technique.)

838.   King, Donald B., and Charles W. Quick, eds., *Legal Aspects
       of the Civil Rights Movement*. 446 pp. Detroit: Wayne State
       Univ. Press, 1965. (See Marion A. Wright, "The Sit–In
       Movement: Progress Report and Proposals," pp. 87–99 and
       William L. Taylor, "Some Observations on the Strategies of
       Protest," pp. 227–35 for a lawyer's view of civil disobedience
       and organized protest. Bibliography.)

839.   Kotz, Nick, and Mary Lynn Kotz, *A Passion for Equality:
       George A. Wiley and the Movement*. 372 pp. New York:
       W.W. Norton, 1977. (Political biography of civil rights and
       welfare rights activist. Ch. 10–19 are on the Congress of
       Racial Equality and ch. 25–32 are on the National Welfare
       Rights Organization. Index. Bibliography.)

840.   Laue, James H., *Direct Action and Desegregation, 1960–1962:
       Toward a Theory of the Rationalization of Protest*. Ed.
       David J. Garrow. 412 pp. Brooklyn NY: Carlson Publishing,
       1989. (Reprint of doctoral dissertation, Harvard University,
       1965. Develops a theory of social movement
       "rationalization" proceeding from relatively spontaneous
       beginnings in the sit-ins of 1960 toward the concretization of
       an ongoing "program" with a focus on voter rights. Of
       particular relevance to the study of nonviolent action are pp.

7–10 and ch. 3–6 which discuss campaigns from Montgomery, Alabama through Albany, Georgia. Appendix C reports various interview responses, including attitudes toward nonviolent action and methods of direct action. Appendix F charts the sit–in wave of early 1960. Index. Bibliography.)

841. Lewis, Anthony, and The New York Times, *Portrait of a Decade: The Second American Revolution.* 322 pp. New York: Random House, 1964. (History of the civil rights movement, 1954–64. See esp. ch. 6 on nonviolent action. Photos. Index.)

842. Lomax, Louis E., *The Negro Revolt.* 271 pp. New York: Harper & Row, 1962. Rev. ed., New York: Signet New American Library, 1963; London: Hamish Hamilton, 1963. (See esp. ch. 8 on the Montgomery Bus Boycott of 1955–56 and ch. 10, 11 on sit–ins and freedom rides.)

843. Louis, Debbie, *And We Are Not Saved: A History of the Movement as People.* 462 pp. Garden City NY: Doubleday, 1970. (Social–psychological history of "the movement" from 1959 to 1968, focusing on internal structure, ideology, and classifications of youth "members." Photos. Appendixes. Bibliography.)

844. Loveland, Anne C., *Lillian Smith: A Southerner Confronting the South: A Biography.* 298 pp. Baton Rouge and London: Louisiana State Univ. Press, 1986. (Biography of Southern writer active in protesting segregation. See ch. 11, 12 on the civil rights movement in early 1960s. Photos. Index.)

845. McAdam, Doug, *Political Process and the Development of Black Insurgency, 1930–1970.* 304 pp. Chicago and London: Univ. of Chicago Press, 1982. (A study of the conditions under which mass protest, or "insurgency," was created and maintained in the cause of civil rights and related issues, especially between 1955 and 1970. Ch. 1–3 discuss several approaches to the study of social movements, including the author's favored "political process" model, while ch. 5–8 described the rise, pursuit, and decline of mass protest in its historical and political setting as it relates to this model.

Appendix 2 contains a chronology of sit–ins in early 1960. Index. Bibliography.)

846.   Meier, August, and Elliott Rudwick, *CORE: A Study in the Civil Rights Movements, 1942–1968.* 563 pp. New York: Oxford Univ. Press, 1973. (A study of one of the leading nonviolent action civil rights organizations. Index.)

847.   Mitchell, Glenford E., and William H. Peace III, eds., *The Angry Black South.* 159 pp. New York: Corinth Books, 1962. (Collection of essays on nonviolent action campaigns from 1957 to 1961. Of particular interest is Robert Brookins Gore, "Nonviolence," on the ethical approach to nonviolent action then current in the civil rights movement.)

848.   Morris, Aldon D., *The Origins of the Civil Rights Movement: Black Communities Organizing for Change.* 354 pp. New York: Free Press, 1984. (Detailed study of desegregation organizations and actions, contending that these originated in the 1953 Baton Rouge bus boycott. Devoted mainly to pre–1960 initiatives, with lengthy case study of Birmingham "mass disruption." Consult index under *boycotts, bus boycotts, direct action, nonviolence,* and *sit–ins,* as well as names of places and leaders. See also concepts of "movement centers" in ch. 3, "movement halfway houses" in ch. 7, and relationship between organization and action in ch. 8. Photos. Index. Bibliography.)

849.   Murphy, Raymond J., and Howard Elinson, eds., *Problems and Prospects of the Negro Movement.* 440 pp. Belmont CA: Wadsworth, 1966. (See Arthur Waskow, "'Creative Disorder' in the Racial Struggle," for effort to develop a perspective on nonviolent means with disruptive effects. Bibliography.)

850.   Muse, Benjamin, *The American Negro Revolution: From Nonviolence to Black Power, 1963–1967.* 345 pp. Bloomington: Indiana Univ. Press, 1968. (Account of black struggle from the 1963 March on Washington to urban violence in 1967 and the U.S. government report issued on them. See ch. 1–3 on the uses

of nonviolent action and ch. 8, pp. 111–27, on school boycotts in 1964. Appendixes. Index.)

851.   Nelson, Hart Michael, "Religiosity of Black Americans: Religious Ideology, Institutional Completeness, and Civil Rights Militancy." 225 pp. Ph.D. diss., Vanderbilt Univ., 1972. (Ch. 4, 5 explore the relationship between religious commitments and support for civil rights actions. Bibliography.)

852.   Peake, Thomas R., *Keeping the Dream Alive: A History of the Southern Christian Leadership Conference from King to the Nineteen–Eighties.* 492 pp. New York, Berne, Frankfurt, and Paris: Peter Lang, 1987. (Parts 1, 2 are on the origins of the SCLC and its activities until 1968, while later sections are concerned with the survival and directions of the organization after the death of M.L. King, Jr. Photos. Appendix. Index. Bibliography.)

853.   Powell, Ingeborg B., "Ideology and Strategy of Direct Action: A Study of the Congress of Racial Equality." 367 pp. Ph.D. diss., Univ. of California, Berkeley, 1965. (Dissertation version of entry 807, containing more extensive discussion of nonviolence as ideology or pragmatic commitment and a case study of a local group. Bibliography.)

854.   Raines, Howell, *My Soul Is Rested: Movement Days in the Deep South Remembered.* 488 pp. New York: Penguin Books, 1983. (Recollections of civil rights movement participants, supporters, opponents, and government officials. Covers CORE as a precursor in 1940s and key events from the Montgomery Bus Boycott of 1955–56 through Alabama and Mississippi campaigns, 1963–65. Insider information and views on many aspects of movement. See index under names and places, *boycotts, civil disobedience, Gandhi, imprisonment, marches, nonviolence, police, sit–ins,* and *violence.* Index.)

855.   Rustin, Bayard, *Down the Line: The Collected Writings of Bayard Rustin.* 355 pp. Chicago: Quadrangle Books, 1971. (Articles and occasional pieces originating from 1942 to 1971.

Section 1 includes accounts of CORE–inspired resistance to Jim Crow laws, including diary of a 1947 proto–freedom ride to "test" segregation. Section 2 contains a report on the Montgomery Bus Boycott, 1957. Index.)

856.   ———, *Strategies for Freedom: The Changing Patterns of Black Protest.* 82 pp. New York: Columbia Univ. Press, 1976. (Historical and prescriptive view of failure of the movement for social change by a prominent advocate of nonviolent means in black struggle. See ch. 1, 2, esp. pp. 14–29 on nonviolent struggle before 1950, pp. 43–44 on segregationist violence, and pp. 48–51 on the 1963 March on Washington. Photos. Index.)

857.   Salter, John R., *Jackson, Mississippi: An American Chronicle of Struggle and Schism.* 248 pp. Hicksville NY: Exposition Press, 1979. (Personal history of Jackson, Mississippi, civil rights campaign from 1961, including references throughout to economic boycott of white businesses.)

858.   Sellers, Cleveland, with Robert Terrell, *The River of No Return: The Autobiography of a Black Militant and the Life and Death of SNCC.* 279 pp. New York: William Morrow, 1973. (See ch. 2–11 for experiences, 1960–66. Index.)

859.   Sitkoff, Harvard, *The Struggle for Black Equality, 1954– 1980.* 259 pp. New York: Hill & Wang, 1981. (Focuses extensively on actions chosen by civil rights movement participants, esp. ch. 2 on Montgomery and early sit–ins, ch. 3 on the sit–ins of 1960–61, and ch. 5 on the Birmingham campaign. Index. Bibliography.)

860.   Sobel, Lester A., ed., *Civil Rights, 1960–66.* 504 pp. New York: Facts on File, 1967. (Very detailed year–by–year chronicle of civil rights protests, court actions, and related activities. Index.)

861.   "Stayed on Freedom." *Southern Exposure* 9, 1 (1981). 128 pp. (Entire issue of *Southern Exposure* magazine devoted to the Civil Rights Movement, primarily consisting of short pieces

with interviews of activists in various campaigns. Carolyn Waters, "Freedom Chronology," pp. 125–27.)

862.   Stoper, Emily Schottenfeld, "The Student Nonviolent Co–ordinating Committee: The Growth of Radicalism in a Civil Rights Organization." 223 pp. Ph.D. diss., Harvard Univ., 1968. (Study of the rapid transformation of goals and political means by SNCC. See pp. 1–11, 18–20 on nonviolent action in SNCC's origins. Pp. 27–43, 170–71, 173, 213–14 contain thoughtful comments on segregationist violence, legalistic repression, and their relation to SNCC's rejection of philosophical nonviolence, its continuation of tactical uses of nonviolent action, and its consideration of violence. Pp. 69–72 are on SNCC in the March on Washington. Bibliography.)

863.   Thompson, Daniel C., *The Negro Leadership Class*. 174 pp. Englewood Cliffs NJ: Prentice–Hall, 1963. (See ch. 7, "Citizenship: Strategies and Techniques," and pp. 132–34, 137–39 on protest and "direct action" options. Index.)

864.   Tushnet, Mark V., *The NAACP's Legal Strategy against Segregated Education, 1925–1950*. 222 pp. Chapel Hill and London: Univ. of North Carolina, 1987. (History of the strategy of change through legal challenge in Southern race relations. See ch. 7 on the coming of a "direct attack" on segregation and ch. 8 on the strategy for *Brown* litigation and beyond. Index. Bibliography.)

865.   Van Der Slik, Jack R., ed., *Black Conflict with White America: A Reader in Social and Political Analysis*. 344 pp. Columbus OH: Charles E. Merrill, 1970. (See part 3 for essays on the protest movement, including Donald von Eschen, Jerome Kirk, and Maurice Pinard, "The Conditions of Direct Action in a Democratic Society," esp. pp. 225–31, for comments on relation between disorder and goal–seeking. Index.)

866.   Waskow, Arthur I., *From Race Riot to Sit–In, 1919 and the 1960s: A Study in the Connections between Conflict and Violence*. 380 pp. New York: Doubleday, 1966. (By comparing episodes of interracial violence in 1919 with the civil rights movement, author explores the concept of replacing violence

with other means of struggle. See ch. 16 for idea of "creative disorder"; essentially nonviolent action in political confrontations. Appendixes. Index. Bibliography.)

867.   Watters, Pat, *Down to Now: Reflections on the Southern Civil Rights Movement.* 426 pp. New York: Pantheon Books, 1971. (Memoirs of the civil rights movement by journalist. The early phase is discussed in part 2 and a detailed account of the 1962 Albany, Georgia campaign is in part 3. Index.)

868.   Westin, Alan F., *Freedom Now! The Civil Rights Struggle in America.* 346 pp. New York: Basic Books, 1964. (Collection of essays and excerpts on civil rights struggle. Part 2 is on historical antecedents. Part 4 is on techniques of struggle. See esp. nos. 10, 11, 23, 25, 26, 34, 37–44. Documents. Bibliography.)

869.   Williams, Robert F., *Negroes with Guns.* Ed. Marc Schleifer. 128 pp. Chicago: Third World Press, 1973. (Memoirs of well-known critic of nonviolence and advocate of violent self-defense in black struggle of 1960s. See Martin Luther King, Jr., "The Social Organization of Non–Violence," pp. 11–15; Truman Nelson, "The Resistant Spirit," pp. 17–36; and ch. 4 on Freedom Riders and the move from nonviolent to violent resistance. Photos. Documents.)

870.   Wilson, James Q., "The Strategy of Protest: Problems of Negro Civic Action." *Journal of Conflict Resolution* 5 (1961): 291–303. (Characterizes black protest in northern cities as an effort by the powerless to wield power; examines the distinction between protest strategies and bargaining strategies.)

871.   Wynn, Daniel W., *The Black Protest Movement.* 258 pp. New York: Philosophical Library, 1974. (See ch. 3–5, 7 for overview of black American protest beginning in the 1930s; made more valuable by comments on the nature of nonviolent means in comparison with violent means, esp. pp. 107–14, 125–29, 149–52, 190–99, 204–8.)

872.   Zinn, Howard, *SNCC: The New Abolitionists.* 286 pp. Boston: Beacon Press, 1965. (Attempts to "catch a glimpse of SNCC

people in action and to suggest the quality of their contribution to American civilization." See esp. pp. 220–24 for an outline of the role of nonviolence in the SNCC agenda, and how it changed according to the violence and brutality that the SNCC activists encountered. Index.)

Montgomery Bus Boycott, 1955–1956

In late 1955, Rosa Parks, who was associated with the local NAACP, was arrested by city police for her refusal to relinquish her bus seat in favor of white passengers. Four days later, a large–scale bus boycott was launched in order to protest the arrest and support demands for change. The boycott held strong for over one year and reportedly cost the bus companies substantially in lost fares. In the end, the boycott was settled through a combination of agreement and court action, meanwhile raising Dr. Martin Luther King, Jr., to his first prominence as a leader.

873. Parks, Rosa with Jim Haskins, *Rosa Parks: My Story*. 192 pp. New York: Dial Books, 1992. (Simply told story of the early life, education, and political activities of the author, largely on the Montgomery Bus Boycott. Ch. 5–7 discuss her association with E.D. Nixon, the local NAACP, and segregated busses in the 1940s and early 1950s; including her trip to Highlander Folk School in 1955. Ch. 8 is on her being arrested for refusing to give up her bus seat to white passengers, and ch. 9, 10 are on the bus boycott. Pp. 174–75 discuss why the author supported tactical nonviolent action despite reservations about Dr. King's views on principled nonviolence. Index.)

874. Robinson, Jo Ann Gibson, *The Montgomery Bus Boycott and the Women Who Started It: The Memoir of Jo Ann Gibson Robinson*. Ed. David J. Garrow. 190 pp. Knoxville TN: Univ. of Tennessee Press, 1987. (Memoirs of participant in Montgomery Bus Boycott and president of Women's Political Council. Editor argues that this group provided initial impetus for boycott. See esp. pp. 22–43 on pre–Rosa Parks boycott campaign. Photos. Documents. Index.)

Sit–Ins and Freedom Rides, 1960–1962

On February 1, 1960, students from a local black college defied Jim Crow in Greensboro, North Carolina by taking seats at a whites–only lunch counter. As word of the "sit–in" spread, the frequency and size of these actions increased, and a new form of direct action came into being. Several of these were notably successful, as was the sit–in in Nashville, Tennessee. A few months later, busloads of activists launched the Freedom Rides. Arguing that segregation of public facilities in interstate commerce violated federal law, the racially–mixed groups of freedom riders insisted on the use of the "white" facilities at bus stations by all passengers. In several places, riders were badly beaten by crowds and busses were burned. These developments coincided roughly with the emergence of SNCC, which provided an organizational framework for the articulation of goals and airing of grievances.

875.   Ahmann, Mathew H., ed., *The New Negro*. 145 pp. Notre Dame IN: Fides Publishers, 1961. (See Diane Nash, "Inside the Sit–Ins and Freedom Rides: Testimony of a Southern Student," ch. 4 for a religiously–oriented view of the Nashville sit–ins and May 1961 freedom ride.)

876.   Garrow, David J., ed., *Atlanta, Georgia, 1960–1961: Sit–Ins and Student Activism*.   195 pp. Brooklyn NY: Carlson Publishing, 1989. (Reprints seven studies of aspects of the movement in Atlanta, focusing primarily on sit–ins and sit–in strategy. Appendix contains "An Appeal for Human Rights," pp. 183–88. Index. Bibliography.)

877.   Industrial Union Department, AFL–CIO, *Tent City . . . "Home of the Brave."* 22 pp. Washington DC: Industrial Union Department, AFL–CIO, [1961?]. (Blacklisted and evicted from their homes after registering to vote, black sharecroppers withdrew to a "tent city" in Fayette City, Tennessee, 1960–61. Photos.)

878.   Kahn, Tom, *Unfinished Revolution*. 64 pp. New York: Socialist Party, Social Democratic Federation, 1960. (Study of early 1960s actions, focusing on channelling of "spontaneity" into nonviolent action as a strategy.)

879.   Oppenheimer, Martin, *The Sit–In Movement of 1960*. Ed.
        David J. Garrow. 222 pp. Brooklyn NY: Carlson Publishing,
        1989. (Reprint of Ph.D. dissertation, Univ. of Pennsylvania,
        1963, then entitled "The Genesis of the Southern Negro
        Student Movement (Sit–In Movement): A Study in
        Contemporary Negro Protest." Studies the factors shaping
        conduct and transformation of sit–ins as a social movement,
        with extensive discussion of influence of organizations.
        Includes precursors and development of movement and ten case
        studies of campaigns, pp. 113–76. Index. Bibliography.)

880.   Peck, James, *Freedom Ride*. 160 pp. New York: Simon &
        Schuster, 1962; New York: Grove Press, 1962. (Foreword by
        James Baldwin. Participant's narrative account of Freedom
        Rides, CORE, and the public perception of them. Includes
        "Sit–Ins: The Students Report," below.)

881.   Peck, Jim, ed., *Sit–Ins: The Students Report*. 16 pp. New York:
        Congress of Racial Equality, 1960. (A short collection of
        personal accounts of the student sit–ins, which were then
        underway in five cities.)

882.   Proudfoot, Merrill, *Diary of a Sit–In*. 204 pp. Chapel Hill
        NC: Univ. of North Carolina Press, 1962. Paperback: New
        Haven CT: College and University Press. (Diary of the
        author's activities in the Nashville, Tennessee sit–ins of
        1960. In addition to the events of the sit–ins themselves, see
        pp. 31–32, 77–78, 108–9, 115, 118, 122, 125–37 on the economic
        boycott or "stay away from downtown" campaign, pp. 53–54,
        109–10 on rules of conduct, and "afterword" for an appraisal.)

883.   Walker, Jack L., "Protest and Negotiation: A Study of Negro
        Political Leaders in a Southern City." 208 pp. Ph.D. diss.,
        State Univ. of Iowa, 1963. (Study of black political
        leadership in Atlanta during and after 1960–61 sit–ins. See
        esp. ch. 3, pp. 166–73. Illustrations. Bibliography.)

884.   White, Robert M., "The Tallahassee Sit–Ins and CORE: A
        Nonviolent Revolutionary Submovement." 271 pp. Ph.D.
        diss., Florida State Univ., 1964. (Study of action and
        organizational structure, contending that nonviolent means

were not innovated but transferred from the CORE repertoire of collective action. On this see discussion of beginnings of the nonviolent concept and CORE auspices, pp. 45–50, 63–69, and ch. 3. Account of actions in ch. 4 and study of organization in ch. 5–7. Bibliography.)

885.   Wolff, Miles, *Lunch at the Five and Ten: The Greensboro Sit-Ins.* 191 pp. New York: Stein & Day, 1970. (Narrative of the first major sit–in in 1960, which maintains [as other accounts do not] that they were initiated by a man named Ralph Johns, pp. 19–29, 36, 96–97. Photos. Bibliography.)

Marches and Mass Protest, 1962–1964

As noted above, mass action largely targeted the cities of the South from 1962 to 1964 in a effort to compel local authorities to negotiate and end some forms of discrimination and segregation. Following an unsuccessful challenge in Albany, Georgia, in 1963 (unsuccessful largely because of the police chief's countermeasures), the SCLC accepted an invitation by the local movement in Birmingham, Alabama. It was in Birmingham that Dr. Martin Luther King, Jr., wrote the "Letter from Birmingham Jail" in which he articulated his theory that "creative disorder" brings about the conditions for settling injustice by bringing the underlying crisis of the system to visibility. In Birmingham, as in other cities, violence by segregationists caused injuries and deaths; here, at least, it also encouraged business and political leaders to reach an accommodation with the movement. In August 1963, 200,000 gathered in the March on Washington, hearing, among other addresses Dr. King's "I Have A Dream" speech.

886.   Dorman, Michael, *We Shall Overcome.* 340 pp. New York: Delacorte Press, 1964. (Journalist's account of civil rights actions in the South from September 1962 to August 1963. See esp. ch. 4 for detailed description of Birmingham marches of 1963.)

887.   Ehle, John, *The Free Men.* 340 pp. New York, Evanston, and London: Harper & Row, 1965. (Account of the personalities

and actions involved in desegregation struggles in Chapel Hill, North Carolina in 1963 and 1964. Illustrations. Photos.)

888.   Garrow, David J., ed., *Birmingham, Alabama, 1956–1963: The Black Struggle for Civil Rights.* 299 pp. Brooklyn NY: Carlson Publishing, 1989. (Reprints three studies, two of which focus on the local movement, its origins and development, and local leader Reverend Fred L. Shuttlesworth. Index.)

889.   ———, ed., *St. Augustine, Florida, 1963–1964: Mass Protest and Racial Violence.* 364 pp. Brooklyn NY: Carlson Publishing, 1989. (Four papers on the event in this Florida city, characterized as among the most violent in opposition to the movement, and as a place where Martin Luther King, Jr., and the SCLC withdrew from a stalemated situation. Includes a report by the Florida Legislative Investigation Committee, pp. 117–326. Index.)

890.   Gentile, Thomas, *March on Washington: August 28, 1963.* 301 pp. Washington DC: New Day Publications, 1983. (Detailed step–by–step description of the 1963 March on Washington for Jobs and Freedom. See esp. ch. 1–5, 8, 12. Photos. Bibliography.)

891.   Good, Paul, *The Trouble I've Seen: White Journalist/Black Movement.* 272 pp. Washington DC: Howard Univ. Press, 1975. (Journalist's personal essays on the 1964 civil rights movement. See pp. 75–103 for detailed discussion of white opposition in St. Augustine, Florida.)

892.   Holt, Len, *An Act of Conscience.* 236 pp. Boston: Beacon Press, 1965. (Personal account of civil rights demonstration and court cases in Danville, Virginia, 1963.)

893.   Thelwell, Michael, *Duties, Pleasures and Conflicts: Essays in Struggle.* 258 pp. Amherst MA: Univ. of Massachusetts Press, 1987. (Part 1 contains fiction; part 2 contains essays on politics and the civil rights movement. See esp. "The August 28th March on Washington: The Castrated Giant" for a critical account of the process of reducing the confrontational and

militant stance of the 1963 march to one of "complete political irrelevance.")

Mississippi Freedom Summer, 1964

National civil rights and voting rights legislation, promoted by President Lyndon Johnson after the assassination of John F. Kennedy, provided encouragement for renewed efforts to bring disenfranchised African–Americans into the electorate. Northern white college students were recruited by SNCC to aid the campaign in Mississippi, exposing them as well as their black co–workers to violence. During the Mississippi Freedom Summer of 1964, three SNCC workers were murdered and others injured or threatened. The Mississippi Freedom Democratic Party, which originated in a protest vote held to show the numbers of potential voters, unsuccessfully challenged the regular party organization for seats at the 1964 Democratic Party convention, illustrating the continuing segregation of Mississippi politics. A significant issue in the Freedom Summer was the place of nonviolence in the movement. Researchers will note that memoirs of the experience discuss participants' doubts about the principles of nonviolence presented to them by trainers, while usually not rejecting the methods they were taught.

894.   Belfrage, Sally, *Freedom Summer*. 246 pp. New York: Viking Press, 1965. (An account of a voter registration campaign in Greenwood, Mississippi, written by a participant.)

895.   Cagin, Seth, and Philip Dray, *We Are Not Afraid: The Story of Goodman, Schwerner, and Chaney and the Civil Rights Campaign in Mississippi*. 500 pp. New York: Macmillan, 1988. (Story of the Freedom Summer of 1964 in Mississippi beginning with the assassination of Goodman, Schwerner, and Chaney, tracing the investigation of their murders and the events of the campaign. Index. Bibliography.)

896.   Holt, Len, *The Summer That Didn't End*. 351 pp. New York: William Morrow, 1965. (Journalistic account of the civil rights activities of 1964, including the Mississippi Freedom Summer Project, ch. 2–5; Freedom Schools, ch. 6; the "White Folks" Project, ch. 7; and their political outgrowths, ch. 8.

Lengthy appendixes include documents on projects, organization, legal issues, and supporting organizations.)

897.   Huie, William Bradford, *Three Lives for Mississippi*. 254 pp. New York: WCC Books, 1965. (Journalist's story of violence against blacks and civil rights movement participants, focusing on the deaths of Schwerner, Chaney, and Goodman. Photos.)

898.   King, Mary, *Freedom Song: A Personal History of the 1960s Civil Rights Movement*. 592 pp. NY: William Morrow, 1987. (Memoirs of white civil rights worker active in voter registration efforts. See ch. 7, "Genesis," esp. pp. 277–79, for a history of nonviolence as a philosophy and how it affected the movement's development, and ch. 8, "Nonviolence," for an analysis of nonviolence as official policy and the problems that it engendered. Photos. Appendixes. Index.)

899.   McAdam, Doug, *Freedom Summer*. 333 pp. Oxford and New York: Oxford Univ. Press, 1988. (Study of activists, actions, and effects of the Mississippi Freedom Summer voting rights project of 1964. See ch. 2 on the character of the activists and the paths that led them to Mississippi, ch. 3 on their experiences, pp. 122–23 on the "abandonment of nonviolence," and ch. 5 on the participants' later uses of their experience. Illustrations. Photos. Appendixes. Index. Bibliography.)

900.   McCord, William, *Mississippi: The Long, Hot Summer*. New York: W.W. Norton, 1965. 222 pp. (Ch. 2–4 recount basic story of the Mississippi Freedom Summer of 1964. See also pp. 193–204 for the debate over means of action. Index.)

901.   Rothschild, Mary Aickin, *A Case of Black and White: Northern Volunteers and the Southern Freedom Summers, 1964–1965*. 213 pp. Westport CT and London: Greenwood Press, 1982. (Account of student shift from nonviolent confrontation to nominally legal voter registration and organization of alternative Democratic party. See ch. 1 on problems of confrontation politics when faced with violence; student discussion of nonviolence, pp. 56–57, 81–82, 109–10, 115, 164; and extensive evidence on effects of segregationist violence,

e.g., pp. 58–61, 97, 119–20, 134–36, 161–63, 166–68. Index. Bibliography.)

902. Sugarman, Tracy, *Stranger at the Gates: A Summer in Mississippi*. 240 pp. New York: Hill & Wang, 1966. (Memoirs of the Mississippi Freedom Summer in 1964 and 1965. In addition to scattered discussion of segregationist violence, see pp. 25–29 on a training session on the "philosophy of nonviolence" and pp. 94–95 for a personal experience of the violence versus nonviolence alternative. Pp. 154–65 describe a demonstration; comment by mayor on "the movement" is in pp. 190–94; and an agricultural labor strike is in pp. 198–201. Illustrations.)

903. Sutherland, Elizabeth, ed., *Letters from Mississippi*. 234 pp. New York, London, and Toronto: McGraw–Hill, 1965. (Collection of letters written by 1964 Mississippi Freedom Summer volunteers involved in nominally legal voter registration activities. Spotty but useful information on segregationist violence and threats, pp. 6–8, 14–15, 25–29, 119–25, 131, 142–46, 149–52, 160, 173, 184–85, 188, 225; and volunteers' fears of it, pp. 8–9, 33, 81, 141–42, 160; and on police actions, pp. 36–38, 80, 84–85, 126–35, 145–46, 182–83. Also discussion of organization and workshops, pp. 13, 105–7, 161–62, on nonviolence as a philosophy and ideology, pp. 12, 29–30, 164; and description and discussion of nonviolent action as a technique, pp. 22, 29–30, 88, 108, 116, 140, 148–49, 154–55, 175–87, 191. Illustrations. Documents.)

Selma, Alabama, Voting Rights Campaign, 1965

The SCLC decided in 1965 to hold a march from Selma to Montgomery, Alabama, as a prelude to a major new voting rights campaign. However, dissension arose between organizations as to the demands and how they would be articulated. Frustration and disillusionment increased after the arrest of Dr. King amidst continuing police brutality. A march from the city to the Montgomery highway across a bridge was charged by mounted officers who clubbed and beat protesters. When activists were murdered, President

Johnson proposed new voting rights legislation to compel state action.
The Selma to Montgomery march finally took place on March 25.

904.   Fager, Charles E., *Selma, 1965: The March That Changed the South.* 2d ed. 257 pp. Boston: Beacon Press, 1985 [orig. publ. 1974]. (Day–by–day narrative of voting rights campaign and Selma–Montgomery march. Includes "Postscript: Selma 1985." Photos. Index. Bibliography.)

905.   Garrow, David J., *Protest at Selma: Martin Luther King, Jr., and the Voting Rights Act of 1965.* 346 pp. New Haven and London: Yale Univ. Press, 1978. (Chronicle of major confrontation at Selma, Alabama, and how it influenced the Voting Rights Act of 1965. Emphasis on media and governmental response. See esp. ch. 7, "The Strategy of Protest and the SCLC at Selma." Illustrations. Photos. Index.)

Massive Resistance

Segregationist opposition to changes in the status of African–
Americans began with the Brown decision and the next year's
Supreme Court command to desegregate public schools with "all
deliberate speed." Some of the methods used in "massive resistance"
to desegregation and the advance of African–American rights include
"avoidance, evasion, and delay," dubious legal doctrines such as state
interposition, mass demonstrations at desegregated schools, boycotts
and closing of public schools, economic boycotts and blacklisting of
African–American activists, and various forms of violence. Many of
these actions were organized by the Citizens' Councils, others by
clandestine groups.

906.   Bartley, Numan V., *The Rise of Massive Resistance: Race and Politics in the South During the 1950s.* 390 pp. Baton Rouge: Louisiana State Univ., 1969. (Study of 1950s massive resistance to public school desegregation, primarily in the South and using largely legal or quasi–legal means. But see ch. 6, 8, 10–15 on other methods, including demonstrations and violence. Illustrations. Photos. Index.)

907.   Blaustein, Albert P., and Clarence Clyde Ferguson, Jr.,
        Desegregation and the Law. 333 pp. New Brunswick NJ:
        Rutgers Univ. Press, 1957. Rev. ed., 359 pp. New York:
        Vintage Books, 1962. (Analysis of massive resistance
        movement in the context of First Amendment rights, court
        precedents, and U.S. jurisprudence. See esp. ch. 15,
        "Avoidance, Evasion, and Delay," for a discussion of legal
        tactics and strategies. Bibliography.)

908.   Carter, Hodding, III, *The South Strikes Back.* 213 pp.
        Westport CT: Negro Universities Press, 1959. (A study of
        white and segregationist resistance to *Brown v. Board of
        Education*, focusing largely on the Citizens' Councils and
        their politics.)

909.   Martin, John Bartlow, *The Deep South Says "Never."* 181 pp.
        New York: Ballantine Books, 1957. (Journalist's account of the
        Citizens' Council movement against integration. Includes
        descriptions of economic retaliation against pro–integration
        blacks, e.g., pp. 29–30, 36, 65–68; and a school boycott by
        whites, pp. 89–93.)

910.   McMillen, Neil R., *The Citizens' Council: Organized
        Resistance to the Second Reconstruction, 1954–64.* 397 pp.
        Urbana, Chicago, and London: Univ. of Illinois, 1971.
        (Although focusing on the organization and ideology of the
        councils, contains some references to their efforts at coercing
        their opponents by violent, threatening, and nonviolent
        means. See esp. pp. 209–15 on use of consumer boycotts.
        Illustrations. Photos. Index. Bibliography.)

911.   Wakefield, Dan, *Revolt in the South.* 128 pp. New York:
        Grove Press; London: Evergreen Books, 1960. (Includes
        journalist's story of White Citizens' Councils and organized
        opposition to desegregation, ch. 1, 2.)

912.   Wilhoit, Francis M., *The Politics of Massive Resistance.* 318
        pp. New York: George Braziller, 1973. (Thorough study of the
        massive resistance movement to oppose and prevent
        desegregation, 1954–64. Ch. 1, 2 discuss the movement's

origins, ch. 6 describes its use of symbolism, and ch. 7, 8 follow its methods in confrontation with federal authority. Index.)

Martin Luther King, Jr., 1929–1968

The son of a minister, Martin Luther King, Jr., trained for the ministry at Morehouse College, Crozer Theological Seminary, and Boston University, where he earned a doctorate. During his training, King read the influential theologians of his time and works by Gandhi and others on nonviolence. King's first settled ministry was in Montgomery, Alabama, where he had been living for eighteen months when the Bus Boycott of 1955–56 began. He was encouraged to lead this movement, which began his career as an activist. After Montgomery, he and other ministers founded the Southern Christian Leadership Council to coordinate direct action, training, and outreach. The SCLC was the primary vehicle through which King's activities described in the historical sections above were carried out. In the course of these actions, his house was bombed, he was arrested several times, and, in April 1968, he was assassinated while in Memphis, Tennessee to support action by African–American workers.

913.   Fisher, William H., *Free At Last: A Bibliography of Martin Luther King, Jr.* 169 pp. Metuchen NJ and London: Scarecrow Press, 1977. (Divided into sections on works by Dr. King, works on him, works in which he figures, and reviews of his books. The first section includes manuscript source and the first three sections include sources from congressional records. Index.)

914.   Pyatt, Sherman E., Comp., *Martin Luther King, Jr.: An Annotated Bibliography.* 166 pp. New York, Westport CT, and London: Greenwood Press, 1986. (See section 4 on "Marches and Demonstrations." Title index.)

Biography

915.   Bennett, Lerone, Jr., *What Manner of Man: Martin Luther King, Jr.* 4th rev. ed. 263 pp. Chicago: Johnson, 1976. Originally published 1964; 2d ed. rev. and enl., 1965; 3d rev.

ed., 1968. (Emphasizes the moral element of King's philosophy and strategy. See index under *Gandhi* and *nonviolence*. Photos. Index.)

916.   Bishop, Jim, *The Days of Martin Luther King, Jr.* 528 pp. New York: G.P. Putnam's Sons, 1971. (Journalist's full–dress biography containing a basic account of King's participation in the movement. Index. Bibliography.)

917.   Branch, Taylor, *Parting the Waters: America in the King Years, 1954–63.* 1062 pp. New York: Simon & Schuster, 1988. (Extremely detailed biography of M.L. King, Jr., and his times, from his family background and call to the ministry until the 1963 March on Washington. Ch. 5 is on the Montgomery Bus Boycott; sit–ins are discussed in ch. 7, 8; Freedom Rides in ch. 11, 12; the Albany, Georgia, campaign in ch. 14; the Birmingham campaign in ch. 18–21; and the March on Washington in ch. 22. Photos. Index.)

918.   Davis, Lenwood G., *I Have a Dream . . . The Life and Times of Martin Luther King, Jr.* 303 pp. Self–published, 1969. (Biography of King as "idealist–realist." See chapters on Montgomery, ch. 6–7; 1957 Prayer Pilgrimage to Washington, ch. 8; Albany, ch. 13; Birmingham, ch. 14; 1963 March on Washington, ch. 15; St. Augustine, ch. 16; Selma, ch. 21–22; and King's anti–Vietnam War activity, ch. 25. Appendixes include "I Have a Dream" text of speech, appendix 5. Index. Bibliography.)

919.   Fairclough, Adam, *To Redeem the Soul of America: The Southern Christian Leadership Conference and Martin Luther King, Jr.* 504 pp. Athens and London: Univ. of Georgia Press, 1987. (History of the SCLC from its founding until the 1970s with chapters on its most significant campaigns, including Montgomery, Albany, Birmingham, Selma, and Chicago. Photos. Index.)

920.   Franklin, John Hope, and August Meier, *Black Leaders of the Twentieth Century.* 383 pp. Urbana IL, Chicago, and London: Univ. of Illinois Press, 1982. (See David L. Lewis, "Martin

Luther King, Jr., and the Promise of Nonviolent Populism," ch. 13. Photos. Index.)

921.   Garrow, David, *Bearing the Cross: Martin Luther King, Jr., and the Southern Christian Leadership Conference.* 800 pp. New York: William Morrow, 1986. (Compendious and detailed biography of Dr. King from 1955 until his death. Chapter–by–chapter accounts of the many campaigns of the SCLC in those years and King's relations with figures active in it. Photos. Index. Bibliography.)

922.   ———, *The FBI and Martin Luther King, Jr.: From "Solo" to Memphis.* 320 pp. New York and London: W.W. Norton, 1981. (Focusing more on the nature of the FBI than King, this study maintains that official conservatism in the face of "radical challenge" explains the FBI's treatment of King. Index.)

923.   King, Coretta S., *My Life with Martin Luther King, Jr.* 372 pp. New York: Holt, Rinehart & Winston, 1969. (Mrs. King's personal reminiscences of her husband and the civil rights movement. Photos.)

924.   Lewis, David L., *King: A Critical Biography.* 460 pp. New York and Washington: Praeger, 1970. (Somewhat critical of King's philosophy and methods. Ch. 3 is on the Montgomery Bus Boycott. See esp. ch. 4, "Satyagraha, Home–Grown," for discussion of the evolution of King's technique of nonviolent action and ch. 5 on tension within the civil rights movement. Ch. 6 is on the Albany campaign, ch. 7 on Birmingham, ch. 9 on Selma, and ch. 11 on Chicago housing campaign. Photos. Index. Bibliography.)

925.   Lokos, Lionel, *House Divided: The Life and Legacy of Martin Luther King.* 567 pp. New Rochelle NY: Arlington House, 1968. (Major thesis is that violence accompanied and was caused by nonviolent campaigns and that the legacy of King is one of lawlessness, with appendix demonstrating the Highlander Folk School to be a communist front. Index.)

926.   Miller, William Robert, *Martin Luther King, Jr.: His Life, Martyrdom, and Meaning for the World.* 319 pp. New York:

Weybright & Talley, 1968. (See esp. ch. 4, "The Seedtime of Nonviolence," esp. pp. 82–85, for King's trip to India and his views on nonviolent action. Ch. 3 is on the Montgomery Bus Boycott, ch. 5 on sit–ins and freedom rides of the early 1960s, ch. 6 on the Albany campaign, ch. 7 on the Birmingham campaign, ch. 8 on the March on Washington, and ch. 9–11 are on campaigns of 1964–65. Illustrations. Photos. Index. Bibliography.)

927.   Oates, Stephen B., *Let the Trumpet Sound: The Life of Martin Luther King, Jr.* 563 pp. New York: Harper & Row, 1982. (Comprehensive biography. See index under *nonviolence, Gandhi, Thoreau, sit–ins, Freedom Rides,* and specific campaigns. Photos. Index.)

928.   Osborne, Charles, ed., *I Have a Dream: The Story of Martin Luther King in Text and Pictures.* 96 pp. New York: Time–Life Books, 1968. (Photoessay with text on King and the civil rights movement. Many photos of actions, including attacks on protesters and police actions. See pp. 6–16 on the Montgomery Bus Boycott, pp. 21–30 on the early 1960s, and pp. 37–67 on the period from Birmingham to Selma.)

929.   Schulke, Flip, ed., *Martin Luther King, Jr.: A Documentary ... Montgomery to Memphis.* 224 pp. New York: W.W. Norton, 1976. (Consult primarily for photos; esp. in ch. 1, 2 on Montgomery Bus Boycott, Freedom Rides, and the sit–in movement; ch. 4 on Birmingham; ch. 9 on voting rights campaign; and ch. 12 on Chicago/Cicero open housing marches. Also includes text of "Letter from Birmingham Jail" and speeches, pp. 214–224. Chronology.)

930.   Westin, Alan F., and Barry Mahoney, *The Trial of Martin Luther King.* 431 pp. New York: Thomas Y. Crowell, 1974. (King's "Letter from Birmingham Jail" was made possible by his refusal to honor an anti–protest injunction and his subsequent arrest. The core of this book, ch. 4–6, is on these events. See also ch. 7–14 on the fate of the case before the Supreme Court and pp. 289–99 on protest, disobedience, and the law. In addition, this work is a study of the uses of legal

and legally tolerated suppression of social movements. Illustrations. Photos. Index. Bibliography.)

931.   Williams, John A., *The King God Didn't Save: Reflections on the Life and Death of Martin Luther King, Jr.* 221 pp. New York: Coward–McCann, 1970. (Black journalist's reflections on King's life and civil rights struggle against the white power structure. Emphasis on the historical role of institutions such as media and religion in determining the success of King's campaigns.)

Interpretation

932.   Ansbro, John J., *Martin Luther King, Jr.: The Making of a Mind.* 366 pp. Maryknoll NY: Orbis Books, 1982. (Account of King's theology, political thought, and their sources. Of importance are ch. 4 on resistance to evil and ch. 6 on King's positions vis–á–vis black thinkers whose ideas conflicted with his own, such as Marcus Garvey and black power theorists, and ch. 7 on King's rejection of violence. Index.);

933.   Garrow, David J., ed., *Martin Luther King, Jr.: Civil Rights Leader, Theologian, Orator.* 3 vols. 1034 pp. Brooklyn NY: Carlson Publishing, 1989. (Collected essays and articles on Martin Luther King, Jr., arranged alphabetically by author. In vol. 1, see Haig Bosmajian, "Rhetoric of Martin Luther King's *Letter from Birmingham Jail,*" pp. 127–44 and James A. Colaiaco, "Martin Luther King, Jr. and the Paradox of Nonviolent Direct Action," pp. 189–202. In vol. 2, see Adam Fairclough, "Martin Luther King, Jr. and the Quest for Nonviolent Social Change," pp. 333–49; Richard Fulkerson, "The Public Letter as a Rhetorical Form: Structure and Style in King's *Letter from Birmingham Jail,*" pp. 379–95; and Mia Klein, "The *Other* Beauty of Martin Luther King, Jr.'s *Letter from Birmingham Jail,*" pp. 569–76. In vol. 3, see Wesley T. Mott, "The Rhetoric of Martin Luther King, Jr.'s *Letter from Birmingham Jail,*" pp. 679–96; Adam Roberts, "Martin Luther King and Nonviolent Resistance," pp. 754–70; Mulford Sibley, "Negro Revolution and Nonviolent Action: Martin Luther King," pp. 796–818; Melinda Snow, "Martin Luther King's

Letter from Birmingham Jail as Pauline Epistle," pp. 857–75; Douglas Strum, "Crisis in the American Republic: The Legal and Political Significance of Martin Luther King's *Letter from Birmingham Jail*," pp. 931–48; and Otis Turner, "Nonviolence and the Politics of Liberation," pp. 997–1008. Index.)

934.　　Hanigan, James P., *Martin Luther King, Jr. and the Foundations of Nonviolence*. 331 pp. Lanham NY and London: University Press of America, 1984. (Critical intellectual biography of King as religious thinker, deriving concepts on nonviolent action in part from this thought. See esp. discussion of the ambiguity of the terms *nonviolent* and *violent* in introduction, and nature of King's principles, ch. 1, 4–9; esp. ch. 6, "The Matter of Means." Index.)

935.　　Lincoln, C. Eric, ed., *Martin Luther King, Jr.: A Profile*. 232 pp. New York: Hill & Wang, 1970. (In addition to essays by Lerone Bennett, Jr., pp. 7–39, and William Robert Miller, pp. 40–71, on the Montgomery Bus Boycott, see critique of the "Letter from Birmingham Jail" by Haig Bosmajian, pp. 128–43; August Meier on "the conservative militant," pp. 144–56; and Louis Lomax on the confrontation of "nonviolence" and "black power," pp. 157–80. Bibliography.)

936.　　Smith, Kenneth L., and Ira G. Zepp, Jr., *Search for the Beloved Community: The Thinking of Martin Luther King, Jr.* 159 pp. Valley Forge PA: Judson Press, 1974. (A study of the intellectual sources of King's thought. Selected bibliography.)

937.　　Walton, Hanes, Jr., *The Political Philosophy of Martin Luther King, Jr.* 137 pp. Westport CT: Greenwood, 1971. (Analysis of King's political philosophy and his role as leader of the "Black Revolution." See pp. 23–28 on application of Gandhian methods to civil rights in the 1940s, pp. 62–69 for King's views on nonviolent civil disobedience, and ch. 4, "The Way of Nonviolence: A Critical View." Author criticizes King's belief in objectless love as unrealistic. See also index under *nonviolence*. Index. Bibliography.)

938. Wasserman, Lois Diane, "Martin Luther King, Jr.: The Molding of Nonviolence as a Philosophy and Strategy, 1955–1963." 147 pp. Ph.D. diss., Boston University, 1972. (Traces foundations of King's philosophy of nonviolence, with emphasis on the influence of Reinhold Niebuhr. Bibliography.)

939. Watley, William D., *Roots of Resistance: The Nonviolent Ethic of Martin Luther King, Jr.* 159 pp. Valley Forge PA: Judson Press, 1985. (On the development and application of King's "nonviolent ethic." Author suggests that nonviolence was both a tactic and a way of life for King. See pp. 55–61 on early Gandhian influence and ch. 5 for "six principles" of Martin Luther King's ethics. Index. Bibliography.)

Works

940. King, Martin Luther, Jr., *Strength to Love.* 159 pp. Philadelphia: Fortress Press, 1981. (Collection of sermons. See ch. 15, "Pilgrimage to Nonviolence," by Coretta Scott King on Martin Luther King and the theory of nonviolent action, pp. 4–5; nonviolence as a "third way," pp. 15–16.)

941. ———, *Stride Toward Freedom.* 230 pp. New York: Harper & Row, 1968. (Primarily about the Montgomery Bus Boycott and the moral basis of nonviolence.)

942. ———, *The Trumpet of Conscience.* 90 pp. New York, Evanston, and London: Harper & Row, 1968. (Canadian Broadcasting Corporation Massey Lectures for 1967. See esp. ch. 4, "Nonviolence and Social Change.")

943. ———, *Where Do We Go from Here: Chaos or Community?* 209 pp. New York and London: Harper & Row, 1967. (Essays on the goals and scope of the civil rights movement following passage of the 1965 Voting Rights Act. Ch. 2 contains King's account of James Meredith's 1966 march and his critique of "black power." Ch. 3 is on white backlash. Ch. 5 outlines future strategies. Appendix. Index.)

944.   ———, *Why We Can't Wait*. 178 pp. New York: Harper &
        Row, 1964. New York: Signet New American Library, 1964.
        (Primarily an account of 1963 Birmingham civil rights
        campaign, with background on the history of discrimination
        against blacks and the state of the civil rights movement.
        Ch. 5 contains "Letter From Birmingham Jail." See index
        under *nonviolence*. Photos. Index.)

945.   Washington, James M., ed., *A Testament of Hope: The
        Essential Writings of Martin Luther King, Jr.* 676 pp. San
        Francisco: Harper & Row, 1986. (Anthology of articles,
        speeches, extracts from books, articles from religious and
        popular magazines, and other writings. Selections in part 1
        address King's concepts of nonviolence and nonviolent action,
        including pieces from 1957–1968. "Letter from Birmingham
        Jail" is in ch. 46. Index. Bibliography.)

Other Movements and Conflicts Since 1960

*The possibility of influencing the direction of societies, governments,
and economies through some combination of direct action methods,
media presence, and pressure politics became thoroughly established
by the end of the 1960s.*

*See also: South Africa: International Relations; Arab League Boycott
of Israel; Chile: Opposition to Allende Government, 1972–1973;
Methods of Nonviolent Action: Sanctuary; Methods of Nonviolent
Action: International Economic Sanctions.*

946.   Miller, Albert Jay, *Confrontation, Conflict, and Dissent: A
        Bibliography of a Decade of Controversy, 1960–1970*. 567 pp.
        Metuchen NJ: Scarecrow Press, 1972. (Partially annotated
        bibliography on social and political conflicts, primarily in
        the U.S. from 1960 to 1970. Sections on confrontation in
        general, student dissent, draft resistance, and "civil
        disobedience, violence, and non–violence." Index.)

947.   Parish, David W., *Changes in American Society, 1960–1978:
        An Annotated Bibliography of Official Government
        Publications*. 438 pp. Metuchen NJ: Scarecrow Press, 1980.

(Selected bibliography exclusively of U.S. government documents, with introduction and finding aids in appendixes. Entries on nonviolent and violent aspects of social change related to race and protest on campus and against the war in Vietnam. See listings under *campus unrest, civil rights, conflicts, peace movement, Students for a Democratic Society, subversion,* and *violence.* Index.)

STUDIES

948.   Alonso, Harriet Hyman, *Peace as a Women's Issue: A History of the U.S. Movement for World Peace and Women's Rights.* Syracuse NY: Syracuse University Press, 1993. (Study of the articulation of feminism, pacifism, and peace action. Ch. 2 traces this connection historically from 1820 into the abolition and suffrage movements. Ch. 3–5 are on the world wars and interwar period, and ch. 6 is on the effects of post-war militant anti–communism. Ch. 7, 8 are on the 1960s–80s and the expansion of peace militancy. Accounts of personalities and protests throughout. Photos. Index. Bibliography.)

949.   Binstock, Robert H., and Katherine Ely, eds., *The Politics of the Powerless.* 340 pp. Cambridge MA: Winthrop Publishers, 1971. (Selections on the "struggles of powerless groups" in American society. See pp. 1–3 on powerlessness, section 5, "Power to the People: Direct Action by the Powerless," and section 6, "Prospects for the Powerless: Philosophies and Strategies.")

950.   Chafetz, Janet Saltzman, and Anthony Gary Dworkin, with the assistance of Stephanie Swanson, *Female Revolt: Women's Movements in World and Historical Perspective.* 270 pp. Totowa NJ: Rowman & Allanheld, 1986. (Study of the emergence of women's movements in the U.S., Europe, and Asia. See ch. 4 for early movements, ch. 5 for movements since the 1960s. Illustrations. Index. Bibliography.)

951.   Epstein, Barbara, *Political Protest and Cultural Revolution: Nonviolent Direct Action in the 1970s and 1980s.* 327 pp.

Berkeley, Los Angeles, and Oxford: Univ. of California Press, 1991. (Historical and thematic history of actors, groups, and campaigns in the "nonviolent direct action movement," identified with those espousing a form of radical politics involving not only nonviolent action as such but commitment to personal, utopian, and decentralized politics. On campaigns and actions, see esp. ch. 2, 3 on the Clamshell and Abalone Alliances, ch. 4 on the Livermore Action Group, and ch. 6 on the politics of moral witness. Ideology, objectives, and the radical context are discussed throughout. Index. Bibliography.)

952.   Ferree, Myra Marx, and Beth B. Hess, *Controversy and Coalition: The New Feminist Movement.* 227 pp. Boston: Twayne Publishers, 1985. (Sociology of current feminism since its 1960s "reemergence." See ch. 4–6, esp. pp. 61–62, 77–78, 94–98, 116, for discussion of alternatives for action, and pp. 78–90, 132–37 for relationships to potentially supportive non-feminist and to anti–feminist groups. Illustrations. Photos. Index. Bibliography.)

953.   Glessing, Robert J., *The Underground Press in America.* 207 pp. Bloomington: Indiana Univ. Press, 1970. Reprint, Westport CT: Greenwood Press, 1984. (Survey of 30 of the more prominent underground publications in the U.S. in the late 1960s. See pp. 3–7 for a definition of "underground"; ch. 2 for a history of the movement, ch. 5 on radical politics, esp. p. 63 for draft resistance organizations; and ch. 6 on underground news services. Includes directory of underground newspapers, pp. 178–90. Illustrations. Index.)

954.   Hershey, Cary, *Protest in the Public Service.* 92 pp. Lexington MA, Toronto, and London: Lexington Books, D.C. Heath, 1973. (Study focusing on protest behavior of "educated labor" in federal agencies in late 1960s. See ch. 2 detailing various actions in which federal personnel were involved. Ch. 3 is on agencies' reaction to employees' participation and pp. 48–50 are on "styles of federal protest." Index. Bibliography.)

955.   Hole, Judith, and Ellen Levine, *Rebirth of Feminism.* 501 pp. New York: Quadrangle Books, 1971. (Accounts of the early

years of contemporary feminism. See discussions of symbolic protest actions in ch. 2 and section 3. Photos. Index. Bibliography.)

956. Leamer, Laurence, *The Paper Revolutionaries: The Rise of the Underground Press*. 220 pp. New York: Simon & Schuster, 1972. (Story of the U.S. "underground" press of 1960s, its precursors and politics. Illustrations. Photos. Index. Bibliography.)

957. Lewis, Roger, *Outlaws of America: The Underground Press and Its Context*. 204 pp. Middlesex, England; Baltimore; Victoria, Australia: Penguin Books, 1972. (Papers on the underground press movement. See ch. 1, 2 for history and description, and ch. 3–5, 13 for focal concerns. Illustrations. Photos. Index. List of underground publications, pp. 179–91.)

958. Love, Janice, *The U.S. Anti–Apartheid Movement: Local Activism in Global Politics*. 296 pp. New York: Praeger, 1985. (Political science study of campaigns to encourage sanctions or divestment. See ch. 1, 2 on methods of groups and sanctions debate. Index. Bibliography.)

959. Nelkin, Dorothy, *Jetport: The Boston Airport Controversy*. New Brunswick NJ: Transaction Books, 1974. (Study of the tension between technological innovation and private interests or environmental concerns, including the quality of the urban residential environment, with a case study of the controversy in the late 1960s and early 1970s over airport expansion in Boston. Includes a discussion of the role of the quasi–public operating authority, local residents' protests, and state efforts at mediation. Index.)

960. Teal, Donn, *The Gay Militants*. 355 pp. New York: Stein & Day, 1971. (Documentation of gay–rights movement in 1969–70, including actions throughout. Documents.)

961. Viorst, Milton, *Fire in the Streets: America in the 1960s*. 591 pp. New York: Simon & Schuster, 1979. (Account of "the phenomenon of social disorder" in the 1960s, with a focus on the civil rights and student movements based on personality

sketches. See ch. 3–7 on civil rights, ch. 9–10 on related post–1964 activity, and ch. 11–12 on anti–Vietnam War movement in 1968. Index. Bibliography.)

962.   West, Guida, *The National Welfare Rights Movement: The Social Protest of Poor Women.* 451 pp. New York: Praeger, 1981. (Participant's history of National Welfare Rights Movement, ca. 1966–75, with emphasis on strategy. See pp. 18–28 on early direct action, pp. 292–303 on "street strategy," and appendix 1 for discussion of social movements. See also index under *strategy.* Index. Bibliography.)

STUDENT MOVEMENTS

Student activist groups predate the 1960s, but it was not until 1963 and 1964 that students coalesced into a political force. The participation of students in Civil Rights Movement activities, such as Mississippi Freedom Summer, focused some on issues of freedom of speech, discrimination, and the like both in the society at large and within the university. The movement against the war in Vietnam engaged students directly as activists and potential participants in the war itself. It provided both a place for alternative politics and the site of struggle among various political tendencies among students.

See also: Movement Against the Vietnam War, 1963–1971, Civil Rights Movement.

963.   Altbach, Philip G., with Robert Graham, *Student Politics and Higher Education in the United States: A Select Bibliography.* 86 pp. St. Louis MO: United Ministries on Higher Education, and Cambridge MA: Center for International Affairs, Harvard Univ., 1968. (Introductory essay by Seymour Martin Lipset. See esp. pp. 12, 28, 30–31, 62–80.)

964.   Aptheker, Bettina, *Higher Education and the Student Rebellion in the United States 1960–1969: A Bibliography.* 50 pp. New York: American Institute For Marxist Studies, 1969.

(References to literature on student protest and politics in the 1960s.)

Studies

965. Altbach, Philip G., and Robert S. Laufer, eds., *Students Protest*. 277 pp. *The Annals of the American Academy of Political and Social Science*, vol. 395 (May 1971). (See esp. Kenneth Keniston and Michael J. Lerner, "Campus Characteristics and Campus Unrest," pp. 39–53 on the rate of violence in protests and "protest–prone students"; Arthur Liebman, "Student Activism in Mexico," pp. 159–70 on the role of force in exacerbating, then crushing, protest; and William John Hanna, "Student Protest in Independent Black Africa," pp. 171–83 which develops a communications model of campus protest, see esp. pp. 176–77 on methods of nonviolent and violent protest. Index.)

966. Astin, Alexander W., Helen S. Astin, Alan E. Bayer, and Ann S. Bisconte, *The Power of Protest: A National Study of Student and Faculty Disruptions with Implications for the Future*. 208 pp. San Francisco, Washington DC, and London: Jossey–Bass, 1975. (Results of a quantitative study of student on–campus protest, ca. 1962–71. Pp. 35–45 identify the incidence, severity, issues, and loci of protest. Ch. 3 models sequences of action, including the role of off–campus police in causing violence. Ch. 4 presents case studies of protests at Beloit College over racial conflict issues, American Univ. student power issues, and anti–war protest at Stanford Univ. Ch. 6 analyzes outcomes. Index. Bibliography.)

967. Avorn, Jerry L., *Up Against the Ivy Wall: A History of the Columbia Crisis*. 307 pp. Ed. Robert Friedman. New York: Atheneum, 1969. (The *Columbia Daily Spectator* history of the Columbia protest and building occupations, April–May 1968. Includes appendixes with reflections by Herbert Deane, "Reflections on Student Radicalism," and Columbia SDS chairperson Mark Rudd, "Symbols of the Revolution." Photos. Chronology. Index.)

968.   Bell, Daniel, and Irving Kristol, eds., *Confrontation: The Student Rebellion and the Universities.* 191 pp. New York and London: Basic Books, 1969. (Reprints essays containing reportage and analysis. See ch. 1 on Berkeley, ch. 2 on San Francisco State, ch. 5, 6 on Columbia, and ch. 7 on Cornell. Index.)

969.   Cohen, Mitchell, and Dennis Hale, eds., *The New Student Left: An Anthology.* 288 pp. Boston: Beacon Press, 1966. (Essays by students active in various movements, edited by editors of student political journal, *The Activist.* See section 2 on student participation in nonviolent action of the civil rights movement and section 3 on Berkeley protest and other agitation of early 1960s.)

970.   Copeland, Alan, and Nikki Arai, eds., *People's Park.* 125 pp. New York: Ballantine Books, 1969. (Photos and chronology, pp. 112–18, of campaign to create a free park out of unused land in Berkeley, California and ensuing conflict. Photos.)

971.   The Cox Commission, *Crisis at Columbia: Report of the Fact–Finding Commission Appointed to Investigate the Disturbances at Columbia University in April and May 1968.* 222 pp. New York: Random House, 1968. (Report of faculty-appointed commission to study Columbia Univ. student actions of April–May 1968. Documents.)

972.   Draper, Hal, *Berkeley: The New Student Revolt.* 246 pp. New York: Grove Press, 1965. (Insider's chronology of the 1964–65 student campaign, from its origin in the banning of certain political activities and continuing through the Free Speech Movement. Second section contains statements and documents. See pp. 39–58 for police car blockade and pp. 107–37 on student strike and aftermath. Documents.)

973.   Erlich, John, and Susan Erlich, eds., *Student Power, Participation, and Revolution.* 254 pp. New York: Association Press, 1970. (Statements and analyses from student writer-activists. Introduction includes excerpts from Port Huron Statement, 1962, pp. 13–18. See selection no. 4 on protest at Univ. of Michigan, October 1965; no. 5 on means of student

power; no. 13 on 1968 Tuskegee Institute protest; no. 14 on San Francisco State College protest, 1966–1968; no. 15 on Columbia Univ. protest; no. 19 on Mission High School strike, 1969; and no. 31 on guerrilla theater in Wisconsin. Documents.)

974.   Exum, William H., *Paradoxes of Protest: Black Student Activism in a White University.* 282 pp. Philadelphia: Temple Univ. Press, 1985. (See pp. 62–88 for detailed description of student–university confrontation and ch. 6–8 for analysis in terms of social movement theory. Index. Bibliography.)

975.   Feuer, Lewis S., *The Conflict of Generations: The Character and Significance of Student Movements.* 543 pp. New York and London: Basic Books, 1969. (History and critique of student movements. Protests, strikes, and demonstrations mentioned throughout. Ch. 1 is an introduction to the author's theory of student movements. See ch. 9 on the Berkeley movement, 1964–66 and pp. 137–40 on a general strike in Russia, 1899. Index.)

976.   Fish, Kenneth L., *Conflict and Dissent in the High School.* 187 pp. New York: Bruce Publishing; London: Collier-Macmillan, 1970. (Examination of high school dissent in 1969. Ch. 2 reports four case studies. Later chapters suggest responses to student protest by teachers and administrators.)

977.   Flacks, Richard, *Youth and Social Change.* 147 pp. Chicago: Markham Publishing Company, 1971. (Pp. 73–102 discuss phases of student dissent in 1960s and questions of authority. Index.)

978.   Foster, Julian, and Durward Long, eds., *Protest! Student Activism in America.* 596 pp. New York: William Morrow, 1970. (Essays and case studies of student protest. Part 1 contains various overviews of activism. Part 3 includes case studies of actions in Indiana, Wisconsin, San Francisco State, Colorado, Princeton, Howard, and Ohio State. See also Ed Schwartz, "On Demonstration," pp. 394–400, and Julian Foster, "Student Protest: Aims and Strategies," pp. 401–18 on the method and strategy of protest demonstrations. Index.)

979.   Glazer, Nathan, *Remembering the Answers: Essays on the American Student Revolt.* 311 pp. New York and London: Basic Books, 1970. Ch. 3, 4, 6 are on the Berkeley conflict of 1964, and ch. 5 discusses "civil disobedience" in the university. Index.)

980.   Grant, Joanne, *Confrontation on Campus: The Columbia Pattern for the New Protest.* 224 pp. New York: New American Library, 1969. (Journalistic account of the Columbia protests of 1968. Photos. Documents. Index.)

981.   Heirich, Max, *The Spiral of Conflict: Berkeley, 1964.* 502 pp. New York and London: Columbia Univ. Press, 1971 [orig. publ. 1968]. (Sociological history of free speech controversy at Berkeley, 1964–65. See ch. 1 for theoretical discussion of analysis of collective action and ch. 20 for application to conflict theory. Descriptions of 26 "episodes" in the conflict in ch. 4–18. See index under *pack–in, picketing, resignations, sit–ins, Sproul Hall,* and *strike.* Photos. Index. Bibliography.)

982.   Light, Donald, Jr., and John Spiegel, with C.J. Lammers, R.S. Laufer, M. Levin, and J.L. Norr, *The Dynamics of University Protest.* 198 pp. Chicago: Nelson–Hall Publishers, 1977. (Theoretical essays on student protest in 1960s. See James L. Norr, "The Organizational Context of Protest," pp. 51–67. Donald W. Light, Jr., "Directed Resistance: The Structure of Tactics in Student Protest," pp. 69–95 is explicitly on the "nature of nonviolent protest" and includes a model on pp. 72–77 of "directed resistance" as contrasted with "passive resistance." See also ch. 5, 7 on faculty and administrative responses to student protests.)

983.   Lipset, Seymour Martin, *Rebellion in the University.* 310 pp. Chicago: Univ. of Chicago Press, 1976 [orig. publ. 1971]. (Sociology of student protest, with two chapters on the history of student activism from the eighteenth century to the 1950s. Index.)

984.   Lipset, Seymour Martin, and Sheldon S. Wolin, eds., *The Berkeley Student Revolt: Facts and Interpretations.* 585 pp. Garden City NY: Anchor Books, Doubleday, 1965.

(Analytical essays and documents on the 1964 Berkeley student protest. See section 3 for chronicle, section 4 for documents and statements, and pp. 519–58 for articles based on survey research.)

985. Mack, Raymond, John P. Morris, and Robert M. O'Neil, *No Heroes, No Villains: New Perspectives on Kent State and Jackson State*. 173 pp. San Francisco and London: Jossey–Bass, 1972. (A study of the implications for academic freedom and higher education of the killings at both institutions. Appendixes.)

986. McGill, William J., *The Year of the Monkey: Revolt on Campus, 1968–69*. 297 pp. New York: McGraw–Hill, 1982. (Memoirs of the Univ. of California, San Diego chancellor, 1968–69, with emphasis on five major campus conflicts. See index under *Anti–war movement, building seizures and break-ins, demonstrations, Free Speech Movement, nonactivist followers, nonviolence, People's Park incident, pressure tactics, strike,* and *student strike.* Photos. Index. Bibliography.)

987. Miller, Michael V., and Susan Gilmore, eds., *Revolution at Berkeley: The Crisis in American Education*. 348 pp. New York: The Dial Press, 1965. (Collection of articles on Berkeley student protest. See A.H. Raskin, "The Berkeley Affair: Mr. Kerr vs. Mr. Savio & Co.," pp. 78–91 for description of conflict, and John Searle, "The Faculty Resolution," pp. 92–104 on resolution of conflict. See also part 3, which includes articles discussing whether direct action tactics were justified. See Sol Stern, "A Deeper Disenchantment," pp. 225–38 for a student account of conflict. See also Colin Miller, "The Press and the Student Revolt," pp. 313–48 for press coverage of events. Chronology, pp. xxiv–xxix.)

988. *On Strike . . . Shut It Down!: A Report on the First National Student Strike in U.S. History: May, 1970*. 133 pp. Chicago: Urban Research Corporation, 1970. (Pp. 1–19 contain an overview of the May 1970 student strikes and protests on 760 college campuses, associated with the Kent State killings. Pp. 20–133 report protest activities on campuses by state.)

989.   Owens, B.D., and Ray B. Browne, eds., *Teach–In: Viability of Change*. 183 pp. Bowling Green OH: Bowling Green Univ. Popular Press, 1970. (Reports and personal reflections on a teach–in at Bowling Green State University, May 1970. See esp. B.D. Owens, "Teach–in," pp. 15–19 and Marvin L. Kumler, "Cooperative Participation In Bowling Green," pp. 21–35 for description; pp. 37–92 for personal reflections. Illustrations. Photos.)

990.   *Parameters of Institutional Change: Chicano Experiences in Education*. 190 pp. Hayward CA: The Southwest Network, 1974. (Informal case studies and conceptual essays on Chicano protests in the late 1960s and early 1970s. See section 1 for case studies, esp. Ray Santana and Mario Esparza, "East Los Angeles Blowouts," pp. 1–9 on 1967–68 school walkouts; and Chicano Students Committee for Justice, "Chicano Demonstrations at New Mexico Highlands University," pp. 33–40. Illustrations.)

991.   President's Commission on Campus Unrest, *The Report of the President's Commission on Campus Unrest*. 537 pp. New York: Arno Press, 1970. (Student protests in the 1960s, including official responses. Special reports on Kent State and Jackson State. Photos. Appendixes. Bibliography.)

992.   Rosenkranz, Richard, *Across the Barricades*. 297 pp. Philadelphia and New York: J.B. Lippincott, 1971. (Journalistic account by participant of April 1968 protest at Columbia Univ., based on interviews.)

993.   Summers, Marvin R., and Thomas E. Barth, eds., *Law and Order in a Democratic Society*. 275 pp. Columbus OH: Charles E. Merrill, 1970. (See three articles on protest on campuses, pp. 203–32; two articles on civil disobedience, pp. 181–202; and H.L. Nieburg, "The Threat of Violence and Social Change," pp. 233–48.)

NATIVE AMERICANS

Many Native American nations retained a variety of rights to land, fishing and hunting, and other things when making treaties with the U.S. and other governments. Sometimes Native Americans have turned to protests and legal tests cases to compel recognition of these rights. One example is "fish–ins," when Indians fish in their traditional places in defiance of laws that restrict them to certain places, times, or methods.

994.   American Friends Service Committee, *Uncommon Controversy: Fishing Rights of the Muckleshoot, Puyallup, and Nisqually Indians.* 232 pp. Seattle and London: Univ. of Washington Press, 1970. (See ch. 5 on fish–in demonstrations, confrontations, and court cases in Washington State in the 1960s over the issue of fishing rights. Illustrations. Index. Bibliography.)

995.   Cohen, Fay G., *Treaties on Trial: The Continuing Controversy over Northwest Indian Fishing Rights.* 229 pp. Seattle and London: Univ. of Washington Press, 1986. (Report prepared for the American Friends Service Committee. On "fish–in" to protest laws, see index under *fish–ins* and *illegal fishing* and esp. pp. 64–66 and ch. 5. Photos include marches and picketing. Index.)

996.   Deloria, Vine, Jr., *Behind the Trail of Broken Treaties: An American Indian Declaration of Independence.* 296 pp. Austin TX: Univ. of Texas Press, 1985. (Titled after a Native American protest caravan of 1972, which ended in occupation and confrontation at Bureau of Indian Affairs offices. See ch. 2, 3 on the development of activism and protest in 1960s, inspired by the civil rights movement. See esp. pp. 25–33, 35–36, 37–39 on protest and site occupation and pp. 46–62 on the protest caravan. Ch. 6 discusses the violent Wounded Knee occupation. Illustrations. Index.)

997.   Steiner, Stan, *The New Indians.* 348 pp. New York and London: Harper & Row, 1968. (See ch. 5 on fish–ins.)

998.   Wilson, Edmund, *Apologies to the Iroquois*. 310 pp. New
        York: Farrar, Straus & Cudahy, 1959. (Tuscaroras' resistance
        to the Power Authority of New York and its planned land
        seizure of 1957–59 are briefly described on pp. 137–68.
        Photos.)

NAZI–SKOKIE CONTROVERSY

*When American Nazis decided to hold marches through the heavily
Jewish suburb of Skokie, Illinois, the residents united to stop them by
nearly any means they could think of. Although the American Civil
Liberties Union supported the free speech aspects of the march,
members resigned rather than be seen to favor Nazis.*

999.   Downs, Donald Alexander, *Nazis in Skokie: Freedom,
        Community, and the First Amendment*. 227 pp. Notre Dame
        IN: Univ. of Notre Dame Press, 1985. (Detailed empirical
        study of efforts by U.S. Nazi group to hold provocative
        marches in a city occupied by many Jewish survivors of
        concentration camps. Includes material on legal challenges
        and counter–actions. See ch. 1–4, esp. ch. 3 on mobilization
        against the Nazi march, including pp. 51–54 on civil
        disobedience and ch. 5–7 on effects. Index.)

1000.   Hamlin, David, *The Nazi/Skokie Conflict: A Civil Liberties
        Battle*. 184 pp. Boston: Beacon Press, 1980. (Journalist's
        account of attempted Nazi marches and opposition. See ch. 4–
        6, including pp. 119–20 on protest resignations from ACLU for
        supporting march as "free speech." Index.)

ANTI–NUCLEAR POWER MOVEMENT

*Construction of nuclear power plants fostered campaigns by people
who challenged either the safety of a specific plant, nuclear safety
in general, or the environmental effects of plants. Organizations and
coalitions pursued a mixture of techniques, including political
lobbying, media campaigns, publicity, and nonviolent demonstrations
and blockades. The effect of some campaigns was to delay construction*

of individual plants, and such campaigns possibly contributed to disenchantment with nuclear power.

1001. Copulos, Milton R., *Confrontation at Seabrook.* 44 pp. Washington DC: The Heritage Foundation, 1978. (Focuses on a May 1977 mass occupation at the Seabrook, New Hampshire, nuclear plant construction site; relates costs imposed by the conflict to overall cost factors.)

1002. Elliot, Dave, with Pat Coyne, Mike George, and Roy Lewis, *The Politics of Nuclear Power.* 141 pp. London: Pluto Press, 1978. (See ch. 9 on strategies of U.S. and British groups and part 3 on political strategies. Bibliography.)

1003. Falk, Jim, *Global Fission: The Battle over Nuclear Power.* 410 pp. Melbourne, Oxford, Auckland, and New York: Oxford Univ. Press, 1982. (Survey of nuclear energy conflicts from 1941 to 1981, focusing on the power of contestants and the issues invoked. See pp. 54–60 on the U.S. protest movement; ch. 5 on the origins of opposition in U.S. and Europe; pp. 125–30 on state responses to protest; pp. 143–46 on the spread of opposition, 1973–75; ch. 9, 10 on international protests; ch. 11 on the Australian movement; ch. 12 on strategy. See also index under *demonstrations* and *occupations.* Index.)

1004. Gyorgy, Anna, *No Nukes: Everyone's Guide to Nuclear Power.* 465 pp. Montreal: Black Rose Books: 1979. (See section 5 on tactics of anti–nuclear groups.)

1005. Price, Jerome, *The Antinuclear Movement.* 207 pp. Boston: Twayne Publishers, 1982. (Overview of history and origins of the anti–nuclear power campaign, with emphasis given to groups and organizations. Ch. 4 discusses "direct action groups" engaging in extralegal actions and analyzes "expressive symbolization." Index. Bibliography.)

1006. Sugai, Wayne H., *Nuclear Power and Ratepayer Protest: The Washington Public Power Supply System Crisis.* 475 pp. Boulder and London: Westview Press, 1987. (Examination of mass mobilization looking at power plant construction, financial failings, and the "ratepayers' revolt" in

Washington state during the 1970s and early 1980s. Identifies
conditions that turn unrest into insurgency and relates these to
the failure of anti–nuclear power organizations to endure.
Appendix. Index. Bibliography.)

NONVIOLENT OPPOSITION TO NUCLEAR WEAPONS

*In anti–nuclear circles in the 1970s and 1980s, the deployment of
greater numbers and more types of weapons combined with fears of
the effects of war (nuclear winter) to create a demand for banning
nuclear weapons. More affirmatively, the proposal for a unilateral
"freeze" on nuclear weapons was believed to lead eventually to their
abandonment. Actions and action choices diverged along these
differing lines of thought. The "freeze" as a policy was, in the view
of some, best advocated by appeals and education of voters and
Congress, who would be alienated by direct action. Others believed
that the danger demanded protest and civil disobedience, or held
political and religious commitments that compelled them to direct
action.*

*See also: Methods of Nonviolent Action: Encampments; Methods of
Nonviolent Action: Blockades and Voyages of Intervention.*

1007. Bennett, Gordon C., *The New Abolitionists: The Story of
Nuclear–Free Zones.* 269 pp. Elgin IL: Brethren Press, 1987.
(History of nuclear weapons free zone movement in U.S. and
internationally. Movement actions include petitions and
symbolic actions. See pp. 27–29 on civil disobedience, pp. 53–
55 on transarmament, ch. 4 on parallels to U.S. abolitionist
movement of 1800s, esp. pp. 98–103 on violent versus
nonviolent means and pp. 106–7 on the "moral embargo" or
isolation. See pp. 181–84 on "extralegality" and
"paralegality" of actions, and pp. 193–95 on boycott as
method of protest. Pp. 220–25 on persuasion and social
movements.)

1008. Dietrich, Jeff, *Reluctant Resister.* 165 pp. Greensboro NC:
Unicorn Press, 1983. (Most of the text consists of letters by
author on his thoughts and experiences in prison after being
sentenced as a result of protests by Orange County Folks for

Peace in 1979. First preface describes the group's activities and second preface describes the Los Angeles County Catholic Worker movement. Photo section contains posters and photos of actions, although the actions themselves and the strategy behind them are left largely unexplained. Photos. Documents.)

1009. Farren, Pat, ed., *What Will It Take to Prevent Nuclear War? Grassroots Responses to Our Most Challenging Question.* 239 pp. Cambridge MA: Schenkman, 1983. (See ch. 12 for briefly stated opinions on the role of action. Illustrations. Photos.)

1010. Laffin, Arthur J., and Anne Montgomery, eds., *Swords into Plowshares: Nonviolent Direct Action for Disarmament.* 243 pp. San Francisco: Harper & Row, 1987. (Collection of essays on civil disobedience and other actions protesting nuclear weapons in the U.S. Ch. 2 is on civil disobedience, which is called "divine obedience" by the authors. Following chapters discuss various Plowshares actions and related topics. Appendix 4 is on civilian–based defense. Photos. Bibliography.)

1011. Loeb, Paul Rogat, *Hope in Hard Times: America's Peace Movement and the Reagan Era.* 322 pp. Lexington MA: Lexington Books, 1987. (Includes accounts of personal experiences in various sorts of actions, including blockades of buildings, marches, public education, and the like. Illustrations. Index.)

1012. McCrea, Frances B., and Gerald E. Markle, *Minutes to Midnight: Nuclear Weapons Protest in America.* 200 pp. Newbury Park CA, London, and New Delhi: Sage Publications, 1989. (Proposes a theory of social movements in "postindustrial" society which is applied to the study of three streams of anti–nuclear action, including the atomic scientists, ban–the–bomb and SANE, and, in ch. 5–7, the nuclear freeze movement. See pp. 159–63 on ideological and organizational issues and the "dilemmas of protest." Appendixes. Index. Bibliography.)

1013. Meyer, David S., *A Winter of Discontent: The Nuclear Freeze and American Politics*. 294 pp. New York: Praeger Publishers, 1990. (Places the Nuclear Freeze Movement in the context of social movements theory and the dynamics of U.S. politics. See ch. 11 on efforts to replace the electorally–oriented strategy of the movement with other forms of action and pp. 254–55 on the "marginalization" of direct action. Index. Bibliography.)

Chapter 3
Asia and the Pacific

If the example of INDIA is excepted, the history of nonviolent action in Asia and the Pacific is practically unknown in the English–speaking world. It is easy to discover, however, that CHINA has an extensive history of nonviolent struggle, more than is documented in this chapter. This includes serious attempts to sanction other states economically through boycotts and reduce the economic influence of outside powers. Much of Asia and all of the Pacific region lie outside what Westerners generally regard as the mainstream of nonviolent action (labor and anti–conscription conflicts in AUSTRALIA and NEW ZEALAND possibly excepted). Nevertheless, conflicts that have given rise to nonviolent action are quite similar to those in the rest of the world, including anticolonial struggles and conflicts over labor organizing, the rights of minorities, and the legitimate powers of the state versus the citizen or subject.

Anti–colonialism has been equally a theme of nonviolent struggle in the Pacific as in Asia, Africa, and Latin America. Two notable and little–known campaigns of nonviolent action were the Parihaka land movement of the Maori (see NEW ZEALAND) and the lengthy O le Mau noncooperation campaign in Western Samoa to resist New Zealand's mandate to rule under the League of Nations (see SAMOA, WESTERN). In recent years, land and the environment, both natural and urban, have been issues of contention in many of the islands, INDIA, AUSTRALIA, and JAPAN.

AUSTRALIA

Most of these works are on economic and labor conflicts, including strikes in the nineteenth and twentieth centuries. Worth noticing is Australian labor's uses of labor boycotts and their development into green bans. Green bans appear to have adapted labor bans (as boycotts are known in BRITAIN, AUSTRALIA, and NEW ZEALAND) into a force for protecting the natural and *social environment by withholding labor from destructive projects. Political conflicts in Australia include the anti–Vietnam War movement and the Queensland Civil Liberties campaign. Environmental conflicts have also arisen as Australia begins to exploit previously–unused natural areas more intensively.*

Labor

Australia has spawned a community of strike researchers in part because it has experienced an active history of strikes and labor boycotts (bans). This history includes a period of "great strikes" in the late nineteenth century. More recently, the strike mechanism has extended into the political arena.

1014.   *Builders' Labourers' Song Book.* 213 pp. Camberwell: Widescope; Carlton South: Australian Building Construction Employees' and Builders' Labourers' Federation, 1975. (Descriptive text, songs, and illustrations on history of protest movements in Australia. Illustrations. Photos. Index of songs.)

1015.   Ebbels, R.N., *The Australian Labor Movement, 1850–1907.* Ed. L.G. Churchward. Reprint. 255 pp. Sydney: Noel Ebbels Memorial Committee, in association with the Australasian Book Society, 1976 [orig. publ. 1960]. (Collection of historical documents. See nos. 34, 35, 45, 62, and part 5, nos. 72–96, on the "great strikes" of 1890–94. Index.)

1016.   Fitzpatrick, Brian, and Rowan J. Cahill, *The Seaman's Union of Australia, 1872–1972: A History.* 363 pp. Sydney: Seaman's Union of Australia, 1981. (See part 1, ch. 2, 3, 7–11, on various maritime strikes, and pp. 209–21 on anti–Vietnam War activities. See index under *bans* and *boycotts.* Illustrations. Photos. Index. Bibliography.)

1017.   Iremonger, Jack, John Merritt, and Graeme Osborne, eds., *Strikes: Studies in Twentieth–Century Australian Social History.* 270 pp. Sydney: Angus & Robertson, in association with the Australian Society for the Study of Labour History, 1973. (Collection of studies covering strike activity, 1903–68, including Broken Hill, post–WWI strikes, and the New South Wales teachers' dispute, 1968. Index.)

1018.   Kennedy, Brian, *Silver, Sin, and Sixpenny Ale: A Social History of Broken Hill, 1883–1921.* 202 pp. Melbourne: Melbourne Univ. Press, 1978. (Ch. 5, 8, 11, 12 offer a history of labor strikes and lockouts in this region of Sydney, 1892–1920. See also pp. 128–29, 136–41 on anti–conscription activities during WWI. Illustrations. Photos. Index. Bibliography.)

1019.   Lockwood, Rupert, *Black Armada.* 352 pp. Sydney South, Australia: Australasian Book Society, 1975. (History of a post–WWII labor boycott campaign, or "black ban," by labor unions that refused to help The Netherlands return to colonial possessions in Indonesia. Characterized as "war without shooting" in the introduction, the campaign from 1945–49 involved refusal of Australian labor to service Dutch ships, work refusals and mutinies by Indonesian and Indian sailors in Dutch vessels, and other inconvenience to Dutch efforts to reestablish themselves. See appendix for list of vessels boycotted, Australian and Asian trade unions involved, and other countries where boycotts resulted. Index.)

1020.   Murphy, D.J., ed., *The Big Strikes: Queensland, 1889–1965.* 303 pp. St. Lucia, Queensland, London, and New York: Univ. of Queensland Press, 1983. (Ch. 1 reviews research on strikes. Part 2 contains essays on fifteen notable Queensland strikes. Index.)

1021.   Rawson, D.W., *Unions and Unionists in Australia.* 166 pp. Sydney, London, and Boston: George Allen & Unwin, 1978. (Ch. 7 discusses the trend of strikes, failure of legal means to control strikes, and new developments such as "political" strikes. Index. Bibliography.)

1022.   Turner, Ian, and Leonie Sandercock, *In Union Is Strength: A History of Trade Unions in Australia, 1788–1983.* 3d ed. 183 pp. Melbourne: Thomas Nelson, 1983 [orig. publ. 1976]. (See pp. 16–19 on the nineteenth century, ch. 3 on "great strikes" of 1890s, pp. 59–62 on the early twentieth century, pp. 68–69 on the general strike of 1917, pp. 70–71 on post–WWI strikes, pp. 87–90 on the 1930s, pp. 103–8 on the 1949 miners' strike, and pp. 122–24 on new tactics since the 1950s. Photos of strikes and demonstrations. Index.)

1023.   Waters, Les, *The Union of Christmas Island Workers.* 170 pp.
         Sydney, London, and Boston: George Allen & Unwin, 1983.
         (See ch. 10, 11 on strikes in 1979 and ch. 12 on background of a
         13–day hunger strike by a supporter of the union in Canberra.
         Photos. Index. Bibliography.)

1024.   Waters, Malcolm, *Strikes in Australia: A Sociological Analysis of
         Industrial Conflict.* 239 pp. Sydney, London, and Boston:
         George Allen & Unwin, 1982. (History of strike patterns in
         Australia and test of a model of strike causation; see ch. 1, 2
         and pp. 43–48 for strike model. Index. Bibliography.)

Environmental Movement

*Citizen action to protect the natural environment is often linked to
construction projects that promise to destroy or severely alter the natural
landscape. One example is the movement in 1982 to prevent hydro–power
damming of the wild Franklin River in Tasmania, a large and relatively
undeveloped island off the southern coast of the continent. Other protests have
attempted to protect threatened species, important natural areas, and
historically significant sites.*

1025.   Green, Roger, *Battle for the Franklin: Conversations with the
         Combatants in the Struggle for South West Tasmania.* 303 pp.
         Sydney and Melbourne: Fontana Books and the Australian
         Conservation Foundation, 1981. (Interviews with actors in the
         S.W. Tasmania dam dispute, including politicians and
         activists. Chronology.)

1026.   Mosely, J.G., and J. Messer, eds., *Fighting for Wilderness: Papers
         from the Australian Conservation Foundation's Third National
         Wilderness Conference, 1983.* 256 pp. Sydney: Fontana Books and
         the Australian Conservation Foundation, 1984. (Protests,
         pickets, blockades and other actions to protect threatened
         natural areas are discussed at least briefly in Rosemary Hill
         and Mike Graham, "Greater Daintree National Park," pp. 7–22;
         Dick Johnson, "Alpine National Park," pp. 45–58; Bob Brown,
         "Wilderness versus Hydro–Electricity in South West
         Tasmania," pp. 59–68, which is something of a how–to manual;

and Penny Figgis, "Out of the Wilderness for the Wilderness Issue?," pp. 227–44. Photos. Appendix.)

1027. Wilderness Society, *Franklin Blockade*. 124 pp. Hobart, Tasmania: The Wilderness Society, 1983. (Participants' descriptions of a large–scale nonviolent direct action to halt the construction of a dam in Tasmania. Includes glossary and chronology. Illustrations. Photos.)

Green Bans

Green bans are boycotts to withhold labor from environmentally–sensitive projects. Both the Australian and British labor traditions use the terms bans or black bans (blacking) for labor boycotts, so green bans were readily named for their environmentalist tinge (entry 1030: 12). With the participation of the leader of the New South Wales Builders' Labourers' Federation, green bans at least temporarily gained enough strength to deprive objectionable projects of labor.

1028. Manning, Peter, and Marion Hardman, *Green Bans*. 128 pp. East Melbourne: Australian Conservation Foundation, [1976]. (Heavily illustrated "personal and polemical" study of green bans, or labor boycotts undertaken to preserve natural or urban environments, by New South Wales Builders' Labourers' Federation. Photos.)

1029. Mundey, Jack, *Green Bans and Beyond*. 154 pp. London, Sydney, Melbourne, Singapore, and Manila: Angus & Robertson, 1981. (Autobiography of New South Wales builders' labourers' union leader, with extensive discussion of green bans spurred by social and environmental issues. See esp. pp. 55–76, 84–117 and consult index under *green bans*. Photos. Index.)

1030. Roddewig, Richard J., *Green Bans: The Birth of Australian Environmental Politics: A Study in Public Opinion and Participation*. 180 pp. Sydney: Hale & Iremonger; Montclair NJ and New York: Allanheld, Osmun/Universe; Washington DC, The Conservation Foundation, 1978. (A study of the transition from the politicized labor boycott, or "black ban," to the defense of urban and natural environments, or "green bans."

Ch. 1–3 are on the making of anti–development bans, based on the willingness of organized labor to withhold its members from environmentally damaging projects; ch. 5, 6 are on the limits of political access and the courts; and ch. 7 is on the political strike, or black ban, as extralegal pressure. Part 3 is on environmental politics, both urban and development oriented, in the 1970s and part 4 assesses green bans. Index.)

Anti–Vietnam War Movement

Australian troops participated in the War in Vietnam because of multilateral treaties with SOUTH VIETNAM and the UNITED STATES, and also because of the government's concern with the politics of the Pacific rim. Australia's movement against involvement included the "moratorium" campaign of 1970 and opposition to conscription for duty in Vietnam.

1031.   Cairns, J.F., M.P., *Silence Kills: Events Leading up to the Vietnam Moratorium 8 May [1970]*. 104 pp. Richmond North: The Vietnam Moratorium Committee, 1970. (Photo and narrative account of demonstrations against the Australian role in Vietnam War, written by chairman of the Vietnam Moratorium Committee. See pp. 9–41 for depiction of marches and pp. 99–104 for editorial reaction. Photos.)

1032.   Findlay, P.T., *Protest Politics and Psychological Warfare*. 63 pp. Melbourne: Hawthorn Press, [1968]. (Effort to link Australia's anti–Vietnam War and anti–conscription movement to Communism. Some information on these movements and the opposition to them, plus views of nonviolent action. See pp. 6–8, 16–19, ch. 4, 5, 8, 9. Photos.)

1033.   King, Peter, ed., *Australia's Vietnam: Australia in the Second Indochina War*. 226 pp. Sydney, London, and Boston: George Allen & Unwin, 1983. (See Michael E. Hamel–Green, "The Resisters: A History of the Anti–Conscription Movement, 1964–1972," ch. 6. Index.)

1034.   Saunders, Malcolm, *A Bibliography of Books, Articles, and Theses on the Australian Peace Movement*. 115 pp. Canberra: Peace Research Centre, Research School of Pacific Studies, Australian

National Univ., 1987. PRC Monograph No. 1. (Definitions, scope, and methods of this selective bibliography are discussed on pp. 1–10, followed by a list of general reference works and histories of Australia. Entries in each chapter are classified as to whether they are "basic references" or "worth consulting." Chapters cover Australia's military history from Crimea to Vietnam, with additional topics on recent interwar periods, Quakers, peace societies, compulsory military training, and conscription. On these last-mentioned topics, see ch. 7, 9, 13. Appendixes.)

Queensland Civil Liberties Campaign

Queensland, Australia's "Deep North," has been the home of both conservative–populist and radical politics. The two clashed in the 1960s and 1970s when Queensland premier Johannes Bjelke–Petersen forbade protest marches. Bjelke–Petersen argued that there was no common–law right to use the public streets for protest and, in the absence of constitutional protections, moved to stop street protests. Among actions used to challenge the ban, protesters held quickie marches and marches that started outside Queensland or on legally–protected university property.

1035.   Brennan, Frank, S.J., *Too Much Order with Too Little Law*. 303 pp. St. Lucia, Queensland: Univ. of Queensland Press, 1983. (Legal–political study of protests before and after the banning of street marches by Queensland's premier Johannes Bjelke–Petersen. See ch. 4 on "protest, disorder, and the abuse of power in Queensland, 1960–79," ch. 5 on police–protester interactions, and ch. 6 on the courts. Index. Bibliography.)

1036.   Plunkett, Mark and Ralph Summy, "Civil Liberties in Queensland: A Nonviolent Political Campaign." *Social Alternatives* [Australia] 1 (1980): 73–90. (Review of the Queensland civil liberties campaign with particular attention to the strategy of nonviolent action and its strengths and shortcomings, as well as the role of the police, third parties, and economics of the movement. Photos.)

1037.   *Social Alternatives* [Australia]. Vol. 5, nos. 3 and 4, 1986. (Journal issues on politics and culture in "populist"

Queensland. See esp., in no. 3, Matthew Foley, "Civil Liberties in Queensland," pp. 54–59. Other articles concerned with industrial relations, racial issues, and politics.)

BURMA

Burma, renamed Myanmar by its military rulers, has experienced both guerrilla and nonviolent opposition to authoritarian government, including the democracy movement of 1988.

1038.   Lintner, Bertil, *Outrage: Burma's Struggle for Democracy*. 2nd ed. 208 pp. London and Bangkok: White Lotus, 1990. Originally published Hong Kong: Review Publishing, 1989. (Descriptive account of protests, strikes, and hunger strikes in the Burma democracy movement of 1988. Ch. 1 discusses the origins of the movement in March 1988, ch. 2 contains material on earlier conflicts and changes of government, and ch. 3–6 are on the development and culmination of the 1988 conflict. Ch. 3–6 in particular recount efforts to conduct "peaceful" demonstrations, followed by violence in reaction to the great violence of police and military in crushing them. Biographies. List of abbreviations. Photos. Chronology. Index.)

CHINA

China has possessed a single central government, although ruled by a variety of overlords, for several thousand years. With the coming of outsiders from Europe in the eighteenth century, China was not only "opened up" economically and culturally to the West but subjected to attempts at domination by European colonial states, the U.S., and Japan. From the time of the Opium Wars of the mid–nineteenth century, the central government was unable to stop outside penetration, often leaving efforts at protecting Chinese autonomy to social movements. As mentioned in the introduction to this chapter, China's history of nonviolent action before the twentieth century is virtually unknown. The introduction of republican government in 1911 dissolved the empire politically, but many Confucian cultural standards persisted. Constitutional change gradually gave more political power to civilian groups and coalitions, which eventually were dominated by the

Guomindang or Nationalist Party. Early in the republican period, China's nonviolent struggles, such as economic boycotts and the May Fourth Movement of 1919, were often attempts to remove foreign domination from political and economic life. China was both the initiator and the target of boycotts to influence political conditions. Beginning around 1905, nationalists tried to restrict Western and Japanese trade infiltration and to defend against outsiders' unjust social policies. Later the United States unsuccessfully tried to exert pressure on China by boycotts after the "loss" of China to communism. With the Japanese invasion, World War II, and creation of the People's Republic, a hiatus began in outsiders' knowledge of nonviolent action in China. In the late 1970s, pro–democracy movements became visible to the outside world when campaigns put up Big Character Posters to publicize their ideas. This trend of mass mobilization and symbolic protest culminated in the Democracy Movement of 1989.

Before 1948

Chinese labor and political forces attempted to protect the country's economy and culture from outside penetration partly through boycotts of foreign goods and ideas. Much of the protest from the republican revolution of 1911 until 1948 is also inseparable from the clashes that would finally lead to the victory of the Chinese Communist Party.

1039. Chesneaux, Jean, *The Chinese Labor Movement, 1919–1927.* Trans. H.M. Wright. 574 pp. Stanford CA: Stanford Univ. Press, 1968. (See ch. 7 on the May Fourth Movement of 1919, ch. 8 on strikes and protests in 1922, ch. 11 on the May Thirtieth Movement of 1925, and ch. 12 on the Canton–Hong Kong strike and boycotts of 1925–26. See also index under *strikes.* Index. Bibliography.)

1040. Cohen, Jerome A., Robert F. Dernberger, and John R. Garson, *China Trade Prospects and U.S. Policy.* 329 pp. New York and London: Praeger, 1971. (See part 1 on the U.S. embargo against China.)

1041. Liao, Kuang–sheng, *Antiforeignism and Modernization in China, 1860–1980: Linkage between Domestic Politics and Foreign Policy.* 333 pp. Hong Kong: Chinese Univ. Press, 1984. (See pp. 58–59, 73–79, 94–97 on boycotts in first half of twentieth century. On antiforeign demonstrations, 1960–80, see pp. 133–51, 183–87, 217–19 and appendix 3. Index. Bibliography.)

1042.   Remer, C.F., with the assistance of William B. Palmer, *A Study of Chinese Boycotts: With Special Reference to Their Economic Effectiveness*. 306 pp. Baltimore MD: Johns Hopkins Univ. Press, 1933. Reprint, New York: Arno Press, 1979. (Study of China's use of the international boycott from 1905 to 1932. Ch. 1–3 introduce boycott in Chinese context and ch. 4–9, 11–14 describe boycotts against foreign states, including the U.S. and Japan. Ch. 10, 14–16 discuss effects of boycotts. Anti–Japan boycott plan, 1931, in appendix 5. Index. Bibliography.)

1043.   Tso, S.K. Sheldon, "The Labor Movement in China." Ph.D. diss., Indiana Univ., 1928. 230 pp. (Study of labor movement in China, ca. 1918–26. See ch. 5, 6 for strike analysis and survey. See also appendix 5 for classification of strikes. Bibliography.)

MAY FOURTH MOVEMENT, 1919

The May Fourth Movement of 1919 is often treated as a cultural renewal and cultural nationalist movement, as it became after its most intense phase was over. Initially, however, it was a student–led direct action campaign to combat the growing and aggressive influence of JAPAN over Chinese affairs (although there were other anti–foreign and anti–Christian themes as well). After anti–Japanese agitation beginning as early as 1915, Chinese students in Japan departed from that country "in a body" in protest and began to agitate in the Chinese universities. Following a mass student march in Peking with a petition to the government on May 4, 1919, the movement escalated into merchant boycotts and labor strikes in several cities lasting several days.

1044.   Chow Tse–tsung, *The May Fourth Movement: Intellectual Revolution in Modern China*. 486 pp. Cambridge: Harvard Univ. Press, 1960. Reprint, Stanford CA: Stanford Univ. Press, 1967. (Detailed history and analysis of the political and cultural movements growing out of Peking students' demonstration on May 4, 1919 against Japanese subjugation of their government. Ch. 1, on the movement's background, discusses anti–Japanese boycotts of 1915 in pp. 23–24 and the "returning–in–a–body" protests of Chinese students studying in Japan on pp. 33–34. In ch. 2, pp. 77–83 discuss student demonstrations and anti–Japanese petitions in May 1918. Ch. 4 describes the May Fourth Incident itself, a large–scale student demonstration and march, and ch. 5 discusses the spread of the movement and subsequent "students' general strike." Ch. 6 details the aid given to the students' movement after arrests began, in the form of merchants' strikes and labor strikes, followed by the resolution of the action phase of the movement. Subsequent chapters demonstrate the enduring political and cultural consequences of the movement and change associated with it. Appendixes include figures on students and universities involved in the May Fourth Incident and labor strikes from 1918 to 1926. Chronology. Index.)

1045. ———, *Research Guide to the May Fourth Movement: Intellectual Revolution in Modern China, 1915–1924.* 297 pp. Cambridge: Harvard Univ. Press, 1963. (Source list and bibliography of materials on the May Fourth Movement and its era in Chinese, Japanese, English, and other languages. See pp. 1–129 for periodical references, many of which are summarized in English. See pp. 215–32, 243–45 for English–language works with some references in French and Russian. Glossary of English equivalents of Chinese terminology, pp. 247–97.)

1046. Kiang, Wen–Han, *The Chinese Student Movement.* 176 pp. Morningside Heights NY: King's Crown Press, 1948. (Ch. 1 is on the May Fourth Movement and its cultural background. Bibliography.)

1047. Scalapino, Robert A., and George T. Yu, *Modern China and Its Revolutionary Process: Recurrent Challenges to the Traditional Order, 1850–1920.* 814 pp. Berkeley, Los Angeles, and London: Univ. of California Press, 1985. (See pp. 456–62 on the course and outcome of the May Fourth Movement, seen as the largest popular mobilization "without resort to large–scale violence" to that time. Photos. Index. Bibliography.)

1048. Schwarcz, Vera, *The Chinese Enlightenment: Intellectuals and the Legacy of the May Fourth Movement of 1919.* 393 pp. Berkeley, Los Angeles and London: Univ. of California Press, 1986. (Follows the intellectuals of the May Fourth Movement and its era until the end of the 1930s. See ch. 1, 2 on cultural aspects of the origins and immediate influence of the movement and ch. 6, "May Fourth as Allegory," on the continuing struggle over its meaning. Glossary. Appendix. Index. Bibliography.)

1049.   Wang, Tsi C., *The Youth Movement in China*. 245 pp. New York NY: New Republic, 1927. (Ch. 10 contains a good deal of detail on collective action in the May Fourth Movement, conceived of as "employing the method of non–resistance, perseverance, and peaceful strikes." See also ch. 11 on movements against Christianity in the same period.)

After 1948

Mao Zedong's Cultural Revolution of the 1970s released forces of discontent among students, peasants, and the urban populations that would challenge the order he had created. In particular, it began a period of student mobilization discussed more fully in the next section.

1050.   Goodman, David S.G., ed., *Groups and Politics in the People's Republic of China*. 217 pp. Armonk NY: M.E. Sharpe, 1984. (Articles on interest groups and internal politics. John P. Burns, "Chinese Peasant Interest Articulation," pp. 126–51 identifies various methods of peasant group self–protection and assertion, including misreporting output, withholding production, demonstrations, and violence.)

1051.   Schell, Orville, *Discos and Democracy: China in the Throes of Reform*. 384 pp. New York: Pantheon Books, 1988. (A journalist's description of and reactions to China in the 1980s. See pp. 201–10 on the Democracy Wall movement of 1977–79 and pp. 211–44 on student demonstrations and demands for democracy at the turn of 1986–87. Also of interest is discussion of democratic ideas in the 1980s in pp. 15–23 and a sketch of Fang Lizhi in pp. 121–39.)

1052.   Spence, Jonathan D., *The Gate of Heavenly Peace: The Chinese and Their Revolution, 1895–1980*. 516 pp. Harmondsworth, Middlesex; New York; Victoria, Australia; Markham, Ontario; and Auckland NZ: Penguin Books, 1982 (orig. publ. 1981).

(Within the context of continued revolutionary trends in China, see pp. 154–60 on the May Fourth Movement of 1919, as both a student protest and a cultural movement, and pp. 405–12 on the Democracy Wall movement of 1978–79. Consult index under *boycotts, strikes,* and *students.* Illustrations. Photos. Index. Bibliography.)

1053.   Stahnke, Arthur A., ed., *China's Trade with the West: A Political and Economic Analysis.* 234 pp. New York, Washington, and London: Praeger, 1972. (See esp. Oliver M. Lee, "U.S. Trade Policy Toward China: From Economic Warfare to Summit Diplomacy," ch. 2. Details the U.S. boycott against China following the revolution and illustrates its ineffectiveness.)

DEMOCRACY MOVEMENT, 1977–1981

Reappraisal of Maoism following Mao Zedong's death in 1976, factional struggles within the party and government, and the suppression of public mourning at the death of Zhou Enlai caused many to reconsider citizen–state relations in the late 1970s. One of the more striking examples of this was the Democracy Movement, in which students and factory workers wrote outspoken criticisms of the state and posted them in prominent places as "Big–Character posters," notably at Beijing's "Democracy Wall." Crowds gathered and stayed even through the night to read, discuss, and record the text of Big–Character posters. For reasons of its own, the government tolerated the democracy movement for several weeks in 1980–81 in the first example of pressure for change from below in contemporary China.

1054.   Barmé, Geremie, and John Minford, eds., *Seeds of Fire: Chinese Voices of Conscience.* 347 pp. Hongkong: Far Eastern Economic Review, 1986. (Selected poems, stories, accounts, plays, drawings, and the like on various themes implying or stating dissent. Section 9 contains pieces by figures connected with the Democracy campaign in 1979, including several on conditions of imprisonment. Photos include a gathering in Tiananmen Square in 1976 and the Democracy Wall in 1979. Appendix.)

1055.   Chang, T.C., C.F. Chen, and Y.T. Lin, eds., *Catalog of Chinese Underground Literature.* 2 vols. Vol. 1, 261 pp. Vol. 2, 273 pp. (Vol. 1 compiles "people's publications" as underground literature, 1978–80. Vol. 2 lists wall posters, underground magazines, and selected pieces from underground literature. Lists and descriptive text in English and Chinese. Illustrations. Documents.)

1056.   I–mu, ed., *Unofficial Documents of the Democracy Movement in Communist China, 1978–1981: A Checklist of Chinese Materials in the Hoover Institution on War, Revolution, and Peace.* 100 pp. Stanford CA: East Asian Collection, Hoover Institution, 1986. (See description of collections, pp. 3–8, and esp. detailed chronology of democracy movement, pp. 11–36.)

1057.   Lin, Yih–tang, comp., *What They Say: A Collection of Current Chinese Underground Publications.* 236 pp. Taipei: Institute of Current China Studies, [1980?]. (English–language texts, nearly all accompanied by a copy of the Chinese original, of wall posters and underground publications from the People's Republic. Introduction discusses the use of wall posters as a traditional method, then by the party and government, and later their use as a method of protest and communication outside regular channels. Pp. viii–ix contain a characterization of types and uses of posters and pp. xix–xxii discuss the Democracy Wall period. Part 1, pp. 1–16, contains color photos of posters from this last period and black–and–white photos or photocopies of others appear in the text. Appendixes.)

1058.   Seymour, James D., ed., *The Fifth Modernization: China's Human Rights Movement, 1978–1979.* 301 pp. Stanfordville NY: Human Rights Publishing Group, 1980. (Documents from the democracy movement of 1978–79, largely on the views of activists. See pp. 11–26 on the course and nature of the movement. Appendix. Index.)

1059.   Widor, Claude, *The Samizdat Press in China's Provinces, 1979–1981: An Annotated Guide.* 157 pp. Hoover Press Bibliography 70. Stanford CA: Hoover Institution, 1987. (Bibliography of eighty–eight unofficial political journals published during the Democracy Movement in both the cities and outlying provinces. Entries arranged geographically and prefaced with brief explanatory histories. Index.)

STUDIES

1060. Garside, Roger, *Coming Alive: China after Mao*. 458 pp. New York, St. Louis, San Francisco, Hamburg, and Mexico City: McGraw–Hill, 1981. (Journalist's essay on Chinese political and social life after Mao. See pp. 8–13 on death of Zhou Enlai and consult index under *Democracy Wall, petitions, poetry,* and *posters*. Photos. Index. Bibliography.)

1061. Goodman, David S.G., *Beijing Street Voices: The Poetry and Politics of China's Democracy Movement*. 208 pp. London and Boston: Marion Boyars, 1981. (Anthology of poetry from Beijing's Democracy Movement during the winter of 1978–79 taken from unofficial publications. See text at beginning of each chapter, esp. pp. 3–20, for introduction to democracy movement and forms of protest. Illustrations. Photos. Index. Bibliography.)

1062. Nathan, Andrew J., *Chinese Democracy*. 313 pp. New York: Alfred A. Knopf, 1985. (An exploration of themes of democracy in Chinese thought since 1895. Discusses the events of the Democracy Movement, 1978–80, and their effect on official thinking and the elections of 1980 in ch. 1, 2, 10. Appendix. Index.)

1063. Ruoxi, Chen, *Democracy Wall and the Unofficial Journals*. 119 pp. Studies in Chinese Terminology, no. 20. Berkeley CA: Center for Chinese Studies, Institute of East Asian Studies, Univ. of California, 1982. (Report on privately published journals connected with the democratic movement centered on the Democracy Wall in Beijing, 1978–81. See ch. 2 for description of democratic movement and posters, spontaneous gatherings, and demonstrations. Ch. 3–9 are on "unofficial journals" and their genesis, publication, major themes, and influence.)

1064. Strand, David, "Political Participation and Political Reform in Post–Mao China (1985)." Copenhagen Discussion Papers No. 6, May 1989. 63 pp. Copenhagen: Center for East and Southeast Asian Studies, Univ. of Copenhagen, 1989. (A distinction among "administered," "autonomous," and "licensed" political participation is introduced in pp. 4–8 and further developed as a characteristic of the 1978–79 Democracy Wall movement and related trends in pp. 29–63.)

DEMOCRACY MOVEMENT, 1988–89

Participants have asserted that the Democracy Movement of 1989, which is primarily associated with the mass occupation of Beijing's Tiananmen Square, was not a direct descendant of the 1978–80 poster campaign. As the entries below reveal, it began with student discussions, organizing, and brief demonstrations as early as the turn of the year in 1987–88. A rapid turn toward confrontation occurred between April and June 1989 when Peking University (Beida) students insisted upon holding marches to commemorate the death of the reformer Hu Yaobang. The subsequent seizure and occupation of the great square grew to enormous proportions and attracted students from the far reaches of China and the support of people from a variety of occupational groups. Throughout, the students pledged their adherence to nonviolence and democracy, although their precise views on either were unclear. Students challenged the government with defiance of martial law, hunger strikes, and symbolic displays such as the Goddess of Democracy statue. After various attempts to stop the movement, the PRC government cracked down violently, killing many in Beijing and once again placing the country under its control.

1065.   Cheng, Chu–yuan, *Behind the Tiananmen Massacre: Social, Political, and Economic Ferment in China.* 256 pp. Boulder CO, San Francisco, and Oxford: Westview Press, 1990. (Places the democracy movement and its outcome within several contexts, including Party politics and the cultural role of intellectuals as protesters. Ch. 6 is on the reasons for the repression of the movement and ch. 7 is on the international reaction. Appendix. Photos. Index.)

1066.   Cherrington, Ruth, *China's Students: The Struggles for Democracy.* 239 pp. London and New York: Routledge, 1991. (History of the student movement and Tiananmen actions, or "Patriotic Democratic Movement." Ch. 4–6 are on student politics through 1988 and ch. 7–9 are on 1989. Appendix 2 contains extracts from leaflets of May 1989.   Index. Bibliography.)

1067. *China in Crisis: The Role of the Military.* 119 pp. Coulsdon, Surrey: Jane's Defence Data, 1989. (Divides into a fairly standard military summary of the People's Liberation Army in the second section and brief pieces on the Tiananmen Square protests and the army's role in them in the first section. Of particular interest on the army and army leaders' motives in the protest period are Jonathan Mirsky, "Revenge of the Old Guard," pp. 3–10; Clare Hollingworth, "Martial Law in Beijing: Causes and Consequences," pp. 11–19; and Paul Beaver and Bridget Harney, "Role of the PLA in Tiananmen Square," pp. 21–30.)

1068. Dukes, Michael S., *The Iron House: A Memoir of the Chinese Democracy Movement.* 180 pp. Layton UT: Gibbs Smith, Publisher, 1990. (Personal account of the Democracy Movement from May 19, 1989 until its end, based in large measure on direct observation, including participation in the Free Speech Triangle and Free Speech Hours at Beijing Univ. Ch. 1, 3–6 are on the pre–crackdown phase and contain transcripts of conversations and big–character posters. Ch. 7, 8 are on the violence and confusion of June 2–4. Ch. 11 is on the subsequent purge and, on p. 148, the "passive resistance" of some who opposed it. Illustrations.)

1069. Editors of Time Magazine, *Massacre in Beijing: China's Struggle for Democracy.* Ed. Donald Morrison. 280 pp. New York: Time Inc. Books, 1989. (Ch. 1 contains an hour–by–hour description of the repression of June 2–4, 1989; ch. 4 is on the origins of the movement and events until late May; and ch. 5, 6 are on the aftermath in China and internationally. Chronology. Glossary. Photos. Index.)

1070. Fathers, Michael, and Andrew Higgins, *Tiananmen: The Rape of Peking.* Ed. Robert Cotrell. 148 pp. London, New York, Toronto, Sydney, and Auckland: *The Independent* in association with Doubleday, 1989. (The events of 1989 from the death of Hu Yaobang on April 15 to the aftermath of the June repression. Photos. Appendix. Index.)

1071. Han Minzhu [pseud.], ed., *Cries for Democracy: Writings and Speeches from the 1989 Chinese Democracy Movement.* Asst. Ed.

Hua Sheng [pseud.]. 401 pp. Princeton: Princeton Univ. Press, 1990. (Brief excerpts from documents and the texts of poems, Big–Character posters, and other sources. Arranged chronologically to cover the movement's origins and protests at the death of Hu Yaobang, the first protest marches, commemoration of the May Fourth Movement of 1919, the hunger strike of mid–May, martial law and the first confrontation with the army, and suppression. Editor's Foreword, pp. xvii–xxi, explains Big–Character posters and the sources of many of the documents in political ephemera. Photos. Index of documents. Index.)

1072.   Hicks, George, ed., *The Broken Mirror: China After Tiananmen*. 526 pp. Harlow, Essex: Longman Current Affairs, 1990. (Essays on various aspects of the Tiananmen events and their aftermath. Selections of interest include Jane Macartney, "The Students: Heroes, Pawns, or Power–Brokers?", pp. 3–23; David Kelly, "Chinese Intellectuals in the 1989 Democracy Movement," pp. 24–51; Geremie Barmé, "Confession, Redemption, and Death: Liu Xiaobao and the Protest Movement of 1989," pp. 52–99; Lucian W. Pye, "Tiananmen and Chinese Political Culture: The Escalation of Confrontation," pp. 162–79; Andrew J. Spano, "Death of a Dream in Rural China," pp. 310–19; and *Asia Watch*, "Punishment Season: Human Rights in China After Martial Law," pp. 369–89. Appendixes are by Joseph Y.S. Chen, titled "A Chronology of Selected Documents and Statements," pp. 475–96, and "Who Was Who During Beijing Spring," pp. 497–509. Index.)

1073.   *June Four: A Chronicle of the Chinese Democratic Uprising*. Trans. Zi Jin and Qin Zhou. 171 pp. Fayetteville and London: Univ. of Arkansas Press, 1989. Originally published in Chinese in Hong Kong by Ming Pao Publishing House, 1989. (Photos and text as compiled by Hong Kong's *Ming Pao* journalists, arranged chronologically. Photos.)

1074.   Li Lu, *Moving the Mountain: My Life in China from the Cultural Revolution to Tiananmen Square*. 211 pp. London: Macmillan, 1990. (Autobiography of a leader of the Democracy Movement. Ch. 8 describes the author's self–initiation into the politics of

China's students in travels from his Nanjing Univ. base; ch. 9, 10 are on his activities until the beginning of the hunger strike; and ch. 11 is on the hunger strike of May 13–19; followed in ch. 12, 13 by the students' refusal to obey martial law, continued protest, and the dispersal of the movement. Photos.)

1075. Liu Binyan, with Ruan Ming and Xu Gang, *"Tell the World"*: *What Happened in China and Why*. Trans. Henry L. Epstein. 195 pp. New York: Pantheon Books, 1989. (Ch. 1 recounts the movement, April–June 1989. In ch. 2, on causes of the movement, pp. 78–85 look at the Democracy Wall Movement of 1978–79. Chronology. Index.)

1076. Simmie, Scott, and Bob Nixon, *Tiananmen Square*. 212 pp. Seattle: Univ. of Washington Press; Vancouver: Douglas & McIntyre, 1989. (Quite detailed chronological account of the student movement, with some attention to its precursors in ch. 1. Photos of demonstrations between pp. 20–21, 116–17. Index.)

1077. Turnley, David, and Peter Turnley, photographers, *Beijing Spring*. 175 pp. New York: Stewart, Tabori & Chang, 1989. (Captioned photos of the Democracy Movement, mostly taken in and around Tiananmen Square, from about May 4 to the end. Photos of action begin on p. 44. Introductory text by Melinda Liu, "Beijing Spring: Loss of the Mandate of Heaven," pp. 25–43.)

1078. Wasserstrom, Jeffrey N. and Elizabeth J. Perry, eds., *Popular Protest and Political Culture in Modern China: Learning from 1989*. 300 pp. Boulder CO: Westview Press, 1992. (Joseph W. Esherick and Jeffrey N. Wasserstrom, "Acting Out Democracy: Political Theater in Modern China," ch. 2 casts the Tiananmen protests as political theater, or "symbol–laden performances whose efficacy lies largely in their power to move specific audiences," and also discusses similar aspects of protest in earlier decades. Jeffrey N. Wasserstrom, "Afterword: History, Myth, and the Tales of Tiananmen," pp. 244–80 identifies and challenges several faulty views of the movement. Index.)

1079. Yi Mu and Mark V. Thompson, *Crisis at Tiananmen: Reform and Reality in Modern China*. 283 pp. San Francisco: China Books and Periodicals, 1989. (A chronicle of the movement from the death of Hu Yaobang to the June days appears in parts 1, 2. Part 3 is on the press in the movement, including efforts to achieve press freedom. Appendix 1 contains various declarations and speeches. Appendix 2 reprints several eyewitness stories. Photos. Chronology. Documents. Index.)

INDIA

During the period from approximately 1919 until 1942, the Indian national movement was dominated by one of the few persons to form a strategic as well as a moral and intellectual approach to nonviolent action, Mohandas K. Gandhi. Nonviolent action challenging British rule actually began earlier than Gandhi's arrival on the scene, notably with the Swadeshi Movement of 1903–1905 in Bengal. However, Gandhi long dominated the chief organizational voice for independence, the Indian National Congress, when it became a direct–action organization during much of the independence campaign. He also gathered influential lieutenants about him who became adept at campaigns of nonviolent action against Britain and in other causes.

Besides their political activity, Gandhi and his followers assisted factory workers, tenant farmers, and India's severely disprivileged "untouchable" castes. The entries here are primarily on the independence struggle and on the person, writings, and ideas of Mohandas K. Gandhi. Historical sections cover the period of significant mobilizations, which are briefly explained in the prefaces. The final sections look at post–independence Gandhian and other social movements, including ecology and anti–state movements.

Nonviolent Struggle in the National Movement

The Indian National Movement was in part an outgrowth of the terrible losses in the great uprising of 1857, when politically divided Indian military forces nearly took control of the country from Britain, only to be defeated. The national movement began as an elite organization in 1885 with the founding of the Indian National Congress. Only after the turn of the twentieth century was direct action contemplated. The entries here compile information both on the contradictory politics of the national movement and the effects of Gandhi and his followers on its development.

1080.   Misra, B.B., ed., with the assistance of Aditya Prasadjha, *Select Documents on Mahatma Gandhi's Movement in Champaran*. 597 pp. Bihar: Government of Bihar, 1963. (Documents from Bihar archives and other sources on the conflict in Champaran, February 1916–May 1918. See list pp. 26–45 and appendixes. Index. Bibliography.)

1081.   Pandey, B.N., ed., *The Indian Nationalist Movement, 1885–1947: Selected Documents*. 272 pp. London and Basingstoke: Macmillan, 1979. (Collected documents with a chronology at beginning of each section. Index. Bibliographical notes.)

1082.   Sen, S.P., ed., *Historical Writings on the Nationalist Movement in India*. 251 pp. Calcutta: Institute of Historical Studies, 1977. (Bibliographical essays, arranged state by state.)

1083.   Sharma, Jagdish Saran, *India since the Advent of the British: A Descriptive Chronology, from 1600 to October 2, 1969*. 817 pp. Delhi: S. Chand, 1970. (Chronological survey of political, social, and cultural history of India. See part 2, 1896–1905; part 3, 1906–18; part 4, 1919–35; and part 5, 1936–47. Index.)

1084.   ———, *Indian National Congress: A Descriptive Bibliography of India's Struggle for Freedom*. 816 pp. Delhi, Jullundur, and Lucknow: S. Chand, 1959. (Detailed, partly annotated bibliography of Congress records and other sources, 1885–1958. Main series is in parts 1, 3; see headings under names of persons, movements, and groups. Exhaustive chronology begins in part 2 and is completed in part 3, pp. 751–52. Documents. Index.)

1085.   Singh, Amar Kaur Jasbir, ed., *Gandhi and Civil Disobedience: Documents in the India Office Records, 1922–1946*. 62 pp. London: India Office Library and Records, 1980. (See the introductory essay on Gandhi and the development of *satyagraha* and civil disobedience campaigns in pp. 1–18. A catalog of records in the India Office, London relating to Gandhi's political career is in pp. 19–47. Index. Bibliography.)

NINETEENTH AND TWENTIETH CENTURIES

The transition of the Indian National Congress from pressure group to direct–action organization is described in great detail in entry 1091. When Indian political leaders considered their options among strategies of action, their thinking was colored by the devastating losses of life and property in the great uprising or "mutiny" of 1857. In its early years, the Indian National Congress consequently restricted itself to "constitutional" political means rather than direct resistance.

1086.   Bartarya, S.C., *The Indian Nationalist Movement*. 409 pp. Allahabad: Indian Press, 1958. (History of the Indian nationalist movement starting in 1857. See pp. 55–64 on Gandhi. Ch. 3 covers 1885–1905; ch. 4, 1905–14; ch. 5, 1914–19; ch. 6, 1919–29; ch. 7, 1929–39; and ch. 8, 1939–47. Index. Bibliography.)

1087.   Coupland, Reginald, *Report on the Constitutional Problem in India*. Part 1, *The Indian Problem, 1833–1935*. 160 pp. Part 2, *Indian Politics, 1936–1942*. 344 pp. Part 3, *The Future of India*. 207 pp. London, New York, Toronto, and Bombay: Oxford Univ. Press, 1942–44. (Sometimes also titled *The Indian Problem: Report on the Constitutional Problem in India*. Parts 1, 2 published separately in 1942 and 1943. Oxford University–sponsored investigation into Indian politics. Part 1 discusses the constitutional background and, in ch. 6–10, examines conflicts from the 1919 struggle over constitutional reform to the aftermath of the Round Table Conference, 1935. Part 2, ch. 3–15 are on provincial government, both under the Congress and non–Congress governments. Ch. 22 is on Gandhi's role in the events of 1942. Appendixes. Indexes.)

1088.   Ghose, Sankar, *Political Ideas and Movements in India*. 558 pp. Bombay, Calcutta, New Delhi, Madras, and Bangalore: Allied Publishers, 1975. (History and analysis of Indian political ideas and movements of the nineteenth and twentieth centuries. See ch. 3, "The Gandhian Path," and ch. 4, "The Struggle for Freedom." Index. Bibliography.)

1089.   Masani, R.P., *Britain in India: An Account of British Rule in the Indian Subcontinent*. 278 pp. London, New York, and Bombay:

Oxford Univ. Press, 1960. (See ch. 6–20 on the period from 1858 to 1948. Photos. Index.)

1090. Mehrotra, S.R., *Towards India's Freedom and Partition*. 322 pp. New Delhi, Bombay, Bangalore, Calcutta, and Kanpur: Vikas Publishing, 1979. (Essays on the political history of India during the nineteenth and early twentieth centuries, with emphasis on independence movements. See ch. 5 on objectives and methods of the Indian National Congress, 1885–1920; ch. 7 on the "home rule" movement; and ch. 8 on Gandhi. Index.)

1091. Pattabhi Sitaramayya, Bhogaraju, *The History of the Indian National Congress, 1885–1935*. 1146 pp. Allahabad: Working Committee of the Congress, 1935. 2 vols. *The History of the Indian National Congress*. Vol. 1, 1885–1935, 690 pp. Vol. 2, 1935–1947, 1116 pp. Bombay: Padma, 1946. Reprint of 2d ed. Delhi: S. Chand, 1969. (The first title originated as a fiftieth-anniversary history and is unchanged except for pagination as vol. 1 of the second ed. In the second ed., vol. 1, see part 2, ch. 5 on the Rowlatt Bills *Satyagraha* of 1919; part 3, ch. 1–4 on the early 1920s; and parts 4, 5 on struggles of 1928–31. Appendix 10–A contains correspondence on the 1930 conflict. In the second ed., vol. 2, see ch. 10–12 on the question of *satyagraha* in 1940; ch. 14 on the Quit India Campaign; and ch. 18, 19 on Gandhi's fast. Appendixes. Indexes.)

1092. Prasad, Bisheshwar, *Bondage and Freedom: A History of Modern India, 1707–1947*. Vol. 2, *Freedom, 1858–1947*. 619 pp. New Delhi and Allahabad: Rajesh Publications, 1979. (History emphasizing "forces that started the movement for freedom by nonviolent methods." See esp. ch. 10 on the Noncooperation Campaign and ch. 11 on the Civil Disobedience Campaign. Index. Bibliography.)

1093. Sarkar, Sumit, *Modern India, 1885–1947*. 486 pp. Delhi, Bombay, Calcutta, Madras: Macmillan India, 1983. (Largely a political history and partly an economic one, focusing on mass movements, their diversity, and movements "from below." Incorporates recent work on caste, class, and popular mobilization. In the pre–Gandhi period, see pp. 53–54 on revenue withholding and pp. 106–24 on the partition of Bengal and the *Swadeshi* Movement of 1905–8. In ch. 5, on 1917–27, see pp. 168–78 on the economics of wartime and post–war claims on India's wealth, pp. 177–87 on Gandhi, and pp. 187–226 on the period from the Rowlatt Satyagraha to the end of the Noncooperation Campaign in 1922. Later sections of the chapter discuss political trends in the subsequent lull. Ch. 6 is almost entirely on the Simon Commission boycott and events associated with the Civil Disobedience Campaign, followed by a look at leftist and rightist trends in Congress politics. In ch. 7, pp. 388–405 are on the Quit India Movement of 1942. Index.)

1094. Suntharalingam, R., *Indian Nationalism: A Historical Analysis.* 471 pp. New Delhi: Vikas Publishing, 1983. 471 pp. (On nationalism, the roles of class and religion, and the history of the Indian National Congress. See ch. 6 on Gandhi, Congress, and the Noncooperation Campaign, esp. pp. 274–86. The Civil Disobedience Campaign and related issues are in pp. 314–36 and pp. 398–415 are on the WWII period. Index.)

INDEPENDENCE STRUGGLE BEFORE THE ARRIVAL OF GANDHI

The Indian National Congress came to dominate the national movement under the leadership of political rivals B.G. Tilak and G.K. Gokhale. On the action front, the primary event of the early twentieth century was a resistance campaign in Bengal (1903–1906) against partition of the province. A leading figure in these events was Bipin Chandra Pal, who is generally seen as an advocate of violence but who also explored nonviolent means in this conflict. Bengal's swadeshi *or self–reliance movement was carried out partly by boycotts on foreign (British) goods and efforts to substitute domestic products for them, a concept that influenced Gandhi in later stages of the independence struggle.*

1095. Dua, R.P., *The Impact of the Russo–Japanese (1905) War on Indian Politics.* 105 pp. New Delhi: S. Chand, 1966. (See ch. 9 on the Bengal *swadeshi* movement in 1905. Index.)

1096. Gopal, Ram, *How India Struggled for Freedom: A Political History.* 469 pp. Bombay: Book Centre, 1967. (See ch. 8 on the Bengal boycotts of 1903–06, including the leadership role of B.C. Pal, and ch. 14–21 on the Gandhi era. Index.)

1097. Sinha, P.B., *Indian National Liberation Movement and Russia, 1905–1917*. 336 pp. New Delhi: Sterling Publishers, 1975. (Study of the historical influence of the Russian Revolution on Indian nationalism. See esp. pp. 280–91 on Gandhi and Tolstoy. Consult index under *boycott, boycott–swadeshi movement, Gandhi, Great October Socialist Revolution, Russian revolution (1905–1907), satyagraha,* and *Tolstoy.* Bibliography.)

1098. Wolpert, Stanley A., *Tilak and Gokhale: Revolution and Reform in the Making of Modern India*. 370 pp. Berkeley and Los Angeles: Univ. of California Press, 1962. (History of the development of Congress until 1919 under the influence of B.G. Tilak and G.K. Gokhale. See esp. ch. 7, 8 on debates of the early twentieth century and the arrival of M.K. Gandhi. Index. Bibliography.)

INDEPENDENCE MOVEMENT, 1907–1947

This section is on the Indian national movement from the end of the Bengal campaigns until 1947. The following section contains entries on more than one aspect of the period, while subsequent sections concern themselves with specific sub–periods. These subperiods coincide with significant campaigns and major transition points in the movement. They include, (1) the rise of Gandhi and the first major satyagraha *in Champaran, (2) the campaign against the Rowlatt Acts and the associated Noncooperation Movement, including the Amritsar Massacre of 1919, (3) the period beginning with the boycott of the Simon commission of inquiry in 1928 and leading to the two phases of the Civil Disobedience Movement and the London Round Table Conference, and (4) the rest of the 1930s and 1940s, including Congress's years as a constitutional power and the Quit India campaign of 1942. See section introductions for more information on these events.*

Gandhi returned to India from South Africa in 1915, pledging his political mentor G.K. Gokhale that he would stay away from politics for a time. During this period he nevertheless engaged a body of followers and began to organize among farmers and labor. Once free from his pledge, Gandhi presented his concept of the nonviolent campaign and its techniques, or satyagraha, to his colleagues as the sovereign weapon in the independence struggle. Debates on strategy were not limited to constitutional versus nonviolent methods because, in the early years of the century, the "terrorists" had maintained, and acted upon their belief, that clandestine violent methods were also effective and legitimate. Although eclipsed for some years, this argument gained great strength in World War II with the formation of the anti–colonial Indian National Army (see entries 1101 and 1105). Nevertheless, Gandhi's influence and his qualities as an organizer and inspirer of talented followers (such as Jawaharlal Nehru and Vallabhbhai Patel) made satyagraha the primary strategy of the Indian National Congress for some years to come, whenever a direct challenge to Britain's policies arose. Several works cited here assess how the Gandhian ascendancy came about and its significance (see entries 1102, 1106, 1117, 1118, and 1128).

1099.   Azad, Maulana A.K., *India Wins Freedom: An Autobiographical Narrative*. 252 pp. Bombay, Calcutta, and Madras: Orient Longmans, 1959. (Written by Muslim Congress leader and later President of India, on the politics of the 1935–48 period. Appendix.)

1100.   Bhattacharya, Buddhadeva, in collaboration with Tarun Kumar Banerjee and Dipak Kumar Das, *Satyagrahas in Bengal, 1921–1939*. 351 pp. Calcutta: Minerva Associates, 1977. (Study of ten local *satyagraha* campaigns, including a case study of the Mahishbathan Salt *Satyagraha* of 1930–31, derived from primary sources, interviews, and field investigations. Index. Bibliography.)

1101.   Bose, Subhas Chandra, *The Indian Struggle, 1920–1942*. 476 pp. New York: Asia Publishing House, 1964. (Written by a popular nationalist leader and advocate of military struggle against British rule.)

1102.   Brown, Judith M., *Modern India: The Origins of an Asian Democracy*. 429 pp. Delhi, Oxford, and New York: Oxford Univ. Press, 1985. (The independence movement seen against the background of economic and political change. See pp. 202–23 on Gandhi's activities to 1922, pp. 255–83 on civil disobedience in 1930–34, pp. 283–306 on Congress's rise to power in the 1930s, and pp. 310–19 on Quit India, 1942. Index.)

1103.   Caveeshar, Sardul Singh, *India's Fight for Freedom: A Critical Survey of the Indian National Movement since the Advent of*

Mahatma Gandhi in the Field of Indian Politics. 2d ed. 480 pp. Lahore: National Publications, 1936. Originally published as *Nonviolent Noncooperation*, 1934. (Early report on the Indian nationalist movement from Gandhi's arrival in India to 1934. Documents in appendixes 7, 8. Photos. Index.)

1104. Chopra, P.N., ed., *India's Struggle for Freedom: Role of Associated Movements.* Assoc. Ed. Xavier Arakal. 5 vols. 843 pp. Delhi: Agam Prakashan, 1985. (Brief histories of groups, organizations, and movements active in politics at the same time as the Indian National Congress. In vol. 1, see ch. 1 on the Home Rule Movement of Annie Besant and the "extremist" Bal Gangadhar Tilak and ch. 2 on the *Swaraj* Party. In vol. 2, ch. 7 discusses peasant unrest in general and ch. 11 is on the *Khudai Khidmatgar* or Servants of God Movement among the Pathans. In vol. 3, regional and political rebellions are covered, including the Indian National Army, as well as social reform campaigns. In vol. 4, the Communist Party, trade unions, and women's organizations are discussed, along with ch. 20 on the *Akali* Movement among Sikhs and its relationship to independence agitation. Index and bibliographies for each selection are in vol. 5.)

1105. Choudhary, Sukhbir, *Growth of Nationalism in India, 1919–1929.* Vol. 2. 639 pp. New Delhi: Trimurti Publications, 1973. (Ch. 1, "Politics of Conflict," contrasts the Gandhian influence in Congress with "Young Revolutionaries" who advocated violence. Documents. Index.)

1106. Das, Durga, *India from Curzon to Nehru and After.* 487 pp. New York: John Day, 1970. (Political memoirs of a journalist. In book 1, ch. 9, 11, 12, discuss Gokhale and Tilak and ch. 13 is on the Noncooperation Campaign of 1921. Book 2 describes "the Gandhian Revolution" of the 1920s and 1930s. Documents. Index.)

1107. Datta, Kalikinkar K., *Renaissance, Nationalism, and Social Changes in Modern India.* 144 pp. Calcutta: Bookland, 1965. (Ch. 3 is on Congress leadership under Tilak, Gokhale, and Lajpat Rai and the Bengal movement of 1905. Ch. 4–7 are on subsequent phases of the independence movement. Bibliography. Index.)

1108.   Dhanagre, D.N., *Agrarian Movements and Gandhian Politics.* 128 pp. Agra: Institute of Social Sciences, Agra Univ., 1975. (A critical view of the role of Gandhi and the Gandhians in shaping and restricting peasant unrest. In reviewing the first major Gandhian rural *satyagraha* in Champaran, author concludes that four features characterized Gandhi's approach to all peasant movements, as follows: preference for minor over fundamental issues, settlement through compromise, representation of prosperous peasants, and cooptation of the poor peasants [pp. 29–30]. Studies include conflicts in Champaran, Kheda, Bardoli, Oudh, and the United Provinces, and the nationwide campaigns of 1920–21 and 1930–32. Glossary. Index.)

1109.   ———, *Peasant Movements in India, 1920–1950.* 254 pp. Bombay, Calcutta, and Madras: Oxford Univ. Press, 1983. (Case studies in the history of agrarian unrest informed in part by classic Marxist views on peasant social structure and revolution. The pre–Gandhian history of rural nationalist action is on pp. 43–49 and pp. 77–82 are on *Khilafat* agitation in Malabar and the associated Moplah Rebellion of 1921. Ch. 4 is entitled "The Bardoli *Satyagraha*: Myth and Reality." The myth is challenged by focusing on Gandhi's methods of revolution as well as his alliance with "rich peasants" over poor. Other chapters are on the Congress in Oudh in the 1920s and the activities of leftist parties from the 1920s to the 1940s. Index. Bibliography.)

1110.   Dwarkadas, Kanji, *India's Fight for Freedom, 1913–1937: An Eyewitness Story.* 480 pp. Bombay: Popular Prakashan, 1966. (Historical memoirs of the independence struggle to the year 1937 by an associate of Annie Besant, with special attention to her activities. See also ch. 10 on the Rowlatt *Satyagraha* and ch. 28–32 on the Civil Disobedience Campaign. Index.)

1111.   Edwardes, Michael, *The Last Years of British India.* 250 pp. London: Cassell, 1963. (Part 2 reviews the independence movement from 1917 to 1947.)

1112. Gopal, Sarvepalli, *Jawaharlal Nehru: A Biography.* Vol. 1, 1889–1947, 398 pp. Vol. 2, 1947–1956, 346 pp. Vol. 3, 1956–1964, 336 pp. Cambridge: Harvard Univ. Press, 1976–1984. (See vol. 1, esp. ch. 3–6, on Nehru's activities as an editor, politician, and Gandhian–faction activist in 1919–22; ch. 9, 10, 12 on the 1930–31 campaign, its preparation, and Nehru's imprisonment; and pp. 260–75, 291–303 on his wartime resistance and jailings. Glossary. Illustrations. Photos. Index. Bibliography.)

1113. Groyer, Sir Maurice, and A. Appadorai, eds., *Speeches and Documents on the Indian Constitution, 1921–1947.* 2 vols. 802 pp. Bombay, London, and New York: Oxford Univ. Press, 1957. (Documents on Indian constitutional questions with an overview in the introduction. On protest and noncooperation, see vol. 1, part 1, nos. 2, 8; part 2, no. 1 [3]; and parts 3, 4. In vol. 2, see part 2, no. 5, and part 4, no. 2. Biographical notes. Index.)

1114. Guha, Arun Chandra, *India's Struggle, Quarter of a Century, 1921–1946.* 2 vols. 890 pp. New Delhi: Government of India, Ministry of Information and Broadcasting, 1982. (Narrative of the Indian nationalist movement by participant. Part 1 focuses on phase of "passive resistance," 1921–39; part 2 is on "active or aggressive resistance," 1940–46.)

1115. Hardiman, David, *Peasant Nationalists of Gujarat: Kheda District, 1917–1934.* 309 pp. Bombay, Calcutta, and Madras: Oxford Univ. Press, 1981. (The politics of elites and peasants as Congress activists and nationalists in the district that spawned the Kheda *Satyagraha* of 1918. Ch. 4 describes nationalist views up to Gandhi's arrival in the area, esp. pp. 79–85. Ch. 5 is on the *satyagraha* and its combination of nationalist politics and cultivator distress; ch. 6 is on Congress organization and Gandhi's relationship with Vallabhbhai Patel; ch. 7 is on the Rowlatt *Satyagraha* and the Non–Cooperation Movement up to 1924; ch. 8 is on the interim between campaigns; and ch. 9 is on the Civil Disobedience Campaign, its phases, and its effects. Of interest, in addition to the details of revenue refusal and noncooperation, is collective emigration or *hijrat* conducted by villagers under repression, see pp. 55–58 on origins and pp. 208–34, 240–41. Glossary. Appendixes. Index. Bibliography.)

1116.   Henningham, Stephen, *Peasant Movements in Colonial India: North Bihar, 1917–1942*. 286 pp. Canberra: Australian National Univ., 1982. (History of peasant unrest in Bihar as the background for Gandhian and nationalist activities. Campaigns cited include the Champaran *Satyagraha*, pp. 46–50; the 1921–23 Noncooperation Movement, pp. 59–69 and ch. 4; the Civil Disobedience campaign of 1930–34, ch. 5; and violence in the Quit India campaign of 1942, ch. 7. Index. Bibliography.)

1117.   Lahiry, Ashutosh, *Gandhi in Indian Politics: A Critical Review*. 221 pp. Calcutta: Firma KLM, 1976. (Critical assessment of the influence of Gandhi on Indian politics from his return to India to independence.)

1118.   Low, D.A., ed., *Congress and the Raj: Facets of the Indian Struggle, 1917–1947*. 513 pp. London: Heinemann Educational Books, Arnold–Heinemann, 1977. (Studies of the politics of the independence conflict, including pieces by David Hardiman, Ravinder Kumar, Brian Stoddart, and David Arnold. Judith Brown writes on Gandhi as a leader, Johannes H. Voight addresses the problems WWII posed for Congress, D.A. Low discusses "civil martial law" in the civil disobedience campaigns, and R.J. Moore writes on British policy throughout the period. Index. Bibliography.)

1119.   Mookerjee, Girija K., *History of Indian National Congress (1832–1947)*. 276 pp. Meerut, Delhi: Meenakshi Prakashan, 1974. (See esp. ch. 12 on Gandhi's entry into Congress politics and part 2 on the independence movement, 1920–47. Documents in appendixes. Index.)

1120.   Nehru, Jawaharlal, *An Autobiography: With Musings on Recent Events*. 618 pp. London: John Lane, The Bodley Head, 1936. 2d ed. 628 pp. London: Bodley Head, 1953. Reprint, Bombay: Allied Publishers, 1962. (Political autobiography drafted in prison, 1934–35. See ch. 7, 10–14 on politics from 1919 to 1921 and ch. 24–38, 40–43, 47–50 on the 1930s. Later chapters describe Nehru's frequent cat–and–mouse style imprisonments in the 1930s. Photos. Appendixes.)

1121. ———, *The Discovery of India*. 490 pp. London: Meridian Books, 1946. 595 pp. New York: John Day, 1946. (A history of Indian culture and Indian nationalism, written in prison in 1942–44. Ch. 8 describes Congress and nationalist politics to 1939 and ch. 9 is on Congress's response to WWII. See esp. sections 5, 6, 10 on civil disobedience and the Quit India campaign.)

1122. ———, *Toward Freedom: The Autobiography of Jawaharlal Nehru*. 440 pp. New York: John Day, 1941. Reprint, Boston: Beacon Press, 1958. (Abridgment of Nehru's autobiography, entry 1122, with similar content. Glossary. Documents in appendixes. Index.)

1123. Pandey, Gyanendra, *The Ascendancy of the Congress in Uttar Pradesh, 1926–34: A Study in Imperfect Mobilization*. 246 pp. Delhi, Oxford, and New York: Oxford Univ. Press, 1978. (Stresses the limitations of the Indian National Congress in its approach to politics and resistance. See ch. 3 on Congress organizing and ch. 4 on propaganda as well as the boycott of the Simon Commission and the proliferation of the Civil Disobedience Campaign. Ch. 7 is primarily on the Civil Disobedience Campaign, focusing on agrarian issues before its inception, its participants, and its decline. Particular attention is given to the peasantry in shaping the movement, as well as Congress's arm's–length treatment of the poor peasants and their issues. Glossary. Appendix. Index. Bibliography.)

1124. Patil, V.T., *Nehru and the Freedom Movement*. 335 pp. New Delhi: Sterling Publishers, 1977. (Critical analysis of Jawaharlal Nehru's contribution to the independence movement. Consult index under *civil disobedience; demonstrations, mass; noncooperation; nonviolence; nonviolent;* and *satyagraha*. Index. Bibliography.)

1125. Ray, Rajat Kanta, *Social Conflict and Political Unrest in Bengal, 1875–1927*. 398 pp. Delhi, Bombay, Calcutta, and Madras: Oxford Univ. Press, 1984. (History of Indian nationalism in Bengal to 1927. See pp. 150–85 on the *swadeshi* movement and revolutionary terror and pp. 246–310 on the Noncooperation Movement of 1919–22. Index. Bibliography.)

1126.   Ross, Alan, *The Emissary: G.D. Birla, Gandhi, and Independence*. 240 pp. London: Collins Harvill, 1986. (Biography of a wealthy industrialist who was Gandhi's benefactor and occasionally his representative in discussions with the government. See chapters in pp. 41–178 on the independence movement era and Birla's relations with Gandhi. Index. Bibliography.)

1127.   Sharma, Radha Krishna, *Nationalism, Social Reform, and Indian Women*. 311 pp. Patna and New Delhi: Janaki Prakashan, 1981. (Study of the relationship between independence agitation and the Indian women's social reform movement, 1921–37. See ch. 2, 3 on women's participation in the nonviolent Gandhian movement and ch. 6 on the movement against *purdah*. Index. Bibliography.)

1128.   Sharp, Gene, *Gandhi Wields the Weapon of Moral Power: Three Case Histories*. 316 pp. Ahmedabad: Navajivan, 1960. (Contains brief studies of Gandhi's Champaran campaign in 1917–18 and his fast in New Delhi in 1948, with a lengthier case study of the 1930–31 independence campaign. Glossary. Index. Bibliography.)

1129.   Suntharalingam, R., *Indian Nationalism: An Historical Analysis*. 471 pp. New Delhi: Vikas Publishing, 1983. (History of Indian nationalism; see esp. ch. 6, "Gandhi and Noncooperation." Index.)

1130.   Sykes, Sir Frederick, *From Many Angles: An Autobiography*. 592 pp. London, Toronto, and Bombay: George G. Harrap, 1942. (See ch. 13–20 on the years 1928 to 1942.)

Gandhi's Return to India and Champaran Campaign

Several Gandhian campaigns were conducted to support tenant farmers and small landholders oppressed by high rents and taxes. The political significance of these struggles was not missed by the Government of India. The first such major conflict was the Champaran Satyagraha of 1917, which was initiated to defend poor indigo workers of the Champaran region of Bihar from excessive rents for their farmland.

1131.   Chaudhury, P.C. Ray, *Gandhiji's First Struggle in India*. 2d ed. 203 pp. Ahmedabad: Navajivan, 1963 [orig. publ. 1955]. (History of the Champaran *Satyagraha* and the government's response. Documents in appendix. Photos. Index. Bibliography.)

1132.   Mittal, S.K., *Peasant Uprisings and Mahatma Gandhi in North Bihar*. 283 pp. Meerut: Anu Prakashan, 1978. (History of peasant movements in North Bihar from the 1800s through Gandhi's time in the region, with attention to the condition of peasants after he left. See ch. 4 on peasant violence in the early twentieth century and ch. 5 on Gandhi's "intervention." Brief oral histories in appendixes. Index. Bibliography.)

1133.   Prasad, Rajendra, *Satyagraha in Champaran*. 2d ed. 224 pp. Ahmedabad: Navajivan, 1949. (The 1917 Champaran campaign as described by Gandhi's co-worker and later president of India. Appendixes. Index.)

1134.   Tendulkar, Dinanath G., *Gandhi in Champaran*. 115 pp. New Delhi: Government of India, Ministry of Information and Broadcasting, Publications Division, 1957. (History of "Gandhi's first *satyagraha* on Indian soil" in 1917, in support of impoverished Bihar indigo workers. Photos.)

Rowlatt Bills Satyagraha and Campaigns to 1928

Britain's post–World War I decision to reform the Indian government led to the Rowlatt Bills of 1919, viewed by many Indians as an attack on basic rights. Gandhi called for resistance, and opposition grew into a national campaign of noncooperation whose objective was to end British rule. Gandhi was arrested and tried in 1922, then jailed for a period. While he intended to maintain nonviolent discipline, political violence in many areas accompanied and even outpaced the nonviolent campaign. In the end, Gandhi withdrew support from the Noncooperation Movement because of this violence and called it off in 1922. The government also employed the army and police in repression of the movement. The Indian National Congress hoped to revive the resistance but found that most of the country could not support further action. Entries here include British government reports on the Noncooperation Movement (entries 1137, 1140, 1152, 1153) and on the Vaikkam (or Vaikom)

Satyagraha of 1924–25, in which Gandhi turned his attention to defending the rights of untouchables (1141, 1149).

1135.   Bahadur, Lal, *Indian Freedom Movement and Thought: Politics of "Pro–Change" versus "No–Change," 1919–1929.* Ed. J.C. Johari. 443 pp. New Delhi, Jalandhar, and Bangalore: Sterling Publishers, 1983. (History of the short–lived Swaraj Party. See ch. 2 on the concept of noncooperation and ch. 3, 4 on the 1920–21 campaign and the Swaraj Party. Index. Bibliography.)

1136.   Bakshi, S.R., *Gandhi and Non–Cooperation Movement, 1920–1922.* 293 pp. New Delhi: Capital, 1983. (History of the Noncooperation Movement against the Rowlatt Bills, 1920–22. See esp. ch. 3 on the boycott of schools and ch. 6 on "the Gandhian technique." Index. Bibliography.)

1137.   Bamford, P.C., *Histories of the Non–Co–operation and Khilafat Movements.* 270 pp. Delhi: Government of India Press, 1925. Reprint, Delhi: Deep Publications, 1974. (Detailed study of these two movements in 1919–22 by a British intelligence official. See ch. 1–6 on the Noncooperation Movement, esp. ch. 6 on the effects of boycotts. Appendix C reprints Congress's instructions to activists on boycotts, *swadeshi*, and organization, pp. 220–22. Index.)

1138.   Brown, Judith, *Gandhi's Rise to Power: Indian Politics, 1915–1922.* 384 pp. Cambridge: Cambridge Univ. Press, 1972. (First of two extended studies of Gandhi's politics; see also entry 1169. Ch. 1 reviews his career in South Africa. Early *satyagrahas* in Champaran, Kaira, and Ahmedabad are discussed in ch. 3; the Rowlatt Bills challenge in ch. 5; and the Noncooperation Movement in ch. 8, 9. Index. Bibliography.)

1139.   Chirol, Sir Valentine, *India.* 352 pp. London: Ernest Benn, 1926. (See ch. 12 on the Rowlatt *Satyagraha* and the Noncooperation Movement and ch. 16, 17 on politics in the following years. Index.)

1140.   Chopra, P.N., ed., *India's Major Non–Violent Movements, 1919–1934: British Secret Reports on Indian People's Peaceful Struggle for Political Liberation.* 188 pp. Delhi: Vision Books, 1979. (Reprints a section of entry 1137 and an anonymous 1936 government report on the Civil Disobedience Movement. Documents in appendixes. Index.)

1141. Desai, Mahadev, *The Epic of Travancore.* 251 pp. Ahmedabad: Navajivan Karyalaya, 1937. (On the Vykom [Vaikkam] *Satyagraha* of 1924–25 to halt discrimination against untouchables. Includes writings and speeches by Gandhi from 1925 to 1937.)

1142. Krishnadas, *Seven Months with Mahatma Gandhi: Being an Inside View of the Non–Co–operation Movement, 1921–1922.* 2 vols. Vol. 1, 449 pp. Triplicane, Madras: S. Ganesan, 1928. Vol. 2, 498 pp. Dighwara, Bihar: Rambinode Sinha, 1928. (Extremely detailed account of Gandhi's movements and activities and other events in 1921–22. Vol. 2, part 7, contains a summary of the Rowlatt Acts resistance. Appendix A has a portion of the Congress report on civil disobedience and appendix B has Gandhi's statement in court.)

1143. Kumar, Nagendra, *Indian National Movement, with Special Reference to the District of Old Saran, Bihar, 1857–1947.* 270 pp. Patna: Janaki Prakashan, 1979. (See appendix 1 for a protest resignation in 1920 and appendix 3 for a 1930 statement on nonpayment of taxes. Documents. Index. Bibliography.)

1144. Kumar, R., ed., *Essays on Gandhian Politics: The Rowlatt Satyagraha of 1919.* 347 pp. London: Oxford Univ. Press, 1971. (Case studies of the regions responding to Gandhi's call to resistance in March 1919.)

1145. MacMunn, Lt. Gen. Sir George, *Turmoil and Tragedy in India: 1914 and After.* 294 pp. London: Jarrolds, 1935. (Views the independence struggle as an essentially violent conflict. See ch. 3, 4, 7 on violence before and during WWI. Ch. 11 discusses the 1919 *satyagraha* and General Dyer's actions at Amritsar. Ch. 15 describes the Civil Disobedience and "Red Shirt" [Servants of God] movements. Photos. Index.)

1146. Minault, Gail, *The Khilafat Movement: Religious Symbolism and Political Mobilization in India.* 294 pp. New York: Columbia

Univ. Press, 1982. (See ch. 3, 4 on Gandhi and the Congress's support for Khilafat agitation among Muslims as issues in the 1920–21 Noncooperation Movement. Index. Bibliography.)

1147.   *Movement: Reminiscences.* 227 pp. New Delhi: Government of India, Ministry of Information and Broadcasting, 1971. (Accounts and reminiscences on the fiftieth anniversary of the Noncooperation Campaign.)

1148.   Pradhan, R.G., *India's Struggle for Swaraj.* 323 pp. Madras: G.A. Natesan, 1930. (History of the independence struggle from its beginnings to October 1929. See esp. ch. 9, 10 on the noncooperation movements, 1920–22, and ch. 12 on the boycott of the Simon commission. Index.)

1149.   Ravindran, T.K., *Vaikkam Satyagraha and Gandhi.* 372 pp. Trichur: Sri Narayana Institute of Social and Cultural Development, 1975. (A history of the Vaikkam [Vykom] *Satyagraha* campaign of 1924–25 in opposition to practices of untouchability. Challenges the standard view of the facts of the case. Documents in appendixes include Gandhi's writings and speeches, a record of his visit to Vaikkam, and official papers. Index.)

1150.   Robb, P.G., *The Government of India and Reform: Policies Towards Politics and the Constitution, 1916–1921.* 379 pp. Oxford: Oxford Univ. Press, 1976. (Ch. 6 discusses government policies and means of "repression." Ch. 7, 8 demonstrate both how repression was used and occasions when the government refrained from using these means against civil disturbances and *satyagraha* in 1920–21. Chronology. Index. Bibliography.)

1151.   Rumbold, Sir Algernon, *Watershed in India, 1914–1922.* 344 pp. London: Athlone Press, Univ. of London, 1979. (A study of the 1914 to 1922 period and the "management of British policy" in both London and India. Ch. 4–7 discuss policy reforms during WWI. Gandhi's 1919 movement and the violence that was its backdrop are discussed on pp. 138–49. Ch. 12, 14–16 detail the 1920–21 Noncooperation Campaign and its effects. Index. Bibliography.)

1152.   Williams, L.F. Rushbrook, *India in 1919: A Report Prepared for Presentation to Parliament in Accordance with the Requirements of the 26th Section of the Government of India Act (5 & 6 Geo. V., Chap. 61)*. 281 pp. Calcutta: Superintendent Government Printing, India, 1920. (See ch. 2 for an official report on the Rowlatt Bills *Satyagraha*, Amritsar Massacre, and other disturbances. Appendix 2 contains the Rowlatt Act text and appendix 7 contains Congress resolutions. Documents. Index.)

1153.   ———, *India in 1920: A Report Prepared for Presentation to Parliament in Accordance with the Requirements of the 26th Section of the Government of India Act (5 & 6 Geo. V., Chap. 61)*. 275 pp. Calcutta: Superintendent Government Printing, India, 1921. (See ch. 2, 3 on Congress and noncooperation. Documents. Index.)

1154.   ———, *India in 1921–1922: A Report Prepared for Presentation to Parliament in Accordance with the Requirements of the 26th Section of the Government of India Act (5 & 6 Geo. V., Chap. 61)*. 368 pp. Calcutta: Superintendent Government Printing, India, 1922. (See ch. 2–4 on noncooperation and political disturbances until Gandhi's arrest in 1922. Documents. Index.)

1155.   Zaidi, A.M., ed., *The Civil Disobedience Enquiry Committee Report, 1922*. 234 pp. New Delhi: Indian Institute of Applied Political Research, 1986. (Report by a group appointed by the Indian National Congress to investigate repression of the Noncooperation Movement and assess the readiness of the country to undertake further acts of civil disobedience. Findings are in ch. 1–5; appendix 1 contains the questionnaire used and appendix 8 contains accounts of repression. Documents.)

Jallianwalla Bagh Massacre, Amritsar, 1919

India was galvanized when a British unit under General Richard Dyer killed many people in Amritsar during the Rowlatt Bills campaign. The exact number killed is unknown, but Fein (entry 1158) supports a figure somewhat over five hundred. Sent there to restore order after the killing of British soldiers, Dyer ordered troops to fire and disperse a protest meeting in an enclosed square, the Jallianwalla Bagh. Many died on the spot. Although the British authorities essentially cleared Dyer, these killings became a focus of Indian anger about British violence for many years to come.

1156.   Datta, V.N., *Jallianwalla Bagh*. 183 pp. Ludhiana: Lyall Book Depot, 1969. (See ch. 1 on Gandhi and *satyagraha*, and ch. 2 on agitation and crowd violence in Amritsar. Ch. 3, 4 recount the massacre and General Dyer's evidence before the Hunter commission on his motives. Photos. Index. Bibliography.)

1157.   Draper, Alfred, *Amritsar: The Massacre that Ended the Raj*. 301 pp. Don Mills, Ontario: General Publishing, 1981. (Tale of massacre and its aftermath. Ch. 2 describes the Rowlatt *Satyagraha* and ch. 4–6 are on General Dyer's actions in Amritsar. Photos. Index. Bibliography.)

1158.   Fein, Helen, *Imperial Crime and Punishment: The Massacre at Jallianwalla Bagh and British Judgment, 1919–1920*. 250 pp. Honolulu: Univ. Press of Hawaii, 1977. (Sociological inquiry into the massacre as an episode of collective violence. Explores the background of British–Indian violence since 1857 and develops a theory of why such extreme punishment of Indian protesters was essentially accepted by the British government. See ch. 2 on the massacre itself and ch. 3, 4 on the background. Ch. 6 discusses subsequent official reports and ch. 7 analyzes Parliament's debates. Index. Bibliography.)

1159.   Furneaux, Rupert, *Massacre at Amritsar*. 183 pp. London: George Allen & Unwin, 1963. (History of massacre, written by journalist specializing in crime. Photos. Index. Bibliography.)

1160.   Horniman, B.G., *Amritsar and Our Duty to India*. 196 pp. London: T. Fisher Unwin, 1920. (Contemporary account and denunciation of Jallianwalla Bagh shootings and General Dyer's "terror" in Amritsar.)

1161.   Ram, Raja, *The Jallianwalla Bagh Massacre: A Premeditated Plan*. Ed. Bal Krishna. 208 pp. Chandigarh: Panjab Univ. Publication Bureau, 1969. 2d ed., 176 pp., 1978. (Presents case that British officials planned massacre. Ch. 4, 5 detail the situation in Amritsar and ch. 6 describes the massacre. Some revision of later chapters in second edition, which adds ch. 7 on official thinking. Appendixes. Bibliography. Index.)

1162.   Swinson, Arthur, *Six Minutes to Sunset: The Story of General Dyer and the Amritsar Affair*. 216 pp. London: Peter Davies, 1964. (Account of massacre and its aftermath, from British viewpoint. See ch. 2 on crowd violence in the city, ch. 3 on the massacre, and ch. 6–10 on reception in Britain. Bibliography. Index.)

Simon Commission, Round Table Conferences, and Civil Disobedience, 1928–1933

The high point of Gandhism and satyagraha as a political force was during the great challenge to British rule of the early 1930s. In the late 1920s, Britain again planned to reform Indian government and dispatched an inquiry commission under Lord Simon to assess local opinion. A nationwide boycott and protest met the commission on arrival in India. In 1930, Gandhi led the Indian National Congress to more aggressive action against British rule, including mass opposition to the tax on salt. The campaign initiated by Gandhi's "Salt March," in which he crossed India on foot to gather sea salt illegally, included a mass "raid" on the Darsana Salt Works. Thus Gandhi launched the 1930–31 Civil Disobedience Campaign to undercut the political and economic basis of British rule. For various reasons, such as violence in the movement and a wish to negotiate with Britain, Gandhi suspended the campaign during the Round Table Conferences in London. When a settlement did not result, he reinitiated Civil Disobedience in 1933. This second phase was suppressed by the government and ended direct political challenges for some years as Congress activists turned instead to constitutional politics. Besides secondary works on the period, entries in this section include several government reports, contemporary journalism, information on the Gandhian struggle in the Bardoli region of Bombay province on behalf of farmers (entries 1170, 1171, 1181) and Gandhi's lengthy fast on behalf of untouchables in 1932 (entry 1184).

1163.   Bakshi, S.R., *Gandhi and Salt Satyagraha*. 181 pp. Kerala: Vishwavidya, 1981. (Chronological study of the salt tax *satyagraha*, 1930. Index. Bibliography.)

1164.   ———, *Simon Commission and Indian Nationalism.* 238 pp. New Delhi: Monshiram Manoharlal Publishers, 1977. (See ch. 3–5 on the origin and spread of the boycott of the Simon commission. Chronology. Index. Bibliography.)

1165.   Brailsford, H.N., *Rebel India.* 262 pp. New York: New Republic, 1931. (Impressions from 1930 visit to India. See ch. 1 on people's motives for following Gandhi.)

1166.   Brockway, A. Fenner, *The Indian Crisis.* 208 pp. London: Victor Gollancz, 1930. (See ch. 9, 10 for contemporary account of civil disobedience campaign and Simon commission.)

1167.   Brown, Judith, *Gandhi and Civil Disobedience: The Mahatma in Indian Politics, 1928–1934.* 414 pp. Cambridge, London, New York, and Melbourne: Cambridge Univ. Press, 1977. (Second of author's works on Gandhi. See also entry 1140. Study of politics following his return to power in Congress ca. 1928. Ch. 3 is on the Salt *Satyagraha* and civil disobedience in 1930, with comments on various measures of their effectiveness. Ch. 4 is on the suspension of civil disobedience, and ch. 6 is on the second phase of civil disobedience in 1932–33. Evidence throughout on the nature and conduct of *satyagraha* and civil disobedience and the behavior of Gandhi, Congress, and the *Raj.* Index. Bibliography.)

1168.   Coatman, J. [John], *India in 1928–1929: A Report Prepared for Presentation to Parliament in Accordance with the Requirements of the 26th Section of the Government of India Act (5 & 6 Geo. V., Chap. 61).* 416 pp. Calcutta: Government of India Central Publication Branch, 1930. (See ch. 1 on strikes and violence during the years covered and ch. 2 on Congress and the arrival of the Simon commission. Documents. Index.)

1169.   Comming, Sir John, ed., *Political India, 1832–1932: A Co-Operative Survey of a Century.* 324 pp. London: Oxford Univ. Press, Humphrey Milford, 1932. (See ch. 10, 11 on Indian leaders; ch. 15, 16 on the Round Table Conference and current politics. Index.)

1170. Desai, Mahadev, *The Story of Bardoli: Being a History of the Bardoli Satyagraha of 1928 and Its Sequel*. 249 pp. Ahmedabad: Navajivan, 1957 [orig. publ. 1929]. (History of 1928 struggle in Bardoli, Bombay Province by agriculturalists resisting revenue increases, largely led by the Gandhian Vallabhbhai Patel. Index.)

1171. Dhanagase, D.N., *Peasant Movements in India, 1920–1950*. 249 pp. Delhi: Oxford Univ. Press, 1983. (See ch. 10, "The Bardoli *Satyagraha*: Myth and Reality." Index. Bibliography.)

1172. Gopal, S., *The Viceroyalty of Lord Irwin, 1926–1931*. 152 pp. Oxford: Clarendon Press, 1957. (See ch. 3 on boycotting the Simon commission and the Bardoli *Satyagraha* and ch. 5, 6 on civil disobedience campaign and settlement. 1935 decree in appendix. Index.)

1173. Grover, D.R., *Civil Disobedience in the Punjab (1930–34)*. 338 pp. Delhi: B.R. Publishing, 1987. (A study of the Civil Disobedience Movement and politics of the Punjab. Includes information on government repression of the movement and the role of the press, both legal and underground. Glossary. Appendixes. Index. Bibliography.)

1174. Henningham, Stephen, "The Contribution of 'Limited Violence' to the Bihar Civil Disobedience Movement." *South Asia* 2 (1979):60–77. (Exploration of the nature and use of "limited amounts" of violence in the movement, defined as "sabotage, intimidation, physical assault, and also social boycott when this was employed to cause grave personal inconvenience." Concludes that such actions were a significant factor in the outcome.)

1175. *India in 1930–1931: A Report Prepared for Presentation to Parliament in Accordance with the Requirements of the 26th Section of the Government of India Act (5 & 6 Geo. V., Chap. 61)*. 752 pp. Calcutta: Government of India Central Publication Branch, 1932. (Ch. 2, pp. 66–129, discusses Congress, the civil disobedience movement, and civil disturbances; pp. 370–80 present evidence on the effects of these conflicts on government finances. Appendixes 2–3 have material on the

Round Table Conference and civil disobedience movements. Documents. Index.)

1176.   *India in 1931–1932: A Report Prepared for Presentation to Parliament in Accordance with the Requirements of the 26th Section of the Government of India Act (5 & 6 Geo. V., Chap. 61).* 238 pp. Calcutta: Government of India Central Publication Branch, 1933. (Ch. 1 details political events from March 1932 to the end of the year; see also appendix 2 for documents on the civil disobedience movement. Index.)

1177.   Irwin, Lord [later Lord Halifax], *Indian Problems: Speeches by Lord Irwin.* 376 pp. London: George Allen & Unwin, 1932. (See pp. 74–115, 290–301, 321–25 on the 1930–31 campaign.)

1178.   Kaur, Manmohan, *Role of Women in the Freedom Movement, 1897–1947.* 287 pp. Delhi and Jullundur: Sterling, 1968. (See ch. 8 on women in the civil disobedience movement of 1930–35 and associated violence in Bengal and ch. 10 on Quit India in 1941–42. Appendix G contains material on conditions of imprisonment for arrested women. Glossary. Index. Bibliography.)

1179.   Malhotra, S.L., *From Civil Disobedience to Quit India: Gandhi and the Freedom Movement in Punjab and Haryana, 1932–1942.* 188 pp. Chandigarh: Punjab Univ., Publication Bureau, 1979. (History of Punjab Province in the independence campaign. See ch. 1, "civil disobedience movement in the Punjab"; ch. 5, "Individual Satyagraha in Punjab (1940–41)"; and ch. 6, "The Quit India Movement." Index. Bibliography.)

1180.   ———, *Gandhi: An Experiment with Communal Politics: A Study of Gandhi's Role in Punjab Politics, 1922–1931.* 248 pp. Chandigarh: Panjab Univ. Publication Bureau, 1975. (See ch. 8, "The Civil Disobedience in the Punjab," pp. 120–41. Index. Bibliography.)

1181.   Mehta, Shirin, *The Peasantry and Nationalism: A Study of the Bardoli Satyagraha.* 215 pp. New Delhi: Manohar, 1984. (History of Bardoli peasant *satyagraha* of 1928. See esp. ch. 3 on local leadership and mobilization, ch. 4 on the Gandhian

Vallabhbhai Patel, and ch. 5 on Bardoli as a local and national issue. Index. Bibliography.)

1182. Miller, Webb, *I Found No Peace: The Journal of a Foreign Correspondent*. 332 pp. New York: Simon and Schuster, 1936. (See ch. 16–19, 21.)

1183. Moore, R.J., *The Crisis of Indian Unity, 1917–1940*. 334 pp. Oxford: Clarendon Press, 1974. (Ch. 4 discusses "the Way of *Satyagraha*" in 1930–31, and pp. 239–96 take up renewal and suppression of opposition in 1932–33. Index. Bibliography.)

1184. Pyarelal [Nair], *The Epic Fast*. 327 pp. Ahmedabad: Mohanlal Maganlal Bhatt, 1932. (Gandhi's "fast unto death" in 1932 about the status of the untouchables.)

1185. Ranga Iyer, C.S., *India in the Crucible*. 336 pp. Reprint, Delhi: Ammol Publications, 1986. (Comment on Indian political reforms, written at time of Simon commission in 1928, as seen against the background of Congress noncooperation. Many comments on Gandhi and noncooperation throughout. Ch. 5 is on *hartal*, protests, and riots upon the arrival of the Simon commission.)

1186. Tomlinson, B.R., *The Indian National Congress and the Raj, 1929– 1942: The Penultimate Phase*. 208 pp. London: Macmillan; Toronto: Macmillan of Canada, 1976. (Study of Congress's response to government reforms, focusing on "constitutional politics." Index. Bibliography.)

From 1933 to Independence in 1947

The beginning of World War II aroused in many Indians the belief that Britain could be forced from the country. Congress followed Gandhi in the Quit India campaign of 1942, involving both personal demonstrations of noncooperation by Gandhi and other leaders and a nationwide civil disobedience campaign. The campaign resulted in both nonviolent and violent actions, to which Gandhi apparently gave an ambivalent response, and was repressed by Britain. Nevertheless, by war's end Britain was ready to withdraw from India. Gandhi later used his influence in an attempt to limit vicious communal violence accompanying the partition of India and Pakistan.

1187.   Bhagat, K.D., *A Decade of Indo–British Relations, 1937–1947.* 521 pp. Bombay: Popular Book Depot, 1959. (Chronology of last years of the *Raj.* See esp. ch. 3–8 on the government, Congress, and Gandhi from 1939–44. Quit India resolution is in appendix 17. Documents. Index. Bibliography.)

1188.   Bhuyan, Aron Chandra, *The Quit India Movement: The Second World War and Indian Nationalism.* 262 pp. New Delhi: Manas Publications, 1975. (Ch. 2, 3, 5 study the development of the campaign and Gandhi's fast. Ch. 4 discusses the "underground resistance movement" that emerged when Congress leaders were arrested in 1942. Index. Bibliography.)

1189.   Chopra, P.N., ed., *Quit India Movement: British Secret Report.* 407 pp. Faridabad, Haryana: Thomson Press (India), 1976. (Reprint, with introduction of report by British official on 1942 campaign. Report itself is followed by extensive "secret evidence," including intercepted letters, statements, and press extracts. Documents. Index.)

1190.   Dwarkadas, Kanji, *Ten Years to Freedom.* 296 pp. Bombay: Popular Prakashan, 1968. (Continuation of entry 1110. See ch. 5 on Quit India and ch. 6–9, 18–19 on Gandhi's activities later in the 1940s. Index.)

1191.   Glendevon, John, *The Viceroy at Bay: Lord Linlithgow in India, 1936–1943.* 288 pp. London: Collins, 1971. (Political biography of viceroy who served during much of WWII. Consult index under *Congress Party* and names of leaders such as *Gandhi, Jinnah, Nehru,* and *Patel,* as well as *civil disobedience* and *satyagraha.*)

1192.   Hutchins, Frances G., *India's Revolution: Gandhi and the Quit India Movement.* 326 pp. Cambridge: Harvard Univ. Press, 1973. (Interpretive history of 1942 campaign based on premise that it forced Britain's withdrawal from India and therefore independence was "revolution," not "gradual constitutional evolution." See ch. 6, "Gandhi as a Revolutionary Leader," and ch. 7–9 on the campaign. Index. Bibliography.)

1193. Mathur, Y.B., *Quit India Movement.* 212 pp. Delhi: Pragati Publications, 1979. (See ch. 1–3 on background and course of campaign in the provinces and ch. 4 on suppression of campaign. Index. Bibliography.)

1194. Mitra, Bejan, and Phani Chakraborty, eds., *Rebel India.* 260 pp. Calcutta: Orient Book, 1946. (Celebration and account of the 1942 uprising following Congress's Quit India resolution, province by province. Appendixes contain the resolution and various speeches, as well as materials on suppression. Photos.)

1195. Pandey, Gyanendra, ed., *The Indian Nation in 1942.* 268 pp. Calcutta and New Delhi: KP Bagchi and Co. for the Centre for Studies in Social Sciences, Calcutta, 1988. (Chronicles by several authors of the Quit India Movement in seven regions of India with attention to organization, actors, and actions. While various common themes emerge, most authors include discussion of the mix of nonviolent and violent means and the relation between violence in the movement and Gandhi's program and intentions. Several authors conclude that Gandhi was willing to risk and accept violence in order to maintain the challenge to Britain. See editor's introduction for summary. Index.)

1196. Panigrahi, D.N., *Quit India and the Struggle for Freedom.* 96 pp. New Delhi: Vikas Publishing House, 1984. (Brief history of Quit India campaign from 1942, with statistics of damages and government repression. Documents in appendixes. See esp. appendixes G and I. Bibliography.)

1197. Rizvi, Goroher, *Linlithgow and India: A Study of British Policy and Political Impasse in India, 1936–1943.* 261 pp. London: Royal Historical Society, 1978. (See pp. 161–67, 206–21 on Quit India and other actions in 1940–42. Index.)

1198. Venkataramani, M.S., and B.K. Shrivastava, *Quit India: The American Response to the 1942 Struggle.* 350 pp. New Delhi:

Vikas, 1979. (Description and analysis of Roosevelt administration response to 1942 Quit India campaign. Index.)

MOHANDAS K. GANDHI (1869–1948)

The following sections contain entries on Gandhi's life, thought, and writings. After spending his childhood in the small principality of Kathiawad, near Bombay, Gandhi later traveled to London to study in law. His emergence as a political figure took place in SOUTH AFRICA, where he remained until 1915. Returning to India, Gandhi became a force in political life and the most influential leader of the Indian National Congress (see introductions to preceding sections) until assassinated in January 1948. Gandhi's ideas on religion, ethics, diet, the "untouchables," simplified economics, and communal living developed alongside his views on nonviolent struggle. The entries here focus upon Gandhi's political significance and his concept of nonviolent action as a technique of political struggle.

See also: South Africa: Gandhi–led Struggles, 1906–1914; India: National Movement.

1199.   Deshpande, Pandurang Ganesh, compiler, *Gandhiana: A Bibliography of Gandhian Literature*. 239 pp. Ahmedabad: Navajivan, 1948. (Bibliography in eight Indian languages and English. Index.)

1200.   Indian Council of Social Science Research, *Mohandas Karamchand Gandhi: A Bibliography*. 379 pp. New Delhi: Orient Longman, 1974. (Classified and annotated bibliography of English–language books on Gandhi published before December 1972. Includes subject, author, and title indexes; each entry offers full table of contents and other information.)

1201.   Kovalsky, Susan Joan, ed., "Mahatma Gandhi and His Political Influence in South Africa, 1893–1914." 27 pp. Mimeo. Johannesburg: Univ. of the Witwatersrand, Department of Bibliography, Librarianship, and Typography, 1971. (Writings by and about Gandhi in his South Africa period, some written at that time but many later. List of sources consulted, p. iii. Index.)

1202.　Satyaprakash, ed., *Gandhiana, 1962–1976*. 184 pp. Gurgaon and
　　　　New Delhi: Indian Documentation Service, 1977. (Bibliography
　　　　of Indian English–language articles, research papers, notes,
　　　　news, and book reviews.)

1203.　Sharma, Jagdish Saran, *Mahatma Gandhi: A Descriptive
　　　　Bibliography, Book One and Two*. 2d ed. 650 pp. New Delhi: S.
　　　　Chand, 1968 [orig. publ. 1955]. (Annotated, primarily English–
　　　　language sources, catalogued by subject. Book 1 contains
　　　　material from Gandhi's birth to 1954. Book 2 compiles items
　　　　from 1954 to 1968. Index.)

Analysis and Interpretation

*Themes that emerge in the following sources include (until recent years) a
generally uncritical acceptance of Gandhi's views and efforts to coopt his
thinking for various causes, such as Marxism, socialism, and the like. Works
here that address political strategy also are generally concerned with
satyagraha and can be located in that way. One should distinguish between
ahimsa, Gandhi's concept of nonviolence and nonharm, and satyagraha, which
includes the strategy and organization of nonviolent struggle. Among the
significant works on satyagraha are entries 1212, 1216–19, 1224, 1228, 1231,
1235, 1237, 1241, 1244, 1246, 1249, 1254, 1259, 1261.*

See also: Ghana, Zambia.

1204.　Agarwal, Shriman Narayan, *Relevance of Gandhian Economics*.
　　　　256 pp. Ahmedabad: Navajivan, 1970. (Includes discussion of
　　　　decentralization, Gandhian socialism, *sarvodaya*, and Marxism.)

1205.　Balasubramanian, R., and T.S. Devadoss, eds., *Gandhian
　　　　Thought*. 194 pp. Madras: Dr. S. Radhakrishnan Institute for
　　　　Advanced Study in Philosophy, Univ. of Madras, 1981. (Papers
　　　　presented at Fourth All–India Conference of the Indian Society
　　　　of Gandhian Studies, January 1979. Emphasis on Gandhian
　　　　views of peace. See esp. ch. 2, 9, 18.)

1206.　Bandyopadhyaya, Jayantanuja, *Social and Political Thought of
　　　　Gandhi*. 415 pp. Bombay: Allied Publishers, 1969. (Social

scientist's critical analysis of Gandhi's thought in the context of the growth of state power and military weaponry. Index.)

1207.   Bhattacharya, Buddhadeva, *Evolution of the Political Philosophy of Gandhi.* 601 pp. Calcutta: Calcutta Book House, 1969. (Marxist examination of Gandhi's thought, including his views on human nature, history, society, economics, *satyagraha*, and political theory. Index.)

1208.   Bedekar, D.K., *Towards Understanding Gandhi.* 172 pp. Bombay: Popular Prakashan, 1975. (Socialist analysis of Gandhi's thought. See ch. 6 on Gandhi's emphasis on nonviolence, pp. 132–34 on *satyagraha*, and pp. 141–43 on relevance for contemporary era. Index. Bibliography.)

1209.   Bissoondoyal, B., *Mahatma Gandhi: A New Approach.* 138 pp. Bombay: Bharatiya Vidya Bhavan, 1981. (Study of Gandhism by a Mauritian, including Gandhi's influence on Mauritian independence movement.)

1210.   Borman, William, *Gandhi and Non–Violence.* 287 pp. Albany: State Univ. of New York Press, 1986. (A "critical exposition and evaluation of Gandhi's philosophy of non–violence." Section 1 is on *ahimsa* and section 2 is on practical application through *satyagraha*. Section 3 contains critical analysis of Gandhi's normative and prescriptive claims on nonviolent conduct and section 4 contains summary and recommendations. Illustrations. Index. Bibliography.)

1211.   Bose, Anima, *Mahatma Gandhi—A Contemporary Perspective.* 96 pp. Delhi: B.R. Publishing, 1977. (Ch. 2 is on Champaran *Satyagraha* of 1917, ch. 3 on the Rowlatt Acts *Satyagraha* of 1919, and ch. 4 on Gandhi's attitudes toward women. Index.)

1212.   Bose, Nirmal Kumar, *Lectures on Gandhism.* 129 pp. Ahmedabad: Navajivan, 1971. (See ch. 3, "An Introduction to *Satyagraha*," including examples of small–scale actions on pp. 24–43; see ch. 8 for a memoir. Index.)

1213.   ———, *Studies in Gandhism.* 2d ed. 358 pp. Calcutta: Indian Associated Publishing, 1947. 3d ed., 1962. 4th ed., 326 pp.

Ahmedabad: Navajivan, 1972 [orig. publ. 1940]. (Essays on economics and politics in Gandhi's thought. Bibliography.)

1214. Brock, Peter, *The Mahatma and Mother India: Essays on Gandhi's Non–Violence and Nationalism*. 223 pp. Ahmedabad: Navajivan, 1983. (Collection of essays on concepts of nonviolent conduct, nationalism, and populism in Gandhi's thought. See ch. 3 for study of 1962 Gandhian *Shanti Sena*, or peace army, and the threat of invasion. Index.)

1215. Chatfield, Charles, ed., *The Americanization of Gandhi: Images of the Mahatma*. 802 pp. New York and London: Garland, 1976. (Collection of magazine articles on images of Gandhi and his relevance for the U.S. See esp. "American Applications: Struggle for Racial Justice," pp. 723–57 and "American Applications: 1968 in *Fellowship Magazine*," pp. 773–802. Illustrations. Photos.)

1216. Chaudhury, P.C. Roy, *Gandhi: The Man*. 264 pp. Mysore: Geetha Book House, 1974. (Study of various facets of Gandhi. See ch. 3, "Gandhi as a Political Strategist." Index. Bibliography.)

1217. Dhawan, Gopi Nath, *The Political Philosophy of Mahatma Gandhi*. 3d ed. 363 pp. Ahmedabad: Navajivan, 1962 [orig. publ. 1946, 2d ed. 1951]. (Study of Gandhi's political philosophy emphasizing technique of *satyagraha*. See ch. 1 on "forerunners," ch. 7–10 on *satyagraha*, and ch. 9 on "the structure of the non–violent state." Index. Bibliography.)

1218. Diwakar, R. [Ranganath] R., *Saga of Satyagraha*. 248 pp. New Delhi: Gandhi Peace Foundation; Bombay: Baratiya Vidya Bhavan, 1969. (Revised and enlarged edition of next entry. Analysis of technique of *satyagraha* in ch. 1–21. Ch. 22–30 describe several *satyagraha* campaigns. Appendixes. Index. Bibliography.)

1219. ———, *Satyagraha: Its Technique and History*. 202 pp. Bombay: Hind Kitabs, 1946. Abridged U.S. ed.: *Satyagraha: The Power of Truth*. 108 pp. Hinsdale IL: Henry Regnery, 1948. (See previous entry. Glossary. Appendixes. Bibliography.)

1220.   Erikson, Erik, *Gandhi's Truth: On the Origins of Militant Nonviolence*. 474 pp. New York: W.W. Norton, 1969; London: Faber & Faber, 1970. (Psychobiography of Gandhi focusing on his identity development to the time of his return to India and its expression in the Ahmedabad strike of 1918. Parts 1, 3 are on the strike and part 2 presents author's view of Gandhi's personality. Part 4 explores aspects of this theory in relation to Gandhi's actions. Index.)

1221.   Fischer, Louis, ed., *The Essential Gandhi: His Life, Works, and Ideas*. 377 pp. New York: Vintage Books, 1962. (Selections from Gandhi's writings with attention to his biography, philosophy, and practice. Index.)

1222.   Gaur, V.P., *Mahatma Gandhi: A Study of His Message of Non–Violence*. 144 pp. New Delhi: Sterling, 1977. (Examination of the concept and practice of "non–violence." Photos. Index. Bibliography.)

1223.   Ghose, Sankar, *Socialism, Democracy, and Nationalism in India*. 503 pp. Bombay, Calcutta, New Delhi, Madras, and Bangalore: Allied Publishers, 1973. (Ch. 1, 2 discuss Gandhi's political method and its use in the independence struggle. Ch. 8, 12 contrast Gandhi with Nehru and various schools of Marxist thought. Index. Bibliography.)

1224.   Gregg, Richard B., *The Psychology and Strategy of Gandhi's Non–Violent Resistance*. 169 pp. Madras: S. Ganesan, 1929. Reprint, New York and London: Garland, 1972. (Preliminary study for entry 2359, *The Power of Non–Violence*. Argues that Gandhi's principle of nonviolent resistance is "universally valid." See esp. ch. 1–3 on psychology of the Gandhian approach.)

1225.   Gupta, Manmathnath, *Gandhi and His Times*. 310 pp. New Delhi: Lipi Prakashan, 1982. (Critical examination of Gandhi's beliefs and actions, contrasting Gandhi with the "revolutionaries." See ch. 4, "Tilting Indian Culture in Favour of Non–Violence," ch. 8 on the Salt March, and ch. 9 on Gandhi and Lord Irwin. Index.)

1226. Holmes, W.H.G., *The Twofold Gandhi: Hindu Monk and Revolutionary Politician.* 144 pp. London: A.R. Mowbray, 1952. (Analysis of Gandhi's dualism. See esp. ch. 5 on fasting and ch. 6–8 on *satyagraha*, its technique, history, and results.)

1227. Hunt, James D., *Gandhi and the Nonconformists: Encounters in South Africa.* 159 pp. New Delhi: Promilla, 1986. (On Gandhi's contacts in England and South Africa with "nonconformist" Protestants [i.e., denominations outside the Church of England]. Information on several of Gandhi's earliest English collaborators, esp. Joseph J. Doke, a supporter in South Africa. Ch. 3 contains a study of a "passive resistance" campaign by Nonconformist churches in England, ca. 1902–6, attempting to prevent encroachment on their conduct of independent church–sponsored schools and conducted by means of protests, demonstrations, and the organized non–payment of taxes. According to the author, it was in connection with this campaign that a British publisher brought out the edition of H.D. Thoreau's "On the Duty of Civil Disobedience" which was later read by Gandhi. Ch. 4 is on the Protestant clergy and Gandhi's efforts in South Africa. Photos. Index. Bibliography.)

1228. Iyer, Raghavan N., *The Moral and Political Thought of Mahatma Gandhi.* 449 pp. New York: Oxford Univ. Press, 1973. (Scholarly examination of basic components of Gandhi's philosophy. See ch. 8 on *ahimsa* and ch. 10, 11 on *satyagraha*. Glossary. Index. Bibliography.)

1229. Karunakaran, K.P., *New Perspectives on Gandhi.* 115 pp. Simla: Indian Institute of Advanced Study, 1969. (Analysis of political influence of Gandhi. Index.)

1230. Khanna, J.K., *Gandhi: On Recent Indian Political Thought.* 279 pp. New Delhi: Ess Ess Publications, 1982. (Study of Gandhi's continuing influence, including influence on Vinoba, J.P. Narayan, and Indian communists and socialists. Index.)

1231. Kripalani, J.B., *Gandhi: His Life and Thought.* 508 pp. New Delhi: Government of India, Ministry of Information and Broadcasting, Publications Division, 1969. (Section 1 on life, section 2 on thought. See ch. 40, "Theory of *Satyagraha*." Appendixes. Index. Bibliography.)

1232.   ———, *Gandhian Thought*. 281 pp. New Delhi: Gandhi Smarak Nidhi; Bombay: Orient Longmans, 1961. (Includes essays from the 1930s written during controversies about Gandhi's approach and Marxism.)

1233.   Lewis, Martin Deming, ed., *Gandhi: Maker of Modern India*. 113 pp. Lexington MA: D.C. Heath, 1965. (Commentary ranging in perspective from Quaker to communist on Gandhi's social and political significance. Bibliography.)

1234.   Lohia, Rammanohar, *Marx, Gandhi, and Socialism*. 550 pp. Hyderabad: Navahind Publications, 1963. (Analysis of the potential beneficial influence of Gandhi's approach on the future development of socialism. Index.)

1235.   Mathur, J.S., and P.C. Sharma, eds., *Facets of Gandhian Thought*. 127 pp. Ahmedabad: Navajivan, 1975. (Essays on the Gandhian concept of nonviolence. See esp. Gene Sharp, "Civil Disobedience in a Democracy," ch. 4; Stuart Nelson, "Gandhian Concept of Non–Violence," ch. 5; M. Al Shafaki, "Gandhi in the Arab World," ch. 9; J.S. Mathur, "Non–Violence and Rapidity of Change," ch. 10.)

1236.   Mukerjee, Hiren, *Gandhiji: A Study*. 2d ed. 225 pp. [New Delhi?]: National Book Agency, 1958. New Delhi: People's Publishing House, 1960. (A communist analysis of Gandhi's political career. Bibliography.)

1237.   Naess, Arne, *Gandhi and Group Conflict: An Exploration of Satyagraha: Theoretical Background*. 172 pp. Oslo: Universitetsforlaget, 1974. (Concentrates on the metaphysics and norms of Gandhi's philosophy. Appendixes. Index. Bibliography.)

1238.   ———, *Gandhi and the Nuclear Age*. 149 pp. Totowa NJ: Bedminster Press, 1965. (Discusses Gandhi's political ethics and compares them with those of Luther, Hobbes, Nietzsche, and Tolstoy. Bibliography.)

1239. Nanda, B.R., *Gandhi and His Critics*. 178 pp. Delhi, Bombay, Calcutta, and Madras: Oxford Univ. Press, 1985. (A collection of essays on Gandhi's thought and his opponents. See ch. 5, 6, 8, 13, 14. Index.)

1240. Panter–Brick, Simone, *Gandhi against Machiavellism: Nonviolence in Politics*. Trans. P. Leon. 240 pp. Bombay, London, and New York: Asia Publishing House, 1966. (Political biography of Gandhi with brief essay in ch. 7 on types of nonviolent action. Index.)

1241. Pattabhi Sitaramayya, B. [Bhogaraju], *Gandhi and Gandhism: A Study*. 2 vols. 520 pp. Allahabad: Kitabistan, 1942. (See vol. 1, part 2 on nonviolence and part 3 on technique of *satyagraha*.)

1242. Power, Paul F., ed., *The Meanings of Gandhi*. 199 pp. Honolulu: East–West Center, Univ. Press of Hawaii, 1971. (See ch. 2 on Gandhi's "lieutenants," ch. 3 on Gandhi in the independence movement, ch. 5 on Gandhi's nonviolence, and ch. 8–10.)

1243. Pradhan, Benudhar, *The Socialist Thought of Mahatma Gandhi*. 2 vols. 766 pp. Delhi: GDK Publications, 1980. (Analysis of Gandhian thought based on premise that he was a "convinced socialist." In vol. 1, see pp. 15–93 for history of Gandhi's socialism, pp. 174–78 on socialism and nonviolence, and ch. 4 on ends and means. In vol. 2, see pp. 404–12 on right to strike, pp. 451–54 on nonviolence and trusteeship, pp. 461–66 on nonviolent coercion, pp. 526–27 on nonviolent revolution, and pp. 575–81 on plea for nonviolence. Photos. Index. Bibliography.)

1244. Prasad, K.M., *Sarvodaya of Gandhi*. 276 pp. New Delhi: Raj Hans, 1984. (Analysis of philosophical roots of Gandhi's view of *sarvodaya*, the "nonviolent society." See ch. 4, "Gandhian Technique of Revolution: *Satyagraha*," esp. pp. 176–92 for typology of methods of nonviolent action. See also index under *satyagraha*.)

1245. Puri, Rashmi–Sudha, *Gandhi on War and Peace*. 244 pp. New York: Praeger Publishers, 1987. (An assessment of Gandhi's anti–war ideas in their development and context. Index. Bibliography.)

1246. Pyarelal [Nair], *Gandhian Techniques in the Modern World*. 2d ed. 66 pp. Ahmedabad: Navajivan, 1959 [orig. publ. 1953]. (Outline of "science of non–violence" as a technique and the possibility of its application. See esp. appendix A, "Armed Invasion and Non–Violent Resistance.")

1247. Radhakrishnan, S., ed., *Mahatma Gandhi: Essays and Reflections on His Life and Work*. 382 pp. London: George Allen & Unwin, 1939. 2nd ed., 557 pp. Norwich, G.B.: Jarrold & Sons, 1949. (Collection of essays and reflections on relevance of Gandhi. Appendixes.)

1248. Ramachandran, G., and T.K. Mahadevan, eds., *Gandhi: His Relevance for Our Times*. 355 pp. Bombay: Bharatiya Vidya Bhavan, 1964. Rev. ed., 393 pp. New Delhi: Gandhi Peace Foundation, 1967. Reprint, Berkeley CA: World without War Council, 1970. (Memorial volume, with contributions by Indian and Western activists and scholars. Photos.)

1249. Ramana Murthi, V.V., *Non–Violence in Politics: A Study of Gandhian Techniques and Thinking*. 246 pp. New Delhi: Frank Bros., 1958. (Part 1 discusses "Gandhian techniques" in his own time, with studies of *satyagrahas*; part 2 analyzes his doctrine. Index. Bibliography.)

1250. Rani, Asha, *Gandhian Non–Violence and India's Freedom Struggle*. 348 pp. Delhi: Shree Publishing House, 1981. (Political biography. Ch. 1 contains history–of–ideas approach to the "genesis, evolution, development, and the application" of Gandhi's version of nonviolence. Ch. 2–5 discuss development and application of his views. Bibliography.)

1251. Rao, M.B., ed., *Mahatma: A Marxist Symposium*. 136 pp. Bombay: People's Publishing House, 1969. (Essays from a Communist Party of India conference.)

1252. Rattan, Ram, *Gandhi's Concept of Political Obligation*. 346 pp. Calcutta: Minerva Associates, 1972. (Study of idea and limits of political obligation in Gandhi's thought. Part 1 is on political obedience and part 2 is on political disobedience, including ch. 8–11 on *satyagraha*. See also appendixes on Gandhi's *satyagraha* movements, imprisonments, and fasts. Index. Bibliography.)

1253. Ray, Annada Sankar, *Yes, I Saw Gandhi*. 205 pp. New Delhi: Gandhi Peace Foundation; Bombay: Bharatiya Vidya Bhavan, 1976. (Personal assessment of Gandhi as thinker and actor. See ch. 6–10, 14, 19.)

1254. Ray, Sibnarayan, ed., *Gandhi, India, and the World: An International Symposium*. 384 pp. Bombay: Nachiketa Publications, 1970. (See pieces by S.P. Aiyar on Gandhi and the Congress "moderates"; Hugh F. Owen on 1920–22 campaign; Stanley Maron on the "non–universality of *Satyagraha*" in modern political conditions; and Maurice Friedman on contrasting power of violence and nonviolence. Index.)

1255. Rudolph, Susanne Hoeber, and Lloyd Rudolph, *Gandhi: The Traditional Roots of Charisma*. 95 pp. Chicago: Univ. of Chicago Press, 1967. (An essay on Gandhi's charismatic authority as located within Indian cultural categories. Ch. 2, "Gandhi and the New Courage," charts some traditions of nonviolent resistance thought in India and their relation to Gandhi.)

1256. Santhanam, K., *Satyagraha and the State*. 96 pp. New York: Asia Publishing House, 1960. (Reflections on the Gandhian method and state power; see ch. 5 on the state and ch. 7–14 on application of *satyagraha* to questions of law, power, and resistance.)

1257. Seshachari, C., *Gandhi and the American Scene: An Intellectual History and Inquiry*. 191 pp. Bombay: Nachiketa Publications Limited, 1969. (Survey of Gandhian thought and its influence upon subsequent American theorists and activists. See ch. 5 for an exploration of the Gandhian method, and ch. 8 for an analysis of the influence of Gandhian thought on the civil rights movement in the U.S. Ch. 9 compares the leadership of Gandhi and Martin Luther King, Jr., as well as the dynamics and difficulties that each leader's respective movement encountered. Index.)

1258.   Sharma, Bishan Sarup, *Gandhi as a Political Thinker*. 164 pp. Allahabad: Indian Press, 1956. (Focuses on Gandhi's political philosophy and views on social and political structure. Bibliography.)

1259.   Sharp, Gene, *Gandhi as a Political Strategist: With Essays on Ethics and Politics*. 357 pp. Boston: Porter Sargent, 1979. (Part 1 contains essays on Gandhi's politics, theory, and contributions to thinking on peace and defense. See also review essays of Erikson, *Gandhi's Truth*, entry 1220, and Bondurant, *Conquest of Violence*, entry 2324. Part 2 contains essays on the relationship between ethics and political struggle, particularly nonviolent struggle. See also comments on Shridharani's *War without Violence*, entry 2344, and on Gandhi's position on WWII at the time of the Quit India campaign of 1942. Bibliography in appendix D.)

1260.   Singh, K.N., *Gandhi and Marx: An Ethico–Philosophical Study*. 176 pp. Patna: Associated Book Agency, 1979. (Critical comparative study of Gandhian and Marxist ethics. See ch. 9, "The Problem of Means and Ends," for discussion of violent vs. nonviolent means. Index. Bibliography.)

1261.   Sonnleitner, Michael W., *Gandhian Nonviolence: Levels of Satyagraha*. 92 pp. New Delhi: Abhinar, 1985. (Examines *satyagraha* as classified into three "levels": method/technique, religious discipline, and soul force. See esp. "*Satyagraha* as Method/Technique," pp. 16–30. Index. Bibliography.)

1262.   Ulyanovsky, Rostislav, *Present–Day Problems in Asia and Africa: Theory, Politics, Personalities*. 240 pp. Moscow: Progress Publishers, 1980 [orig. publ. in Russian, 1978]. (Soviet theoretical essay on national liberation struggles. Section on Gandhi, pp. 163–96.)

1263.   Winslow, Jack C., and Verrier Elwin, *Gandhi: The Dawn of Indian Freedom*. 224 pp. New York, Chicago, London and Edinburgh: Fleming H. Revell, [1931]. (Essays on Indian independence and Gandhi. See ch. 3, "The Meaning of Satyagraha," esp. pp. 110–11. Index.)

Biography

Gandhi's biographers usually divide his life into several phases. After his early years, London studies, and South African experience, he entered the ruling clique of the Indian National Congress and was later eclipsed after the losses of the Noncooperation Movement. Again in prominence during the lead–up to the Civil Disobedience Movement, he withdrew somewhat from politics until 1942, at that time becoming the moral, if not political, leader of the final push toward independence. Works on the time before his return to India include Bhattacharya, Devanesan, Doke, Green, Hunt, Pyarelal, and Rolland. Those primarily on the period from 1919 to 1944 include Bolton, Bose, Karaka, Pyarelal, Raman, Walker, and Watson. Those on the last years include Gandhi and Pyarelal.

1264. Alexander, Horace, *Gandhi Through Western Eyes.* 218 pp. Philadelphia PA: New Society Publishers, 1984 [orig. publ. 1969]. (Biography and memoirs by British acquaintance of Gandhi from 1928–1948. See pp. 38–42 on non–cooperation campaign of 1920–1922, ch. 7 on "Quit India" campaign (1939–1945). See also index under *civil disobedience* and *satyagraha.* Appendix (pp. 189–211) contains letters from Gandhi to author. Index.)

1265. Ashe, Geoffrey, *Gandhi.* 404 pp. New York: Stein & Day, 1968. (Popular biography. Illustrations. Index. Bibliography.)

1266. Bhattacharya, Bhabani C., *Mahatma Gandhi.* 236 pp. New Delhi: Arnold–Heinemann, 1977. (Gandhi as seen through his reading, writing, and contacts with writers. See ch. 6 on his reaction to Thoreau, ch. 9 on *satyagraha*, and ch. 18 for comments on the pamphlet *Hind Swaraj* of 1908, entry 1328.)

1267. Bolton, Glorney, *The Tragedy of Gandhi.* 326 pp. London: George Allen & Unwin, 1934. (Critical journalistic biography of Gandhi. See pp. 15–20 for condemnation of Gandhi, ch. 7 on *satyagraha* in South Africa, and ch. 10 on civil disobedience movement. Index.)

1268. Bose, Anima, *Mahatma Gandhi: A Contemporary Perspective.* 96 pp. Delhi: B.R. Publishing, 1977. (Ch. 3 contains a history of the

Champaran *Satyagraha* of 1917 and ch. 4 studies the Rowlatt
Acts resistance in 1919. Index.)

1269.   Brown, Judith M., *Gandhi: Prisoner of Hope*. 440 pp. New Haven
         and London: Yale Univ. Press, 1989. (Biography of Gandhi that
         stresses his politics, personality, and spiritual strivings.
         Accounts of his public and political life are chronological; see
         index under *ahimsa* and *Gandhi: attitudes* for his concepts and
         their development. Photos. Index.)

1270.   Dalal, C.B., *Gandhi, 1915–1948: A Detailed Chronology*. 210 pp.
         Bombay: Bharatiya Vidya Bhavan, 1961. Reprint, New Delhi:
         Gandhi Peace Foundation, 1971. (Chronology of Gandhi's
         years in Indian politics, with separate indexes for places and
         names. See also list of Gandhi's fasts and imprisonments, p.
         204. Appendixes. Index. Bibliography.)

1271.   Devanesan, Chandsan D.S., *The Making of the Mahatma*. 432 pp.
         Madras: Orient Longmans, 1969. (Biography of Gandhi in his
         formative years, up to age forty. Ch. 1–3 describe the cultural
         and familial milieu of Kathiawad, ch. 5 is on the South African
         experience, and ch. 6 is a critique of *Hind Swaraj* [entry 1328].
         Focuses on East–West cultural conflict in Gandhi's life. Index.
         Bibliography.)

1272.   Doke, Joseph J., *M.K. Gandhi: An Indian Patriot in South Africa*.
         97 pp. London: London Indian Chronicle, 1909. Reprint, 103
         pp. Madras: G.A. Natesan, 1919. (Biography of Gandhi and
         account of "passive resistance" by Indians in South Africa.
         Writer was an early supporter of Gandhi. Section on Gandhi's
         political life begins on p. 33. See esp. pp. 83–88 on the concept
         of passive resistance [in the Natesan ed., pp. 86–93].)

1273.   Easwaran, Eknath, *Gandhi the Man*. 184 pp. 2d ed. Petaluma
         CA: Nilgiri Press, 1978 [orig. publ. 1973]. (Heavily illustrated
         biography of Gandhi. See appendix, "How *Satyagraha* Works,"
         by Timothy Flinders. Photos. Index.)

1274.   Edwardes, Michael, *The Myth of the Mahatma: Gandhi, the
         British, and the Raj*. 270 pp. London: Constable, 1986. (Part 4

contains a debunking account of episodes in Gandhi's life.
Illustrations. Photos. Index.)

1275. Fischer, Louis, *Gandhi: His Life and Message for the World.* 192
pp. New York: Mentor, New American Library, 1954.
(Biography stressing Gandhi's personal, religious, and political
development. Index.)

1276. ———,*The Life of Mahatma Gandhi.* 558 pp. New York: Harper
& Bros., 1950. London: Jonathan Cape, 1951. Reprint, New
York: Collier Books, 1969. Reprint, New York: Harper & Row,
1983. (Part 1 is on Gandhi's life and thought in the South
Africa period and part 2 is on his political life in India, 1915–
46. Photos. Index.)

1277. Gandhi, Manubehn, *The Lonely Pilgrim: Gandhiji's Noakhali
Pilgrimage.* 273 pp. Ahmedabad: Navajivan, 1964. (Account of
Gandhi's efforts to stop Hindu–Muslim riots in Noakhali,
Bengal, December 1946–March 1947.)

1278. Gas, Durga, ed., *Gandhi in Cartoons.* 240 pp. Ahmedabad:
Shantilal H. Shah, Navajivan Trust, 1970. (112 historical
cartoons on Gandhi from exhibition at Gandhi Museum, New
Delhi, April 1969. Many have period reactions to his politics
from South Africa on. See esp. the cartoons on pp. 17, 29, 31,
33, 37, 55, 57, 63, 65, 75, 149, 207, 239.)

1279. Gopalaswami, K., *Gandhi and Bombay.* 566 pp. Bombay: Gandhi
Smarak Nidhi and Bharatiya Vidya Bhavan, 1969. (Study of
Gandhi's activities in, and influence on, Bombay. Photos.
Index. Bibliography.)

1280. Gray, R.M., and Manilal C. Parekh, *Mahatma Gandhi: An Essay
in Appreciation.* 136 pp. London: Student Christian Movement,
[1924]. (Biography of Gandhi through early 1920s. See ch. 7, 8
on the noncooperation campaign. Illustrations. Photos. Index.)

1281. Green, Martin, *The Origins of Nonviolence: Tolstoy and Gandhi
and Their Historical Settings.* 256 pp. University Park PA and
London: Pennsylvania State Univ. Press, 1986. (Parallel
biographies tracing the roots of Gandhi's and Tolstoy's

philosophies of nonviolence, focusing on intellectual
development. See pp. 1–7 for direct contact between the two
and ch. 9–12 for Gandhi exclusively. Index. Bibliography.)

1282.   Hunt, James D., *Gandhi in London*. 264 pp. New Delhi: Promilla,
         1978. (London as a site of Gandhi's education and political
         activity. See pp. 14–20 on legal studies; ch. 3, 9 on trips to
         London from South Africa, including pp. 137–42 on his
         reaction to the women's suffrage campaign; and ch. 7 on 1931.
         Illustrations. Photos. Index. Bibliography.)

1283.   Jack, Homer A., ed., *The Gandhi Reader: A Source Book of His Life
         and Writings*. 532 pp. Bloomington: Indiana Univ. Press, 1956.
         (Collection of excerpts from writings by Gandhi and his
         contemporaries, arranged as a biography. See esp. ch. 3, 4 on
         South Africa, ch. 10 on the 1930 Salt March, and ch. 12 on the
         1932 fast. Index. Bibliography.)

1284.   Karaka, D.F., *Out of Dust*. 7th ed. 258 pp. Bombay: Thacker,
         1968 [orig. publ. 1940]. (Journalistic biography of Gandhi.)

1285.   Keer, Dhananjay, *Mahatma Gandhi: Political Saint and Unarmed
         Prophet*. 819 pp. Bombay: Popular Prakashan, 1973. (Political
         biography. Index.)

1286.   Kripalani, J.B., *Gandhi: His Life and Thought*. 508 pp. New Delhi:
         Government of India, Ministry of Information and
         Broadcasting, Publications Division, 1970. (Part 1 is a standard
         biography, followed by "an integral approach" to Gandhi's
         thought in part 2. Ch. 40 discusses idea of *satyagraha*.
         Documents in Appendixes. Index. Bibliography.)

1287.   ———, *The Gandhian Way*. 3d ed. 184 pp. Bombay: Vora, [orig.
         publ. 1945]. (Essays by Congress leader from 1930s. See part
         two on "non–violence" and Congress, including essay "Non–
         Violent Revolution," and ch. 14, "The Gandhian Way.")

1288.   Kulkami, V.B., *The Indian Triumvirate: A Political Biography of
         Mahatma Gandhi, Sardar Patel, and Pandit Nehru*. 728 pp.
         Bombay: Bharatiya Vidya Bhavan, 1969. (See ch. 2–7 on

Gandhi and ch. 8–12 on his collaborator Vallabhbhai Patel. Index.)

1289. Mehta, Ved, *Mahatma Gandhi and His Apostles*. 260 pp. New York: Viking Press, 1977. (Journalistic biography of Gandhi and Gandhians. See esp. pp. 33–46, 56–68 on living Gandhians. See also *"Satyagraha* in South Africa," pp. 119–30; *"Satyagraha* in India," pp. 131–54; and "Nonviolence: Brahmacharya and Goat's Milk," pp. 179–213. Index.)

1290. Moon, Penderel, *Gandhi and Modern India*. 312 pp. New York: W.W. Norton, 1969. (Straightforward political biography. Comments on the ambiguity of Gandhi's position on nonviolence appear on pp. 279–85. Glossary. Index. Bibliography.)

1291. Namboodiripad, E.M.S., *The Mahatma and the Ism*. Rev. ed. 132 pp. Calcutta: National Book Agency, 1981 [orig. publ. 1958]. (Marxist–Leninist corrective to standard views, based on Tendulkar's *Mahatma*, entry 1303. See esp. ch. 13–15 for appraisal of Gandhism.)

1292. Nanda, B. [Bal] R., *Mahatma Gandhi: A Biography*. 542 pp. Boston: Beacon Press; London: George Allen & Unwin, 1958. (Book 1, ch. 1–15, describe Gandhi's South Africa years; book 2, his "emergence" as a leader up to 1922; book 3, the 1930s and Gandhi's varied interests of those years; and book 4, the WWII years and after. Glossary. Index. Bibliography.)

1293. Payne, Robert, *The Life and Death of Mahatma Gandhi*. 703 pp. New York: E.P. Dutton; London: Bodley Head, 1969. (Extended political and spiritual biography, depending heavily on Gandhi's own writings. Glossary. Photos. Chronology. Index. Bibliography.)

1294. Polak, H. [Henry] S.L., H.N. Brailsford, and Lord Pethick–Lawrence, *Mahatma Gandhi*. 320 pp. London: Odhams Press, 1949. (Divides Gandhi's life into early years, 1849–1914; middle years, 1915–39; and last years, 1939–48. Author Polak was a South Africa collaborator of Gandhi. Illustrations. Index.)

1295.   Prasad, Rajendra, *At the Feet of Mahatma Gandhi.* 335 pp. New York: Asia Publishing House, 1961. (Combines personal memoir and political biography, beginning with the Champaran campaign. Index.)

1296.   Pyarelal [Nair], *The Epic Fast.* 328 pp. Ahmedabad: Mohanlal Maganlal Bhatt; New York: Universal, 1932. (Account of Gandhi's September 1932 "fast unto death" to protest treatment of untouchables. Includes excerpts from speeches and writings by Gandhi and others. Chronology.)

1297.   ———, *Mahatma Gandhi: The Early Phase.* 854 pp. Ahmedabad: Navajivan, 1965. (Detailed biography of Gandhi from birth until his return to South Africa from a visit to India in 1896. Writer was warden of extensive collection of Gandhiana from which much of account is taken. Illustrations. Photos. Documents in appendixes. Index.)

1298.   ———, *Mahatma Gandhi: The Last Phase.* 2 vols. Vol. 1, 750 pp. Vol. 2, 887 pp. Ahmedabad: Navajivan, 1956–58. 2d ed. 2 vols. Vol. 1, 367 pp., 1965. Vol. 2, 375 pp., 1966. (Detailed biography of Gandhi from his release from prison in 1944 until his death. Writer was warden of extensive collection of Gandhiana from which much of account is taken. Vol. 1 occasionally bound as two books. Photos. Glossary. Index.)

1299.   Raman, T.A., *What Does Gandhi Want?* 117 pp. New York, London, and Toronto: Oxford Univ. Press, 1942. (Record of Gandhi's statements on WWII with excerpts from writings and speeches, 1939–42. See index under *nonviolence.* See also appendix 1, "Gandhi's Passive Resistance Movements" and appendix 2, "Hunger Strikes." Photos. Index.)

1300.   Rolland, Romain, *Mahatma Gandhi: The Man Who Became One with the Universal Being.* Trans. Catherine D. Groth. 250 pp. New York and London: Century, 1924. (Impressionistic early biography of Gandhi up to the noncooperation movement of 1919–22. Bibliography.)

1301.   Sheean, Vincent, *Lead, Kindly Light.* 374 pp. New York: Random House, 1949. (Journalistic account of author's trips to

India, Gandhi's actions, and his relationship to Hinduism. See ch. 4, "The Way of Action," and appendix, "Forerunners of Gandhi." Index. Bibliography.)

1302. Shirer, William L., *Gandhi: A Memoir.* 255 pp. New York: Simon & Schuster, 1979. (Journalistic biography/memoir of Gandhi. Photos. Index.)

1303. Tendulkar, Dinanath G., *Mahatma: Life of Mohandas Karamchand Gandhi.* 8 vols. Vol. 1, 1869–1920, 338 pp. Vol. 2, 1920–29, 394 pp. Vol. 3, 1930–34, 327 pp. Vol. 4, 1934–38, 330 pp. Vol. 5, 1938–40, 355 pp. Vol. 6, 1940–45, 315 pp. Vol. 7, 1945–47, 426 pp. Vol. 8, 1947–48, 336 pp. Bombay: Vithalbai K. Javeri & D.G. Tendulkar, 1951–54. Rev. ed., New Delhi: Government of India, Ministry of Information and Broadcasting, Publications Division, 1960–63. (Very detailed biography of Gandhi, relying heavily on his own writings. Photos. Documents. Appendixes. Indexes.)

1304. *Trial of Gandhiji.* 268 pp. Ahmedabad: V.R. Shah, Registrar, High Court of Gujarat, 1965. (Gujarat State High Court records of March 13, 1922, trial. Includes evidence, statements, and transcripts. Introduction by J.M. Shelat gives a history of events surrounding the trial. Plates contain facsimiles of documents. Illustrations. Index.)

1305. Walker, Roy, *Sword of Gold: A Life of Mahatma Gandhi.* 200 pp. London: Indian Independence Union, 1945. (See ch. 2, 3 on South Africa struggles, ch. 7 on 1930 civil disobedience campaign, and ch. 9 on other campaigns of the early 1930s. Photos.)

1306. Watson, Blanche, ed., *Gandhi and Non–Violent Resistance: The Non–Co–Operation Movement of India: Gleanings from the American Press.* 549 pp. Madras: Ganesh, 1923. (Collection of journalism on Gandhi by American, English, and Indian writers.)

1307. Watson, Francis, *The Trial of Mr. Gandhi.* 288 pp. London: Macmillan, 1969. (History of Gandhi's trial in 1922 is in ch. 2–4. Index.)

1308.   Woodcock, George, *Mohandas Gandhi.* 133 pp. New York: Viking Press, 1971. (Short critical biography. Index. Bibliography.)

Memoirs

Associates of Gandhi began to write memoirs of him as early as his South Africa years. Some of the entries here are interpretations of Gandhi, but those by Birla, who was Gandhi's occasional go–between, and Nehru also offer impressions of his methods.

1309.   Birla, Ghanshyam Das, *Bapu: A Unique Association.* 4 Vols. Vol. 1, 1924–34, 480 pp. Vol. 2, 1935–36, 381 pp. Vol. 3, 1937–39, 366 pp. Vol. 4, 1940–47, 464 pp. Bombay: Bharatiya Vidya Bhavan, 1977. (Collection of correspondence with Gandhi and Mahadev Desai. Author was a wealthy industrialist and financial supporter of Gandhi's campaigns. Photos.)

1310.   ———, *In the Shadow of the Mahatma: A Personal Memoir.* 337 pp. Bombay, Calcutta, and Madras: Orient Longmans, 1953. (Political memoir and collection of correspondence with Gandhi, Desai, and British politicians. Documents. Index.)

1311.   Chandiwala, Brijkrishna, *At the Feet of Bapu.* 345 pp. Ahmedabad: Navajivan, 1954. (Reminiscences of an aide to Gandhi, especially during his later years. Glossary. Index.)

1312.   Gandhi, Manubehn, *Last Glimpses of Bapu.* Trans. Moti Lal Jain. 348 pp. Delhi, Agra, and Jaipur: Shiva Lal Agarwala, 1962. (Diary of associate of Gandhi, detailing his life in 1947–48. See ch. 13–19 on fast in early 1948. Illustrations. Photos. Documents.)

1313.   Nehru, Jawaharlal, *Nehru on Gandhi: A Selection, Arranged in the Order of Events, from the Writings and Speeches of Jawaharlal Nehru.* 150 pp. New York: John Day, 1948. (Memoirs of work with Gandhi. Index.)

1314. Reynolds, Reginald, *A Quest for Gandhi*. 215 pp. Garden City NY: Doubleday, 1952. (Memoirs of British member of Gandhi's ashram.)

1315. Watson, Francis, *Talking of Gandhiji: Four Programmes for Radio First Broadcast by the British Broadcasting Corporation*. 141 pp. London, New York, and Toronto: Longmans, Green, 1957. (Scripts of four radio broadcasts in 1956, based upon interviews with Indian leaders. Photos.)

Works

Gandhi's writings have been collected in their entirety, as far as can be determined, in ninety volumes (entry 1321). Of the many other selections cited here, those actually issued by Gandhi (rather than edited selections) include entries 1320, 1322, 1336. Other useful volumes for the study of Gandhi in his historical context include records of correspondence and petitions addressed to the British government (entries 1317, 1326, 1327, 1333); speeches, addresses, and other correspondence (entries 1318, 1331, 1343, 468, 474, 476, 477); and collected articles from the journal Young India from 1919 to 1926 (entries 1325, 1343—1346).

See also: South Africa: Gandhi–led Struggles.

1316. Bose, Nirmal Kumar, ed., *Selections from Gandhi*. 311 pp. Ahmedabad: Navajivan, 1948. (Extracts from writings before 1942, with isolated later additions. See esp. ch. 3, "Fundamental Beliefs and Ideas"; ch. 10, "India's Freedom: Ways and Means"; ch. 11, "Nonviolence"; ch. 13, "*Satyagraha*"; and ch. 14, "The Life of the *Satyagrahi*." Index.)

1317. *Correspondence with Mr. Gandhi: August 1942–April 1942*. 125 pp. New Delhi: Government of India, Manager of Publications, 1944. (Correspondence during the Quit India phase, as published by the imperial government. See esp. "the 'fast' correspondence," pp. 5–13, and the "'Congress Responsibility' Letters," pp. 33–115. Does not completely overlap with entry 1326.)

1318. Desai, Mahadev H., *Day–to–Day with Gandhi (Secretary's Diary)*. Trans. Hemantkumar G. Nilkanth. Ed. Narhari D. Parikh. 4

vols. Vol. 1, November 1917–March 1919, 400 pp. Vol. 2, April 1919–October 1920, 400 pp. Vol. 3, October 1920–January 1924, 400 pp. Vol. 4, January 1924–November 1924, 388 pp. Varanasi: Sarva Seva Sangh Prakashan, 1968–69. (Each volume combines, in varying proportions, Desai's diary with copies of Gandhi's correspondence. Documents in appendixes. Indexes.)

1319.   Gandhi, Mohandas K., *All Men Are Brothers*. 196 pp. Paris: UNESCO; New York: Columbia Univ. Press, 1958. Ahmedabad: Navajivan, 1960. Reprint, Chicago: World without War Publications, 1972. (Selected texts from Gandhi's writings, arranged by topic. See ch. 3 on "means and ends" and ch. 4 on *ahimsa*. Glossary. Bibliography.)

1320.   ———, *An Autobiography; or, the Story of my Experiments with Truth*. First published in Gujarati, 2 vols., 1927 and 1929. Pagination varies. English–language eds., 391 pp. Ahmedabad: Navajivan, 1940. 640 pp., 1948. Reprint, Washington DC: Public Affairs Press, 1954. Current U.S. edition, 528 pp. Boston: Beacon Press, 1957 and later. (Self–emphasis on ascetic, psychological, dietary, and religious concerns, requiring careful comparison with other writings, biographies, and studies. Index.)

1321.   ———, *The Collected Works of Mahatma Gandhi*. 90 vols. Vol. 1, 1884–96, 343 pp. Vol. 2, 1896–97, 413 pp. Vol. 3, 1898–1903, 498 pp. Vol. 4, 1903–05, 520 pp. Vol. 5, 1905–06, 520 pp. Vol. 6, 1906–07, 560 pp. Vol. 7, January–December 1907, 576 pp. Vol. 8, January–August 1908, 603 pp. Vol. 9, September 1908–November 1909, 668 pp. Vol. 10, November 1909–March 1911, 580 pp. Vol. 11, April 1911–March 1913, 666 pp. Vol. 12, April 1913–December 1914, 700 pp. Vol. 13, January 1915–October 1917, 646 pp. Vol. 14, October 1917–July 1918, 580 pp. Vol. 15, August 1918–July 1919, 538 pp. Vol. 16, August 1919–January 1920, 581 pp. Vol. 17, February–June 1920, 616 pp. Vol. 18, July–November 1920, 515 pp. Vol. 19, November 1920–April 1921, 604 pp. Vol. 20, April–August, 1921, 567 pp. Vol. 21, August–December, 1921, 603 pp. Vol. 22, December 1921–March 1922, 544 pp. Vol. 23, March 1922–May 1924, 606 pp. Vol. 24, May–August, 1924, 615 pp. Vol. 25, August 1924–January 1925, 640 pp. Vol. 26, January–April 1925, 607 pp. Vol.

27, May–July 1925, 492 pp. Vol. 28, August–November 1925, 508 pp. Vol. 29, November 1925–February 1926, 482 pp. Vol. 30, February–June 1926, 618 pp. Vol. 31, June–November 1926, 594 pp. Vol. 32, November 1926–January 1927, 631 pp. Vol. 33, January–June 1927, 517 pp. Vol. 34, June–September 1927, 579 pp. Vol. 35, September 1927–January 1928, 575 pp. Vol. 36, February–June 1928, 503 pp. Vol. 37, July–October 1928, 453 pp. Vol. 38, November 1928–February 1929, 464 pp. Vol. 39, February 1929, 563 pp. Vol. 40, February–May 1929, 462 pp. Vol. 41, June–October 1929, 605 pp. Vol. 42, October 1929–February 1930, 554 pp. Vol. 43, March–June 1930, 480 pp. Vol. 44, July–December 1930, 497 pp. Vol. 45, December 1930–April 1931, 494 pp. Vol. 46, April 16–June 17, 1931, 451 pp. Vol. 47, June–September 1931, 478 pp. Vol. 48, September 1931–January 1932, 542 pp. Vol. 49, January–May 1932, 577 pp. Vol. 50, June–August 1932, 499 pp. Vol. 51, September 1–November 15, 1932, 505 pp. Vol. 52, November 1932–January 1933, 483 pp. Vol. 53, January–March 1933, 538 pp. Vol. 54, March 6–April 22, 1933, 527 pp. Vol. 55, April 23–September 15, 1933, 494 pp. Vol. 56, September 16, 1933–January 15, 1934, 550 pp. Vol. 57, January 16–May 17, 1934, 540 pp. Vol. 58, May 18–September 15, 1934, 496 pp. Vol. 59, September 16–December 15, 1934, 490 pp. Vol. 60, December 16, 1934–April 24, 1935, 505 pp. Vol. 61, April 25–September 30, 1935, 506 pp. Vol. 62, October 1, 1935–May 31, 1936, 507 pp. Vol. 63, June 1–November 2, 1936, 450 pp. Vol. 64, November 3, 1936–March 14, 1937, 478 pp. Vol. 65, March 15–July 31, 1937, 506 pp. Vol. 66, August 1, 1937–March 31, 1938, 510 pp. Vol. 67, April 1–October 14, 1938, 478 pp. Vol. 68, October 15, 1938–February 28, 1939, 518 pp. Vol. 69, March 1–July 15, 1939, 501 pp. Vol. 70, July 16–November 30, 1939, 464 pp. Vol. 71, December 1, 1939–April 15, 1940, 480 pp. Vol. 72, April 16, 1940–September 11, 1940, 500 pp. Vol. 73, September 12, 1940–April 15, 1941, 504 pp. Vol. 74, April 16–October 10, 1941, 432 pp. Vol. 75, October 11, 1941–March 31, 1942, 488 pp. Vol. 76, April 1–December 16, 1942, 491 pp. Vol. 77, December 17, 1942–July 31, 1944, 508 pp. Vol. 78, August 1–December 31, 1944, 452 pp. Vol. 79, January 1–April 24, 1945, 464 pp. Vol. 80, April 25–July 16, 1945, 479 pp. Vol. 81, July 17–October 31, 1945, 492 pp. Vol. 82, November 1, 1945–January 19, 1946, 484 pp. Vol. 83, January 20–April 13, 1946, 476 pp. Vol. 84, April 14–July 15, 1946, 532 pp. Vol. 85, July 16–October

20, 1946, 550 pp. Vol. 86, October 21, 1946–February 20, 1947, 526 pp. Vol. 87, February 21–May 24, 1947, 586 pp. Vol. 88, May 25–July 31, 1947, 520 pp. Vol. 89, August 1–November 10, 1947, 555 pp. Vol. 90, November 11, 1947–January 30, 1948, 598 pp. Delhi: Government of India, Ministry of Information and Broadcasting, Publications Division, 1958–84. (Exhaustive collection of Gandhi's written works, both published and unpublished, from all known sources. Strictly chronological. Glossary. Photos. Documents. Index.)

1322.   ———, *Constructive Programme, Its Meaning and Place*. 2d ed. 31 pp. Ahmedabad: Navajivan, 1945 [orig. publ. 1941]. (Gandhi's presentation of his program of development and social–service work as necessary for the independence struggle and as basic training for "civil disobedience.")

1323.   ———, *Ethics of Fasting*. 123 pp. Ed. Jag Parvesh Chander. Lahore: India Printing Works, 1944. (Writings on fasts and their motives, 1920–43, with introduction touching on fasting as "self–purification" and as pressure.)

1324.   ———, *For Pacifists*. 106 pp. Ed. Bharatan Kumarappa. Ahmedabad: Navajivan, 1949. (Selection compiled by editor on occasion of convention of "pacifists"; many on concepts of nonviolence and nonviolent action.)

1325.   ———, *Freedom's Battle, Being a Comprehensive Collection of Writings and Speeches on the Present Situation*. 2d ed. 341 pp. Madras: Ganesh, 1922. (Pieces from *Young India*. See section 2 on the Khilafat movement, section 4 on *Swaraj*, and section 8 on the Noncooperation movement. Index.)

1326.   ———, *Gandhiji's Correspondence with the Government, 1942–44*. 2d. ed. 360 pp. Ed. Pyarelal [Nair]. Ahmedabad: Navajivan, 1945. (Correspondence between Gandhi and British officials during his imprisonment, August 1942–July 1944. Part 2, section B, and parts 3, 4 are on Gandhi's 1943 fast. Appendixes include articles by Gandhi, Nehru, Patel, and others. Documents.)

1327. ——, *Gandhiji's Correspondence with the Government 1944–47.* 375 pp. Ed. Pyarelal [Nair]. Ahmedabad, Navajivan, 1959. (From May 1944 to August 1947. Of interest is part 4, section U, "About Operation of Economic Sanction Against South Africa." Appendixes. Documents.)

1328. ——, *Indian Home Rule.* 2d ed. 136 pp. Madras: Ganesh, 1919 [orig. publ. 1908]. 2d ed. 102 pp. Triplicane, Madras: S. Ganesan, 1921, 1922. First Navajivan version is reprint of second edition under title *Hind Swaraj;* or, *Indian Home Rule.* 80 pp. Ahmedabad: Navajivan, 1938. Rev. ed., 110 pp., 1939. (First serialized in Gujarati in South Africa under the title *Hind Swaraj.* Gandhi's first major piece of writing, a pamphlet advocating India's freedom from Britain. Takes the form of a dialogue advocating the view that India is responsible for its subjection to Britain and contrasting "brute force" against "passive resistance" as means of gaining freedom.)

1329. ——, *In Search of the Supreme.* Ed. V.B. Kher. 3 vols. Vol. 1, 388 pp. Vol. 2, 344 pp. Vol. 3, 356 pp. Ahmedabad: Navajivan, 1961. (Gandhi's theology. In vol. 1, see esp. selections 58–70 on noncooperation with evil and selections 192–221 on fasting. In vol. 2, see esp. section 1, part 3, on *ahimsa,* and section 4, "Politics and Religion." Index.)

1330. ——, *The Law and the Lawyers.* Ed. S.B. Kher. 246 pp. Ahmedabad: Navajivan, 1962. (Selections from Gandhi's personal experience as a lawyer in sections 1 and 2, his trials in section 3, and his thoughts on lawyers and *satyagraha* in section 4. Index.)

1331. ——, *Letters to Sardar Vallabhbhai Patel.* Trans. and ed. Valji Govindji Desai and Sudarshan V. Desai. 250 pp. Ahmedabad: Navajivan, 1957. (Gandhi's correspondence with key collaborator Patel. See translator's note for references to relevant selections. Index.)

1332. ——, *The Moral and Political Writings of Mahatma Gandhi. Volume I: Civilization, Politics, and Religion. Volume II: Truth and Non–Violence. Volume III: Non–Violent Resistance and Social Transformation.* Ed. Raghavan Iyer. Vol. I, 625 pp. Vol. II, 678 pp. Vol. III, 641 pp. Oxford: Clarendon Press, 1986. (Vol. 1 includes influences on Gandhi's ideas [section 3] and the complete text of *Hind Swaraj* [section 4; also entry 1328]. Vol. 2 compiles writings on *ahimsa* or nonviolence in section 4. Vol. 3 opens with collected pieces on *satyagraha* and related topics such as civil disobedience, fasting, and other methods of nonviolent action, and closes with texts on *sarvodaya*, the Gandhian systematics of societal change. Index. Bibliography.)

1333.   ———, *My Appeal to the British*. Ed. Anand T. Hingorani. 79 pp. New York: John Day, 1942. (Record of petitions to British from April 26 to July 26, 1942.)

1334.   ———, *My Picture of Free India*. Ed. Anand T. Hingorani. 230 pp. Bombay: Bharatiya Vidya Bhavan for Anand T. Hingorani, 1965. (Gandhi's conception of *swaraj*. See ch. 30, "The Non–Violent State," and ch. 31, "The Non–Violent Defence." Glossary. Bibliography.)

1335.   ———, *My Religion*. Ed. Bharatan Kumarappa. 160 pp. Ahmedabad: Navajivan, 1958 [orig. publ. 1955]. (In addition to writings on religion, see ch. 25, part B, "Direct Action," and part C, "In Place of War." Index.)

1336.   ———, *Nonviolence in Peace and War*. 3d ed. Vol. 1, 512 pp. Ahmedabad: Navajivan, 1948 [orig. publ. 1942]. Vol. 2, 403 pp. Ahmedabad: Navajivan, 1949. (Collected writings and talks on nonviolent responses to diverse Indian and international problems. Index.)

1337.   ———, *Non–Violent Resistance*. New York: Schocken Books, 1967. Indian edition entitled *Satyagraha: Non–Violent Resistance*. Ed. Bharatan Kumarappa. 406 pp. Ahmedabad: Navajivan, 1951. (Collected articles and summaries of speeches on the nonviolent technique.)

1338.   ———, *Sarvodaya: The Welfare of All*. Ed. Bharatan Kumarappa. 200 pp. Ahmedabad: Navajivan, 1954. (Expanded selection of Gandhian texts on *sarvodaya*. See esp. section 6 on *satyagraha* and conflict. Part 2 contains pieces by Vinoba Bhave and others. Index.)

1339. ———, *Satyagraha in South Africa*. Trans. Valji Govindji Desai. 511 pp. Triplicane, Madras: S. Ganesan, 1928. 2d ed., 351 pp. Ahmedabad: Navajivan, 1951. Rev. 2d ed., 511 pp. Ahmedabad: Navajivan, 1950. (Gandhi's personal account of Indian struggles against British colonial racial policies in South Africa and the development of his technique. Index.)

1340. ———, *Stonewalls Do Not a Prison Make*. Ed. V.B. Kher. 231 pp. Ahmedabad: Navajivan, 1964. (Gandhi's writings on "prison code" for *satyagrahis* are in part 1, experiences in South African jails in part 2, and experiences in Indian jails in part 3. Chronology. Index.)

1341. ———, *Teachings of Mahatma Gandhi*. Ed. Jag Parvesh Chander. 620 pp. Lahore: Indian Printing Works, 1945. (Selections from Gandhi, arranged as a philosophical dictionary.)

1342. ———, *True Education*. 267 pp. Ahmedabad: Navajivan, 1962. (See section 2, ch. 11–14, 17, 21, 22, for Gandhi's advice to students on participation in resistance. Index.)

1343. ———, *Writings and Speeches of Mahatma Gandhi Relating to Bihar, 1917–1947*. Ed. K.K. Datta. 341 pp. Patna, Bihar: Government of Bihar, 1960. (Speeches and excerpts from *Young India* and correspondence. See section 1 on Champaran and section 2 on Noncooperation movement of 1920–21. Photos. Glossary. Index.)

1344. ———, *Young India, 1919–1922*. 1199 pp. Triplicane, Madras: S. Ganesan, 1922; New York: B.W. Huebsch, 1923. (Gandhi's pieces from journal *Young India*, primarily on the Noncooperation movement, with essay on the movement by Rajendra Prasad. Index.)

1345. ———, *Young India, 1922–1924*. 1286 pp. Triplicane, Madras: S. Ganesan, 1924. (Material from the period of Gandhi's imprisonment.)

1346. ———, *Young India, 1924–1926*. 1352 pp. Triplicane, Madras: S. Ganesan, 1927. 984 pp. New York: Viking Press, 1927. (Section 2 compiles writings on the noncooperation movement and

related topics. Section 5 on "*satyagraha* and nonviolence"
includes several items on the Vykom [Vaikkam] *Satyagraha*.)

1347.   Mathur, J.S., and A.S. Mathur, eds., *Economic Thought of
         Mahatma Gandhi*. 666 pp. Allahabad: Chaitanya Publishing
         House, 1962. (Comprehensive collection of Gandhi's writings
         on economic philosophy. See detailed table of contents and
         index under *boycott, civil disobedience, lockout, noncooperation,
         nonviolence, nonviolent, picket, satyagraha, satyagrahi*, and *strike*.
         Index.)

1348.   Merton, Thomas, ed., *Gandhi on Nonviolence: Selected Texts from
         Gandhi's Nonviolence in Peace and War*. 82 pp. New York: New
         Directions, 1965. (Selections from Gandhi with an introduction
         by the editor.)

1349.   Nag, Kalidas, ed., *Tolstoy and Gandhi*. 136 pp. Patna: Pustak
         Bhandar, 1950. (The Gandhi–Tolstoy correspondence and
         related material.)

1350.   Prabhu, R.K., and U.R. Rao, eds. *The Mind of Mahatma Gandhi*.
         2d ed. 226 pp. London: Oxford Univ. Press; Ahmedabad:
         Navajivan, 1946 [orig. publ. 1945]. 3d ed., 589 pp. Ahmedabad:
         Navajivan, 1976. (Collection of excerpts. See ch. 5 on
         nonviolence and ch. 6 on *satyagraha*. Glossary. Chronology.
         Index.)

1351.   Rajagopalachari, C., and J.C. Kumarappa, eds., *The Nation's
         Voice*. 340 pp. Ahmedabad: Navajivan Press, 1932. (Texts of
         Gandhi's speeches in England, 1931, with comments by
         Mahadev Desai. Index.)

1352.   Shokla, Chandrashanker, *Conversations of Gandhiji*. 134 pp.
         Bombay: Vora, 1949. (Gandhi's speeches and dialogues,
         September 1933–July 1934, as collected by temporary secretary.
         Mostly on work with the *harijan* problem, but see ch. 8–10, 14,
         18, 19, 40, 46. Index.)

KHAN ABDUL GHAFFAR KHAN (1890–1988)

Abdul Ghaffar Khan, the "frontier Gandhi" of what is now Pakistan, rates a biographical section for the uniqueness of his position. Under the influence of Gandhi, Ghaffar Khan organized the warlike Pathans of the Northwest Frontier as early as 1919. As Muslims, the Servants of God did not accept Gandhi's Hindu message but rather his concepts of nonviolence and uncompromising resistance, a resistance in which they suffered greatly. Ghaffar Khan remained influential among his people after Pakistan's independence and was imprisoned for many years because he rejected that nation's constitution.

1353.   Andrews, C.F., *The Challenge of the North–West Frontier*. 208 pp. London: Allen & Unwin, 1937. (See ch. 7 on the "frontier movement" as it stood at the time. Index.)

1354.   Easwaran, Eknath, *A Man to Match His Mountains: Badshah Khan, Nonviolent Soldier of Islam*. 240 pp. Petaluma CA: Nilgiri Press, 1984. (Popular biography of Abdul Ghaffar Khan. See esp. his activities among Pathan Servants of God and with Gandhi in pp. 83–85, 103–13, 125–28, 131–36, and ch. 12, 13, 14. Chronology. Photos. Index. Bibliography.)

1355.   Khan, Khan Abdul Ghaffar, *My Life and Struggle: Autobiography of Badshah Khan as Narrated to K.B. Narang*. Trans. Helen H. Borman. 248 pp. Delhi: Orient Paperbacks, Hind Pocket Books, [1969]. (Memoirs, with accounts of several *satyagrahas* and imprisonments. See esp. origin of Pathan Khudai Khidmatgar or Servants of God, pp. 93–97; their nonviolent actions and repression; and Khan's response to partition, pp. 196–213.)

1356.   Pyarelal [Nair], *A Pilgrimage for Peace: Gandhi and Frontier Gandhi among N.W.F. Pathans*. 216 pp. Ahmedabad: Navajivan, 1950. (Story of Gandhi's 1938 visit to the Pathans of the North–West Frontier Province with Abdul Ghaffar Khan. See appendix, "Quintessence of *Satyagraha*." Photos. Index.)

1357.   ———, *Thrown to the Wolves*. 164 pp. Calcutta: Eastlight Book House, 1966. (Political biography of Abdul Ghaffar Khan. See ch. 7 on origins of Servants of God, section 2 on activities with

Gandhi, and ch. 18–20 on Khan's opposition to Pakistan constitution. Photos. Appendixes. Index.)

1358.   Spain, James W., *The Way of the Pathans*. 190 pp. London: Robert Hale, 1962. 2nd ed., Karachi, London, and New York: Oxford Univ. Press, 1973. (Study of Pathan history and culture. See pp. 90–93 for a visit to Abdul Ghaffar Khan in prison. Photos. Index.)

1359.   Tendulkar, D.G., *Abdul Ghaffar Khan: Faith Is a Battle*. 550 pp. Bombay: Popular Prakashan for the Gandhi Peace Foundation, 1967. (See pp. 56–360 on Abdul Ghaffar Khan's role in the Indian independence struggle and pp. 406–65 on partition. Glossary. Index. Bibliography.)

1360.   Yunus, Mohammad, *Frontier Speaks*. 204 pp. Bombay: Hind Kitabs, 1947. (Ch. 3 discusses Abdul Ghaffar Khan and ch. 7 discusses nonviolence and the Pathans. Appendixes. Index.)

SARVODAYA AND OTHER POST–GANDHIAN MOVEMENTS

India's turbulent and violent post–independence history has nevertheless included two trends of nonviolent action and resistance. In one of these, those influenced by Gandhi's ideas on economics and simplicity conducted the "sarvodaya" movement, which combined his ideas with a call for nonviolent revolution. More recently, social movements concerned with the natural environment and the effects of development and changes both on the environment and the livelihood of the people have turned to nonviolent protest and defiance of the state.

1361.   Desai, Narayan, *A Hand Book for Shanti Sainiks*. 54 pp. Rajghat, Varanasi, India: Sarva Seva Sangh Prakashan, 1963. (Handbook for training Shanti Sena members for *sarvodaya* movement. Gives outlines of organization and practical advice in sketchy form. Of interest are ch. 2 on "corporate discipline," ch. 13 on "dealing with disturbances," and ch. 20 on "nurturing the movement." Bibliography.)

1362.   Narayan, Jayaprakash, *Towards Total Revolution*. Ed. Brahmanand. Vol. 1, *Search for an Ideology*, 268 pp. Vol. 2,

Politics in India, 307 pp. Vol. 3, *India and Her Problems,* 193 pp. Vol. 4, *Total Revolution,* 226 pp. Bombay: Popular Prakashan, 1978. (By leader in independence struggle and post–Gandhian movements. In vol. 1, see pp. xviii–lxxviii on Narayan's participation in independence movement, 1929–48; pp. xcii–cxlv on post–Gandhian nonviolent movements; and ch. 6, 8, 15, 16, 18–21. In vol. 2, see ch. 39, 43, 50 on *sarvodaya*. In vol. 3, see ch. 2 on right to strike, and ch. 7 on student action. In vol. 4, see ch. 20, 22, 25. Index.)

1363. Omvedt, Gail, *We Will Smash this Prison! Indian Women in Struggle.* 196 pp. London: Zed Press, 1980. (Account of women organizing for social change in India during the 1970s. Author describes, among other actions, the method of *ghereos,* or surrounding of officials until demands are met. See ch. 2, 5, 7, 8 and pp. 2, 79, 82, 94–95 on *ghereos.* Documents.)

1364. Ostergaard, Geoffrey, *Nonviolent Revolution in India.* 419 pp. Sevagram: J.P. Amrit Kosh; New Delhi: Gandhi Peace Foundation, 1985. (History of *sarvodaya* movement from Gandhi's death to 1982, with emphasis on "strategy and tactics" and leaders Vinoba and J.P. Narayan. Introduction discusses concept of nonviolent revolution. Index. Glossary.)

1365. Ostergaard, Geoffrey, and Melville Currell, *The Gentle Anarchists: A Study of the Leaders of the Sarvodaya Movement for Non–Violent Revolution in India.* 421 pp. Oxford: Clarendon Press, 1971. (Case study of *Sarvodaya* movement, a Gandhian program for development and societal change, and *bhoodan* or land–gift campaign. See esp. ch. 1, section 1, ch. 5, on organizational elements, and ch. 6 on strategy and tactics. See also index under leaders and concepts. Index. Bibliography.)

1366. Routledge, Paul, *Terrains of Resistance: Nonviolent Social Movements and the Contestation of Place in India.* 170 pp. Westport CT and London: Praeger, 1993. (Empirical and theoretical study of the joint influences of development and the state, locality, and nonviolent action in Indian social movements. Ch. 3 studies the Baliapal movement against removal of a population to construct a missile range in Orissa and ch. 4 is on the Chipko environmental movement. On theory and the relations among nonviolent action and power, locality and place, and the study of conflict, see ch. 2, 6. Index. Bibliography.)

1367.   Sarin, Manohar Lal, *The Case of Goa (1961) and the Controversy Regarding Gandhian Non–Violent Resistance (Satyagraha) and International Law Involved in It.* 605 pp. Ph.D. diss. Philipps–Universität, Marburg/Lahn, 1973. (Dissertation examining Indian 1961 military takeover of Portuguese Goa and issues involving the U.N. Charter, international law, and Gandhian nonviolent struggle. See pp. 62–74, ch. 3, part 3, and esp. ch. 5 on *satyagraha* campaign for independence in Goa. Bibliography.)

1368.   Shepard, Mark, *Gandhi Today: The Story of Mahatma Gandhi's Successors.* 146 pp. Washington DC and Cabin John MD: Seven Locks Press, 1987. (Ch. 2 is on Vinoba Bhave and Jayaprakash Narayan, ch. 3 is on Narayan Desai, and ch. 4 is on the Chipko ecological defense movement. Photos. Index.)

JAPAN

Reasons that Japan is not considered a likely place for nonviolent struggle include its history of civil violence and the perception of its people as deferential and compliant toward authority. However, the premodern Japanese peasantry used traditional methods of nonviolent protest and appeal (including personal self–sacrifice in protest) alongside traditions of revolt. In the post–war period, Japanese labor and students experimented with nonviolent means in addition to political violence. Also, peace and conflict researcher Takeshi Ishida has criticized Western concepts of nonviolent action from a Japanese viewpoint.

See also: China: May Fourth Movement, 1919; Korea: Under Japanese Domination.

1369.   Apter, David E., and Nagayo Sawa, *Against the State: Politics and Social Protest in Japan.* 250 pp. Cambridge and London: Harvard Univ. Press, 1984. (Authors use the enduring Sanrizuka protest movement against construction of Narita

International Airport on farmland to explore issues of violence and protest in democratic systems. Thorough examination of motives for acceptance and employment of limited collective violence by movement. See esp. ch. 4 for overview of movement and ch. 10, "Reflections on Protest." Photos. Index.)

1370. Bakke, E. Wight, *Revolutionary Democracy: Challenge and Testing in Japan.* 343 pp. Hamden CT: Archon Books, 1968. (See ch. 8, "Direct Action Politics," for a view of demonstrations as a response to failure of established institutions to provide channels for expression. Index. Bibliography.)

1371. Battistini, Lawrence H., *The Postwar Student Struggle in Japan.* 167 pp. Tokyo and Rutland VT: Charles H. Tuttle, 1956. (Ch. 4–6 describe the several phases of student political activity from 1948 to 1955, focusing on Zengakuren. Discussion of nonviolent and violent student strikes and demonstrations in each chapter. Index. Bibliography.)

1372. Beer, Lawrence Ward, *Freedom of Expression in Japan: A Study in Comparative Law, Politics, and Society.* 415 pp. Tokyo, New York, and San Francisco: Kodansha International, 1984. (Author discusses the history and present context of public expression and its limits. See ch. 2, 3 on the history of law regarding expression, protest, and its control. Of interest is the discussion of labor "dispute activities," such as various kinds of partial work refusals, one–person labor refusals, and mass poster gluing, pp. 215–19. Appendix. Index.)

1373. Bix, Herbert, *Peasant Protest in Japan, 1590–1884.* 296 pp. New Haven and London: Yale Univ. Press, 1986. Detailed study of regional peasant uprisings, often combined with or preceded by petitions, flight, and protests. See pp. xix–xxv on the typology of protest and xxxiii–xxxv on the character of the *gimin* or martyr. Glossary. Index. Bibliography.)

1374. Borton, Hugh, *Peasant Uprisings in Japan of the Tokugawa Period.* 2d ed. 219 pp. New York: Paragon, 1968. Originally published, *Transactions of the Asiatic Society of Japan (Second Series)* 16 (1938). (Gives accounts of nonviolent land desertions, violence, and other forms of peasant uprising such as wrecking of officials' residences. Appendixes. Bibliography.)

1375.   Hane, Mikiso, *Peasants, Rebels, and Outcastes: The Underside of Modern Japan*. 297 pp. New York: Pantheon, 1982. (See pp. 193–204 on women silk workers' strikes in the 1920s and 1930s. Index.)

1376.   Ishida, Takeshi, *Japanese Political Culture: Change and Continuity*. 173 pp. New Brunswick and London: Transaction Books, 1983. (Analytical essays on Japanese political culture. Ch. 8, "The Significance of Nonviolent Direct Action: A Japanese Perspective," criticizes several views of nonviolent action and offers an alternative concept with examples from recent Japanese history. See also other chapters in part 3, "Essays in Peace Research." Index.)

1377.   Koschmann, J. Victor, ed., *Authority and the Individual in Japan: Citizen Protest in Historical Perspective*. 318 pp. Tokyo: Univ. of Tokyo Press, 1978. (See J. Victor Koschmann, "Introduction: Soft Rule and Expressive Protest," pp. 1–30, on relationship between obedience and protest in Japanese culture. Index.)

1378.   Krauss, Ellis S., Thomas P. Rohlen, and Patricia G. Steinhoff, eds., *Conflict in Japan*. 417 pp. Honolulu: Univ. of Hawaii Press, 1984. (Collection of essays on conflict theory and conflict case studies in Japan. See essays on labor, student, and "status" conflict—the tea pourers' revolt—in ch. 6, 8, 9. Index.)

1379.   Neary, Ian, *Political Protest and Social Control in Pre–war Japan: The Origins of Buraku Liberation*. 250 pp. Manchester, England: Manchester Univ. Press, 1989. (On the struggle of the quasi-ethnic "outcast" sector of Japanese society known as the Burakumin in protesting their unequal status and the government's counter–policy. Among the methods used by Burakumin are "thorough denunciation campaigns" against those who malign them. Photos. Glossary. Appendix. Index. Bibliography.)

1380.   O'Barr, Jean F., ed., *Perspectives on Power: Women in Africa, Asia, and Latin America*. 130 pp. Durham NC: Duke Univ. Center for

International Studies, 1982. (Susan J. Pharr, "Tea and Power: The Anatomy of a Conflict," pp. 37–49 discusses a brief "tea-pourers' rebellion" in Japan; while Audrey Wipper, "Riot and Rebellion Among African Women: Three Examples of Women's Political Clout," pp. 50–72, has several examples of a traditional repertoire of insult, social boycott, and women's *charivari*.)

1381. Smith, Henry DeWitt, II, *Japan's First Student Radicals*. 341 pp. Cambridge: Harvard Univ. Press, 1972. (See pp. 22–30 on transformation of random actions into protest and strikes; ch. 3 on organizations and protest in the 1920s; ch. 7–8 on suppression of activism in 1920s and 1930s, esp. pp. 215–19 on student strike organization; and pp. 286–88 for a comment on appearance of the *"Gewalt* technique" of limited street violence. Illustrations. Photos. Index. Bibliography.)

1382. Vlastos, Stephen, *Peasant Protests and Uprisings in Tokugawa Japan*. 184 pp. Berkeley, Los Angeles, and London: Univ. of California Press, 1986. (See comment on pp. 2–3 on relation between violent and nonviolent action and ch. 3 on "direct-appeal movements" and "demonstrating in force" during the early Tokugawa period. Index. Bibliography.)

Opposition to the Security Treaty of 1960

Japan's security agreement with the United States, in which Japan was an anti–Soviet bulwark, came up for renegotiation and renewal in 1960. The ruling Liberal Democratic Party wished to put a treaty through quickly, but other parties and radical students opposed it fiercely. Minority parties held parliamentary boycotts to block the treaty, but the focus of attention was on mass demonstrations by students and their allies under the main nationwide student organization, Zengakuren.

1383. Cary, James, *Japan Today: Reluctant Ally*. 211 pp. New York: Frederick A. Praeger, 1962. (See ch. 8, 11, 12 on the 1960 Security Treaty Crisis. Index.)

1384. Dowsey, Stuart J., ed., *Zengakuren: Japan's Revolutionary Students*. 269 pp. Berkeley CA: Ishi Press, 1970. (Written by

Japanese students, ca. 1969. Haradon Hisato, "The Anti–Ampo Struggle," discusses *Zengakuren* participation in 1960, including effort of "Mainstream *Zengakuren*" to shape movement actions. Bibliography.)

1385.   Packard, George R., III, *Protest in Tokyo: The Security Treaty Crisis of 1960*. 423 pp. Princeton NJ: Princeton Univ. Press, 1966. (See ch. 7, 8 on petitions, parliamentary boycott, strikes, and demonstrations of May–June 1960, with much attention to the role of *Zengakuren* and other organizations. Photos. Documents. Index. Bibliography.)

1386.   Scalapino, Robert A., and Junnosuke Masumi, *Parties and Politics in Contemporary Japan*. 190 pp. Berkeley and Los Angeles: Univ. of California Press, 1962. (See ch. 5 for case study of the 1960 Security Treaty Crisis in relation to party politics. Index.)

1387.   Takayanagi, Shunichi, and Kimitada Miwa, eds., *Postwar Trends in Japan: Studies in Commemoration of Rev. Aloysius Miller, S.J.* 272 pp. Tokyo: Univ. of Tokyo Press, 1975. (See Kazuko Tsurumi, "Student Movements in 1960 and 1969: Continuity and Change," esp. pp. 209–11, for reasons for violence in later demonstrations and pp. 196, 222–23 for effects of refraining from violence in 1969 demonstrations.)

Environmental Conflict

Industrial development has caused a great deal of degradation to the environment in many areas, and government often has not taken preservation as a necessary priority. Protests against the change in the social environment as well as the natural environment have been associated with development. As in many societies, objection to environmental pollution and degradation has not been the majority position, but Iijima compiles a record of citizen protest dating back as much as three centuries.

1388.   Iijima, Nobuko, ed., *Pollution Japan: Historical Chronology*. 401 pp. Tokyo: Asahi Evening News, 1979. (A chronology of environmental damage and its human costs. Parts 3, 4, on the 1945–75 era, detail "citizen movements," environmental issues, and the actions of business and government. Scattered information under the heading "environmental issues" on protests dating to the early Tokugawa period.)

1389. McKean, Margaret A., *Environmental Protest and Citizen Politics*. 291 pp. Berkeley, Los Angeles, and London: Univ. of California Press, 1981. (Study of Japanese "citizens' movements" against industrial pollution and their mobilization, beliefs, and methods. See ch. 1, 3, 4, 7; esp. pp. 149–63, on methods. Methodological appendix. Index. Bibliography.)

1390. Steiner, Kurt, Ellis S. Krauss, and Scott C. Flanagan, eds. *Political Oppositions and Local Politics in Japan*. 486 pp. Princeton NJ: Princeton Univ. Press, 1980. (See part 3 on citizens' environmental protest movements in the 1960s and 1970s. Index.)

1391. Strong, Kenneth, *Ox against the Storm: A Biography of Tenaka Shoze: Japan's Conservationist Pioneer*. 232 pp. British Columbia: Univ. of British Columbia Press, 1977. (Biography of politician and activist leader of peasants' anti–pollution campaign, late 1800s to early 1900s. Protests included petitions, demonstrations, and other actions. See esp. ch. 7–9. Illustrations. Photos. Bibliography.)

Labor

Radical Japanese labor has both threatened and used mass strikes, including in one case the threat of a general strike. Japanese labor has more often employed modified forms of the strike such as slow–downs or working to rule. See also entries 1378, 1380 on noncooperation by women required to serve tea to their colleagues.

1392. Hanami, Tadashi, *Labor Relations in Japan Today*. 253 pp. Tokyo, New York, and San Francisco: Kodansha International, 1979. (Japanese labor disputes in the legal context. See ch. 5 for a theory of disputes. Discussion of political strikes and labor strikes is in ch. 4, part 3, and ch. 7. Ch. 8 discusses collective action alternatives to strikes, including modified strikes, and ch. 9 looks at the role of factory occupations and violence in

labor actions and students' "mass bargaining." Index.
Bibliography.)

1393.   Moore, Joe, *Japanese Workers and the Struggle for Power, 1945–1947*. 305 pp. Madison: Univ. of Wisconsin Press, 1983. (Historical and interpretive study of the Japanese labor movement in the immediate post–WWII period, focusing on radical labor, *Zaibatsu* industrialists, and the occupation government. Chapters are arranged so as to reflect the back–and–forth of workers' collective action and industrialists' response. Of interest are pp. 7–17 on the "apparatus of control" and ch. 2, 4–6, 8 on workers' organizations and actions, including discussion of "production control" as a form of union action approximating a takeover of production and pp. 229–43 on the failed general strike movement of early 1947. Consult index under *demonstrations, industrial sabotage* [i.e., by industry against labor], *production control, rice rallies, strikes,* and *struggle committees.* Index. Bibliography.)

1394.   Scalapino, Robert, *The Early Japanese Labor Movement: Labor and Politics in a Developing Society*. 304 pp. Berkeley CA: Univ. of California Institute of East Asian Studies, Center for Japanese Studies, 1983. (Study of Japanese labor organization and the effects that industrialization and the infusion of Western ideas had on Japanese labor relations in the formative stages of its modern period. Index. Bibliography.)

KOREA

Nonviolent methods, especially mass demonstrations, have been part of Korean political life since the late nineteenth century. They have been used to address internal discord and in resistance to foreign domination, both from JAPAN and the West. Most entries in this section are on the independence movement of 1919, a largely unsuccessful nonviolent movement against Japanese dominion. Following Korea's formal independence from Japan in 1945, demonstrations and other methods were employed against Korean rulers who were perceived as unjust or dictatorial. Readers familiar with Korean politics will also know of the regularity of street violence between students and police during a succession of military–dominated regimes.

Precolonial

Intellectuals were in the vanguard of protest movements against the influence of Japan and the West before Japan acted to consolidate its colonial position in Korea. These movements led near the turn of the century to protests and organizing among the literati and to the Tonghak rebellion and peasant violence.

1395.   Deuchler, Martina, *Confucian Gentlemen and Barbarian Envoys: The Opening of Korea, 1875–1885.* 310 pp. Seattle and London: Univ. of Washington Press, 1977. (History of Korea's treaty relations with Japan and the West in late nineteenth century. See esp. pp. 104–107, "Confucian Reaction: The Literati Movement of 1881," for an account of Korean intellectuals' protest movement against foreign cultural encroachment. Appendix. Index. Bibliography.)

1396.   Kim, C.I. Eugene, and Han–Kyo Kim, *Korea and the Politics of Imperialism, 1876–1910.* 260 pp. Berkeley and Los Angeles: Univ. of California Press, 1967. (Analyzes cultural and political effects of Japanese annexation of Korea in the early twentieth century. See esp. ch. 7, "The Reform Movement and Its Aftermath, 1896–1904," which chronicles the growth of the Independence Club, a movement that galvanized "massive popular support which at times was strong enough to force the government to grant political concessions." Pp. 112–14 examine the movement's methods and analyze its failure. Appendix. Bibliography.)

1397.   Noh, Jong–Sun, *Religion and Just Revolution: Third World Perspective.* 218 pp. Seoul: Voice Publishing House, 1987. (Prominent Korean theologian's examination of the roles of violence and nonviolence in the Tonghak Movement ["people's struggle for justice"] which began in the late nineteenth century in order to reunite Korea's political and cultural ideals with its religious traditions. Argues that the Western model of violence and nonviolence as mutually exclusive is not appropriate for examining Korean use of nonviolent methods. Photos. Appendix. Index. Bibliography.)

Under Japanese Domination

Japan gradually increased its control over Korea and became the colonial power in that land in the early years of the twentieth century. In March 1919, a group of Korean activists declared the independence of their country and simultaneously called for peaceful demonstrations in support. Crowds chanting the slogan mansei, *or long life, demonstrated against the Japanese throughout the country. The Korean movement apparently had no considered strategy except to remain nonviolent and to demonstrate. Many demonstrators were injured or killed when Japanese forces attacked the crowds with great violence. The movement was subdued within days and was followed by nationalist agitation and occasional student strikes or demonstrations in the following decades.*

1398.   Choi, Woonsang, *The Fall of the Hermit Kingdom*. 179 pp. Dobbs Ferry NY: Oceana Publications, 1967. (See brief description in ch. 4 of appeals and protests in 1905 against annexation. Index. Bibliography.)

1399.   Choy, Bong–youn, *Korea: A History*. 474 pp. Rutland VT and Tokyo: Charles E. Tuttle, 1971. (See ch. 7 on 1919 demonstrations against Japanese rule, described as a "nationwide peaceful uprising," and student revolt of 1929–30. Ch. 13 is on student revolution against Syngman Rhee, 1960. Index. Bibliography.)

1400.   Chung, Henry, *The Case of Korea: A Collection of Evidence on the Japanese Domination of Korea, and on the Development of the Korean Independence Movement*. 367 pp. New York, Chicago, London, and Edinburgh: Fleming H. Revell, 1921. (Ch. 11–14 discuss the independence movement and suppression of March 1919 demonstrations. Accounts of demonstrations and repression in appendix 7. Photos. Index.)

1401.   Cynn, Hugh Heung–Wo, *The Rebirth of Korea: The Reawakening of the People, Its Causes, and the Outlook*. 272 pp. New York: Abingdon Press, 1920. (See ch. 1–3 on the demonstrations for independence in March 1919 and the repression they prompted. Illustrations. Appendixes.)

1402. *The Independence Movement in Korea: A Record of Some Events of the Spring of 1919: Reprinted from the Japan Chronicle.* 72 pp. Kobe, Japan: Japan Chronicle, 1919. (News reports containing references to "passive resistance," tax protests, and *mansei* slogan with emphasis on repression and cruelties.)

1403. Kendall, Carlton W., *The Truth about Korea.* 104 pp. 2d ed. San Francisco: Korean National Association, 1919. (Brief history of Japanese rule. See pp. 24–33 on 1919 movement and documents on pp. 47–93, including international appeals and declaration of independence. Photos. Bibliography.)

1404. Ki–baik Lee, *A New History of Korea.* Trans. Edward W. Wagner and Edward J. Schultz. 474 pp. Cambridge: Harvard Univ. Press; Seoul: Ilchokak, Publishers, 1984. (Author's name is sometimes spelled differently in other editions. In ch. 14, parts 1–4 explain the background of the independence movement and part 5 briefly describes the March First Movement of 1919. Ch. 15 describes changes in Japanese policy occasioned by the nationalist movement and, in parts 3, 4, collective resistance to colonialism. A very brief account of the April Revolution of 1960 is on pp. 384–85. Photos. Index.)

1405. Kim, C.I. Eugene, and Dorothea E. Mortimore, eds., *Korea's Response to Japan: The Colonial Period, 1910–1945.* 349 pp. [n.p.], Center for Korean Studies, Western Michigan Univ., 1977. (Proceedings of 1974 Conference on Korea. See esp. Oh Kon Cho, "Resistance Theaters and Motion Pictures," which examines resistance sentiment as manifest in Korean drama, and C.I. Kim, "Nationalist Movements and Students," which analyzes the role of students in the March 1 movement of 1919 and the subsequent student strikes. Appendix. Index.)

1406. Lee, Chong–Sik, *The Politics of Korean Nationalism.* 342 pp. Berkeley and Los Angeles: Univ. of California Press, 1963. (Political history of Korean nationalist movements, late nineteenth and early twentieth centuries. On nonviolent aspects before 1919 see pp. 25–28, 64–66, 75. Section 3, esp. ch. 7, discusses March 1 movement; see pp. 141, 150–51, 243–44, 248–50, 252, 255–56. Index.)

1407.   McKenzie, F.A., *Korea's Fight for Freedom*. 320 pp. New York and London: Fleming H. Revell, 1919. (See ch. 4, 14–17 about nonviolent action and the independence movement. Pp. 247–50 contain text of the "Proclamation of Korean Independence," which denounced violence.)

1408.   Nahm, Andrew C., *Korea, Tradition and Transformation: A History of the Korean People*. 583 pp. Elizabeth NJ and Seoul: Hollym International, 1988. (Ch. 8 discusses political and cultural nationalism under Japanese domination, including the March First Movement and self–sufficiency campaigns. The 1960 revolution is discussed on pp. 434–36. Photos of the March First Movement are on p. 269 and Appendix F contains the 1919 declaration of independence. Chronology. Appendixes. Index.)

1409.   Oliver, Robert T., *Syngman Rhee: The Man behind the Myth*. 380 pp. New York: Dodd, Mead, 1954. (Biography of former President of Korea. See ch. 7 on Rhee's part in "protest without revolution" during the March 1 movement. Photos. Index.)

1410.   Sohn, Pow–key, Kim Chol–choon, and Hong Yi–sup, *The History of Korea*. 363 pp. Seoul, Korea: Korean National Commission for UNESCO, 1970. (See part 5, ch. 3 for brief discussion of March 1 movement of 1919 and repression. Some statistics included. Photos. Index. Bibliography.)

1411.   Sunoo, Harold Hak–won, *Korea: A Political History in Modern Times*. 343 pp. Columbia MO: Korean–American Cultural Foundation; Seoul, Korea: Kunkuk Univ. Press, [n.d.]. (See pp. 214–20 on 1919 movement; esp. p. 219 for negative assessment of nonviolent action and pp. 241–42 on student strikes of 1929. Photos. Documents. Index. Bibliography.)

1412.   Young, A. Morgan, *Japan in Recent Times, 1912–1926*. 347 pp. Westport CT: Greenwood Press, 1973 [orig. publ. 1929]. (See ch. 15 for a brief description of the Korean movement from the viewpoint of the Japanese administration.)

Post–Independence

Two focal points of Korean protest were in 1960, when demonstrations brought about the downfall of Syngman Rhee, and in 1984, when a student uprising in the city of Kwangju was dealt with by severe repression by the army in which many died. The number killed in the Kwangju Uprising was not revealed, but it apparently ran to several hundred.

1413. Clark, Donald N., ed., *The Kwangju Uprising: Shadows over the Regime in South Korea.* 101 pp. Boulder and London: Westview Press, 1988. (Essays explaining the demonstrations, repression, and related issues. Includes culturally–based interpretations of the confrontation and a reconstruction of the U.S. role. Appendix, pp. 83–92, contains official account of the uprising as delivered by the defense minister in 1985. Chronology. Index.)

1414. Hidaka, Rokuro, *The Price of Affluence: Dilemmas of Contemporary Japan.* Trans. and ed. Gavan McCormack. 176 pp. Tokyo, New York, and San Francisco: Kodansha International, 1984. Originally published as *Sengo Shiso o Kangaeru.* Tokyo: Iwanami Shoten, 1980. (Ch. 7 contains reflections on relationship between Japan's 1960 Security Treaty conflict and Korea's April Revolution. See pp. 132–35 for concept of violence–free revolution of Ham Sok Hon.)

1415. Kim, Chong Lim, *Political Participation in Korea: Democracy, Mobilization and Stability.* 238 pp. Santa Barbara CA and Oxford: Clio Books, 1980. (See Sungjoo Han, "Student Activism: A Comparison between the 1960 Uprising and the 1971 Protest Movement," ch. 7, for a study of changes in student protest politics in Korea. Index.)

1416. Rhee, Young–Pil, *The Breakdown of Authority Structure in Korea in 1960: A Systems Approach.* 120 pp. Seoul: Seoul National Univ. Press, 1982. (Originally a doctoral dissertation, this work attempts to explain the dynamics of the 1960 protests as a failure of self regulation on the part of the political system, based upon a notion of the mutually reinforcing effects of coercive repression and collective action. See esp. ch. 3–6 on the revolt of 1960 as discussed against this model. Index. Bibliography.)

1417.   Warnberg, Tim, "The Kwangju Uprising: An Inside View." *Korean Studies* 11 (1987): 33–57. (Diary of the Kwangju demonstrations, violence, and repression of May 1980 with an assessment of various justifications and explanations.)

NEW ZEALAND (AOTEAROA)

New Zealand's history of nonviolent action is split into two diverging paths. Firstly, settlement of the country by Europeans was associated with conflict both with and among the Polynesian inhabitants, the Maori. (The Maori word for their homeland, Aotearoa or Long White Cloud, is used here also.) Very significant is a lengthy period of protest and noncooperation that followed the end of the Maori Wars and came to be called the Parihaka Rebellion (see below). The second path was in some ways very European, because the settlers of New Zealand brought with them traditions of labor organizing and action from Great Britain, including strikes, bans (labor boycotts), and the like, as well as conscientious objection.

In more recent years, New Zealand activists were in the forefront of the campaign to boycott sports with South African teams, especially in attempting to stop tours by South African teams.

See also: Western Samoa: Mau Movement, Methods of Nonviolent Action: Blockades and Voyages of Intervention.

Maori Resistance and the Parihaka Movement

The Maori Wars of the mid–nineteenth century resulted in the deaths of many Maori, usually in wars against one another. This helped consolidate the European hold on the islands and extend settler claims to land and authority. Organized nonviolent opposition, especially against land–taking, began about 1870 under the leadership of Whiti–O–Rongomai (also know as Te Whiti), who led the Parihaka Movement. Considered a kind of prophet among his people, Te Whiti instructed them in innovative methods of nonviolent opposition, including plowing up land that had been claimed by Europeans as a symbolic way of showing that it still belonged to the Maori. Although suppressed at its home base in Parihaka by the army, the movement remained alive and spawned other protests and resistance into the twentieth century.

1418. Caselberg, John, ed., *Maori Is My Name: Historical Maori Writings in Translation.* 152 pp. Dunedin: John McIndoe, 1975. (Ch. 4–12 contain speeches given at protest meetings, petitions, and war manifestoes. Ch. 13 is on the Parihaka story of "passive resistance." See esp. pp. 133–36 for Te Whiti's sayings. Bibliography.)

1419. Cowan, James, *The New Zealand Wars: A History of the Maori Campaigns and the Pioneering Period.* Vol. 2, *The Hauhau Wars, 1864–72.* 560 pp. Wellington: R.E. Owen, 1956. (See story of Parihaka, pp. 476–91. Illustrations. Photos. Index.)

1420. Mamak, Alexander, and Ahmed Ali, *Race, Class, and Rebellion in the South Pacific.* 144 pp. Sydney, London, and Boston: George Allen & Unwin, 1979. (Of significance are brief case studies of the Parihaka Rebellion, pp. 107–14, and aboriginal protests in Australia, 1960s, pp. 114–26. Index. Bibliography.)

1421. Mitcalfe, Barry, *Nine New Zealanders.* 72 pp. Christchurch: Whitcombe & Tombs, 1963. (See pp. 51–59 on Te Whiti and Parihaka. Illustrations.)

1422. Scott, Dick, *Ask That Mountain: The Story of Parihaka.* 216 pp. Auckland: Heinemann/Southern Cross, 1975. Reprint, 1981. (History of Whiti–O–Rongomai and the lengthy Maori nonviolent resistance to European land–taking, beginning 1869 and continuing intermittently for at least thirty years. See ch. 4, pp. 179–81, on the Maori protest plowing of seized lands, which was recorded as late as 1898. Illustrations. Photos. Index.)

1423. Simpson, Tony, *Te Riri Pakeha: The White Man's Anger.* 256 pp. Waiura, Martinborough: Alister Taylor, 1979. (See pp. 190–200 on Parihaka rebellion. Illustrations. Photos. Index. Bibliography.)

1424. Williams, John A., *Politics of the New Zealand Maori: Protest and Cooperation, 1891–1909*. 204 pp. Seattle and London: Univ. of Washington Press, 1969. (See ch. 3, "Postwar Maori Protest Movements, 1870–97," on Te Whiti and Parihaka; ch. 4 on extralegal "Maori Parliament"; and ch. 9, "The Renewal of Organized Maori Protest, 1905–9." Photos. Index. Bibliography.)

Recent Maori Politics

The Maori people have pursued several forms of political expression in modern New Zealand, including attempts to protect land holdings and fishing rights, and have formed various organizations to do this, including the protest-political group Mana Motuhake.

1425. Hazelhurst, Kayleen M., *Political Expression and Ethnicity: Statecraft and Mobilisation in the Maori World*. 222 pp. Westport CT and London: Praeger, 1993. (Consult index under "protest actions" and "protest movements" for Maori participation in demonstrations and other actions in the context of their political objectives. Ch. 6 on the Mana Motuhake political group includes accounts of protests by group members. Index. Bibliography.)

1426. Walker, Ranginui, *Ka Whawhai Tonu Motu: Struggle Without End*. 334 pp. Auckland NZ: Penguin Books, 1990. (History of the Maori, their culture and politics. Ch. 5–7 are on the wars of the nineteenth century, the following chapters on survival and self–assertion, and ch. 11, 12 on the various forms and issues of more recent Maori activism, including Mana Motuhake. See pp. 156–59, 181–85 on Te Whiti and Rua Kenana, another "prophet" of separate development. Photos. Index. Bibliography.)

Conscientious Objection

1427. Grant, David, *Out in the Cold: Pacifists and Conscientious Objectors in New Zealand during World War II*. 270 pp.

Auckland: Reed Methuen Publishers, 1986. (Heavily illustrated history of religiously–motivated pacifists and their tribulations. Ch. 1 describes opposition to conscription in WWI and organizing in the interwar years, while ch. 2, 3 detail pacifists' efforts to speak and protest in the early war years and the government's measures to stop them. Ch. 5–7 are largely on the treatment of pacifists in prison camps and their responses, including noncooperation and hunger strikes. Photos. Index. Bibliography.)

Protest Against Sports with South African Teams

South Africa's segregated sports teams were subject to a United Nations–declared boycott which led to protests by New Zealanders in the 1960s through early 1980s. Activists tried to stop New Zealand teams from hosting visiting South African teams, even though many people involved in sports wanted to continue South African tours. New Zealand activists held extensive protests in the streets and at stadiums trying to halt a tour by the South African national rugby team in 1981.

See also: Methods of Nonviolent Action: Sports Boycotts.

1428. *Operation Rugby: 19 July–13 September 1981.* 130 pp. plus annexes. Wellington: New Zealand Police, Police Headquarters, 1982. (Police report on activities during efforts to halt tour of South African rugby team, July 19–September 13, 1981. Opposition included nonviolent and violent demonstrations and marches and other actions. See introduction, photos, and annex W for chronology of events.)

1429. Newnham, Tom, *A Cry of Treason.* 185 pp. Palmerston North: Dunmore Press, 1978. (Activist's account of 1976 conflict over New Zealand's position on South African apartheid policy in sports, focusing on January softball team visit to New Zealand and boycotts and protests at Montreal Olympics. Includes guerrilla theater, demonstrations, haunting, and the like. Photos. Index.)

1430. ———, *Apartheid Is Not a Game.* 89 pp. Auckland, N.Z.: Graphic Publications, 1975. (Numerous accounts of anti–

apartheid movement's nonviolent action in opposition to New Zealand's participation in sports with South Africa, including boycotts, skywriting, and nonviolent invasion of matches. Illustrations. Photos.)

1431.   ———, *By Batons and Barbed Wire: A Response to the 1981 Springbok Tour of New Zealand.* 96 pp. Auckland: Real Pictures, 1983 [orig. publ. 1981]. (Photos and text on the effort to halt a tour by the South African rugby team and enforce the international boycott of S.A. sports teams. Text shows that an initial success in barricading a field hardened the determination to go through with the tour and that of police to escalate their methods. See "Police and Protest Tactics," pp. 78–81 for a summary of this. Photos.)

1432.   Shears, Richard, *Storm Out of Africa: The 1981 Springbok Tour of New Zealand.* 154 pp. Auckland, N.Z.: Macmillan, 1981. (Journalists' story of protests surrounding 1981 South African rugby team tour of New Zealand. Ch. 9 examines violence in protests. Photos.)

Labor and Agriculture

New Zealand's own accounts of labor conflicts often focus on significant strikes or the sweep of labor history and organizing. Among the conflicts reported on in these entries are a five–month long dockworkers' strike in 1951 and agricultural issues.

1433.   Bassett, Michael, *Confrontation '51: The 1951 Waterfront Dispute.* 264 pp. Wellington: A.H. & A.W. Reed, 1971. (History of five–month dock strike and government attempts to declare strikes illegal and use emergency powers. Focuses on strategy of both sides in strike. Illustrations. Photos. Index.)

1434.   Holland, H.E., "Ballot Box," and R.S. Ross, *The Tragic Story of the Waihi Strike.* 202 pp. Wellington: The "Worker" Printery, 1913. Reprint, Dunedin: Hocken Library, 1928. (Pro–labor account of Waihi miners' and workers' union strike of 1912. Photos. Documents.)

1435.   Howells, John M., Noel S. Woods, and F.J.L. Young, eds., *Labour and Industrial Relations in New Zealand*. 331 pp. Victoria, Australia: Sir Isaac Pitman, 1974. (Symposium on industrial relations. Part 3 is on industrial conflict. See especially ch. 8, 9 on strike frequency and legal issues. Consult index under *strikes* and *lockouts*. Index.)

1436.   Roth, Bert, and Janny Hammond, *Toil and Trouble: The Struggle for a Better Life in New Zealand*. 180 pp. Auckland: Methuen, 1981. ("Picture book" of New Zealand labor and strikes since 1840. Illustrations. Photos. Documents. Index.)

1437.   Roth, H., *Trade Unions in New Zealand: Past and Present*. 180 pp. Wellington: A.H. & A.W. Reed, 1973. (History of New Zealand labor disputes in pp. 3–90. Consult index under *strike, right to,* and *strikes*. Index. Bibliography.)

1438.   Scott, Dick, *151 Days: History of the Great Waterfront Lockout and Supporting Strikes, February 15–July 15, 1951*. 206 pp. Reprint, Christchurch: Labour Reprint Society, 1977. 1st ed., 1952. Abridged ed., 1954. (Unionists' official report on dock strikes. Illustrations. Photos. Documents. Index.)

1439.   Slee, June, *Bloody Friday: An Account of the Southland Farmers' Protest*. 48 pp. Dunedin: John McIndoe, 1979. (Photos and text on sheep farmers' protest against being left with unwanted sheep raised for slaughter. See pp. 1–24 on protest by driving sheep to slaughter through town of Invercargill and pp. 3, 4, 20, 30–46 on conflict between farmers and unionized freezer plant workers, both of which exchanged "bans." Photos. Documents.)

THE PHILIPPINES

Revolution of 1986

The presidency of Ferdinand Marcos engendered much opposition during the 1970s and 1980s. Little was organized nonviolent action, although the left held several election boycotts. Direct action against Marcos began when

*former senator and political prisoner Benigno Aquino returned to the country
from the U.S. and was immediately assassinated at the airport on August 21,
1983. His legacy of opposition passed to his widow, Corazon Aquino, who ran
against Marcos in a "snap" presidential election in early 1986. After Marcos
claimed victory through evident fraud, Mrs. Aquino declared herself the
genuine winner and prepared her followers for demonstrations and civil
disobedience. Before these could begin, disaffected military officers of the
Reform the Army group (RAM), mutinied against Marcos and took over a
military camp near Manila. The rebellious soldiers were prepared for a violent
showdown but became the rallying point for the "People Power" forces of
Aquino during the events of February 22–25, 1986. Protests and
demonstrations accelerated until a mass blockade of the streets prevented loyal
forces from confronting the rebel military. This effectively stopped Marcos's
organized response, and, as demonstrations continued, he fled to the United
States. Mrs. Aquino then assumed the presidency.*

1440.   Aguirre, Col. Alexander P., *A People's Revolution of Our Time:
        Philippines, February 22–25, 1986.* 116 pp. Quezon City: Pan–
        Service Master Consultants, 1986. (Ch. 1 is on the military
        reform movement and ch. 2 discusses the soldiers' revolt as led
        by Enrile and Ramos and its plans to defend the occupation of
        Camp Crame. See pp. 24–26 on human blockades, pp. 32–34 on
        "military actions that turned the tide," and pp. 36–38 on
        marines' and soldiers' decision not to fire on civilians.
        Chronology. Appendixes.)

1441.   Arillo, Cecilio T., *Breakaway: The Inside Story of the Four–Day
        Revolution in the Philippines, February 22–25, 1986.* 288 pp.
        Manila: CTA & Associates, 1986. (A quite detailed chronicle of
        the Philippines revolution from the military side, drawn
        substantially from military sources including officers' reports
        and letters of various kinds, intelligence reports, and other
        military reports. Ch. 1–4 provide a day–by–day account,
        followed by a ch. 5 summarizing the origins of the revolt, ch. 6
        on People Power, and ch. 7, "RAM: Toward a Unique Martial
        Tradition." Photo section, pp. 184–275. Index. Bibliography of
        primary sources mentioned above, pp. 276–78.)

1442.   Bonner, Raymond, *Waltzing with a Dictator: The Marcoses and
        the Making of American Policy.* 570 pp. Revised ed., New York:
        Vintage Books, 1988 [orig. publ. 1982]. (An account of the

Marcos years with emphasis on the U.S. and U.S. personalities. See ch. 14 on the assassination of Benigno S. Aquino and its immediate aftermath, including pp. 345–46 on the demonstrative funeral held for him. Ch. 6 is on Marcos's "snap election" of 1986, including pp. 412–15 on the election–monitoring group NAMFREL and pp. 419–22 on vote–counting fraud and work stoppage by computer workers. See also pp. 439–45 on the conversion of Generals Ramos and Enrile to the Aquino camp and U.S. deliberations during the February Revolution. Index. Bibliography.)

1443.   Bresnan, John, ed., *Crisis in the Philippines: The Marcos Era and Beyond.* 298 pp. Princeton NJ: Princeton Univ. Press, 1986. (See Carl H. Lande, "The Political Crisis," ch. 5 for introductory overview of period from the Aquino assassination to 1986. Index.)

1444.   Chapman, William, *Inside the Philippines Revolution.* 288 pp. New York and London: W.W. Norton, 1987. (See pp. 229–49 on the National Democratic Front and the Communist Party of the Philippines in electoral protests and boycotts in the 1970s and 1980s and their decision to boycott the 1986 election as well, judged an error by the author. Index.)

1445.   Elwood, Douglas J., *Philippines Revolution 1986: Model of Nonviolent Change.* 60 pp. Quezon City, Philippines: New Day Publisher, 1986. (Brief history and analysis of the revolution seen as applied nonviolent action. See pp. 5–6 on the question of political power; pp. 24–29 on the role of the local peace movement and training conducted by Hildegard Goss–Mayr, Jean Goss–Mayr, and Richard Deats; and pp. 35–36 on "nonviolence theory." Appendix B reprints an anonymous statement on "creative nonviolence" from 1983. Photos. Appendixes.)

1446.   Fenton, James, "The Snap Revolution." *Granta* 18 (1986):33–155. (Journalist's story of his experiences during the revolution. See esp. pp. 42–48 on the election boycott and demonstrations; pp. 58–62, 66–69 on NAMFREL and the election controversy; and pp. 108–55, "The Snap Revolution." Photos.)

1447.   Joaquin, Nick, *The Quartet of the Tiger Moon: Scenes from the People Power Apocalypse.* 112 pp. Manila: Book Stop, 1986. (Day–by–day account of the nonviolent revolution, interspersed with many photos. See esp. pp. 43–46 for accounts of masses of people bringing tanks to a halt. Photos.)

1448.   Johnson, Bryan, *The Four Days of Courage: The Untold Story of the People Who Brought Marcos Down.* 290 pp. New York: Free Press, 1987. (Day–by–day account focusing on RAM and Cardinal Jaime Sin and the Catholic Church. See ch. 2–3 for RAM's coup preparations before 1986. See ch. 6–16 on military revolt, demonstrations, and fighting. Illustrations. Photos. Chronology. Index.)

1449.   Komisar, Lucy, *Corazon Aquino: The Story of a Revolution.* 290 pp. New York: George Braziller, 1987. (Pp. 3–5, 37–50 discuss Benigno Aquino's career in opposition to Marcos and pp. 52–60 describe beginnings of Corazon Aquino's political career. Pp. 93–103 are on her plans for action after the election and pp. 105–23 are on the RAM mutiny and demonstration. Illustrations. Index.)

1450.   Mamot, Patricio R., *People Power: Profile of Filipino Heroism.* 208 pp. Quezon City: New Day, 1986. (Engaged account of February Revolution, based on news articles and interviews. On concept of "people power" and nonviolent action, see pp. 11–15, 19–20, 29–30, 32, 40–41, 120–22, 153–55, 189–91. Photos.)

1451.   Mercado, M.A., ed., *People Power: The Philippine Revolution of 1986: An Eyewitness History.* 320 pp. Manila: James B. Reuter, S.J. Foundation, 1986. (Oral history of the revolution, including eyewitness accounts by Corazon Aquino, Juan Ponce Enrile, Fidel Ramos, and Cardinal Jaime Sin. Photos. Appendix.)

1452.   Ordonez, Marcelo, *People Power: A Demonstration of the Emerging Filipino Ideology.* 46 pp. Quezon City: Sampaguita Printing Press, 1986. (Monograph by Filipino social scientist that explores cultural and historical bases of "people power." Contains manifesto of suggestions for maintaining future peace and self–determination. Bibliography.)

1453. Schwenk, Richard L., *Onward, Christians! Protestants in the Philippines Revolution*. 102 pp. Quezon City: New Day Publishers, 1986. (Reviews the contributions of evangelical Protestants of a variety of denominations to People Power actions, with emphasis on "nonviolence as a Christian phenomenon." Glossary. Chronology. Photo section, pp. 57–90.)

1454. Simons, Lewis M., *Worth Dying For*. 320 pp. New York: William Morrow, 1987. (Focuses mainly on the history of Marcos' extravagance and political ineptitude as a backdrop to the four–day revolution. See esp. pp. 288–295 for description of "people power" demonstration and the Marcos flight. Photos. Index.)

1455. Soriano, Marcelo B., *The Unused Guns of the 4–Day EDSA Revolt*. 101 pp. Quezon City: The author, 1986. (Presents a corrective to the view that no armed civilians were involved in the revolt at the EDSA barracks, as summarized in ch. 13 which offers impressions of militarized civilians prepared to support the military rebellion. Appendixes.)

1456. Univ. of Santo Tomas Social Research Center, *The Philippine Revolution and the Involvement of the Church*. 99 pp. Manila: Social Research Center, Univ. of Santo Tomas, 1986. Monograph no. 4. (See pp. 8–19 for description and chronology of revolution, p. 22 for people blocking tanks, pp. 5, 91–92 on "non–violence." Photos. Documents.)

1457. UST Social Research Center, *The Philippine Revolution and the Involvement of the Church*. 99 pp. Manila: Social Research Center, Univ. of Santo Tomas, 1986. SRC Monograph 4. (Provides social scientific views on the claim that the Catholic Church was intimately involved in election monitoring and the revolution and led in its adoption of "active nonviolence." Photos.)

1458. Yap, Miguela Gonzalez, *The Making of Cory*. Quezon City: New Day Publishers, 1987. 266 pp. (In addition to pp. 48–49 on a prison hunger strike by Benigno Aquino and pp. 74–83 on the aftermath of his assassination, see pp. 96–103 and ch. 7 on the elections of 1986, including pp. 126–30 on Corazon Aquino's ideas for "civil disobedience." Ch. 8 is on the revolution of February 1986, including discussion of RAM's anticipated coup and a chronicle of events. Photos. Appendix. Bibliography.)

TIBET

Tibet is considered by China as part of its realm. China has suppressed the traditional culture of the country, driven out its leadership, and encouraged immigration by ethnic Chinese (Han). Demonstrations and resistance have also been met with repression.

1459.   Kelly, Petra K., Gert Bastian, and Pat Aiello, eds., *The Anguish of Tibet*. 382 pp. Berkeley CA: Parallax Press, 1991. (Collected pieces, documentation, and personal accounts on all aspects of China's position in Tibet and opposition to it, both internal and international. Includes articles on methods of repression, suppression of national identity, and similar issues. See Christa Meindersma, "Eyewitness: Lhasa Demonstrations—1988," pp. 245–47 and Susanne Maier, "Eyewitness: Lhasa Demonstrations—1989," pp. 248–51. Photos. Appendixes. Bibliography.)

WESTERN SAMOA

Mau Movement Against New Zealand Mandate, 1919–1936

The following entries are on a twelve–year campaign of protest and noncooperation, against a colonial government, which is practically unknown outside the Pacific region. While Germany had been the first colonial power in Western Samoa, New Zealand received a mandate from the League of Nations to govern the islands, which was challenged by the pro–independence O le Mau movement. The movement conducted demonstrations and boycotts and constructed alternative political institutions to undercut New Zealand's power. Led by a traditional chief, Tamasese, the movement survived the violent death of its leader when troops fired into a crowd and went on to support a period of noncooperation and resistance. It is noteworthy that these sources have few preconceptions about nonviolent action and offer much detail about the means and measures of the movement and their effects.

1460. Davidson, J.W., *Samoa Mo Samoa: The Emergence of the Independent State of Western Samoa.* 467 pp. Melbourne, London, Wellington, and New York: Oxford Univ. Press, 1967. (See ch. 5, esp. pp. 118–56, on the O le Mau movement of 1926–38 and its effect on independent government, incl. pp. 122, 130–33, 137–38, 141–42 on various nonviolent means used. Index.)

1461. Field, Michael J., *Mau: Samoa's Struggle against New Zealand Oppression.* 262 pp. Wellington, N.Z.: A.H. & A.W. Reed, 1984. (Detailed history of Samoan resistance against New Zealand government, headed by the Mau organization. See ch. 6–14; esp. ch. 8, which discusses the "passive resistance" policy of Mau on pp. 99–106. Illustrations. Photos. Index. Bibliography.)

1462. Hempenstall, Peter J., *Pacific Islanders under German Rule: A Study in the Meaning of Colonial Resistance.* 264 pp. (Ch. 2 studies resistance in Samoa under German colonialism prior to WWI. See also ch. 8, "Resistance: Conservatism and Innovation," and ch. 9, "The Social Dynamics of Protest." Index. Bibliography.)

1463. Hempenstall, Peter, and Noel Rutherford, *Protest and Dissent in the Colonial Pacific.* 200 pp. Suva: Institute of Pacific Studies, Univ. of the South Pacific, 1984. (Ch. 1 is a case study of the Western Samoa protest and resistance movements under both German and New Zealand domination. See also ch. 2 for an economic protest movement in Tonga and ch. 3 for a 1959 labor strike in Fiji. Photos. Index. Bibliography.)

1464. Keesing, Felix M., *Modern Samoa: Its Government and Changing Life.* 506 pp. London: George Allen & Unwin, 1934. (Analysis of Samoan government under League of Nations mandate and before. See pp. 152–57, 177–91 on Mau movement. Illustrations. Index. Bibliography.)

1465. Rowe, N.A., *Samoa under the Sailing Gods.* 339 pp. London and New York: Putnam, 1930. (Ch. 20–23 contain a chronological account of government and opposition in early Mau years, up to the death of Tamasese in 1929. Written by opponent of New Zealand mandate. Detailed account of demonstration at time of Tamasese's death is on pp. 275–78. Photos. Index. Bibliography.)

VIETNAM

Opposition to South Vietnamese Government

The "third force" or "third way" was shorthand for religious and political opposition to the government of South Vietnam and sometimes also to the National Liberation Front (NLF). A loose coalition of religious groups, students, and others was strongest from about 1963 to 1967. The roots of the third force lay in the clash of Buddhists and the government of Ngo Dinh Diem in 1963. The Catholic Diem family tried to limit Buddhists' right to hold religious ceremonies freely in public, quickly escalating to severe punishments when they resisted. Buddhists replied with demonstrations in the capital, Saigon. Although they renounced violence, some Buddhists and their supporters decided on public self–immolation as a sign of their unyielding protest. In November 1963, military forces raided many pagodas in the middle of the night, beating and arresting many monks. After this episode, the U.S. turned against the regime and supported a coup d'état that took place soon after, and in which the Diem brothers were killed.

1466.   Arnold, Lynn, et al., *Hoa Binh: The Third Force and the Struggle for Peace in Vietnam: A Report by Four Australian University Students Who Recently Visited South Vietnam.* 44 pp. Melbourne, Australia: Aquarius Editorial Committee of Melbourne University War Resisters International for the Federal Pacifist Council, [1970]. (The report of International Fellowship of Reconciliation Team that went to Saigon in July 1970 to investigate the Buddhists, students, lawyers, unionists, and other urban groups who had been struggling for peace and an end to foreign intervention since the time of Diem. Photos.)

1467.   Boyle, Richard, *The Flower of the Dragon: The Breakdown of the U.S. Army in Vietnam.* 282 pp. San Francisco: Ramparts Press, 1972. (Journalist's story of experiences in Vietnam. See pp.

147–80 for protest voyage of vessel *Prajna* by the Coconut Monk, Dao Dua, 1968. See also pp. 192–200 on student protest and pp. 85–90, 222–36 on U.S. soldiers' refusal to enter combat. Photos.)

1468. Fitzgerald, Frances, *Fire in the Lake: The Vietnamese and the Americans in Vietnam*. 491 pp. Boston: Little, Brown, 1972. (See ch. 3, pp. 129–35, ch. 8, 9, pp. 301–02, 420 on Buddhist resistance. Index. Bibliography.)

1469. Gheddo, Piero, *The Cross and the Bo–Tree: Catholics and Buddhists in Vietnam*. Trans. Charles Underhill Quinn. 368 pp. New York: Sheed & Ward, 1970. (Study of religious aspects of Vietnamese conflict quite critical of Buddhists. See pp. 178–88, 191–201 on Buddhist actions in 1963; pp. 272–76 on 1966, and pp. 310–15, 347–51 on the "third way." See also pp. 204–5, n. 26, for discussion of self–immolation.)

1470. Halberstam, David, *The Making of a Quagmire*. 323 pp. New York: Random House, 1965. (Ch. 13–15, 17 discuss Buddhist and student protests and the origins of the coup against Diem.)

1471. Hammer, Ellen J., *A Death in November: America in Vietnam, 1963*. 373 pp. New York: E.P. Dutton, 1987. (Discussion of Buddhist protests, self–immolation, and pagoda raids in 1963 on pp. 110–18, 134–52, 159–68. Index.)

1472. Hassler, Alfred, *Saigon, U.S.A.* 291 pp. New York: Richard W. Baron, 1970. (Account by executive director of Fellowship of Reconciliation on Buddhist movement for peace in Vietnam, its relation to U.S. peace movement, and the "U.S. Study Team on Religious and Political Freedom in Vietnam." Documents. Index.)

1473. Kahin, George McT., *Intervention: How America Became Involved in Vietnam*. 550 pp. New York: Alfred A. Knopf, 1986. (The 1963 Buddhist clashes with the Diem government are discussed on pp. 148–53 and continued Buddhist involvement in demonstrations and politics in the years following are on pp. 227–30, 233–34, 267–71, 294–96. The "Struggle Movement" of 1966 is described on pp. 414–32. Index.)

1474.   Lacouture, Jean, *Vietnam: Between Two Truces*. Trans. Konrad
        Kellen and Joel Carmichael. 295 pp. New York: Random
        House, 1966. Originally published in French as *Le Vietnam entre
        deux paix*. Paris: Editions du Seuil, 1965. (See part 3, ch. 1, pp.
        108–11, and part 6, ch. 2, on the Buddhists and their political
        role in South Vietnam in the mid–1960s. Index.)

1475.   Luce, Don, and John Sommer, *Viet Nam: The Unheard Voices*.
        336 pp. Ithaca and London: Cornell Univ. Press, 1969.
        (Personal experiences of two International Voluntary Service
        volunteers. See ch. 6 on the "struggle movement" and ch. 12 on
        student movements. Photos. Index.)

1476.   Nhat Hanh, Thich, *Vietnam: Lotus in a Sea of Fire*. 115 pp. New
        York: Hill & Wang, 1967. (Places Buddhist war resistance in
        Vietnam, ca. 1963–67, in context of religion and history. See pp.
        76–91 on peace movement, including 1965 peace petition.
        Appendixes.)

1477.   *The Pentagon Papers: The Defense Department History of the
        United States Decision–Making on Vietnam*. The Senator Gravel
        Edition, vol. 2. 834 pp. Boston: Beacon Press, 1971. (See ch. 4,
        esp. pp. 201–52, on the effects of the Buddhist campaign, and
        its repression, on U.S. policy towards the Diem regime. Photos.
        Glossary. Appendix.)

1478.   Roberts, Adam, "Buddhism and Politics in South Vietnam."
        The World Today [London] 21 (1965): 240–50. (Account of
        Buddhist political involvement and its technique in opposition
        to Diem government.)

1479.   ———, "The Buddhists, the War, and the Vietcong." *The World
        Today* [London] 22 (1966): 214–22. (Study of the implications of
        Buddhist adoption of nonviolent methods in politics for their
        role in South Vietnamese anti–government forces.)

1480.   Schechter, Jerrold, *The New Face of Buddha: Buddhism and
        Political Power in Southeast Asia*. 300 pp. New York: Coward–
        McCann, 1967. (See ch. 8 on political ideas and personalities
        and ch. 9–11 on the rise and fall of Buddhist dissent in
        Vietnam, 1963–66. Photos.)

1481.   Warner, Denis, *The Last Confucian*. 274 pp. New York: Macmillan, 1963. Reprint. 327 pp. Baltimore, Harmondsworth, England, and Ringwood, Australia: Penguin Books, 1964. (See ch. 13 on Diem and the Buddhists.)

1482.   Wirmark, Bo, *The Buddhists in Vietnam: An Alternative View of the War*. 42 pp. Belgium: War Resisters' International, 1974. (Account of Vietnamese Buddhist peace movement, and "implications of the Buddhist position in its political context." See esp. pp. 9–13, 19–25. Illustrations. Photos. Documents.)

Prison Camp Resistance in North Vietnam

In defending themselves against the total control exerted by their captors and its psychological effects, U.S. servicemen held prisoner in North Vietnam developed many means of resistance and protest, some of which are shown in the following entries.

1483.   Denton, Jeremiah A., Jr., with Ed Brand, *When Hell Was in Session*. 192 pp. Lake Wylie SC: R.E. Hopper and Associates, 1982. (Memoirs of a POW, with many examples of spirited resistance to North Vietnamese prison authorities.)

1484.   Mulligan, James A., *The Hanoi Commitment*. 298 pp. Virginia Beach VA: RIF Marketing, 1981. (Memoir of U.S. POWs and their resistance in captivity. See esp. pp. 219–25 for noncooperation and a fast and pp. 237–39 for a "church service revolt." Photos.)

Chapter 4
Europe

Although researchers cannot generalize about nonviolent action in a continent as diverse as Europe, there are some points that characterize the region's common history. For one thing, Europe is the home of the concept of "passive resistance," which is an older term than nonviolent action but has a similar meaning (see Huxley, entry 1588 for a history of this idea). With this concept to draw on, Europeans shared a common thread in their employment of noncooperation and resistance for over a century and a half. Consequently, the researcher finds various national experiences in the use of nonviolent action early in the nineteenth century (see GREAT BRITAIN), at the time of the Revolutions of 1848 (see HUNGARY), and at the end of the century (see FINLAND).

Another source of nonviolent action and its traditions has been the labor movement. In some European states, debates over the proper means of action in labor conflicts, which often encompassed nonviolent action, also originated in the early nineteenth century and perhaps earlier. The labor movements of the various countries developed the strike and various forms of limited or disguised strikes, boycotts, picketing, and all sorts of marches, parades, and symbolic speech used to support their movements.

Both of the factors in European history just discussed are associated with state–making and the creation of a modern economy in the past two centuries. Two other, more recent, events loom large in European history since 1930. One is Nazism and resistance to the German occupation of Europe from 1939 to 1945, while the other is dissent and opposition against the Soviet state after 1917 and opposition in its East European empire from World War Two until the late 1980s. In both of these examples, it may seem at first as if there was no place for nonviolent action. This is especially true of Germany's implacable war against the Jews of Europe. Yet nonviolent action, both open and disguised, was an important feature of both of these. In the case of the Holocaust, this was associated with the hiding and rescue of Jews and "illegal" immigration into Palestine (see Chapter 1). In the Soviet world, it included open, if sporadic, protest even within the U.S.S.R. itself, often conducted by religious groups and intellectuals.

OPPOSITION AND RESISTANCE TO NAZI OCCUPATION, 1939–1945

Entries in this section are on resistance, both individual and collective, in Nazi–occupied Europe from 1939 to 1945. Of course, much resistance in Europe was military or para–military, and it was often closely associated with governments in exile or allied forces. Protest, noncooperation, disguised disobedience, and strikes sometimes contributed to attempts to reduce the scope and powers of Nazi methods. Some of these had the goal of protecting the remnants of national sovereignty (see THE NETHERLANDS), while other nations tried to prevent Nazism from extending its grasp further once it was in command (see NORWAY). Some nonviolent action was simply the result of desperation and in an attempt to keep people alive. This section also contains some entries on nonviolent action in the hiding, flight, and rescue of Jewish victims of the Nazis, of which there is more below.

See also: Bulgaria, Denmark, France, Hungary, the Netherlands, Norway, Poland, Romania, Palestine: "Illegal" Immigration of Jews During British Mandate, 1944–1948.

1485.   Bramstedt, E.K., *Dictatorship and Political Police: The Technique of Control by Fear.* 275 pp. New York: Oxford Univ. Press, 1945. (Study of the history of repression and Fascist and Nazi methods of control and repression. Ch. 2–4 discuss the SS, Gestapo, and political concentration camps. Part IV, on "terror and resistance," includes ch. 5 on Socialist and church resistance in Germany and ch. 6 on the occupied countries, with studies of the Netherlands, underground press, and "passive resistance" in Norway. See pp. 44–48, 59–61, 142–143, 186 for discussion of *agents provocateurs.* Index.)

1486.   *European Resistance Movements, 1939–1945: First International Conference on the History of the Resistance Movements Held at Liege–Bruxelles–Breendonk, 14–17 September 1958.* 410 pp. Oxford: Pergamon Press, 1960. (Articles in French, German, and English. See L. de Jong, "Anti–Nazi Resistance in the

Netherlands," pp. 137–49; J. Haestrup, "Exposé," pp. 150–62, on resistance in Denmark; and Philip Friedman, "Jewish Resistance to Nazism: Its Various Forms and Aspects," pp. 195–214.)

1487. *European Resistance Movements, 1939–1945: Proceedings of the Second International Conference on the History of Resistance Movements Held at Milan, 26–29 March 1961.* 663 pp. Oxford: Pergamon Press, 1964. (Articles in French and English. This volume focuses largely on resistance movement contacts with allied governments. See J. Haestrup, "Denmark's Connection with the Allied Powers during the Occupation," pp. 282–97; S. Kjelstadli, "The Resistance Movement in Norway and the Allies [1940–1945]," pp. 324–39; and L. de Jong, "The Dutch Resistance Movement and the Allies [1940–1945]," pp. 390–465. Photos. Index of names.)

1488. Haestrup, Jorgen, *European Resistance Movements, 1939–1945: A Complete History.* 567 pp. Westport CT and London: Meckler, 1981. (Thorough synthesis and review of the nature and actions of WWII resistance movements. Ch. 1, 2 are on problems of definition, method, and the composition of resistance. See also ch. 3 on "Forms of Civil Disobedience"; i.e., nonviolent resistance methods that ranged from symbolic protest to noncooperation and strikes, and pp. 218–36 on illegal newspapers. Although little is concluded on effects, see pp. 78, 82, 98, 101, 103, 107–8, 126–27, 131, 140, 144. Illustrations. Index. Bibliography.)

1489. Laska, Vera, *Women in the Resistance and in the Holocaust: The Voices of Eyewitnesses.* 345 pp. Westport CT and London: Greenwood Press, 1983. (Collected personal accounts. See ch. 2 on Denmark, ch. 3 on the Netherlands, and ch. 6–7 on organized assistance to Jews. Illustrations. Photos. Index. Bibliography.)

1490. Michel, Henri, *The Shadow War: Resistance in Europe, 1939–1945.* 416 pp. London: Andre Deutsch, 1972. Originally published as *La Guerre de l'Ombre.* Paris: Bernard Grasset, 1970. (Detailed discussion of resistance movements, para–military and nonviolent. See esp. ch. 12, "Passive and Administrative

Resistance," as well as pp. 76–80, 82–84, 224–29. Chronology.
Index. Bibliography.)

1491.   Miller, Russell, and the editors of Time–Life Books, *The
         Resistance*. 208 pp. Alexandria VA: Time–Life Books, 1979.
         (Photo–history concerned mostly with military resistance, but
         see photos on pp. 8–17; pp. 30–39 on the clandestine press; pp.
         128, 130, 134–37 on Danish rescue of Jews; and pp. 138–49 on
         Dutch hiding of Jews. Illustrations. Photos. Index.
         Bibliography.)

1492.   Riess, Curt, *Underground Europe*. 325 pp. New York: Dial Press,
         1942. (Collected narratives of wartime resistance, most
         involving sabotage, assassination, and undergrounds.)

1493.   Rings, Werner, *Life with the Enemy: Collaboration and Resistance
         in Hitler's Europe, 1939–1945*. Trans. J. Maxwell Brownjohn. 280
         pp. Garden City NY: Doubleday, 1982. (Journalistic account of
         techniques of occupation used by German forces, 1939–45 and
         responses to them, especially collaboration and resistance. See
         pp. 27–31 on Denmark's "legalistic tricks," pp. 153–88 on
         nonviolent resistance, and pp. 265–67 on the efficacy of para-
         military resistance. Illustrations. Photos. Index. Bibliography.)

1494.   Semelin, Jacques, *Unarmed Against Hitler: Civilian Resistance in
         Europe, 1939–1943*. 198 pp. Westport CT: Praeger, 1993.
         (Thorough study of "civil resistance" [as opposed to "the
         Resistance"] in Nazi–occupied Europe, covering the years from
         the beginning of warfare until the Allied advances threatened
         German control from without. In addition to analytical
         chapters on the nature of occupation control measures, the
         influence of social solidarity, public opinion, and legitimacy,
         see ch. 2 on definitions, ch. 3 on noncooperation, ch. 7 on
         repression, ch. 7 on genocide, and ch. 9 on the question of
         effectiveness and outcomes. Methodological appendix. List of
         cases categorized by method employed, pp. 261–63. Index.)

1495.   Seth, Ronald, *The Undaunted: The Story of Resistance in Western
         Europe*. 327 pp. New York: Philosophical Library, 1956. (Brief,
         popular–style accounts of resistance in nine countries, often
         para–military and sabotage, as well as some nonviolent

resistance and Special Operations Executive activities. Bibliography.)

1496. Snoek, Johan M., *The Grey Book: A Collection of Protests against Anti–Semitism and the Persecution of Jews Issued by Non–Roman Catholic Churches and Church Leaders during Hitler's Rule.* 341 pp. Assen, the Netherlands: Koninklijke Van Gorcum, 1968. (Chronicle containing many extracts from documents. See esp. pp. 13–24 on the causes and results of church protests; part 3 on the war years, esp. ch. 21–26, 29 on countries where some assistance was given to Jews; and ch. 23 on countries where the "churches kept silent." Documents. Bibliography.)

1497. Toynbee, Arnold, and Veronica M. Toynbee, eds., *Survey of International Affairs, 1939–1946.* Vol. 4, *Hitler's Europe.* 730 pp. London, New York and Toronto: Oxford Univ. Press, 1954. (See pp. 34–42 on German internal opposition, pp. 126–53 on law and repression, pp. 327–37 on Italy, pp. 400–33 on resistance in Vichy France, and part 5 on occupation and resistance in Western European countries. Index.)

Jewish Resistance

Jewish resistance in the Holocaust took several forms, conditioned by the overwhelming military power of Nazi Germany and local collaborator regimes, by the breadth of the campaign to destroy European Jewry, and by the refusal of non–Jews to interfere with the Holocaust or resist its extension. The entries below point to some resistance that penetrated the death camps themselves and to episodes of hiding and of rescue of victims. In some states, such as FRANCE and BULGARIA, there were limits on direct Nazi control and opportunities occasionally arose for protest and noncooperation. Perhaps best known among these are the actions of non–Jews in protecting and transporting Jews escaping from the Holocaust. Some states, such as DENMARK, were able to thwart the deportation of Jews to an extent. Likewise, Jewish groups were able to operate on the margins of Nazi control to carry out rescues

See also Palestine: "Illegal" Immigration of Jews During British Mandate.

1498.   Bauer, Yehuda, *The Jewish Emergence from Powerlessness*. 103 pp.
         Toronto, Buffalo, and London: Univ. of Toronto Press, 1979.
         (See pp. 26–40, "Forms of Jewish Resistance during the
         Holocaust," which argues that there was much nonviolent and
         violent resistance. See esp. pp. 26–27 on definitions of
         resistance and pp. 34–40 for examples of "unarmed active
         resistance." Index.)

1499.   ————, *They Chose Life: Jewish Resistance in the Holocaust*. 63 pp.
         New York: The American Jewish Committee, 1973. (See ch. 5,
         pp. 32–39, on nonviolent resistance and noncooperation.
         Photos.)

1500.   Fein, Helen, *Accounting for Genocide: National Responses and
         Jewish Victimization during the Holocaust*. 468 pp. New York:
         Free Press; London: Collier Macmillan, 1979. (Historical–
         sociological study of the structure of genocide against
         European Jews and the Jewish response to the Holocaust. See
         ch. 1 for discussion of structures of genocide and pp. 114–118
         for Christian protests against oppression of Jews. See esp. ch. 6
         for "social defense movements" in Denmark, Belgium, and
         Bulgaria. See also ch. 10 on the Netherlands and ch. 11 on
         Hungary. Appendixes. Index. Bibliography.)

1501.   Latour, Anny, *The Jewish Resistance in France, 1940–1944*. Trans.
         Irene R. Ilton. 287 pp. New York: Holocaust Library, 1970. (See
         particularly material on the saving of children and adults, pp.
         60–93, 113–19, 130–38, and pastor Andre Trocmé, pp. 138–45.
         Photos. Chronology. Index.)

1502.   Marrus, Michael, ed., *The Nazi Holocaust: Historical Articles on
         the Destruction of European Jewry*. 9 books in 15 volumes.
         Westport CT and London: Meckler, 1989. (Collection of articles
         on nearly every imaginable aspect of the Holocaust. On
         resistance, rescue, and related issues, see articles in the list that
         follows. Book 4, *The "Final Solution" Outside Germany*, vol. 1,
         418 pp. Louis de Jong, "Jews and non–Jews in Nazi–Occupied
         Holland," pp. 129–45; Leni Yahil, "Methods of Persecution: A
         Comparison of the 'Final Solution' in Holland and Denmark,"
         pp. 169–90; Jean Ancel, "Plans for the Deportation of the
         Rumanian Jews and Their Discontinuation in Light of

Documentary Evidence (July–October 1942)," pp. 334–73; and Nissan Oren, "The Bulgarian Exception: A Reassessment of the Salvation of a Jewish Community," pp. 393–416. Book 5, *Public Opinion and Relations to the Jews in Nazi Europe*, vol. 1, 450 pp. Philip Friedman, "Was There an 'Other Germany' during the Nazi Period?," pp. 3–45; Ian Kershaw, "The Persecution of the Jews and German Popular Opinion in the Third Reich," pp. 86–114; Otto Dov Kulka, "'Public Opinion' in Nazi Germany and the 'Jewish Question'," pp. 115–38. Book 5, *Public Opinion and Relations to the Jews in Nazi Europe*, vol. 2, 336 pp. This volume contains part 3 of book 5, entitled "Support for Jews," and includes Moshe Bejski, "The 'Righteous Among the Nations' and Their Part in the Rescue," pp. 451–76; Samuel P. Oliner, "The Need to Recognize the Heroes of the Nazi Era," pp. 477–85; Joseph Kermish, "The Activities of the Council for Aid to Jews ('Zegota') in Occupied Poland," pp. 485–516; Teresa Prekerowa, "The Relief Council for Jews in Poland, 1942–1945," pp. 517–32; Hugo Valentin, "Rescue and Relief Activities in Behalf of Jewish Victims of Nazism in Scandinavia," pp. 533–60; Leni Yahil, "The Uniqueness of the Rescue of Danish Jewry," pp. 561–69; Tatiana Brustein–Berenstein, "The Historiographic Treatment of the Abortive Attempt to Deport the Danish Jews," pp. 570–607; Lawrence Baron, "The Dynamics of Decency: Dutch Rescuers of Jews during the Holocaust," pp. 608–26; Louis de Jong, "Help to People in Hiding," pp. 627–69; and Daniel Carpi, "The Rescue of Jews in the Italian Zone of Occupied Croatia," pp. 670–730. Book 7, *Jewish Resistance to the Holocaust*. 563 pp. Yehuda Bauer, "Forms of Jewish Resistance during the Holocaust," pp. 34–48 [esp. pp. 42–48]; Konrad Kwiet, "Problems of Jewish Resistance Historiography," pp. 49–69 [esp. pp. 66–69]; Yitzhak Arad, "Jewish Family Camps in the Forest: An Original Means of Rescue," pp. 214–40; Helmut Eschwege, "Resistance of German Jews against the Nazi Regime," pp. 385–428; Arnold Paucker, "Some Notes on Resistance," pp. 429–42; Hillel J. Kieval, "Legality and Resistance in Vichy France: The Rescue of Jewish Children," pp. 482–509; Haim Avni, "The Zionist Underground in Holland and France and the Escape to Spain," pp. 510–45. Book 8, *Bystanders to the Holocaust*, vol. 3, 468 pp. Steven Kobla, "Sweden's Attempts to Aid Jews, 1939–1945," pp. 1173–97. Book 9, *The End of the Holocaust*. 733 pp. Dalia

Ofer, "The Rescue of European Jewry and Illegal Immigration to Palestine in 1940—Prospects and Reality: Berthold Storfer, and the Mossad Le'Aliyah Bet," pp. 199–222; Leni Yahil, "The Scandinavian Countries to the Rescue of Concentration Camp Prisoners," pp. 356–97; Leni Yahil, "Raoul Wallenberg—His Mission and His Activities in Hungary," pp. 398–444.)

1503.   Suhl, Yuri, ed., *They Fought Back: The Story of the Jewish Resistance in Nazi Europe.* 327 pp. New York: Schocken, 1967. London: Macgibbon & Kee, 1968. (Collection of short historical pieces on Jewish resistance all over Europe, mostly armed struggle and armed uprisings. See Yuri Suhl, "Chief Physician Remba," pp. 82–84 for description of a rescue operation undertaken by Suhl posing as a doctor and Matei Yulzari, "The Bulgarian Jews in the Resistance Movement," pp. 275–81. Index.)

1504.   Syrkin, Marie, *Blessed Is the Match: The Story of Jewish Resistance.* 361 pp. Philadelphia: Jewish Publication Society of America, 1947. (Popular style account of violent and nonviolent resistance and rescue and protection of Jews. See especially ch. 2, 3, 6, 9.)

Hiding and Rescue of Jews

Some non–Jews in nearly every country occupied by the Nazis tried to assist persecuted Jews by hiding them or helping them to move to safer places, often at the risk of the rescuers' own lives.

See also: Bulgaria, Denmark, Palestine: "Illegal" Immigration of Jews During British Mandate.

1505.   Bartoszewski, Wladyslaw, and Zofia Lewin, *The Samaritans: Heroes of the Holocaust.* Ed. Alexander T. Jordan. 442 pp. New York: Twayne, 1970. (Personal accounts, with a good deal of scattered detail, of aid to Jews in Poland. Of interest are accounts of the use of false papers, including a Gestapo counter–plot to entrap resisters and escapees, and various testimonials of survivors. Index of names.)

1506. Friedenson, Joseph, and David Kranzler, *Heroine of Rescue: The Incredible Story of Recha Sternbuch, Who Saved Thousands from the Holocaust*. 335 pp. Brooklyn NY: Mesorah Publications, 1984. (Biography of couple who aided rescue efforts during and after WWII. On wartime organizing and methods, see ch. 1, 3, 5–7, 9. Photos. Documents. Index.)

1507. Gutman, Yisrael, and Efraim Zuroff, eds., *Rescue Attempts during the Holocaust*. 684 pp. Jerusalem: Yad Vashem, 1977. (See pp. 289–331 on Lithuania, pp. 603–15 on Belgium and France, and pp. 627–47 for a discussion of personalities. See also limited comments on the rescue of "over 98 percent" of Danish Jews, pp. 617–25. Documents. Index.)

1508. Szonyi, David M., ed., *The Holocaust: An Annotated Bibliography and Resource Guide*. 396 pp. New York: KTAV Publishing House for the National Jewish Resource Center, 1985. (See pp. 80–92 for entries on Jewish rescue efforts, church resistance in Germany, and aid to Jews.)

1509. Yahil, Leni, *The Holocaust: The Fate of European Jewry, 1932–1945*. 808 pp. New York and Oxford: Oxford Univ. Press, 1990. (Detailed, wide–ranging study of the destruction of the Jews of Europe, beginning from the Nazi taking of power. Rescue and resistance are discussed in various places, most notably in ch. 19–21 which detail survival and rescue operations. Ch. 20 in particular discusses rescues from Denmark, Finland, and Bulgaria and the efforts of Jewish organizations, while ch. 21 describes ransom negotiations and the Wallenberg mission. Appendix. Index. Bibliography.)

PROTEST AND DISSENT SINCE 1945

These references discuss protest movements in several European countries after 1945, many of which are associated with anti–Soviet politics. See also sections on individual countries below.

1510. Brinton, William, and Alan Rinzler, eds., *Without Force or Lies: Voices from the Revolution of Central Europe in 1989–90*. 495 pp.

San Francisco: Mercury House, 1990. (Short pieces on various aspects of the movements of 1989 and 1990. Of some interest are Václav Havel, "The Power of the Powerless," pp. 43–127; Edith Anderson, "Town Mice and Country Mice: The East German Revolution," pp. 170–92; Adam Michnik, "The Moral and Spiritual Origins of Solidarity," pp. 239–50; Václav Havel, "Four Essays," pp. 265–80; and George Paul Csicsery, "The Siege of Nógrádi Street, Budapest, 1989," pp. 289–302 which is largely on the flight of Germans from the DDR.)

1511.   Bugajski, Janusz, and Maxine Pollack, *East European Fault Lines: Dissent, Opposition, and Social Activism*. 333 p. Boulder CO: Westview, 1989. (Summarizes and assesses a variety of the approaches taken by oppositions in the countries of Soviet–dominated Eastern Europe. Ch. 2 is on the origins and meaning of dissidence in these states and on government methods of halting dissent. Ch. 3 is specifically on conflict strategies and the factors that shape them; see pp. 79–90 on "unorganized dissent and non–violence." The following chapters take up themes that appear across states, such as human rights activism, religious dissent, and the economic and cultural spheres as sources of opposition. Index.)

1512.   Curry, Jane Leftwich, ed., *Dissent in Eastern Europe*. 227 pp. New York: Praeger, 1983. (Collection of essays on dissent in various European nations. For general Eastern European dissent, see ch. 1, 8, 12, 13. Index.)

1513.   Ash, Timothy Garton, *The Magic Lantern: The Revolution of 89 Witnessed in Warsaw, Budapest, Berlin and Prague*. 156 pp. New York: Random House, 1990. (See "Budapest: The Last Funeral," pp. 47–60 on the demonstrative reinterment of Imre Nagy and its political significance; "Berlin: Wall's End," pp. 61–77 on the East German demonstrations of 1989 and the opening of the wall; and "Prague: Inside the Magic Lantern," pp. 78–130 for a day–by–day account of Civic Forum and the change of government in Czechoslovakia.)

1514.   Kaltefleiter, Werner, and Robert L. Pfaltzgraff, eds., *The Peace Movements in Europe and the United States*. 211 pp. London and

Sydney: Croom Helm, 1985. (Brief essays on peace movements in Europe and the U.S. Index.)

1515. Mastny, Vojtech, ed., *East European Dissent.* Vol. 1, 1953–64, 296 pp. Vol. 2, 1965–70, 259 pp. New York: Facts on File, 1972. (Vol. 1 contains accounts of internal dissent in East Europe from journalistic sources, covering Czechoslovakia, pp. 21–22; the GDR, pp. 10–21, 33–34, 164–75; Hungary, pp. 99–157, 192–93; Poland, pp. 79–87, 162–64, 175–77, 191–92, 202–3, 256; and the U.S.S.R., pp. 22–23, 76–79, 193–94, 226–27, 238–39. Vol. 2 contains detailed historical accounts of anti–Soviet dissent, including defections, demonstrations, protests, riots, and similar actions. Countries covered include Czechoslovakia, pp. 55–58, 75–102, 166–88, 230–34; Poland, pp. 22–26, 114–17, 188–89, 218–24; and the U.S.S.R., pp. 11, 14, 37–42, 120–31, 149–64, 209–18. Photos. Index.)

1516. Rochon, Thomas R., *Mobilizing for Peace: The Antinuclear Movements in Western Europe.* 232 pp. Princeton NJ: Princeton Univ. Press, 1988. (Demographic analysis of European peace movements, which maintains that movements represent feasible and innovative programs rather than simply being a reaction to adversity in their respective political contexts. Index.)

AUSTRIA

Under Nazi Domination

Although it was the first nation taken over by Nazi Germany, Austria's collaboration with the Nazi system and also its resistance have only recently become issues of note for the outside world. Religiously–motivated noncooperation and refusal to serve in the military were of some significance, especially among the Bibelforscher or Jehovah's Witnesses.

1517. Luza, Radomir V., *The Resistance in Austria, 1938–1945.* 366 pp. Minneapolis: Univ. of Minnesota Press, 1984. (Overview of opposition and resistance in Austria, combining discussion of nonviolent and violent means. See esp. pp. 8–13 for definitions and review of resistance and ch. 6 for brief discussion of Jehovah's Witnesses' refusal to obey conscription. Index. Bibliography.)

1518. Maass, Walter B., *Country Without a Name: Austria Under Nazi Rule, 1938–1945.* 178 pp. New York: Frederick Ungar, 1979. (Describes rise of Nazism in Austria and the subsequent resistance, which is characterized as sporadic and unorganized. See esp. pp. 30–40 for reasons for the failure of resistance, which author attributes in part to the lack of Allied support. See index under *underground* for further examples. Photos. Index. Bibliography.)

1519. Zahn, Gordon C., *In Solitary Witness: The Life and Death of Franz Jägerstätter.* 284 pp. New York, Chicago, and San Francisco: Holt, Rinehart & Winston, 1964. (Biography of Franz Jägerstätter, an Austrian Catholic conscientious objector who committed nearly total personal noncooperation against Nazi political changes and military conscription. Extracts from his writings throughout. Photos. Bibliography.)

THE BALTICS

The Baltic countries of Estonia, Lithuania, and Latvia have fallen within the orbit of Russia for many years and were formally part of the Soviet Union until winning their freedom in 1989. Both culturally and religiously different from RUSSIA, much of their "dissent" during the 1960s through 1980s was along those lines. With the rise of Gorbachev and his changes in the Soviet system, the Baltic states developed autonomous political movements that led to their independence. In Latvia and Lithuania in particular, continuing Russian presence has led to fears of possible invasion and associated preparation for civil resistance should it take place.

1520. Bourdeaux, Michael, *Land of the Crosses: The Struggle for Religious Freedom in Lithuania, 1939–78.* 359 pp. Devon, England: Augustine, 1979. (Description and documentation of church protests against suppression, persecution, and dissent of the Lithuanian church. See esp. ch. 4, 5, 10–12 on protests, *samizdat,* and suppression. Illustrations. Photos. Documents. Index.)

1521.   Clemens, Walter C., Jr., *Baltic Independence and Russian Empire.* 346 pp. New York: St. Martin's Press, 1991. (History of the Baltic states "bridge" between East and West from the end of WWII, arguing that nonviolent resistance was one of their basic policy programs leading toward independence. See ch. 8–12 on the 1988–90 period, including demonstrations, other nonviolent actions of the time, problems of intra–Baltic politics, and, in ch. 13, the question of Soviet "concessions or crackdown." Index.)

1522.   Eglitis, Olgerts, *Nonviolent Action in the Liberation of Latvia.* 72 pp. Cambridge MA: Albert Einstein Institution, 1993. Albert Einstein Institution Monograph No. 5. (Essay on the actions of 1987–90 that led to the virtual independence of Latvia and of 1990–91 in which the populace defended its independence against encroachment by Soviet "Black Berets" forces. Six appendixes contain documents from the latter period, including detailed guidelines prepared at the time of the August 1991 coup attempt in Russia on the conduct of a nonviolent defense against usurpation; appendix IV, pp. 52–65.)

1523.   Oleszchuk, Thomas C., *Political Justice in the USSR: Dissent and Repression in Lithuania, 1969–1987.* 221 pp. Boulder CO: East European Monographs, 1988. (A study of national dissent in Lithuania and its punishment under Soviet legal standards. See ch. 3 on the dissidents and ch, 4, 5 on legal procedure and case outcomes. Ch. 7 discusses why the punishment of dissenters is not as severe as otherwise might be expected. Ch. 8, 9 review the treatment of dissent in the period of rapid changes in top leadership and of Gorbachev. Appendix. Index.)

1524.   Senn, Alfred Erich, *Lithuania Awakening.* 294 pp. Berkeley and Los Angeles: Univ. of California Press, 1990. (Detailed account of Lithuanian opposition politics from the summer of 1987 through 1990, focusing on the organization Sajudis and its role. See esp. ch. 4–9. Photos. Index.)

1525.   Silde, Adolfs, *Resistance Movement in Latvia*. Supplemented by
        Gunars Rode, *Latvia before the Helsinki Agreement (1962–1975)*.
        95 pp. Stockholm: Latvian National Foundation, 1985 (orig.
        publ. 1972). (The discussion by Silde, pp. 5–70, divides
        resistance into armed resistance, passive resistance, and
        spiritual resistance. See pp. 26–51 on nonviolent "passive"
        resistance including demonstrations, haunting officials and
        Soviet soldiers, written protests, and the like and pp. 52–57 on
        "spiritual" or cultural resistance. The appended piece by Rode
        includes information on economic resistance, "feigned
        ignorance," express protest involving writings and
        demonstrations, protest against the Soviet invasion of
        Czechoslovakia, prison protests, and other topics. Appendixes.
        Index.)

1526.   Vardys, V. Stanley, *The Catholic Church, Dissent, and Nationality
        in Soviet Lithuania*. 349 pp. Boulder CO: East European
        Quarterly, 1978. Distributed by Columbia Univ. Press, New
        York. (See ch. 9–11 on religious protest, repression, and public
        opinion. Documents in appendix. Index. Bibliography.)

BULGARIA

Saving of Bulgarian Jews

*Bulgaria was one of the few occupied European countries in which a large
proportion of Jews were saved from the Holocaust. The Bulgarian state, which
was basically pro–German, passed a law that tried to place Jews under local,
rather than Nazi, jurisdiction. There were also demonstrations and
clandestine actions by Bulgarian civilians, including the Communist Party, to
resist Nazi encroachment and persecution of Jews.*

1527.   Chary, Frederick B., *The Bulgarian Jews and the Final Solution,
        1940–1944*. 246 pp. Pittsburgh: Univ. of Pittsburgh Press, 1972.
        (See ch. 3, 4 on planned deportation of Jews and ch. 5 on why it
        failed. Pp. 145–51 discuss demonstrations held at the time
        planned for deportation. Appendixes. Indexes. Bibliography.)

1528.   Hirschmann, Ira A., *Life Line to a Promised Land*. 214 pp. New York: Vanguard Press, 1946. (Focuses on the escape route for Jews from the Balkans via Turkey to Palestine.)

1529.   Oliver, Khaim, *We Were Saved: How the Jews in Bulgaria Were Kept from the Death Camps*. 2d ed. 211 pp. Sophia, Bulgaria: Sophia Press, 1978 [orig. publ. 1967]. (Overview of Bulgarian opposition to Nazism, the Protection of the Nation Act, and efforts to prevent deportation of Jews, focusing on role of Communist Party. See esp. pp. 54–58, 106–12, 155–73, 180–204 on protests in support of Jews. Illustrations. Photos.)

1530.   Tamir, Vicki, *Bulgaria and Her Jews: The History of a Dubious Symbiosis*. 314 pp. New York: Sepher–Hermon Press for Yeshiva Univ. Press, 1979. (Places WWII experience in context of long history of Jewish presence. See ch. 4, "Fascist Bulgaria and the Jews During World War II," esp. pp. 167–78, on oppression under the Law for the Defense of the Nation, and pp. 198–216 on protest and resistance. Some detail on organizations, less on actions. Illustrations. Photos. Index.)

CZECHOSLOVAKIA

German Rule, 1938–1945

Like other Nazi–occupied countries, Czechoslovakia developed a wide array of resistance methods during World War II. These included setting up a government–in–exile, large–scale boycotts of German goods, and sabotage of supply and information networks.

1531.   *Czechoslovakia Fights Back: A Document of the Czechoslovak Ministry of Foreign Affairs*. 210 pp. Washington DC: American Council on Public Affairs, 1943. (History of occupied Czechoslovakia from 1938 to 1942. See ch. 10 on acts of opposition in early years of occupation, individual noncooperation and symbolic protest, as well as violence and sabotage. Documents. Index.)

1532.   Hronek, Jiri, *Volcano under Hitler: The Underground War in Czechoslovakia*. 141 pp. London: "The Czechoslovak" Independent Weekly, 1941. (Chronicle of Czechoslovakian resistance methods. Written during the occupation, it advocates passive resistance and sabotage as the only effective means of countering the Nazis. See esp. ch. 6, 8, 10, 12, 15–17 for accounts of boycotts, railway and factory sabotage, and student revolts. Illustrations.)

1533.   Mastny, Vojtech, *The Czechs under Nazi Rule: The Failure of National Resistance, 1939–1942*. 274 pp. New York and London: Columbia Univ. Press, 1971. (History of repression and resistance to Nazi occupation with scattered accounts of nonviolent and violent resistance. See pp. 4–5, 107–22, 178–79, 223 on nonviolent resistance. Index. Bibliography.)

Dubcek Period and Warsaw Pact Invasion, 1968–1969

The Czechoslovak Communist Party undertook a program of reform and limited democratization in 1968 under its leader, Alexander Dubcek. This "Prague Spring" excited the people of the country with the idea that democracy might be possible and promised to serve as an example other Eastern European countries (such as POLAND). Perceiving a threat to its international order, the U.S.S.R. directed an invasion of Czechoslovakia in August, ostensibly under Warsaw Pact direction. In order to protect their autonomy, the Czechoslovakian populace participated in a campaign of direct and indirect resistance lasting from the time of the invasion until the Spring of 1969, by which time the reformers had been replaced with hard–liners.

1534.   Hejzlar, Zdenek, and Vladimir V. Kusin, *Czechoslovakia 1968– 1969: Chronology, Bibliography, Annotation*. 316 pp. New York and London: Garland, 1975. (See chronology, esp. pp. 75–148, for references to nonviolent action in the resistance from August 1968. Bibliography concentrates on "Prague Spring" revitalization movement, but see pp. 261–316 for multilingual bibliography on Czechoslovakian reform and resistance.)

1535.   Parrish, Michael, *The 1968 Czechoslovak Crises: A Bibliography, 1968–1970*. 41 pp. Santa Barbara CA: American Bibliographical Center, Clio Press, 1971. (References in several languages, many on the invasion and resistance. Section 1 compiles book–length entries, section 2 contains documents, and sections 3, 4 contain references to articles and periodicals. Index.)

STUDIES

1536.   Bloomfield, Jon, *Passive Revolution: Politics and the Czechoslovak Working Class, 1945–1948*. 290 pp. New York: St. Martin's Press, 1979. (Explores the role of Czechoslovakian mass organizations, their influence on the emergence of the Communist Party of Czechoslovakia, and their impact on subsequent political events, including the 1968 invasion. Index. Bibliography.)

1537.   Chapman, Colin, *August 21st: The Rape of Czechoslovakia*. 123 pp. Philadelphia and New York: J.B. Lippincott, 1968. (Brief popular account of the invasion and resistance in August and September. Photos.)

1538.   Eidlin, Fred H., *The Logic of "Normalization": The Soviet Intervention in Czechoslovakia of 21 August 1968 and the Czechoslovak Response*. 278 pp. New York: Columbia Univ. Press, 1980. (Analysis of societal dynamics of resistance to Soviet intervention. See esp. ch. 2, 3, 5. Index. Bibliography.)

1539.   Ello, Paul, ed., *Czechoslovakia's Blueprint for "Freedom," "Unity, Socialism and Humanity": Dubcek's Statements: The Original and Official Documents Leading to the Conflict of August 1968*. 304 pp. Washington DC: Acropolis Books, 1968. *Dubcek's Blueprint for Freedom: His Original Statements Leading to the Invasion of August 1968*. 352 pp. London: William Kimber, 1969. (Contains four important Communist Party of Czechoslovakia documents from April to August 1968. 1969 Publication contains a profile of Dubcek by Hugh Lunghi.)

1540.   French, A. [Alfred], *Czech Writers and Politics, 1945–1969*. 435 pp. Boulder CO: East European Monographs, 1982; distributed by Columbia Univ. Press. (Focuses on literature, but with comments on the effects of the death of Jan Palach, pp. 335–64. Documents. Index. Bibliography.)

1541.   Golan, Galia, *Reform Rule in Czechoslovakia: The Dubcek Era,*
         1968–1969. 327 pp. Cambridge: Cambridge Univ. Press, 1973.
         (Ch. 10, 11 discuss resistance in 1968–69. Index. Bibliography.)

1542.   Horsky, Vladimir, *Prag 1968: Systemveränderung und*
         Systemverteidigung. 534 pp. Stuttgart: Ernst Klett Verlag;
         Munich: Kosel–Verlag, 1975. (Authoritative study of the
         democratization movement and later resistance to the Warsaw
         Pact invasion and occupation. In German, with brief English
         summary. Index. Bibliography.)

1543.   Hruby, Peter, *Fools and Heroes: The Changing Role of Communist*
         Intellectuals in Czechoslovakia. 265 pp. New York: Pergamon
         Press, 1980. (See pp. 102–7 on workers' nonviolent action
         before and during the Soviet invasion. Index. Bibliography.)

1544.   Josten, Josef, *Unarmed Combat: As Practised in Czechoslovakia*
         since August 1968. 88 pp. Delhi: D.K. Publishing House, 1973.
         (Study of Czechoslovakian nonviolent resistance; includes
         documents, posters, leaflets, and slogans. Photos.
         Bibliography.)

1545.   Journalist M, *A Year Is Eight Months.* 201 pp. Garden City NY:
         Doubleday, 1970. Originally published as *Die Kontrollierte*
         Revolution. Germany: Paul Zsolnay Verlag, 1969. (Journalist's
         description of the invasion and the events leading up to it. See
         ch. 19–21 for step–by–step account of occupation and
         resistance until late August 1968. Chronology. Index.
         Bibliography.)

1546.   Kaplan, Frank L., *Winter into Spring: The Czechoslovak Press and*
         the Reform Movement, 1963–1968. 208 pp. New York: Columbia
         Univ. Press, 1977. (See pp. 148–62 on media role in
         Czechoslovakia's nonviolent resistance. Index. Bibliography.)

1547.   Levy, Alan, *Rowboat to Prague.* 531 pp. New York: Grossman
         Publishers, 1972. Reprinted as *So Many Heroes.* 388 pp.
         Sagaponack NY: Second Chance Press, 1980. (Personal memoir
         of invasion and resistance. See ch. 12–16 on the August 1968
         invasion and ch. 17–21 on occurrences in the autumn of 1968
         and first half of 1969.)

1548. Littell, Robert, ed., *The Czech Black Book*. 303 pp. New York: Praeger, 1969. (Documents from various Czechoslovakian sources arranged as a narrative of resistance from 20 to 27 August 1968. Originally compiled by a committee of the Czechoslovak Academy of Sciences as a rejoinder to the Soviet *White Book*, entry 1550. Appendixes.)

1549. Mlynar, Zdenek, *Nightfrost in Prague: The End of Humane Socialism*. Trans. Paul Wilson. 300 pp. New York: Karz, 1980. Originally published as *Nachtfrost*. Cologne: Europäische Verlagsanstalt, 1978. (Ch. 3 contains an insider's account of the activities of higher Czechoslovakian leadership at time of the invasion, including evidence of their limited knowledge of the resistance. See pp. 148–51, 176, 184, 198–200, 206–09 for comments on resistance, its effects on Soviet forces, and "brief political victory" before the Moscow protocol signing. Photos. Index.)

1550. *On Events in Czechoslovakia: Facts, Documents, Press Reports, and Eye–Witness Accounts*. 168 pp. Moscow: Press Group of Soviet Journalists, 1968. (Soviet publication issued in September 1968 to discredit Czechoslovakian resistance and justify the invasion and occupation. Known in Czechoslovakia as the *White Book*. Photos.)

1551. Paul, David W., *The Cultural Limits of Revolutionary Politics: Change and Continuity in Socialist Czechoslovakia*. 308 pp. New York: Columbia Univ. Press, 1979. (See ch. 8, "From Svejk to Dubcek: The Humor and Pathos of Political Nonviolence.")

1552. Pelikan, Jiri, *Socialist Opposition in Eastern Europe: The Czechoslovak Example*. Trans. Marian Sling, V. Tosek, and R. Tosek. 116 pp. London: Allison & Busby, 1976. (See pp. 25–60 on tactical errors of Communist Party leadership and opposition since 1969.)

1553. Randle, Michael, April Carter, and others, *Support Czechoslovakia*. 64 pp. London: Housmans, for the War Resisters International, 1968. (Brief description of Czechoslovak resistance and protests in other Warsaw Pact countries combined with personal accounts by War Resisters

International [WRI] volunteers of demonstrations conducted by them in the U.S.S.R., Bulgaria, Hungary, and Poland. Origins of these demonstrations described on pp. 17–23 and the actions themselves on pp. 24–54. Appendix 2 is a training "briefing" for the WRI protesters.)

1554.   Remington, Robin A., ed., *Winter in Prague: Documents on Czechoslovak Communism in Crisis*. 473 pp. Cambridge MA and London: MIT Press, 1969. (A valuable collection of documents on democratization in 1968, Soviet pressures and responses, the invasion, world Communist reaction, resistance, and accommodation. Index. Bibliography.)

1555.   Renner, Hans, *A History of Czechoslovakia since 1945*. 200 pp. Trans. Evelien Hurst–Buist. London and New York: Routledge, 1989. Originally published in Dutch as *Geschiednis van Tjechoslowakie na 1945*. (Ch. 4–6 are on the events of 1968–69. Includes some detail in pp. 71–76 to support the conclusion that, with reference to the first days of occupation, "the fact that the plans of the occupying forces misfired should be ascribed especially to . . . non–violent national resistance," p. 75. Index. Bibliography.)

1556.   Schwartz, Harry, *Prague's 200 Days: The Struggle for Democracy in Czechoslovakia*. 274 pp. New York: Praeger, 1969. (Primarily on democratization before the invasion. Index. Bibliography.)

1557.   Skilling, H. Gordon, *Czechoslovakia's Interrupted Revolution*. 922 pp. Princeton: Princeton Univ. Press, 1976. (See pp. 760–92 on nonviolent resistance and the failure to encourage collaboration effectively.)

1558.   Suvorov, Viktor, *The Liberators*. 202 pp. London: Hamish Hamilton, 1981. (Bitter memoir of service in the Soviet military by an officer who served in the Czechoslovakian intervention. See pp. 135–60 on preparations for invasion and pp. 158–202 for observations on its conduct.)

1559.   Sviták, Ivan, *The Czechoslovak Nightmare, 1968–1969: Bureaucratic Dictatorship*. 110 pp. Chico CA: Graphic Fox, 1978.

(Articles by leading dissident intellectual on the Prague Spring and Soviet invasion. See pp. 30–36, 52–63. Illustrations.)

1560.   Szulc, Tad, *Czechoslovakia since World War II*. 503 pp. New York: Viking Press, 1971. (See ch. 18–19 on occupation and opposition, 1968–69. Index. Bibliography.)

1561.   Valenta, Jiri, *Soviet Intervention in Czechoslovakia, 1968: Anatomy of a Decision*. 208 pp. Baltimore and London: Johns Hopkins Univ. Press, 1979. (Employs "bureaucratic–politics paradigm" to review factors leading to Soviet invasion of Czechoslovakia and its costs. See conclusions, pp. 154–64.)

1562.   Wechsberg, Joseph, *The Voices*. 113 pp. Garden City NY: Doubleday, 1969. (An account of clandestine radio broadcasts by the resistance begins on p. 29.)

1563.   Windsor, Philip, and Adam Roberts, *Czechoslovakia, 1968: Reform, Repression, and Resistance*. 200 pp. New York: Columbia Univ. Press; London: Chatto & Windus, 1969. (Part 2, ch. 4–8, describe resistance to Warsaw Pact intervention from 20 August to the "truce" of October 1968. Documents in appendixes.)

1564.   Zeman, Zbynek A.B., *Prague Spring: A Report on Czechoslovakia, 1968*. 169 pp. New York: Hill and Wang; Harmondsworth, England; Baltimore; and Victoria, Australia: Penguin Books, 1969. (Report on the 1968 "programmed revolution" up to 20 August. Chronology.)

Charter 77 Movement

1977 was the Year of Political Prisoners. In this year, a group of Czechoslovakian dissidents documented their government's abuses of prisoners and violations of the United Nations Human Rights covenant. The document came to be known as Charter 77 and reached a worldwide audience. The campaigners themselves were subject to arrest and repression but maintained their protests for several years after, including their work to document "everyday repression."

1566.   *Human Rights in Czechoslovakia: The Documents of Charter '77—1977–1982*. 246 pp. Washington DC: Congress of the United States, Commission on Security and Cooperation in Europe, 1982. Mimeo. (Section 1 contains Charter 77 documents relating to the Madrid conference; Section 2 contains Charter 77 documents no. 1–26, with some exclusions, dated from 1977–1982; and section 3 contains various documents from 1982 including two on Poland. Index. Bibliography.)

1567.   *Palach Press Bulletin*. London: Palach Press, February 1976–April 1982. (Frequently appearing collection of news, documents, and document summaries with coverage of Czechoslovakian dissent.)

1568.   Precan, Vilem, ed., *Human Rights in Czechoslovakia: A Documentation, September 1981–December 1982*. 115 pp. Paris: International Committee for the Support of Charter 77 in Czechoslovakia, in cooperation with the Help and Action Coordination Committee, 1983. (Section 1 documents human rights violations from September 1981–December 1982. Appendix B contains various protests, with several by VONS, the Czechoslovakian human rights committee. Appendix D contains a chronology of actions "in defense of human rights" in the period concerned. Index. Bibliography.)

1569.   *White Paper on Czechoslovakia*. 269 pp. Paris: International Committee for the Support of Charter 77 in Czechoslovakia, 1977. (Collected Charter 77 documents.)

STUDIES

1570.   Bugajski, Janusz, *Czechoslovakia: Charter 77's Decade of Dissent*. 118 pp. The Washington Papers 125. New York, Westport, and London: Praeger, 1987. (A review of Charter 77 in its origins, composition, activities, and effects. In addition to early chapters on the group's start, personnel, and history, see ch. 5 on other movements. Ch. 6, on "repression and reprisal," includes a history of the government's measures against Charter 77 and a discussion of the methods used. Documents in appendix. Index.)

1571. Heneka, A., Frantisek Janouch, Vilem Precan, and Jan Vladislav, eds., *A Besieged Culture: Czechoslovakia Ten Years after Helsinki*. Trans. Joyce Dahlberg. 300 pp. Stockholm and Vienna: Charter 77 Foundation and International Helsinki Federation for Human Rights, 1985. (Czechoslovakian intellectuals describe their experiences, some as a result of Charter 77 activities, on pp. 59–122. "Chronicle of Everyday Repression" on pp. 183–262. Documents. Photos. Index.)

1572. Josten, Josef, *Czechoslovakia: From 1968 to Charter 77—A Record of Passive Resistance*. 22 pp. *Conflict Studies* 86, August 1977. London: Institute for the Study of Conflict, 1977. (Brief survey that includes accounts of ostracism of Soviet troops and intervention by *agents provocateurs* during the nonviolent resistance. Utilizes the Charter 77 movement to argue that "passive resistance," originating in 1968, continued. See pp. 4–13 on resistance from August 1968 into the early 1970s. Documents.)

1573. Keane, John, ed., *The Power of the Powerless: Citizens against the State in Central–Eastern Europe*. 228 pp. Armonk NY: M.E. Sharpe, 1985. (Presentation of the significance of Charter 77 by campaign members, dating originally to 1979. See Vaclav Havel, "The Power of the Powerless"; Miroslav Kusy, "Chartism and 'Real Socialism' "; Peter Uhl, "The Alternative Community as a Revolutionary Avant–Garde"; and Josef Vohryzek, "Thoughts inside a Tightly Corked Bottle." Documents.)

1574. Kusin, Vladimir V., *From Dubcek to Charter 77: A Study of "Normalization" in Czechoslovakia, 1968–1978*. 353 pp. Edinburgh: Q Press, 1978. (Personal, analytical history of dissent in Czechoslovakia. See pp. 11–13, 20, 24–30, 30–37, 58–59 on invasion and opposition in 1968–69; pp. 110, 145–69, 196–98 on dissent and organizing to the mid–1970s, and part 4 on dissent and opposition connected with Charter 77. Index. Bibliography.)

1575. Kyncl, Karol, and Ivan Kyncl, *After the Spring Came Winter*. Trans. George Theiner. 105 pp. Stockholm: Askelin & Hägglund and Charta 77 Foundation, 1985 [orig. publ. 1983].

(Highly personal insiders' account of Charter 77, the related group VONS, or the Committee to Defend the Unjustly Prosecuted, and their members during the period roughly between 1977 and 1989. Much detail on Charter 77 members and their activities and punishments, on police surveillance and arrests, and on cultural work related to the movement. Heavily illustrated with photos of activists, meetings and events, protest symbols, and the police.)

1576.   Riese, Hans–Peter, ed., *Since the Prague Spring: The Continuing Struggle for Human Rights in Czechoslovakia.* Trans. Eugen Loebl. 208 pp. New York: Random House, 1979. (Collection of documents of the Charter 77 movement, including text of Charter 77 on pp. 11–14, other documents and statements of the Charter 77 group, and letters to Czechoslovakian officials and figures outside Czechoslovakia. See appendix for discussion of Charter 77 and signers.)

1577.   Skilling, H. Gordon, *Charter 77 and Human Rights in Czechoslovakia.* 363 pp. London, Boston, and Sydney: George Allen & Unwin, 1981. (Text with extensive collection of documents. See esp. author's description of the Charter 77 group's tactics in ch. 4; "independent civic action", individual *samizdat*, appeals, flying demonstrations, and a hunger strike in ch. 6; and discussion of "parallel structures," pp. 183–85, and their relation to human rights claims, pp. 186–91. Of interest among documents are text of Charter 77, pp. 209–12; various statements by Charter 77 group; statements on Poland and the U.S.S.R., pp. 277–82; and statement on a protest hunger strike, pp. 310–12. Documents. Index. Bibliography.)

DENMARK

Occupation and Rescue of Danish Jews, 1939–1945

Once Denmark was occupied at the beginning of general European war in 1940, British and Allied policy encouraged sabotage and low–level paramilitary action in resistance. On several occasions, the Danes preferred nonviolent forms of resistance. The most notable of these was the rescue of the great majority of Danish Jewry and their transportation in small boats to neutral Sweden, which was done in 1943. In 1944, the people of Copenhagen held a mass strike, the "people's strike," trying to dislodge the German grip.

1578. Bennett, Jeremy, *British Broadcasting and the Danish Resistance Movement: A Study of the Wartime Broadcasts of the BBC Danish Service, 1940–1945.* 266 pp. Cambridge: Cambridge Univ. Press, 1966. (Describes role of BBC in encouraging adoption of British resistance policy in Denmark, focusing largely on sabotage. Photos. Index. Bibliography.)

1579. Flender, Harold, *Rescue in Denmark.* 281 pp. New York: Simon & Schuster; London: W.H. Allen, 1963. (Story of Jewish rescue and anti–deportation resistance.)

1580. Haestrup, Jorgen, *Secret Alliance: A Study of the Danish Resistance Movement, 1940–1945.* Trans. Alison Borch–Johnson. 3 vols. Vol. 1, 269 pp. Vol. 2, 352 pp. Vol. 3, 374 pp. Odense, Denmark: Odense Univ. Press, 1976–77. Originally published in Danish as *Kontakt med England 1940–1943.* (Primarily concerned with British–sponsored military and sabotage units. See vol. 2, pp. 89–117, 248–57 on problems of communication under repression and pp. 320–52 on Copenhagen General Strike of 1944.)

1581. Hansen, Holger Horsholt, *Triumph in Disaster.* 64 pp. London: His Majesty's Stationery Office, 1945. (See pp. 16–45 about the general strike in Copenhagen. Photos.)

1582. Lampe, David, *The Savage Canary: The Story of Resistance in Denmark.* 236 pp. London: Cassell, 1957. (Chronicles Danish quasi–military resistance. See ch. 7 on the Jewish rescue and ch. 10 on the "people's strike" of June–July 1944. Photos. Index.)

1583. Petrow, Richard, *The Bitter Years: The Invasion and Occupation of Denmark and Norway, April 1940–May 1945.* 403 pp. New York: William Morrow, 1974. (Popular account of occupation in Denmark and Norway. See ch. 8 on Norway's civilian resistance and ch. 12–15, 19 on Denmark's resistance and the rescue of Danish Jews. Photos. Index. Bibliography.)

1584.   Ryan, Michael D., ed., *Human Responses to the Holocaust: Perpetrators and Victims, Bystanders and Resisters*. Papers of Conference on the Church Struggle and the Holocaust. 278 pp. New York and Toronto: Edwin Mellen Press, 1981. (Jorgen Glenthoj, "The Little Dunkerque: The Danish Rescue of Jews in October 1943," pp. 93–119, describes the politics of open and disguised noncooperation in the hiding and transportation of Jews sought by Nazis. Photos. Bibliography.)

1585.   Thomas, John Oram, *The Giant–Killers: The Story of the Danish Resistance Movement, 1940–1945*. 320 pp. London: Michael Joseph, 1975. (Although focusing largely on U.K.–sponsored semi–military resistance, contains material on the underground press, ch. 5; rescue of Jews, ch. 7–8; some material on the people's strike, pp. 20–22, 24, 87–88, and a students' "Ten Commandments" for noncooperation, pp. 92–93. Illustrations. Photos. Index.)

1586.   Werstein, Irving, *That Denmark Might Live: The Saga of the Danish Resistance in World War II*. 143 pp. Philadelphia: Macrae Smith, 1967. (Examples of symbolic protest and noncooperation, pp. 8–9, 10–11, 18–22. See esp. ch. 7 on rescue of Jews and ch. 8 on the general strike of June–July 1944. Photos. Index.)

1587.   Yahil, Leni, *The Rescue of Danish Jewry: Test of a Democracy*. 538 pp. Philadelphia: Jewish Publication Society of America, 1983 [orig. publ. 1969]. (Consult ch. 5–7 and conclusion on the background, organization, and conduct of 1943 rescue of Danish Jewry by sea. Illustrations. Photos. Index. Bibliography.)

FINLAND

The Russian government, which essentially ruled Finland, annulled the Finnish constitution in 1901 to prepare for the political and cultural "Russification" of Finland. Finnish nationalists resisted encroachments on both grounds, largely following the underground group Kagal. This group advocated using noncooperation not only against Russia but also against Finns who consented to the Russian imposition of power. Over ten years of resistance included the "great strike" of 1905, which coincided with the Russian Revolution of that year. Note that Huxley connects the thought and action of Finnish defenders of their constitutional order and national identity with advocates of passive resistance elsewhere in Europe.

1588. Huxley, Steven Duncan, *Constitutional Insurgency in Finland: Finnish "Passive Resistance" against Russification as a Case of Nonmilitary Struggle in the European Resistance Tradition.* 284 pp. Helsinki, Finland: Finnish Historical Society, 1990. (This study is divided so as to cover four topics, including observations on the study of resistance and nonviolent action in part 1; terminology and technique of "passive resistance" in part 2; a detailed original case study of the Finish resistance in its origins, conduct, and outcomes in parts 3, 4; and a brief critique of this case's relevance to the concept of "nonmilitary struggle" in part 5. Of interest within these topical sections are the critique of the concept of nonviolent action, pp. 16–23, and historical Finnish national views on resistance and "passive revolution," esp. those of Johan Vilhelm Snellman, pp. 4–16, 23–29, 98–106. In addition, part 3 on passive resistance includes observations on this term and its usage by twentieth century thinkers as well as tracing the term from circa 1819 into the twentieth century, pp. 47–61, and its relationship to traditions in European and American views of popular resistance, pp. 61–77. Within the case study itself, in addition to pages cited above, see pp. 106–19 on the transmission of Hungary's national resistance of 1848–67 into Finnish strategies; the "constitutional insurgency" in its action phase in the years 1893–1905, pp. 143–230; and assessment of the outcome, pp. 231–52. Index. Bibliography.)

1589.   Jackson, J. Hampden, *Finland.* 243 pp. New York: Macmillan, 1940. (See ch. 4, 5 for incidents of Finnish civilian resistance to Russification. Ch. 4 covers events surrounding the Russian revolution of 1905 and ch. 5 covers the era of the Bolshevik revolution. Index. Bibliography.)

1590.   Jutikkala, Eino, with Kauko Pirinen, *A History of Finland.* Trans. Paul Sjöblom. Rev. ed. 293 pp. New York: Praeger, 1972 [orig. publ. 1962]. (Ch. 9, pp. 228–48, follows Finland's conflicts with Russia from protests and noncooperation against conscription to the aftermath of the "great strike" of 1905. Index.)

1591.   Kirby, D.G., *Finland in the Twentieth Century.* 253 pp. Minneapolis: Univ. of Minnesota Press, 1979. (Ch. 2 discusses the conduct of noncooperation and of violence and the debate over both as means of resistance in the two "periods of oppression," 1900–1917. Index. Bibliography.)

1592.   ———, ed. and trans., *Finland and Russia, 1808–1920: From Autonomy to Independence: A Selection of Documents.* 256 pp. London and Basingstoke: Macmillan, 1975. (Pp. 80–117 contain documents on resistance to Russification and the "great" general strike of 1905.)

1593.   Mazour, Anatole G., *Finland between East and West.* 298 pp. Princeton NJ, New York, Toronto and London: D. Van Nostrand, 1956. (See esp. ch. 2 on nationalism and "passive resistance" before 1917. Photos. Appendixes. Index. Bibliography.)

1594.   Paasivirta, Juhani, *Finland and Europe: International Crises in the Period of Autonomy, 1808–1914.* Trans. Anthony F. Upton and Sirkka R. Upton. Ed. D.G. Kirby. 220 pp. London: C. Hurst, 1981. (Pp. 166–98 discuss the history of Russification and Finnish resistance, 1890–1906. Index. Bibliography.)

1595.   Puntila, L.A., *The Political History of Finland, 1809–1966.* Trans. David Miller. 248 pp. Helsinki: Otava Publishing, 1975. (See ch. 3, 4 on Finnish nationalism during the period of Russification, including comments on the rationale for noncooperation, pp. 65–66, and the "great strike" of 1905, pp. 71–72. Index.)

FRANCE

France's turbulent and, as one student of the country calls it, "contentious"
history has included conflicts waged by just about every possible form of
action. Generally, documentation of nonviolent action in France in English is
limited and because of this turbulent history, evidence of it is usually
combined with discussions of violence and other forms of struggle. Among the
topics reflected below are labor, farmers', and feminist struggles, and recent
events concerned with issues of the environment and nuclear power.

1596.   Heinz, Grete, and Agnes F. Peterson, *The French Fifth Republic:*
        Continuity and Change, 1966–1970: An Annotated Bibliography.
        125 pp. Stanford CA: Hoover Institution Press, Stanford Univ.,
        1974. (Mostly French–language sources, annotated in English.
        Alphabetic arrangement requires using index; consult under
        civilian–military relations, generals' Putsch, May 1968, May 1968
        student revolt, military service, conscientious objectors, pacifism,
        strikes, students, trade unions, and *women's rights.* See also next
        entry. Author, Subject, and Title Index.)

1597.   ———, *The French Fifth Republic: Establishment and Consolidation*
        1958–1965. 170 pp. Stanford CA: Hoover Institution Press,
        Stanford Univ., 1970. (See previous entry. Consult index under
        civilian–military relations, generals' Putsch. Author, Subject, and
        Title Index.)

Studies

1598.   Berger, Suzanne, *Peasants against Politics: Rural Organization in*
        Brittany, 1911–1967. 300 pp. Cambridge: Harvard Univ. Press,
        1972. (See pp. 115, 191–92, 199, 205, 206, 208, 209 for accounts
        of peasant demonstrations and their political effects. Index.
        Bibliography.)

1599.   Cerny, Philip G., ed., *Social Movements and Protest in France.* 226
        pp. London: Frances Pinter, 1982. (See ch. 2, esp. pp. 24–34, on
        student protests after May 1968; ch. 8, esp. pp. 187–95, on labor
        action in Brittany; and ch. 9 on anti–nuclear activities,
        including a brief description of the debate over violence after

the Malville anti–nuclear power demonstration, pp. 207–08.
Index.)

1600. Hallie, Philip, *Lest Innocent Blood Be Shed*. 304 pp. New York,
       Hagerstown MD, San Francisco and London, 1979. (An
       account of the sheltering of Jewish refugees, especially
       children, in Vichy France by the people of the Protestant
       village of Le Chambon. Focuses in large part on the
       personalities and activities of the pastor, André Trocmé, and
       his collaborators. The story of Le Chambon's path from minor
       acts of noncooperation to offering refuge to Jews takes up ch.
       3–11. Of interest are the role of the Friends Service Committee,
       pp. 124–37; the Le Chambon system, ch. 7; and evidence that a
       German functionary restrained the army from an attack on Le
       Chambon because it presented a different kind of resistance
       than did violence, p. 245. The reflections of the author, an
       ethicist, follow. Photos. Index.)

1601. Hanagan, Michael P., *The Logic of Solidarity: Artisans and
       Industrial Workers in Three French Towns, 1871–1914*. 261 pp.
       Urbana, Chicago, and London: Univ. of Illinois Press, 1980.
       (Studies of strikes and "strike waves" in three communities of
       the Stéphanois region of the Loire, undertaken to explore the
       nature of coalitions between skilled artisans and industrial
       workers and the effects of differing forms of work on social
       protest. Ch. 3, "Economic Structure and Strike Activity,"
       models the form and context of strikes and ch. 4, 5, 6 explore
       the structure of various artisanal and industrial trades and
       their relation to coalitions, militancy, and strikes. In ch. 6, pp.
       167–71 detail a 1911 "general strike." Photos. Appendix. Index.
       Bibliography.)

1602. Hause, Steven C., with Anne R. Kenney, *Women's Suffrage and
       Social Politics in the French Third Republic*. 381 pp. Princeton NJ:
       Princeton Univ. Press, 1984. (Ch. 3, 4, 6 discuss French
       feminism's consideration of the problem of collective action,
       with descriptions of pre–WWI demonstrations and mock
       voting in ch. 6. Illustrations. Photos. Index. Bibliography.)

1603. Howorth, Jolyon, and Patricia Chilton, eds., *Defence and Dissent
       in Contemporary France*. 264 pp. London and Sydney: Croom

Helm; New York: St. Martin's Press, 1984. (Part 2, "Voices of Dissent," includes Claude Bourdet, "The Rebirth of a Peace Movement"; Christian Mellon, "Peace Organizations in France Today"; and Tony Chafer, "Ecologists and the Bomb." See pp. 209–11 on nonviolent organizations in France; see also index under *civil defence, conscientious objection, Larzac, May 1968, non–violence, pacifism,* and *peace movements.* Index. Bibliography.)

1604.   Kedward, H.R., *Resistance in Vichy France: A Study of Ideas and Motivation in the Southern Zone, 1940–1942.* 311 pp. Oxford: Oxford Univ. Press, 1978. (On the concept of resistance and the illegal press, see pp. 91–94, 123–30, and ch. 8. On protests, see pp. 160–63, 180–84, and ch. 9, "Popular Protest," esp. pp. 215–19 on patriotic demonstrations and pp. 221–24 on hunger protests. Illustrations. Index. Bibliography.)

1605.   Kesselman, Mark, ed., *The French Workers' Movement: Economic Crisis and Political Change.* Trans. Edouardo Diaz, Arthur Goldhammer, and Richard Shyrock. 350 pp. Boston and London: George Allen and Unwin, 1984. (Analysis of contemporary French labor movement, tracing its modern history and examining its current political challenges. Index. Bibliography.)

1606.   Nelkin, Dorothy, and Michael Pollack, *The Atom Besieged: Extraparliamentary Dissent in France and Germany.* 198 pp. Cambridge and London: MIT Press, 1981. (Sociological study of anti–nuclear movements, their origins, methods, and impact on politics. See esp. ch. 5, 6, 8–10, 12, 14. Illustrations. Photos.)

1607.   Perrot, Michelle, *Workers on Strike: France, 1871–1890.* Trans. Chris Turner, with the assistance of Erica Carter and Claire Laudet. 321 pp. Leamington Spa, Hamburg, and New York: Berg, 1987. (Detailed study of strikes in France, 1871–90, with emphasis on components of strike process. See ch. 4 on strike methods and ch. 7, 8 on collective behavior aspects of strikes.)

1608.   Rawlinson, Roger, *Larzac: A Victory for Nonviolence.* 43 pp. London: Quaker Peace & Service, 1983. (Brief history of the Larzac peasants' struggle against land taking for a military base. See pp. 11–12 on the influence of Lanza del Vasto and Abbé Jean Toulat on the choice of nonviolent means. Photos.)

1609.   Touraine, Alain, Zsuzsa Hegedus, Francois Dubet, and Michel Wieviorka, *Anti–Nuclear Protest: The Opposition to Nuclear Energy in France*. Trans. Peter Fawcett. 202 pp. Paris: Editions de la Maison des Sciences de L'Homme; Cambridge: Cambridge Univ. Press, 1983. Originally published as *La Prophétie Anti–Nucléaire*. Paris: Editions du Seuil, 1980. (Study of anti–nuclear energy movement, using Touraine's method of "sociological intervention to force self–analysis by movement actors." See ch. 2 on origins, esp. pp. 22–25 on demonstrations in 1974–76; ch. 4 on "the struggles," esp. pp. 60–64; and pp. 81–83 on the dramatic failure of the 1977 Malville demonstration. Bibliography.)

1610.   Watt, Richard M., *Dare Call It Treason*. 344 pp. New York: Simon & Schuster, 1963. (See esp. ch. 11, 12, 16 on mutinies and ch. 13, 14 on reactions to them by the army and General Pétain. Photos. Index. Bibliography.)

1611.   Williams, John, *Mutiny 1917*. 257 pp. London, Melbourne and Toronto: William Heinemann, 1962. (See ch. 7, 8, 11, 12 on army mutiny and ch. 9, 10 on mutiny agitation on the home front. Photos. Index. Bibliography.)

Algiers Generals' Putsch, 1961

This attempted coup d'état was initiated by generals who plotted to derail the independence of Algeria. Assuming the loyalty of the troops to their commanders, the generals attempted to seize control within Algeria and defy the authority of President Charles DeGaulle. A significant factor in thwarting these plans was provided by military draftees who refused orders and stayed in their barracks, in part at the behest of DeGaulle himself.

1612.   Henissart, Paul, *Wolves in the City: The Death of French Algeria*. 508 pp. New York: Simon & Schuster, 1970. (Ch. 4–6 review the generals' plot of 1961. Ch. 6, pp. 108–10, 114–17, discusses noncooperation by the troops and the generals' reaction. Index. Bibliography.)

1613. Kelly, George Armstrong, *Lost Soldiers: The French Army and Empire in Crisis, 1947–1962.* 404 pp. Cambridge: MIT Press, 1965. (See pp. 309–29 on the Algiers Putsch of April 1961, including characterization on p. 323 of the draftees' resistance as a "sit–down strike." Index. Bibliography.)

1614. Menard, Orville D., *The Army and the Fifth Republic.* 265 pp. Lincoln NE: Univ. of Nebraska Press, 1967. (See pp. 205–12 on de Gaulle's call to noncooperation and its effects. Photos. Index. Bibliography.)

1615. O'Ballance, Edgar, *The Algerian Insurrection, 1954–1962.* 231 pp. London: Faber & Faber, 1967. (See esp. pp. 177–80, 184–85 on anti–Putsch protest and noncooperation. Illustrations. Index.)

1616. Roberts, Adam, "Civil Resistance to Military Coups." *Journal of Peace Research* 12 (1975): 19–36. (Inquiry into role of civilian nonviolent resistance in contributing to the defeat of military takeover attempts, with case examples from the Kapp Putsch of 1920 in Germany and the Algiers Generals' Revolt.)

1617. Talbott, John, *The War without a Name: France in Algeria, 1954–1962.* 305 pp. New York: Alfred A. Knopf, 1980. (See pp. 207–11 on soldiers' noncooperation during Putsch. Index. Bibliography.)

Events of May 1968

Student demonstrations were held in many parts of Europe in 1968, often against the Vietnam War. In May 1968, a student revolt quickly spread from the new university complex at Nanterre to the universities of Paris and other cities. The conflict soon involved the occupation of university buildings by students, street fighting, and political radicalization. While many Paris students were committed to a deliberate strategy of violence and street fighting from behind barricades, workers who joined the revolt instead occupied factory premises in what was often termed a general strike. In Paris, the students' building occupations continued after the street conflicts while strikes and other actions by workers themselves outlasted the student revolt.

1618.   Wylie, Laurence, Franklin D. Chu, and Mary Terrall, *France: The Events of May–June 1968: A Critical Bibliography*. 118 pp. Cambridge: Harvard Univ. Council for European Studies, 1973. (Annotated bibliography of sources in English and French. Index.)

STUDIES

1619.   Absalom, Roger, *France: The May Events, 1968*. 96 pp. London: Longman, 1971. (Extracts from news articles and documents. See esp. ch. 1, 5, 6, 9. Selection 20 describes "techniques of demonstrations" and a photo on p. 89 shows a street barricaded with apples in the autumn of 1967. Photos.)

1620.   Bourges, Hervé, *The French Student Revolt: The Leaders Speak*. Trans. B.R. Brewster. 112 pp. New York: Hill & Wang; Paris: Editions du Seuil, 1968. (Interviews with student leaders on details of the movement, with a certain amount of information on the relation between violent and nonviolent actions and "mass spontaneity." Chronology.)

1621.   Brown, Bernard E., *Protest in Paris: Anatomy of a Revolt*. 240 pp. Morristown NJ: General Learning Press, 1974. (See esp. ch. 1 for a chronology of events and outline of major groups that played a part and ch. 4 for an analysis of the protest's strategy and direction. Index. Bibliography.)

1622.   Cohn–Bendit, Daniel, and Gabriel Cohn–Bendit, *Obsolete Communism: The Left–Wing Alternative*. Trans. Arnold Pomerans. 256 pp. New York, St. Louis, and San Francisco: McGraw–Hill, 1968. (See section 1, ch. 1, 2, and pp. 116–32, 152–63.)

1623.   Gretton, John, *Students and Workers: An Analytical Account of Dissent in France, May–June 1968*. 320 pp. London: Macdonald, 1969. (Analysis of the causes and course of student and worker activism culminating in the events of May 1968. See in general ch. 2–6, esp. pp. 77–81, on initial student tactics; pp. 82–89, 95–96, 110–12 on the beginnings of violence in Paris and factors in its continuation; pp. 176–84, 192–94 on the general strike; pp.

180–90, 197–200 on isolation and suppression of students; and ch. 6 on the factory occupations. Document 15 is a student leaflet asking citizens to provide "the force of onlooking eyes" as an aid against repression. Illustrations. Index. Bibliography.)

1624. Hoyles, Andrée, *Imagination in Power: The Occupation of Factories in France in 1968*. 72 pp. Nottingham: Spokesman Books, 1973. (Survey research on French strikes and occupations, May–June 1968, with individual case studies throughout. See ch. 4 on the process of occupation and pp. 42–44 on leaflets, posters, and films.)

1625. Labro, Philippe, *"This Is Only a Beginning."* Trans. Charles Lam Markmann. 400 pp. New York: Funk & Wagnalls, 1969. Originally published as *Editions et Publications Premiéres* 2 (1968). (Primarily from interviews and documents. See pp. 37–56, 60–62 on Cohn–Bendit, pp. 173–238 on "the shock waves," pp. 239–306 for statements by trade unionists, and pp. 311–23 for interview with student leader. Glossary of groups.)

1626. Schnapp, Alain, and Pierre Vidal–Naquet, *The French Student Uprising, November 1967–June 1968: An Analytical Record*. Trans. Maria Jolas. 654 pp. Boston: Beacon Press, 1971. Abridged and updated. Originally published as *Journal de la Commune Etudiante: Textes et Documents Novembre 1967–Juin 1968*. Paris: Editions du Seuil, 1969. (Collection of documents with notes and introduction focusing on the student movement. Of interest are discussions of growing international demonstrations in early 1968, pp. 70–85; Nanterre beginnings, pp. 95–140; and documents on the Paris actions, ch. 2, 3. Ch. 5, "Forms and Means of Action," includes documents on violence in pp. 325–32 and occupations in pp. 332–55. Photos. Index. Bibliography.)

1627. Seale, Patrick, and Maureen McConville, *Red Flag/Black Flag: French Revolution, 1968*. 252 pp. New York: G.P. Putnam's Sons, 1968. (Journalists' accounts of 1968 events. See esp. ch. 6, 7, 9, 11 on students and professionals and ch. 10 on "the great strike." Photos. Index.)

1628.   Singer, Daniel, *Prelude to Revolution: France in May 1968.* 434 pp. London: Jonathan Cape, 1970. (Journalists' account of May events. See esp. part 3 on workers' takeover of momentum from students. Index.)

1629.   Touraine, Alain, *The May Movement: Revolt and Reform. May 1968: The Student Rebellion and Workers' Strikes—The Birth of a Social Movement.* Trans. Leonard F.X. Mayhew. 373 pp. New York: Random House, 1971. Reprint, New York: Irvington Publishers, 1979. (Account and analysis of May 1968 events. See index under *barricades, Cohn–Bendit, demonstrations, factory occupations, general strikes, student movements, violence,* and *workers.* Index.)

GERMANY

Before 1945

WORLD WAR I MUTINIES

Like the military forces of FRANCE, German soldiers and sailors rebelled against the brutality of the war with mutinies. After several years of war, dissident organizing grew within the Imperial German Navy, resulting in a mutiny in August 1917 that included noncooperation and resistance. German naval mutinies had a more political and radical character than the French army mutinies did.

1630.   Horn, Daniel, *The German Naval Mutinies of World War I.* 346 pp. New Brunswick NJ: Rutgers Univ. Press, 1969. (See ch. 3 for organization of enlisted men's movement of dissent and ch. 4 for August 1917 mutiny and soldiers' strike. Index. Bibliography.)

1631.   Woodward, David, *The Collapse of Power: Mutiny in the High Seas Fleet.* 240 pp. London: Arthur Barker, 1973. (Ch. 3 is on unrest and mutiny of 1917 in the German fleet. Index.)

KAPP PUTSCH, 1920

The legitimacy of the Weimar Republic was widely rejected, especially in army circles, in the turmoil following World War I. In 1920, a group of military officers and disaffected civil servants attempted to overthrow the government with the assistance of paramilitary Free Corps units. While fleeing Berlin, the legal government appealed for popular refusal to obey or assist the conspirators. This appeal was honored, aided by labor strikes and street demonstrations, and the Putsch collapsed after several days. Despite deaths inflicted by the Putsch supporters, labor and the Berlin populace remained defiant until the Free Corps withdrew.

1632. Daniels, H.G., *The Rise of the German Republic*. 292 pp. London: Nisbet, 1927. New York: Charles Scribner's Sons, 1928. (See ch. 9, esp. pp. 132–47. Illustrations. Index. Bibliography.)

1633. Eyck, Erich, *A History of the Weimar Republic*. Vol. 1, *From the Collapse of the Empire to Hindenberg's Election*. Trans. Harlan P. Hanson and Robert G.L. Waite. 373 pp. Cambridge: Harvard Univ. Press, 1962. (See pp. 148–52 on the Kapp Putsch and factors in its defeat and ch. 8 on the *Ruhrkampf* and associated political developments. Index.)

1634. Halperin, S. William, *Germany Tried Democracy: A Political History of the Reich from 1918 to 1933*. 567 pp. New York: Thomas Y. Crowell, 1946. Reprint, Hamden CT and London: Archon Books, 1965. (See ch. 12 on the Kapp Putsch and ch. 17, 18 on the Ruhr occupation. Index. Bibliography.)

1635. Waite, Robert G.L., *Vanguard of Nazism: The Free Corps Movement in Postwar Germany, 1918–1923*. 344 pp. Cambridge: Harvard Univ. Press, 1952. (See ch. 6 on Free Corps participation in the Kapp Putsch. Appendix. Index. Bibliography.)

1636. Wheeler–Bennett, John W., *The Nemesis of Power: The German Army in Politics, 1918–1945*. 829 pp. New York: St. Martin's Press, 1954. 2d ed., London: Macmillan, 1984. (In 2d ed., see pp. 73–81 on the army role in the Kapp Putsch of 1920 and pp. 102–10 on the Ruhr occupation. Discussion of "resistance circles" and the plot of June 1944 appears in part 3, ch. 3–7. Photos. Chronology. Documents. Index. Bibliography.)

RUHRKAMPF, 1923

The Ruhrkampf was a resistance movement against foreign military power, one whose key actors were primarily civilians. In January 1923, France and Belgium sent forces into the Ruhr region of Germany, its industrial core, to extract reparations that Germany owed from World War I but had not adequately paid. The Franco–Belgian expedition was thwarted in its early days when a coalition of industrialists, labor, and government officials refused to assist its efforts in any way. After a lengthy stalemate, France and Belgium were able to develop methods of repression and control that threatened the integrity of the resistance. At the same time, Weimar Germany was suffering hyperinflation, exacerbated by the need to support the Ruhrkampf financially. In a conflict further complicated by Communist uprisings, nationalist sabotage groups, and French–inspired nationalist movements on the western side of the Rhine, Germany called off the resistance in September.

1637.   Cornebise, Alfred Emile, "Some Aspects of the German Response to the Ruhr Occupation, January–September 1923." 215 pp. Ph.D. diss., Univ. of North Carolina at Chapel Hill, 1966. (Focuses on intra–governmental aspects of the German conduct of resistance. See ch. 3, 6, 7 for a distinction between passive and active resistance and ch. 4 on the subsidy of resistance. Bibliography.)

1638.   Gedye, G.E.R., *The Revolver Republic: France's Bid for the Rhine*. 255 pp. London: Arrowsmith, 1930. (British reporter's view of the Rhineland occupation, Ruhr resistance, and Rhineland separatism. See ch. 4–7 on the *Ruhrkampf* and ch. 8 on the separatists in the same period. Photos.)

1639.   Greer, Guy, *The Ruhr–Lorraine Industrial Problem: A Study of the Economic Inter–Dependence of the Two Regions and Their Relation to the Reparation Question*. 328 pp. New York: Macmillan, 1925. (Study of the economic and political problems caused by dividing the Rhine–region industrial zone between France and Germany at end of WWI. See ch. 4–6 for background to the

Ruhr occupation and ch. 7 for an assessment of its causes and effects. Appendixes. Index. Bibliography.)

1640. Lenoir, Nancy R., "The Ruhr in Anglo French Diplomacy: From the Beginning of the Occupation until the End of Passive Resistance." 400 pp. Ph.D. diss., Univ. of Oklahoma, 1972. (Primarily on the diplomacy of the Ruhr occupation and international entanglements, with particular attention to France. Appendixes. Bibliography.)

1641. Tillett, Ben, A. Creech–Jones, and Samuel Warren, *The Ruhr: The Report of a Deputation from the Transport and General Workers Union*. 62 pp. London: Labour Publishing, 1923. (Report by an investigative team of British labor unionists, with special attention to the economic effects of occupation and resistance up to June 1923. Statistics supplied in text and appendixes. List of interviewees. Index.)

1642. Toynbee, Arnold J., *Survey of International Affairs, 1924*. 528 pp. London: Humphrey Milford, Oxford Univ. Press, 1926. (Part 2, section A, discusses international aspects of the reparations problem, occupation of the Ruhr, and the Dawes Plan. See esp. pp. 268–300 on the Ruhr struggle and pp. 323–39 on international negotiations from the German diplomatic initiative of 2 May 1923 to the end of resistance. Index.)

1643. Tuohy, Ferdinand, *Occupied, 1918–1930: A Postscript to the Western Front*. 318 pp. London: Thornton Butterworth, 1931. (See ch. 16, pp. 184–202, for a journalist's recounting of the Ruhr occupation and resistance. Index.)

Opposition and Resistance to Nazism

The concepts of resistance and opposition have broadened by historians in recent years as they apply to opposing the Nazi system within Germany. Recent works regard nonconformity, low–level noncooperation, and other measures as kinds of opposition and do not limit themselves to Communist and military resistance, such as the June 1944 plot to kill Hitler. In addition, some works argue that certain Nazi policies were thwarted by opposition (including campaigns to do away with the handicapped and to remove religious symbols from schools in Catholic areas).

See also: Europe: Opposition and Resistance to Nazi Occupation, 1939–1945.

1644.   Almond, Gabriel A., ed., *The Struggle for Democracy in Germany.* 345 pp. Chapel Hill: Univ. of North Carolina Press, 1949. (See Wolfgang N. Kraus and Gabriel A. Almond, "Resistance and Repression under the Nazis," ch. 2 and Gabriel A. Almond and Wolfgang N. Kraus, "The Social Composition of German Resistance," ch. 3. Index.)

1645.   Andreas–Friedrich, Ruth, *Berlin Underground, 1938–1945.* Trans. Barrows Mussey. 312 pp. New York: Henry Holt, 1947. (Personal account of resistance and Jewish rescue work, by a member of the "Uncle Emil" resistance group.)

1646.   Bentley, James, *Martin Niemöller.* 253 pp. Oxford: Oxford Univ. Press, 1984. (Biography of prominent activist in German Protestant opposition to Nazification, 1933–35. Niemöller led Pastors' Emergency League and other groups and carried on protest individually from 1935 until his arrest and imprisonment in 1937. See esp. ch. 5–8. Photos. Index. Bibliography.)

1647.   Boehm, Eric H., *We Survived: Fourteen Histories of the Hidden and Hunted of Nazi Germany.* 320 pp. New Haven CT: Yale Univ. Press, 1949. Reprint, Santa Barbara CA, Denver CO, and Oxford: ABC–Clio Information Services, 1966 and 1985. (Epilogues added in 1966 and 1985. See ch. 10 for a narrative of the *Rote Kapelle* leaflet group. Index.)

1648.   Bundeszentrale für politische Bildung, *Germans against Hitler, July 20, 1944.* Trans. Allan Yahraes and Lieselotte Yahraes. 360 pp. Bonn: Press and Information Office of the Federal Government of Germany, 1964. (Focuses chiefly on officers' rebellion against Hitler. See ch. 2 on resistance "circles" and ch. 6, 7 on "spirit" and beliefs of resistance. Photos. Index. Bibliography.)

1649.   Fraenkel, Heinrich, *The German People versus Hitler*. 370 pp. London: George Allen & Unwin, 1940. (Estimate of nature and methods of opposition to the Nazi regime, combining economic and political acts of opposition. Appears to have been written to gain support for the idea that not all Germans accepted Hitler. See ch. 3–7, 14, 15, 19, 21, 22; esp. pp. 79–98 on labor, pp. 240–52 on underground broadcasting, and pp. 297–302 on disguised resistance. Brief bibliography.)

1650.   Gallin, Mary Alice, *Ethical and Religious Factors in the German Resistance to Hitler*. 231 pp. Washington: Catholic Univ. of America Press, 1955. (Inquiry into motivations of resistance to Nazism. See esp. ch. 2 on the role of individual conscience, ch. 5 on the right of resistance, and conclusions, pp. 198–202. Index. Bibliography.)

1651.   Graml, Hermann, Hans Mommsen, Hans–Joachim Reichhardt, and Ernst Wolf, *The German Resistance to Hitler*. Trans. Peter Ross and Betty Ross. 281 pp. Berkeley: Univ. of California Press, 1970. (See throughout on resistance organizations and Hans–Joachim Reichhardt, "Resistance in the Labor Movement," pp. 149–92, on extreme difficulties faced by Social Democratic and Communist opposition. Index.)

1652.   Hoffman, Peter, *German Resistance to Hitler*. 169 pp. Cambridge and London: Harvard Univ. Press, 1988. Originally published as *Widerstand gegen Hitler: Probleme des Umsturzes*. Munich: Piper Verlag, 1979. (Brief review of what is known on the composition, thought, and actions of resistance groups, with special attention to assassination attempts. See ch. 2–3 on early Nazi repression and preparation of the legal and bureaucratic mechanisms of repression. Note discussion of boycott of Jews and international reaction to it, p. 37. Ch. 4 describes the spectrum of civilian groups that operated in resistance to the regime. Author concludes, p. 127, that resistance "succeeded only in demonstrating its existence and its readiness to stand up and be counted." Index. Bibliography of English–language sources.)

1653.   ———, *The History of the German Resistance, 1933–1945*. 847 pp. Cambridge MA: MIT Press, 1977. Originally published as

Widerstand, Staatsstreich, Attentat. Munich: Piper Verlag, 1969. (As the original German title implies, this history focuses largely on coup plans and conspiracies, with particular attention to the assassination attempt on Hitler of July 1944. On other issues, pp. 6–17 discuss the failure to mount a resistance in 1933 and Nazi efforts to obviate this, and ch. 2 sets the stage for later developments by discussing resistance attitudes and groups. Appendix. Index. Bibliography.)

1654.   Jansen, Jon B., and Stephan Weyl [pseud.], *The Silent War: The Underground Movement in Germany.* Trans. Anna Caples. 357 pp. Philadelphia and New York: J.B. Lippincott, 1943. (See ch. 2–5 on the tasks and problems of underground organizations and ch. 3, 6 on repression.)

1655.   Kershaw, Ian, *Popular Opinion and Political Dissent in the Third Reich: Bavaria, 1933–1945.* 425 pp. Oxford: Clarendon Press, 1983. (History of dissent against Nazi policies among farmers, industrial labor, and the middle class. In addition to accounts of their "overwhelmingly verbal" dissent, see ch. 8 on popular protest against euthanasia and the removal of crucifixes from schools. Index. Bibliography.)

1656.   Leuner, Heinz D., *When Compassion Was a Crime: Germany's Silent Heroes, 1933–1945.* 164 pp. London: Oswald Wolff, 1966. (Primarily recounts acts of individual resistance and assistance to victims of the Nazi system. Chronology. Bibliography.)

1657.   Lewy, Guenter, *The Catholic Church and Nazi Germany.* 416 pp. New York and Toronto: McGraw–Hill, 1964. (Part 1 studies Hitler's successful effort to counter the church's ban on Nazism and the subsequent "great reconciliation" of church and Nazi state. See also part 2, ch. 6–8 on church conformity to Hitler's policies; esp. ch. 6, section 2, entitled "Tactics of Adaptation," for a trenchant criticism of the decision not to oppose Hitler's rule. Ch. 9 discusses Catholic protests against sterilization and euthanasia, ch. 10 studies Catholicism and the destruction of the Jews, and ch. 11, "The Problem of Resistance," briefly recounts protest, public opinion, and the organized resistance. Appendix. Index.)

1658. Manvell, Roger, and Heinrich Fraenkel, *The Canaris Conspiracy: The Secret Resistance to Hitler in the German Army*. 268 pp. New York: David McKay, 1969. (On the background and preparation of failed takeover plots. See part 1 for material on General Beck and part 2, sections 1 and 2, for some discussion of other resistance groups. Photos. Chronology. Index. Bibliography.)

1659. Merson, Allan, *Communist Resistance in Nazi Germany*. 372 pp. London: Lawrence & Wishart, 1985. Atlantic Highlands NJ: Humanities Press International, 1986. (History of resistance by the German Communist Party and associated groups from the Nazi seizure of power in 1933 to 1945. The unpreparedness of the party in 1933 is discussed in pp. 20–26, and ch. 3 is on protests at that time and suppression of the party as a legal entity. Ch. 4 includes discussion of the Gestapo and methods of repression on pp. 47–66 and Communist party methods on pp. 62–67. Ch. 4 is on political action, propaganda, and the press until ca. 1935. Later chapters detail the crisis of survival of the later 1930s and opposition groups in the war years. This includes, in ch. 13, discussion of the Schulze–Boysen–Harnock group or "Rote Kapelle," and the Herbert Baum group. Mention of leafletting, underground press, disguised publications, and similar methods throughout. Glossary. Index. Bibliography.)

1660. Nicosia, Francis R., and Lawrence D. Stokes, *Germans against Nazism: Nonconformity, Opposition, and Resistance in the Third Reich*. 435 pp. New York and Oxford: Berg Publishers, 1990. (Historical essays on aspects of dissent, opposition, and social discontent as resistance to Nazism and Nazi policies from the rise of Hitler to the end of WWII.)

1661. *Persecution and Resistance under the Nazis*. 500 pp. London: Institute of Contemporary History, 1978. The Wiener Library Catalogue Series no. 7. (Catalogue of holdings of Wiener Library, London. Reprint of original 1949 catalogue with extensive updates. See section 3 on German resistance in general, section 4 on the occupied countries, and section 5, subsections D and E on Jewish resistance. Appendix 2 lists

illegal pamphlets from Germany after 1933, many under
disguised titles, some originating outside the country.)

1662.   Peukert, Detlev J.K., *Inside Nazi Germany: Conformity,
        Opposition, and Racism in Everyday Life*. Trans. Richard
        Deveson. 288 pp. New Haven and London: Yale Univ. Press,
        1987. Originally published as *Volksgenossen   und
        Gemeinschaftsfremde: Anpassung, Ausmerze und Aufbegehren
        unter dem Nationalsozialismus*. Cologne: Bund–Verlag, 1982.
        (Everyday life and popular discontent under National
        Socialism in Germany. See ch. 5–8; see also index under
        *conflicts within Third Reich, go–slows at work, "grumbling,"
        nonconformist and dissident behavior, popular opposition, protest,
        refusals, resistance movement, strikes*, and *"swing [big–band music]
        movement."* Illustrations. Photos. Index. Bibliography.)

1663.   ———, "Ruhr Miners under Nazi Repression, 1933–1945,"
        International Journal of Oral History 1 (1980): 111–27. (Partly
        methodological and partly on the effects of Nazi repression
        and the state–sponsored rationalization of the work process,
        this article also has observations on "passive resistance" by
        left–wing miners and the continuation of opposition under
        repression.)

1664.   Peterson, Edward, *The Limits of Hitler's Power*. 472 pp.
        Princeton NJ: Princeton Univ. Press, 1969. (A study of the
        capacity of various groups to "divert" Nazi policy from its
        course in greater or lesser measure. Includes studies of five
        urban regions and of village life to discover sources of
        opposition and "diversion" as well as obedience. See ch. 9 for
        conclusion, esp. comment on resistance on pp. 436–37 and on
        "loyal disobedience" on pp. 449–51. Index. Bibliography.)

1665.   Rasmussen, Larry L., *Dietrich Bonhoeffer: Reality and Resistance*.
        222 pp. Nashville and New York: Abingdon Press, 1972.
        (Theological and biographical study of Bonhoeffer's decision
        to reject his pacifism and support the assassination attempt of
        July 1944 on Hitler, with discussion of means of resistance, pp.
        45–55, 187–96, and Bonhoeffer's pacifism, part 1, ch. 2; part 2,
        ch. 1, 2; and Appendix A, on Bonhoeffer and Gandhi. Index.)

1666. Rothfels, Hans, *The German Opposition to Hitler: An Assessment*. 166 pp. London: Oswald Wolff, 1961. (See pp. 27–31 on "degrees of non–conformity" and pp. 45–124 for a history of resistance groups. Index.)

1667. Stachura, Peter D., ed., *The Shaping of the Nazi State*. 304 pp. London: Croom Helm; New York: Barnes & Noble, 1978. (See Jeremy Noakes, "The Oldenburg Crucifix Struggle of November 1936: A Case Study of Opposition in the Third Reich," pp. 210–33, for a study of symbolic protest and noncooperation in the Catholic opposition to deconsecration of schools and the effects of opposition on party leadership. Index.)

1668. Stoltzfus, Nathan A., "Social Limitations on the Nazi Dictatorship: The Rosenstraße Protest and the Case of German–Jewish Intermarriage." 379 pp. Ph.D. dissertation, Harvard University, 1993. (Uses the demonstration in Berlin's Rosenstraße, March 1943, as a key event for the discussion of Nazi policies and the limits placed on them by society. In this case, described in ch. 6, the German non–Jewish spouses of Jewish men arrested in a final sweep of the Jews of Berlin gathered in front of the prison for several days, a protest that ended when the government determined to release the people it had seized. Bibliography.)

1669. Zahn, Gordon C., *German Catholics and Hitler's Wars: A Study in Social Control*. 232 pp. New York: Sheed and Ward, 1962. (A study of conformity rather than of resistance, this inquiry begins by looking into the fate of the Catholic peace movement after the advent of Hitler. Part 2 studies the role of the bishops and the cases of Cardinals von Gaulen, Faulhaber, and Gröber [identified with opposition to Hitler] and Bishop Rarkowski [a supporter of the state]. Author concludes that despite personal heroism and acts of resistance "at no time was the German Catholic population released [by the bishops] from its moral obligations to obey the legitimate authority of the National Socialist rulers," p. 73.)

1670. Zassenhaus, Hiltgunt, *Walls: Resisting the Third Reich: One Woman's Story*. 248 pp. Boston: Beacon Press, 1974.

(Autobiography of a German woman who assisted political prisoners during the 1940s.)

1671.   Zeller, Eberhard, *The Flame of Freedom: The German Struggle against Hitler*. Trans. R.P. Heller and D.R. Masters. 471 pp. Coral Gables FL: Univ. of Miami Press, 1969. (Early chapters include material on military opposition and noncooperation; others focus on the assassination attempt of July 20, 1944. Bibliography.)

WEISSE ROSE

The self–named White Rose group (Weisse Rose) were Munich University students led by brother and sister Hans and Sophie Scholl. White Rose activists distributed or posted anti–Hitler leaflets in Munich and other cities until they were arrested on being detected. Perhaps because their protests coincided with the German defeat at Stalingrad, the Scholls and others in their group were executed in February 1943.

1672.   Bayles, William, *Seven Were Hanged: An Authentic Account of the Student Revolt in Munich University*. 80 pp. London: Victor Gollancz, 1945. (Early account of the White Rose group as told by a student who had fled Germany. Pp. 15–67 recount the origins, actions, and trial of members. Pp. 69–77 contain a personal account of the announcement of German defeat at Stalingrad and the execution of White Rose members.)

1673.   Dumbach, Annette E., and Jud Newborn, *Shattering the German Night: The Story of the White Rose*. 259 pp. Boston and Toronto: Little, Brown, 1986. (History of the White Rose group and its relationship with the German resistance movement in general. See esp. ch. 7–10, 13–18, and "Aftermath." Index. Bibliography.)

1674.   Hanser, Richard, *A Noble Treason: The Revolt of the Munich Students against Hitler*. 319 pp. New York: G.P. Putnam's Sons, 1979. (Popular account of White Rose. See ch. 7, 9; including spontaneous demonstrations at the Univ. of Munich, 1943. Index.)

1675. Scholl, Inge, *The White Rose: Munich, 1942–1943.* Trans. Arthur R. Schultz. 2d ed. 160 pp. Middletown CT: Wesleyan Univ. Press, 1983. First English version entitled *Students Against Tyranny.* Originally published as *Die Weisse Rose.* Frankfurt: Verlag der Fri. Hefte, 1952. (Basic account of the White Rose by a Scholl family member. See pp. 30–52, 68–72, and concluding remarks, pp. 96–98. Documents include White Rose leaflets, pp. 73–93. Photos.)

1676. Vinke, Hermann, *The Short Life of Sophie Scholl.* Trans. Hedwig Pachter. 210 pp. New York: Harper & Row, 1984. (Popular account based largely on interviews, which are excerpted in the text. See esp. pp. 106–60.)

Federal Republic of Germany

The pre–1989 Federal Republic is known more for its struggle against acts of terror and the anti–radical actions it undertook than for nonviolent opposition. This is partly because of gaps in the record and future research should point up both the protests against repressive measures and nonviolent protest.

1677. Burns, Rob, and Wilfried van der Will, *Protest and Democracy in West Germany: Extra–Parliamentary Opposition and the Democratic Agenda.* 325 pp. Houndmills, Basingstoke and London: Macmillan Press, 1988. (On issues, groups, and movements active beyond the bounds of regular constitutional politics in the post–WWII Federal Republic, focusing in particular on trends of thought among "critical intellectuals." Chapters on peace protest both early and recent, student and feminist politics, the "citizens' initiatives" or activist pressure groups of the 1970s–80s, and the Green Party. Of interest are pp. 55–64 on political violence and the state's responses in the 1960s; pp. 76–77, 91–96 on disarmament and the Easter Marches; and pp. 109–15 on student provocations and demonstrations. In ch. 5 on citizens' initiatives, see pp. 175–78 on the occupation and renovation of housing; pp. 178–83 on the suppression of radicalism; pp. 189–92 on the campaign against expanding Frankfurt airport; and pp. 194–204 on protests against nuclear power plants and the issues raised there. In ch. 6, see throughout on peace organizations and actions, esp. pp. 224–29. Authors comment on violence in intended nonviolent actions in several places, esp. pp. 191, 198–202. Glossary. Chronology. Index. Bibliography.)

GREEN MOVEMENT

The notable exceptions to the idea that little nonviolent opposition took place in the FRG were anti–nuclear protest and the Green movement. As noted in the sources below, Greens participated in support for urban groups who took over abandoned housing, environmentalist actions, and anti–nuclear politics. In addition, the Green Party adopted "nonviolence" as a plank in the party platform.

1678.   Capra, Fritjof, and Charlene Spretnak, in collaboration with Rödiger Lutz, *Green Politics*. 244 pp. New York: E.P. Dutton, 1984. (On the Green Party's adoption of "nonviolence" in a particular sense as a party goal, see pp. 43–47; see also pp. 70–80 on peace movement actions.)

1679.   Papadakis, Elim, *The Green Movement in West Germany*. 230 pp. London and Canberra: Croom Helm; New York: St. Martin's Press, 1984. (Study of Green odyssey from ecology to politics. See ch. 4 on environmental action, pp. 123–30 on urban squatters, and ch. 7 on peace–oriented actions. Index. Bibliography.)

1680.   Pilat, J.F., *Ecological Politics: The Rise of the Green Movement*. The Washington Papers. Vol. 8, no. 77. 72 pp. Beverly Hills and London: Sage Publications, 1980. (See ch. 4 on demonstrations, ch. 6 for discussion of anti–nuclear activities in various countries, and appendix 2 for chronology of anti–nuclear demonstrations. Bibliography.)

German Democratic Republic

EAST BERLIN UPRISING, 1953

Occurring within the first decade of the Soviet–dominated East European political and economic order, the Berlin revolt of June 1953 is considered in some of the works here to have resulted from the conditions that order imposed on labor. The revolt was relatively brief, consisting largely of a declared general strike and a march by labor in the streets of East Berlin. It was soon suppressed but, as study of more recent events in Eastern Europe reveals, lived in the popular memory.

1681. Bendix, Reinhardt, *Work and Authority in Industry: Ideologies of Management in the Course of Industrialization*. 466 pp. New York: John Wiley & Sons; London: Chapman & Hall, 1956. (See ch. 6, esp. pp. 387–400, for a study of methods of control over industrial work as a factor in the June 1953 uprising and subsequent normalization. Index.)

1682. Brandt, Heinz, "The East German Popular Uprising, 17 June 1953." *The Review: Quarterly Studies* 2 (October 1959): 91–109. Imry Nagy Institute for Political Research, Brussels. (Describes the causes of the uprising, laying blame primarily on Walter Ulbricht. See esp. pp. 102–9 on collective action against the ruling Social Unity Party.)

1683. Brant, Stefan, *The East German Rising, 17th June 1953*. Trans. Charles Wheeler. 202 pp. London: Thames & Hudson, 1955. New York: Praeger, 1957. Originally published as *Der Aufstand*. (See ch. 6–11 on the uprising, esp. pp. 62–79 for account of the general strike and march through East Berlin. Illustrations. Photos.)

1684. Hildebrandt, Rainer, *The Explosion: The Uprising behind the Iron Curtain*. Trans. E.B. Ashton. 198 pp. Boston: Little, Brown; Toronto: Duell, Sloan and Pearce, 1955. (Day–by–day narrative of the June uprising and its aftermath, based on personal accounts by participants, including a Soviet officer. Photos.)

1980S AND BERLIN WALL

One of the first and best–known of the mass movements against a communist government, the East German opposition movement found its roots in a combination of trends that had begun several years earlier. One factor was intellectual resistance by people on the left such as Robert Havemann and Rudolf Bahro, while a second was the "unofficial" anti–nuclear and peace movement. Direct action began when thousands of Germans emigrated illegally through Hungary, which had declared its border open. This was followed by demonstrations in several cities led in part by the group New Forum. Despite some violence against the protesters, the government determined that it could not repress the people massively and began a series of back–pedaling maneuvers that included appointing moderate prime ministers and opening the Berlin Wall in the face of demonstrations there.

1685.   Bornstein, Jerry, *The Wall Came Tumbling Down: The Berlin Wall and the Fall of Communism*. 95 pp. New York: Arch Cape Press, 1990. (Photo–essay on demonstrations at and around the Berlin Wall in 1989 and the opening of east–west passage through the wall, combined with a history of the wall and accounts of protests and changes of government in several Eastern European countries. Chronologies. Photos.)

1686.   Keithly, David M., *The Collapse of East German Communism: The Year the Wall Came Down, 1989*. 241 pp. Westport and London: Praeger, 1992. (Assessment of the reasons for the events of 1989, in parts 1 and 2, and the process they followed. See esp. ch. 10 on the combination of mass exit and opposition demonstrations in the autumn of 1989; ch. 11, "People Without Fear," on the effects of demonstrations on the government; and ch. 12 on the opening of the Berlin Wall. See also pp. 222–26 on why the regime did not repress the demonstrations. Index. Bibliography.)

1687.   Neckermann, Peter, *The Unification of Germany or the Anatomy of a Peaceful Revolt*. 112 pp. Boulder CO: East European Monographs, 1991. Monograph no. 33. (Ch. 1, 2 review the events of 1989–90, while the conclusion, pp. 82–84, argues that one of the three factors conducive to German reunifcation was that "discipline and nonviolence removed the communist regime's option to use brute force," thereby preventing its ability to end the protests and "survive.")

1688. Philipsen, Dirk, *We Were the People: Voices from East Germany's Revolutionary Autumn of 1989.* 417 pp. Durham NC and London: Duke University Press, 1993. (Collected interviews with GDR activists and political figures involved in the transformation of the state. See esp. ch, 1, 3 and part 3 for the author's assessment and activists' reflections. Chronology, 1945–1990, pp. 385–401. Index. Bibliography.)

1689. Sandford, John, *The Sword and the Ploughshare: Autonomous Peace Initiatives in East Germany.* 111 pp. London: Merlin/European Nuclear Disarmament, 1983. (On activities of autonomous peace movement, see ch. 4, esp. pp. 58–67, 70–75, postscript, and associated documents, pp. 89–99. Chronology.)

1690. Woods, Roger, *Opposition in the GDR under Honecker, 1971–1985: An Introduction and Documentation.* Trans. Christopher Upward. 257 pp. New York: St. Martin's Press; London: Macmillan, 1986. (Ch. 3 is on the problem of defining and describing "opposition" and ch. 4 is on opposition in the GDR. Ch. 5 evaluates the strength and significance of opposition. See documents from the unofficial peace movement, nos. 30–38. Consult index for Rudolf Bahro, Wolf Biermann, and Robert Havemann. Chronology. Documents. Index. Bibliography.)

GREAT BRITAIN

Researchers have documented Britain's history of nonviolent action very thoroughly, although not always with the intention of doing so. In addition to traditional forms of protest and opposition to the effects of social change and the strengthening of the powers of elites and the central state, industrial conflict has strongly marked British history. Use of the word strike goes far back in British labor history and it is possible that the great strike of 1842 was the world's first general strike. The petition campaigns of the 1830s and 1840s to introduce the People's Charter of rights also was promoted by discussion and use of many means of nonviolent action. In more recent times, Britain has appeared to itself to be unusually strike–prone. Nonviolent action has not been limited to strikes and labor disputes but has also been a feature of struggles over basic rights (women's suffrage), peace and arms races (from interwar pacifism to Greenham Common), and similar movements.

Before 1900

Protest before the modern era was considered so threatening to the state and established order that little distinction was made between violent and nonviolent methods. Buried in the history of British protest, however, are several episodes of protest and noncooperation. One of the most striking is the movement for the People's Charter, or Chartism, of the 1830s and 1840s. Chartists circulated several petitions demanding that Parliament respect their charter of rights, held mass meetings, and developed the idea of a complete cessation of work—a general strike?—during a month held sacred to the cause.

1691.   Slack, Paul, ed., *Rebellion, Popular Protest, and the Social Order in Early Modern England*. 339 pp. Cambridge: Cambridge Univ. Press, 1984. (Articles from the journal *Past and Present*. See David Rollison, "Property, Ideology, and Popular Culture in a Gloucestershire Village, 1660–1740," ch. 14, for a description of "groaning" as a public act of communal censure. Index.)

1692.   Thompson, Dorothy, *The Chartists*. 399 pp. London: Temple Smith, 1984. (History of the People's Charter movement in mid–nineteenth century Britain. Introduction explains author's reservations on viewing Chartism as a political movement in which success or failure were significant categories. Ch. 1 discusses several "reforms" that excited opposition before the drafting of the Charter, such as labor reforms, the Irish Coercion Act of 1833, and the "collapse and crushing" of union organization and strikes. See throughout on Chartism's extraparliamentary methods, esp. ch. 2 on underground "unstamped" newspapers that published in defiance of stamp duties; ch. 3 on the origins of the Charter petition, national convention, and "grand national holiday" ideas and the repression they drew upon them in 1839; ch. 4 on the Newport Rising; ch. 11 on strikes of 1842; and ch. 13 on the "third petition" and London demonstrations of 1848. Appendix. Index. Bibliography.)

1693. Thompson, Dorothy, ed., *The Early Chartists*. 307 pp. London and Basingstoke: Macmillan; Columbia: Univ. of South Carolina Press, 1971. (Documents on Chartism, 1838–40. Of interest are selections 4–8, 16 on meetings and petitions; selection 17 on placards and counter–placards; selection 18 on the "General Convention of the Industrious Classes" of 1839; selection 20 for two arguments in opposition to the "Sacred Month" [general strike] idea; and following selections on confrontations with the authorities. Index. Bibliography.)

Women's Suffrage Movement

The women of the Pankhurst family were a central part of "militant" women's suffrage in Britain and the organization they created, the Women's Social and Political Union (WSPU). The suffrage cause is also associated with property destruction and a reputation for violence, even though little direct violence was done. Methods included campaigns of window–breaking, arson, and personal attacks. As entry 1699 suggests, violence was partly a response to violence received by activists, but suffragists also used many nonviolent means. In addition to demonstrations and protest theater, a notable example is noncooperation and hunger strikes in prison by several activists. The government resorted to feeding prisoners forcibly and "cat and mouse" prosecutions, when protesters were released from prison and then arrested again after they had recovered their strength. In addition to these, some suffragists performed highly dramatic acts of personal sacrifice in hopes of strengthening the cause.

1694. Holledge, Julie, *Innocent Flowers*. 194 pp. London: Virago Press, 1981. (Descriptive history of Actresses' Franchise League and the involvement of actresses and playwrights in suffrage activities. See part 2, ch. 3, 4, and part 3, ch. 6, on the development of political and protest theater. Part 4 contains three suffrage propaganda plays. Photos. Bibliography.)

1695. Kenney, Annie, *Memories of a Militant*. 308 pp. London: Edward Arnold, 1924. (Autobiography of a member of the Militant Movement for Women's Suffrage in Britain. Photos.)

1696.   Lytton, Constance, *Prison and Prisoners: Some Personal Experiences*. London: William Heinemann, 1914. 337 pp. (Memoir of Women's Social and Political Union [WSPU] activist. A noblewomen released from prison after a hunger strike because of her rank, she disguised herself as a working woman in future protests and was forcibly fed many times on subsequent prison hunger strikes. See ch. 3–5, 11–13.)

1697.   Metcalfe, A.E., *Woman's Effort: A Chronicle of British Women's Fifty Years' Struggle for Citizenship, 1865–1914*. 363 pp. Oxford: B.H. Blackwell, 1917. (Contrasts "constitutional" and "militant" methods. See parts 2–4. Illustrations. Documents. Index.)

1698.   Morgan, David, *Suffragists and Liberals: The Politics of Woman Suffrage in England*. 184 pp. Totowa NJ: Rowman & Littlefield, 1975. (Ch. 2–9 discuss liberal governments' conduct toward the woman suffrage question in light of various forms of "militancy" and parliamentary politics, 1906–14. Index. Bibliography.)

1699.   Morrell, Caroline, *Black Friday: Violence against Women in the Suffragette Movement*. 61 pp. London: Women's Research and Resources Centre Publications, 1981. (Examination of violence by police and crowds against suffrage demonstrators. Includes important information on the role of this violence in turning the WSPU toward property destruction and "violence" as its policy. See ch. 5, 6. Photos. Bibliography.)

1700.   Pankhurst, Christabel, *Unshackled: The Story of How We Won the Vote*. Ed. Lord Pethick–Lawrence of Peaslake. 284 pp. London: Hutchinson, 1959. (A first–hand account of the militant years of the women's suffrage movement 1905–14. Photos. Index.)

1701.   Pankhurst, Emmeline, *My Own Story*. 364 pp. London: Eveleigh Nash, 1914. Reprint, New York: Source Book Press, 1970. (Memoir and detailed account of Women's Social and Political Union's actions, reasoning behind tactics, and relation to British law and politics. See book 1, ch. 3, 4; book 2, ch. 1–5, 7, 8; and pp. 356–63. Photos.)

1702. Pankhurst, E. Sylvia, *The Suffragette: The History of the Women's Militant Suffrage Movement, 1905–1910.* 502 pp. New York: Sturgis & Walton, 1912. (History of the suffrage movement dating from the founding of the WSPU to 1910. Contains some material not in the following entry, including a first–hand account of a prison hunger strike, pp. 393–95. Photos.)

1703. ———, *The Suffragette Movement: An Intimate Account of Persons and Ideals.* 631 pp. London and New York: Longmans, Green, 1931. Reprint, New York: Kraus, 1971. Reprint, London: Virago, 1977. (A first accounting by Emmeline Pankhurst's daughter, with history of WSPU to 1910. See book 2, ch. 2, 4, 6, 8; book 3, ch. 1–5. Photos.)

1704. Pethick–Lawrence, Emmeline, *My Part in a Changing World.* 354 pp. London: Victor Gollancz, 1938. (Account by treasurer of the WSPU. See ch. 10–22, esp. 283–85, for criticism of the Pankhursts and ch. 19 on Conspiracy Trial costs. Photos.)

1705. Raeburn, Antonia, *The Militant Suffragettes.* 269 pp. London: Michael Joseph, 1973. (History of suffragism from 1905 to WWI. Ch. 1–3 discuss organization and demonstrations up to the large–scale imprisonments of 1908. Ch. 5 is on the first phase of militancy, ch. 7 is on the Black Friday suppression of women's protests in 1910, and ch. 8–12 are on attacks on property, other militancy, and the Cat and Mouse Act. Photos. Chronology. Index. Bibliography.)

1706. Rosen, Andrew, *Rise Up, Women! The Militant Campaign of the Women's Social and Political Union, 1903–1914.* 312 pp. London and Boston: Routledge & Kegan Paul, 1974. (See esp. ch. 4, 8–10 on the beginnings of "militancy," ch. 13 on the acceptance of violence and property destruction as means, and ch. 16–19 on the arson campaign. Photos. Index. Bibliography.)

1707. Rover, Constance, *Women's Suffrage and Party Politics in Britain, 1866–1914.* 240 pp. London: Routledge & Kegan Paul; Toronto: Univ. of Toronto Press, 1967. (Analysis of the political impact of suffragism and its methods. See ch. 6, 7, 9, esp. pp. 80–94, on extralegal tactics as well as pp. 94–101 on "violence." Bibliography. Documents.)

1708.   Strachey, Ray, *The Cause: A Short History of the Women's Movement in Great Britain*. 429 pp. Portway and Bath: Cedric Chivers, 1974 [orig. publ. 1928]. U.S. ed., *Struggle: The Stirring Story of Woman's Advance in England*. 429 pp. New York: Duffield, 1930. (See ch. 6, 14–19 on the suffrage movement, 1865–1918. Photos. Appendixes. Index.)

1709.   Tremain, Rose, *The Fight for Freedom for Women*. 151 pp. New York: Ballantine Books, 1973. (See ch. 6, 7, 9 on the origins of British suffrage tactics and WSPU methods. Illustrations. Photos.)

Soldiers' Protests, 1917–1919

Like the servicemen of France and Germany, British soldiers and sailors protested conscription and conditions in the military during and after World War I by demonstrations and strikes.

1710.   Gill, Douglas, and Gloden Dallas, *The Unknown Army*. 178 pp. London: Verso, 1985. (Study of British army unrest in and just after WWI. See esp. ch. 6–12 on dissent and various soldiers' strikes, 1917–19. Index.)

1711.   Rothstein, Andrew, *The Soldiers' Strikes of 1919*. 114 pp. London and Basingstoke: Macmillan, 1980. (Examines protest movement in the armed forces against post–WWI conscription. Ch. 3, "The Soldiers Intervene," details demonstrations at British bases in France, India, and England. See ch. 4, "They Understood Nothing," for an assessment of the movement's effects. Index.)

Conscientious Objection and Inter–War Peace Movement

Researchers studying conscientious objection should distinguish among pacifism, legal conscientious objector status, and the active refusal to accept conscription. While pacifism refers to the conviction that war is an unacceptable method of settling international disputes (whatever the source of this conviction), legal conscientious objector status is recognition by the government that an individual is exempt from military service based upon holding certain convictions. Direct refusal of conscription may not actually be motivated by pacifism but also by other reasons for rejecting war and the power of the state to conscript troops and make war. These entries contain material on groups that fought against conscription and warfare (the No–Conscription Fellowship and the Peace Pledge Union), the actions and fate of individual conscription refusers, and the treatment of radical refusers during wars that most other citizens considered justified.

1712. Barker, Rachel, *Conscience, Government, and War: Conscientious Objection in Great Britain, 1939–1945.* 174 pp. London, Boston, and Henley: Routledge & Kegan Paul, 1982. (Attempt at a "more objective and dispassionate" study of conscientious objection in Great Britain during WWII. See p. 5 on the distinction between conscientious objection and civil disobedience. Ch. 1 describes the growth of a "mass pacifist movement" into the 1930s and ch. 6 examines the fate of conscientious objectors in prison, under "cat and mouse" prosecutions, and in the military. Index. Bibliography.)

1713. Ceadel, Martin, *Pacifism in Britain, 1914–1945: The Defining of a Faith.* 342 pp. Oxford: Clarendon Press, 1980. (History of ideas and actions of British pacifism in the era of the world wars. Pp. 1–8 distinguish between absolute and situational opposition to war. See pp. 37–46 on conscientious objection in WWI; pp. 88–101, 248–65 on reactions to Gandhi and concepts of nonviolent resistance in the 1930s; and pp. 154–63 on the issue of sanctions against Hitler, 1934–35. See also index under *conscientious objection* and *pacifism*, and individuals and organizations by name. Index. Bibliography.)

1714. Morrison, Sybil, *I Renounce War: The Story of the Peace Pledge Union.* 108 pp. London: Sheppard Press, 1962. (Personal story of the Peace Pledge Union and its initiator, Dick Sheppard. See ch. 1–3 on activities before WWII and ch. 4 for reaction to WWII. Photos. Appendixes. Index.)

1715. Robbins, Keith, *The Abolition of War: The "Peace Movement" in Britain, 1914–1919.* 255 pp. Cardiff: Univ. of Wales Press, 1976. (See ch. 1 on the pre–war peace movement, which includes pp. 22–23 on Labour's consideration of a "general strike" against war; and ch. 4–6 and pp. 207–10 on the No–Conscription Fellowship. Index. Bibliography.)

1716. Vellacott, Jo, *Bertrand Russell and the Pacifists in the First World War*. 326 pp. New York: St. Martin's Press, 1981. (Study of Russell and the No–Conscription Fellowship during WWI. See index under *Allen, Reginald Clifford; Brockway, Archibald Fenner; Childs, General Sir Wyndham; hungerstriking; No–Conscription Fellowship; Russell, Bertrand;* and *Society of Friends*. Index. Bibliography.)

Labor

With at least 250 years of strike history, British labor has attempted, or indeed invented, nearly every form of strike and has given serious attention to questions of strike strategy, discipline, and the role of nonviolent versus violent conduct in confrontations. Strikes and strike frequency in Britain has been linked to the kinds of work discipline used in industry, attempts by proprietors and managers to manage or prevent strikes, and to non–economic motives of strikes, such as influencing policy and defending gains.

1717. Clegg, Hugh Armstrong, *The System of Industrial Relations in Great Britain*. 3rd ed. 517 pp. Oxford: Basil Blackwell, 1976. (Ch. 7 is on strikes and their incidence and causes, with attention to unsanctioned and sanctioned strikes. Index.)

1718. Frow, R., E. Frow, and Michael Katanka, *Strikes: A Documentary History*. 257 pp. London: Charles Knight, 1971. (Anthology from various sources, including many period documents, on British strikes from the 1750s to the 1920s, with descriptions, songs and verse, and illustrations. Pp. 195–222 contain a 1929 document by the Red International of Labour Unions, "Strike Strategy and Tactics." Photos. Index.)

1719. McCord, Norman, *Strikes*. 142 pp. Oxford: Basil Blackwell, 1980. (History of strikes, ca. 1800–1970, as affected by the changing industrial system. Index.)

1720. McKelvey, Jean Trepp, *Dock Labor Disputes in Great Britain: A Study in the Persistence of Industrial Disputes*. 59 pp. New York

State School of Industrial and Labor Relations, Cornell Univ. Bulletin No. 23 (1953). (Brief study of British dockers' strikes from the Great Dock Strike of 1887 into the post–WWII period, focusing on efforts to change the hiring system in hope of ending the tendency to strike. Appendix.)

1721.   Smith, Harold, comp., *The British Labour Movement to 1970: A Bibliography*. 250 pp. London: Mansell Publishing, 1981. (Selected books and journal articles on labour history. See pp. 200–6 on strikes and pp. 207–9 on the general strike of 1926. Other sections contain references to histories and research sources, Chartism and associated labor conflicts, organizations, and cooperatives. Index.)

NINETEENTH CENTURY

There are two important themes reflected in these entries. First, it was in the nineteenth century that lengthy and widespread strikes first arose, notably the great "general strike" of 1842 in the cotton mills. Second, one of the first truly significant people's movements in the English–speaking world, the People's Charter movement or Chartism, coincided with the development of the strike. Indeed, the two are related, because Chartism sought to speak for the laboring people. In addition, Chartism proposed the concept of a "national holiday" or "sacred month," when all the producing classes of the country would halt their labors to dramatize and reconsider their contribution to the system.

1722.   Dutton, H.I., and J.E. King, *"Ten Per Cent and No Surrender"*: *The Preston Strike, 1853–1854*. 283 pp. Cambridge: Cambridge Univ. Press, 1981. (Very detailed history of a lengthy strike and lockout in the textile industry with observations on its social–economic context. Many references to mass meetings and strike–support activities as well as to decision of strikers to remain "peaceable," e.g., pp. 113, 127, 134, plus sanctions used, pp. 64–65, and the effects of provocations, p. 133. Index. Bibliography.)

1723.   Foster, John, *Class Struggle and the Industrial Revolution: Early Industrial Capitalism in Three English Towns*. 346 pp. London: Weidenfeld and Nicholson, 1974. (History of industrialism, conflict, and the resulting "liberalization" of labor relations in typical English industries before 1850. See pp. 48–51 on collective action from 1818 to 1834, pp. 112–18 on the general strike of 1842 in the cotton industry, and pp. 140–49 for a summary of "mass action." Appendixes. Index.)

1724.   Jenkins, Mick, *The General Strike of 1842*. 326 pp. London: Lawrence & Wishart, 1980. (Concludes that the 1842 general strike originated in Chartist and labor ideas developing for some years. Describes conduct of strike and efforts by leaders to limit looting, property damage, and violence, most of which occurred in process of spreading the strike or in clashes with troops firing on meetings or processions. Illustrations. Documents in appendixes. Index.)

1725.   Quinault, R., and J. Stevenson, eds., *Popular Protest and Public Order: Six Studies in British History, 1790–1920*. 242 pp. London: George Allen & Unwin, 1974. (See F.C. Mather, "The General Strike of 1842," pp. 115–40.)

1726.   Tilly, Louise A., and Charles Tilly, eds., *Class Conflict and Collective Action*. 260 pp. Beverly Hills and London: Sage Publications, 1981. (Brian R. Brown presents a structural interpretation of the general strike of 1842 as the "first political mass strike of modern times" in "Industrial Capitalism, Conflict, and Working Class Contention in Lancashire, 1842," pp. 111–42.)

1727.   Webb, Sidney, and Beatrice Webb, *The History of Trade Unionism*. 784 pp. New York: Kelly, 1965 [orig. publ. 1894]. Revised ed., NY: Longmans, Green, 1920. (History of the British trade union movement. See p. 46 on the origin of the term *strike*. Consult index under the names of occupations and organizations to locate discussion of various strikes and other collective action. Appendixes. Index.)

TWENTIETH CENTURY

The professionalization of police and the state's willingness to take a hand in strike control are stressed in these entries. Strikers have consistently tried to demonstrate, in effect, that industry and the state can neither dispense with their services nor easily force them back to work. Sources assembled here explore the ways in which industry and government have tried to limit their dependency on labor and to compel a return to work on acceptable terms.

1728. Geary, Roger, *Policing Industrial Disputes: 1893 to 1985*. 171 pp. Cambridge: Cambridge Univ. Press, 1985. (History of the use and control of violence by the state as an option in confronting strikers from the Wales coal lockout of 1893 to the miners' strike of 1984. Index.)

1729. Jeffery, Keith, and Peter Hennessey, *States of Emergency: British Governments and Strikebreaking since 1919*. 320 pp. London: Routledge & Kegan Paul, 1983. (History of the British government's system of maintaining services during major strikes, 1919–82, as a form of strikebreaking. See esp. ch. 5 on the 1926 general strike and ch. 9 for evaluation. Appendixes. Index. Bibliography.)

1730. Marson, Dave, *Children's Strikes in 1911*. 35 pp. History Workshop Pamphlets, no. 9. Oxford: Routledge & Kegan Paul, 1973. (Pamphlet history of school children's strikes in at least 62 towns in 1911. Photos. Documents.)

1731. Melling, Joseph, *Rent Strikes: Peoples' Struggle for Housing in West Scotland, 1890–1916*. 130 pp. Edinburgh: Polygon Books, 1983. (History of early housing protest in Scotland. See ch. 6–9 on labor strikes and rent strikes of 1915. Illustrations. Photos. Index.)

1732. Raynes, J.R., *Coal and Its Conflicts: A Brief Record of the Disputes between Capital and Labour in the Coal Mining Industry of Great Britain*. 342 pp. London: Ernest Benn, 1928. (History of industrial relations in mining, with strikes mentioned throughout. See esp. ch. 5–11 on the period from 1893 to 1913, ch. 15 on the coming of the general strike of 1926, and ch. 16–

18 on the general strike itself and associated coalfield disputes. Index.)

1733.   White, Joseph L., *The Limits of Trade Union Militancy: The Lancashire Textile Workers, 1910–1914*. 272 pp. Westport CT and London: Greenwood Press, 1978. (Social history of strikes and lockouts seen in context of work organization and causes of strikes. See pp. 7–11 for comments on recent interpretations of strikes and ch. 5–8 for descriptive material. Index.)

General Strike, May 1926

The general strike of May 1926 was a sympathetic strike because a dispute in the mining industry led the Trades Union Congress to declare a wider strike to support the miners. The ten–day strike was tenaciously fought by strikers and the government. In addition to using police and military forces (although relatively little violence), the government recruited volunteers among students and the middle class to maintain services. Labor relied on local councils to propagate the strike and to organize picketing and strikers' aid. Both labor and government presented their case in newspapers published for this purpose, the government's being edited by strike opponent Winston S. Churchill. Collapsing in the face of government intransigence, the general strike was followed by a lengthy lockout of the miners whose cause it had championed.

1734.   Arnot, R. Page, *The General Strike, May 1926: Its Origin and History*. 245 pp. London: Labour Research Department, 1926. Reprint, New York: Augustus M. Kelley, 1967. Reprint, East Ardsely, Wakefield, West Yorkshire: E P Publishing, 1975. (On events of the strike, with sketches of the preceding twelve months. See esp. part 2 for a day–by–day account of the strike. Documents.)

1735.   Burns, Emile, *The General Strike, May 1926: Trades Councils in Action*. 191 pp. London: Labour Research Department, 1926. Reprint, London: Lawrence & Wishart, 1975. (Based on questionnaires about the strike returned by 152 localities. Describes the organization of pickets, meetings, and tasks of organizing the strike. See pp. 95–191 for the full text of replies. Analysis discusses categories such as organization, pp. 11–25,

75–83, 85–90; meetings, communication, and morale, pp. 27–54, 61–68; and relief and assistance to strikers, pp. 26, 55–60, 69–74. Illustrations. Documents.)

1736. Citrine, Lord [Walter McLellan Citrine], *Men and Work: An Autobiography*. 384 pp. London: Hutchinson, 1964. (For a memoir and diary of general strike by a Trades Union Congress leader, see ch. 9–11. Photos. Index.)

1737. Farman, Christopher, *The General Strike, May 1926*. 305 pp. London: Rupert Hart–Davis, 1972. (Detailed history of the strike, especially in its political aspects. Photos. Appendixes. Bibliography.)

1738. Florey, R.A., *The General Strike of 1926: The Economic, Political and Social Causes of that Class War*. 222 pp. London: John Calder, 1980. New York: Riverrun Press, 1981. (Reviews the history of general strikes, 1842–1926, with emphasis on official anti–Communism, British fascism, and class conflict. See ch. 7 on the conduct of the 1926 general strike. Documents in appendixes, including strike plan in appendix 7. Illustrations. Bibliography. Index.)

1739. Gilbert, Martin, *Winston S. Churchill*. Vol. 5, *The Prophet of Truth, 1922–1939*. 1167 pp. Boston: Houghton Mifflin, 1977. (See ch. 9, 10 on Churchill and the government anti–strike newspaper, *British Gazette*. Photos. Index.)

1740. ———, *Winston S. Churchill*. Vol. 5, Companion: Part I, Documents, *The Exchequer Years: 1922–1929*. 1504 pp. Boston: Houghton Mifflin, 1981. (See pp. 691–721 for documents on Churchill's activities during the strike, including meeting minutes and articles for the *British Gazette*. Biographical index.)

1741. Haigh, R.H., D.S. Morris, and A.R. Peters, eds., *The Guardian Book of the General Strike*. 175 pp. Aldershot, Hants.: Wildwood House, 1988. (Reports from the *Manchester Guardian* edited into a daily record stretching from April 30 to May 21, 1926. Includes introductory chapter on background and some brief comments in text. Chronology.)

1742.   Jones, Thomas, *Whitehall Diary*. Vol. 2, 1926–1930. Ed. Keith
        Middlemas. 311 pp. London: Oxford Univ. Press, 1969. (Diary
        and documents of Prime Minister Stanley Baldwin's cabinet
        secretary and confidant. Particularly strong on the weeks
        before the strike; see pp. 7–53. Appendixes. Index.)

1743.   Kibblewhite, Liz, and Andy Rigby, *Aberdeen in the General
        Strike*. 31 pp. Aberdeen: Aberdeen People's Press, 1977.
        (Includes discussion of efforts to prevent violence and the role
        of volunteer strikebreakers, pp. 12–14, and personal accounts
        of experiences in the general strike, pp. 19–31. Photos.)

1744.   Large, Marion, ed., *The Nine Days in Birmingham: The General
        Strike, 4–12 May 1926*. 43 pp. Birmingham: Birmingham Public
        Libraries Social Sciences Division, 1976. (On the effects of the
        strike in Birmingham. See pp. 17–21 on the strikers' and
        government's newspapers, pp. 24–30 on police tactics, pp. 33–
        34 on the "second wave" of the strike and its ending, and pp.
        36–37 on the employers' counter–attack. Documents.)

1745.   Martin, Kingsley, *The British Public and the General Strike*. 127
        pp. London: Leonard & Virginia Woolf, 1926. (Examination of
        the ideas involved in the conflict.)

1746.   Mason, Anthony, *The General Strike in the North East*. 116 pp.
        Occasional Papers in Economic and Social History no. 3. Hull:
        Univ. of Hull Publications, 1970. (Local history of the
        organization and immediate effects of the general strike in the
        Newcastle region, with attention to government and strikers'
        efforts to countervail each other. See pp. 65–75 on the
        relationship between picketing and violence and pp. 82–85 on
        the press. Illustrations. Index. Bibliography.)

1747.   Middlemas, Keith, and John Barnes, *Baldwin: A Biography*. 1149
        pp. London: Weidenfeld & Nicholson, 1969. (Strongest on the
        government's role in events leading to the strike, see ch. 15.
        Photos. Appendixes. Index.)

1748.   Morris, Margaret, *The General Strike*. 479 pp. Harmondsworth
        and Baltimore MD: Penguin Books, 1976. (History of the
        general strike and its origins. Parts 1, 4 are on the strike itself

with a special study on regional events added on pp. 379–439. See throughout on organization of the strike. Pp. 69–76 are on the use of military forces in the strike; pp. 11–14, 390–96 are on strike breakers; pp. 76–77, 387–88 on the special constables [anti–strike volunteers]; and pp. 243–44, 249–53 are on the BBC. See also pp. 76–78 on the Defense Corps' lack of violence in strike; pp. 78–86, 241–44 on strikers' methods of communication; and p. 90 for the strike committee's call to avoid violence. Photos and period drawings. Index.)

1749. Mowat, Charles Loch, *Britain between the Wars: 1918–1940*. 694 pp. London: Methuen, 1955. (Ch. 6 presents a history of the coal strike and general strike of 1926 based on the thesis that the general strike "marked the end, not the beginning of a time of unrest and possible revolution following WWI." Bibliography.)

1750. Murray, John, *The General Strike of 1926: A History*. 208 pp. London: Laurence & Wishart, 1951. (Class struggle view of strike. See ch. 5 on the strike itself. Index. Bibliography.)

1751. Nearing, Scott, *The British General Strike: An Economic Interpretation of Its Background and Its Significance*. 186 pp. New York: Vanguard Press, 1926. (Early study of the nine day strike. Appendixes. Documents. Bibliography.)

1752. Noel, Gerard, *The Great Lock–Out of 1926*. 239 pp. London: Constable, 1976. (See ch. 5, 7, 8, 11, 14, 15. "Informal sketch" of miners' industrial action from the beginnings of the general strike to the end of their separate actions and the mine–owners' "lockout." Photos. Index. Bibliography.)

1753. Phillips, G.A., *The General Strike: The Politics of Industrial Conflict*. 388 pp. London: Weidenfeld & Nicholson, 1976. (Analytical history of the conduct and effects of the general strike, stressing its shortcomings, and of union and government interaction during the strike. See counterpoint presented in ch. 6, 7 on the conduct of the strike by each side, including p. 146 on Red Money [strike funds from Soviet sources], pp. 153–60 on anti–strike volunteers, and pp. 160–62, 201–6 on the police and violence. See also ch. 8 on the press and broadcasting; ch. 9 on local organization, including p. 206 for an assessment of nonviolent conduct; ch. 10 on calling off the strike; and ch. 11 on its effects. Documents in appendix. Index. Bibliography.)

1754.   Renshaw, Patrick, *Nine Days in May: The General Strike*. 11 pp. of text plus 134 plates. London: Eyre Methuen, 1975. (Photo essay with brief introduction, stressing the role of volunteer strikebreakers and the military.)

1755.   Rhodes James, Robert, ed., *Memoirs of a Conservative: J.C.C. Davidson's Memoirs and Papers, 1910–1937*. 446 pp. London: Weidenfeld & Nicholson, 1969. (Documents and memoirs edited together into a narrative. See ch. 11, primarily on government publishing and broadcasting during the strike and the use of the military and volunteers. Pp. 227–32 discuss the government view of the strike as revolutionary challenge to authority. Photos. Index. Bibliography.)

1756.   Skelley, Jeffrey, ed., *The General Strike, 1926*. 412 pp. London: Lawrence & Wishart, 1976. (Anthology. Especially useful are part 2 for region–by–region accounts and part 3 for personal reminiscences. See also pp. 71–94 on the role of the Communist Party in the strike. Chronology.)

1757.   Symons, Julian, *The General Strike: A Historical Portrait*. 259 pp. London: Cressett Press; Chester Springs PA: Dufour, 1957. (Detailed history of the general strike. Part 1 describes the background and part 2 the period immediately before the strike began. In the subsequent narrative, see esp. ch. 2–4 on the stoppage and restoration of transport; ch. 11, 12 on media; and ch. 17 on the settlement, or "surrender," that halted the strike. Photos. Appendixes. Bibliography.)

1758.   Trory, Ernie, *Brighton and the General Strike*. 32 pp. Brighton: Crabtree Press, 1975. (See eyewitness accounts of the "Battle of Lewes Road," pp. 25–31.)

1759.   ———, *Soviet Trade Unions and the General Strike*. 48 pp. Brighton: Crabtree Press, 1975. (On money from the Soviet Union and the dispute over accepting it. Bibliography.)

Protests and Hunger Marches by the Unemployed

Mass marches by people protesting the effects of economic hardship began in the depression of the 1930s and have reappeared as recently as the 1970s and 1980s.

1760.   Hannington, Wal, *Unemployed Struggles, 1919–1936: My Life and Struggle amongst the Unemployed.* 328 pp. Reprint, New York: Barnes & Noble, 1973. Originally published London: Lawrence & Wishart, 1936. (See esp. ch. 3, 4, 11 on demonstrations and hunger marches by the unemployed. Photos of marches and other actions.)

1761.   Kingsford, Peter, *The Hunger Marchers in Britain, 1920–1939.* 244 pp. London: Lawrence & Wishart, 1982. (Study of national hunger marches in 1920–39 by the unemployed. See ch. 1 for organization of the unemployed and on the issues of violence, p. 15, and "direct action," pp. 21–22. Ch. 2–8 detail various marches from 1922–36 and ch. 9 is on mass protest. Ch. 10 takes up the problem for the unemployed of facing the options of "acceptance of their lot, revolt, or the exercise of organised pressure" as options. Photos. Index.)

1762.   Pickard, Tom, *Jarrow March.* 120 pp. London and New York: Allison & Busby, 1982. (History of an October 1936 march of the unemployed from Jarrow to London to petition the House of Commons. See introduction for a brief description and pp. 81–118 on the march. Illustrations. Photos. Documents.)

Labor Since 1945

Labor conflict after World War II was shaped by several factors. Notable among these were Britain's relative economic decline and the changing place of government in the economy. Because of the first factor, labor often found itself on the defensive and innovated alternatives to the classic strike in response, such as sit–ins and occupations. Likewise, the Conservative Party government of Margaret Thacher and John Major pursued very different policies than its predecessors, including privatization and closing state–run enterprises. The results were several decades of confrontation (see entry 1765) and the reputation of Britain as a uniquely strike–prone society (see entry 1769).

1763.   Arnison, Jim, *The Million Pound Strike*. 85 pp. London: Lawrence & Wishart, 1971. (Pamphlet–style report of a 1970 industrial strike in Stockport, England. See ch. 4, which describes a stone–throwing demonstration and its effects; material in ch. 5, 7, 11 on harassment of strikebreakers; ch. 7 on picketing and some characters; and ch. 9, 11 on the "blacking" of the factory by unions.)

1764.   Coates, Ken, *Work–ins, Sit–ins and Industrial Democracy: Implications of Factory Occupations in Great Britain in the Early 'Seventies*. 175 pp. Nottingham: Spokesman Press, 1981. (Discusses various plant occupations and sit–ins related to the closing of industrial facilities, lay–offs, and the like in 1971–75. Along with several accounts of occupations, the appendix to ch. 7 reprints an employer's reaction plan from 1975. Glossary. Appendixes. Index. Bibliography.)

1765.   Durcan, J.W., W.E.J. McCarthy, and G.P. Redman, *Strikes in Post–War Britain: A Study of Stoppages of Work Due to Industrial Disputes, 1946–1973*. 464 pp. London: George Allen & Unwin, 1983. (Comprehensive, statistically based study of the "pattern" of strikes and their likely causes, with description, analysis, and policy commentary. Esp. useful for strike statistics and inter–industry case studies, ch. 2–6, 8–10, and the effort to diagnose economic versus non–economic impetus to go on strike, ch. 7, 12. Authors stress the nature of strike as a sanction throughout. Appendixes. Index. Bibliography.)

1766.   Friedman, Henry, and Sander Meredeen, *The Dynamics of Industrial Conflict: Lessons from Ford*. 386 pp. London: Croom Helm, 1980. (Account of women's strike for equal pay as viewed by various participants, followed by analysis of its effects. Index. Bibliography.)

1767.   Hemingway, John, with William Keyser, *Who's in Charge? Worker Sit–ins in Britain Today*. 67 pp. Oxford: Metra Oxford Consulting, 1975. (Consulting group's study of worker sit–ins in Great Britain in 1975 based upon interviews. Classifies sit–

ins into two types, redundancy and industrial relations, pp. 10–42.)

1768. Pitt, Malcolm, *The World on Our Backs: The Kent Miners and the 1972 Miners' Strike*. 216 pp. London: Lawrence & Wishart, 1972. (An insider's chronicle. See ch. 6–9 on the strikers' method of shifting the locus of conflict from the pits to distribution points by conducting mass pickets preventing the commercial movement of coal. Chronology. Index.)

1769. Turner, H.A., *Is Britain Really Strike-Prone? A Review of the Incidence, Character and Costs of Industrial Conflict*. 48 pp. Univ. of Cambridge, Dept. of Applied Economics, Occasional Papers no. 20. Cambridge: Cambridge Univ. Press, 1969. (Policy-oriented inquiry into the British propensity for strikes and their effects. See esp. ch. 5, 6 on the impact of strikes.)

Miners' Strike of 1984

The turbulent miners' strike was a direct and bitter confrontation between the miners' union and the Thatcher government. It was a struggle in which the issues were overshadowed by the struggle itself, which included mass picketing by strike supporters, confrontations between massed police and pickets, spreading of the action beyond the pits to coal distribution points, and bitter negotiations. As an example of all-out conflict, both by labor and the state, this strike is among the most significant examples in recent times.

1770. Adeney, Martin, and John Lloyd, *The Miners' Strike, 1984–5: Loss Without Limit*. 319 pp. London: Routledge & Kegan Paul, 1986. (Journalists' account of personalities and actions in the strike, including observations on intra-union strife, the authorities, the reasons for the strike, and its ending. Ch. 7 is largely on mass picketing. Index.)

1771. Benyon, Huw, ed., *Digging Deeper: Issues in the Miners' Strike*. 252 pp. London: Verso, 1975. (See John McIlroy, "The Police and the Pickets: The Law Against the Miners," ch. 5; Kim Howells, "Stopping Out: The Birth of a New Kind of Politics," ch. 7; and Loretta Loach, "We'll Be Here Right to the End . . . and After: Women in the Miners' Strike," ch. 9.)

1772.   Fine, Bob, and Robert Miller, eds., *Policing the Miners' Strike*. 243 pp. London: Lawrence & Wishart, 1985. (Essays on political and legal aspects of police action in the miners' strike of 1984–85, including observations on the use of police to restrict the effectiveness of mass picketing. Index.)

1773.   Goodman, Geoffrey, *The Miners' Strike*. 213 pp. London and Sydney: Pluto Press, 1985. (Focuses on the sources of failure in the 1984–85 miners' strike and the roles played by the state, police, unions, and pickets. See ch. 2 for thesis that the Thatcher government sought a test of strength with the miners and ch. 4–7 on confrontation and violence. Chronology. Index.)

1774.   Samuel, Ralph, Barbara Bloomfield, and Guy Boanas, *The Enemy Within: Pit Villages and the Miner's Strike of 1984–1985*. 260 pp. London and New York: Routledge & Kegan Paul, 1986. (Primarily personal accounts, including interviews, journals, and letters. See esp. pp. 92–99 for an organizer's speech and ch. 6, 8 on support organizations. Illustrations. Photos. Index.)

1775.   *Thurcroft: A Village and the Miners' Strike: An Oral History*. 276 pp. Nottingham and Atlantic Highlands NJ: Spokesman, 1986. (Oral history of activists in Thurcroft, South Yorkshire during the 984–85 miners' strike. Ch. 2 is on the beginning of the strike; ch. 3 is on flying pickets, mass pickets, and violence among pickets, police, and strikebreakers; ch. 4 is on the strike in the village proper; and ch. 5 is on women's organization. Photos. Index.)

Political Protest and Conflict Since 1945

Among the many political protests and conflicts that stand out in British history since 1945, the anti–nuclear weapons movement stands out. Partly descended from movements originating after WWI, it took on its own coloration with the demand to do away with nuclear weapons entirely and, during the 1980s, to prevent United States deployment of missiles in Britain.

1776.   Arrowsmith, Pat, ed., *To Asia in Peace: The Story of a Non–Violent Action Mission to Indo China*. 188 pp. London: Sidgwick & Jackson, 1972. (Personal narrative by members of a January

1968 delegation to Cambodia intended to halt the bombing of that country by making themselves into potential victims. Organizational difficulties of such an undertaking are discussed throughout. Documents.)

1777.   Benewick, Robert, and Trevor Smith, eds. *Direct Action and Democratic Politics*. 324 pp. London: George Allen & Unwin, 1972. (See esp. Peter Cadogan, "From Civil Disobedience to Confrontation," ch. 10 and Peter Herin, "Direct Action and the Springbok Tours," ch. 12. Index.)

1778.   Bouchier, David, *The Feminist Challenge: The Movement for Women's Liberation in Britain and the USA*. 263 pp. London: Macmillan, 1983. New York: Schocken, 1984. (Comparative study of feminism in these two societies since the 1960s. See esp. ch. 2, 4 and pp. 143–44, 160–64, 193–94, 217–23. Index.)

1779.   Minnion, John, and Philip Bolsover, *The CND Story: The First 25 Years of CND in the Words of the People Involved*. 149 pp. London: Allison & Busby, 1983. (Collection of short articles by forty members of the Coalition for Nuclear Disarmament [CND], with an introductory historical overview by editors. Photos. Appendixes. Bibliography.)

1780.   Taylor, Richard, and Colin Pritchard, *The Protest Makers: The British Nuclear Disarmament Movement of 1958–1965 Twenty Years On*. 190 pp. Oxford; Elmsford NY; Willowdale, Ontario; and Pott's Point, New South Wales: Pergamon Press, 1980. (History of the early years of mass action by the CND. Illustrations. Photos. Index. Bibliography.)

1781.   Taylor, Richard, and Nigel Young, eds. *Campaigns for Peace: British Peace Movements in the Twentieth Century*. 308 pp. Manchester: Manchester Univ. Press, 1987. (Papers on the history, ideology, and actions of British movements against warfare and armaments. See esp. Nigel Young, "War Resistance and the British Peace Movement since 1914," ch. 3; Martin Ceadel, "The Peace Movement between the Wars: Problems of Definition," ch. 5; Michael Randle, "Non–violent Direct Action in the 1950s and 1960s," ch. 7; and Josephine

Eglin, "Women and Peace: From the Suffragists to the Greenham Women," ch. 10. Index.)

HUNGARY

Revolution of 1848 and Movements Against Austrian Rule, 1848–1867

The Hungarian nation fought against Austria's domination from the 1840s until a settlement between the two was reached in the 1860s. In the Revolution of 1848, Hungarian liberals held an early form of demonstration as the revolution mobilized. After the suppression of the revolution, Hungarians resorted to "passive resistance" against the extension of the power of the Austrian throne, finally accepting a compromise solution in which the imperial power remained united but Austria and Hungary were governed individually.

1782.   Deak, Istvan, *The Lawful Revolution*. 436 pp. New York: Columbia Univ. Press, 1979. (See ch. 2 on March 1848. Photos. Index. Bibliography.)

1783.   Deme, Laszlo, *The Radical Left in the Hungarian Revolution of 1848*. 172 pp. Boulder CO: East European Quarterly, 1976. (See ch. 3 on the demonstrations of 15 March 1848. Index. Bibliography.)

1784.   Griffith, Arthur, *The Resurrection of Hungary: A Parallel for Ireland, with Appendices on Pitt's Policy and Sinn Fein*. 170 pp. Dublin: Whelan & Son, 1918. (An Irish nationalist reflects on Hungary's nineteenth–century resistance. See esp. pp. 16–68 on "passive resistance." Policy statement on Sinn Fein follows in Appendix 2.)

1785.   Stroup, Edsel Walter, *Hungary in Early 1848: The Constitutional Struggle against Absolutism in Contemporary Eyes*. 261 pp. Buffalo NY and Atlanta GA: Hungarian Cultural Foundation, 1977. (See ch. 2 on the first phase of the Revolution of 1848, as well as pp. 87–88, 100–102, and ch. 6 on demonstrations in March of that year. Illustrations. Photos. Index. Bibliography.)

1786. Taylor, A.J.P., *The Habsburg Monarchy, 1809–1918: A History of the Austrian Empire and Austria–Hungary.* Rev. ed., 279 pp. London: Hamish Hamilton, 1948 [orig. publ. 1941]. Reprint, 304 pp. Harmondsworth, England and Baltimore: Penguin Books, 1964. (See ch. 4–6 on the Revolution of 1848 and ch. 7–11 on Hungarian resistance until the dual monarchy was created in 1866–67. Index. Bibliography.)

Rescue of Hungarian Jews, 1944–1945

Hungarian Jews had relatively little help from their countrymen, partly because many Hungarians supported and assisted the Nazi occupation. However, it was in Hungary that a daring experiment was made in using nominally neutral bodies to protect a threatened population. In 1944–45 [check dates] Raoul Wallenberg, Swedish envoy in Budapest, and the less well-known Swiss consul Charles Lutz took it on themselves to find and protect Jews in danger of deportation to the death camps. Wallenberg and Lutz gave some of these people protective passes that the Nazis often recognized as valid, which saved the lives of many.

1787. Bierman, John, *Righteous Gentile: The Story of Raoul Wallenberg, Missing Hero of the Holocaust.* 218 pp. New York: Viking Press, 1981. (See ch. 4, pp. 50–55, and ch. 6–10 on Wallenberg's methods in Budapest. Photos. Bibliography.)

1788. Braham, Randolph L., *The Politics of Genocide.* 2 vols. 1269 pp. New York: Columbia Univ. Press, 1981. (Completely detailed political history of the Jews of Hungary and their destruction, often stressing that Nazi personnel were entirely dependent upon assistance from regular and irregular Hungarian forces in accomplishing this genocide. See ch. 29, "Rescue and Resistance," on attempts to transport Hungarian Jews beyond the grasp of the Holocaust and on the difficulties of resistance. This and other chapters also discuss rescue efforts by the embassy personnel of neutral countries, including Sweden and Switzerland. Consult index under *Lutz, Charles; Wallenberg, Raoul; neutral states; protective passes;* and *IRC* [International Red Cross]. Photos. Appendixes. Documents. Indexes.)

1789.   Lester, Elenore, *Wallenberg: The Man in the Iron Web*. 183 pp.
        Englewood Cliffs NJ: Prentice–Hall, 1982. (See pp. 5–8 and ch.
        5–9 on Wallenberg in Hungary. Photos. Appendix. Index.)

1790.   Marton, Kati, *Wallenberg*. 243 pp. New York: Random House,
        1982. (See ch. 3–20 on the Wallenberg mission. Photos. Index.
        Bibliography.)

1791.   *Raoul Wallenberg: Dossierdokumentation från Beskikningen,
        Budapest och Utrikesdepartementet, 1944–1957*. 49 vols.
        Stockholm: Utrikesdepartementet, 1980–1982. (Mimeographed
        collection of photocopied documents, arranged
        chronologically, on Raoul Wallenberg and his case, many of
        them from official Swedish sources. Documents in Swedish,
        English, French, German, and Russian. Note: no titles or
        publication information appear on the document volumes
        themselves.)

1792.   Rosenfeld, Harvey, *Raoul Wallenberg: Angel of Rescue*. 261 pp.
        Buffalo NY: Prometheus Books, 1982. (See pp. 25–29 on the
        origins of the rescue work and ch. 3–7 on Wallenberg's
        activities in Hungary, as well as pp. 37–40, 62–63 on Swiss
        consul Charles Lutz. Appendixes. Index. Bibliography.)

1793.   Werbell, Frederick E., and Thurston Clarke, *Lost Hero: The
        Mystery of Raoul Wallenberg*. 284 pp. New York: McGraw–Hill,
        1982. (Journalists' story of Wallenberg with a good deal of
        detail on his activities in Hungary. Photos. Index.
        Bibliography.)

Revolution, 1956–1957

*Dissent against Communist rule in Hungary began about 1953, first among
professional writers and students. In October 1956, the Hungarian
government decided to rebury wartime partisan Laszlo Rajk, previously
ignored as a non–Communist, in a hero's grave. The ceremony broke out into
demonstrations, which continued in Budapest itself, accompanied by petitions
and demands for reform. The nonviolent phase of the Revolution of 1956 was
soon supplanted when activists seized arms and took over the government.
The Soviet Union successfully crushed the revolt and reimposed Soviet–*

supported rule, during which action two brief general strikes were held in November and December.

1794. Aczel, Tamas, ed., *Ten Years After: The Revolution in the Perspective of History.* 253 pp. London: MacGibbon & Kee, 1966. New York: Holt, Rinehart & Winston, 1967. (See esp. appendixes by Stephen Barley, "Bibliography of the Hungarian Revolution" and "Hungary: A Chronology of Events, 1953–65.")

1795. Aczel, Tamas, and Tibor Meray, *The Revolt of the Mind: A Case History of Intellectual Resistance behind the Iron Curtain.* 449 pp. New York: Praeger, 1959. (First–hand account of dissent and opposition to Soviet domination by the Hungarian Writers' Association, 1953–59. Biographies in appendix.)

1796. Aptheker, Herbert, *The Truth about Hungary.* 256 pp. New York: Mainstream, 1957. (Study of the role of communists and the Soviet Union in post–WWII Hungary. See ch. 6, 7 on grievances before the revolt and ch. 8, 9 on the revolt itself, including a discussion of demonstrations in the first days and their relation to later fighting.)

1797. Barber, Noel, *Seven Days of Freedom: The Hungarian Uprising 1956.* 268 pp. London: Macmillan, 1973. (Covers violent and nonviolent struggle Oct. 23–Nov. 23. Appendix I contains student manifesto of 19 October 1956. Photos. Appendixes. Bibliography.)

1798. Beke, Laszlo, *A Student's Diary: Budapest, October 16–November 1, 1956.* Ed. and trans. Leon Kossar and Ralph M. Zoltan. 125 pp. New York: Viking Press, 1957. (See esp. pp. 15–36 on the student demonstrations of October and the decision by students and their allies to seize and use weapons.)

1799. Fetjö, François, *Behind the Rape of Hungary.* 355 pp. New York: David McKay, 1957. (In part 1, see pp. 114–16 on the funeral of Laszlo Rajk and ch. 4 on intellectual dissenters. Part 2, ch. 1 is on the early days of the revolution. Pp. 252–99 are on the Kadar government from its inception to the liquidation of the revolution. Chronology.)

1800.   Helmreich, Ernst C., *Hungary*. 466 pp. New York: Praeger, 1957. Reprint, Westport CT: Greenwood Press, 1973. (See Neal V. Buhler, "The Hungarian Revolution," pp. 352–89; esp. pp. 353–58 on writers' and students' protests and the October demonstrations. Appendixes. Index. Bibliography.)

1801.   Kecskemeti, Paul, *The Unexpected Revolution: Social Forces in the Hungarian Uprising*. 178 pp. Stanford CA: Stanford Univ. Press, 1961. (Analysis of forces of dissent in post–1953 Hungary. See esp. pp. 63–70 on writers' "insubordination" and opposition; pp. 76–82 on the demonstrative funeral of Rajk and the martyrs of the wartime underground and student politics; and pp. 106–18 on demonstrations and the beginning of the 1956 fighting. Index. Bibliography.)

1802.   Lasky, Melvin J., ed., *The Hungarian Revolution: Story of the October Uprising as Recorded in Documents, Dispatches, Eye–Witness Accounts, and World–Wide Reactions*. 318 pp. London: Martin Secker & Warburg; New York: Praeger, 1957. (See entries on pp. 37–55. Photos. Documents.)

1803.   Lomax, Bill, *Hungary, 1956*. 222 pp. London: Allison & Busby, 1976. (A description of opposition after 1953 and the events of the revolution. See ch. 1, 2 on precursors and the early days of the revolution and ch. 5 on Workers' Councils and the general strike of November 1956. Chronology. Index. Bibliography.)

1804.   Meray, Tibor, *Thirteen Days that Shook the Kremlin: Imre Nagy and the Hungarian Revolution*. Trans. Howard L. Katzander. 290 pp. London: Thames & Hudson, 1959. U.S. edition entitled *Thirteen Days that Shook the Kremlin*. New York: Frederick A. Praeger, 1959. (Book 2 is on the revolution up to 4 November 1956, esp. pp. 85–91 on the demonstrations of 23 October and first violent clashes. See pp. 245–46 on the "double power" of Kádár and the Workers' Councils in November 1956.)

1805.   Mikes, George, *The Hungarian Revolution*. 192 pp. London: Andre Deutsch, 1957. (Pp. 64–96 discuss writers, students, and nationalist dissent, the first demonstrations, and the beginning of armed clashes. "The Hunger Strike of a Nation," pp. 162–75, describes strikes and general strike in opposition to the Kádár government. Photos. Index.)

1806. Pryce–Jones, David, *The Hungarian Revolution*. 127 pp. London: Ernest Benn, 1969. (Brief illustrated account of background and the Hungarian conflict. See esp. pp. 54–112 and photos, pp. 54, 59, 64–68, 77, 80–83. Index.)

1807. Urban, George, *The Nineteen Days: A Broadcaster's Account of the Hungarian Revolution*. 361 pp. London, Melbourne, and Toronto: Heinemann, 1957. (See esp. ch. 1, 2 on writers, students, and the first days of the revolution. Photos. Appendixes. Index.)

1808. Váli, Ferenc A., *Rift and Revolt in Hungary: Nationalism versus Communism*. 590 pp. Cambridge: Harvard Univ. Press, 1961. (See ch. 18–20 for the beginnings of opposition and on the revolution until the first Soviet intervention. See also pp. 392–95 on the brief general strike of December 1956 and the dissolving of opposition organizations. Note attention on pp. 261–66 to the Polish events of 1956 as they related to the Hungarian uprising. Index. Bibliography.)

1809. Zinner, Paul E., *Revolution in Hungary*. 380 pp. New York and London: Columbia Univ. Press, 1962. Reprint, Freeport NY: Books for Libraries Press, 1972. (See ch. 8, 9 on intellectuals and, on pp. 227–35, the first demonstrations and petitions. Ch. 10–14 discuss the revolution itself. Index.)

IRELAND

Famine, emigration, and dispossession from the land were factors in increasing agrarian strife in nineteenth–century Ireland. Reform movements, such as the Tenants' League, appeared to show that amelioration alone could not gain committed popular support. In 1879, a public protest by tenant farmers resulted in decreased rents, prompting the formation of the Irish National Land League with the purpose of supporting tenants throughout the country. The Land League developed a great variety of methods of protest and noncooperation to control rents and evictions. These included rent refusal, establishing parallel courts, and boycotting persons. The League began as a movement of moral suasion and was opposed to violent methods. As the landowners and imperial government turned to more forceful methods, the League increasingly turned to sanctions and pressure, and as tensions increased so did the incidence of violence.

Land League Era

1810.   Becker, Bernard H., *Disturbed Ireland: Being the Letters Written During the Winter of 1880–81*. 338 pp. London: Macmillan, 1881. (Collected letters by English journalist intended as a "purely descriptive" account of the upheaval. See especially ch. 3, 15, 18. Ch. 6 is on Captain Boycott.)

1811.   Bew, Paul, *C.S. Parnell*. 152 pp. Dublin: Gill and Macmillan, 1980. (See ch. 3 on Parnell in the years of the Land League struggle, with some judgements on his ideology and conduct. Index. Bibliography.)

1812.   ———, *Land and the National Question in Ireland, 1858–87*. 307 pp. Dublin: Gill and Macmillan, 1978. (See ch. 4–9 on Land League, esp. pp. 91–97, 110–14, 121–34, ch. 8; and pp. 196–201 for variations on the "no–rent" approach. Emphasis on tactics and strategy. Appendixes. Index. Bibliography.) .

1813.   Clancy, James J., *The Land League Manual*. 331 pp. New York: Thomas Kelly, 1881. (See esp. pp. 1–29 on the Land League. Appendix. Index.)

1814.   Comerford, R.V., *The Fenians in Context: Irish Politics and Society, 1848–82*. 272 pp. Dublin: Wolfhound Press; Atlantic Highlands NJ: Humanities Press, 1985. (See Ch. 8 on the Land League of 1879–82. Index. Bibliography.)

1815.   Davitt, Michael, *The Fall of Feudalism in Ireland; or, The Story of the Irish Land League Revolution*. 751 pp. London and New York: Harper, 1904. Reprint, Shannon: Irish Univ. Press, 1970. (See ch. 12–30 on the Land League, as recounted by a leader of that movement partly responsible for its strategy. Bibliography on Davitt included in reprint edition.)

1816. Foster, R.F., *Charles Stewart Parnell: The Man and His Family*. 403 pp. Atlantic Highlands NJ: Humanities Press; Sussex: Harvester Press, 1976. (Material on Fanny Parnell and women's activities; consult index under *Ladies' Land League* and *Land League*. Index. Bibliography.)

1817. James, Sir Henry, Q.C., M.P., *The Work of the Irish Leagues*. 862 pp. London, Paris, New York, and Melbourne: Cassell, 1890. (Text of 12–day speech given by author during court inquiry, combining "a history of the origins, principles, and actions of the Leagues, with an outline of the political events occurring in Ireland during the period of their existence." See esp. pp. 268–93 for James' account of the origins of the boycott.)

1818. Lloyd, Clifford, *Ireland under the Land League: A Narrative of Personal Experiences*. 243 pp. Edinburgh and London: William Blackwood, 1892. (Memoir of British "resident magistrate," ca. 1880–81, stressing Land League violence. Of interest are descriptions of the author's activities in opposing the "mob" and supporting the collection of rents, ch. 6–9.)

1819. Locker–Lampson, G., *A Consideration of the State of Ireland in the Nineteenth Century*. 699 pp. London: Archibald Constable, 1907. (Study of social, economic, and political history of Ireland during most of the century. See index under *Land League* and *boycotting*. See also p. 380 and pp. 634–36 on the origin of the term "boycott." Appendixes.)

1820. Lyons, F.S.L., *Charles Stewart Parnell*. 704 pp. New York: Oxford Univ. Press, 1977. (For coverage of several topics on the Land League, see index under *boycott, proposed; Irish National Land League; Ladies' Land League; Manifesto "To the People of Ireland"; new departure; no–rent manifesto;* and *Plan of Campaign*. See also pp. 134–38 on the invention of the systematic boycott. Photos. Index.)

1821. Marlow, Joyce, *Captain Boycott and the Irish*. 319 pp. New York: Saturday Review Press, E.P. Dutton; London: Andre Deutsch, 1973. (On Charles C. Boycott, the Land League, and the origin of the systematic boycott. See ch. 10–19 on Parnell's designation of the boycott, the struggle with Captain Boycott, and aftermath. Illustrations. Photos. Appendixes. Index. Bibliography.)

1822.   Moody, T.W., *Davitt and the Irish Revolution, 1846–82*. 674 pp. (Biography of the republican leader Michael Davitt. See ch. 8–12 for a detailed history of Land League agitation and Davitt's part in it, including pp. 418–21 on the origins of the boycott. Appendixes. Index. Bibliography.)

1823.   Morley, John, *The Life of William Ewart Gladstone*. 3 vols. Vol. 1, 1809–1859, 660 pp. Vol. 2, 1859–1880, 666 pp. Vol. 3, 1880–1898, 641 pp. London: Macmillan, 1903 and 1909. (On boycotting, rent refusal, evictions, the Land League, and changes in Home Rule plans. See esp. vol. 3, pp. 47–48, 57, 59, 66, 199, 243–44, 300–301, 352, 372, 379–80, 398, 401–03, 410. Chronologies. Appendixes. Index in vol. 3.)

1824.   O'Brien, R. Barry, *The Life of Charles Stewart Parnell, 1846–1891*. 2 vols. New York: Haskell House, 1968 [orig. publ. 1898]. (See vol. 1, ch. 9, 11–13 on the Land League, boycotting and the no-rent movement, and Parnell's parliamentary support of the movement until his suspension and arrest. Appendix. Index.)

1825.   O'Hegarty, P.S., *A History of Ireland under the Union: 1801 to 1922*. 811 pp. London: Methuen, 1952. (See especially ch. 43–45 on the Land League and ch. 60–83 on the Sinn Fein movement, including the development of parallel government in the Dail. Ch. 61 discusses Arthur Griffith's development of parliamentary boycott and parallel government policies out of the "Hungarian analogy" and pp. 757–59 assess Sinn Fein's becoming "goaded" out of its policy of "long–term passive resistance" by British "suppression." Epilogue to 1927. Index.)

1826.   Palmer, Norman D., *The Irish Land League Crisis*. 340 pp. New Haven: Yale Univ. Press; London: Oxford Univ. Press, 1940. (Includes detailed treatment of means of resistance and the boycott and data on parallel government. On the origin of the term "boycott," see pp. 197–212. See ch. 10 on boycotts as the Land League's "most powerful weapon of attack" and subsequent chapters on the League and government up to its suppression, including pp. 298–300 on the No–Rent Manifesto. Index.)

1827. Sheehy–Skeffington, Francis, *Michael Davitt: Revolutionary, Agitator, and Labour Leader.* 291 pp. London: T. Fisher Unwin, 1908. (Biography of the Land League leader by a fellow nationalist. See especially ch. 5, 6.)

1828. Ward, Margaret, *Unmanageable Revolutionaries: Women and Irish Nationalism.* 296 pp. London: Pluto Press, 1983. (See ch. 1 for the Ladies' Land League and debates over methods. Index.)

Nationalism and Republicanism Before 1919

The Sinn Fein (Ourselves Alone) organization began with founder Arthur Griffith's proposal in 1905 for a nonviolently–created and self–governing Ireland. In his concept, Ireland could still be under the British Crown but not subject directly to Parliament as it had been since 1800. The Sinn Fein movement grew rapidly and, in a change from Griffith's conception, conducted a military uprising in 1916. The Easter Rising had limited support at the time, but Britain's repressions created a sense of martyrdom that confirmed in many people the need for a paramilitary force to fight Britain. A Sinn Fein parliament, the Dáil Eireann, was also convened as the group evolved into an extra–legal parallel government. Sinn Fein, the Dáil, and other parties later split over a question similar to that raised by Griffith, whether they could accept professed loyalty to the Crown while conducting self–government, a question that led to a bitter civil war.

1829. Colum, Padraic, *Arthur Griffith.* 400 pp. Dublin: Browne & Nolan, 1959. U.S. ed. *Ourselves, Alone! The Story of Arthur Griffith and the Origins of the Irish Free State.* New York: Crown Publishers, 1959. 400 pp. (Political biography of Griffith and his numerous associates. See pp. 78–80 for his interest in Hungary's "Passive Resistance." Part two discusses the development of Sinn Fein into a parallel government and the organization of the Dáil Eireann.)

1830. Davis, Richard, "The Advocacy of Passive Resistance in Ireland, 1916–1922." *Anglo–Irish Studies, Humanities Press* 3 (1977): 35–55. (Summarizes points in entry 1831, below.)

1831.   ———, *Arthur Griffith and Non–Violent Sinn Fein*. 253 pp.
          Dublin: Anvil Books, 1974. (Political biography of Irish
          moderate nationalist Griffith to 1917, with extensive discussion
          of Irish contribution to theories of revolutionary nationalism
          and its methods of struggle. Shows Griffith's awareness of
          Hungarian nonviolent struggle in 1848 in pp. 18, 21, 92, 100–
          107, 113–16, and that Indian nationalists were in turn aware of
          Irish experience, esp. pp. 91–93, 96. On development of a
          theory of "passive resistance," see ch. 6 and pp. 147–50, 153–55.
          On controversy over violent versus nonviolent means, see pp.
          70–73, 91–98, 124–25. Epilogue on Irish contributions to
          guerrilla struggle. Photos. Index. Bibliography.)

1832.   Fox, R.M., *Louie Bennett: Her Life and Times*. 123 pp. Dublin:
          Talbot Press, [1957]. (Popular biography of Louie Bennett,
          pacifist, suffragist, union organizer in Ireland. See ch. 4, 5, 7, 8.)
          Bennett, Louie

1833.   Gaughan, J. Anthony, *Austin Stack: Portrait of a Separatist*. 408
          pp. Mount Merrion, County Dublin: Kingdom Books, 1977.
          (See ch. 5, pp. 74–101, on Stack's hunger strikes under
          imprisonment, 1917–19. Photos. Index. Bibliography.)

1834.   Levenson, Leah, *With Wooden Sword: A Portrait of Francis
          Sheehy–Skeffington, Militant Pacifist*. 282 pp. Boston:
          Northeastern Univ. Press; Dublin: Gill & Macmillan, 1983.
          (Biography of Irish nationalist and supporter of feminism and
          passive resistance, summarily executed during 1916 Easter
          Rising. See ch. 11 on anti–conscription and anti–war activities
          and prison hunger strike, and ch. 13 on his relationship to the
          Rising. Illustrations. Index. Bibliography.)

1835.   O'Hegarty, P.S., *Sinn Fein: An Illumination*. 56 pp. London:
          Maunsel, 1919. (Includes discussion of the role of Arthur
          Griffith and Sinn Fein as a nonviolent struggle movement. See
          esp. ch. 4 on the Sinn Fein policy of denying British
          sovereignty.)

1836.   ———, *The Victory of Sinn Fein: How It Won It, and How It Used
          It*. 218 pp. Dublin: Talbot Press; London: Simpkin, Marshall,

Hamilton, Kent, 1924. (See ch. 6,7 on the formation of the Dáil Eireann as an extralegal government, esp. pp. 36–37 for the assessment that the whole–hearted support for the Irish served to "paralyze" the British government. See also ch. 9 on change in Griffith's thought after 1916 and ch. 10 on the boycott of goods from Ulster. Appendix.)

1837. Wright, Arnold, *Disturbed Dublin: The Story of the Great Strike of 1913–14*. 348 pp. London: Longmans, Green, 1914. (Antagonist's story of lengthy strike in dockyards and transport led by James Larkin. See ch. 12–17, 21–22 on course of strike, interventions, and associated violence. Index.)

IRELAND, NORTHERN

Northern Ireland is known for the protracted and extreme violence that has characterized its struggles. After a period of being relatively quiet, as far as open conflict is concerned, Northern Ireland's current series of conflicts began in the late 1960s when activists raised the banner of civil rights and nonviolent action, only to be severely repressed. Since that time, both Catholic–Nationalist and Protestant–Loyalist forces have very explicitly adopted a policy of violence, including bombing campaigns, attacks on troops and civilians, assassinations, kneecapping, and other acts. Both sides have turned to protest and noncooperation when it appeared to suit them. On the Loyalist side, this was the case in general strikes in 1974 and 1977. For the IRA, it involved protests by political prisoners that led to prison hunger strikes in 1980–81 in which several activists died. A third force, partly representing political views that diverged from the IRA and partly representing revulsion at violence and its effects, coalesced briefly in the Peace People movement in the 1970s. Attempts at intergroup reconciliation as such are not included here.

1838. Deutsch, Richard, and Vivien Magowan, *Northern Ireland 1968–73: A Chronology of Events*. Vol. 1 (1968–71), 180 pp. Vol. 2 (1972–73), 209 pp. Belfast: Blackstaff Press, 1973. *Northern Ireland, 1968–74: A Chronology of Events*. Vol. 3 (1974), 209 pp. Belfast: Blackstaff Press, 1975. (Very complete calendar of the Northern Ireland conflict, with brief descriptions of each event noted. Consult index under the names of groups, persons, and actions. See vol. 3, pp. 54–83, on the general strike and governmental crisis of May 1974. Photos. Index. Bibliography.)

STUDIES

1839.   Bleakley, David, *Peace in Ulster*. 132 pp. London, Oxford: Mowbrays, 1972. (A political activist and one–time member of the Northern Ireland cabinet discusses organizations, covenants, and efforts to reduce violence. See esp. ch. 6 on a local peace committee. Photos.)

1840.   ———, *Saidie Patterson: Irish Peacemaker*. 118 pp. Belfast: Blackstaff Press, 1980. (See esp. pp. 70–91 on "peace" and women's activism. Illustrations. Photos. Index.)

1841.   Buckland, Patrick, *A History of Northern Ireland*. 195 pp. Dublin: Gill and Macmillan, 1981. (Ch. 6 discusses politics during the government of Terence O'Neill; esp. pp. 118–31 on NICRA, PD, and their Paisleyist antagonists. The Ulster Workers Council general strike of 1974 is reviewed on pp. 170–73. Index.)

1842.   Bufwack, Mary S., *Village without Violence: An Examination of a Northern Irish Community*. 193 pp. Cambridge MA: Schenkman, 1982. (Anthropological study of a Northern Irish community. While focusing largely on the avoidance of violence, it gives some attention to alternatives to violence, e.g., ch. 1, 2, 6, 9. See esp. pp. 22–26 on "Strategies and Tactics." Illustrations. Appendix.)

1843.   Elliot, R.S.P., and John Hickie, *Ulster: A Case Study in Conflict Theory*. 180 pp. London: Longman, 1971. (See pp. 49–62 for a review of violence and nonviolent action in the civil rights campaign. Index.)

1844.   Gallagher, Eric, and Stanley Worrall, *Christians in Ulster, 1968–1980*. 241 pp. Oxford, New York, Toronto, and Melbourne: Oxford Univ. Press, 1982. (For a discussion of the role of organized religion in conflicts around the civil rights marches, the 1974 general strike, and prisoners and peace campaigns, see ch. 3, 6, 7, 8, 11. Index. Bibliography.)

1845. McKeown, Ciaran, *The Passion of Peace*. 319 pp. Belfast: Blackstaff Press, 1984. (Autobiography of involvement in the civil rights movement during 1960s and the Peace People group in 1970s. The earlier campaign is discussed on pp. 43–55. See esp. the author's view of "nonviolent tactics," pp. 49–52, and the Burntollet Bridge affair, pp. 53–55. Peace People and the difficulties of such a group are discussed on pp. 138–244, 259–end. Pp. 157–65, 197–201, 210–12 are on marches, and pp. 109–13 discuss the general strike of 1974. Index.)

1846. Shivers, Lynne, and David Bowman, S.J., *More than the Troubles: A Common Sense View of the Northern Ireland Conflict*. 244 pp. Philadelphia PA: New Society Publishers, 1984. (Ch. 6 charts organized efforts at conflict intervention and reconciliation. See pp. 139, 187–88, 194–200 for authors' view of the relevance of nonviolent action. Photos. Index. Annotated bibliography.)

1847. Sullivan, Eileen A., and Harold A. Wilson, eds., *Conflict in Ireland*. 262 pp. Gainesville FL: [n.p.], 1976. (Papers from a 1974 Univ. of Florida Symposium entitled "Violence in Northern Ireland." Paul F. Power, "Civil Protest as an Alternative to Violence," pp. 169–83, analyzes explicitly conscious nonviolent action during the 1964–74 period.)

1848. Target, G.W., *Bernadette: The Story of Bernadette Devlin*. 384 pp. London, Sydney, Auckland, and Toronto: Hodder & Stoughton, 1975. (Biography of the civil rights activist and Member of Parliament. See ch. 5, 6, 7 on the civil rights movement era and p. 337 on Devlin's employment at 10 Downing Street of the traditional Irish method of fasting outside the house of a debtor. Photos. Index.)

1849. White, Barry, *John Hume: Statement of the Troubles*. 292 pp. Belfast: Blackstaff Press, 1984. (Well–informed political biography of the activist and political leader. See ch. 6 on 1968–69 demonstrations, including comments on Hume's role in their nonviolent aspects and organizations. See ch. 7 on violence in 1969 and pp. 113–17 on the Alternative Assembly and the impact of the internment unit. See pp. 119–23 on Bloody Sunday in 1972 and Hume's politics thereafter; pp. 128–30 on the 1972 prison hunger strike; ch. 6 on the 1974 loyalist general strike; p. 199 on a subsequent strike; and ch. 18 on the 1980 hunger strikes. Scattered discussion in later chapters of various parties' boycotts of the legislature. Index.)

1850.   Wilson, Tom, *Ulster: Conflict and Consensus*. 330 pp. Oxford and New York: Basil Blackwell, 1989. (History of Ulster province as a part of the British possessions in Northern Ireland, written by a participant in economic and development issues. See ch. 15 on the Civil Rights protests of 1968 and their relation to later civil violence, pp. 181–84 on the Ulster Workers' Council general strike of 1974, and pp. 188–89 on the hunger strikes of 1981. Chronology. Appendixes. Indexes. Bibliography.)

Civil Rights Campaign and People's Democracy, 1967–1972

This campaign focused on the social consequences of British control of Northern Ireland and arose during the period 1967–1968. Largely Catholic in composition and student led at first, the People's Democracy organization and its civil rights campaign sought to achieve full civil rights through nonviolent action. A British civil rights commission (Cameron Commission) was established by the government to investigate and British troops were sent in, partly to protect demonstrators attacked by supporters of the status quo. An attack by Protestant militants on a 1969 march from Belfast to Londonderry at the Burntollet Bridge is a notable example. Nonviolent action was soon abandoned as an explicit strategy. Rioting and violence increased through 1972 when, in the "Bloody Sunday" massacre, civil rights marchers were killed and the British imposed direct rule over the province.

1851.   Arthur, Paul, *The People's Democracy, 1968–1973*. 159 pp. Belfast: Blackstaff Press, 1974. (Chronological account of the People's Democracy [PD] organization and its role in the civil rights movement, 1968–70. Often assumes events are known to the reader. See ch. 1 on its early actions, the effect of violent suppression of the Belfast–Derry march in creating "counter–

violence," and PD unsureness of the nature of nonviolent action. See ch. 2 on clashes in 1969 and ch. 3 on changes in goals during 1969–70 plus local campaigns, pp. 89–96. Documents. Index. Bibliography.)

1852. De Paor, Liam, *Divided Ulster*. 2d ed. 251 pp. Harmondsworth: Penguin Books, 1971. (In addition to a discussion of the Land League of the nineteenth century in pp. 51–56 and a 1907 strike on pp. 61–62, see pp. 151, 157–61 and ch. 6, 7 on the civil rights movement of 1968–69. Illustrations. Index.)

1853. Devlin, Bernadette, *The Price of My Soul*. 206 pp. London: Andre Deutsch, 1969. (Political autobiography of the Northern Ireland activist and one–time member of parliament. See ch. 6–10 on civil rights activities, esp. pp. 91–98, 108–12 on early marches and ch. 9 on the march attacked at Burntollet Bridge. For thoughts on nonviolent means, see pp. 96–97, 117, and for shift to violence, see pp. 195–98 and ch. 14.)

1854. Egan, Bowes, and Vincent McCormack, *Burntollet*. 2d ed. 68 pp. London: LRS Publishers, 1969. (Report on the planned four–day march organized by People's Democracy in January 1969 and the attacks on it, culminating in the Burntollet Bridge affair. Contends that violence at Burntollet Bridge was prepared in advance and indicts the police for participating in it. Photos.)

1855. Government of Northern Ireland, *Disturbances in Northern Ireland*. 124 pp. Belfast: Her Majesty's Stationery Office, 1969. (Cameron Commission report on the civil rights campaigns of 1968 and early 1969. Contains details of specific marches and other actions. See esp. ch. 3–10, 15 and appendixes 7, 10, 12. Illustrations. Documents.)

1856. Hastings, Max, *Barricades in Belfast: The Fight for Civil Rights in Northern Ireland*. 211 pp. New York: Taplinger, 1970. (Journalist's account of the events of 1968–69. See index under *Apprentice Boys of Derry; Civil Rights Association and Movement; Devlin, Miss Bernadette; Dungammon;* and *People's Democracy.* Photos. Index.)

1857.   ———, *Ulster, 1969: The Fight for Civil Rights in Northern Ireland*. 203 pp. London: Victor Gollancz, 1970. (On marches, demonstrations, and increasing violence in Northern Ireland, 1968–69. See ch. 2–4 on 1968 marches and the Burntollet affair, and pp. 100–101, 106–7, 110–11 on the loss by civil rights organizations of the ability to prevent violence in demonstrations. Photos.)

General Strike of 1974

Extralegal nonviolent action has not been restricted to Catholics but included a successful 1974 general strike by Protestants. In that year, the British government once again introduced reform plans that appeared to threaten the unique position of Northern Ireland's Protestant majority. By practically shutting down all economic life and services within the province, the Loyalist forces compelled the government to put these plans on the shelf. A second strike in 1977 was much less effective.

1858.   Bruce, Steve, *God Save Ulster: The Religion and Politics of Paisleyism*. 308 pp. Oxford: Clarendon Press, 1986. (See pp. 108–9, 113–15 on the 1974 and less successful 1977 general strikes. Appendix. Index.)

1859.   Darby, John, and Arthur Williamson, eds., *Violence and the Social Services in Northern Ireland*. 205 pp. London: Heinemann Educational Books, 1978. (See Louis Boyle, "The Ulster Workers' Council Strike, May 1974," pp. 155–64 on social-welfare problems and the community response to the strike. Other chapters treat the impact of protracted conflict and violence on services. Chronology. Index. Bibliography.)

1860.   Fisk, Robert, *The Point of No Return: The Strike Which Broke the British in Ulster*. 264 pp. London: Andre Deutsch, 1975. (Account of 1974 Ulster Workers' Council strike that toppled the Stormont government. Chronology in Appendix 1. Photos. Index.)

1861.   Smyth, Clifford, *Ian Paisley: Voice of Protestant Ulster*. 206 pp. Edinburgh: Scottish Academic Press, 1987. (See pp. 92–94, 106–

14 on the 1974 general strike, lessons drawn from it, and efforts
to repeat it in 1977. Index. Bibliography.)

1862. [Ulster Workers' Association], "The Ulster General Strike
[1974]." 2d ed. 55 pp. Mimeo. [Londonderry, Northern
Ireland]: n.p., 1977 [orig. publ. 1974]. (Strike bulletins of the
Ulster Workers' Association, a group supporting the strike
from the Left which was not connected to Ulster Workers
Council. Documents.)

Peace People and Campaign Against Political Violence

*Random deaths resulting from violence between the Catholic–Nationalist
forces, Protestants, and British troops were the occasion of a movement
against violence—organized partly by the Peace People led by Mairead
Corrigan and Betty Williams—in the 1970s. Like many movements against
violence, this group foundered on the question of its wider purpose and
dissolved after a relatively short life.*

1863. Deutsch, Richard, *Mairead Corrigan/Betty Williams.* 219 pp.
Woodbury NY: Barron's, 1977. (Journalist's account of the
Peace People organization, 1976–77, from its spontaneous
beginnings in protests against deaths caused by violence to its
later organizational crises. See esp. ch. 1, 3–7. Illustrations.
Photos. Documents.)

1864. O'Donnell, Dalry, *The Peace People of Northern Ireland.* 122 pp.
Victoria, Australia: Widescope, 1977. (Informal description of
the Northern Ireland "Peace Movement." See ch. 4–6 on
marches and rallies against sectarian violence and ch. 7 for
personal accounts by participants.)

Prison Protests and Hunger Strikes of 1980–81

*Imprisoned members of the Irish Republican Army (IRA) and other
paramilitary groups had generally been granted a special status as political
offenders before the 1970s. IRA members refused to accept the withdrawal of
this status, which included the requirement to wear prison uniforms and take*

prison jobs. They conducted a "blanket protest," by wearing only a blanket instead of a uniform, and "dirty protest," which involved making the cell blocks as filthy as possible. Conducted with a bitterness that belies their names, these protests evolved into a mass hunger strike in the prison where the IRA members were held. Led by Bobby Sands, a second group of hunger strikers refused to yield in any way, as did the British government headed by Margaret Thatcher. In the end, ten died, Sands included, before the hunger strikes stopped.

1865.   Bartlett, Jonathan, ed., *Northern Ireland.* 167 pp. New York: H.W. Wilson, 1983. The Reference Shelf, vol. 54, no. 6. (See section 2 for articles on the Maze Prison hunger strikes of 1981 and some history of hunger strikes in Ireland. Bibliography.)

1866.   Beresford, David, *Ten Men Dead: The Story of the 1981 Irish Hunger Strike.* 334 pp. New York: Atlantic Monthly Press, 1989 (orig. publ. in Britain by Grafton Books, 1987). (Recounts the second Northern Ireland prisoners' hunger strike of 1981, interspersed with fictionalized account of prison life and with citations from prisoners' letters smuggled to IRA leadership outside.)

1867.   Coogan, Tim Pat, *On the Blanket: The H Block Story.* 271 pp. Dublin: Ward River Press, 1980. (Story of the IRA prisoners on blanket protests and dirty protests.)

1868.   Feehan, John M., *Bobby Sands and the Tragedy of Northern Ireland.* 151 pp. Dublin and Cork: Mercier Press, 1983. (Popular biography of Bobby Sands. See ch. 5, 6 on his hunger strike.)

1869.   O'Malley, Padraig, *Biting at the Grave: The Irish Hunger Strikes and the Politics of Despair.* 330 pp. Boston: Beacon Press, 1990. (An inquiry into the origins, conduct, and effects of the IRA prison hunger strikes of 1980–81 that emphasizes three interrelated contexts: the religious, the psychological, and the mythic; in addition to their grounding in Anglo–Irish and inter–Irish conflicts. The first section recounts the course of prison protests and hunger strikes, with comments in pp. 22–23 and elsewhere on such protests as the adoption of a suffering greater than the adversary could itself inflict. Glossary. Chronology. Index. Bibliography.)

ITALY

Protest in Italy has been influenced by trends in Marxist thought about the ends and methods of opposition, largely associated with the violence of the Red Brigades in the 1970s and 1980s. It has also involved nonviolent action in political, environmental, and anti–weapons protest. This is especially true of social activist Danilo Dolci who originated a variety of means of direct action in leading Sicilians to oppose Mafia influence and overcome their poverty.

1870. Lotta Continua, *Take over the City.* 36 pp. London: Rising Free, n.d. (Descriptions of Italian rent strikes and other mass actions intended to secure better living conditions for workers, many organized by *Lotta Continua* and other communist and socialist organizations. Illustrations. Photos. Bibliography.)

1871. Mangione, Jerre, *A Passion for Sicilians: The World Around Danilo Dolci.* 384 pp. New Brunswick NJ and Oxford: Transaction Books, 1985. Orig. publ. New York: William Morrow, 1968. Reprint entitled *The World Around Danilo Dolci.* New York: Harper & Row, 1972. (Memoirs and biography of Dolci. See pp. 2–6 on "reverse strike" of 1956 and ch. 5 on Roccamera occupation of the piazza. Other actions of 1963–1964 discussed throughout.)

1872. McNeish, James, *Fire Under the Ashes: The Life of Danilo Dolci.* 256 pp. Boston: Beacon Press, 1969, and London: Hodder and Staughton, 1965. (Traces development of Dolci's career as an activist. See esp. ch. 17, pp. 131–134, for Gandhi's influence on Dolci, and pp. 223–227 for description of Dolci's method of active nonviolence. Photos. Index. Bibliography.)

1873. Tarrow, Sidney, *Democracy and Disorder: Protest and Politics in Italy, 1965–1975.* 400 pp. Oxford: Clarendon Press, 1989. (Methodologically sophisticated study of recent protest events in Italy, including both nonviolent and violent forms, which reveals the sources, means, and outcomes of collective action in that country as well as contributing to the study of the topic in general. Part 1 dissects the protest environment into sources, means ["repertoire of contention"], action and opponent groups, and objectives. Parts 2, 3 look first at the major institutional players of students, labor, and religion, and second, at three sets of organizations, the extraparliamentary opposition, a leftist action group in Tuscany, and the radical political group Lotta Continua. Part 4 addresses "outcomes" including the violence from 1969 into the 1980s, protest and political institutionalization, and "disorder and democracy." Methodological appendixes. Index. Bibliography.)

Resistance to Fascism and War

Fascism suppressed most organized opposition well into the WWII years, leaving only underground channels. However, the combination of anti-fascism, self-awareness, and a willingness to help led to the survival of many Italian Jews in a country dominated by, and occupied for some months by, Nazi Germany.

1874.   Luzzatto, Riccardo, *Unknown War in Italy*. 135 pp. London: New Europe, 1946. (Report on semi–military and civilian "mass resistance" in Italy beginning ca. 1943. See esp. pp. 21–27, 43, 55–56, 79–82 on strikes and protests. Documents.)

1875.   Rosengarten, Frank, *The Italian Anti–Fascist Press, 1919–1945: From the Legal Opposition Press to the Underground Newspapers of World War II*. 263 pp. Cleveland: Case Western Reserve Univ. Press, 1968. (See ch. 3 for anti–fascist underground from 1925 to 1939, pp. 95–112 on "methodology of underground journalism," and pp. 112–21 on functions of underground press. Index. Bibliography.)

1876.   Wilhelm, Maria, *The Other Italy: Italian Resistance in World War II*. 272 pp. New York: Norton, 1988. (Traces the development of a unified resistance against Fascism. Chronology of events pp. 22–29. See esp. ch. 9, "The Unification of the Resistance" for strategy used to forge disparate groups into a more formidable political whole. References to passive resistance throughout. Photos. Illustrations. Index. Bibliography.)

1877.   Zuccotti, Susan, *The Italians and the Holocaust: Persecution, Rescue, and Survival*. 334 pp. New York: Basic Books, 1987. (A study of various facets of the high survival rate of Italy's

Jewish population under the Mussolini government and the German occupation regime. Includes extended discussion of Jewish self–help and activism in anti–fascist organizations, rescue and assistance by non–Jewish Italians, and the roles of religious, officials, and the military. See esp. ch. 1, 4–11, 13. Anecdotal evidence throughout on rescue, flight, and hiding of Jews and noncooperation and subterfuge to protect them; see esp. ch. 10 on this. Photos. Index.)

THE NETHERLANDS

Nazi Occupation, 1940–1945

In 1937, the government of The Netherlands passed laws that forbade civil servants from cooperating with any occupying power, beyond necessary limits (entry 1886). Never effectively made known, they were of little help when the country was taken over by Nazi Germany. Despite this, noncooperation, protest, and, strikes were aimed at Nazi power. In retaliation against 1944 railroad strikes, organized by resistance groups outside the country, the Germans blocked most transportation and practically starved the population during the Hunger Winter of 1944–45. In addition, despite a very early strike to protest anti–semitism in 1941, Christian society and the churches took some time to develop views on their responsibility to aid Dutch Jewry. Even when assisted, the majority of Jews were deported, but some were hidden and saved or transported from the country.

See also: Europe: Opposition and Resistance to Nazi Occupation, 1939–1945.

1878. Simoni, Anna E.C., ed., *Publish and Be Free: A Catalogue of Clandestine Books Printed in the Netherlands, 1940–1945, in the British Library.* 289 pp. The Hague: Martinus Nijhoff, in association with British Museum Publications for the British Library, London, 1975. (Catalog and annotated bibliography of May 1970 exhibition of Dutch clandestine publishing, with translations of titles into English, descriptive annotations, and biographical sketches of authors. See introduction for history, esp. pp. 1–5. Illustrations. Index of publishers.)

STUDIES

1879.   Boolen, J.J., and J.C. Van Der Does, *Five Years of Occupation: The Resistance of the Dutch against Hitler–Terrorism and Nazi–Robbery*. 122 pp. N.p.: D.A.V.I.D, [1945?]. (Pamphlet written near the end of the war. See pp. 31–32 on resistance to forced labor levies; pp. 38–60 on oppression and resistance of religion, students, and medical and legal groups; and pp. 104–19 on the then–current Hunger Winter of 1944–45. Written by order of the Secretary–General of the Department of Education, Arts and Sciences, and printed on The Secret Press of D.A.V.I.D., apparently in the still–occupied Netherlands, spring 1945.)

1880.   de Jong, Louis, and Joseph W.F. Stoppelman, *The Lion Rampart: The Story of Holland's Resistance to the Nazis*. Ed. and trans. Joseph W.F. Stoppelman. 336 pp. New York: Querido, 1943. (Wartime account of Dutch resistance. See ch. 2–7 on the German system in the Netherlands, ch. 10 on Dutch Jewry, ch. 11, 12 on aspects of resistance by political groups and students, pp. 287–90 on the underground press, and pp. 336–37 on "passive resistance." Photos. Appendixes. Documents. Index. Bibliography.)

1881.   Posthumus, N.W., ed., "The Netherlands under Nazi Occupation." 232 pp. *The Annals of the American Academy of Political and Social Science* 245. Philadelphia: American Academy of Political and Social Science, 1946. (Entire issue devoted to articles on society, economy, and social life during occupation. Many selections contain brief mention of opposition, but see H.C. Troow, "The Resistance of the Netherlands Churches," pp. 149–61, and W.F. Noordhoek Hegt, "The Resistance of the Medical Profession," pp. 162–68. Index.)

1882.   Presser, Dr. J., *Ashes in the Wind: The Destruction of Dutch Jewry*. Trans. Arnold Pomerans. 556 pp. London: Souvenir Press, 1968. Originally published in the Netherlands as *Ondergang*. The Hague: Staatsuitgeverij, 1965. (Many brief accounts of resistance and protest in context of extermination of Dutch Jews. See esp. pp. 20–24, 27–29, 45–57, 89, 144–48, 278–84, 301–5, and ch. 6. Illustrations. Photos. Index.)

1883. Ryan, Michael D., ed., *Human Responses to the Holocaust: Perpetrators and Victims, Bystanders and Resisters*. Papers of conference "The Church Struggle and the Holocaust." 284 pp. New York and Toronto: Edwin Mellen Press, 1981. (See Pieter de Jong, "Responses of the Churches in the Netherlands to the Nazi Occupation," pp. 121–43, for a personal account of the growth of awareness of cooperation with occupiers as a problem; church protest against persecution of Jews in February 1943, pp. 121, 124–33, 135–36; and student refusal to sign loyalty oath, p. 136. Photos. Bibliography.)

1884. Sijes, B.A., *De Februari–Staking: 25–26 Februari 1941*. 237 pp. The Netherlands: Martinus Nijhoff, 1954. (History of Amsterdam strike against anti–Semitic measures and Nazi terrorism on February 25–26, 1941. In Dutch, with English summary on pp. 215–28. Documents and photos in text. Index.)

1885. Warmbrunn, Werner, *The Dutch Under German Occupation, 1940–1945*. Stanford CA: Stanford Univ. Press; London: Oxford Univ. Press, 1963. (Part 3 is on the Dutch response to occupation. See esp. ch. 7 on strikes of 1941 and 1943, pp. 138–146 on 1944 railroad strike, pp. 146–153 on resistance to loyalty pledge in universities, pp. 153–156 on medical "resignations", and ch. 11 on the underground press. Bibliography.)

1886. Woodruff, John H., *Relations Between the Netherlands Government–in–Exile and Occupied Holland during World War II*. 152 pp. Boston: Boston Univ. Press, 1964. (See pp. 8–9, 16–19 on *Ordinances of 1937*, which, although not well publicized, established legal limits to civil–servant collaboration; pp. 25–27 on definitions of resistance; pp. 30, 44–57, 77–96 on clandestine organizations; and pp. 71–76 on 1944 rail strike organized by government–in–exile.)

NORWAY

Nazi Occupation and Fascist Rule, 1940–1945

When Nazi Germany occupied Norway in 1940, both military and nonmilitary resistance came into being. Germany installed Norwegian Vidkun Quisling as its puppet–ruler in occupied Norway, charging him with establishing a "corporatist" Nazi model state in Norway. Part of this plan involved coordinating all kinds of occupational groups into state organizations that would inculcate Nazi views. A state–directed teachers' organization was intended to play a key role, along with organizations of athletes, clergy, and others. The bulk of teachers refused to take part, as did athletes and clergy. Much of the repression that followed fell on the teachers, but, by standing fast, they prevented the effective action of the corporate state.

1887.   Adamson, Hans C., and Per Klein, *Blood on the Midnight Sun.* 282 pp. New York: W.W. Norton, 1964. (Includes accounts of the evacuation of Norway's gold reserves, the sinking of a ship with heavy water aboard, and underground organizations. Photos. Bibliography.)

1888.   Andenaes, Johannes, Olav Riste, and Magne Skodvin, *Norway and the Second World War.* 168 pp. Oslo: Johan Grundt Tanum, 1966. (Analysis of the phenomenon of collaboration with Nazis. See esp. pp. 67–71, "The Strength of the Resistance" for brief outline of the resistance movement. Photos. Index. Bibliography.)

1889.   Fen, Ake, *Nazis in Norway.* 157 pp. New York: Penguin Books, 1943. (By a young reporter who worked with the underground press. See esp. ch. 5–14 for an early description of occupation and resistance up to June 1942.)

1890.   Gjelsvik, Tore, *Norwegian Resistance, 1940–1945.* 234 pp. Trans. Thomas Kingston Derry. London: C. Hurst, 1979. Originally published as *Hjemme Fronten: Den Sivile Motstand Under Okkupasjonen, 1940–1945.* Oslo: J.W. Cappelens, 1977. (Personal history advocating the view that resistance was aimed at preventing a collaborator government from throwing Norway into the war on Germany's side, pp. 14, 130. On organizational factors, see pp. 14–19, 48–55. Many references to nonviolent protest and noncooperation, including resignations, pp. 22, 26–27; the sports strike, pp. 17, 23–26; students' and teachers' noncooperation, pp. 33–34, 58–65, 112–18; strikes, pp. 45–48, 172–75, 195–97; and conscription refusal, pp. 130, 137–41, 143–45, 149–53. See also pp. 31–33 and ch. 3 on *holdningskampen*, translated here as "standfast struggles." Illustrations. Photos. Index.)

1891.   Höye, Bjarne, and Trygve M. Ager, *The Fight of the Norwegian Church against Nazism.* 180 pp. New York: Macmillan, 1943. (Report on state church's resistance to incorporation into fascist state. See ch. 3 on bishops' statements, boycott of radio, and participation in protests. See also pp. 88–92, 99–101 on bishops' and pastors' resignations; ch. 10, 11 on "free church"; and other protests on pp. 115–16, 141–43. Appendix contains pastoral letter by bishops, February 1941.)

1892.   Johnson, Amanda, *Norway, Her Invasion and Occupation.* 382 pp. Decatur GA: Bowen Press, 1948. (On protest and noncooperation episodes, see pp. 90, 132–34, 138–44, ch. 7, 9, 11, 12. Ch. 12 is on the teachers' resistance. Index. Bibliography.)

1893.   Myklebost, Tor, *They Came as Friends.* Trans. Trygve M. Ager. 297 pp. Garden City NY: Doubleday, Doran, 1943. (A popular contemporary account of resistance by churchmen, teachers, and others, up to autumn 1942.)

1894.   Petrow, Richard, *The Bitter Years: The Invasion and Occupation of Denmark and Norway, April 1940–May 1945.* 403 pp. New York: William Morrow, 1974. (See ch. 8–11, 16, 19, 20. Popular style account without footnoted sources.)

1895.   Riste, Olav, and Berit Nökleby, *Norway, 1940–45: The Resistance Movement.* 93 pp. Oslo: Johan Grundt Tanum, 1970. (Brief history of civilian and military resistance. See esp. pp. 21, 23–28, 33–36, 41–46 on civilian resistance, including resignations, strikes, and protests; as well as photos pp. 17, 21, 43, 45. Index.)

1896. Royal Norwegian Government Information Office, *Norway's Schools in the Battle for Freedom*. 52 pp. London: Hodder and Stoughton, for the Royal Norwegian Government Information Office, [1942]. (Wartime report on teachers' resistance and public support, including texts of statements, pp. 21–28, and children's symbolic protests, pp. 42–46.)

1897. Royal Norwegian Government Information Office, *The Norwegian Church Struggle*. 68 pp. London, 1943. (Wartime pamphlet on the ongoing resistance of the Norwegian churches and clergy.)

1898. Royal Norwegian Government's Press Representatives, *Norway's Teachers Stand Firm*. 32 pp. Washington DC, 1942. (Content similar to entry 1899 but more polemical. Documents.)

1899. Sharp, Gene, "Tyranny Could Not Quell Them: How Norway's Teachers Defeated Quisling During the Nazi Occupation and What It Means for Unarmed Defence Today." 43 pp. London: Peace News, [1959] 1963. (Popular–style account of Norwegian teachers' resistance to state plan to establish a Fascist–controlled teachers' organization as a foundation of the corporatist state and as an instrument for ideological indoctrination. Illustrations. Photos.)

1900. Skodvin, Magne, "Norway in the Second World War." Pp. 178–87 in Harald L. Tvereras, ed., *Humaniora Norvegica: The Year's Work in Norwegian Humanities*. 252 pp. Oslo: Akademisk Forlag, 1954. (Brief review of history and literature of Norway's WWII experience; most references in Norwegian. Bibliography.)

1901. Wabey, William, *Look to Norway*. 242 pp. London: Secker & Warburg, 1945. (An early account of Fascist rule and Norwegian resistance.)

1902. Worm–Möller, Jacob, *Norway Revolts against the Nazis*. 152 pp. London: Lindsay Drummond, 1941. (Very early period report on Norwegian resistance to Nazi invasion until 1941. See pp. 73–78 and ch. 7 for numerous accounts of nonviolent noncooperation by citizenry; also Bishops' letter of protest, January 1941, in appendix 5. Documents. Photos.)

POLAND

Poland has been first in many things in the twentieth century, from being the first country invaded by the Germans at the start of WWII to the first country to conduct a successful challenge to Communist rule. In WWII, Poland suffered a very high level of civilian casualties in Nazi extermination and reprisal campaigns, which was true of Jews and non–Jews alike. This unquestionably influenced the nature and conduct of the resistance, which was essentially an exile and underground struggle. After the war years, the Soviet imposed Communist government met challenges from the workers in 1956, 1970, 1971, 1976, and finally in 1980 with the Solidarity strikes. Suppressed by martial law in 1981, Solidarity survived underground and formed the basis of a parallel power that emerged at the end of the decade to take over as the government collapsed.

Nazi Occupation and Fascist Rule, 1940–1945

After the 1939 German invasion of Poland that began World War II, Polish political organizations were forced underground. They later coalesced into the primary anti–Nazi organization, the Armia Kraieva (AK), or Home Army. Polish leftists also formed a People's Army out of small localized resistance units. Thus, Poland went through the war with a divided resistance movement in which nonviolent resistance was a minor factor. Also, while Polish assistance to threatened Jews was limited, entries below contain some information on hiding and rescue work.

1903. Bartoszewski, Wladyslaw, and Zofia Lewin, eds., *Righteous among Nations: How Poles Helped the Jews, 1939–1945*. 921 pp. London: Earlscourt Publications, 1969. (Efforts to demonstrate and document Polish work to save and assist Jews during occupation, containing many personal statements and lengthy documents section. Index.)

1904. Gross, Jan Tomasz, *Polish Society under German Occupation: The Generalgouvernement, 1939–1944*. 351 pp. Princeton NJ:

Princeton Univ. Press, 1979. (In addition to chapters on the nature of collaboration and on the Home Army and underground as social movement and quasi–state, see in ch. 9 "Terror and Obedience," a contribution to thought about the effectiveness of repression. Index. Bibliography.)

1905.   Karski, Jan, [pseud.] *Story of a Secret State*. 391 pp. Boston: Houghton Mifflin, 1944. (Written by a member of the Polish underground about both violent and nonviolent resistance.)

1906.   Korbonski, Stefan, *The Polish Underground State: A Guide to the Underground, 1939–1945*. Trans. Marta Erdman. 243 pp. New York: Columbia Univ. Press, 1978. (Ch. 10 discusses the inclusion of civil resistance into the underground, a boycott of German measures deemed "socially harmful or damaging to the national substance," which was in part conducted nonviolently. Index. Bibliography.)

1907.   Tec, Nechama, *When Light Pierced the Darkness: Christian Rescue of Jews in Nazi–Occupied Poland*. 262 pp. New York and Oxford: Oxford Univ. Press, 1986. (On rescue of Jews by non–Jews in WWII era, focusing on Poland with discussion of other examples in pp. 7–11. See ch. 2–4. Theory developed in ch. 10. Illustrations. Documents. Index. Bibliography.)

Political and Labor Struggles Since 1956

Strikes and conflict between industrial workers and the government occurred in 1956, 1970–71, and 1976. Often there was violence when strikers attacked Party offices and the police, and the strikes were violently and effectively repressed. In 1970–71, some shipyard workers tried an alternative form of strike by staying in their work place rather than taking to the streets. By the mid–1970s, students and intellectual dissenters also began to suffer from the suppression of their movements and considered making common cause with workers. Among the organizations that resulted was the Committee for the Defense of the Workers (KOR), which was primarily staffed by intellectuals and encouraged the creation of unofficial labor organizations. In the late 1970s, workers formed free trade union committees, especially in the shipyards of Gdansk.

DOCUMENTS

1908. *Committee in Support of Solidarity Reports.* [U.S.] Nos. 1–. 1982–1988. (Documents from a variety of Polish sources on Solidarity underground, repression, continued protests, and Polish politics in the martial law period.)

1909. *Palach Press Bulletin.* London: Palach Press, February 1976–April 1982. (Document source. Irregularly–appearing bulletin of news, documents, and document summaries from Eastern Europe; coverage of Poland in no. 7, July 1977, to no. 9, March 1978.)

1910. *Poland Watch Digest,* Journal of the Poland Watch Center, Washington DC. (Articles on Polish and Eastern European issues; covers martial law period with some comments and documentation on earlier struggle.)

1911. *Uncensored Poland News Bulletin.* London: Information Center for Polish Affairs (U.K.), 1980–. (Document source. Regularly appearing bulletin of news and documents covering Solidarity and related movements; some in Polish, much in English.)

1912. Preibisz, Joanna M., ed., *Polish Dissident Publications: An Annotated Bibliography.* General ed. Jane Leftwich Curry. 395 pp. New York: Praeger, 1982. (Bibliography of periodicals, books, and documents from Polish sources available to the editors, dating ca. 1976–August 1980. Of greatest use to readers of Polish, but each entry abstracted in English. Consult index under names of persons and organizations, dates of events [alphabetized by month and year], and subject headings such as human rights, hunger strikes, and strikes. Includes incidental information on dissent in other East European countries. Journals entered include *Robotnik* and *Solidarnosc.* Books include Stefan Kawalec on KOR's origins, collections of KOR documents, a Jacek Kuron anthology, and Janusz Rozek on peasant activism. Documents include those of pre–Solidarity labor groups, peasant activism, KOR–KSS, other "social self–defense" groups, student activism, and hunger strikes. Index.)

1913.   Twierdochlebow, W.J., "Solidarnosc: A Biblio–historiography of the Gdansk Strike and the Birth of the Solidarity Movement." 76 pp. Photocopy. Menlo Park, CA: Center for the Study of Opposition in Poland, 1983. (A "highly personal work," abstracting and commenting on sources in several languages. Intends to point out and correct leftist bias and other errors. Most useful for Polish–language material.)

STUDIES

1914.   Bernhard, Michael H., *The Origins of Democratization in Poland: Workers, Intellectuals, and Oppositional Politics, 1976–1980*. 298 pp. New York: Columbia Univ. Press, 1994. (Study of Polish politics from the factory strikes of June 1976 to the winter of 1979–80, with attention to the founding and role of the organization KSS–"KOR." Ch. 5 is on KOR's "improvising" of a strategy and methods to defend workers' rights after repression in the 1976 strikes and ch. 7 is on the regrowth of workers' "oppositional politics" in the following years. Index. Bibliography.)

1915.   ———, "The Strikes of June 1976 in Poland." *Eastern European Politics and Societies* 1 (1987): 363–92. (Account and analysis of widespread one–day strikes aimed at forcing retraction of price increases by government. Reconstructs the events of major strikes with stress on the implications of this conflict for the political development of opposition.)

1916.   Blazynski, George, *Flashpoint Poland*. 379 pp. New York: Pergamon Press, 1979. (Detailed view of political events of 1970s. Some hour–by–hour and day–by–day accounts of 1970, 1976 events. See esp. ch. 2–4, 8, 9, 11–15. Index. Bibliography.)

1917.   Brumberg, Abraham, ed., *Poland, Genesis of a Revolution*. 336 pp. New York: Vintage Books, 1983. (Background to Solidarity era. See Alex Pravda, "The Workers," ch. 6 and Jozef Sreniowski, "In Praise of Strikes," pp. 165–69. Index.)

1918.   *Dissent in Poland: Reports and Documents in Translation, December 1975–July 1977*. 200 pp. London: Association of Polish

Students and Graduates in Exile, 1977. (See esp. preface, protest documents in section 1, 1976 strikes in section 4, and KOR activities in section 5. Chronology, June 1976–June 1977. Documents.)

1919. Dziewanowski, M.K., *Poland in the Twentieth Century*. 309 pp. New York: Columbia Univ. Press, 1977. (See pp. 177–98 for review of the conflicts of 1956–70. Index.)

1920. Karpinski, Jacub, *Count–Down: The Polish Upheavals of 1956, 1968, 1970, 1976, 1980. . . .* Trans. Olga Amsterdamska and Gene Moore. 220 pp. New York: Karz–Cohl Publishers, 1982. (Polish reform and change efforts, 1945–79. On 1956, see pp. 49–53, 57–58, 61–68; on 1968, see pp. 110–16, 118–38; on 1970, see pp. 158–60, 164–66; and on 1976, see pp. 192–94. Index.)

1921. Laba, Roman, *The Roots of Solidarity: A Political Sociology of Poland's Working–Class Democratization*. 247 pp. Princeton NJ: Princeton University Press, 1991. (Study of the prehistory and development of the Solidarity movement which focuses very strongly on the self–motivation of the workers. See both introduction and ch. 9 for the author's theory of political action and challenge to the idea that the intellectuals led the way to Solidarity. Ch. 1, 2 are on the strikes of 1970, ch. 6 is on "grass roots" development of the capacity for resistance, ch. 7 is on ritual and symbolism in the movement, and ch. 8 is on ideology. Photos. Index. Bibliography.)

1922. Lewis, Flora, *A Case History of Hope: The Story of Poland's Peaceful Revolutions*. 281 pp. Garden City NY: Doubleday, 1958. (Looks at protest movements of June and October 1956 in context of general political situation. See ch. 5, 6, 8, 9, 11, 12.)

1923. Polish Helsinki Watch Committee, *Prologue to Gdansk: A Report on Human Rights by the Polish Helsinki Watch Committee*. Cohn, Ludwig, et. al., Members of the Polish Helsinki Watch Committee, and Co–Workers of the Intervention Bureau of the Social Self–Defense Committee "KOR," eds. 155 pp. [New York]: U.S. Helsinki Watch Committee, [1981]. (Documents police and the state's response to dissent, as seen by KOR, in the vocabulary of human rights. Information about activities of

KOR and "Polish Democratic Opposition," before 1980. See ch. 2, sections 4 and 5, and ch. 3, esp. section 5 on police reprisals, searches, and assaults on activists, including Adam Michnik, pp. 118–28. Documents. Index.)

1924. Raina, Peter, *Political Opposition in Poland, 1954–1977*. 551 pp. London: Poets & Painters Press, 1978. (History of dissident intellectuals in Poland, with documents on relevant organizations, legal defenses, and government responses. Documents. Bibliography.)

1925. ———, *Independent Social Movements in Poland*. 632 pp. London: London School of Economics and Political Science, 1981. (Documentary account of activities of several dissident and opposition groups between ca. 1977 and 1980, with introduction and some commentary. Includes documents on police repressions, rural activism, KOR [pp. 183–310], independent academic courses, early free trade unions [pp. 370–89], and Solidarity from July–September 1980 [pp. 435–624]. Documents. Index. Select bibliography.)

1926. Syrop, Konrad, *Spring in October: The Story of the Polish Revolution of 1956*. 219 pp. London: Weidenfeld & Nicholson; New York: Praeger, 1957. (Account of political events of 1956, including workers' protests and riots; see ch. 3–6, 12, 15. Pp. 48–52, 72–76 cover workers' actions in June; and pp. 133–39, 141–43, 170–78, those of October. Photos. Index.)

1927. Tökés, Rudolf L., ed. *Opposition in Eastern Europe*. 330 pp. Baltimore MD and London: Johns Hopkins Univ. Press, 1979. (See Jacques Rupnik, "Dissent in Poland, 1968–78: The End of Revisionism and the Rebirth of Civil Society," pp. 60–112, and Alex Pravda, "Industrial Workers: Patterns of Dissent, Opposition, and Accommodation," pp. 209–62. Index.)

1928. Triska, Jan F., and Charles Gati, eds., *Blue–Collar Workers in Eastern Europe*. 318 pp. London, Boston, and Sydney: George Allen & Unwin, 1981. (See Jan de Weydenthal, "Poland: Workers and Politics," pp. 187–208. Index.)

1980s

The 1980s began with the "Polish August" of Solidarity's first strikes and the conversion of the traditional "workers' veto" into an organized power. Solidarity's own internal difficulties and increased government intransigence under General Jaruzelski culminated in its suppression and martial law at the end of 1981. While Solidarity activists attempted to organize underground, society as a whole withdrew more and more its effective participation in the institutions of government and the economy. As the 1980s closed, Solidarity was again legalized under a compromise with the government that eventuated finally in the disappearance of the Communist regime.

1929. Kaminski, Bartomiej, *The Collapse of State Socialism: The Case of Poland*. 264 pp. Princeton NJ: Princeton University Press, 1991. (Study of the Polish state and institutions in the 1980s. Although largely on the state itself and its failure to achieve "normalization," see ch. 4 on "negative legitimation" and the development of the "workers' veto" before 1980, and ch. 6 on the "withdrawal" of society and the state from existing structures. Appendix. Index. Bibliography.)

1930. Koralewicz, Jadwiga, Ireneusz Bialecki, and Margaret Watson, ed., *Crisis and Transition: Polish Society in the 1980s*. 184 pp. (Sociological studies with a focus on public opinion and also on interpretive–theoretical analysis of the Polish social and state order. See Jadwiga Koralewicz, "Changes in Polish Social Consciousness during the 1970s and 1980s: Opportunism and Identity," pp. 3–25 on personal responses to "external coercion"; Jadwiga Staniszkis, "The Political Articulation of Property Rights: Some Reflections on the 'Inert Structure'," pp. 53–79, esp. the section beginning on p. 72 subtitled "paradoxes of revolt"; and Wlodzimierz Pankow, "The Solidarity Movement, Management, and the Political System in Poland," pp. 111–29. Bibliography.)

1931. Michta, Andrew A., *Red Eagle: The Army in Polish Politics*. 270 pp. Stanford CA: Hoover Institution Press, 1990. (An institutional study of the political role of the Polish army with emphasis on General Wojciech Jaruzelski and the events of 1980–81. Proposes that the political uses of the army were central to its construction under the post–WWII government.

In addition to chapters on the institution itself, see pp. 50–52, 67–74 on pre–1980 civil conflict. Ch. 5 traces the martial law idea in the first eight months of Solidarity, ch. 6 is on the government in 1981, ch. 7 is on martial law, ch. 8 is on the role of the U.S.S.R., and ch. 9 is on the attempted "normalization" of the 1980s. Index. Bibliography.)

1932.   Monticone, Ronald C., *The Catholic Church in Communist Poland, 1945–1985: Forty Years of Church–State Relations*. 227 pp. Boulder CO: East European Monographs, 1986. (Includes discussion of the tension between church and state in the 1970s on pp. 63–74 and protests and strikes in 1980 on pp. 96–105. The church's role as "mediator" between society and the state in 1980–81 is the subject of ch. 4 and the martial law period is discussed in ch. 5. Index. Bibliography.)

1933.   Walesa, Lech, *A Way of Hope*. 325 pp. New York: Henry Holt, 1987. Originally published in French as *Un chemin d'éspoire*. (Memoirs of Lech Walesa with some material from other activists. Recollections of the events of 1968 are on pp. 53–54 and of 1970 on pp. 59–78. The origins of the free trade unions and the strikes of August 1980 are on pp. 99–138, with Solidarity's growth to the time of the Bydgoszcz affair to p. 204. An account of the martial law period to the death of Father Jerzy Popieluszko follows. Photos. Chronology. Index.)

1934.   Wiatr, Jerzy J., *The Soldier and the Nation: The Role of the Military in Polish Politics, 1918–1985*. 204 pp. Boulder CO and London: Westview Press, 1988. (See ch. 9 on the military from August 1980 until martial law began and ch. 10 on "restabilization" after 1981. Index. Bibliography.)

1935.   Zielonka, Jan, *Political Ideas in Contemporary Poland*. 210 pp. Aldershot UK, Brookfield VT, Hong Kong, Singapore, and Sydney: Avebury, 1989. (In addition to chapters on the ideas and visions of KOR, the Polish Catholic Church, and Solidarity, see ch. 4, "Solidarity's Strategy of Social Change" on its nonviolent approach. Students of the technique of nonviolent action will be interested in pp. 93–103, 107–10, and notes 1, 41, 42, and especially the points in note 53. Index. Bibliography.)

SOLIDARITY, 1980–1981

Factory–occupation strikes in July–August 1980 in Gdansk gave rise to the Inter–Factory Strike Committee (MKS), which negotiated demands with a government team and became the core of the trade union Solidarity. Developing into a broad–scale movement, Solidarity used strikes and other weapons of protest in a running conflict with the government. After a period of apparent successes, Solidarity ran into difficulties and the government felt strong enough to ban it and declare martial law in December 1981.

1936. Albright, Madeleine Korbel, *Poland: The Role of the Press in Political Change*. 162 pp. New York: Praeger, 1983. The Washington Papers 102, vol. 11. (See pp. 17–19 on underground press, 1976–80; pp. 20–25, 34–38, and ch. 5 on Solidarity media and role in spreading information on strikes.)

1937. Andrews, Nicholas G., *Poland, 1980–1981: Solidarity Against the Party*. 363 pp. Washington DC: National Defense Univ. Press, 1985. (General history of Solidarity. Ch. 7–15 focus on Solidarity–party interaction and ch. 6, 9, 11 discuss Soviet reactions and influence. Photos. Appendixes.)

1938. Ascherson, Neal, *The Polish August: The Self–Limiting Revolution*. 281 pp. New York: Viking Press, 1982. (Reviews rise of Solidarity in context of Polish politics since 1945.)

1939. Ash, Timothy Garton, *The Polish Revolution: Solidarity, 1980–1982*. 396 pp. London: Jonathan Cape, 1983. (Journalist's narrative of August 1980–December 1981 events. Among other points see pp. 38–67 on Gdansk strikes, pp. 79–84 on confrontation over Solidarity's registration, pp. 244–60 on martial law's beginnings, p. 280 on moral protest, and p. 282 on nonviolent conduct. Chronology. Index. Bibliography.)

1940. Bielasiak, Jack, and Maurice Simon, eds., *Polish Politics: The Edge of the Abyss*. 381 pp. New York: Praeger, 1984. (See esp. Jack Bielasiak, "The Evolution of Crisis in Poland," pp. 1–28, for worker shift from violence to occupation strikes, pp. 14–17; Christine M. Sadowski, "Bread and Freedom: Workers' Self–Government Schemes in Poland," pp. 96–117, on role of riots and strikes of 1970s and aftermath, pp. 104–13; and T. Anthony

Jones, David Bealmer, and Michael D. Kennedy, "Public Opinion and Political Disruption," pp. 138–68. Index.)

1941.   Biondi, Lawrence, S.J., and Frank Mocha, ed., *Poland's Solidarity Movement*. 236 pp. Chicago: Loyola Univ. of Chicago, 1984. (Conference papers on the origins, nature, and prospects of Solidarity. George E. Lerski, "Nonviolent Solidarity," pp. 79–88 grapples with aspects of nonviolent resistance in Solidarity and Irene Dubicka–Morawska, "Solidarity and Determination: Solidarity International, the Group of Delegates, and the Nationwide Resistance Committee ('OKO')," pp. 111–30 offers an account of organization under martial law.)

1942.   *The Birth of Solidarity: The Gdansk Negotiations, 1980.* Trans. A. Kemp–Welch. 220 pp. London: Macmillan, 1983. (Full text of negotiations between Inter–Factory Strike Committee and government delegates, 23–31 August 1980; with Tadeus Kowalik, "Experts and the Working Group," pp. 143–67; and biographies, pp. 201–8. Index.)

1943.   *The Book of Lech Walesa*. 203 pp. New York: Simon & Schuster, 1982. Originally published as *Walesa*. Gdansk: Wydawnictwo Morskie, 1981. (Anthology of personal memoirs. See esp. ch. 2, 3, 5–9.)

1944.   Bromke, Adam, *Poland: The Last Decade*. 189 pp. Oakville, Ontario: Mosaic Press, 1981. (Articles on opposition in Poland. See ch. 7, 12–14, 17.)

1945.   De Weydenthal, Jan B., Bruce D. Porter, and Kevin Devlin, *The Polish Drama: 1980–1982*. 359 pp. Lexington MA and Toronto: Lexington Books, 1983. (Written by Radio Free Europe researchers. Ch. 1–3 contain accounts of August 1980– December 1981 situation. See esp. pp. 6–26 on Solidarity's rise; pp. 62–72 on early 1981 strikes; pp. 79–84, 92–94 on protest, strikes, and coming of martial law. Ch. 7 discusses Eurocommunist response to Solidarity and its methods. Index.)

1946. *Gdansk 1980: Pictures from a Strike.* 63 pp. London: Puls Publications, 1981. (Photos of Gdansk shipyard strike, 14–31 August 1980. Material on conduct of strike, public support, communication, and role of religion. Chronology. Documents.)

1947. Hough, Jerry F., *The Polish Crisis: American Policy Options.* 80 pp. Washington DC: The Brookings Institution, 1982. (Review of political situation in Poland, plus analysis of economic weapons potentially usable by U.S. to influence events. See pp. 60–68.)

1948. International Metalworkers Federation, *Report of a Visit to Poland, 3–11 December 1980.* 70 pp. Geneva: International Metalworkers Federation, [1981]. (Interviews and visits to locations of Solidarity activity. Photos. Documents.)

1949. Johnson, A. Ross, *Poland in Crisis.* 72 pp. Santa Monica, CA: Rand Corporation, 1982. Rand Note #N–1891–AF. (Views Solidarity's history in light of Polish crises and Soviet pressure on Polish party. Considers Solidarity the "first mass nonviolent challenge to Soviet domination," p. 4. See also pp. xi–xix, 4–8, 25 for analysis of actions.)

1950. Lipski, Jan Jozef, *KOR: A History of the Workers' Defense Committee in Poland, 1976–1981.* 571 pp. Berkeley, Los Angeles and London: Univ. of California Press, 1985. (Detailed history of KOR [later KSS–KOR] by active member. For KOR activities and the sanctions against them, see table of contents and index under *beatings, blacklisting, Charter of Workers' Rights, collective letters, communiques, demonstrations, detentions, dismissals, fast, fines, hunger strikes, leaflet campaigns, opposition movement, police, property: confiscate/appropriated, searches, strikes, student movements,* and *workers;* as well as names of persons, places, organizations, and events. Of interest are pp. 70–72 on principle of nonviolence, pp. 161–65, 389–92, and 413–17 on innovative fasts inspired in part by examples of M.K. Gandhi and M.L. King, Jr.; also pp. 424–31 on KOR role in 1980 strikes including ideas on "tactics of striking." KOR statements in appendixes. Index.)

1951.   MacDonald, Oliver, ed., *The Polish August: Documents from the Beginnings of the Polish Workers' Rebellion: Gdansk, August 1980.* 177 pp. Seattle WA: Left Bank Books, 1981. 2nd ed. Originally published in *Labour Focus on Eastern Europe,* vol. 4, nos. 1–3 (1980). (Documents and interviews on 1980 events. See esp. Gdansk strike bulletin issues, 20–31 August 1980, pp. 27–101, including statement "What to Demand and How to Conduct Strikes," pp. 31–32. Glossary. Chronology.)

1952.   MacShane, Denis, *Solidarity: Poland's Independent Trade Union.* 172 pp. Nottingham, England: Spokesman, 1981. (Narrative account of Solidarity as a trade union to mid–1981. See pp. 14–15 on logic of the strike, ch. 3 on leadership, ch. 4 on KOR before 1980, ch. 5 on actions to date of Bydgoszcz clash, and ch. 10 on Solidarity press. 1979 workers' rights charter in appendix.)

1953.   Malcher, George C., *Poland's Politicized Army.* 303 pp. New York: Praeger, 1984. (Ch. 7 on Solidarity's impact on army, ch. 9 and appendix E on condemnation of Solidarity before martial law, ch. 11 on conduct of martial law, and ch. 13 on resistance. Appendixes. Index. Bibliography.)

1954.   Mason, David S., *Public Opinion and Political Change in Poland, 1980–1982.* 275 pp. Cambridge, London, New York, New Rochelle, Melbourne, and Sydney: Cambridge Univ. Press, 1985. (Public opinion toward protest, Solidarity, and the state, and changes in it, are discussed in ch. 4, 5, 7, 9. Index. Bibliography.)

1955.   Myant, Martin, *Poland: A Crisis for Socialism.* 250 pp. London: Lawrence & Wishart, 1982. (Follows interplay between official policies and citizens' expectations and actions from 1945 to 1981. Chronology.)

1956.   Persky, Stan, *At the Lenin Shipyard.* Vancouver, BC: New Star Books, 1981. (Circumstantial account, focusing largely on personalities, of period from August 1980 to April 1981. Text of Gdansk Agreement in appendix. Photos.)

1957.   Persky, Stan, and Henry Flam, eds., *The Solidarity Sourcebook.* 255 pp. Vancouver, BC: New Star Books, 1982. (Anthology of articles about Solidarity, some by Solidarity members. Chronology. Bibliography.)

1958.   Potel, Jean–Yves, *The Promise of Solidarity.* Trans. Phil Markham. 257 pp. New York: Praeger, 1982. Also published as *The Summer before the Frost: Solidarnosc in Poland.* London: Pluto Press, 1982. (Journalist's account of Solidarity's inception. Material from interviews and personal narrative, some text of negotiations. Appendixes contain Twenty–One Demands, notes on persons and organizations, chronology.)

1959.   Raina, Peter, *Poland 1981: Towards Social Renewal.* 480 pp. London, Boston and Sydney: George Allen & Unwin, 1985. (Documentation, with introductory essays, of Solidarity and some related movements, ca. August 1980–December 1981. Ch. 1 discusses many confrontations of the period, including "warning" strikes. See ch. 1–3, 5, 10, 12–15; esp. ch. 3 on the Bydgoszcz clash and ch. 5, 13 on Solidarity's program. Documents. Bibliography.)

1960.   Robinson, William F., ed., *August 1980: The Strikes in Poland.* 447 pp. Munich: Radio Free Europe Research, 1980. (Articles compiled from material prepared for broadcast on Radio Free Europe, August–September 1980. Includes documents from mid–August to mid–September 1980.)

1961.   Ruane, Kevin, *The Polish Challenge.* 344 pp. [London?]: British Broadcasting Corporation, 1982. (Chronological account, 1976–81, stressing government and union activities; much text from reports, speeches, and announcements. Photos. Index.)

1962.   Sanford, George, *Polish Communism in Crisis.* 259 pp. London and Canberra: Croom Helm, 1983. New York: St. Martins Press, 1983. (Institutional analysis of Polish state, dilemmas of reform, and response to Solidarity, 1980–81. Skeptical of considering Solidarity primarily as a movement for democratization. See observations on limits of effective pressure for reform, pp. 8–11, and Solidarity case study to

April 1981, pp. 48–52, 75–76, 100–105, 126–27, 154–60. Glossary. Index. Bibliography.)

1963. Singer, Daniel, *The Road To Gdansk: Poland and the U.S.S.R.* 256 pp. New York: Monthly Review Press, 1981. (Analysis of dissident movement, mostly written shortly before Gdansk strike, with description of Solidarity's first weeks. See ch. 3 and Postscript. Index.)

1964. ———, *The Road To Gdansk: Poland and the U.S.S.R.* 2d ed. 272 pp. New York and London: Monthly Review Press, 1982. (Adds chapter chronicling Solidarity's efforts at being "more than a union" through 1981 to declaration of martial law.)

1965. Staniszkis, Jadwiga, *Poland's Self–Limiting Revolution.* Ed. Jan T. Gross. 364 pp. Princeton NJ: Princeton Univ. Press, 1984. (Author, a Polish sociologist, was an adviser to union negotiators in Gdansk, August 1980. This work discerns patterns in Polish society that create, modify, and absorb protest. See esp. introduction, ch. 1–3, 9, and epilogue. Index.)

1966. Starski, Stanislaw, *Class Struggle in Classless Poland.* 253 pp. Boston: South End Press, 1982. (Comments on the Polish struggle, largely from August 1980 to November 1981, by a Solidarity member.)

1967. Szajkowski, Bogdan, *Next to God . . . Poland: Politics and Religion in Contemporary Poland.* 274 pp. London: Frances Pinter, 1983. (On role of church in politics and protest. See esp. chs. 2, 3. Index. Selected bibliography.)

1968. Teague, Elizabeth, *Solidarity and the Soviet Worker: the Impact of the Polish Events of 1980 on Soviet Internal Politics.* 378 pp. London, New York, and Sydney: Croom Helm, 1988. (Studies official and rank–and–file responses to Solidarity's actions, including efforts to manage and limit expressions of discontent within the U.S.S.R.. See ch. 3 on workers' protest and strikes and their sparseness, ch. 8 on Soviet public opinion, and ch. 9 on *samizdat* expression. Index. Bibliography.)

1969. Touraine, Alain, Francois Dubet, Michael Wieviorka, and Jan Strzelecki, *Solidarity: The Analysis of a Social Movement: Poland 1980–1981*. Trans. David Denby. 203 pp. Cambridge, London, and New York: Cambridge Univ. Press, 1983. (Focuses on causes and internal structures of Solidarity, based largely on research into rank–and–file opinion. See esp. pp. 37–40 on August 1980 strike; pp. 49–59 on popular action; pp. 74–76 on role of the Bydgoszcz affair; ch. 5, pp. 103–36, "The Militants Analyze Their Own Action"; and ch. 8, "Resistance," particularly pp. 180–82, on rejection of confrontation in December 1981. Index. Brief bibliography.)

1970. Triska, Jan F., and Charles Gati, eds., *Blue–Collar Workers in Eastern Europe*. 318 pp. London, Boston and Sydney: George Allen & Unwin, 1981. (See George Kolankiewicz, "Poland, 1980: The Working Class Under 'Anomic Socialism,'" pp. 136–56. Index.)

1971. Tymoski, Andrzej, ed. and trans., *The Strike in Gdansk: August 14–31, 1980*. 56 pp. New Haven CT: Don't Hold Back, 1981. (Excerpts from Solidarity strike bulletin. Photos.)

1972. Walendowski, Tadeusz, *The Polish Workers' Movement and Human Rights*. 30 pp. New York: U.S. Helsinki Watch Committee, 1980. (Text of Gdansk Agreement and chronology of events, July–October 1980. Documents.)

1973. Weschler, Lawrence, *Solidarity: Poland in the Season of Its Passion*. 238 pp. New York: Simon & Schuster, 1982. (Journalist's chronological account of Solidarity. Illustrations. Photos. Documents.)

1974. Woodall, Jean, *The Socialist Corporation and Technocratic Power*. 294 pp. Cambridge, London and New York: Cambridge Univ. Press, 1982. (See Postscript placing 1980 strikes in context of difficulties of internal reform. Index. Bibliography.)

MARTIAL LAW AND AFTER, 1981–1989

Martial law ("state of war" in Polish terminology) permitted the suppression of many dissident organizations. Activists attempted to continue a level of resistance in prisons, with great difficulty, while some Solidarity activists advocated the creation of an underground that would work to create an alternative civil society. The early 1980s saw not only the survival of the Solidarity underground but also many symbolic expressions of the society's continuing rejection of the governing system. The underground persisted even after the lifting of martial law in 1983 and contributed to the dismantling of the regime in 1988.

1975. Kaufman, Michael T., *Mad Dreams, Saving Graces: Poland: A Nation in Conspiracy.* 270 pp. New York: Random House, 1989. (Journalist's reflections on experiences in Poland in the mid–1980s. Many anecdotes on Solidarity figures, their actions, and popular resistance. See ch. 6 on Solidarity's resistance during the period underground, esp. pp. 92–100 on the role and development of the nonviolent strategy.)

1976. Labedz, Leopold, and the staff of *Survey* magazine, eds., *Poland Under Jaruzelski.* 447 pp. New York: Charles Scribner's Sons, 1984. (Anthology of brief documents, proposals, and commentary from Poland, many from underground sources, on martial law and problems of conducting resistance. See esp. pp. 11–16 on the strike under martial law by Poleski; pp. 61–79 on protests and the founding of KOR by Lipski; pp. 145–49 on not signing security pledges by Michnik; pp. 150–59 for symposium on resistance by Kuron, Bujak, and Kulerski; pp. 221–34 on documentation and government response by Filipowicz; pp. 262–67 on Solidarity's response to martial law by Mianowicz; p. 297 on nonviolent discipline by Bujak; pp. 278–86 on government repression; and pp. 287–90, 300–307, 309–10, 406–23 for other pieces on post–1981 protest. Documents. Index.)

1977. Lineberry, William P., ed., *Poland.* 169 pp. New York: H.W. Wilson, 1984. The Reference Shelf, vol. 56, no. 2. (See articles by John Darnton and Robert Ball and section 3, including p. 157 on removal of crucifixes from schools and church resistance. Bibliography lists periodical articles, 1980–84.)

1978. Michnik, Adam, *Letters from Prison and Other Essays*. 354 pp. Ed. Maya Latynski. Berkeley, Los Angeles, and London: Univ. of California Press, 1985. (Essays arranged in reverse chronological order on subjects that include Solidarity and the logic of personal and collective resistance after the declaration of martial law. See esp. "On Resistance: A Letter from Bialoleka, 1982," pp. 41–63; "Letter from Gdansk Prison 1985," pp. 76–99; comments on Solidarity and its strategy in section 2; and comments on earlier movements in section 3. Index.)

1979. Mur, Jan [pseud.], *A Prisoner of Martial Law: Poland: 1981–1982*. 311 pp. Trans. Lillian Vallee. San Diego, New York, and London: Harcourt Brace Jovanovich, Publishers, 1984. (Journal and reflections of a Solidarity activist interned from the declaration of martial law until August 1982. Includes some information on internees' noncooperation with the expected behavior for prisoners, protests and demands, organizing, and news of the outside world. Author's activities after release, and continued news of detainees, begins on p. 235. See index under *hunger strikes, Solidarity [NSZZ]*, and *Strzebielinek internment camp*. Photos. Index.)

1980. *Poland Under Martial Law: A Chronology of Events, 13 December 1981–30 December 1982*. Comp. Roman Stefanowski. Radio Free Europe Research, 1 July 1983. (Chronology of events, with appendixes. See appendix 2 on strikes during the period covered and appendix 3 on demonstrations.)

1981. Polish Helsinki Watch Committee, *1984: Violations of Human Rights in Poland*. 131 pp. Ed. Eric Chernoweth. Trans. Ewa Eliasz Brantley and Agnieska Kolakowska. New York and London: Committee in Support of Solidarity (U.S.) and Information Centre for Polish Affairs (U.K.), 1985 [orig. publ. 1984]. (Carefully categorized accounting of state methods of repression, nonjudicial punishment, and violation of rights in judicial and other proceedings in Poland during the first nine months of 1984. Sections 5, 6, 9–12 are of interest regarding the political situation of the time and the "amnesty" of 1984 is detailed in section 13.)

1982. ———, *Poland Under Martial Law*. Trans. Catherine A. Fitzpatrick, Irene Lasota, and Sonia Sluzar. 340 pp. [New York]: U.S. Helsinki Watch Committee, 1983. (Documentation by underground Solidarity group of eighteen months of martial law. Ch. 2, 5, 6, 9 discuss martial law powers and use against Solidarity and its allies. Ch. 4 describes anti–Solidarity publicity. See esp. pp. 38–43 on martial law powers, p. 47 for disavowal of violence by Solidarity, and pp. 207–26 on suppression of strikes and demonstrations after 12 December 1981. Note: authorship not same as entry 1980.)

1983. *Repressions in Poland: State of War*. 113 pp. Brussels: Coordinating Office Abroad of NSZZ "Solidarnosc," [1983?] (Report on martial law focusing on the arrest and internment of Solidarity activists. See pp. 12–13 on internment protests and hunger strikes. Majority of text consists of appendixes containing government decrees, protests, descriptions and denunciations of prison conditions, personal experiences, and the like. Appendixes.)

1984. Sanford, George, *Military Rule in Poland: The Rebuilding of Communist Power, 1981–1983*. 288 pp. New York: St. Martin's Press, 1986. (Study of causes of Polish military takeover of power in December 1981 and subsequent mass repression from 1981–83. See pp. 15–19 on cause of 1980–81 crisis, ch. 3 on military and 1980–81 crisis, ch. 7 on opposition, focusing on Solidarity underground. Index. Bibliography.)

1985. [Toch, Marta], *Reinventing Civil Society: Poland's Quiet Revolution, 1981–1986*. A Helsinki Watch Report. 103 pp. New York and Washington DC: U.S. Helsinki Watch Committee, 1986. (Report on the creation and maintenance of Polish "independent or alternative society" as a basis for resisting the regime. In the introduction, a Solidarity activist describes this approach as "fighting without violence," p. 13. Examples of individual methods of protests and noncooperation are scattered throughout. See also chapters on professionals' boycotts and noncooperation, independent educational programs and research, the resistance and Solidarity press, protest postage stamps with Solidarity symbolism, distribution of audiotapes as a "sound newspaper," and the like.)

1986. Tymowski, Andrzej, ed. and trans., *Solidarity Under Siege*. 70 pp. New Haven, CT: Advocate Press, 1982. (Brief documents and interviews. See pp. 19–20 for text of martial law decree; pp. 44–63 for Solidarity discussion of resistance, including Kuron's thesis. Photos. Documents.)

1987. [Weiser, Irit], *Poland: Three Years After: A Report on Human Rights in Poland*. 105 pp. New York and Washington: Lawyers Committee for International Human Rights, 1984. (Includes the legal basis for martial law and repressive violence and chapters on limits placed on labor organizing, freedom of expression, academic freedom, and freedom of association.)

1988. Weschler, Lawrence, *The Passion of Poland: From Solidarity Through the State of War*. 281 pp. New York: Pantheon, 1984. (Expansion of entry 1975. See esp. pp. 101–7, 115, 129–30, 152, 158, 176, 195. Photos. Chronology. Documents in appendixes.)

1989. Zalewska, Magda, Henryk Gawinski, and John Taylor, *Solidarity Underground: Free Trade Unionism in Poland Today*. A Polish Solidarity Campaign Special Report. 24 pp. London: Polish Solidarity Campaign, 1983. (Pamphlet on the Solidarity underground and the underground society.)

ROME, ANCIENT

As a literate society, Rome recorded some of the opposition it experienced and its treatment of it, including the acts of Christian martyrs remembered by later generations.

1990. Bainton, Roland H., *Christian Attitudes toward War and Peace: A Historical Survey and Critical Re–evaluation*. 299 pp. Nashville: Abington Press, 1978 [orig. publ. 1960]. (Survey of Christian pacifism, just war beliefs, and the Crusades. See ch. 5 on pacifism of early Christians in Roman Empire and ch. 10 on the historic peace churches. Illustrations. Index.)

1991. Frend, W.H.C., *Martyrdom and Persecution in the Early Church: A Study of a Conflict from the Maccabees to Donatus*. 625 pp. Oxford:

Basil Blackwell, 1965. (Focuses on persecution of Christians in Rome before Constantine. See ch. 1, 3, 7–13 on Christians' refusal to recant their religion under persecution; consult index under *anti–militarism* for early Christian pacifism. Index. Bibliography.)

1992.   Horsley, Richard A., *Jesus and the Spiral of Violence: Popular Jewish Resistance in Roman Palestine.* 355 pp. New York: Harper & Row 1987. (Examines political situation of Jews in Roman Palestine and their resistance. See esp. part 2, "Popular Jewish Nonviolent Resistance," for descriptions of resistance methods (popular protest, refusal to pay tax, etc.) and part 3, "Jesus and Nonviolent Social Revolution" for a critical evaluation of the implications of Jesus' social philosophy, especially regarding violence and nonviolence. Index.)

1993.   Ricciotti, Giuseppe, *The Age of Martyrs: Christianity from Diocletian to Constantine.* Trans. Rev. Anthony Bull. 305 pp. Milwaukee WI: Bruce Publishing, 1959. (A semi–popular account of persecutions. See pp. 63–227.)

1994.   Yuge, Toru, and Masaoki Doi, eds., *Forms of Control and Subordination in Antiquity.* 625 pp. Tokyo: Univ. of Tokyo Press, 1988. Published jointly by the Society for Studies on Resistance Movements in Antiquity [Tokyo, Japan] and E.J. Brill [New York and Leiden, the Netherlands]. (Proceedings of the International Symposium for Studies on Ancient Worlds. Explores ancient social paradigms in order to illuminate current issues. See esp. Evans, "Resistance at Home: The Evasion of Military Service in Italy during the Second Century B.C.," pp. 121–140; Rubinsohn, "Macedonian Resistance to Roman Occupation in the Second Half of the Second Century B.C.," pp. 141–158; and Oh, "The Early Christians' Attitude Toward Military Service," pp. 523–529.)

RUSSIA

Russia, its empire, its successor states, and the neighbors it dominated as satellites have been marked during this century by a series of upheavals, including the two revolutions of 1905 and 1917, the Soviet state and the dissent it both sparked and repressed, and the recreation of a Russian state in the late 1980s. Both revolutions of the early part of the century included a period of nonviolent, or partly nonviolent struggle. Between the Bolshevik revolution and the 1960s lies a period in which little detail of dissent is known, except for the Leninist and Stalinist repressions of any opposition which included the creation of the prison camp system. Dissent reemerged in Russia as political dissidence and as the Jewish "refuseniks" in the 1960s and as religious and nationalist strivings in the states of its Eastern European empire.

Russian Revolution

1995. Carpenter, Kenneth E., ed., *Russian Revolutionary Literature Collection, Houghton Library, Harvard University: A Descriptive Guide and Key to the Collection on Microfilm.* 220 pp. New Haven CT: Research Publications, 1976. (Catalogue of Harvard's collection of Russian revolutionary literature before 1920. Includes books, pamphlets, broadsides, periodicals, and leaflets. Name and title indexes.)

1996. Crisp, Olga, and Linda Edmondson, eds., *Civil Rights in Imperial Russia.* 321 pp. Oxford: Clarendon Press, 1989. (Essays on various aspects of civil rights in nineteenth and early–twentieth century Russia. Of interest are D.C.B. Lieven, "The Security Police, Civil Rights, and the Empire, 1855–1917," pp. 235–62 and Linda Edmondson, "Was There a Movement for Civil Rights in Russia in 1905?", pp. 263–85. Index.)

1997. Edmondson, Linda Harriet, *Feminism in Russia, 1900–17.* 197 pp. London: Heinemann Educational Books, 1984. (On suffrage actions, notably in the period of the revolution of 1905. See ch. 2, 3, esp. pp. 35–36, 47–49, 70–78; and on pacifism in WWI, see pp. 158–62. Index. Bibliography.)

1998. Olgin, Moissaye J., *The Soul of the Russian Revolution.* 423 pp. New York: Henry Holt, 1917. (Impressionistic contemporary study of the "the Russian nation in action." See part 2 on 1905, ch. 33 on the rebirth of collective action in 1901–14, and ch. 35, 36 on the beginnings of the revolution in 1917. Illustrations. Statistical appendixes. Index.)

REVOLUTION OF 1905–1906

Unrest by peasants, workers, and non–Russian nationalities increased at the beginning of the twentieth century, especially during a wave of large strikes in 1903. In 1905, strikes were accompanied by demonstrations and protests, spreading rapidly to contribute to a revolutionary situation. Fostered politically by liberals and Social Democrats who demanded the formation of a legislative assembly (Duma), the revolution gained impetus from Russia's losses in the war against Japan. In early 1905, a large protest procession under the leadership of the priest Father Gapon tried to deliver a petition to the emperor at the palace in St. Petersburg. The marchers were massacred by troops, which led to further distrust and pressure on the emperor. As strikes and protests continued, including mass strikes in July, the emperor agreed to call a Duma. Later in 1905, Bolsheviks organized a general strike in Moscow, which was actually an armed uprising that was soon repressed. Unrest continued through 1906 and although the Duma survived, the imperial government gradually set it aside and regained many of its former powers.

1999.   Ames, Ernest O.F., ed., *The Revolution in the Baltic Provinces of Russia: A Brief Account of the Activity of the Lettish Social Democratic Workers' Party*. 98 pp. London: Independent Labour Party, 1907. (Written anonymously, with focus on Latvian revolutionaries from 1897 to 1906. See ch. 6 for debate on pros and cons of violent uprisings and ch. 8–17 on the 1905 revolution before the outbreak of systematic violence. Photos.)

2000.   Baring, Maurice, *A Year in Russia*. 319 pp. London: Methuen: New York: Dutton, 1907. (Covers August 1905 to August 1906.)

2001.   Baron, Samuel H., *Plekhanov: The Father of Russian Marxism*. 389 pp. Stanford CA: Stanford Univ. Press, 1963. (Ch. 14 surveys and interprets Plekhanov's reaction to 1905. Bibliography.)

2002.   Bing, Edward J., ed., *The Letters of Tsar Nicholas and Empress Marie: Being the Confidential Correspondence Between Nicholas II, Last of the Tsars, and His Mother, Dowager Empress Maria Feodorovna*. 311 pp. London: Ivor Nicholson & Watson, 1937. (See pp. 183–221 for selected letters and explanatory text. Photos. Index.)

2003. Bonnell, Victoria E., *Roots of Rebellion: Workers' Politics and Organizations in St. Petersburg and Moscow, 1900–1914.* 560 pp. Berkeley, Los Angeles, and London: Univ. of California Press, 1983. (Part 2 is on organized labor in the 1905 revolution and part 3 is on labor organizing in following years. See index under *boycotts, demonstrations,* and *strikes and workplace conflicts.* Photos. Index. Bibliography.)

2004. Charques, Richard, *The Twilight of Imperial Russia.* 250 pp. London: Oxford Univ. Press, 1958. (See ch. 6 on 1905; consult index under *strikes* for references to the labor unrest in political movements, 1896–1917. Index. Bibliography.)

2005. Edelman, Robert, *Proletarian Peasants: The Revolution of 1905 in Russia's Southwest.* 195 pp. Ithaca and London: Cornell Univ. Press, 1987. (Examines peasant involvement in the 1905 revolution and dispels myth that peasant revolts were ill-conceived and ineffective. See esp. ch. 3, "A Strike Movement: Demands and Tactics" for conditions which sparked rebellions, esp. pp. 94–99, which give examples of how peasant reactions changed in accordance with worsening conditions. Index.)

2006. Engelstein, Laura, *Moscow, 1905: Working–Class Organization and Political Conflict.* 308 pp. Stanford CA: Stanford Univ. Press, 1982. (See ch. 5 on September strike movement and ch. 6, 7 on October general strike. See also pp. 64–67 on January–February 1905 strikes and protest activity, and pp. 71–72 on student protests in September 1905. Consult index under *strikes* for references arranged by month. Index. Bibliography.)

2007. Futrell, Michael, *Northern Underground: Episodes of Russian Revolutionary Transport and Communications Through Scandinavia and Finland, 1863–1917.* 240 pp. London: Faber & Faber, 1963. (On 1905–06, see pp. 44–84. Ch. 5–7 are on the revolutionary period. Appendix. Biographical Notes.)

2008. Galai, Shmuel, *The Liberation Movement in Russia 1900–1905.* 325 pp. Cambridge: Cambridge Univ. Press, 1973. (History of "zemstvo radicalism" and intelligentsia's role; see pp. 113–15 on the suppression of the Kazan Square demonstration of early

1901 and following pages on the question of violence. Also ch. 6, 7, 9, 10 on pre–1905 agitation and ch. 11, 12 on the Revolution of 1905. Index. Bibliography.)

2009.   Gapon, George, *The Story of My Life*. 261 pp. New York: E.P. Dutton, 1906. (Father Gapon's apologia. Appendix contains text of the St. Petersburg Workmen's petition of January 22, 1905.)

2010.   Gurko, V.I., *Features and Figures of the Past: Government and Opinion in the Reign of Nicholas II*. Trans. Laura Matveev; ed. J. E. Wallace Sterling, Xenia J. Eudin, and H.H. Fisher. 760 pp. Stanford CA: Stanford Univ. Press, 1939. (See esp. ch. 15–21. The author was an assistant minister of the Interior and member of the Russian State Council. Appendix. Index.)

2011.   Harcave, Sidney, *First Blood: The Russian Revolution of 1905*. 316 pp. New York: Macmillan, 1964. (Ch. 3 discusses the Putilov factory strike and Bloody Sunday. Ch. 4–7 follow the phases of the revolution from January to December 1905. See esp. pp. 99–116 on the effects of Bloody Sunday; pp. 152–56 on the strike movement; pp. 168–91 on strikes resulting from government attempts at suppression of the revolution, including the October general strike; and pp. 220–41 on the question of armed uprisings in the last stages. Appendixes. Index. Bibliography.)

2012.   Harper, Samuel N., *The Russia I Believe In: The Memoirs of Samuel N. Harper, 1902–1941*. 279 pp. Chicago: Univ. of Chicago Press, 1945. (Selections from Harper's letters, contemporary notes, and diary from St. Petersburg and Vyborg, pp. 26–51.)

2013.   Healy, Ann Erickson, *The Russian Autocracy in Crisis, 1905–1907*. 314 pp. Hamden CT: Archon Books, 1981. (Surveys demonstrations and strikes, failure of second general strike, and nonviolent response to dissolution of the Duma. See ch. 2, 3, 11. Index. Bibliography.)

2014.   Hough, Richard, *The Potemkin Mutiny*. 190 pp. New York: Pantheon Books, 1961. (Popular account of *Potemkin* mutiny and its role in the Revolution of 1905 along the Black Sea coast. See pp. 48–55 on strikes and the beginnings of street fighting in Odessa. Photos.)

2015. Kaplan, Simon, *Once a Rebel*. 311 pp. New York and Toronto: Farrar & Rinehart, 1941. (Special attention to condition and plight of Jews. See esp. pp. 197–214 on October strike.)

2016. Keep, John L.H., *The Rise of Social Democracy in Russia*. 334 pp. London, New York, and Bombay: Oxford Univ. Press, 1963. 334 pp. (Focuses on the role played by the Social Democratic Party. See ch. 5, 7 on January 1904 to December 1905. Bibliography.)

2017. King, David, and Kathy Porter, *Images of Revolution: Graphic Art from 1905 Russia*. 128 pp. New York: Pantheon Books, 1983. (Graphics of protest, denunciation, and opposition from periodicals of the 1905 revolution, with introduction and photos. Bibliography.)

2018. Luxemburg, Rosa, *The Mass Strike, the Political Party and the Trade Unions*. Trans. Patrick Lavin. 227 pp. New York: Harper Torchbooks, 1971. (Essay written in 1906 which explores the role that the general strike played in the 1905 revolution. Analyzes various tactical issues involved; e.g., the role of leadership and the importance of mass participation. Also contains "The Junius Pamphlet: The Crisis in German Social Democracy," a 1915 essay that laments the destruction unleashed by WWI and its effects on the party.)

2019. McClelland, James C., *Autocrats and Academics: Education, Culture, and Society in Tsarist Russia*. 150 pp. Chicago and London: Univ. of Chicago Press, 1979. (Ch. 5 examines student activism in the 1905 revolution. Index. Bibliography.)

2020. Miliukov, Pavel Nikolaevich, *Russia and Its Crisis*. 589 pp. Chicago: Univ. of Chicago Press, 1906. (Expansion of lectures held in 1903, important for cultural, economic, and political background and comments on the beginning of the Revolution of 1905. See ch. 7. Index.)

2021. Nevinson, Henry W., *The Dawn in Russia; or, Scenes in the Russian Revolution*. 2nd ed. 371 pp. London and New York: Harper & Brothers, 1906. Reprint, New York: Arno Press and The New York Times, 1971. (British journalist's account of events of 1905 revolution. References to general strike throughout. See esp. pp. 77–80 for plan to close out bank accounts in order to cripple the state. Ch. 9, "The Days of Moscow—I," describes the immediate effects of the strike. Passive resistance and noncooperation efforts in honor of the Bloody Sunday martyrs are described on pp. 229–230. Appendix contains texts of Duma declarations, including a plea to the public to refuse to pay soldiers and a decree that the government betrayed the consent of the people and was therefore illegitimate. Illustrations. Photos. Appendix. Index.)

2022. Oldenburg, S.S., *Last Tsar: Nicholas II, His Reign & His Russia*. Vol. 2. *The Years of Change: 1900–1907*. Trans. Leonid I. Mihalap and Patrick J. Rollins; ed., Patrick J. Rollins. 239 pp. Gulf Breeze FL: Academic International Press, 1977. (See pp. 154–73 on strikes and other actions that caused the Czar to create the national Duma. Illustrations. Photos. Documents. Index and Bibliography in vol. 4.)

2023. Robinson, Geroid Tanquary, *Rural Russia under the Old Regime: A History of the Landlord–Peasant World and a Prologue to the Peasant Revolution of 1917*. 342 pp. New York: Macmillan, 1932. (Ch. 9, 10 contain material on role of peasants in 1905 revolution. Appendix. Index. Bibliography.)

2024. Sablinsky, Walter, *The Road to Bloody Sunday: Father Gapon and the St. Petersburg Massacre of 1905*. 414 pp. Princeton NJ: Princeton Univ. Press, 1976. (See ch. 6 on the strikes of early 1905 and origin of procession to the emperor; pp. 185–92 on the petition; and ch. 8, 9 on Bloody Sunday. Text of petition in appendix 2. Index. Bibliography.)

2025. Schapiro, Leonard, *The Communist Party of the Soviet Union*. 686 pp. New York: Random House; London: Eyre & Spottiswoode, (2d ed.) 1970. (See ch. 3, esp. pp. 64–70, on Bolsheviks and the 1905 revolution and ch. 9, esp. pp. 161–169,

on Bolshevik organizational activities to the aftermath of the
July demonstrations. Photos. Index. Appendixes.)

2026. Schneiderman, Jeremiah, *Sergei Zubatov and Revolutionary
Marxism: The Struggle for the Working Class in Tsarist Russia*. 401
pp. Ithaca NY: Cornell Univ. Press, 1976 [orig. publ. 1970].
(Chronicles the Czarist government's attempts to secure the
political loyalty of Russian workers in the period immediately
preceding the Revolution of 1905. See esp. ch. 12–13 for
detailed analysis of the Odessa general strike of 1903 and its
political effects. Photos. Index. Bibliography.)

2027. Schwarz, Solomon M., *The Russian Revolution of 1905: The
Workers' Movement and the Formation of Bolshevism and
Menshevism*. Trans. Gertrude Vakar. 361 pp. Chicago and
London: Univ. of Chicago Press, 1967. (Focuses primarily on
Social Democratic activities and politics during the revolution.
Appendix. Index.)

2028. Seton–Watson, Hugh, *The Decline of Imperial Russia, 1855–1914*.
406 pp. New York: Praeger; London: Methuen, 1952. (Ch. 7,
"The Days of Liberty," covers events from the Baku strike and
Bloody Sunday to the dissolution of the Duma in 1907. Index.
Bibliography.)

2029. Trotsky, Leon, *1905*. Trans. Anya Bostock. 488 pp. New York:
Random House, 1971. (Written from 1908 to 1909, with a focus
on then–recent events of Oct.–Dec. 1905. References to strikes
and consolidation of a national workers' movement
throughout. See esp. ch. 6, "January 9th," and ch. 7, "The Strike
in October," for accounts of Bloody Sunday [depicting Gapon
as a "political and moral nonentity"] and the wave of strikes
which followed and eventually culminated in the Petersburg
Soviet. Index.)

2030. Urussov, Prince Serge Dmitriyevich, *Memoirs of a Russian
Governor*. Trans. and ed. Herman Rosenthal. 181 pp. London
and New York: Harper, 1908. (Contains 1903–04 background.)

2031. Wolfe, Bertram D., *Three Who Made a Revolution: A Biographical
History*. 4th ed. 659 pp. New York: Dial Press, 1964. (Ch. 16,

"Police Socialism," is on the coming of the Revolution of 1905, esp. pp. 281–86. Ch. 17, 18 are on exile politics and the 1905 revolution; also pp. 318–31 are on the general strike of October 1905 and its aftermath. Photos. Index.)

REVOLUTION OF 1917, FEBRUARY–JULY

The Russian Revolution of 1917 began with strikes and factory occupations in both Moscow and St. Petersburg in February and March. These led to political instability, especially because of the country's privations and losses in World War I, and eventually to the capitulation of the emperor. In the confused period that followed, parties agreed only with difficulty on continuing mass action, although the streets, cities, and countryside were turbulent with protest and discussion. Disagreements among the parties led to the near–collapse of a great anti–war protest planned for June 1917 in St. Petersburg, while workers concentrated largely on wage and factory–management issues. The Bolsheviks exploited these divisions to take power in their coup d'état of October 1917.

2032.   Chamberlin, William H., *The Russian Revolution, 1917–1921*. Vol. 1, 511 pp. New York: Macmillan, 1965 [orig. publ. 1935]. (Ch. 4–17 survey events from the February Revolution to the start of the Civil War after the Bolshevik *coup d'etat*. See esp. ch. 9 on the defeat of the attempted *coup d'etat* by General Kornilov. Photos. Appendix. Index and bibliography in vol. 2.)

2033.   Hasegawa, Tsuyoshi, *The February Revolution: Petrograd, 1917*. 652 pp. Seattle and London: Univ. of Washington Press, 1981. (Study of the labor revolt in Petrograd that escalated into the Revolution of 1917. See esp. part 3 for a detailed description of the sequence of events, beginning with the International Women's Day demonstration. Conclusion includes a shortened synopsis of events. Illustrations. Photos. Appendixes. Index. Bibliography.)

2034.   Katkov, George, *Russia, 1917: The February Revolution*. 489 pp. New York: Harper & Row; London: Longmans, 1967. (Argument based largely on role of German interests in revolutionary unrest. See pp. 88–95 on Petrograd strikes of February 1916 and ch. 10, esp. pp. 248–71, on strikes, demonstrations, and the beginnings of armed clashes between strikers and police in that city a year later. Photos. Glossary. Appendix. Index. Bibliography.)

2035. Keep, John L.H., *The Russian Revolution: A Study in Mass Mobilization.* 614 pp. New York: W.W. Norton, 1976. (See pp. 59–63 on February 1917 industrial strikes and ch. 14 on peasants' "passive resistance" to requisitions. Glossaries. Chronology. Index. Bibliography.)

2036. Koenker, Diane, *Moscow Workers and the 1917 Revolution.* 420 pp. Princeton NJ: Princeton Univ. Press, 1981. (Historical exploration of role of Moscow workers in the 1917 revolution. See esp. ch. 8 on strikes of March–October 1917, and index under *strikes.* Index. Bibliography.)

2037. Robinowich, Alexander, *Prelude to Revolution: The Petrograd Bolsheviks and the July 1917 Uprising.* 299 pp. Bloomington IN and London: Indiana Univ. Press, 1968. (See ch. 3 on inability of competing groups to agree on anti–war demonstration for 10 June 1917, and pp. 97–106 on demonstration of 18 June; photo facing p. 104. Photos. Index.)

2038. Smith, S.A., *Red Petrograd: Revolution in the Factories, 1917–1918.* 347 pp. Cambridge: Cambridge Univ. Press, 1983. (Study of impact of revolution on factory life in Petrograd in 1917–18 and workers' struggle for control of factories. See pp. 48–53 on strike activity during WWI, ch. 3 on eight–hour day and wage disputes, pp. 171–74 on workers' refusal to evacuate factories, and pp. 190–200 on "social composition of labour protest and labour organization." See also index under *strikes.* Index. Bibliography.)

2039. Trotsky, Leon, *The History of the Russian Revolution.* Trans. Max Eastman. 3 vols. Vol. 1, *The Overthrow of Czarism.* Vol. 2, *The Attempted Counter–Revolution.* Vol. 3, *The Triumph of the Soviets.* 1295 pp. London: Victor Gollancz, 1934. Reprint, Ann Arbor MI: Univ. of Michigan Press, 1957; London: Gollancz, 1965. (In vol. 1, ch. 7–9 describe the February 1917 revolution, ch. 11 is on the history of the idea of "dual power," and ch. 22 offers a view of the June 18, 1917 demonstration. In vol. 2, ch. 9, 10 discuss the Kornilov coup, including pp. 744–48 on the effects of noncooperation in confusing the anti–revolutionary forces. Glossary. Chronology. Appendixes. Index.)

Political Opposition and Prison Camp Strikes

The system of prison and labor camps, established in the 1920s and 1930s, received many new inmates during and after World War II. Foreign Communists and refugees, prisoners of war, and many genuine or suspected opponents of Stalin were included. Although little is known about them, it is evident that labor strikes and uprisings occurred in several camps, particularly at Vorkuta in 1953.

2040.   Barton, Paul, "The Strike Mechanism in Soviet Concentration Camps." *International Commission against Concentration Camp Practices Monthly Information Bulletin* 4 (1955): 19–27. (Journal later titled *Saturn Monthly Review*. Brief review of strikes in Soviet penal camps, 1935–53, including mention of 1936 hunger strike at the Vorkuta camp.)

2041.   "The Ninety–Six Day Strike in the Norilsk Camps." *International Commission against Concentration Camp Practices Monthly Information Bulletin* 4 (1955): 28–35. (Journal later titled *Saturn Monthly Review*. Very brief abstract of information on strike [1953?] at Norilsk camp complex, as reported by Japanese prisoners.)

2042.   Schapiro, Leonard, *The Origin of the Communist Autocracy: Political Opposition in the Soviet State, First Phase, 1917–1922*. 2d. ed. 397 pp. Cambridge: Harvard Univ. Press, 1977 [orig. publ. 1954]. (A study of Leninist consolidation and the removal of opposition inside and outside the Communist Party. See part 2 on Social Revolutionaries, left–wing Bolsheviks, and Mensheviks in the very first years of the revolution and part 3 on Lenin's destruction of internal opposition in the early 1920s. Appendixes. Index. Bibliography.)

2043.   Scholmer, Joseph, "The Transformation of the Soviet Concentrationary System." *Saturn Monthly Review* 2 (1956): 32–45. (See esp. pp. 39–44 on the "great strikes.")

2044.   ———,*Vorkuta*. 204 pp. London: Weidenfeld & Nicholson,
1954. New York: Holt, Rinehart & Winston, 1955. (Memoir of
Vorkuta by a German held there; see ch. 11 on the Vorkuta
strike, including thoughts on reasons for repression not being
total, p. 235.)

Political Dissent, 1960 to 1980s

*Soviet "dissent" from 1960 until Gorbachev's time was not a single
phenomenon. Perhaps because conditions under Nikita Khruschev permitted
some opportunity to speak out, groups began to express their dissent. They
were variously composed of intellectuals, Jews wanting to emigrate to Israel,
Christians dissenting against suppression of the churches, and others. Their
methods of protest, communication, and organization varied. Some Jews, for
example, became the "Refuseniks"—those "refused" the right of emigration
and punished for having applied for it. Intellectual and religious dissenters
became experts on samizdat (underground publication of their writings) and
similar methods. Dissent was also expressed in song and its dissemination on
underground tapes, leafletting and demonstrations, hunger strikes, and
simply in noncooperation. The state used a variety of methods to suppress and
punish. In addition to imprisonment, it resorted to holding dissidents in
psychiatric hospitals where they were subjected to drug injections and, as in
the case of the outstanding physicist Andrei Sakharov and his spouse Elena
Bonner, exile to cities far from their homes. The entries below include dissent
in Ukraine. The Baltic states of Lithuania and Latvia are listed above,
although of course they shared many issues with Russia proper.*

2045.   *A Chronicle of Current Events*. London: Amnesty International,
February 1971 to 1983. (Journal of the Soviet civil rights
movement. Text translated from Russian original. Nos. 22, 23,
27 also contain bibliography of English–language sources.
Photos. Index.)

2046.   *A Chronicle of Human Rights in the U.S.S.R.*, nos. 1–48. New
York: Khronika Press, November 1972 to April 1983. (Source of
information from Soviet dissident sources on political actions,
prisoners, psychiatric treatment, and protests from within and
outside the U.S.S.R. Relies in part on *A Chronicle of Current
Events*.)

2047. Cohen, Stephen F., ed., *An End to Silence: Uncensored Opinion in the Soviet Union from Roy Medvedev's Underground Magazine Political Diary.* 375 pp. New York, London: W.W. Norton, 1982. (Articles from *samizdat Political Diary* [1964–71]. See preface on history of magazine and Roy Medvedev and pp. 17–21 on its genesis. Ch. 3 compiles condemnations of "Neo-Stalinism" and ch. 4 is on "Currents of Soviet Opinion and Dissent." Documents. Index.)

2048. Medvedev, Roy A., ed., *The Samizdat Register.* 314 pp. Trans. Brian Pearce, Tamara Deutscher, Ellen Wood, Vera Magyar. New York: W.W. Norton; Toronto: George G. McLeod, 1977. (Essays from the *samizdat* journal *XX Century*, mostly commenting on the early history of the U.S.S.R. and its failures.)

2049. ———, ed., *The Samizdat Register II.* 323 pp. London: Merlin Press, 1981. (See previous entry. In addition to pieces on Stalinism, democracy, and Zinoviev and Kamenev, see reviews by Medvedev of Andre Sakharov's *My Country and the World* and the third volume of Alexander Solzhenitsyn's *The Gulag Archipelago*.)

2050. Reddaway, Peter, ed., *Uncensored Russia: The Human Rights Movement in the Soviet Union.* Trans. Peter Reddaway. 499 pp. London: Jonathan Cape, 1972. (Translation of the *samizdat* journal *Chronicle of Current Events* [April 1968–December 1969] into sections reorganized by subject. In the introduction, see pp. 17–24 on origins of *samizdat* and the "democratic movement." In addition to description of certain trials and the fate of individuals such as Grigorenko and Marchenko, see part 4 on the protests and treatment of nationalities and religious groups and part 6 on activities outside Moscow. Of particular interest are the many references to prison–camp hunger strikes and to December 5 demonstrations in Red Square; also pp. 95–126 on Red Square demonstrations in support of Czechoslovakia; and pp. 249–69 on demonstrations, hunger strikes, and resettlement efforts by Crimean Tartars. Photos. Index of names only.)

2051. Reve, Karl Van Het, ed., *Dear Comrade: Pavel Litvinov and the Voices of Soviet Citizens in Dissent*. 199 pp. New York, London, Toronto, and Tel Aviv: Pitman Publishing, 1969. (Parallel Russian and English texts of several documents. Includes two documents by Pavel Litvinov, who took part in efforts to protest the treatment of Alexander Ginsburg, Andrei Sinyavski, and Yuli Daniel. Also included, without table of contents or index, are the texts of various communications to Litvinov by other dissidents, who are left unnamed. Document 1 is a transcript from memory of Litvinov's interrogation by the KGB in 1967. Document 18 is a protest co–signed by Litvinov and Daniel's wife, Larisa Bogoraz. See editor's introduction and notes for background and explanations.)

2052. de Boer, S.P., E.J. Driessen, and H.L. Verhaar, eds., *Biographical Dictionary of Dissidents in the Soviet Union, 1956–1975*. 697 pp. The Hague, Boston, and London: Martinus Nijhoff, 1982. (Biographies of "unofficial, oppositionist Soviet Citizens," which includes "dissident activity" for each entry.)

2053. Liber, George, and Anna Mostovych, comp., *Nonconformity and Dissent in the Ukrainian SSR, 1955–1975: An Annotated Bibliography*. 245 pp. Cambridge MA: Harvard Ukrainian Research Institute, Harvard Univ., 1978. (Divided into two sections, one of primary and Soviet secondary sources catalogued alphabetically by subjects, most of which are the names of persons and groups, and one of selected secondary sources. The first section contains English–language notes on the content of each entry, while the second contains many entries in English. List of sources consulted, pp. xxxi–xxxix. Appendix. Index.)

2054. Woll, Josephine, in collaboration with Vladimir G. Treml, *Soviet Dissident Literature: A Critical Guide*. 289 pp. Boston: G.K. Hall, 1983. (Selective bibliography of *samizdat* material published abroad with some annotations. See introductory essay, esp. pp. xiv–xix on "dissent and *samizdat*." Index.)

STUDIES

2055.   Alexeyeva, Ludmilla, *Soviet Dissent: Contemporary Movements for National, Religious, and Human Rights.* 543 pp. Middletown CT: Wesleyan Univ. Press, 1985. Originally published in Russian as *History of Dissent in the U.S.S.R.* New York: Khronika, 1984. (Compendium of information and analysis of social and political dissent in U.S.S.R. since the "first open protest" of Tartar nationalism in early 1960s, written by well-informed member of the human rights movement. Divides dissent into nationalist, religious, emigration, and economic rights streams. Especially strong are ch. 10 on the Jewish movement, and ch. 16 on *samizdat* communication and suppression. Illustrations. Photos. Index.)

2056.   Amalrik, Andrei, *Notes of a Revolutionary.* 360 pp. New York: Alfred A. Knopf, 1982. (Memoirs of dissident writer of *Will the Soviet Union Survive until 1984?* See ch. 3–9 on participation in a petition drive, pp. 23–27; its aftermath for him, and his hunger strikes, pp. 235–37, 249–58. Illustrations.)

2057.   Azbel, Mark Iakovlevich, *Refusenik: Trapped in the Soviet Union.* 526 pp. Boston: Houghton Mifflin, 1981. (Autobiography of physicist denied permission to emigrate from U.S.S.R. Contains discussion of Soviet dissent and trials, pp. 191–204, 213–19, 243–45; extralegal conferences on science and Jewish culture, e.g., pp. 331–44, 431–51, 469–71; and refusenik hunger strike of 1973, pp. 301–15. Photos. Index.)

2058.   Babyonyshev, Alexander, *On Sakharov.* Trans. Guy Daniels. 312 pp. New York: Alfred A. Knopf, 1982. (Some of Sakharov's writings are reprinted in part 3. See also personal statements of fellow–dissidents, esp. those by Maria Petrenko–Podyapolskaya, Larisa Bogoraz, Anatoly Marchenko, and Maksudov, "What Do You Think of Sakharov?: The Results of a Selective Survey," pp. 111–18. Documents.)

2059.   Bloch, Sidney, and Peter Reddaway, *Psychiatric Terror: How Soviet Psychiatry Is Used to Suppress Dissent.* 510 pp. New York: Basic Books, 1977. (Detailed study of use of psychiatric methods in suppression of dissent. See Tarsis case, pp. 65–73;

Grigorenko case, pp. 102–20; Goranevskaya case, pp. 127–47, ch. 6, 9; and discussion of international opposition in ch. 10. Appendixes include Vladimir Bukovsky and Semyon Guzman, "Manual on Psychiatry for Dissenters," pp. 419–440, *samizdat* which offers advice on use of psychiatry in cases of dissent and "practical recommendations on tactics." Photos. Index.)

2060. Bonavia, David, *Fat Sasha and the Urban Guerrilla: Protest and Conformism in the Soviet Union*. 193 pp. New York: Atheneum, 1973. (Journalistic, somewhat impressionistic, account of dissent and conformism in U.S.S.R., 1969–72. See "The Direct Approach," pp. 10–24, on dissenters; "Pavel," pp. 25–37, on individual dissenter; "Samizdat," pp. 74–84; and "Jews," pp. 100–118, on Jewish dissidents.)

2061. Bourdeaux, Michael, *Faith on Trial in Russia*. 192 pp. London: Hodder & Stoughton, 1971. (Ch. 2 describes a demonstration and delegation by Baptists in May 1966; ch. 4–6 discuss Baptist leaders and their trials and imprisonment, focusing on Georgi Vins. Further Readings.)

2062. ———, *Religious Ferment in Russia: Protestant Opposition to Soviet Religious Policy*. 266 pp. London, Melbourne, and Toronto: Macmillan; New York: St. Martin's Press, 1968. (Study of Baptists and evangelical Christians; see 1963 American embassy petitions, pp. 16–19; and many instances of Baptist demonstrations, illegal baptism and prayer groups, and illegal leaflets. Appendix 2 contains data on religious prisoners. Index.)

2063. Browne, Michael, ed., *Ferment in the Ukraine: Documents by V. Chornovil, I. Kandyba, L. Lukyanenko, V. Moroz, and Others*. 285 pp. London and Basingstoke: Macmillan, 1971. (Introduction, pp. 1–28, contains history of Ukrainian dissent. See written protests and statements in parts 2–5. Index. Bibliography.)

2064. Brumberg, Abraham, ed., *In Quest of Justice: Protest and Dissent in the Soviet Union Today*. 491 pp. New York, Washington, and London: Praeger, 1970. (Mostly documents, including political analysis, appeals, and protests; but see also Abraham Brumberg, "The Rise of Dissent in the U.S.S.R.," pp. 3–14; and

Stephen M. Weiner, "Socialist Legality on Trial," pp. 39–51, including pp. 40–42 on protest of perceived injustice in trials.)

2065.   Bykovsky, Vladimir, *To Build a Castle: My Life as a Dissenter*. Trans. Michael Scammell. 438 pp. New York: Viking Press, 1979. (Memoir of prison and political life. See pp. 30–31, 34–42 on prison noncooperation, hunger strikes, and mass complaints; pp. 74–75 on social view of protest; pp. 145–56, 161 on 1961 Mayakovsky Square poetry readings; pp. 249–50 for arrest for leafletting for 1965 Pushkin Square demonstration; pp. 277–81 on 1967 demonstration; pp. 302–5 on trials of 1967. Also much information on psychiatric treatment and imprisonment as response to dissent.)

2066.   Chalidze, Valery, *The Soviet Human Rights Movement: A Memoir*. 62 pp. New York: The Jacob Blaustein Institute for the Advancement of Human Rights, 1984. (Memoir by well-known Soviet dissident, co–founder of Soviet Human Rights Committee. See pp. 19–26 for his assessment of group and its achievements. Documents in Appendix 1.)

2067.   Cohen, Richard, *Let My People Go! Today's Documentary Story of Soviet Jewry's Struggle to Be Free*. 286 pp. New York: Popular Library, 1971. (Reports and documents on Jewish dissent in late 1960s and early 1970s, including events surrounding the Brussels Conference of February 1971. See pp. 13–23 on the Simchat Torah demonstrations and pp. 229–34 on the Moscow Presidium sit–in and hunger strike in 1971. Illustrations. Photos. Documents.)

2068.   Connor, Walter D., *Socialism's Dilemmas: State and Society in the Soviet Bloc*. 299 pp. New York: Columbia Univ. Press, 1988. (See essays on the relationship between Soviet dissent and modernization in ch. 2, workers and intellectuals in ch. 8, "Workers and Power," ch. 9 which includes a discussion of "action direct and indirect," and thoughts on intellectual trends in Eastern European dissentin ch. 11.)

2069.   Etkind, Efim, *Notes of a Non–Conspirator*. Trans. Peter France. 265 pp. Oxford, London, and New York: Oxford Univ. Press, 1978. (Memoir of a literary and cultural dissenter who, among other offenses, was accused of hiding a manuscript of Alexander Solzhenitsyn's *The Gulag Archipelago*. Appendixes.)

2070.	Feldbrugge, F.J.M., *Samizdat and Political Dissent in the Soviet Union*. 267 pp. Leyden, the Netherlands: A.W. Sijthoff, 1975. (In addition to studying political positions connected with practitioners of *samizdat* political journalism, author addresses the beginnings of *samizdat*, ch. 1; its role as political opposition, ch. 2; and official repression, ch. 6. Index.)

2071.	Gerstenmaier, Cornelia, *The Voices of the Silent*. Trans. Susan Hecker. 587 pp. New York: Hart, 1972. (Documents in pp. 309–545 include appeals, open letters, and descriptions of events. Index.)

2072.	Gilbert, Martin, *The Jews of Hope*. 247 pp. London and Basingstoke: Macmillan, 1984. (Journalistic account of the "refuseniks," Jewish dissenters refused the right to emigrate. Profiles of individuals and their experiences in several chapters; discussion of protest letters, hunger strikes, illegal teaching of Hebrew, pamphlets, illegal meetings, etc. throughout. Photos. Index.)

2073.	Gorbanevskaya, Natalia, *Red Square at Noon*. Trans. Alexander Lieven. 285 pp. London: André Deutsch, 1972. (Account by participant of arrest, trial, and sentencing of those involved in 25 August 1968 demonstration in Red Square against the Soviet invasion of Czechoslovakia.)

2074.	Hopkins, Mark, *Russia's Underground Press: "The Chronicle of Current Events."* 223 pp. New York: Praeger, 1983. (Journalist's account of "The Chronicle of Current Events," Soviet underground bulletin of the human rights movement. Appendix A: Chronology. Appendix B: "Chronicle" contents. Index. Bibliography.)

2075.	*Human Rights in the Soviet Un. n*, Joint Committee on Foreign Affairs and Defence, Parliament of the Commonwealth of Australia. 232 pp. Canberra, Australia: Australian Government Publishing Service, 1979. (Report of findings on human rights in U.S.S.R., detailing repression of minorities and dissent movement. See esp. pp. 87–97 on Jewish refuseniks, ch. 8 on right to protest and dissident movement and repression, and ch. 10 on Western support of Soviet human rights movement. Illustrations.)

2076.   Klose, Kevin, *Russia and the Russians: Inside the Closed Society.* 350 pp. New York and London: W.W. Norton, 1984. (Journalist's account of lives of several Soviet dissidents, primarily the family of Andrei Sakharov and Elena Bonner, and of Alexei Nikitin and Anatoli Koryagin. See ch. 11 on Sakharov and Bonner's "political fasting." Index. Bibliography.)

2077.   Litvinov, Pavel, *The Demonstration in Pushkin Square.* 128 pp. Boston: Gambit, 1969. (Documents of trials following brief demonstration in 1967, with descriptions of event and motivations in trial testimony throughout.)

2078.   Marchenko, Anatoly, *From Tarusa to Siberia.* 139 pp. Royal Oak MI: Strathcona, 1980. (Memoir of a non–political arrestee and his prison journey to dissidence and a prison–camp hunger strike. Photos. Documents.)

2079.   Medvedev, Roy A., *On Soviet Dissent: Interviews with Piero Ostellino.* Trans. William A. Parker and George Saunders. 158 pp. New York: Columbia Univ. Press, 1980. Originally published in Italian as *Intervista sul dissenso in URSS.* Rome: Giuseppe Laterza & Figli, 1977. (More on the conditions rather than the methods of dissidence; See esp. ch. 1–3, 10 and brief discussion of role of public opinion in U.S.S.R.; p. 145, in connection with U.S. boycott of Olympic games. Documents. Index.)

2080.   Ploss, Sidney I., *Moscow and the Polish Crisis: An Interpretation of Soviet Policies and Intentions.* 182 pp. Boulder CO and London: Westview Press, 1986. (A study based on the formal analysis of Soviet "propaganda" of various sorts and its nuances, designed to detect Soviet leaders' intentions during the Polish events of 1980–81. Contains evidence that an invasion of Poland was unlikely and that the "rollback" of Solidarity's gains with later encouragement of a declaration of martial law was the chief policy. Chronology in appendix. Index.)

2081. Plyushch, Leonid with a contribution by Tatyana Plyushch, *History's Carnival: A Dissident's Autobiography*. Trans. Marco Carynnyk. 446 pp. New York and London: Harcourt Brace Jovanovich, 1979. First published by Editions du Seuil, 1977. (On Ukrainian dissidence and repression, see ch. 10, and sections 3 and 4, including discussion of psychiatric hospitalization in ch. 19, 20. Index.)

2082. Podrabinek, Alexander, *Punitive Medicine*. Trans. Alexander Lehrman. 236 pp. Ann Arbor: Karona Publishers, 1980. (In addition to scattered references to treatment of dissident political prisoners, there is a mention, pp. 40, 45, of Western psychiatrists boycotting Soviet counterparts. Contains "white list" of prisoners, ch. 11, and "black list" of physicians and others. Photos.)

2083. Rainbolt, William R., *The History of Underground Communication in Russia since the Seventeenth Century*. 95 pp. Palo Alto CA: R. & E. Research Associates, 1979. (Historical study of the communication of dissident thought representative of *raskol*, or the chasm between the government and the governed. See ch. 5, 6 on *samizdat*. Bibliography.)

2084. Rass, Rebecca, with the collaboration of Morris Brafman, *From Moscow to Jerusalem: The Dramatic Story of the Jewish Liberation Movement and Its Impact on Israel*. 256 pp. New York: Shengold Publishers, 1976. (Chronological journalistic account of the growth of the Jewish movement of 1967–75 and its effect on Israeli involvement in the emigration issue.)

2085. Rigby, T.H., Archie Brown, and Peter Reddaway, *Authority, Power and Policy in the USSR: Essays Dedicated to Leonard Shapiro*. 207 pp. London and Basingstoke: Macmillan, 1980. (See Peter Reddaway, "Policy towards Dissent since Khruschev," pp. 155–92 which reviews the various areas of dissent in the Soviet Union, policy making, and policy change. Index.)

2086.   Rothberg, Abraham, *The Heirs of Stalin: Dissidence and the Soviet Regime.* 448 pp. Ithaca NY and London: Cornell Univ. Press, 1972. (Dissent beginning in the de–Stalinization period is divided into artistic, political, and scientific strands, with details of ideas, organizations, and repression. The first of these, discussed in part 2, includes the cases of Joseph Brodsky, Andre Sinyavsky, Yuli Daniel, and Alexander Solzhenitsyn [also the topic of several other sections]. The second, in part 3, includes protest against the invasion of Czechoslovakia and the cases of Anatoly Kuznetsov and Andre Amalrik, as well as discussion of psychiatric methods of repression. Zhores Medvedev and Andre Sakharov are discussed in part 4. Index. Bibliography.)

2087.   Rubenstein, Joshua, *Soviet Dissidents: Their Struggle for Human Rights.* 319 pp. Boston: Beacon Press, 1980. (Historical look at dissent and noncooperation, dissenters, and the Soviet state's response from the late 1950s. Thorough coverage of personalities and their fate. Index. Bibliography.)

2088.   Sakharov, Andrei, *Memoirs.* 773 pp. Trans. Richard Lourie. London, Sydney, Auckland, and Johannesburg: Hutchinson, 1990. (Autobiography to 1986 and Sakharov's release from exile in Gorky, with section 2 being generally concerned with his political activities and punishments. On Sakharov's hunger strikes, see pp. 411–13, 468–87, 557–75, 599–603. On his exile to Gorky, see pp. 510–618. Consult index under headings including *Chronicle of Current Events, Czechoslovakia, dissident, dissident movement, dissidents, Helsinki Groups, human rights, Human Rights Committee, human rights movement, KGB, political prisoners, press, psychiatric hospitals, Pushkin Square demonstrations* and the names of Soviet leaders, dissident figures, and publications. Appendixes include protests and, in appendix C, statements on Sakharov's 1984 hunger strike. Glossary of names. Index. Bibliography.)

2089.   ———, *Sakharov Speaks.* Ed. Harrison E. Salisbury. 251 pp. London: Collins & Harvill Press, 1974. (Collection of Sakharov's writings, including famous essay "Progress, Coexistence, and Intellectual Freedom," pp. 55–114.)

2090. Saunders, George, ed., *Samizdat: Voices of the Soviet Opposition*. 464 pp. New York: Monad Press, 1974. (Original texts and documents on and from Soviet dissent, apparently dating from as early as 1957. See editor's introduction, "Currents in the Soviet Opposition," pp. 15–44 and section prefaces on periods and themes of dissent. Of particular interest are Brigitte Gerland, "Vorkuta [1950–53]: Oppositional Currents and the Mine Strikes," pp. 217–34 and "Debate on Tactics" in the form of several related pieces from *Chronicle of Current Events*, 1970–71, pp. 445–53. Photos. Appendix. Index.)

2091. Schapiro, Leonard, ed., *Political Opposition in One–Party States*. 289 pp. London and Basingstoke: Macmillan, 1972. (Articles from the journal *Government and Opposition*, ca. 1967–1972, mostly on the Soviet sphere. David E. Powell, "Controlling Dissent in the Soviet Union," pp. 201–16 discusses the legal and political sanctions used to punish dissent in the U.S.S.R. as of the early 1970s. Index.)

2092. Schatz, Marshall S., *Soviet Dissent in Historical Perspective*. 214 pp. Cambridge: Cambridge Univ. Press, 1980. (Presents Soviet dissent as the continuation of pre–revolutionary traditions among the intelligentsia. In addition to ch. 2–4 on the intelligentsia and its themes, see ch. 5 on Khruschev's attack on Stalin and literary dissent, ch. 6 on the Sinyavsky–Daniel trial, and ch. 7, 8 on dissidents and their ideas. Index. Bibliography.)

2093. Schroter, Leonard, *The Last Exodus*. 432 pp. New York: Universe Books, 1974. (Study of the Jewish resistance in the Soviet Union. Describes nonviolent action used against repression and for permission to emigrate. See esp. ch. 21, "Tactics of Confrontation," for examples of resistance methods. Appendix. Index.)

2094. Sharlett, Robert, "Dissent and Repression in the Soviet Union and Eastern Europe: Changing Patterns since Khruschev." *International Journal* 33 (1978): 763–95. (Journal issue entitled *Prague 1968: The Aftermath*. This article reviews the "dialectic" of dissent and repression in the U.S.S.R., Czechoslovakia, and Poland, adopting the view that "dissent cannot be divorced from its constant companion—repression." See pp. 765–71 on several forms of repression, pp. 771–75 on dissent, and the following pages on changes in policies of repression during the Brezhnev era.)

2095.   Shatz, Marshall S., *Soviet Dissent in Historical Perspective*. 224 pp. Cambridge: Cambridge Univ. Press, 1980. (See ch. 6 on the Sinyavsky–Daniel trial, incl. mention of a Red Square demonstration, pp. 126–128, and ch. 7. Index. Bibliography.)

2096.   Shindler, Colin, *Exit Visa: Detente, Human Rights and the Jewish Emigration Movement in the U.S.S.R.*. 310 pp. London: Bachman & Turner, 1978. (History of Jewish emigration movement in context of great–power relationships. See preface and ch. 1 on early phases of movement, ch. 5–7 on later phases. Consult index under *demonstrations, Hebrew language, hunger strikes, sit-ins*, and topics related to trials and repression. Lengthy quotations from documents in text. Photos. Index. Bibliography.)

2097.   Shtromas, Alexander, *Political Change and Social Development: The Case of the Soviet Union*. 173 pp. Frankfurt and Bern: Verlag Peter Lang, 1981. (Beginning with a reminder that "overt dissent" is not identical with "political opposition," author reviews dissent after 1956, ch. 1; and develops typology, ch. 3. See pp. 12–16 on *samizdat* and trials and protests it engendered, and pp. 82–87 on "extra–structural dissent." Index.)

2098.   Simon, Gerhard, *Church, State, and Opposition in the U.S.S.R.*. 258 pp. London: C. Hurst, 1974. Originally published in German as *Die Kirchen in Russland: Berichte, Dokumente*. München: Manz, 1970. (See ch. 4–6 on churches and the state, documents in ch. 7. Index. Bibliography.)

2099.   Smith, Gerald Stanton, *Songs to Seven Strings: Russian Guitar Poetry and Soviet "Mass Song."* 285 pp. Bloomington: Indiana Univ. Press, 1984. (First section is on accepted "mass song," pp. 70–86 on convict and prison camp songs, second section on self–publication via *magnitizdat* and four artists. Photos. Index. Bibliography.)

2100. Sobchak, Anatoly, *For a New Russia: The Mayor of St. Petersburg's Own Story of the Struggle for Justice and Democracy.* 191 pp New York: Free Press; London: HarperCollins, 1992. (Personal account of Russian politics and change, 1988–90. Ch. 5 is on a commission, of which the author was a member, investigating the killing of demonstrators in Tbilisi, Georgia, in 1989, and ch. 8 is on the "first little Putsch" planned in Leningrad late in that same year. *Epilogue* is a comment on the attack by Russian troops in Vilnius, Lithuania, and *Afterword* is on the August 1991 St. Petersburg coup, both of which occurred after the main narrative closes. Photos of "Bloody Sunday" in Vilnius are between pp. 128–29. Index.)

2101. Spechler, Dina R., *Permitted Dissent in the U.S.S.R.: Novy Mir and the Soviet Regime.* 316 pp. New York: Praeger, 1982. (Although not a study of nonviolent action, this historical study of the phases of post–Stalinist dissent contributes to understanding factors in toleration, repression, and self–limitation of dissent and opposition. See esp. introduction, ch. 1, and ch. 6 for conceptual treatments. Index. Bibliography.)

2102. Tökés, Rudolf L., ed., *Dissent in the U.S.S.R.: Politics, Ideology, and People.* 467 pp. Baltimore and London: Johns Hopkins Univ. Press, 1975. (See ch. 1 on repression; ch. 6 on religious dissent; and esp. Howard L. Biddulph, "Protest Strategies of the Soviet Intellectual Opposition," ch. 2, on resources, publics, and methods; and Gene Sosin, "Magnitizdat: Uncensored Songs of Dissent," ch. 8, on dissemination of tape–recorded songs of protest and cultural criticism. Illustrations. Index.)

2103. Verba, Lesya, and Bohdan Yase, eds., *The Human Rights Movement in Ukraine: Documents of the Ukrainian Helsinki Group, 1976–1980.* 277 pp. Baltimore, Washington DC, and Toronto: SMOLOSKYP, 1980. (Collection of documents originated by Ukrainian group for promotion of rights under Helsinki agreement; individual manifestos, memoranda, petitions and appeals, account of members' 1977 trial findings, pp. 203–50; and biographical notes, pp. 251–65. Photos. Index.)

2104. Weeks, Albert L., *Andrei Sakharov and the Soviet Dissidents: A Critical Commentary.* 89 pp. New York: Monarch Press, 1975.

(Brief examination of Sakharov's political writings with background on the dissident movement. Bibliography.)

2105. Yakobson, Sergius, and Robert V. Allen, *Aspects of Intellectual Ferment and Dissent in the Soviet Union.* 86 pp. Washington DC: US Government Printing Office, 1968. (Review of human rights–oriented dissent and its literary aspects, ca. 1958–1966.)

PART II

STUDIES OF
NONVIOLENT ACTION
AND RELATED FIELDS

Chapter 5
Methods and Dynamics of Nonviolent Action

Section I
Methods of Nonviolent Action

The methods of nonviolent action are simply its most basic component parts, the kinds of actions that people choose or find themselves doing when they take part in nonviolent conflict. Other terms could be used, such as forms or types of nonviolent action, but the concept of methods communicates the idea that groups use these means in order to accomplish something. They might be letting off steam, raising an issue publicly, making an appeal, bringing some sort of pressure to bear, imposing a cost on their adversary, or something similar. In any case, it is the methods that make up the discrete, separate behaviors that go together to compose nonviolent action. (The discussion and classification here follows Gene Sharp, The Politics of Nonviolent Action, entry 2343).

A glance through the following pages shows that methods of nonviolent action are grouped into three categories; methods of nonviolent protest and persuasion, methods of noncooperation, and methods of nonviolent intervention. Because the forms of noncooperation are so multiple, and the areas of human life they appear in so varied, these methods are subdivided into social, economic, political and sometimes psychological types. Readers should be cautious in using the idea of methods and remember that the categories are not intended to indicate the tactics or strategy of nonviolent action (which are more a question of how the methods are selected and applied in real conflicts) nor are they intended to relate directly to the mechanisms of change in nonviolent struggle that are explained in section two of this chapter.

The Politics of Nonviolent Action identifies nearly two hundred methods, but there are certainly more than this because new circumstances and technologies create opportunities to think up new methods. For example, some users of this book will remember the idea of samizdat from the Soviet dissident movements of the 1960s through 1980s. Samizdat is illegal or secret self–publishing of a book or text of some kind. The Russian and Baltic dissidents also developed magnitizidat, which is copying the illegal material— such as a protest song—onto an audio cassette to distribute it. Chinese student protesters of the 1980s did something similar by reading the wording of protest posters onto cassettes and sending them to cities or universities far away so that protesters there could be informed.

Other new technology has given rise to new ways to use old methods. The walk–out or quickie strike is not new, but it was used in a new way in the Philippines February Revolution of 1986 when computer operators who feared that an election was being stolen walked out suddenly, leaving no one to enter presumably fraudulent vote totals into the computers. As these examples show, much can be learned about nonviolent action from studying the methods, but they are most important as they fit into some ongoing struggle.

Users will need to consult other sections of this research guide if they want to explore methods of nonviolent action thoroughly; consult the subject index under the names of methods. Since each work is listed only once, many references to methods of nonviolent action are in the chapters on different countries and regions. The sections here include the works that are most particularly about a certain method rather than a specific country or region. Lastly, the methods are grouped somewhat differently here than in The Politics of Nonviolent Action, so that generally similar methods are listed together and individual methods listed separately only if there are enough entries to warrant this.

METHODS OF PROTEST AND PERSUASION

Methods of nonviolent protest and persuasion are means of expression and symbolic display, usually group or collective in nature. Like all methods of nonviolent action, they aim at influencing the course and outcome of a conflict in ways that are not provided for in the usual procedures for settling disputes that a political system might have. As symbolic communication, they can take on a very large number of forms. They may be based on speech or writing, but also on music and song, theater, or the images of art and visual expression. Indeed, they may simply be based on the human body or masses of bodies, as are marches, demonstrations, processions, and protest funerals. The rhetorical and persuasive aspects of these methods are often very clear and direct, as in

Dr. Martin Luther King, Jr.'s renowned "Letter from Birmingham City Jail" (1963; entry 945). Alternatively, the communication may be indirect or even occult, relying largely on symbols that will be best understood by a certain target audience (see, for example, entry 2111 on the symbolism of British trade union banners and entry 2099 on Russian prison and protest songs). Because of these factors, the audiences for methods of nonviolent protest and persuasion are often multiple, and researchers must be careful to avoid assuming that they are a direct communication from a protest group to the authorities or major adversary. In using the entries that follow, note that many methods of protest and persuasion appear in the sections on particular struggle only, often because there is as yet no analytical literature on them. This is true, for example of protest funerals, even though they have been significant in the coming of the 1956 Revolution in HUNGARY and the students' Democracy Movement of 1989 in CHINA.

See also: Russia: Political Dissent, 1960–1980s.

Symbols and Statements

Formal statements, rhetoric, and speechmaking clearly begin at the borderline of normal political behavior but extend beyond into all sorts of symbolic expression of protest. They include written or oral expressions of opinion, dissent, or support for a certain policy, both by individuals and groups, as well as visual symbols of dissent. They include underground press, posters and art, and other displays. Some of these may be crude, even gathering their effect from their crudeness, while others become highly–developed symbolic forms that express the identity, commitments, and grievances of those who display them.

See also: Russia: Political Dissent, 1960–1980s.

2106. Boase, Paul H., ed., *The Rhetoric of Protest and Reform, 1878–1898.* 354 pp. Athens OH: Ohio Univ. Press, 1980. (History of speechmaking during the era of "protest and reform" in U.S. See, in part 1, Malcolm O. Sillars, "The Rhetoric of the Petition in Boots," ch. 1 on Coxey's Army and the 1894 march on Washington to protest unemployment. In part 2, see Donald H. Ecroyd, "The Populist Spellbinders," ch. 6. In part 3, entitled "Women Take Up the Cause of Reform," see esp. pp. 196–201 on "methods of persuasion" and pp. 201–07 on the rhetoric of suffrage movement. Index.)

2107.   Bormann, Ernest G., ed., *Forerunners of Black Power: The Rhetoric of Abolition*. 248 pp. Englewood Cliffs NJ: Prentice–Hall, 1971. (Collection of speeches and addresses by abolitionists, represented as "radical rhetoric." See "The Rhetoric of Abolition," pp. 1–37, analyzing speeches as method of protest, and "The Abolitionist Rhetorical Tradition in Contemporary America," pp. 231–41, on rhetoric as protest in civil rights and black power movements. Index. Bibliography.)

2108.   Danky, James P., *Undergrounds: A Union List of Alternative Periodicals in Libraries of the United States and Canada*. 206 pp. Madison WI: State Historical Society of Wisconsin, 1974. (List of alternative periodicals, broadly defined as politically and culturally "to the left of center." Listed by title and state. Photos.)

2109.   Evans, David, and Sylvia Gohl, *Photomontage: A Political Weapon*. 128 pp. London and Bedford, England: Gordon and Fraser Gallery, 1986. (Collection of twentieth–century posters and photomontage intended as satire and political commentary or to promote an ideology. Special attention in the introduction and plates section 1 to the role of John Heartfield in originating the technique of protest montage. Illustrations. Index. Bibliography.)

2110.   Fisher, Randall M., *Rhetoric and American Democracy: Black Protest through Vietnam Dissent*. 303 pp. Lanham MD, New York and London: University Press of America, 1985. (Analysis of the rhetoric of political movements and rhetorical action in black protest, anti–radicalism, and conflict over the war in Vietnam. See esp. ch. 5 on rhetoric of nonviolent civil rights movement, ch. 10 for chronicle of anti–Vietnam War movement, and ch. 11 on the "ethos of dissent" in the anti–war movement. Illustrations. Bibliography.)

2111.   Gorman, John, *Banner Bright: An Illustrated History of the Banners of the British Trade Union Movement*. 184 pp. London: Allen Lane, 1973. (Innovative study of trade union banners as carriers of statements and symbolism. See pp. 27–37 on the symbols, their sources, and some uses; pp. 24–25 on fate of banners in action; and photos of banners in demonstrations and parades in pp. 67–68, 101, 103, 110, 112, 114, 116, 119, 128–29, 134–48, 153, 157, 167, 172–74, 179. Heavily illustrated with photos and drawings. Index.)

2112. Harlow, Barbara, *Protest Literature*. 234 pp. New York and London: Methuen, 1987. (Study of representative themes from various cultural sources including Palestinian, several African peoples, and Latin America. Ch. 2 is on resistance poetry, ch. 3 is on resistance narrative, and ch. 4 is on prison memoirs. Index. Bibliography.)

2113. Kunzle, David, *Posters of Protest: The Posters of Political Satire in the U.S., 1966–1970*. 160 pp. Santa Barbara CA: Art Galleries, Univ. of California, Santa Barbara, 1971. (Catalogue of pictorial satire and protest in posters of the late 1960s, with history of protest art and commentary on "revolutionary style." Illustrations. Index. Bibliography.)

2114. Posener, Jill, *Spray It Loud*. 96 pp. London: Routledge & Kegan Paul, 1982. (Photo–essay, mostly on using spray paint to express protest messages that symbolically deride, modify, or challenge the intended message of billboards, advertising, and posters. Includes a copy of a card with advice on what to do when arrested for this offense. Photos.)

2115. Rickards, Maurice, ed., *Posters of Protest and Revolution*. 112 pp. Somerset, England: Adams & Dart, 1970. (Illustrated book of political protest posters. See introduction for brief overview of history of posters of protest beginning with Martin Luther in 1517. Of interest for nonviolent protest and persuasion are posters nos. 2, 3, 5–7, 15, 20, 22, 32–36, 83, 84, 86, 87, 91, 93, 94, 107, 117, 118, 135–38, 151, 153, 165, 177, 187–95, 198, 205–11, 213, 216, 218–27. Illustrations. Index.)

2116. Watson, Francis M., Jr., *The Alternative Media: Dismantling Two Centuries of Progress*. 134 pp. Rockford IL: Rockford College Institute, 1979. (See ch. 1 for discussion of how "underground" press became "alternative press" in early 1970s. See also ch. 3 on politics of alternative press. Index.)

2117.   White, Stephen, *The Bolshevik Poster*. 152 pp. New Haven and London: Yale Univ. Press, 1988. (Examination of Russian propaganda poster art from the revolutionary and civil war periods, including a history of the political poster in Russia. Illustrations.)

Music, Song, and Theater

Protest songs and protest theater are among those methods of nonviolent protest and persuasion whose audience is likely to be the supporters of a cause rather than its adversaries or the uncommitted public. Mobilized groups may use theater to keep up morale and to put their grievances in an easily–understood and symbolic form. Much the same is true of protest songs and music, which serve the functions of encouraging people to join in and of teaching them the attitudes and policies of the group in addition to spreading the word.

See also: United States: Industrial Workers of the World.

2118.   Carawan, Guy, and Candie Carawan, eds., *We Shall Overcome! Songs of the Southern Freedom Movement*. 112 pp. New York: Oak Publications, 1963. (Collection of songs from the civil rights movement, with sections on songs from sit–ins, freedom rides, voter registration efforts, and campaigns in Albany GA and Birmingham AL. Photos.)

2119.   Coult, Tony, and Baz Kershaw, eds., *Engineers of the Imagination: The Welfare State Handbook*. 227 pp. London and New York: Methuen, 1983. (Handbook on history, techniques, and events of "Welfare State International," an alternative theater company founded in 1968 in Britain. See Sue Fox, "Street and Outdoor Performance," pp. 31–41 and Luk Mishalle, "Music," pp. 41–57 for advice on organizing. Ch. 4 is on core techniques. Ch. 5 is on events staged by Welfare State International. Illustrations. Photos. Bibliography.)

2120. Denisoff, R. Serge, *Sing a Song of Social Significance*. 2d ed. 255 pp. Bowling Green OH: Bowling Green State Univ. Popular Press, 1983. (Analytical study of protest songs and "songs of persuasion." See pp. 1–18 for a definition of the protest song. Emphasis on historical roots of American protest songs. Bibliography)

2121. ———, *Songs of Protest, War & Peace: A Bibliography & Discography*. Rev. ed. 70 pp. Santa Barbara CA and Oxford: ABC–Clio, 1973. (Includes books, periodicals, songbooks, publications, and discography. See esp. section 5, pp. 39–42 on songs of war and peace from *Sing Out!*, 1950–64; section 6, pp. 42–47 on songs from *Broadside*, 1962–72; and section 7, pp. 47–52 for a discography of American protest songs. Index.)

2122. Denisoff, R. Serge, and Richard A. Peterson, eds., *The Sounds of Social Change*. 332 pp. Chicago: Rand McNally, 1972. (Anthology of articles on music as protest. See esp. R. Serge Denisoff, "The Evolution of the American Protest Song" and "Music in Social Movements"; Richard Brazier, "The Industrial Workers of the World 'Little Red Songbook'"; R. Serge Denisoff and Mark Levine, "Brainwashing or Background Noise: The Popular Protest Song"; and John P. Robinson and Paul M. Hirsch, "Teenage Response to Rock and Roll Protest Songs." Index.)

2123. Goorney, Howard, and Ewan MacCall, eds., *Agit–prop to Theatre Workshop*. 205 pp. Manchester, England: Manchester Univ. Press, 1986. (Collection of scripts by political playwrights, 1930–1950. See Introduction, pp. ix–lvii, and Epilogue, pp. 199–205 for discussion of history and nature of "revolutionary theatre." Illustrations. Photos.)

2124. Greenway, John, *American Folksongs of Protest*. 348 pp. Philadelphia: Univ. of Pennsylvania Press, 1953. (History and typology of protest folksongs. Introduction discusses genesis and structure of protest song and ch. 1 gives a historical survey. Other chapters are on protest songs of farmers and black workers. Ch. 8 contains biographical sketches of song writers. See also appendix for discography of songs of social and economic protest, pp. 311–27. Index. Bibliography.)

2125.   Hampton, Wayne, *Guerrilla Minstrels*. 306 pp. Knoxville: Univ. of Tennessee Press, 1986. (Biographical sketches of John Lennon, Joe Hill, Woody Guthrie, and Bob Dylan in context of U.S. "protest song culture." Illustrations. Photos. Discography. Index. Bibliography.)

2126.   Itzin, Catherine, *Stages in the Revolution: Political Theatre in Britain Since 1968*. 399 pp. London: Eyre Methuen, 1980. (History of British political theater, 1968–78. Descriptions of theater in protest against a variety of issues throughout. See esp. pp. 39–50 on the AgitProp Street Players. Chronology of productions, pp. 363–389. Index.)

2127.   Kivnick, Helen Q., *Where is the Way: Song and Struggle in South Africa*. 378 pp. New York: Penguin Books, 1990. (Song in its multitude of forms in post–traditional African life in South Africa, including a section on the song contests of migrants and hostel dwellers. Part 6, "In Protest," discusses the place of protest song in the movements of the 1980s and some functions served by song in the movements. Appendix on pp. 350–63 contains discography.)

2128.   Lesnick, Henry, ed., *Guerrilla Street Theater*. 442 pp. New York: Bard Books, Avon Books, 1973. (Collection of articles, notes, statements, scripts from guerrilla and street theater organizations around the U.S. Text interspersed with artistic pieces describing various groups and their intentions. See "Introductory Notes to Guerrilla/Street Theater," pp. 11–25. Illustrations. Photos.)

2129.   Lomax, Alan, comp., *Hard Hitting Songs for Hard–Hit People*. Notes on songs by Woody Guthrie. Music transcribed and ed. by Pete Seeger. 368 pp. New York: Oak Publications, 1967. (Songs of working people in the U.S. with text and photos. See pp. 119, 139–143, 150–152, 178–183, 239–254, 268–271, 281–283, 286–291, 295–299, 302–303, 306–308, 314–319, 322–328, 332–333, 346–349 for songs on strikes and other labor action, pp. 350–353 for anti–war songs. Photos. Index of songs.)

2130.   Luziaraga, Gerardo, ed., *Popular Theater for Social Change in Latin America*. 432 pp. Los Angeles CA: Univ. of California at

Los Angeles, Latin American Center Publications, 1978. (Articles in Spanish or English on popular theater in various countries. Theodore Shank and Adele Edling Shank, "Chicano and Latin American Alternative Theater," ch. 15 includes protest–oriented theater such as *Teatro Campesino* from California—once associated with the United Farm Workers— and its use of myth in protest theater. Index.)

2131.   Miller, Judith Graves, *Theater and Revolution in France since 1968.* 169 pp. Lexington KY: French Forum, 1977. (See esp. ch. 3 on the role of theater in the events of May 1968. Bibliography.)

2132.   Palmer, Roy, *The Sound of History: Songs and Social Comment.* 361 pp. Oxford and New York: Oxford Univ. Press, 1988. (A study of folksongs in broadsides and the oral tradition and themes of social commentary, memory, and protest contained in song. Thematic sections include "protest and deference" in rural life, pp. 37–42; strikes, pp. 107–17; "rough music" and ceremonies of denunciation, pp. 197–98. Also political protest and comment, ch. 7 and war and peace, ch. 8. Illustrations include an anti–enclosure song, p. 43; strikers' documents, pp. 114–15; rough music, p. 205; Chartist songs, pp. 248–49; a Poor Law protest, p. 250; and "Never Flog Our Soldiers," p. 294. Photos. Discography. Indexes. Bibliography.)

2133.   Perris, Arnold, *Music as Propaganda: Art to Persuade, Art to Control.* 247 pp. Westport CT and London: Greenwood Press, 1985. (Music for propaganda and persuasion. See ch. 8 on popular music in the 1960s, focusing on the U.S. Index. Bibliography.)

2134.   Philbin, Marianne, ed., *Give Peace a Chance: Music and the Struggle for Peace.* 122 pp. Chicago: Chicago Review Press, 1983. Catalog of the Exhibition at the Peace Museum, Chicago. (Collection of items focusing on peace–oriented popular and protest music. See esp. pieces by Jerome Rodnitzky and R. Serge Denisoff. Illustrations. Photos. Bibliography.)

2135.   Rodnitzky, Jerome L., *Minstrels of the Dawn: The Folk–Protest Singer as a Cultural Hero.* 192 pp. Chicago: Nelson–Hall, 1976. (Examination of the history of American folk–protest, with emphasis on the evolution of the protest song and four writer-performers who became "cultural heroes" during the 1960s: Woody Guthrie, Joan Baez, Phil Ochs, and Bob Dylan. Photos. Discography. Index. Bibliography.)

2136.   Stourac, Richard, and Kathleen McCreery, *Theatre as a Weapon: Workers' Theatre in the Soviet Union, Germany and Britain, 1917–1934.* 336 pp. London and New York: Routledge & Kegan Paul, 1986. (History of the workers' theater movements in U.S.S.R. [Blue Blouse], Germany [Agitprop Theatre], and Great Britain [Workers' Theatre Movement] and theoretical description of methods utilized in these groups. See index under *agitation, agitprop, dramaturgy, form–content relationship, General Strike, hunger marches, living newspaper, marches, mass spectacles, montage, music, posters, propaganda, repression, satire, song,* and *visualization/making visible.* Illustrations. Photos. Appendixes. Index. Bibliography.)

Assemblies, Marches, and Processions

These methods vary greatly in the numbers and kinds of people likely to assemble and in their relationship to the continuing dispute. They share the character of presenting the physical presence of the participants in a symbolic manner, either by their numbers (as in mass marches and demonstrations) or by situating themselves in a significant place (as in a strike picket line at the gates of a factory or mine). Participants may symbolically blockade or occupy an area also, as picketers do when they call on others not to cross the line. Of course, they may shift at some point toward actual physical occupation of a place, a transition to methods of nonviolent intervention.

See also for examples: South Africa; Chile; Canada: Labor; United States: Women's Suffrage Movement; United States: Movement Against the Vietnam War; United States: Labor; United States: Struggle for Desegregation and Civil Rights; Australia: Queensland Civil Liberties Campaign; China: Democracy Movement, 1988–1989; India; Japan: Opposition to the Security Treat of 1960; Germany: 1980s and Berlin Wall; Great Britain: Women's Suffrage Movement; Great Britain: Protests and Hunger Marches by the Unemployed; Ireland, Northern: Civil Rights Campaign and People's Democracy.

2137. Davis, Susan G., *Parades and Power: Street Theater in Nineteenth–Century Philadelphia*. 235 pp. Philadelphia: Temple Univ. Press, 1986. (On street theater and parades as political action. Ch. 4 is on parades of poor and working class Philadelphians, see esp. pp. 96–103 on political protest. Ch. 5 is on workers' parades; see esp. pp. 132–43 on strike parades. Illustrations. Index.)

2138. Deming, Barbara, *Prison Notes*. 205 pp. New York: Grossman, 1966. (Diary of peace marchers' confrontations in Albany GA, 1964.)

2139. Egerton, Henry C., *Handling Protest at Annual Meetings*. 76 pp. New York: The Conference Board, 1971. (Report on 1970 annual meetings of 17 major corporations at which protest occurred and recommendations for managing conflict. Appendix C contains reports of six such meetings. Documents.)

2140. Etzioni, Amitai, *Demonstration Democracy*. 108 pp. New York, London, and Paris: Gordon & Breach, 1970. (Analysis of the role of demonstrations in U.S. political life.)

2141. Gilbert, Norman, "The Mass Protest Phenomenon: An Examination of Marches on Washington." 173 pp. Ph.D. diss., Northern Illinois Univ., 1972. (A study of large–scale protest based on comparison of six marches on Washington, DC, 1894–1970. Discusses the relationship among protest, established institutions, and political beliefs where the "strategy of non–violent protest" is used. Bibliography.)

2142. Gilbert, Tony, *Only One Died: An Account of the Scarman Inquiry into the Events of 15th June 1974, in Red Lion Square, when Kevin Gately Died Opposing Racism and Fascism*. 254 pp. London: Kay Beauchamp, [1975]. (Report of public inquiry into death of a participant in a counter–demonstration against the British National Front, June 15, 1974. Illustrations. Photos.)

2143. Halloran, James D., Philip Elliot, and Graham Murdock, *Demonstrations and Communication: A Case Study*. 330 pp. Harmondsworth, Middlesex: Penguin, 1970. (Based on a case study of an October 1968 London demonstration against U.S.

involvement in Vietnam. Maintains that media reportage duplicated pre–existing prejudices and concentrated upon the few violent events while ignoring overwhelmingly peaceful march. Questions whether marchers are motivated to remain peaceful when not perceived as such. Index.)

2144.   Kahn, Peggy, Norman Lewis, Rowland Livock, and Paul Wiles, with John Mesher, *Picketing: Industrial Disputes, Tactics, and the Law*. 223 pp. London, Boston, Melbourne, and Henley: Routledge & Kegan Paul, 1983. (Sophisticated study of the nature and choice of "tactics" in industrial conflict within the context of recent British legislation aimed in part at controlling picketing. See esp. ch. 4 on the concept of tactics in disputes, the cases discussed in ch. 6–9, and analysis of influence of law on tactics in ch. 10. Consult index on *blacking, Grunwick, mass picketing, picketing, police, Saltley,* and *secondary actions.* Index. Bibliography.)

2145.   Lehmann, Jerry, *We Walked to Moscow*. 88 pp. Raymond NH: Greenleaf Books, 1966. (Story of an anti–war march from San Francisco to Moscow, 1960–61. Illustrations.)

2146.   Lyttle, Bradford, *You Come with Naked Hands: The Story of the San Francisco to Moscow March for Peace*. 246 pp. Raymond NH: Greenleaf Books, 1966. (Story of origin, organization, and conduct of 1960–61 peace march across U.S., Europe, and U.S.S.R. Diaries and reports excerpted throughout. Appendixes follow ch. 1 and some other chapters. Photos. Documents.)

2147.   Mason, Henry L., *Mass Demonstrations against Foreign Regimes: A Study of Five Crises*. 98 pp. Tulane Studies in Political Science 10 (1966). (Natural history approach to "mass demonstrations" in the form of three strikes in the Netherlands under Nazi occupation in 1941, 1943, and 1944; outbreak of the Hungarian revolution of 1956; and demonstrations in Panama in 1964 against U.S. domination. Analysis of underlying and immediate factors and leadership groups, followed by discussion of the outbreak, spread, and repression of the demonstrations. Epilogue discusses the relationship between these demonstrations, wider resistance, and government policy.)

2148. Ralph, Chris, *The Picket and the Law*. 22 pp. London: Fabian Society, 1977. (Fabian Society pamphlet on the history and current status of law regarding picketing. See historical review in pp. 3–9 and ch. 4 on "protest" pickets. Bibliography.)

2149. *Rights in Concord: The Response to the Counter–Inaugural Protest Activities in Washington, D.C., January 18–20, 1969.* 125 pp. Washington DC: Task Force on Law and Law Enforcement to the National Commission on the Causes and Prevention of Violence, [1969]. (Report of January 18–20, 1969 demonstration, with interviews and photographs, pp. 1–78. Focuses largely on policing and social–control aspects of the demonstrations. Description of preparations by protesters and police and discussion of events are on pp. 79–120. Illustrations. Photos.)

2150. Salstrom, Paul, *Manual on Peace Walks*. 27 pp. Raymond NH: Greenleaf Books, 1967. (Short manual based on peace walks held ca. 1960–62; contains practical advice on logistics and a discussion of the mystique bred in peace walks.)

2151. Waskow, Arthur I., *The Worried Man's Guide to World Peace*. 219 pp. New York: Doubleday, 1963. (Among the "levers" making possible impacts on government decisions toward peace, author discusses demonstrations and "direct action" in pp. 152–170. Index.)

METHODS OF NONCOOPERATION

In considering the methods of noncooperation, one is concerned with relatively deliberate withdrawal from usual, expected, or even mandatory participation in some relationship, activity, institution, or regime with which the activists are engaged in some conflict. In keeping with the observation, dating back at least to Henry David Thoreau in the mid–nineteenth century, that participation is cooperation and cooperation is therefore furtherance of some objective or policy of another, noncooperation is generally aimed at limiting the effectiveness of an adversary's actions by reducing the assistance necessary to achieve the object. The classification of subtypes must therefore depend upon the kind of relationship that is attenuated. If the relationship or institution in question is social, involving perhaps expected assistance or deference or perhaps some sort of voluntary common activity, the noncooperation is social. If the relationship is economic, as it involves labor and employer or buyer and seller, perhaps, the type of noncooperation is economic. If the relationship in question is political, such as that involving citizenship or the expectations of political membership, the noncooperation is political. Thus, it is the form of association that is the source of the noncooperation that is in question when classifying these methods, not the objective. The objective may be political, for example, but the source of the noncooperation, social in such a case as the conduct of a social boycott against officials.

Methods of Social Noncooperation

While methods of social noncooperation are many, relatively few are discussed at length in any literature. Here we are limited primarily to sports boycotts, both against South Africa and at the Olympic Games, and the U.S. sanctuary movement of the 1980s. One of the most notable forms of social noncooperation is ostracism or social boycott, which involves stripping persons of all claim to be treated normally in social life and includes refusing to speak to someone, turning of backs, refusal to offer assistance or to sell goods to them.

See also for examples: United States: Blacklisting in Entertainment; Ireland: Land League Era.

2152. Foley, Karen Sue, *The Political Blacklist in the Broadcast Industry.* 498 pp. New York: Arno Press, 1979. Reprint of Ph.D. dissertation, Ohio State Univ., 1972. (Historical study of the blacklist era in the U.S. Ch. 2, 3 discuss origins, methods, and industry responses to pressure. Documents. Bibliography.)

2153. Fuchs, Estelle, *Pickets at the Gates.* 205 pp. New York: Free Press; London: Collier–Macmillan, 1966. (Designed for use in teacher education. Part 2 studies a 1965 school boycott "protesting *de facto* segregation" in New York City with participant interviews. Documents. Bibliography.)

2154.   Vaughn, Robert, *Only Victims: A Study of Show Business Blacklisting*. 355 pp. New York: G.P. Putnam's Sons, 1972. (History of House Committee on Un–American Activities and show business. See p. 19 for definition and consult index under *blacklisters*. Documents. Index. Bibliography.)

SPORTS BOYCOTTS

Apartheid SOUTH AFRICA tried to maintain contacts with other nations through sports even after it was made the object of economic sanctions. It concentrated especially on European–dominated countries of the British Commonwealth. In several of these countries, most notably NEW ZEALAND (AOTEAROA) boycotts were put into effect and actively pursued by anti–apartheid forces. The other major example here is the U.S.–led boycott of the 1980 Olympic Games in order to sanction the U.S.S.R. for its war in Afghanistan.

See also: New Zealand (Aotearoa): Protests Against Sports with South African Teams.

2155.   Edwards, Harry, *The Revolt of the Black Athlete*. 203 pp. New York: Free Press, 1969. (Popular account of black protest connected with sports. See esp. the campaign to boycott and ban South African participation in competitions, pp. 56, 59, 92–97, and 1968 Olympic Games protest, ch. 3–5. Photos. Index. Bibliography.)

2156.   Hoberman, John, *The Olympic Crisis: Sport, Politics and the Moral Order*. 167 pp. New Rochelle NY: Aristide D. Caratzas, 1986. (Argues that sports boycotts reduce the strength of the "Olympic Movement." Sports boycotts are discussed on pp. 6–7, 16–27. Ch. 3 is on the 1980 Moscow Olympics and American boycott. Epilogue is on Soviet "non–participation" in 1984 Los Angeles Olympics. Illustrations. Photos. Index. Bibliography.)

2157.   Kanin, David B., *A Political History of the Olympic Games*. 161 pp. Boulder CO: Westview Press, 1981. (History of the games, including a proposed boycott of the 1936 Berlin Olympics, pp. 53–55; protests of South African sports apartheid, pp. 97–102;

and the Moscow Olympics in 1980, which the U.S. boycotted, ch. 7. Index.)

2158.   Lapchick, Richard, *The Politics of Race and International Sport: The Case of South Africa.* 268 pp. Westport CT and London: Greenwood Press, 1975. (Examines protests and boycotts against South African participation in numerous sports, including boycott and protests by black Americans. See esp. ch. 4. Documents. Index. Bibliography.)

2159.   Ramsamy, Sam, *Apartheid: The Real Hurdle: Sport in South Africa and the International Boycott.* 107 pp. London: International Defence and Aid Fund for Southern Africa, 1982. Revision of Joan Buckhill, *Race Against Race.* 77 pp. London: International Defence and Aid Fund, 1976. (Ch. 7 is on the boycott "weapon." Illustrations. Photos. Documents.)

2160.   Redmond, Gerald, ed., *Sport and Politics.* 218 pp. Champaign IL: Human Kinetics Publishers, 1986. (See ch. 19 on Canadian boycott of 1980 Moscow Olympic games and ch. 20 for Soviet boycott of 1984 Los Angeles Olympic games.)

2161.   Woods, Donald, *Black and White.* 142 pp. Dublin: Ward River Press, 1981. (See pp. 23–27, 52–127, 139–42 for memoirs and analysis of relationship between sports and politics in South Africa and effects of international boycotts. Author, ex–editor of *Daily Dispatch*, was an official of non–racial sports associations.)

Methods of Economic Noncooperation

Economic noncooperation involves refusing to take action to provide some kind of economic benefit or advantage to another. It may be a boycott, which means refusal to buy from, sell to, or engage in specific economic arrangements with another. It may likewise be the withholding of rents, services, taxes, labor, or any of a variety of economically–significant contributions. Political as well as economic conditions may determine the relative commonness of the many possible methods. At a given time, labor boycotts may be both common and reasonably successful in meeting their aims, while at others they may be rare. This may be for economic reasons (that is, whether they gather enough commercial effect to influence business policy) or for political ones (for example, whether they are punished by law as undue interference with business or restraint of trade). As will be discussed below, international economic sanctions and labor strikes have been most intensively studied to determine the reasons for their variations in frequency and effects.

See also for examples: Nigeria: Women's War of 1929 and Other Women's Struggles; Iran: Tobacco Boycott and Revolution, 1891–1909; United States: Anti–Nazi Boycott; United States: Montgomery Bus Boycott; Australia: Green Bans; India: Nonviolent Struggle in the National Movement.

2162.   Brill, Harry, *Why Organizers Fail: The Story of a Rent Strike.* 192 pp. Berkeley, Los Angeles, London: Univ. of California Press, 1971. (Empirical study of 14–month public housing rent strike organized by four black militants belonging to a "Neighborhood Action Committee" in 1965–66.)

2163.   Burghardt, Stephen, ed., *Tenants and the Urban Housing Crisis.* 241 pp. Dexter MI: New Press, 1972. (Part 1 contains brief studies of rent strikes and part 4 considers "strategy and tactics," including rent strikes, "squat–ins," and other methods. See esp. ch. 11–13.)

2164.   Durland, William, *People Pay for Peace: A Military Tax Refusal Guide for Radical Religious Pacifists and People of Conscience.* Rev. ed. 104 pp. Colorado Springs: Center Peace Publishers, 1982. (Combines religiously–oriented justifications for tax refusal with a how–to section and primer on the legal process incurred by tax refusers. An interview with a refuser is on pp. 30–32, followed by examples of support letters. Appendix.)

2165.   Galenson, Walter, *Labor in Norway.* 373 pp. Cambridge: Harvard Univ. Press, 1949. (See ch. 6 on the use of boycotts by the Norwegian labor movement and efforts to outlaw them. Appendixes.)

2166.   Hedemann, Ed, *Guide to War Tax Resistance.* 125 pp. 3rd ed., New York: War Resisters League, 1986 [orig. publ. 1981]. (Introduction to reasons for tax resistance on pp. 9–14. See esp. "How to Resist," pp. 25–39; "History of War Tax Resistance in the U.S.," pp. 63–69; "Global War Tax Resistance," pp. 70–75;

personal histories of resisters, pp. 76–95; and "Resistance Actions," pp. 96–100. Illustrations. Documents. Index.)

2167.   Laidler, Harry W., *Boycotts and the Labor Struggle: Economic and Legal Aspects*. 488 pp. Reprint, New York: Russell & Russell, 1968 [orig. publ. 1913]. (See part 1, ch. 2 on "modern forms" of boycotts. Index. Bibliography.)

2168.   Powelson, Jack, *Holistic Economics and Social Protest*. 32 pp. Wallingford PA: Pendle Hill Publications, 1983. Pendle Hill Pamphlet No. 252. (Raises questions about the occasionally negative effects of nonviolent economic protest in an attempt to develop a "holistic" strategy of economic protest. See esp. pp. 16–20 on boycotts.)

2169.   Smith, N. Craig, *Morality and the Market: Consumer Pressure for Corporate Accountability*. 351 pp. London and New York: Routledge, 1990. (Examination of the potential and actual influence of consumers over markets and businesses. Discusses "ethical purchase behaviour" aimed at encouraging social and political responsibility in business and closely examines organized consumer boycotts. Ch. 5 relates the "boycott tactic" to concepts of "nonviolent direct action" and offers a historical view. Ch. 7 focuses on the history of consumer boycotts of business, their conduct, and factors in effectiveness. Ch. 8 contains five brief case studies and ch. 9 reviews management strategies. Appendix B lists sixty–five recent cases. Appendixes. Index. Bibliography.)

2170.   Sullivan, Leon H., *Build Brother Build*. 192 pp. Philadelphia: Macrae Smith, 1969. (Pp. 68–69 and ch. 4 are on the "Selective Patronage Program" in Philadelphia between 1959–63, which selectively boycotted businesses to encourage them to hire blacks. Photos. Index.)

2171.   Wolman, Leo, *The Boycott in American Trade Unions*. 148 pp. Baltimore: Johns Hopkins Press, 1916. Reprint, New York: Arno & The New York Times, 1971. (Ch. 2 gives a history of the boycott, ch. 3 is on materials boycotts, ch. 4 on commodities boycotts, ch. 1, 5 describe the mechanism of the boycott, and ch. 6 is on legal aspects. Index.)

INTERNATIONAL ECONOMIC SANCTIONS

International economic sanctions do not precisely constitute a method of nonviolent action in themselves since they often involve a mixture of embargoes, boycotts, financial blockades, diplomatic nonrecognition and other methods of inflicting costs on an adversary. Sanctions episodes do share in common the attempt to use (or threaten) the withdrawal of economic benefits in pressuring some target state to alter its policies. If colonial conflicts between a colony and its foreign rulers can be considered international, then the history of international economic sanctions in modern times commences in the autumn of 1765 when the British North American colonies carried out the first of three campaigns of commercial pressure against Britain designed to compel the alteration of imperial laws (in this case, the Stamp Act). More recently, Mussolini's Italy, the European government of Rhodesia (now ZIMBABWE), and SOUTH AFRICA have been among many states made the target of sanctions.

See also for examples: South Africa: International Relations; Zimbabwe (Southern Rhodesia); Arab League Boycott of Israel; OPEC Oil Boycott (Embargo), 1973; Chile: Opposition to Allende Government; United States: American Colonial Resistance and the Independence Movement, 1765–1775; United States: Embargo and Nonintercourse, 1807–1812; China: Before 1948.

2172.　Ayubi, Shaheen, Richard E. Bissell, Nana Amu–Brafih Korsah, and Laurie A. Lerner, *Economic Sanctions in U.S. Foreign Policy.* 86 pp. Philadelphia: Foreign Policy Research Institute, 1982. (Case studies of U.S. attempts at trade coercion. Ch. 1 discusses meaning and purpose of economic sanctions. Case studies on Iran, Soviet Union, South Africa, and Rhodesia. See pp. 83–86 for policy recommendations.)

2173.　Baer, G.W., *The Coming of the Italian–Ethiopian War.* 404 pp. Cambridge: Harvard Univ. Press, 1967. (See ch. 8–10 for British mistrust of the League of Nations as an effective body in connection with sanctions and ch. 12 for the sanctions declaration. Index. Bibliography.)

2174.　Barros, James, *Britain, Greece, and the Politics of Sanctions: Ethiopia, 1935–1936.* 248 pp. London: Royal Historical Society; Atlantic Highlands NJ: Humanities Press, 1982. (History of

Greek sanctions against Italy during the Italo–Ethiopia crisis of 1935–36 and the effect of Britain on Greek policy. See pp. 12–24 on 1935 demonstrations in Greece and ch. 4, 5 on sanctions. Index. Bibliography.)

2175.   Bonsal, Philip W., *Cuba, Castro, and the United States*. 288 pp. London: Univ. of Pittsburgh Press, 1971. (See ch. 16 on U.S. economic sanctions against Cuba. Bonsal was U.S. Ambassador to Cuba, 1959–60.)

2176.   Brockway, Thomas, *Battles without Bullets: The Story of Economic Warfare*. 95 pp. New York: Foreign Policy Association, 1939. (Maintains that economic means were substituted for conventional war in the relations among antagonistic states in the 1930s. See brief comments on boycotts and embargoes, pp. 87–88.)

2177.   Clark, Evans, ed., *Boycotts and Peace: A Report by the Committee on Economic Sanctions*. 381 pp. New York and London: Harper, 1932. (An examination of the potential of international economic sanctions to maintain peace. Appendixes.)

2178.   DeLancey, Mark W., *African International Relations: An Annotated Bibliography*. 365 pp. Boulder CO: Westview Press, 1981. (Consult index under *sanctions* for periodical literature on Rhodesian and South African sanctions to 1978.)

2179.   Doxey, Margaret P., *Economic Sanctions and International Enforcement*. 162 pp. London and New York: Oxford University Press, 1971. (Discusses the development of international sanctions, problems of enforcement, responses to sanctions, and their use against specific countries. Selected Bibliography.)

2180.   Ellings, Richard J., *Embargoes and World Power: Lessons From American Foreign Policy*. 176 pp. Boulder and London: Westview Press, 1985. (Analysis of "strategic embargoes" and other economic sanctions in post–WWII period. Contains case study of Western embargo against communist countries and comparative study of 107 actual and threatened embargoes; see pp. 161–63 for list. Introduction and ch. 1, 2 give theoretical foundation. Ch. 4 discusses dynamics of strategic embargo,

1947–83. Ch. 5 discusses American use of economic sanctions. Index. Bibliography.)

2181.   Galtung, Johan, "On the Effects of International Economic Sanctions with Examples from the Case of Rhodesia." *World Politics* 19 (1967): 378–416. (Review of the standard assumptions about the relationship between sanctions and change of behavior, combined with objections to this "naive" view based on Rhodesia's reactions to sanctions imposed after UDI.)

2182.   Healy, Dermot, *The Grain Weapon.* 50 pp. *Centrepieces* 1 (1982). (Occasional paper arguing for the success of the U.S. grain embargo against the U.S.S.R. as imposed under President Carter and the possibility of future political influence from the same source. See pp. 15–16 on the three conditions of "grain linkage–leverage diplomacy," followed by a discussion of each.)

2183.   Hoffman, Frederick, "The Functions of Economic Sanctions: A Comparative Analysis." *Journal of Peace Research* 2 (1967): 140–60. (Analysis of the political motives for conducting economic sanctions stressing their function in relieving tension within international organizations, rather than efficacy strictly understood. Case studies of League of Nations debate on sanctioning Italy in 1935 and United Nations consideration of Rhodesia in 1965. Appendixes.)

2184.   Hufbauer, Gary Clyde, and Jeffrey J. Schott, assisted by Kimberly Ann Elliott, *Economic Sanctions in Support of Foreign Policy Goals.* 102 pp. Policy Analyses in International Economics 6. Washington DC: Institute for International Economics, 1983. (See also next entry. Drawing their conclusions from an extensive sample of case studies, the authors analyze the structure of a "sanctions episode" in ch. 2 and the relevant political and economic variables involved in the conduct and effects of sanctions in ch. 4, 5. Ch. 6 reduces the policy lessons of this research into nine commandments and a series of "do's and don'ts." Appendix B describes the authors' method for estimating the costs of sanctions. Bibliography.)

2185.   ———, *Economic Sanctions Reconsidered: History and Current Policy*. 753 pp. Washington DC: Institute for International Economics, 1985. (Comprehensive analysis of the use of economic sanctions in foreign policy, reviewing over 100 cases of sanctions, 1914–83. Represents data base from which previous entry is derived. General bibliography is on pp. 93–95 and individual bibliographies follow each case.)

2186.   Khan, Haider Ali, *The Political Economy of Sanctions against Apartheid*. 115 pp. Boulder CO and London: Lynne Rienner Publishers, 1989. (Employs the Social Accounting Matrix to model and assess the economic effects of sanctions upon South Africa. Ch. 3 is on the "logic" of sanctions, ch. 4 is on trade sanctions, and ch. 5 is on disinvestment. Appendix. Index. Bibliography.)

2187.   Leyton–Brown, David, ed., *The Utility of Economic Sanctions*. 320 pp. London and Sydney: Croom Helm, 1987. (Conference papers on cases of sanctions and related issues. Topics include League of Nations and U.N. sanctions, East–West disputes, and Middle East conflicts. Part 4, on consequences for states of imposing sanctions, contains pieces on costs to the U.S. of food and technology [oil pipeline] embargoes, part 5 has papers on costs to third parties, and part 6 contains two papers on lessons regarding sanctions as policy. Index.)

2188.   Licklider, Roy, *Political Power and the Arab Oil Weapon: The Experience of Five Industrial Nations*. 343 pp. Berkeley, Los Angeles, and London: Univ. of California Press, 1988. (Study of the Middle East policies of five nations who were the targets of the oil embargoes of 1973–74 and the potential power and influence of the embargo in policy change. Ch. 1 contains an explanation and critique of concepts of international economic sanctions and power, followed by case studies of sanctions effects in the Netherlands, Great Britain, Canada, Japan, and, at some length, the U.S. The last chapter assesses the effect of sanctions and other efforts at international "coercion" on policy behavior within the context set in ch. 1. Index. Bibliography.)

2189. Losman, Donald J., *International Economic Sanctions: The Cases of Cuba, Israel, and Rhodesia.* 156 pp. Albuquerque: Univ. of New Mexico Press, 1979. (Uses the theory of international trade to help interpret the U.S. embargo against Cuba since its revolution, Arab states' boycott of Israel, and collective sanctions against Rhodesia after UDI, with particular attention to unintended effects of the failure of embargoes to sanction their targets effectively. Ch. 6 concludes that the episodes studied here "failed to accomplish their political ends, and it seems unlikely that economic measures alone will fare better in the future." Index. Bibliography.)

2190. Lundborg, Per, *The Economics of Export Embargoes: The Case of the U.S.–Soviet Grain Suspension.* 127 pp. London and New York: Croom Helm, 1987. (Quantitative modeling and discussion of various types of economic sanctions with emphasis on export embargoes, their efficiency, and ramifications. See ch. 3 for 1980 U.S. embargo on grain shipments to the U.S.S.R. Appendix. Index. Bibliography.)

2191. Ninic, Miroslav, and Peter Wallensteen, eds., *Dilemmas of Economic Coercion: Sanctions in World Politics.* 250 pp. New York: Praeger, 1983. (Eight essays on aspects of international sanctions, with an introductory note and pieces on the effects of sanctions, on food sanctions, and East–West sanctions. Of particular interest are Jerrold D. Green, "Strategies for Evading Sanctions," and Peter Wallensteen, "Economic Sanctions: Ten Modern Cases and Three Important Lessons." Index.)

2192. Paarlberg, Robert, *Food Trade and Foreign Policy: India, the Soviet Union, and the United States.* 266 pp. Ithaca NY and London: Cornell Univ. Press, 1985. (Denies the assertion that food trade is a source of power and pressure in the international sphere. See ch. 1 on the belief in "food power" and ch. 5, 6 for studies of U.S. partial food embargo against India, 1965–67, and grain embargo against U.S.S.R., 1980–81, as tests of "coercive potential" of food trade weapon. Index. Bibliography.)

2193. The Royal Institute of International Affairs, *International Sanctions.* 247 pp. London, New York, and Tokyo: Oxford Univ. Press, 1938. (Assessment of 1935–36 League of Nations sanctions experience in the case of Italy's invasion of Ethiopia. See ch. 2 for definitions and ch. 3–9 for discussion of the separate components of the sanctions against Italy, including diplomatic sanctions, raw materials and oil embargo, and financial sanctions. Ch. 16 discusses "the determination of the aggressor," ch. 17 looks at problems of international coordination, and ch. 18 assesses the 1935–36 sanctions episode. Appendixes. Index.)

2194.   U.S. Congress. House. Committee on Foreign Affairs. Subcommittee on Europe and the Middle East. *An Assessment of the Afghanistan Sanctions: Implications for Trade and Diplomacy in the 1980s.* 133 pp. Washington, DC: U.S. Government Printing Office, 1981. (Assessment of U.S. economic sanctions against U.S.S.R. following invasion of Afghanistan, in form of partial grain embargo and the Olympic boycott. See pp. 23–52 on grain embargo and pp. 79–93 on Olympic boycott.)

2195.   Wallensteen, Peter, "Characteristics of Economic Sanctions." *Journal of Peace Research* 3 (1968): 248–67. (Study of cases of economic sanctions, 1932–67. After examining various theories explaining the degree of success based upon the orientation of action toward the sender, receiver, and environment, author concludes that "economic sanctions have been unsuccessful as a means of influence in the international system.")

2196.   Walters, F.P., *A History of the League of Nations.* 833 pp. London, New York, and Toronto: Oxford Univ. Press, 1960 [orig. publ. 1952]. (See ch. 2 for discussion of the influence of pacifism on inception of League and ch. 32 on treaties attempting to set up the "machinery of peace." See ch. 53, esp. pp. 656–88, on the decision for sanctions during the Italian adventure in Ethiopia, their conduct, and their abandonment. See also pp. 232–37 for observations on League inaction during the Franco–Belgian occupation of Germany's Ruhr region in 1923. Appendix. Index.)

2197.   Weintraub, Sidney, ed., *Economic Coercion and U.S. Foreign Policy: Implications of Case Studies from the Johnson Administration.* 234 pp. Boulder CO: Westview Press, 1982. (Theory and case studies of "economic pressure" in U.S.

relations with other states. Theory section focuses on motives, methods, and effects; ch. 1, 2, 4. Case studies include U.S. efforts between 1963 and 1967 to influence the U.A.R., India, and South Africa. Index.)

STRIKES

As much of the literature cited here has found, distinguishing strikes from lockouts in retrospect, and especially using aggregated data, is nearly impossible. A strike is the deliberate and often organized temporary cessation of labor by wage earners, while a lockout is a temporary cessation of employment by wage payers. The works compiled here address to questions of particular interest to students of nonviolent action, the causes of strikes and the dynamics of strikes. Strikes and lockouts may be caused by primarily economic issues, such as labor's judgement of its value on the market as opposed to what the employer is willing to pay. Some works also find non-economic causes of strikes, such as change in the patterns of authority and autonomy between labor and employer. In the dynamics of strikes, attention is given to the organization and maintenance of strikes, the capacity of strikes to sanction an adversary effectively, and procedures for bringing strikes to a close.

See also for examples: Canada: Labor; United States: Labor; Australia: Labor; Japan: Labor; New Zealand (Aotearoa): Labor and Agriculture; Great Britain: Labor; Poland: Solidarity.

2198. Baer, Walter E., *Strikes: A Study of Conflict and How to Resolve It.* 260 pp. New York: AMACOM, 1975. (Written from the viewpoint of management's wish to avoid or control strikes. See ch. 1 for a view of strikes as a problem, ch. 5 on breaches of no-strike clauses, ch. 6 on violence in strikes, and ch. 7 on wildcat strikes. Documents in appendixes. Index.)

2199. Barbash, Jack, *The Practice of Unionism.* 465 pp. New York: Harper & Brothers, 1956. (Attempts a comprehensive theory of union organization and functions in the 1930s and 1940s. See esp. ch. 10, "Strikes, Picket Lines, and Boycotts," for a discussion of various forms of these methods as "the decisive weapons . . . to give meaning to collective bargaining." Of interest are pp. 217–20, 232–34 on types of strikes and pp. 227–

30 on the causes of violence on picket lines. Pp. 234–45 discuss the "management" and strategy of strikes and factors in the power of strikes. Note also the author's view that, at the time, "nothing very much has been written about the strike as a run–of–the–mill union activity rather than a social upheaval," p. 442. Index.)

2200.   Batstone, Eric, Ian Boraston, and Stephen Frenkel, *The Social Organization of Strikes*. 236 pp. Oxford: Basil Blackwell, 1978. (Divides into two micro–level studies; one of the sociology of strikes within a plant and the other of the development of a "near–strike." Ch. 2 discusses the social definition of the strike; ch. 3 its relation to sources of power, esp. pp. 41–44 on alternatives; and ch. 6 its dynamics. See also ch. 10–13 on mobilization in a bargaining situation. Index. Bibliography.)

2201.   Chamberlain, Neil W., and Jane Metzger Schilling, *The Impact of Strikes: Their Social and Economic Costs*. 257 pp. New York: Harper & Brothers, 1954. (Policy–oriented study contemplating the possibility of governmental "strike–control." Discussion based on a model of strike effects on the public in ch. 2, 3, which is applied to post–WWII strikes in coal, rail, and steel industries, ch. 4–10. Index.)

2202.   ———, *Social Responsibility and Strikes*. 293 pp. New York: Harper & Brothers, 1953. (Study of the societal response to strikes. Ch. 5–8 discuss public opinion and the effects of strikes; ch. 9–15 discuss "direct," "indirect," and "legal" sanctions to control strikes; and ch. 12, 13 present case studies of two lengthy strikes in which public and governmental interventions occurred. Index.)

2203.   Crouch, Colin, *Trade Unions: The Logic of Collective Action*. 251 pp. Glasgow: Fontana Paperbacks, 1982. (Examination of modern British trade unions. See ch. 3, "The Means of Collective Action," which deals extensively with ways in which worker organization may be used against employers and how methods such as strikes and picketing can be planned for optimum effect. Index. Bibliography.)

2204.   Edwards, P.K., *Strikes in the United States, 1881–1974*. 336 pp. Oxford: Basil Blackwell, 1981. (Statistical study of factors in strike trends and their relation to governmental regulation ["institutionalisation" in the British sense] in an "exceptionally" strike–prone nation. Appendixes on statistics and methods. Index.)

2205.   Fantasia, Rick, *Cultures of Solidarity: Consciousness, Action, and Contemporary American Workers*. 304 pp. Berkeley, Los Angeles, and London: Univ. of California Press, 1988. (Qualitative sociological study of class consciousness as an emergent property of industrial life and of the conflicts related to it, with the strike seen as both a result of and setting for class consciousness. Ch. 1 is concerned with theories of solidarity and strikes and ch. 2 with the changing history of unionism and strike activity in the U.S. in the twentieth century and with interpretations of industrial relations. These are followed by case accounts of wildcat strikes in a metal–working factory in ch. 3 and the community context of a strike in ch. 5. Ch. 6 is on implications for the study of micro–level social process and collective action. Appendix. Index. Bibliography.)

2206.   Gennard, John, *Financing Strikers*. 184 pp. London and Basingstoke: Macmillan, 1977. (Views the question of who bears economic costs of striking in context of U.K. social policy. Includes a model of the provision of strike benefits, ch. 4, esp. pp. 60–63, and comments on the "state subsidy" theory of strikes in Britain, ch. 7. Index. Bibliography.)

2207.   Gentel, William D., and Martha L. Handelman, *Police Strikes: Causes and Prevention*. 267 pp. Washington DC: U.S. Department of Justice, National Institute of Justice, 1980. (Case studies and analysis of five police strikes, 1975–1976. See ch. 6 for a summary of the causes and typical events of strikes. Bibliography.)

2208.   Gould, William R., IV, *Strikes, Dispute Procedures, and Arbitration: Essays on Labor Law*. 313 pp. Westport CT and London: Greenwood Press, 1985. (Collected essays. See ch. 1 on "substitutes for the strike weapon" and ch. 4, 8 on other aspects of strikes. Ch. 5, 6 are on the labor injunction. Index.)

2209.   Gouldner, Alvin W., *Wildcat Strike*. 179 pp. Yellow Springs OH: Antioch Press, 1954. (Locates the causes of the wildcat strike studied here in the shift from traditional to rationalized organization of work. See pp. 2–6 on the strike and ch. 9, "Rudiments of a Theory of Group Tensions.")

2210.   Griffin, John Ignatius, *Strikes: A Study in Quantitative Economics*. 319 pp. New York: Columbia Univ. Press, 1939. Columbia Univ. Studies in History, Economics, and Public Law, no. 451. Reprint, New York: AMS Press, 1968. (Early statistical study of strikes and strike outcomes. See pp. 19–28 on problems of definition and measurement. Also of interest are ch. 4 on causes and results of strikes, ch. 5 on unionization and the trend of strikes, and ch. 10 comparing this study with others. Statistical appendixes. Bibliographies list state and federal reports on labor conflict to ca. 1938.)

2211.   Griffiths, Toni, *The Teachers' Strike*. 29 pp. London: National Union of Teachers, 1971. (Account of 1969–70 teachers' strikes in England and Wales, with emphasis on organization of publicity, including photos of marches, vigils, display of banners from boats, and other devices.)

2212.   Hall, Fred S., *Sympathetic Strikes and Sympathetic Lockouts*. 118 pp. New York: Columbia Univ. Press, 1898. Columbia Univ. Studies in History, Economics and Public Law, vol. 10, no. 1. (Distinguishes sympathetic strikes as a general phenomenon from the sympathetic strike movement of the 1880s. Author contends that such strikes are caused by the "indiscretion of young unions" not yet sobered by defeats. See ch. 1, esp. pp. 16–28 on definition; ch. 2 on causal and temporal origins of sympathetic strikes; ch. 3 for classification of sympathetic strikes and lockouts; and ch. 4 for cases from several countries. Selected bibliography includes official publications of several governments on strikes to ca. 1895 and materials on selected strikes in the U.S., U.K., Australia, and France.)

2213.   Hartley, Jean, John Kelly, and Nigel Nicholson, *Steel Strike: A Case Study in Industrial Relations*. 209 pp. London: Batsford Academic and Educational, 1983. (Sociological account of 1980 steel strike in U.K., focusing on picketing as a primary activity, ch. 4–6, and union–committee organization of strike actions, ch. 7–9. Closing overview, ch. 11, analyzes strike as a "fighting organization." Index. Bibliography.)

2214. Hartmann, George W., and Theodore Newcomb, eds., *Industrial Conflict: A Psychological Interpretation*. 583 pp. New York: Cordon, 1939. Reprint, New York: Arno, 1977. (Anthology on social–psychological aspects of industrial conflict. See Keith Sward, "The Johnston Strike of 1937: A Case Study of Large–Scale Conflict," ch. 4 which concludes that organized "third parties" opposed to the strike "held the balance of power" in this conflict; "An Employer and an Organizer View the Same Series of Conflicts," ch. 5; T. Swann Harding, "Strikes are Anachronistic," ch. 19 which proposes to end strikes by scientific means; and Sheldon Menefee, "Propaganda and Symbol Manipulation," ch. 20. Index.)

2215. Hicks, J.R., *The Theory of Wages*. 247 pp. London: Macmillan, 1932. (Economic explanation of the increase in the power of trade unions and government intervention in setting wages. See ch. 7 on strikes and lockouts, esp. pp. 141–47, 154–58 on "concession" and "resistance" curves.)

2216. Hiller, E.T., *The Strike: A Study in Collective Action*. 304 pp. Chicago: Univ. of Chicago Press, 1928. (Life–cycle approach to strikes as "ordeal by battle." See ch. 2 on definition and ch. 3–17 on process of the strike. Ch. 6 is on maintaining order and ch. 7, 8 are on morale. Ch. 9, section 2 and ch. 10, sections 3, 4 are on controlling strike breakers. Ch. 11, 12 take up "tactics" and methods of coercion available to both parties. See also ch. 12 on political strikes and ch. 13 on "the mythical general strike" and its failure. Appendix. Index. Bibliography.)

2217. Hyman, Richard, *Strikes*. 218 pp. N.p. [Glasgow?]: Fontana/Collins, 1972. 2nd ed., 1977. (Written from the viewpoint of the British industrial relations system. Of most general significance are pp. 19–24, 52–56 on mechanics and varieties of action; pp. 23–36 on measurement of trends and costs of strikes; pp. 36–43 on the wildcat strike as a normal event; and pp. 109–15, 131–32 on the rationality of strike action. Index. Bibliography.)

2218.   Ingham, Geoffrey K., *Strikes and Industrial Conflict: Britain and Scandinavia*. 95 pp. London and Basingstoke: Macmillan, 1974. (Argues that comparative strike frequencies are explainable by the degree of organization of industries, employers, and labor. See pp. 25–33, 35–37, 50–60 and ch. 5 on causes of strikes and ch. 2 for a review of the work of Arthur M. Ross and Paul T. Hartman, to which this study is a response. Bibliography.)

2219.   Jackson, Michael P., *Strikes*. 232 pp. Sussex: Wheatsheaf Books; New York: St. Martin's Press, 1987. (An introduction to the statistical study of strikes, with comparisons of strike activity in various nations, esp. Australia, the U.S., and the U.K. Ch. 4, a review of theories of strike trends, separately discusses the institutional thesis, the political factors thesis, and economic factor explanations of strikes, followed in ch. 5 by industrial relations theories of strike conflict. Ch. 6 reviews thinking on the personal, social, and economic effects of strikes. Index. Bibliography.)

2220.   Kerr, Clark, John Dunlop, Frederick T. Harbison, and Charles A. Myers, *Industrialism and Industrial Man*. 331 pp. Cambridge: Harvard Univ. Press, 1960. (In the context of a theory of industrialization, authors discuss "universal responses of workers" in the form of strikes and protest, pp. 202–15. Index.)

2221.   Knowles, K.G.J.C., *Strikes: A Study in Industrial Conflict: With Special Reference to British Experience between 1911 and 1945*. 330 pp. Oxford: Basil Blackwell; New York: Philosophical Library, 1952. (The work that founded post–WWII British thought on strikes, with much suggestive and informed comment on strikes as a phenomenon. See esp. pp. 2–19 on the nature of strikes, ch. 2–4 on causes and correlates of strikes, and ch. 5 on consequences, including pp. 249–50 for a theory of strike outcomes. Index.)

2222.   Kornhauser, Arthur, Robert Dubin, and Arthur Ross, eds., *Industrial Conflict*. 551 pp. New York, Toronto, and London: McGraw–Hill, 1954. (Original source of Clark Kerr and Abraham Siegel, "The Interindustry Propensity to Strike—An International Comparison," pp. 189–212 which relates strike proneness to the social environment of labor. See also Arthur

M. Ross, "The Natural History of the Strike," pp. 23–36 on U.S. unionism and strikes and Albert Rees, "Industrial Conflict and Business Fluctuations," pp. 213–20 on strike cycles. Index.)

2223. McIlroy, John, *Strike! How to Fight. How to Win.* 228 pp. London: Pluto Press, 1984. (Manual on how to conduct strikes effectively. See ch. 3, 4, 7, 9, 11–13 on strike process under British conditions. Ch. 6, 10 discuss alternatives to strikes and auxiliary measures such as overtime bans, work to rule, and brief and selective strikes. Ch. 8 is on occupation strikes. Index. Bibliography.)

2224. Mullins, Walter G., *Strike Defense Manual.* 142 pp. Houston, London, Paris, and Tokyo: Gulf Publishing, 1980. (Proposing that "the power of the strike lies simply in the fact that it is feared," the author presents a manual for contending against a strike. Index.)

2225. Neal, Richard G., and Craig D. Johnston, *Countering Strikes and Militancy in School and Government Services.* 192 pp. Richard Neal Associates, 1982. ("A practical guide for coping with Public Employee strife." See ch. 2 for comparison of government and industrial strikes, ch. 4 on causes of strikes, ch. 9 on picketing, ch. 12 on "preemptive measures," ch. 14 on coping with the strike, and ch. 15 on communications during strikes.)

2226. Nicholson, J. Shield, *Strikes and Social Problems.* 238 pp. London: Adam and Charles Black; New York: Macmillan, 1896. (See ch. 1 for an 1893 address on "Strikes and a Living Wage," prompted by the English coal strike of that year, proposing an economic view of strikes as a "peculiar way of doing business" and an evil. Index.)

2227. Shorter, Edward, and Charles Tilly, *Strikes in France, 1830–1968.* 428 pp. Cambridge, London, New York, and Melbourne: Cambridge Univ. Press, 1974. Reprint, 1978. (Analytical study of the incidence of French strikes focusing on how the strike has changed along with economic and social change. See ch. 3–5 on strike data and Appendix A on method. Index. Bibliography.)

2228.   Steuben, John, *Strike Strategy*. 320 pp. New York: Gaer Associates, 1950. (Suggests ways to prepare for and to conduct a strike effectively. Bibliography.)

2229.   Vagts, Christopher R., and Robert B. Stone, *Anatomy of a Teacher Strike: Case History of Teacher Militancy and How a Board of Education Coped with It*. 254 pp. West Nyack, NY: Parker, 1969. (Case study of Huntington, Long Island teachers' strike in 1968 by superintendent of schools and Board of Education consultant. See ch. 4–6 on strike itself and "the strategy of winning public sympathy." Documents.)

2230.   Walsh, Kenneth, *Strikes in Europe and the United States: Measurement and Incidence*. 230 pp. London: Frances Pinter, 1983. (Cross–national statistical study of strike rates and effects, 1971–82. Summary chapters on trends, causes, duration, strike–proneness, and the relation of strikes to unions and the industrial relations system. See pp. 3–6, 15–22 on types of strike–related actions, pp. 22–39 on measures of strike and lock–out activity, and appendix for publications containing country–by–country data. Index.)

2231.   Warner, W. Lloyd, and J.O. Low, *The Social System of the Modern Factory: The Strike: A Social Analysis*. 245 pp. Yankee City Series, vol. 4. New Haven: Yale Univ. Press; London: Oxford Univ. Press, 1947. (Anthropological–sociological analysis of a community–wide strike in one industry, 1933, tracing its causes to change in skill hierarchies and social control. See ch. 3 on phases of the strike and ch. 1, 2, 5–8 on causes. Appendixes. Index.)

2232.   Webb, Sidney, and Beatrice Webb, *The History of Trade Unionism*. Rev. ed. 784 pp. New York: Kelly, 1965 [orig. publ. 1894]. (History of British trade union movement. See p. 46 on the origin of the term *strike* and consult index under names of occupations and organizations to locate discussion of various strikes and other actions. Appendixes. Index.)

2233.   Wheeler, Hoyt N., *Industrial Conflict: An Integrative Theory*. 293 pp. Columbia: Univ. of South Carolina Press, 1985. (Presents a theory of industrial conflict incorporating perspectives from various more general conflict theories. Among the "pillars" of conflict discussed are "readiness to aggressive action," ch. 6 and "collective aggressive action," ch. 7. See also ch. 2 for a review of the strike study literature. Index.)

2234.   Wright, Carroll D., *The Battles of Labor*. 220 pp. Philadelphia: George W. Jacobs, 1906. (Lectures tracing strikes to ancient times. Ch. 3 contains general description of the great strikes of the late nineteenth century and ch. 4 comments on then-current issues, including law, pp. 103–107; the role of force and violence, pp. 194–200; and the boycott, pp. 200–203.)

Slow–Downs

Slow–down strikes are one example among many of restricted strikes, where the employees work slowly and ineffectively yet remain in the workplace. As may be seen from the entries below, slow–downs are often considered a form of labor sabotage by researchers.

See also: United States: Industrial Workers of the World.

2235.   Brown, Geoff, *Sabotage: A Study in Industrial Conflict*. 402 pp. Nottingham: Bertrand Russell Peace Foundation for Spokesman Books, 1977. (Sociological study of sabotage broadly defined, primarily worker slow–downs. Focuses on British labor from the eighteenth century to 1976. Discussion of strikes, boycotts, slow–downs, and sabotage throughout. See esp. ch. 3 on the role of sabotage in the thought of the Industrial Workers of the World. Index.)

2236.   Cohen, Stanley, ed., *Images of Deviance*. 255 pp. Middlesex, England; Baltimore MD; and Victoria, Australia: Penguin Books, 1971. (See Laurie Taylor and Paul Walton, "Industrial Sabotage: Motives and Meanings," pp. 219–45, based on a broad definition of sabotage as "rule–breaking which takes the form of conscious action or inaction directed towards the mutilation or destruction of the work environment." This includes slow–downs and other noncooperation.)

2237.   Hammett, Richard S., Joel Seidman, and Jack London, "The Slowdown as a Union Tactic," *Journal of Political Economy* 65 (1957): 126–34. (Brief review of the nature and conduct of the labor slow–down as a "pressure device.")

2238.   Veblen, Thorstein, *The Engineers and the Price System*. 151 pp. New York: B.W. Huebsch, 1921. Reprint, New York: Harcourt, Brace & World, 1963. (See ch. 1 for theoretical essay on industrial sabotage, defined as "peaceable or surreptitious manoeuvers of delay, obstruction, friction, defeat" and "conscientious withdrawal of efficiency" as performed by employees, employers, and businesses.)

GENERAL STRIKES

The general strike consists of a widespread cessation of work, usually in several industries at once and often undertaken in an attempt to shut down economic activities throughout a city or region. The general strike has been as much an idea or ideology, often connected with revolutionary politics, as a reality. Dating to as early as 1842, general strikes have occurred in many countries of the world, although they have generally been of short duration.

See also for examples: Kenya; Nigeria; Palestine: General Strike, 1936; Canada: Winnipeg General Strike, 1919; United States: Great Strike of 1977; United States: Pullman Strike and Rail Boycotts of 1894; United States: General Strikes; Denmark; France: Events of May 1968; Germany: Kapp Putsch; Germany: East Berlin Uprising, 1953; Great Britain: Before 1900; Great Britain: General Strike, May 1926; Ireland, Northern: General Strike of 1974; Russia: Revolution of 1905.

2239.   Crook, Wilfrid H., *Communism and the General Strike*. 483 pp. Hamden CT: Shoestring Press, 1960. (Updated version of the ideas in next entry, with a more polemical cast. Subdivides general strikes into economic, political, and revolutionary types. See ch. 2 on early general strikes, including the relationship of the English general strike of 1842 to Chartism. Case studies include economic general strikes in Sweden, Canada, Britain, and the U.S.; political general strikes in Belgium, France, Germany, the Netherlands, Italy, East Germany, and Haiti; and revolutionary general strikes in imperial Russia, Germany, Spain, Argentina Denmark, and Hungary. Appendix also contains numerous very brief descriptions of other general strikes. Part 3 presents assessment and theory. Appendix. Index. Bibliography.)

2240. ————, *The General Strike: A Study of Labor's Tragic Weapon in Theory and Practice*. 649 pp. Chapel Hill: Univ. of North Carolina Press, 1931. (See also previous entry. Historical and theoretical study of general strikes, 1842–1930. See pp. vii–viii for definitions and ch. 2, 7 on concepts of the general strike. Contains historical studies of general strikes in Great Britain in 1842 and 1926, ch. 1, 9–13; Belgium in 1913, ch. 3; Swedenin 1902 and 1909, ch. 4; the Netherlands in 1903, ch. 5; Russia in 1905, ch. 6; Germany in 1920, ch. 14; and Seattle and Winnipeg in 1919, ch. 15. Appendix includes documents on the British general strike of 1926. Index. Bibliography.)

2241. Goodstein, Phil H., *The Theory of the General Strike from the French Revolution to Poland*. 337 pp. Boulder CO: East European Monographs, 1984. (History of ideas. Reviews interplay between the general strike as concept and as fact, ca. 1720–1914, with epilogue briefly describing several general strikes, 1919–1968. See pp. 1–4 for definitions. Includes question of violent versus nonviolent general strikes. Index. Bibliography.)

2242. Industrial Workers of the World, *The General Strike for Industrial Freedom*. 48 pp. Chicago: Industrial Workers of the World, 1933. (IWW pamphlet proposing "the General Strike" as only the method to achieve industrial freedom. See pp. 2–3, 8–9 for criticism of armed insurrection and pp. 32–36 explaining the general strike.)

2243. Katsiaficas, George, *The Imagination of the New Left: A Global Analysis of 1968*. 323 pp. Boston: South End Press, 1987. (Political account of the international New Left in 1968, focusing on two case studies of actions seen by the author as general strikes; that of May 1968 in France, ch. 3, and the 1970 student strike in the U.S., ch. 4. See also ch. 1 for an analysis of the New Left as an interconnected world–historical movement and ch. 2 for descriptions of the movements of 1968 around the world. Documents in Appendix. Index.)

2244.   Lewis, Arthur D., *Syndicalism and the General Strike: An Explanation*. 320 pp. London: T. Fisher Unwin, 1912. (Study of syndicalist concept of strikes and general strikes. Primarily on France and the ideas of Georges Sorel, with chapters on Italy, Germany, and England. Index. Bibliography.)

Methods of Political Noncooperation

Political noncooperation means the withholding of cooperation or compliance with the expected or required standards of conduct in political office or within the political system. The area of political noncooperation has increased in various parts of the world with the expansion of state power and citizenship rights. In other words, some states may now expect and enforce greater obedience from their citizens while the citizens themselves may either defend their perceived political rights or attempt to keep parts of their life free of government interference.

See also for examples: Ghana; Kenya; Nigeria; South Africa; Zambia; Iran; Palestine: Palestinians and the Intifada; Brazil: Military Rule, 1964–1985; El Salvador, Guatemala: Civic Strike, 1944; Canada: Doukhobors; United States: American Colonial Resistance and the Independence Movement, 1765–1775; United States: Cherokee Resistance to Removal; United States: Dorr Rebellion, 1841–1842; United States: Opposition to War and Expansionism; United States: Struggle for Desegregation and Civil Rights; Australia: Queensland Civil Liberties Campaign; India: Nonviolent Struggle in the National Movement; Korea: Under Japanese Domination; New Zealand (Aotearoa): Maori Resistance and the Parihaka Movement; Philippines: Revolution of 1968; Western Samoa: Mau Movement Against New Zealand Mandate; Europe: Hiding and Rescue of Jews; Bulgaria; Czechoslovakia: Dubcek Period and Warsaw Pact Invasion, 1968–1969; Denmark; Finland; France: Algiers Generals' Putsch, 1961; Germany: Kapp Putsch, 1920; Germany: Ruhrkampf, 1923; Ireland: Land League Era; Norway; Russia: Political Dissent, 1960 to 1980s.

CIVIL DISOBEDIENCE

Civil disobedience usually means deliberate disobedience of illegitimate laws in order to protest them or prevent them from becoming effective. As may be seen in the following citations, this may be group or individual and it may be direct or indirect (disobedience of unobjectionable laws used in service of an illegitimate purpose). In the West, the idea of civil disobedience is associated historically with Henry David Thoreau, who proposed in 1848 that resistance by a minority could "clog" the machinery of government. Mohandas Gandhi (see INDIA) also advocated the idea, although he saw civil disobedience as only part of a strategy of nonviolent struggle. Civil disobedience as a concept has gradually expanded its meaning to imply mass or group disruption (possibly illegal) aimed at preventing an illegitimate or unjust policy from proceeding. Likewise, thinkers who question or reject the legitimacy of disruptive civilian struggle have associated civil disobedience with more generalized disobedience of the law. They have argued in turn that civil disobedience is not acceptable because of the degradation of law and order that it engenders.

See also: United States: Opposition to War and Expansionism; United States: Struggle for Desegregation and Civil Rights; United States: Anti–Nuclear Power Movement; United States: Nonviolent Opposition to Nuclear Weapons; China: Democracy Movement: 1988–1989; India: Nonviolent Struggle in the National Movement; Legal Aspects of Nonviolent Action.

2245. Arendt, Hannah, *Crises of the Republic.* 240 pp. New York: Harcourt Brace Jovanovich, 1972. (Collected political essays. See pp. 49–102 for "Civil Disobedience" and pp. 103–98 for "On Violence" [entry 2571]. Index.)

2246. Ball, Terence, *Civil Disobedience and Civil Deviance.* 49 pp. Beverly Hills CA and London: Sage Publications, 1973. (Essay on historical aspects of the justification for civil disobedience, highlighting three major modes of justification: liberalism, ch. 2; Thoreauvian radicalism, ch. 3; and the sociology of deviant behavior, ch. 4, which claims that civil disobedience is potentially functional social deviance. Bibliography.)

2247. Bay, Christian, and Charles C. Walker, *Civil Disobedience: Theory and Practice.* 50 pp. Montreal: Black Rose Books, 1975. (Preface by Dimitrios Roussopoulos contains a brief history of civil disobedience. Bay's essay, pp. 13–30, presents a theoretical analysis of the concept of civil disobedience. Walker's "Civil Disobedience: Practice," pp. 32–47, presents a short training or organizing manual for civil disobedience as a method of nonviolent action. Pp. 48–50 contain brief descriptions of nine Canadian cases.)

2248.   Bedau, H.A., ed., *Civil Disobedience in Focus*. 217 pp. London and New York: Routledge, 1991. (Collected essays and sources. Of interest are H.A. Bedau, "Civil Disobedience and Personal Responsibility," ch. 3 which contains a discussion of "Thoreau's Principle" justifying resistance; Herbert J. Storing, "The Case Against Civil Disobedience," ch. 5 which mounts an attack on Martin Luther King, Jr.'s version of civil disobedience as "irrelevant"; Joseph Raz, "Civil Disobedience," ch. 11; and Brian Smart, "Defining Civil Disobedience," ch. 12. Index.)

2249.   Bedau, Hugh Adam, ed., *Civil Disobedience: Theory and Practice*. 282 pp. New York: Pegasus, 1969. (Collection of essays and analyses of the concept of civil disobedience. Includes Henry David Thoreau, "Civil Disobedience." Part 2 contains five articles on civil disobedience in the civil rights movement. See esp. William L. Taylor, "Civil Disobedience: Observations on the Strategies of Protest," pp. 98–105 for a legal analysis and Louis Waldman, "Civil Rights—Yes: Civil Disobedience—No," pp. 106–15 for a critique of M.L. King, Jr.'s, strategy. Part 3 contains articles on civil disobedience against war and nuclear weapons and part 4 presents articles on the ethical, political, and legal justification of civil disobedience. Index.)

2250.   Childress, James F., *Civil Disobedience and Political Obligation: A Study in Christian Social Ethics*. 250 pp. New Haven and London: Yale Univ. Press, 1971. (Within the context of a moral–ethical inquiry, author develops a definition and concept of civil disobedience, ch. 1, and discusses its application, ch. 4. See esp. "problems of definition," pp. 1–12 and "forms and means of resistance," pp. 202–25. Index.)

2251.   Chipman, Lauchan, Michael Hamel–Green, and others, *Conscience and the Law*. 87 pp. South Yarra, Victoria: Heinemann Educational Australia, 1974. (Debate counterposing a legalist defense of the primacy of authority against activists' defense of civil disobedience. See esp. pp. 23–28, 46–62. Bibliography.)

2252. *Civil Disobedience*. 32 pp. Santa Barbara CA: Center for the Study of Democratic Institutions, 1966. (Pamphlet containing papers presented at conference of attorneys on the concept of civil disobedience. See esp. papers by Harrop A. Freeman for classification and discussion of legal aspects, Raghavan N. Iyer on Gandhi and civil disobedience, and Harry Kalven, Jr. on Thoreau.)

2253. *Civil Disobedience, 1969–1970: A Compilation of the Original DICTA Published by The Virginia Law Weekly*. 126 pp. Charlottesville: Virginia Law Weekly DICTA, 1970. (Brief essays on legal aspects of civil disobedience. See esp. pieces by Bodenheimer, McKay, Keeton, and Hartt on concepts. Articles by Friedland, Morsell, Selden, and Sax are on then–current conflicts. Rotko and Marshall write from the official's viewpoint and Sahid writes on a "Game Theory of Violence," pp. 101–10.)

2254. Coffin, William Sloane, Jr., and Morris I. Leibman, *Civil Disobedience: Aid or Hindrance to Justice?* 93 pp. Washington: American Enterprise Institute for Public Policy Research, Rational Debate Series, 1972. (Debate between Coffin, who advocates for civil disobedience, and Leibman, who advocates working for change within the political and legal system.)

2255. Cohen, Carl, *Civil Disobedience: Conscience, Tactics, and the Law*. 222 pp. New York and London: Columbia Univ. Press, 1971. (Discusses the nature and justification of civil disobedience and the place of punishment in considering its legal status. See pp. 10–22 on civil disobedience as public protest and ch. 3 for a classification of civil disobedience. Consult index under *tactics*. Index.)

2256. Cox, Archibald, Mark DeWolfe Howe, and J.R. Wiggins, *Civil Rights, the Constitution, and the Courts*. 76 pp. Cambridge: Harvard Univ. Press, 1967. (Archibald Cox, "Direct Action, Civil Disobedience, and the Constitution," pp. 2–29, explores nonviolent action from the lawyer's viewpoint; see esp. classification problems on pp. 5–11 and rule of law issues, pp. 19–29.)

2257. Dixit, R.D., *Civil Disobedience: A Philosophical Study.* 104 pp. Delhi: GDK Publications, 1980. (Philosophical analysis of civil disobedience as a method of political protest. See ch. 3 on Thoreau, ch. 4 on Gandhi, and pp. 55–60 for discussion of violent versus nonviolent action. Index. Bibliography.)

2258. Fortas, Abe, *Concerning Dissent and Civil Disobedience.* 68 pp. New York: New American Library, 1968. (Reasons against the use of civil disobedience in public conflicts as marshaled by U.S. Supreme Court justice.)

2259. Goldwin, Robert A., ed., *On Civil Disobedience: Essays Old and New.* 145 pp. Chicago: Rand McNally, 1969. (See, in response to Thoreau and King, Harris L. Wofford, Jr., "Law as a Question: The Uses and Abuses of Civil Disobedience," pp. 79–94 and Herbert J. Storing, "The Case against Civil Disobedience," pp. 95–120.)

2260. Haksar, Vinit, *Civil Disobedience, Threats and Offers [Gandhi and Rawls].* 58 pp. Oxford and New York: Oxford Univ. Press, 1986. (Explores the "similarities and dissimilarities" between Gandhi and John Rawls on "persuasive" civil disobedience in liberal regimes in ch. 1. Noncooperation is discussed in ch. 2 and "coercive proposals" in ch. 3, both in the context of justifications for coercive versus persuasive actions.)

2261. Hall, Robert T., *The Morality of Civil Disobedience.* 162 pp. New York, Evanston, San Francisco, and London: Harper & Row, 1971. (See pp. 13–17 and ch. 2 for definition and clarification. Ch. 3 contains theoretical framework for considering the moral justification of civil disobedience. Pp. 87–93 discuss nonviolent versus violent action. Ch. 5 applies theory to specific cases, including Birmingham 1963, pp. 109–114; war tax resistance, pp. 114–21; and a 1969 "D.C. Nine" action protesting Dow Chemical's production of napalm, pp. 122–27. Index. Bibliography.)

2262. Harris, Paul, ed., *Civil Disobedience.* 296 pp. Lanham MD: University Press of America, 1989. (An anthology of sources primarily concerned with the combined political, moral, and legal issues associated with civil disobedience in constitutional systems. Editor's introduction includes a six–part definition of civil disobedience, pp. 4–14, and is also concerned with the issue of justification. Among essays included that may not be readily available elsewhere are Herbert J. Storing, "The Case Against Civil Disobedience," ch. 3; Alan Gewirth, "Civil Disobedience, Law, and Morality: An Examination of Justice Fortas' Doctrine," ch. 5; Clyde Frazier, "Between Obedience and Revolution," ch. 11; Wilson Carey McWilliams, "Civil Disobedience and Contemporary Constitutionalism," ch. 12; and Paul F. Power, "Civil Disobedience as Functional Opposition," ch. 13. Index. Bibliography.)

2263. Held, Virginia, Kai Nielson, and Charles Parsons, eds., *Philosophy & Political Action.* 282 pp. New York, London, and Toronto: Oxford Univ. Press, 1972. (Essays edited for the New York Group of the Society for Philosophy and Public Affairs. See part 2, "Defiance of the State," for articles on civil disobedience and dissent. See esp. Virginia Held, "On Understanding Political Strikes," ch. 4 which gives a philosophical analysis of political strikes of various kinds and a discussion of civil disobedience. Also of interest is Gordon J. Schochet, "The Morality of Resisting the Penalty," on criminal responsibility for civil disobedience. See also part 1 for essays on revolution, including an ethical defense of violence by Joseph Margolis, ch. 2. Index.)

2264. Kent, Edward, ed., *Revolution and the Rule of Law.* 181 pp. Englewood Cliffs NJ: Prentice–Hall, 1971. (Essays on dissent and the democratic ideal of the rule of law. Includes M.L. King, Jr., "Letter from Birmingham City Jail," pp. 12–29; John Rawls, "The Justification of Civil Disobedience," pp. 30–45; Virginia Held, "Civil Disobedience and Public Policy," pp. 92–110; Michael Walzer, "The Obligation to Disobey," pp. 111–29; and Alfred G. Meyer, "Political Change Through Civil Disobedience in the U.S.S.R. and Eastern Europe," pp. 130–48. See also Robert Paul Wolff's essay "On Violence," pp. 60–76 for a philosophical examination of the justification of violence for social change. Bibliography.)

2265. Macfarlane, Leslie J., *Political Disobedience.* 95 pp. London and Basingstoke: Macmillan Press, 1971. (Broad–brush analysis of the range of politically–oriented "disobedience," both violent and nonviolent. See pp. 28–33 contrasting paradigmatic figures advocating nonviolent and violent disobedience and ch. 4, esp. pp. 45–46. Bibliography.)

2266. Madden, Edward H., *Civil Disobedience and Moral Law in Nineteenth–Century American Philosophy*. 214 pp. Seattle and London: Univ. of Washington Press, 1968. (Study in the history of moral and reform thought in the U.S and the problems of slavery and civil disobedience, broadly understood, ca. 1825–70. Index. Bibliography.)

2267. Manning, Robert, and Michael Janeway, eds., *Who We Are: An ATLANTIC Sampler on the United States and Vietnam*. 378 pp. Boston and Toronto: Little, Brown Atlantic Monthly Press Book, 1969. (See Charles Wyzanski, Jr., "On Civil Disobedience," and Leo Tolstoy, "Advice to a Draftee.")

2268. Murphy, Jeffrie G., ed., *Civil Disobedience and Violence*. 151 pp. Belmont CA: Wadsworth, 1971. (Collected essays on civil disobedience from philosophical viewpoint. Among those not readily accessible elsewhere are pieces by John Rawls, Sidney Hook, and Kropotkin. See also a brief piece by the editor dating from a 1967 teach–in, "The Vietnam War and the Right to Resistance," pp. 64–72. Bibliography.)

2269. Pennock, J. Roland, and John W. Chapman, eds., *Political and Legal Obligation: Nomos XII*. 455 pp. New York: Atherton Press, 1970. (Final section contains essays on civil disobedience, including James Luther Adams, "Civil Disobedience: Its Occasions and Limits," pp. 293–331; Kent Greenawalt, "A Contextual Approach to Disobedience," pp. 332–69; and Gerald C. MacCallom, Jr., "Some Truths and Untruths about Civil Disobedience"; and portions of Mark R. MacGuigan, "Obligation and Obedience," pp. 46–54.)

2270. Singer, Peter, *Democracy and Disobedience*. 150 pp. Oxford: Clarendon Press, 1973. (Philosophical analysis of the forms of limited disobedience which the author views as compatible with a model democratic society. See pp. 72–84 on disobedience for publicity and pp. 92–104 on conscientious objection. Appendix contains application of theory to disobedience to Northern Ireland. Index.)

2271. Smith, Michael P., and Kenneth L. Deutsch, eds., *Political Obligation and Civil Disobedience: Readings.* 431 pp. New York: Thomas Y. Crowell, 1972. (Collects many basic writings with particular attention to ethical issues. See esp. pieces by Sibley, ch. 2; Frankel, Power, and Bay, in section 3; Walzer, ch. 23; and Dworkin, ch. 27.)

2272. Thoreau, Henry David, "Resistance to Civil Government"; also known as "Civil Disobedience" and "On the Duty of Civil Disobedience." (Essay on the rationale for resistance to government taken from a lecture given by the author in Concord, Massachusetts in 1848, during the Mexican War. Originally printed under the title "Resistance to Civil Government" in the journal *Aesthetic Papers* [1849]. Reprinted after the author's death in Henry David Thoreau, *A Yankee in Canada, with Anti–Slavery and Reform Papers* [1866] under the title "Civil Disobedience." It is not known if Thoreau selected or authorized the latter title, nor is the origin of the alternate title "On the Duty of Civil Disobedience" known to be connected to Thoreau. In this essay, Thoreau argues that unthinking and self–interested cooperation with evil conditions is the primary obstacle to reform of unjust, although lawful, practices. In arguing for opposition to such practices, Thoreau observes that breaking the laws upon which injustice rests serves as "a counter friction" to the "machine" that produces it and further that even a minority of citizens is "irresistible when it clogs by its own weight." Thoreau also discusses his theory of the state, conscience, and the reasons why people avoid civil disobedience, as well as his own experience. Although Thoreau's observations upon "friction" are often taken to result from his principles and his theory of conscientious action, they deserve to be viewed as empirical observations testable as such. Henry David Thoreau, *Reform Papers.* Ed. Wendell Glick. 403 pp. Princeton: Princeton Univ. Press, 1973, contains an authoritative edition of the text of "Resistance to Civil Government," pp. 63–90. See note on the editing of the essay, which concludes that there is no evidence that Thoreau chose the alternative title "Civil Disobedience" and which is entirely silent on the title "On the Duty of Civil Disobedience." Other available editions of this work include the following: *A Yankee in Canada, with Anti–Slavery and Reform Papers*. 286 pp. New York: Greenwood Press, 1969 [orig. publ. 1866, reprint 1892]. *On the Duty of Civil Disobedience*. 21 pp. Introduction by Gene Sharp. London: Peace News, 1963. *The Variorum Civil Disobedience*. Ed. Walter Harding. 91 pp. New York: Twayne, 1967. *Walden or, Life in the Woods and On the Duty of Civil Disobedience*. 256 pp. New York: New American Library, 1960. *Walden and Civil Disobedience*. 431 pp. Harmondsworth, England, New York, Ringwood, Victoria, Australia, Markham, Ontario, and Auckland, New Zealand: Penguin, 1983.)

2273.   Van den Haag, Ernest, *Political Violence and Civil Disobedience*. 123 pp. New York, Evanston, San Francisco, London: Harper & Row, 1972. (Essays on civil disobedience, pp. 3–49, and political violence, pp. 53–123. See esp. pp. 14–22 on arguments for disobedience, pp. 29–32 on coercive versus persuasive civil disobedience, pp. 56–57 on nonviolent defiance, and pp. 60–64 on coercion and violence. Appendixes.)

2274.   Walzer, Michael, *Obligations: Essays on Disobedience, War, and Citizenship*. 244 pp. Cambridge MA: Harvard Univ. Press, 1970. (See section 1 for essays on the nature of obligation and civil disobedience. Index.)

2275.   Weber, David R., ed., *Civil Disobedience in America: A Documentary History*. 318 pp. Ithaca NY: Cornell Univ. Press, 1978. (Primary documents by American proponents of what has become known as civil disobedience, including selections on the colonial period, mid–nineteenth century nonresistance, disobedience to the 1850 Fugitive Slave Law, women's rights actions from 1848 to 1917, the civil rights movement, and twentieth century war resistance. Index.)

2276.   Whittaker, Charles E., and William Sloane Coffin, Jr., *Law, Order, and Civil Disobedience*. 168 pp. Washington DC: American Enterprise Institute for Public Policy Research, 1967. (Debate between the position that mass law breaking is never justified and a religiously–oriented defense of resisting specific injustices, with text of spectators' challenges and debaters' responses.)

2277. Woodcock, George, *Civil Disobedience*. 69 pp. Toronto: Canadian Broadcasting Corporation, 1966. (Text of radio addresses exploring the past of civil disobedience in both Eastern and Western [English] traditions of thought and action. Index.)

2278. Zashin, Elliot M., *Civil Disobedience and Democracy*. 368 pp. New York: Free Press, 1972. (An analysis of whether civil disobedience is compatible with liberal democracy. See ch. 4 on definition and ch. 5–8 for analysis of conduct and effects of nonviolent action. Index. Selected bibliography.)

2279. Zinn, Howard, *Disobedience and Democracy: Nine Fallacies on Law and Order*. 124 pp. New York: Random House, 1968. (Reply to Fortas [entry 2260]. Zinn defines civil disobedience as "deliberate violation of law for a vital social purpose" and assumes that civil disobedience may be violent.)

2280. Zwiebach, Burton, *Civility and Disobedience*. 241 pp. Cambridge, London, New York and Melbourne: Cambridge Univ. Press, 1975. (Justificatory essay on civil disobedience based on an expanded theory of obligation. Author suggests that civility and obligation can only be justified by the creation of a "common life," which is "the theoretical foundation for judging the rightness of obligations imposed by public authority." He defines four basic categories of rights [citizenship, freedom, equality, and accountability] and concludes that civil disobedience is a political right and justified as part of the common life. See part 2 on disobedience and esp. ch. 8 where author argues for a permissive treatment of disobedience in the courts. Index.)

SANCTUARY

Sanctuary means offering the shelter and protection of a church or religious institution to persons who are, or might be, subject to arrest. Sanctuary in this sense rests upon the claim that sanctified places can with some authority be considered refuges from civil power. References here are mostly on the U.S. sanctuary movement of the 1980s that protected Central Americans who departed their home countries and entered the U.S. without the sanction of law.

2281.   Bau, Ignatius, *This Ground Is Holy: Church Sanctuary and Central American Refugees.* 288 pp. New York and Mahwah NJ: Paulist Press, 1985. (History of movement by North American churches to provide sanctuary for Central American refugees and the historical roots of sanctuary. See ch. 1 for introduction, ch. 2–3 for legal implications, ch. 5 for early religious traditions of sanctuary, ch. 6 for sanctuary in British history, and ch. 7 for sanctuary in U.S. history. Bibliography.)

2282.   Corbett, Jim, *The Sanctuary Church.* 42 pp. Wallingford PA: Pendle Hill Publications, 1986. Pendle Hill Pamphlet No. 270. (Essay on North American church movement to give sanctuary to Central American refugees.)

2283.   Golden, Renny, and Michael McConnell, *Sanctuary: The New Underground Railroad.* 214 pp. Maryknoll NY: Orbis Books, 1986. (Account of North American sanctuary movement with personal stories and history. See esp. ch. 2, 6 on group structure and problems of action. Photos.)

2284.   MacEoin, Gary, ed. *Sanctuary: A Resource Guide for Understanding and Participating in the Central American Refugees' Struggle.* 217 pp. Cambridge MA, San Francisco, Hagerstown MD, Philadelphia, London, Mexico City, São Paolo, Singapore, and Sydney: Harper & Row, 1985. (Papers from a symposium on this movement, many of which are on theological justifications for sanctuary, its history, and its relationship to the human rights question. Appendix.)

2285.   Thomas, Maria H., ed., *Sanctuary: Challenge to the Churches.* 89 pp. Washington DC: The Institute on Religion and Democracy, 1986. (Presentations and discussion from an October 1985 conference on sanctuary with emphasis on justifying sanctuary of Central American refugees.)

NONCOOPERATION IN GOVERNMENT AND MILITARY

Officials, functionaries, employees, and others serve the ends of government or private organizations (perhaps with a governmental mandate) through their expertise and assistance. They may have various reasons for withholding this participation, including reservations about the objectives of the organization. Likewise, their nonparticipation may be disguised or open, complete or partial. Two areas of noncooperation that involve professionals include resignation in protest and whistleblowing (revealing illegal or immoral activities), but mutinies and refusal of orders are a military version of noncooperation.

See also: United States: Professionals' Strikes; Philippines: Revolution of 1986.

2286.   Bowman, James S., Frederick A. Ellison, and Paula Lockhart, *Professional Dissent: An Annotated Bibliography and Resource Guide.* 322 pp. New York and London: Garland Publishing, 1989. (Classified bibliography on "whistle–blowing and dissent" and related topics. Early sections compile references on whistle–blowing in business, government, and the professions, followed by a review of several relevant literatures, including legal documents. Index.)

2287.   Bryant, Clifton D., *Khaki–Collar Crime: Deviant Behavior in the Military Context.* 388 pp. New York: Free Press; London: Collier Macmillan, 1979. (See ch. 5 for discussion of individual and group noncompliance with military norms, including deliberately ineffective behavior, pp. 141–45; criticism of authority, pp. 156–59; failure to obey orders, pp. 160–61; and mutiny, pp. 163–68. Index. Bibliography.)

2288.   Everett, Melissa, *Breaking Ranks.* 242 pp. Philadelphia PA and Santa Cruz CA: New Society Publishers, 1989. (Journalistic oral histories of ten men who resigned in protest from careers in the military, weapons industries, intelligence, and other areas of the foreign policy establishment. Ch. 11 contains discussion of the factors contributing to their individual conversions. Ch. 12 examines the contemporary anti–militarism movement in the U.S. and the role of "insiders' protests.")

2289.   Glazer, Myron Peretz, and Penina Mygdal Glazer, *The Whistleblowers: Exposing Corruption in Government and Industry.* 286 pp. New York: Basic Books, 1989. (Views employees who call attention to misdeeds of their employers as "ethical resisters" and traces the origins of their activities to the 1960s. Ch. 1, 2 discuss recent history of whistleblowing, ch. 3 locates source of ethical standards informing whistleblowers in their training as professionals, and ch. 4 explores influence of strong beliefs on the capacity to expose wrongdoing. Ch. 5 identifies several types of sanctions available to punish whistleblowers, including blacklisting, dismissal, transfer to another job, and personal harassment and sexual exploitation. Ch. 7 discusses the press, lawmakers, and organized interest groups as allies of the whistleblower. Appendix. Index.)

2290.   Lamb, Dave, *Mutinies: 1917–1920.* 32 pp. Oxford and London: *Solidarity*, [1977]. (Brief history of British and Canadian army and navy mutinies during WWI. Photos. Illustrations. Documents.)

2291.   Nader, Ralph, Peter J. Petkas, and Kate Blackwell, eds., *Whistle Blowing: A Report of the Conference on Professional Responsibility.* 302 pp. New York: Grossman Publishers, 1972. (Conference papers on whistle blowing, including accounts of personal experience as well as theory, history, and description of the process. See ch. 19, "To Blow the Whistle," on the recommended method. Appendixes. Index.)

2292.   Weinstein, Deena, *Bureaucratic Opposition: Challenging Abuses at the Workplace.* 145 pp. New York and Oxford: Pergamon Press, 1979. (On strategies aimed at changing bureaucracies in public and private organizations from within. See ch. 4 on "strategies and tactics," esp. pp. 88–99 on "direct action." Index. Bibliography.)

2293.   Weisband, Edward, and Thomas M. Franck, *Resignation in Protest: Political and Ethical Choices Between Loyalty to Team and Loyalty to Conscience in American Public Life.* 236 pp. New York: Grossman, 1975. (On the style, motives, and personal costs of resignations in protest in the U.S. federal government, with comparisons based on British experiences. See ch. 2 on examples and limits of protest resignations, ch. 3 on the costs involved, and an Anglo–American comparison in ch. 4. Ch. 1, 5–7 discuss the issues of group loyalty and individual autonomy raised by the study. Appendixes. Index.)

2294. Westin, Alan F., ed., *Whistle Blowing! Loyalty and Dissent in the Corporation*. 181 pp. New York: McGraw–Hill, 1981. (Personal accounts by people who disclosed dangerous or illegal practices, refused commands and expectations they considered illegitimate, protested harassment or discrimination, and the like. Index.)

METHODS OF NONVIOLENT INTERVENTION

In any of a variety of ways, methods of nonviolent intervention interfere with or directly modify the workings of an institution. Usually, nonviolent intervention disrupts the established order or status quo in some visible way. This may be psychological, by placing a burden of choice on an adversary that must be resolved in some way, or it may be physical, social, economic, or political.

Psychological Intervention

FASTS AND HUNGER STRIKES

Fasts of moral pressure and hunger strikes are forms of psychological intervention. Their clear intent is to place their object (a person or group) in a position that requires them to take some action to prevent the fast from going too far. Fasts may be symbolic in their effect, presenting an appeal, or more directly intended to compel the adversary toward some action.

See also for examples: Bolivia; China: Democracy Movement, 1988–1989; India: Nonviolent Struggle in the National Movement; India: Mohandas K. Gandhi; Great Britain: Women's Suffrage Movement; Northern Ireland: Prison Protests and Hunger Strikes of 1980–81; Russia: Political Dissent, 1960–1980s.

2295.   Brooks, Svevo, John Burkhart, Dorothy Granada, and Charles Gray, *A Guide to Political Fasting*. 2d ed. 57 pp. Cottage Grove OR: Larry Langdon Publications, 1982 [orig. publ. 1980]. (Describes the "art of fasting" and how to use it. Bibliography.)

2296.   Kritzer, Amelia, *Fasting*. 71 pp. Haverford PA: Nonviolent Action Project of the Center for Nonviolent Conflict Resolution, Haverford College, [1972]. (A "guide" to fasting [9 pp.] bound with studies of fasts in Washington DC in 1970 and 1971 and outside a Pennsylvania prison in 1969. Photos. Documents. Bibliography.)

2297.   Rogers, Eric N., *Fasting: The Phenomenon of Self-Denial*. 160 pp. Nashville TN and New York: Thomas Nelson, 1976. (Review of the phenomenon of fasting, distinguishing between religious or health-oriented fasts and fasting in protest. See esp. ch. 13, "What Makes it Work?" Index.)

Physical Intervention

Physical intervention is characterized by persons attempting to interfere with other activities or institutional processes. It includes sit–ins, obstruction, and the nonviolent occupation, or attempted occupation, of places.

See also for examples: Palestine: Illegal Immigration of Jews During British Mandate, 1944–1948; United States: Quaker "Invasion" of Massachusetts; United States: Movement Against the War in Vietnam, 1963–1971; United States: Student Movements; United States: Anti–Nuclear Power Movement; United States: Nonviolent Opposition to Nuclear Weapons; Australia: Environmental Movement; China: Democracy Movement, 1988–1989; India: Simon Commission, Round Table Conferences, and Civil Disobedience, 1928–1933; India: Mohandas K. Gandhi; Japan; New Zealand (Aotearoa): Maori Resistance and the Parihaka Movement; New Zealand (Aotearoa): Protests Against Sports With South African Teams; Philippines: Revolution of 1986.

ENCAMPMENTS

A relatively recent method of nonviolent intervention has been establishing encampments at some location in order to create a presence, monitor activities, or actually to interfere with some activity.

2298.   Cataldo, Mima, Ruth Putter, Bryna Fireside, and Elaine Lytle, *The Women's Encampment for a Future of Peace and Justice: Images and Writings.* 108 pp. Philadelphia: Temple Univ. Press, 1987. (Text and photos on Romulus NY encampment beginning in 1983. See introduction for the organization of the camp, including pp. 15–17 on counter–demonstrators. Ch. 2, 3 are on logistics and ch. 4, 5 and pp. 39, 49, 54–58 on actions associated with the encampment. Illustrations. Photos. Documents.)

2299.   Cook, Alice, and Gwyn Kirk, *Greenham Women Everywhere: Dreams, Ideas and Actions from the Women's Peace Movement.* 127 pp. London: Pluto Press, 1983. (Account of Women's Peace Camp, Greenham Common, England with personal contributions. See esp. pp. 38–62 on various nonviolent actions taken by the women, pp. 63–79 on elements and issues of nonviolence, and pp. 91–107 on the relationship of media to the camp. Photos.)

2300.   Harford, Barbara, and Sarah Hopkins, *Greenham Common: Women at the Wire.* 179 pp. London: Women's Press, 1984. (Narrative edited from diaries, recollections, and statements. Contains description and discussion of motivations, symbolism employed, arrests and imprisonment, and public opinion. See "Dateline," pp. v–viii and ch. 4, 7, 11. Photos. Bibliography.)

2301.   Participants of the Puget Sound Women's Peace Camp, *We Are Ordinary Women: A Chronicle of the Puget Sound Women's Peace Camp.* 115 pp. Seattle WA: Seal Press, 1985. (Photo essay on peace camp that began in September 1982 containing drawings, excerpts from journals, and trial testimony.)

SIT–INS AND OCCUPATIONS

Sit–ins and occupations occur when participants physically occupy a location. While the motives and effects vary greatly, sit–ins and occupations establish a presence that may interfere in the normal operations of an institution.

See also for examples: United States: Sit–Down Strikes, 1930s; United States: Student Movements; United States: Sit–Ins and Freedom Rides, 1960–1962.

2302.   Greenwood, John, *Worker Sit–ins and Job Protection: Case Studies of Union Intervention.* 120 pp. Farnborough, England: Gower Press, 1977. (Studies labor sit–down strikes as a response to "redundancy" job loss in U.K. and other countries. See ch. 3, 7–8 for analysis and ch. 5–6 on the Lip Factory sit–in in France, 1973. Index. Bibliography.)

2303.   Lofland, John, and Michael Fink, *Symbolic Sit–Ins: Protest Occupations at the California Capital.* 112 pp. Washington DC: University Press of America, 1982. (A study of sit–ins by interest groups chiefly conducted as symbolic protest, classified by the authors as pack–ins, lone–ins, one–night stands, spirited sieges, and long–term vigils. See ch. 1 on types of struggle and ch. 8 for conclusions on dynamic factors. Index.)

2304.   *Sit–ins and Work–ins.* 39 pp. London: Institute of Personnel Management, National Committee on Employee Relations, 1976. (Advice on conflict management for U.K. companies experiencing sit–ins during industrial changes of 1970s. See esp. pp. 2–5, 11–16, and catalogue of cases in Appendix 1.)

BLOCKADES AND VOYAGES OF INTERVENTION

As early as the 1950s, voyagers have undertaken to interfere with or prevent certain seagoing activities by interposing themselves and their vessels. This has included sailing into nuclear test areas, placing a vessel between a whale–hunting ship and its quarry, and massed blockades of ports and facilities.

2305.   Bigelow, Albert, *The Voyage of the Golden Rule: An Experiment with Truth.* 286 pp. Garden City NY: Doubleday, 1959.

(Account of a protest voyage into a Pacific nuclear testing site. Appendixes.)

2306.   Boardman, Elizabeth Jelinek, *The Phoenix Trip: Notes on a Quaker Mission to Haiphong.* 174 pp. Burnsville NC: Celo Press, 1985. (Story of 1967 Phoenix Project to deliver medical supplies to North and South Vietnam civilians. See Lynne Shivers, "Analysis of Peace Agency: A Quaker Action Group," pp. ix–xiii and Appendix A for letters condemning and supporting the trip. Photos.)

2307.   Brown, Michael, and John May, *The Greenpeace Story.* 160 pp. London: Dorling Kindersley, 1989. (Photos and text chronicling Greenpeace campaigns from their origins to the mid–1980s. Voyages to protest or prevent nuclear testing by sailing vessels into test areas in the Pacific are chronicled in several chapters. See esp. ch. 1, 2 on the first voyages to Amchitka Island, Alaska, and ch. 3, 4 and pp. 77–79 on the *Vega* voyages to the Moruroa Atoll test site maintained by France. Ch. 9, 10 contain sections on protest voyages against the disposal of nuclear waste materials at sea. Ch. 11 is on the *Rainbow Warrior* voyage to New Zealand in preparation for a protest at Moruroa and that vessel's sinking by French agents. Other chapters discuss voyages for the protection of marine mammals and other activities against pollution and nuclear power. Photos. Index.)

2308.   Cargill, Gavin, *Blockade '75: The Story of the Fishermen's Blockade of the Ports.* Glasgow, Scotland: Molendinar Press, 1976. (Story of 1975 U.K. fishing–boat blockade of ports to protest economic losses. "Diary" in part 3. Illustrations. Photos.)

2309.   Hunter, Robert, *To Save a Whale: The Voyages of Greenpeace.* 119 pp. San Francisco: Chronicle Books, 1978. (Story of early Greenpeace campaigns to protest whaling in mid–1970s. Discusses early history of Greenpeace anti–testing campaign and genesis of anti–whaling campaigns. See also confrontation with Soviet whalers, pp. 34–51, and campaign of 1976, pp. 68–111. Photos.)

2310.   ———, *Warriors of the Rainbow: A Chronicle of the Greenpeace Movement.* 454 pp. New York: Holt, Rinehart and Winston,

1979. (Journalistic history of first seven years of Greenpeace movement by a member. See index under specific voyages and boat names.)

2311.   McTaggart, David, with Robert Hunter, *Greenpeace III: Journey into the Bomb*. 372 pp. London: Collins, 1978. (Memoir by captain of sailing vessel *Vega* in attempt to halt French atmospheric testing of nuclear weapons by positioning itself in the fallout area during a test. Illustrations. Photos.)

2312.   Mitcalfe, Barry, *Boy Roel: Voyage to Nowhere*. 154 pp. Auckland, New Zealand: Alister Taylor, 1972. (Story of voyages of New Zealand ships into French bomb testing areas, 1972. See also voyage of *Greenpeace III*, pp. 132–137. Photos.)

2313.   Newnham, Tom, *Peace Squadron: The Sharp End of Nuclear Protest in New Zealand*. 60 pp. Auckland: Graphic Publications, 1986. (Lively and committed account of waterborne New Zealand "nuclear–free zone" activists who sailed, rowed, and paddled into the paths of nuclear–power vessels in order to prevent their entry into port. Photos.)

2314.   The Sunday Times Insight Team, *Rainbow Warrior: The French Attempt to Sink Greenpeace*. 302 pp. London, Melbourne, Auckland, Johannesburg: Hutchinson, 1986. (Journalistic account of French demolition of Greenpeace ship. Ch. 8 includes early protest voyages and history of Greenpeace. Ch. 9 is on the Pacific anti–nuclear testing protests. Illustrations. Photos. Index.)

2315.   Taylor, Richard K., *Blockade: A Guide to Non–Violent Intervention*. 175 pp. Maryknoll NY: Orbis Books, 1977. (Participants' account of 1971 nonviolent campaign protesting U.S. military and economic aid to Pakistani dictatorship. Part 1 chronicles attempt to blockade Pakistani freighters with canoes and kayaks. Part 2 contains a "manual" for nonviolent direct action. Appendixes outline strategies for recruitment, media relations, sign and leaflet production, and fundraising. Photos.)

Section II
Dynamics of Nonviolent Action

Dynamics are the processes that occur during actual conflicts in which nonviolent action is used, especially as they either increase or decrease the likelihood that activists will achieve a conclusion acceptable to them. Dynamics include preparation, training, strategy, and organization and the kinds of interactions that conflict groups have with their adversaries, their supporters, and third parties who may be hostile, neutral, or indifferent. Lastly, dynamics refers also to the steps and stages that bring about a conclusion, particularly the mechanisms of change that may operate when successes are achieved.

TECHNIQUE AND CONCEPTS OF NONVIOLENT ACTION

Whether viewed from a historical or definitional perspective, it is evident that nonviolent action is neither a simple nor a completely distinctive concept. In the minds of many people, nonviolent action is associated with nonviolence, peace, justice, pacifism, human rights, and other ideas. In order to develop a manageable concept of nonviolent action as a means of action in conflicts, therefore, it is necessary to determine what is distinctive about nonviolent action as opposed to these other ideas and concepts (see the Introduction for more on these points). This section is therefore concerned with nonviolent action as such, reserving consideration of nonviolence, peace movements, and the like for another chapter.

2316. Bergfeldt, Lennart, "Nonviolent Action: State of the Literature." Uppsala, Sweden. Uppsala Univ., Department of Peace and Conflict Research. Report No. 20. 1979. 55 pp. (Critical review of twenty works, which range in depth from opinion articles to full–fledged scholarly studies, judged by their ability to meet criteria explained on pp. 7–8. These criteria include the theoretical development of the works and of the topic in general, which are discussed on pp. 40–46.)

2317.   Blumberg, Herbert H., "An Annotated Bibliography of Serials
        Concerned with the Non–Violent Protest Movement."
        Sociological Abstracts 17 (1969): pp. xxi–xlx. (List of newsletters,
        journals, and other serial publications likely to contain
        information on groups using nonviolent action or on
        nonviolent action in general. Annotated.)

2318.   Carter, April, David Hoggett, and Adam Roberts, eds.,
        Nonviolent Action: A Selected Bibliography. Revised and enlarged
        edition. 84 pp. London: Housmans; Haverford PA: Center for
        Nonviolent Conflict Resolution, Haverford College, 1970.
        (Selected, annotated entries on concepts and history of
        nonviolent action. Sections A–C compile entries on theory and
        methods and section D on case studies.)

2319.   *Nonviolence: An Annotated Bibliography*. 41 pp. Cornell Univ.
        Libraries Bibliography Series, Number 4, April, 1971. (Selective
        annotated bibliography of books, journal articles, pamphlets,
        leaflets, and tapes with sections on "philosophy of
        nonviolence," nonviolent action, pacifism, and conscientious
        objection. Section entitled "nonviolent action for change," pp.
        17–25, contains entries on training, the U.S. civil rights
        movement, and some international leaders of nonviolent
        conflict.)

2320.   Pickus, Robert, and Robert Woito, *To End War: An Introduction:
        Ideas, Books, Organizations, Work That Can Help*. Rev. ed. 332 pp.
        New York: Harper & Row, 1970. (Bibliography with
        introductory essays for each section. See esp. section 9,
        "Conscientious Objection and the Draft"; section 10, "Social
        Change: The Nonviolent Approach"; section 11, "Political
        Processes and the Peace Effort"; and section 12, "Peace
        Research.")

2321.   Woito, Robert, *To End War: A New Approach to International
        Conflict*. 755 pp. New York: Pilgrim Press, 1982. (Sixth revised
        edition of a work first published in 1967 as an annotated
        bibliography and revised in 1970 [entry 2320]. Text and
        annotated bibliography present a non–military security
        strategy. See pp. 105–6 on civilian–based defense, pp. 129–31
        on international sanctions, pp. 259–60 on Soviet dissidents, pp.

399–400 on conscientious objection, p. 400 on political obligation, pp. 408–9 on pacifism, ch. 16 on nonviolent approaches to social change, pp. 531–33 on citizen peace movements, and ch. 21 for resources for individual nonviolent action to end war. Title and author indexes.)

Technique of Nonviolent Action

The technique approach to nonviolent action takes a social–scientific and historical view of the methods and dynamics of nonviolent action as a technique of struggle in acute conflicts. The technique approach focuses upon questions of causal factors in the inception of nonviolent struggle and the factors promoting the selection of nonviolent means but stresses to a somewhat greater extent the study of the processes during the course of conflict and their relationship to the outcomes and effects of nonviolent action. Technique–oriented studies generally place greater emphasis on the development of concepts and theories that attempt to explain the dynamics of nonviolent action based upon measurable factors and the collection and analysis of comparative data.

2322.   *"Analysis of Nonviolence in Theory and Fact,"* Sociological Inquiry 38 (1968): 1–93. (Special issue on nonviolent action. Papers include A. Paul Hare, "Nonviolent Action from a Social-psychological Perspective," pp. 5–12, which analyzes three cases by combining George C. Homans's "exchange theory" and other approaches to interpersonal behavior; Sidney I. Perloe, David S. Olton, and David L. Yaffe, "The Effect of Nonviolent Action on Social Attitudes," pp. 13–22, which applies social–psychological theories of attitude change to nonviolent action; Judith Stiehm, "Nonviolence Is Two," pp. 23–30, which distinguishes between principled nonviolence and pragmatic nonviolence; George Lakey, "Technique and Ethos in Nonviolent Action: The Woman Suffrage Case," pp. 37–42, which presents a case study of the Woman's Party in the U.S.; Herbert H. Blumberg, "Accounting for a Nonviolent Mass Demonstration," pp. 43–50, which gives an account of a 1963 civil rights demonstration in Durham NC; Inge Powell Bell, "Status Discrepancy and the Radical Rejection of Nonviolence," pp. 51–64, which presents results of interviews with members of Congress of Racial Equality from 1961–1963;

Paul E. Wehr, "Nonviolence and Differentiation in the Equal Rights Movement," pp. 65–76, which traces the effects of increasing ideological differentiation on the strategy of nonviolent action in the civil rights movement; and Herbert H. Blumberg, "A Guide to Organizations, Books and Periodicals Concerned With Nonviolence," pp. 77–93, which includes a brief annotated bibliography.)

2323.   Bond, Douglas G., "Alternatives to Violence: An Empirical Study of Nonviolent Direct Action." 384 pp. Ph.D. dissertation, Univ. of Hawaii, 1985. (Empirical study using factor analysis and regression analysis of 72 cases of nonviolent action. Research aims both to understand the dimensions of nonviolence, by classifying types of nonviolence based on the "underlying patterns of variance," and to explore the relationship between characteristics and outcomes of nonviolent action. Ch. 2 presents the conceptual framework and research design. Ch. 3 discusses the historical cases chosen and rationale behind the choices. Ch. 4 presents variables; see esp. p. 63 for list. Ch. 5–8 discuss results. See esp. ch. 9 for discussion of findings on the perception, efficacy, and meanings of nonviolence. Appendix 1 contains case sketches. Bibliography.)

2324.   Bondurant, Joan V., *Conquest of Violence: The Gandhian Philosophy of Conflict*. 269 pp. Princeton NJ: Princeton Univ. Press, 1958; Berkeley CA: Univ. of California Press, 1965. Rev. ed. 281 pp. Princeton NJ: Princeton Univ. Press, 1988. (Systematization of Gandhi's views on conflict process and the role of *satyagraha*. Ch. 1, 2 discuss core ideas and their application. Case studies on local Gandhian campaigns at Vykom [Vaikkam], Bardoli, and Ahmedabad and national *satyagrahas* against the Rowlatt Bills and salt laws are in following chapters. Case studies support analysis of extent to which practice of *satyagraha* met Gandhi's criteria. Ch. 6 contrasts Gandhian political concepts with Western theory. Revised ed. includes a new preface and an epilogue on the implications of nonviolent action in the Gandhian mode. Glossary. Bibliography. Index in revised ed.)

2325.   Bruyn, Severyn T., and Paula M. Rayman, eds., *Nonviolent Action and Social Change*. 316 pp. New York: Irvington, 1981. (Essays and case studies on nonviolent action. See introduction by Bruyn and Rayman; Severyn T. Bruyn, "Social Theory of Nonviolent Action: A Framework for Research in Creative Conflict," ch. 1; and George Lakey, "Sociological Mechanisms of Nonviolence: How It Works," ch. 2 which discusses the concept of mechanisms of change. Part 2 presents U.S. case studies, including accounts of protests of the 1963 invasion of Cuba, the United Farm Workers, a 1963 peace walk in Albany, Georgia, and the anti-nuclear power movement. Part 3 includes chapters on Danilo Dolci, African nonviolent action, and Norwegian and Czech resistance to the Nazis. See also ch. 11 on civilian-based defense by Gene Sharp, ch. 12 on feminism and nonviolence, and ch. 13 on theater and nonviolent action. Index. Bibliography.)

2326.   Case, Clarence Marsh, *Non–Violent Coercion: A Study in Methods of Social Pressure*. 423 pp. New York and London: Century, 1923. Reprint, New York: Garland Publishing, 1972. (Early sociological study of nonviolent action. In addition to chapters on principled traditions of "nonviolence," see ch. 8–9 on conscientious objectors in WWI; ch. 10–11 for a discussion of "psycho–social traits of non–violent resistants"; ch. 12–13 on "passive resistance"; ch. 14–15 on contemporary conscientious objection; ch. 16 on demonstrations and strikes; ch. 17 on industrial boycotts; ch. 18 on political and social boycotts; ch. 19 on Gandhian "soul-force"; ch. 20 on Gandhian noncooperation; and ch. 21 on persuasion and coercion in social action. Index.)

2327.   De Crespigny, Anthony, "The Nature and Methods of Non–violent Coercion," *Political Studies* 12 (1964): 256–65. (Analysis of coercion as a mode of political action and classification of principal methods of nonviolent coercion, defined as attempts to limit freedom of choice which do not involve threat or use of physical force. Primary methods discussed include boycott, strike, and civil disobedience.)

2328.   Galtung, Johan, "On the Meaning of Nonviolence." Pp. 341–377 in *Peace, War and Defence: Essays in Peace Research*. Vol. 2.

472 pp. Copenhagen: Christian Ejlers, 1976. (Definitional and theoretical essay developing the concept of "nonviolence" from action theory with analysis of "negative and positive influence" and sanctions derived therefrom.)

2329. Goldstein, Arnold P., Edward G. Carr, William S. Davidson II, Paul Wehr, and collaborators, *In Response to Aggression: Methods of Control and Prosocial Alternatives.* 560 pp. New York and Oxford: Pergamon Press, 1981. (Paul Wehr, "Aggressive Nonviolence," ch. 11 defines its subject as "defensive behavior having a hostile intent but using nonviolent means to reach its goals." A case study of Danish anti–Nazi resistance is in pp. 481–90, followed by analysis of the place of communication and organization in this resistance. Index.)

2330. Hare, A. Paul, and Herbert H. Blumberg, eds., *Nonviolent Direct Action: American Cases: Social–Psychological Analyses.* 575 pp. Washington: Corpus Books, 1968. (Short articles and excerpts on U.S. experience of nonviolent struggle from WWII to the late 1960s accompanied by analyses of the nature, psychology, and conditions of nonviolent action. Part 2 and ch. 19, 20 discuss the civil rights movement and part 3 contains accounts of peace voyages, marches, and demonstrations. Analytical contents include A. Paul Hare, "Introduction to Theories of Nonviolence," pp. 1–30; Gene Sharp, "Types of Principled Nonviolence," pp. 273–313; George Lakey, "The Mechanisms of Nonviolent Action," pp. 381–93; Martin Oppenheimer, "Towards a Sociological Understanding of Nonviolence," pp. 394–406; Judith Stiehm, "Nonviolence Is Two," pp. 447–74; Herbert H. Blumberg, "Accounting for a Nonviolent Mass Demonstration," pp. 475–91, and A. Paul Hare, "Nonviolent Direct Action from a Social–Psychological Perspective," pp. 513–30. An updated version of Herbert H. Blumberg, "A Guide to Organizations, Books, and Periodicals Concerned with Nonviolence; Annotated Bibliography" appears in appendix. Index.)

2331. Horsburgh, H.J.N., *Non–violence and Aggression: A Study of Gandhi's Moral Equivalent of War.* 207 pp. London: Oxford Univ. Press, 1968. (Presents a Gandhian alternative to armed force as an instrument of justice in the form of *satyagraha* or nonviolent resistance. Ch. 2 presents the bases of *satyagraha*, see esp. pp. 41–54 for a discussion of means and ends and pp. 54–59 on "creative conflict." Ch. 3, "The Practice of Satyagraha," contains a discussion of the preparations for nonviolent struggle, pp. 60–76, nonviolent technique, pp. 76–87, and brief illustrative case studies, pp. 87–94. Ch. 4–5 examine the nature of a nonviolent civilian defense. Author gives an assessment of *satyagraha* in ch. 6. Index.)

2332.   Lakey, George R., *Non Violent Action: How It Works.* 23 pp. Wallingford PA: Pendle Hill Pamphlet No. 129, 1963. (Brief introduction to nonviolent action.)

2333.   ———, "The Sociological Mechanisms of Non–Violent Action," in *Peace Research Reviews* 2, 6 (Dec. 1968): 1–98. Oakville, Ont.: Canadian Peace Research Institute. (Identifies "coercion, conversion and persuasion" as sociological mechanisms of nonviolent action in ch. 2. See also ch. 3–5 on characteristics of "the nonviolent actor," opponents, and third–party publics. Bibliography.)

2334.   de Ligt, Bartélemy, *The Conquest of Violence: An Essay on War and Revolution.* 306 pp. New York and London: Garland, 1972. Reprint of the 1937 edition [orig. publ. 1935]. (Analysis of violent and nonviolent revolutionary means. Thesis is that violent means in social revolution contradict ethical and political ends of socialism and that there are effective nonviolent alternatives. Ch. 1–3, 5 are on violence. See esp. ch. 6 on the effectiveness of nonviolent struggle, ch. 7 for historical examples, ch. 8 for an analysis of violent and nonviolent means in revolutionary struggles, and ch. 9–14 for an application of the principles of nonviolent struggle to conflicts in Russia, Spain, and Hitler's Germany. Ch. 11 examines the League of Nations and the application of sanctions. Ch. 12 discusses violent and nonviolent defense against Hitler. Pp. 269–85 present a "Plan of Campaign Against All War and All Preparation for War," in peace time and war time, both individual and collective. Appendixes. Index. Bibliography.)

2335.   Lofland, John, *Protest: Studies of Collective Behavior and Social Movements.* 349 pp. New Brunswick NJ and Oxford:

Transaction Books, 1985. (Studies of social protest, collective behavior, and religious and political movements. See introduction for "conceptions of protest," including nonviolent action. See ch. 12, "Social Struggle and the Protest Occupation," for discussion of "protest struggle" as distinct from violent struggle and "polite struggle"; see esp. pp. 265–69 on the form of extended sit–in termed a protest occupation. Ch. 14 is on "crowd lobbying," the assembling of large numbers of protesters to lobby public officials. Ch. 15 is on symbolic sit–ins for various political reasons at the Sacramento, California, capitol building. Author distinguishes among "pack–ins," "lone–ins," "one night stands," "spirited sieges," and "long term vigils." Index. Bibliography.)

2336. Miller, William Robert, *Nonviolence: A Christian Interpretation*. 380 pp. New York: Association Press, 1964. Reprint, New York: Schocken Books, 1966. (Topics discussed in the first two parts include the meanings of nonviolence and violence, three types of "generic nonviolence" [nonresistance, passive resistance, and nonviolent direct action], nonviolent revolution, *ahimsa*, and Christian nonviolence. More explicitly on the technique of nonviolent action, the author discusses levels of motivation, civil disobedience, nonviolent national defense, the idea of an intervention–oriented nonviolent brigade, strategic phases in nonviolent action, and nonviolent training and discipline. The third part presents cases of nonviolent action by converted Moravian Indians in the U.S. in 1782; Hungary, 1859–67; Finland, 1898–1905; Danish and Norwegian resistance to Nazi occupation, 1940–43; South African resistance in the 1950s; Ghana in 1950; the U.S. civil rights movement after 1955; and various episodes identified as "spontaneous nonviolence." Glossary. Index. Bibliography.)

2337. Molnar, Andrew L., with Jerry M. Tinker and John D. LeNoir, *Human Factors Considerations of Undergrounds in Insurgencies*. 291 pp. Washington DC: Special Operations Research Office, the American Univ., 1965. (Authors discuss techniques and organization of "passive resistance" in section on "underground psychological operations" in ch. 10.)

2338. Nakhre, Amrut W., *Social Psychology of Nonviolent Action: A Study of Three Satyagrahas.* 207 pp. Delhi: Chanakya Publications, 1982. (Based on case studies of three Indian campaigns; in Bardoli [1928], Rajkot [1938–39], and Pardi [1953–64]. Tests the concept that an internalized ideology of nonviolence is needed to motivate nonviolent conduct during action, finding that the rank–and–file adopted nonviolence as an ethic and pattern of life while leaders adopted it as a technique. Tables. Index. Bibliography.)

2339. Pelton, Leroy H., *The Psychology of Nonviolence.* 291 pp. New York, Oxford, and Sydney: Pergamon Press, 1974. (Effort to place the effects of nonviolent action within a psychological context. Ch. 2 discusses cognitive aspects of attitudes and attitude change. Ch. 3, 5–7 apply these to the workings of nonviolent protest and noncooperation, stressing attitude change and reconciliation. Index. Bibliography.)

2340. Roberts, Adam, ed., *Civilian Resistance as a National Defense: Nonviolent Action Against Aggression.* 320 pp. Harrisburg PA: Stackpole Books, 1968. Originally published as *The Strategy of Civilian Defense: Non–violent Resistance to Aggression.* 320 pp. London: Faber & Faber, 1967. Reprint, *Civilian Resistance as a National Defense.* 367 pp. Harmondsworth, Middlesex and Baltimore MD: Penguin Books, 1969. (Papers on the concept and history of national defense conducted using nonviolent action by the civilian populace. See part 1 for essays on military attack, *coups d'etat,* and totalitarian regimes. Part 2 contains Gene Sharp, "The Technique of Non–violent Action," ch. 4; Wolfgang Sternstein, "The *Ruhrkampf* of 1923: Economic Problems of Civilian Defence," ch. 5; Magne Skodvin, "Norwegian Non–violent Resistance during the German Occupation," ch. 6; Jeremy Bennett, "The Resistance against the German Occupation of Denmark, 1940–45," ch. 7; Theodor Ebert, "Non–violent Resistance to Communist Regimes?," ch. 8, a study of the 1953 East Berlin uprising; and B.H. Liddell Hart, "Lessons from Resistance Movements: Guerrilla and Non–violent," ch. 9. Part 3 takes up the policy of "civilian defense," with Adams Roberts, "Civilian Defence Strategy," ch. 10, and "Transarmament to Civilian Defence," ch. 13; Theodor Ebert, "Organization in Civilian Defence," ch. 11;

April Carter, "Political Conditions for Civilian Defence," ch. 13; and Thomas Schelling, "Some Questions on Civilian Defence," ch. 14. Index.)

2341.   Seifert, Harvey, *Conquest by Suffering: The Process and Prospects of Nonviolent Resistance.* 207 pp. Philadelphia: Westminister Press, 1965. (Ethical examination of nonviolent resistance as a method for social change, as seen from a Christian perspective. Ch. 1 outlines nonviolent resistance, specifying three methods; noncooperation, civil disobedience, and self–suffering. Ch. 2 examines the dynamics of resistance, emphasizing the struggle between resisters, opponents, and third parties. See also ch. 5 for a Christian evaluation of nonviolent resistance and ch. 6 for a discussion of factors contributing to success or failure. For views on whether nonviolent resistance is coercive, see index under *coercion* and *persuasion*. Index.)

2342.   Sharp, Gene, *Exploring Nonviolent Alternatives.* 161 pp. Boston: Porter Sargent, 1970. (Introductory essay on nonviolent action. Brief case descriptions in ch. 1 include 1940 Norwegian anti–Nazi sports strike, Indian nonviolent resistance, El Salvador in 1944, Russia in 1953, and the U.S. civil rights movement. Ch. 2 is on the technique of nonviolent action, ch. 3 is on civilian–based defense, ch. 4 is on research, ch. 5 offers a list of 85 cases of nonviolent action categorized by issue, and ch. 6 gives a course curriculum for civilian–based defense. Selected readings list is on pp. 133–59.)

2343.   ———, *The Politics of Nonviolent Action.* 902 pp. Boston: Porter Sargent, 1973. Paperback in three vols. entitled *Power and Struggle, The Methods of Nonviolent Action,* and *The Dynamics of Nonviolent Action.* (Comprehensive study containing the first complete statement of the technique of nonviolent struggle in social and political conflicts emphasizing its unique theory of power, methods of action, dynamics in conflict situations, and factors in the success and failure of nonviolent action. Historic references throughout. Part 1 presents an introduction to nonviolent action. Ch. 1 examines the nature and control of political power and focuses on the social roots of power, the nature of obedience, and the role of consent in presenting the beginnings of a theory of the control of political power through nonviolent action. Ch. 2 introduces nonviolent action as a technique of struggle, discussing characteristics of nonviolent action and giving case histories to illustrate the potential of the technique. Part 2 classifies and describes 198 distinct methods of nonviolent action. Ch. 3 contains the methods of nonviolent protest and persuasion. Ch. 4–7 contain methods of noncooperation; ch. 4 examines methods of social noncooperation, ch. 5 examines economic boycotts and ch. 6 examines the strike, both as types of economic noncooperation. Ch. 7 examines the methods of political noncooperation, including civil disobedience of "illegitimate" laws. Ch. 8 presents the methods of nonviolent intervention, distinguishing between psychological, physical, social, economic, and political intervention. Part 3 analyzes the dynamics of nonviolent action. Ch. 9 describes the groundwork for nonviolent action, focusing primarily on preparation and basic strategy. Ch. 10 examines the repression that nonviolent challenge provokes. Ch. 11 argues that solidarity and discipline are necessary to fight repression. Ch. 12 is on "political jiu–jitsu," the process by which nonviolent actionists cause the violence of the opponent's repression to be exposed in the worst possible light, thereby shifting opinion and support from the opponent to the nonviolent actionists. Ch. 13 presents three ways by which success is achieved in a nonviolent struggle; conversion, accommodation, and nonviolent coercion. Ch. 14 discusses the effects of nonviolent action on the nonviolent group and on power relations. Appendix contains a summary of factors determining the outcome of nonviolent struggles. Index. Bibliography.)

2344.   Shridharani, Krishnalal, *War without Violence: A Study of Gandhi's Method and Its Accomplishments.* 351 pp. New York: Harcourt, Brace, 1939. Rev. ed., 299 pp. Bombay: Bharatiya Vidya Bhavan, 1962. Reprint of 1939 ed.: New York, London: Garland Publishing, 1972. (Discusses the technique of *satyagraha*, its origins and applications, and compares it to war. Index. Bibliography.)

Concepts and Studies of Nonviolent Action

Entries compiled here include a variety of views on studying nonviolent action and related questions. Several relate nonviolent struggle to problems of peace, freedom and democracy, and the moral or transformational objectives of the actors.

2345.   Albert, David H., *People Power: Applying Nonviolence Theory.* 64 pp. Philadelphia: New Society Publishers, 1985. (A simplified introduction to several issues in the use of nonviolent action, including brief chapters on definition, issues of power, noncooperation, and strategy [for which see pp. 55–59]. Bibliography.)

2346.   Archer, Jules, *Resistance.* 222 pp. Philadelphia: Macrae Smith, 1973. (Brief popular–style introduction to nature and problems of resistance, predominantly nonviolent. Index. Bibliography.)

2347.   Barkan, Steven E., "Strategic, Tactical, and Organizational Dilemmas of the Protest Movement against Nuclear Power." *Social Problems* 27 (1979): 19–37. (Examines four factors in strategic choice that concern anti–nuclear power campaigns, as exemplified by Clamshell Alliance activists in protests in Seabrook NH in the 1970s. Among these factors are the understanding and objects of "civil disobedience and nonviolence," pp. 26–28, and legal implications of tactical choices.)

2348.   Bell, Ralph Graham, *Alternative to War.* 83 pp. London: James Clarke, 1959. (Personal essay describing and advocating "active nonviolent resistance" as an alternative to pacifism and militarism. See ch. 5 for description of the concept. Ch. 6 is on effective resistance against totalitarianism, ch. 7 is on resistance by oppressed people against own government, and ch. 8 is on international disputes and nonviolent resistance. See also ch. 9 on questions of organization and training of nonviolent forces.)

2349.   Bondurant, Joan V., ed., in association with Margaret W. Fisher, *Conflict: Violence and Nonviolence.* 206 pp. Chicago and New York: Aldine Atherton, 1971. (Essays on violent and nonviolent modes of conducting conflict. See Bondurant, "The

Search for a Theory of Conflict," ch. 1. Roy Finch, "The New Peace Movement," ch. 2, describes ideology and actions of peace activists following WWII in the U.S. Harry Prosch, "Limits to the Moral Claim in Civil Disobedience," ch. 3, and Darnell Rucker, "The Moral Ground of Civil Disobedience," ch. 4, present opposing views of the ethics of civil disobedience. See H.L. Niebing, "The Threat of Violence and Social Change," ch. 5, for discussion of the role of threats of violence in social change in political systems. Eugene V. Walter, ch. 6, is on violence and terrorism. Bondurant, "Creative Conflict and the Limits of Symbolic Violence," ch. 8, is on Gandhian nonviolent action and its relation to symbolic violence. Gene Sharp, "The Technique of Nonviolent Action," ch. 11, includes 84 cases of nonviolent action, pp. 163–169. See Thomas C. Schelling, "Some Questions on Civilian Defense," ch. 12. Margaret W. Fisher, "Contrasting Approaches to Conflict," ch. 13, contains discussion of Gandhian *satyagraha* as mode for conducting conflict. Index.)

2350. Carter, April, *Direct Action and Liberal Democracy.* 169 pp. New York: Harper & Row, 1973. (Views the protest movements of the 1960s as part of a long tradition of English and American efforts to influence government from outside, beginning at least with John Wilkes ca. 1763. Ch. 4, "Violence and Power," discusses the vulnerabilities of nonviolent action, pp. 85–93, and ch. 5 studies civil disobedience. Index. Bibliography.)

2351. Center for Research on Aggression, Syracuse Univ., *Prevention and Control of Aggression.* 366 pp. New York: Pergamon Press, 1983. (See Neil H. Katz with Kathleen L. Uhler, "An Alternative to Violence: Nonviolent Struggle for Change," ch. 10 for introduction to nonviolent action with case studies of Seabrook nuclear power plant protests, 1976–1978 and the Iranian Revolution of 1979. Index.)

2352. Charitanya, Krishna, *The Sociology of Freedom.* 451 pp. New Delhi: Manohar, 1978. (Extended essay on author's concept of freedom and politics. See references to nonviolent action included throughout and ch. 10, "Politics for Moral Man." Index.)

2353. Charny, Israel W., ed., *Strategies Against Violence: Design for Nonviolent Change.* 417 pp. Boulder CO: Westview Press, 1978. (Compendium of articles on subjects ranging from discussion of the violent or nonviolent personality to international peace proposals, not based on an expressed concept of nonviolent action. Of interest are Elise Boulding, "The Child and Nonviolent Social Change," ch. 4 on the socialization of "children who become altruists, activists, and nonviolent shapers of the future"; "Personal Commitment to Nonviolent Social Change [A *Playboy* Interview of Joan Baez]," ch. 6; and A. Paul Hare, "Dealing With Collective Violence [With Examples from India and Kent State]," ch. 13.)

2354. Dellinger, Dave, *Revolutionary Nonviolence.* 390 pp. Indianapolis and New York: Bobbs–Merrill, 1970. (Collected essays, 1943–1970, by a prominent radical pacifist.)

2355. Estey, George F., and Doris A. Hunter, eds., *Nonviolence: A Reader in the Ethics of Action.* 287 pp. [Boston]: Ginn, 1971. (Reader on ethical aspects of nonviolence as they relate to action, with short selections from and about Thoreau, Gandhi, and King, as well as challenges and reflections. Brief bibliography and "film project" notes at end of each section.)

2356. Fahey, Joseph, and Richard Armstrong, eds., *A Peace Reader: Essential Readings on War, Justice, Non–Violence and World Order.* 477 pp. New York and Mahwah NJ: Paulist Press, 1987. (Textbook survey of historical and contemporary readings on peace, nonviolent action, and world order. Section 3 is entitled "Non–violence: Philosophy and Strategy" and includes basic selections by M.L. King, Jr., Gandhi, and others, most notably in the context where "nonviolence" is viewed as a commitment. Reprints Gene Sharp, "Investigating New Options in Conflict and Defense," pp. 109–25 and "The Techniques of Nonviolent Action," pp. 300–6, as well as Christopher Kruegler and Patricia Parkman, "Identifying Alternatives to Political Violence: An Educational Imperative," pp. 248–59.)

2357. Feminism and Nonviolence Study Group, *Piecing It Together: Feminism and Nonviolence.* 58 pp. Devon, England: Feminism and Nonviolence Study Group, 1983. (Advocates feminist view of nonviolent action and the system in which it ought to operate. See esp. definition and viewpoint, pp. 29–30; critique of concept of self–suffering as a primarily masculine ideal, pp. 34–36; and occasions for use of nonviolent action, ch. 3. Photos. Bibliography.)

2358. Goodman, Paul, ed., *Seeds of Liberation*. 551 pp. New York: George Braziller, 1964. (Parts 2 and 3 include essays on nonviolence, war, civil rights, and colonialism by diverse authors.)

2359. Gregg, Richard, *The Power of Nonviolence*. 2nd ed. 192 pp. New York: Schocken, 1966 [orig. publ. 1935]. (A thorough revision of the author's pre–WWII arguments. The Gandhi–influenced Gregg argues that "moral jiu–jitsu," conversion of the opponent, and persuasion are the key sources of success of nonviolent action. Ch. 4, 5 discuss "mass nonviolence," ch. 7 proposes nonviolent resistance as a substitute for war, and ch. 10, 11 are on training. Index.)

2360. Guinan, Edward, ed., *Peace and Nonviolence: Basic Writings*. 174 pp. New York, Paramus, and Toronto: Paulist Press, 1973. (Of interest are pieces by Cesar Chavez, ch. 7; William Sloan Coffin, ch. 8; Danilo Dolci, ch. 11; Hildegard Goss–Mayr, ch. 16; Nhat Hanh, ch. 18; and A.J. Muste, ch. 27.)

2361. Hall, Gladys Walton, Grace C. Clark, and Michael A. Creedon, eds., *Advocacy in America: Case Studies in Social Change*. 205 pp. Lanham MD, New York, and London: University Press of America, 1987. (See Jessie J. Harris, "Nonviolence as a Strategy for Change: Charleston Hospital Strike," pp. 63–80 for a case study of a 1969 strike employing the repertoire of the civil rights movement. Index.)

2362. Hare, A. Paul, and Herbert H. Blumberg, eds., *Liberation without Violence: A Third–Party Approach*. 367 pp. London: Rex Collings, 1977. (Case studies of nonviolent action in several conflicts and the role of third parties. Part 1 contains accounts and analyses of the 1930 Indian Salt *Satyagraha* and the 1963 Birmingham, Alabama, civil rights campaign, reflections by

Helder Camara on Brazilian resistance, and an account of resistance in Larzac, France, to the expansion of an army base onto farm land. Part 2 contains reflections by Narayan Desai on intervention in Indian riots, a Quaker intervention into racial conflict in 1970, a rally at Kent State University in 1971, and the 1973 American Indian protest in Wounded Knee, South Dakota. Part 3 contains a 1959 Sahara anti–French atomic testing protest, Charles Walker's account of "nonviolence in Eastern Africa," a 1970 action by Puerto Ricans protesting U.S. Naval testing on the island of Culebra, and 1971 "Operation Omega" attempting to sail relief supplies to East Bengal. Part 4 contains accounts of 1966–68 resistance in Nagaland, 1969–70 riots on the Caribbean island of Curacao and subsequent implementation of an institute to study nonviolent social change, and conflict resolution attempts in Cyprus, 1972–74. Part 5 discusses the editors' model of a third-party approach to nonviolent social change. Index. Extensive bibliography.)

2363.   Holmes, Robert L., ed., *Nonviolence in Theory and Practice*. 208 pp. Belmont CA: Wadsworth Publishing, 1990. (Based upon the view that nonviolent action is an expression of the ethic of rejection of violence as such, the editor compiles readings both on nonviolence as an ethic and on nonviolent action as a practice. Readings on practice included here that are not readily available elsewhere include Liane Norman Elison, "Molly Rush and the Plowshares Eight," pp. 105–12; Allan Solomonow, "Living Truth: A Jewish Perspective," pp. 153–55; Mubarak Awad, "Nonviolent Resistance: A Strategy for the Occupied Territories," pp. 155–63; Liane Norman Elison, "Peace through Strength," pp. 164–67; R. Scott Kennedy, "The Druze of the Golan: A Case of Nonviolent Resistance," pp. 193–203; and Richard Deats, "The Philippines: The Nonviolent Revolution that Surprised the World," pp. 203–6. Bibliography.)

2364.   Hope, Marjorie, and James Young, *The Struggle for Humanity: Agents of Nonviolent Change in a Violent World*. 305 pp. Maryknoll NY: Orbis Books, 1977. (Biographical sketches with some useful material on Lanza del Vasto, Danilo Dolci, Cesar

Chavez, Thich Nhat Hanh, and Kenneth Kaunda. Photos. Index. Bibliography.)

2365. Kelman, Herbert C., *A Time to Speak: On Human Values and Social Research.* 349 pp. San Francisco: Jossey–Bass, 1968. (Part three examines the role of the social scientist as a participant in social action. See esp. ch. 9, "The Relevance of Nonviolent Action," which gives emphasis to nonviolent action in the civil rights movement, and ch. 10, "Political Dissent in a Crisis Atmosphere," on dissent and McCarthyism in the U.S. See also pp. 315–32 on the function of dissent, esp. pp. 327–32 on civil disobedience. Index. Bibliography.)

2366. Kool, V.K., ed., *Perspectives on Nonviolence.* 283 pp. New York: Springer–Verlag, 1990. (Papers from a 1988 conference, primarily concerned with personality, interpersonal and societal relationships. On nonviolent action, see Neil Katz, "Evaluation Research of Nonviolent Action," ch. 12; Amy Hubbard "'Killing the Messenger': Public Perceptions of Nonviolent Protest," ch. 13; and Leonard Gambrell, "Nonviolence and International Relations: A Conceptual Analysis of Power from Scholarship in Nonviolent Action," ch. 29. Index.)

2367. Kumar, Satish, ed., *School of Non–Violence.* 72 pp. London: Christian Action and Housmans, 1969. (Collection of addresses and course abstracts given at the London School of Non–Violence. See Geoffrey Ashe, "The Philosophy of Non–Violence," on British historical roots and influence of Gandhi; Vinoba Bhave, "The Politics of Non–Violence"; and Fred Blum, "Non–Violent Sociology.")

2368. Lynd, Staughton, ed., *Nonviolence in America: A Documentary History.* 535 pp. New York: Bobbs–Merrill, 1966. (Collection of essays and documents presenting the philosophy and history of "nonviolence" in America. See introduction on historical roots and connections of nonviolent action. Part 1 is on Quaker resistance and part 2 is on the abolition movement. In part 2, see esp. Adin Ballou, "Christian Non–Resistance," ch. 6; H.D. Thoreau, "Civil Disobedience," ch. 7; and Elihu Burritt,

"Passive Resistance," ch. 9. Part 3 is on anarchists in the late 1800s and early 1900s. Ch. 15 includes letters from imprisoned women's suffragists in 1917. Part 5 is on WWI conscientious objectors. Ch. 20 is on sit–down strikes in labor movements. Part 7 is on WWII conscientious objectors. Part 8 is on post–WWII "direct action for peace," which includes A.J. Muste, "Of Holy Disobedience," ch. 25. Part 9 is on the civil rights movement and part 10 is on "nonviolent revolution." Index.)

2369.   McAllister, Pam, ed., *Reweaving the Web of Life: Feminism and Nonviolence.* 454 pp. Philadelphia: New Society Publishers, 1982. (Essays, reflections, and other pieces devoted to exploring linkages between feminist theory and experience and nonviolent conduct. Illustrations. Photos. Index. Bibliography.)

2370.   McAllister, Pam, *You Can't Kill the Spirit.* 237 pp. Philadelphia PA and Santa Cruz CA: New Society, 1988. (Collected brief accounts illustrating women's use of nonviolent action. See pp. 8–9 on "tactical nonviolence," pp. 9–13 for a criticism of classic texts on nonviolent action for neglecting women's actions, and pp. 13–15 for stories of resistance. Ch. 1 includes the Mothers of the Plaza de Mayo in Argentina, Japanese women's peace movement, and the Greenham Common peace camp. Ch. 2 includes South African women's resistance, the Cuban Mothers March of 1957, the Australian Anzac Day protest in 1981–82, and the Women's Pentagon Action in 1980–81. Ch. 3 contains stories of women's rights actions, ch. 4 focuses on labor, and ch. 5 is on tax resistance. Ch. 6 contains stories of actions involving symbolic protest such as graffiti, pp. 99–106, and pouring blood, pp. 106–12. Ch. 7 focuses on song as nonviolent action. Ch. 9 includes movements promoting rights of race, gender, and sexual orientation. Ch. 10 focuses primarily on mass obstruction conducted by women in the 1871 Paris Commune and the 1986 Philippine revolution. Ch. 11 emphasizes humor in nonviolent action. Chronology, pp. 203–9 and geography, pp. 219–25.)

2371.   Satha–Anand, Chaiwat, "The Nonviolent Prince." 361 pp. Ph.D. dissertation, Univ. of Hawaii, 1981. (Author presents a "nonviolent paradigm" to replace the contemporary "violent paradigm." This study attempts to provide rulers with nonviolent alternatives by using the metaphor of Machiavelli's *The Prince*, which connotes ideas of practicality and reliance on one's own capability. Ch. 4 contains *The Nonviolent Prince* in 13 chapters which outline guidelines for nonviolent strategies for dealing with elites, the people, and international opponents using conversion, persuasion, and nonviolent coercion. See esp. ch. 11 on taking hostages as a form of nonviolent defense. Two critiques of this treatise follow. The final chapter makes a plea for a nonviolent political science. Bibliography.)

2372. Seeley, Robert A., *The Handbook of Non–Violence*. 344 pp. Westport CT: Lawrence Hill; Great Neck NY: Lakeville Press, 1986. (Includes Aldous Huxley, *An Encyclopedia of Pacifism*. Both Huxley's work and Seeley's additions, printed successively here, are organized as philosophical dictionaries of movements, concepts, and interpretations relevant to anti–war sentiment, pacifism, and nonviolent action. Index of *Encyclopedia*, pp. 101–4. Bibliography.)

2373. Sibley, Mulford Q., *The Quiet Battle: Writings on the Theory and Practice of Non–violent Resistance*. 390 pp. New York: Doubleday Anchor Books, 1963. Reprint, Boston: Beacon Press, 1969. (Compilation of readings organized into sections on "foundations," "nonviolent action in the absence of specific principled commitments," and "principled nonviolent action." In part 1, see excerpt from Etienne de la Boétie on voluntary servitude and pieces by Case and Gregg. In part 2, see de Ligt on the effectiveness of nonviolent struggle and case material on ancient times, the nineteenth century, and twentieth century Norway and U.S.S.R. Part 3 contains case material on early and contemporary America, South Africa, and two pieces on war and defense. Index.)

2374. Simpson, Dick, and George Beam, *Strategies for Change: How to Make the American Political Dream Work*. 258 pp. Chicago: Swallow Press, 1976. (See ch. 6, "Nonviolent Issue Strategies," for argument against strategies of riots, violent confrontation, demonstrations, and lobbying and proposal for "nonviolent issue campaigns" that include boycotts and civil disobedience. See also pp. 140–54 on a 1969–70 Chicago anti–pollution campaign, pp. 155–58 evaluating that campaign, and ch. 8 on strategy. Illustrations. Photos. Documents. Index. Bibliography.)

2375.   Stiehm, Judith, *Nonviolent Power: Active and Passive Resistance in America*. 132 pp. Lexington MA, Toronto, and London: D.C. Heath, 1972. (Essay distinguishing two forms of "nonviolent resistance," individual and group, with an inquiry into their backgrounds and effects. Stresses motives to behave nonviolently rather than strategy of nonviolent action. Index. Bibliography.)

2376.   Templin, Ralph T., *Democracy and Nonviolence: The Role of the Individual in World Crisis*. 334 pp. Boston: Porter Sargent, 1965. (Critical political essay on democracy in the U.S. which presents an argument regarding "systematic and democratic nonviolent resistance to the genocidal tendencies of the age." Author sees nonviolent resistance as part of the fulfillment and function of the duty of democratic citizenship. See ch. 13 on Gandhi's influence, ch. 14 on the power of "active love," ch. 15 on nonviolent revolution, and ch. 16 on civil disobedience as a method of nonviolent resistance. Ch. 17 includes brief discussion of pacifism and its role in nonviolent national defense. Appendixes. Index.)

2377.   Weinberg, Arthur, and Lila Weinberg, eds., *Instead of Violence: Writings by the Great Advocates of Peace and Nonviolence Throughout History*. 486 pp. New York: Grossman, 1963. (Excerpts and brief statements divided into sections on recent, WWII–era, WWI–era, nineteenth century, and early thoughts on peace and opposition to war. Bibliography.)

PREPARATIONS FOR NONVIOLENT STRUGGLE

Groundwork of some kind has often prepared the way for nonviolent struggle, even when it appears to be spontaneous. Planning, training, and discipline in particular are thought by some theorists and advocates to contribute to the effectiveness of nonviolent campaigns.

Manuals and Handbooks

Manuals, handbooks, and primers below provide practical knowledge and advice on conducting nonviolent campaigns. They contain views on choosing tactics and strategies, training exercises, and grassroots organizing methods.

2378. Alinsky, Saul D., *Rules for Radicals: A Practical Primer for Realistic Radicals.* 196 pp. New York: Random House, 1971. (A guide to creating organizations to combat entrenched power structures. Recommends the use of a variety of means, both within and outside the framework of nonviolent action.)

2379. American Friends Service Committee, Nonviolent Action Training Program, *Action Guide on Southern Africa.* 3d ed. 59 pp. Philadelphia: American Friends Service Committee, [n.d.]. (Booklet describing proposed action campaigns to protest South African policies. Section 1 describes possible actions, many based on "economic leverage," and section 2 offers advice on organizing. See appendix C for examples of action, esp. a short description of a protest at tennis cup match, pp. 53–55. Photos. Bibliography.)

2380. Coover, Virginia, Ellen Deacon, Charles Esser, and Christopher Moore, *Resource Manual for a Living Revolution.* 343 pp. Philadelphia: New Society Press, 1977. (Manual for the conduct of change–oriented collective action, with many exercises and tools. Emphasis is on groups, training, organizing, and strategy. Bibliographies on pp. 18–21, 22–25, 38–41, 96–98, 127, 150, 199–200, 244–47. Photos. Index.)

2381. Hedemann, Ed, ed., *War Resisters League Organizer's Manual.* Rev. ed. 222 pp. New York: War Resisters League, 1986 [orig. publ. 1981]. (See Ed Hedemann, "Nonviolence," pp. 11–15, second section on "Basic Organizing Techniques," pp. 136–44 on leaflets and posters, and fifth section on "Action." Illustrations. Photos. Documents. Index. Resource lists throughout.)

2382. Huehnefeld, John, *The Community Activist's Handbook: A Guide to Organizing, Financing, and Publicizing Community Campaigns.* 160 pp. Boston: Beacon Press, 1970. (The mechanics of organizing to press for local–level change, assuming a limited use of nonviolent techniques. See pp. 45–48 on "the protest demonstration" and advice for thinking through the conduct of a demonstration and part 3 on "the show down" and virtues of *ad hoc* organizations.)

2383.   Kahn, Si, *Organizing: A Guide for Grassroots Leaders*. 387 pp. New York: McGraw–Hill, 1982. (Manual on grassroots organizing by union and community organizer. See esp. ch. 2 on leadership, ch. 8 on strategy, ch. 10 on tactics, and ch. 11 on training. Index.)

2384.   Oppenheimer, Martin, and George Lakey, *A Manual for Direct Action*. 139 pp. Chicago: Quadrangle, 1965. ("Practical training manual for nonviolent direct action," with focus on civil rights movement in the U.S. and emphasis on strategy and tactics. See esp. ch. 6 which describes workshops on direct action and ch. 7 on tactics. Ch. 11 addresses debate between armed defense and nonviolent action. Illustrations. Appendixes. Index.)

2385.   Walzer, Michael, *Political Action: A Practical Guide to Movement Politics*. 125 pp. Chicago: Quadrangle Books, 1971. (Guide to participation in citizens' political action, written by activist and professor of government. See esp. pp. 88–90, 96–104, 108–11.)

2386.   Wilcox, Fred, ed., *Grass Roots: An Anti–nuke Source Book*. 185 pp. Trumansburg NY: Crossing Press, 1980. (An organizing manual consisting of brief articles on methods of opposition to nuclear power. Includes discussion of nonviolent methods and other options.)

Organizing and Community Organizations

The tactics, strategies, and preparations for nonviolent action may involve methods developed by community grassroots organizing groups. In addition, such groups may advocate and use nonviolent action as a part of their approach to social change.

2387. Alinsky, Saul, *Reveille for Radicals*. 235 pp. New York: Vintage Books, 1969 [orig. publ. 1946]. (Part 2 discusses organizing and action in conflicts. See esp. ch. 8, "Conflict Tactics." Index. Bibliography.)

2388. Bailey, Robert, Jr., *Radicals in Urban Politics: The Alinsky Approach*. 187 pp. Chicago and London: Univ. of Chicago Press, 1974. (See ch. 4–6 on community organizations and their methods, esp. pp. 83–91 on the "protest approach" and a critique of the belief that change via protest "requires media involvement." Index. Bibliography.)

2389. Boyte, Harry C., Heather Booth, and Steve Max, *Citizen Action and the New American Populism*. 215 pp. Philadelphia: Temple Univ. Press, 1986. (Focuses on group "citizen action" and presents the case for organization as a source of civic empowerment. See ch. 3. Photos. Index.)

2390. Brager, George, Harry Specht, and James L. Torczyner, *Community Organizing*. 441 pp. New York: Columbia Univ. Press, 1987. (Study of the historical background, process, sponsoring organizations, and tactics of community organizing from a social welfare viewpoint. See part 4 on tactics, esp ch. 12 and pp. 226–339 for a discussion of tactics in social change activism, and ch. 16 on "direct action and disruption." Index.)

2391. Delgado, Gary, *Organizing the Movement: The Roots and Growth of ACORN*. 269 pp. Philadelphia: Temple Univ. Press, 1986. (History of the Association of Community Organizations for Reform Now [ACORN] since its inception in 1970 with an analysis of community organizing by an experienced member. Ch. 2 is on ACORN's roots in the movements of the 1960s. See also pp. 29–30 on tactics, pp. 78–79 for a table on individual ideology and activist roles, and pp. 203–06 on resource mobilization. See index under *collective social action, demonstrations, leadership, protest,* and *tactics*. Photos. Index. Bibliography.)

2392. Doughton, Morgan J., *PeoplePower: An Alternative to 1984!* 278 pp. Bethlehem PA, Philadelphia, and Washington DC: Media

America, 1976. (Personal view of anti–poverty work and community organizing based on the concept that participation fosters community power. See ch. 3 on self–help and action. Illustrations.)

Training

Training, which includes education and the development of skills and attitudes believed important for successful nonviolent action, has increasingly become used in campaigns and struggles. Training dates back at least to the early campaigns of Mohandas Gandhi and was used prominently in the U.S. civil rights movement.

2393.   Randle, Michael, and Gene Sharp, "Annotated Bibliography on Training For Non–Violent Action and Civilian–Based Defence," *UNESCO Yearbook on Peace and Conflict Studies* (1981): 63–180. Westport CT: Greenwood Press; Paris: UNESCO, 1981. (References to books, manuscripts, notes, and other sources on "preparation for particular tasks within the framework of non–violent action and civilian defence." See introduction by Randle, pp. 65–78.)

STUDIES

2394.   Gregg, Richard B., *A Discipline for Non–Violence*. 31 pp. Wallingford, PA: Pendle Hill, [1940]. Pendle Hill Pamphlet No. 11. (Outlines program of "physical discipline for non–violence" based on military training and emphasizing manual work.)

2395.   ———, *Training for Peace: A Programme for Peace Workers*. 36 pp. London: George Routledge & Sons (Peace Pledge Union), [1936]. (Pamphlet advocating Gregg's view of nonviolent struggle as a policy of the Peace Pledge Union to provide an alternative to war. See pp. 1–5 for rationale, following pages for group or "team" organization and goals of training.)

2396.   Olson, Theodore W., and Lynne Shivers, *Training for Nonviolent Action*. 40 pp. [London]: War Resisters International, [1970].

(Pamphlet introduction to training for nonviolent action. Photos. Documents. Bibliography.)

2397.   Walker, Charles C., ed., *Training for Nonviolent Action: Some History, Analysis, Reports of Surveys*. 76 pp. Haverford PA: Nonviolent Action Research Project of the Center for Nonviolent Conflict Resolution, Haverford College, [1973]. (Collection of essays and brief descriptions on training theory, conducting a workshop, and evaluating training. Bibliography, pp. 18–22.)

LEGAL ASPECTS OF NONVIOLENT ACTION

The formal legal system and nonviolent action may intersect in several ways, including deliberate or unintended breaches of law by participants, arguments over legal justifications of nonviolent challenges, and punishment of activists by the state. In addition, the police forces and the courts may be the mechanisms through which the state administers, sanctions, or suppresses nonviolent action. Lastly, legal challenges and strategies may be viewed by participants either as supplements to or alternatives to nonviolent action.

See also for examples: South Africa: Struggles Against the Racial System; Arab League Boycott of Israel; United States: Antislavery Movements and Abolitionism; United States: Opposition to War and Expansionism; United States: Pullman Strike and Rail Boycotts of 1894; United States: Industrial Workers of the World; United States: Blacklisting in Entertainment; United States: Struggle for Desegregation and Civil Rights; United States: Nazi–Skokie Controversy; United States: Anti–Nuclear Power Movement; United States: Nonviolent Opposition to Nuclear Weapons; Australia: Queensland Civil Liberties Campaign; Great Britain: Women's Suffrage Movement; Great Britain: Conscientious Objection and Inter–War Peace Movement; Ireland, Northern: Civil Rights Campaign and People's Democracy, 1967–1972; Norway: Against Fascist Rule and Nazi Occupation, 1940–1945; Poland: Martial Law and After, 1981–1989; Methods of Nonviolent Action: Civil Disobedience.

2398.   Bassiouni, M. Cherif, ed., *The Law of Dissent and Riots*. 498 pp. Springfield IL: Charles C Thomas, 1971. (Essays on legal aspects of conflict and contention. See part 3 on civil disobedience and law, part 5 on police "use of force" against riots, and ch. 13 on "regulation of demonstrations." Bibliography.)

2399.   Becker, Theodore L., ed., *Political Trials*. Indianapolis and New York: Bobbs–Merrill, 1971. (Essays on various political trials. See ch. 7 on Soviet dissidents Sinyavsky and Daniel and ch. 8 on the Chicago conspiracy trial. Index.)

2400.   Belknap, Michael R., ed., *American Political Trials*. 316 pp. Westport CT and London: Greenwood Press, 1981. (See Daniel Novak, "The Pullman Strike: Debs, Darrow, and the Labor Injunction," ch. 6. See also chapters on anti–communist trials and the Chicago conspiracy trial. Index. Bibliographic essay.)

2401.   Bickel, Alexander M., *The Morality of Consent*. 156 pp. New Haven CT and London: Yale Univ. Press, 1975. (Essays on civil disobedience and constitutional law in U.S. See ch. 3 on protest and permitted speech and ch. 4 for three short essays on legality and civil disobedience. Index. Bibliography.)

2402.   Boyle, Francis Anthony, *Defending Civil Resistance Under International Law*. 378 pp. Dobbs Ferry NY: Transnational Publishers, 1987. (Manual for attorneys who wish to introduce evidence of U.S. governmental violations of international law as a defense issue in trials of persons charged as a result of nonviolent protests against nuclear weapons, Central America, and South Africa policies. See ch. 1 on the claim of a constitutional right to "nonviolent civil resistance" against breaches of international law, esp. pp. 5–8 on the concept of nonviolent civil resistance in contradistinction to civil disobedience. Ch. 2 contains attorneys' guidelines for conducting an international law defense by arguing that nonviolent civil resistance is a permitted act. Ch. 4–6 contain trial materials for cases in the named areas. Appendix. Index. Bibliography.)

2403.   Christenson, Ron, *Political Trials: Gordian Knots in the Law*. 303 pp. New Brunswick NJ and Oxford: Transaction Books, 1986. (Categorization and historical analysis of trials raising political issues. See model on p. 12. Ch. 5 discusses trials of "dissenters"; pp. 183–84 briefly discuss the 1922 trial of Gandhi. Index. Bibliography.)

2404. Cord, Robert L., *Protest, Dissent and the Supreme Court.* 303 pp. Cambridge MA: Winthrop Publishers, 1971. (Introduction and court opinions on "free speech" issues covering anti–war and draft protests from 1919 to 1970, pp. 36–84; protest in public places, 1963–1969, pp. 176–261; and protest on private property, including three 1963 sit–in cases, pp. 270–86, and a picketing case, pp. 287–99. Documents.)

2405. Dorsen, Norman, and Leon Friedman, *Disorder in the Court: Report of the Bar Association of the City of New York, Special Committee on Courtroom Conduct.* 432 pp. New York: Pantheon Books, 1973. (Study and recommendations for legal control of "disorderly trials," see ch. 3, 4, 5 on disorder in trials and ch. 6, pp. 111–18, for regulation of acts of protest during trials, including "passive disrespect" and noncooperation. Index.)

2406. Elliff, John T., *Crime, Dissent, and the Attorney General: The Justice Department in the 1960s.* 276 pp. Beverly Hills and London: Sage Publications, 1971. (While ch. 3, on "black militancy," mostly concerns federal response to violence and fears of violence, pp. 112–20 discuss Justice Department activities in the 1968 Poor People's Campaign Washington tent city. Ch. 4 contains detailed discussion of legal response to anti–war protest, 1965–69, including activities of the Selective Service System and two presidential administrations. See also ch. 5 "domestic intelligence surveillance." Index.)

2407. Gotlieb, Gideon, "Vietnam and Civil Disobedience," pp. 597–615 in Richard Falk, ed., *The Vietnam War and International Law,* vol. 2. 1240 pp. Princeton NJ: Princeton Univ. Press, 1969. (Essay on legal issues raised by breaches of law in opposition to war in Vietnam. Index.)

2408. Greenberg, Jack, *Litigation for Social Change: Methods, Limits, and Role in Democracy.* 64 pp. New York: Association of the Bar of the City of New York, 1974. (Lecture by experienced civil rights litigator on campaigns to change legal structures as an "instrument of social change." See esp. pp. 12–15 on the campaign leading to *Plessy v. Ferguson* and pp. 16–23 on the school desegregation cases. Index. Bibliography.)

2409.   Hewitt, Patricia, *The Abuse of Power: Civil Liberties in the United Kingdom*. 295 pp. Oxford: Martin Robertson, 1982. ("Peaceful Protest and Public Assembly," ch. 5 is on the logic, law, and policy of legal control of demonstrations, protests, and other collective action in Britain. Index.)

2410.   Kadish, Mortimer R., and Stanford H. Kadish, *Discretion to Disobey: A Study of Lawful Departures from Legal Rules*. 241 pp. Stanford CA: Stanford Univ. Press, 1973. (Jurisprudential depiction of the conditions under which persons acting as officials or as citizens are justified under the law in disobeying legal commands and rules. Ch. 3, 4 attempt to establish a concept of "legitimated disobedience" relevant to nonviolent action and civil disobedience and legal defenses for these actions. Index.)

2411.   Kirchheimer, Otto, *Political Justice: The Use of Legal Procedure for Political Ends*. 452 pp. Princeton NJ: Princeton University Press, 1961. (Historical and political study of the uses of courts and trials to suppress political activity. Ch. 4 is on legal repression of organizations, ch. 6 is on the individual before the court in political cases, and ch. 11 contains a section on the "strategy of political justice," pp. 417–22. Index. Bibliography.)

2412.   Sibley, Mulford Q., *The Obligation to Disobey: Conscience & the Law*. 119 pp. New York: Council on Religion and International Affairs, 1970. (See esp. ch. 3, "Individual Conscience and the Law" for argument that conscientious disobedience to law is not a threat to the legal order.)

2413.   Turk, Austin T., *Political Criminality: The Defiance and Defense of Authority*. 231 pp. Beverly Hills, London, and New Delhi: Sage Publications, 1982. (Ch. 2 is on the criminalization of political acts and ch. 3 is on the acts themselves. See esp. pp. 99–108, which categorize political resistance as dissent, evasion, disobedience, or violence. See also ch. 4 on the social–control response to political crimes. Index. Bibliography.)

APPLICATIONS OF NONVIOLENT STRUGGLE

Sources compiled in this section provide examples of efforts to apply ideas about nonviolent action, its strategies, and its possible effects to specific conflict situations. They include particularly concepts of civilian–based or "social" defense and of nonviolent revolution.

2414.   Dunn, Ted, ed., *Alternatives to War and Violence—A Search*. 196 pp. London: James Clarke, 1963. (Papers from 1961 conference in Colchester, England. See Richard Hauser, "Training For Peace," pp. 119–28 on group training techniques for action and research to promote peace and disarmament; Arlo De Vere Tatum, "World Peace Brigade," pp. 129–34 on training of a "world peace brigade" for nonviolent action; Gene Sharp, "Facing Totalitarianism Without War," pp. 135–48 on nonviolent resistance to totalitarian regimes; Anthony Weaver, "Direct Action and Civil Disobedience in Britain—A Justification," pp. 149–55, on nonviolent action as extra–parliamentary power; and Ranganath R. Diwakar, "Satyagraha," pp. 186–96.)

2415.   Galtung, Johan, *The True Worlds: A Transnational Perspective*. 469 pp. New York: Free Press, 1980. (Diagnosis and critique of the contemporary world system with a framework containing strategies for action attempting to create a "true world" based on liberation and security from violence. See pp. 139–49 on nonviolent revolution and pp. 205–15 on "nonmilitary defense." Appendix. Index.)

2416.   Hare, A. Paul, and Herbert H. Blumberg, eds., *A Search for Peace and Justice: Reflections of Michael Scott*. 255 pp. London: Rex Collings, 1980. (Reflections on the process and effectiveness of nonviolent action by participant and strategist Michael Scott, based on interviews conducted by the editors from 1977 to 1980. Ch. 1 contains his views on nonviolent action. Ch. 3–14 each focus on a specific action, presenting description and Scott's evaluation; see pp. viii–x for evaluation model. See esp. chapters on 1946 passive resistance in Durban, South Africa; Namibian resistance since 1946; the 1959 "Sahara

Protest Team" against French atomic testing; the World Peace Brigade in Rhodesia, 1962–1964; resistance by the Cold Comfort Farm protest group in Zimbabwe [Rhodesia] from 1972; and Scott's participation in the Campaign for Nuclear Disarmament from 1960. See also his article, "Pacifism Is Not Enough," pp. 218–24, on nonviolent direct action in the peace movement. Index. Bibliography.)

2417.   Huxley, Aldous, *Ends and Means: An Inquiry into the Nature of Ideals and into the Methods Employed for Their Realization.* 386 pp. New York and London: Harper & Brothers, 1937. (A critique of violence and centralization in social change.)

2418.   Kumar, Mahendra, *Violence and Nonviolence in International Relations.* 256 pp. Delhi, India: Thomson Press, 1975. (Attempt to develop "theory of nonviolence in international relations." Ch. 2 describes the "secularization of nonviolence" and ch. 3–5 examine violence between states. Ch. 6–8 are on applying "nonviolence" to international relations. Index. Bibliography.)

2419.   Smoke, Richard, with Willis Harman, *Paths to Peace: Exploring the Feasibility of Sustainable Peace.* 111 pp. Boulder and London: Westview Press, 1987. (A primer on traditional and alternative approaches to international conflict resolution and prevention. See pp. 47–54 on nonviolent civilian resistance and pp. 58–61 on the concept of "peaceful invasions." Index.)

2420.   Stephenson, Carolyn M., ed., *Alternative Methods for International Security.* 243 pp. Washington DC: University Press of America, 1982. (Exploration of alternatives to currently–favored approaches to security policy. See esp. article by Stephenson arguing for a revised conception of security systems, pp. 29–36; Gene Sharp, "Making the Abolition of War a Realistic Goal," pp. 127–40; and Beverly Woodward on nonviolent struggle and defense, pp. 141–49. See pp. 210–212 for a brief literature review on nonviolent action. Illustrations.)

2421.   Weaver, Anthony, *War as a Method of Settling Disputes Outmoded: A Guide to Thought and Action.* 62 pp. London: Housmans, 1960. (Pamphlet essay on nonviolent action as alternative to war. Pp. 38–47, on nonviolent resistance, discuss several British cases and concepts briefly, as do pp. 60–62 on protests in the U.K. against nuclear weapons in the 1950s. Bibliography, pp. 9–15.)

Civilian–Based Defense

Civilian–based defense (CBD) represents a specific application of the theory of nonviolent action to concerns of national defense. Civilian–based defense proposes the use of nonviolent noncooperation and defiance by a population against internal usurpation or foreign invasion as an alternative to traditional military defense policies. In the case of invasion, advocates of CBD argue that the resisting nation may aim to deny an attacker its goals and objectives and make it impossible to rule a nation as a means of deterrence and defense. In the case of usurpation, advocates argue that coups d'état and other unconstitutional seizures of state power could be defeated by similar means. European researchers are generally also concerned with the "social" aspects of CBD, including the assertion of minority rights, gender and racial equity, and the defense of progressive values.

2422.   Alternative Defense Commission, *Defence Without the Bomb: The Report of the Alternative Defence Commission*. 278 pp. New York: Taylor & Francis, 1983. (Evaluation and advocacy of British defense without nuclear weapons. See ch. 7, 8 for discussion of civilian–based defense. Bibliography.)

2423.   Alternative Defense Commission, *Without the Bomb: Non–Nuclear Defense Policies for Britain*. 92 pp. London: Paladin Books and Granada Publishing, 1985. (Shorter, updated version of previous entry. Index.)

2424.   American Friends Service Committee, *In Place of War: An Inquiry into Unarmed National Defense*. 115 pp. New York: Grossman, 1967. (Introduction to concepts of civilian–based defense. See ch. 1 for views on nonviolent action, ch. 2 on training, ch. 3 on organization and strategy, and ch. 4 for an evaluation. Selected bibliography.)

2425.   ———, "Speak Truth to Power: A Quaker Search for an Alternative to Violence." 71 pp. NPL: American Friends Service Committee, 1955. (Pamphlet prepared for the AFSC on the application of principles of nonviolence to international conflict in the nuclear era. See esp. ch. 4, "Alternatives to Violence," and ch. 6, "The Politics of Non–Violence.")

2426.   Boserup, Anders, and Andrew Mack, *War Without Weapons: Non–Violence in National Defence*. 194 pp. New York: Schocken Books, 1974. (Analysis of "civilian defence." See introduction and ch. 1 for theory and concepts related to defense and conflict. Ch. 2, 3 on methods and organizational problems of civilian defence. Ch. 4 examines the analogy with guerrilla warfare. Ch. 5 is on issue of repression. Ch. 6, 7 contain historical case studies of resistance against occupation and against military coups. Ch. 9 is on combining civilian and military defense. Ch. 10 is on "non–violent defence in classical strategic theory." Brief guide to the literature. Index.)

2427.   Fischer, Dietrich, *Preventing War in the Nuclear Age*. 236 pp. Totowa NJ: Rowman & Allanheld, 1984. (Discussion of concrete measures to prevent war. Ch. 9 is on transarmament. Ch. 10 discusses nonmilitary defense with emphasis given to dissuasion of attacks. See also ch. 12 on forms of power and resistance. Appendix. Index. Bibliography.)

2428.   Galtung, Johan, "On the Strategy of Nonmilitary Defense." Pp. 378–426 in *Peace, War and Defence: Essays in Peace Research*. Vol. 2. 472 pp. Copenhagen: Christian Ejlers, 1976. (Essay on concept of civilian–based defense.)

2429.   Gress, David, *Peace and Survival: West Germany, the Peace Movement, and European Security*. 266 pp. Stanford CA: Hoover Institution Press, 1985. (See comments on concept of "civilian defense" with review of Daniel Frei's counter–arguments, pp. 80–82. Index. Bibliography.)

2430.   Hancock, W.K., *Four Studies of Peace and War in This Century*. 129 pp. London, New York and Ibadan: Cambridge Univ. Press, 1961. (Four lectures on the stated topic, with ch. 3 being a Gandhi–influenced commentary on "non–violence." In the context of a retelling of Gandhi's South Africa years, author maintains [p. 57] that "technique" was the Gandhian contribution and later [pp. 84–92] addresses the contribution of

Gandhi's ideas as "an alternative to armed conflict or preparedness for it," with additional discussion of the civilian–based defense proposals of King–Hall. Appendix.)

2431. Hollins, Henry B., Averill L. Powers, and Mark Sommer, *The Conquest of War: Alternative Strategies for Global Security.* 224 pp. Boulder CO and London: Westview Press, 1989. (Part 1 contains chapters on several proposals for replacing or controlling war without reliance on current means. Ch. 8, "Civilian–based Defense: The Strength of Bare Hands and Stubbornness," offers a somewhat sketchy introduction to the basic concepts of civilian–based defense. Index. Bibliography.)

2432. Kennan, George F., *Russia, The Atom and the West.* 116 pp. New York: Harper, 1957. (See pp. 60–65 on combined policy of paramilitary actions and "civil resistance" in case of attempted Communist take–overs in Western Europe.)

2433. King–Hall, Commander Sir Stephen, *Common Sense in Defence.* 48 pp. London: K–H Services; Nyack NY: Fellowship of Reconciliation, 1960. (Booklet summarizing and updating entry 2436 in popular form.)

2434. ———, *Defence in the Nuclear Age.* 223 pp. London: Victor Gollancz, 1958. Nyack NY: Fellowship of Reconciliation, 1959. (British military thinker's argument for shifting British defense policy to one based on the "practice of non–violence." Part 2 proposes a nonviolent, civilian–based system of defense implemented by a created European Treaty Organization. Part 3 discusses nonviolent civilian defense in context of attempted occupation. See esp. pp. 187–95 for historical examples and ch. 12 on training for implementation of civilian–based defense.)

2435. ———, *Power Politics in the Nuclear Age: A Policy for Britain.* 224 pp. London: Victor Gollancz, 1962. (Presents argument for Britain to abandon nuclear weapons and develop a "power policy" of nonviolent civilian defense. See ch. 5 on "non–violent power," ch. 13 for implementation of this new defense policy, ch. 14 on Soviet reaction to this policy, and ch. 15 on nonviolent resistance to Soviet occupation.)

2436.   Kruegler, Christopher, "Liddell Hart and the Concept of Civilian–Based Defense." 185 pp. Ph.D. dissertation, Syracuse Univ., 1985. (On the concept of civilian–based defense and its development, in particular the role played by Captain Sir Basil Liddell Hart. Ch. 2 presents a typology of approaches to war, peace, and national security issues. Ch. 3 traces the pre–Liddell Hart intellectual roots of civilian–based defense. Ch. 5 outlines the distinction between "morally based pacifism" and "strategic nonviolence," referring specifically to Liddell Hart's writings. Ch. 6 examines the specific concept of civilian–based defense. Ch. 7 presents the development of the concept after 1964. Bibliography.)

2437.   Mahadevan, T.K., Adam Roberts, and Gene Sharp, eds., *Civilian Defence: An Introduction.* 265 pp. Bombay: Bharatiya Vidya Bhavan; New Delhi: Gandhi Peace Foundation, 1967. (Attempt to formulate effective nonviolent alternative to traditional national defense. See ch. 2, "Gandhi's Defense Policy," and ch. 3, "Resisting Totalitarianism without War," by Sharp. Part Two provides introduction to civilian–based defense. See esp. Jerome D. Frank, "Psychological Problems in the Elimination of War," ch. 5, for examination of motivational and psychological obstacles to elimination of war and the implementation of nonviolent resistance. See ch. 9–11 on preparation and methods. Ch. 12, 13 by Theodor Ebert examine the stages of a resistance campaign and the factors contributing to success. Appendixes. Index.)

2438.   Olson, Theodore, and Gordon Christiansen, *Thirty–One Hours: The Grindstone Experiment.* 107 pp. Toronto: Canadian Friends Service Committee, 1966. (Report, analysis, and documentation of Grindstone simulation experiment 1965. Includes description, narrative, evaluation, analytical articles, and documents. In this exercise, professed pacifists are presented with a hostile military takeover and attempt to defend themselves according to their beliefs. Documents. Photos.)

2439.   Sharp, Gene, *Making Europe Unconquerable: The Potential of Civilian–based Deterrence and Defense.* 190 pp. Cambridge MA: Ballinger Publishing, 1985. (Presentation of nonviolent civilian–based deterrence and defense policy against possible

Soviet attack on Western Europe. Ch. 2 examines question of civilian–based defense for Western Europe and includes case studies of Kapp Putsch of 1920, Ruhr conflict of 1923, Warsaw Pact's Czechoslovakian invasion of 1968, and a list of other cases, pp. 42–43. Ch. 3 gives analysis of "transarmament" defined as "changing over from a military system to a civilian–based defense system." Ch. 4 is on preventing attack [deterrence] and ch. 5 on defense by previously organized nonviolent action; see esp. pp. 89–90 on nonviolent *blitzkrieg*, pp. 91–94 on communication and warning, and p. 97 for list of possible defense weapons. Ch. 6 on successful defense against attack, see esp. pp. 112–115 on defeating *coup d'etat*. Ch. 7 suggests steps to promote civilian–based defense. Index. Bibliography.)

2440.   ———, *National Security Through Civilian–Based Defense*. 93 pp. Omaha NE: Association for Transarmament Studies, 1985. (Booklet introduction to civilian–based defense as alternative to military deterrence policies. See esp. pp. 16–18 on "direct defense by civilians," pp. 19–22 on the history and dynamics of nonviolent action, pp. 22–23 on transarmament, p. 28 on forms of noncooperation, and pp. 41–46 for suggestions on promoting civilian–based defense. Pp. 57–92 present 59 "research areas and policy studies.")

2441.   Sider, Ronald J., and Richard K. Taylor, *Nuclear Holocaust and Christian Hope*. 428 pp. London, Sydney, Auckland, and Toronto: Hodder and Stoughton, 1982. (See section 4, "Biblical Faith and National Defence" on "nonmilitary defence," including pp. 264–87 on historical cases of nonviolent action, ch. 14 on theory of civilian–based defence, and ch. 15 on the application of civilian–based defense. Appendixes. Bibliography.)

2442.   Sommer, Mark, for the Exploratory Project on the Conditions of Peace, *Beyond the Bomb: Living Without Nuclear Weapons*. 180 pp. Massachusetts(*sic*): Expro Press, 1985. Distributed by the Talman Co., New York City. (See discussion of nonviolent action and its role in defense policy, pp. 67–85. Index.)

2443.   Sveics, V.V., *Small Nation Survival: Political Defense in Unequal Conflicts.* 271 pp. Jericho NY: Exposition Press, 1970. ("Political defense," as proposed here, includes but is not limited to nonviolent means. See esp. pp. 50–69, critique of violence and control in pp. 105–24, and ch. 6, 8, 9. Bibliography.)

2444.   Wright, Quincy, William M. Evan, and Morton Deutsch, eds., *Preventing World War III: Some Proposals.* 460 pp. New York: Simon and Schuster, 1962. (Collected essays on arms races, international tensions, and related topics. See Arne Naess, "Nonmilitary Defense," pp. 123–135, for a very early proposal for a defense system based upon nonviolent action and Jerome D. Frank, "Human Nature and Nonviolent Resistance," pp. 192–205, which stresses the psychological tasks in replacing war with nonviolent means.)

Nonviolent Revolution

Nonviolent revolution may be defined as the disintegration or radical modification of a regime by means of mass nonviolent action. Often, the nonviolent revolutionary holds that social inequities are sufficiently deep and entrenched to warrant a radical change in individuals and society brought about by nonviolent revolution. Nonviolent struggles may be framed within a nonviolent revolutionary strategy synthesizing a belief in principled nonviolence or pragmatic nonviolent action with a desire for radical change. Such ideas often take inspiration from activists and thinkers such as Mohandas Gandhi and A.J. Muste.

See also: Resistance and Revolution.

2445.   Desai, Narayan, *Towards a Non–Violent Revolution.* 167 pp. Rajghat, Varanasi: Sarva Seva Sangh Prakashan, 1972. (Study of *shanti sena*, or peace army, and intervention by nonviolent means in India. Photos. Index. Bibliography.)

2446.   Lakey, George, *Strategy for a Living Revolution.* 234 pp. New York: Grossman, 1973. Paperback: San Francisco: W.H. Freeman, 1973. (Presentation of strategy and tactics for nonviolent "civilian insurrection" for radical change in the U.S. Author suggests important stages are cultural preparation, building organizational strength, propaganda of the deed, political and economic noncooperation, and intervention and parallel institutions. Ch. 2 contains brief case studies of nonviolent revolutions, including France 1968, El Salvador 1944, and Guatemala 1944. See pp. 72–77 on building affinity groups of resistance, pp. 103–9 on the strategy of nonviolent actions which create dilemmas for opponent. Ch. 6 is on political and economic noncooperation. Ch. 7 is on intervention and parallel institutions. Pp. 180–86 are on nonviolent defense. Ch. 9 addresses objections to nonviolent revolution. Index.)

2447. Lanza del Vasto, *Warriors of Peace*. Trans. Jean Sidgwick. Ed. Michel Random. 226 pp. New York: Alfred A. Knopf, 1974. (Essays by French Gandhian leader. Section 1 discusses his theory of nonviolence, including an essay on nonviolence and self–defense. Section 2 covers campaigns in Europe, 1957–65, plus an essay on nonviolence in Western history. Extensive scattered references to fasts for moral pressure and Gandhi–style fasts.)

2448. Swomley, John M., Jr., *Liberation Ethics*. 243 pp. New York: Macmillan; London: Collier–Macmillan, 1972. (A discussion of the ethical and practical problems of revolution, the limitations of violence, and nonviolent alternatives.)

Section III
Pacifism, Principle, and War

In empirical terms, most nonviolent struggle is chosen for pragmatic or practical reasons. There are also various religious and ethical values and belief systems which reject violence on grounds of principle. Concepts like "pacifism" or "nonviolence" thus have been used to describe a wide variety of concepts and actions. Sharp [entry 1259] classifies principled nonviolence into six categories, nonresistance, active reconciliation, moral resistance, selective nonviolence, satyagraha, and nonviolent revolution. Aspects of those beliefs relating specifically to principles and their views on violence, war, and participation in war are compiled below. These references are not intended to be exhaustive but are selected as they relate to knowledge of nonviolent action.

PACIFISM AND PRINCIPLED NONVIOLENCE

Pacifism and principled nonviolence are broader streams of thought than either war resistance or nonviolent revolution alone, combining these streams with other ideas. The following works may either advocate, analyze, or discuss the history of the organized pacifist tradition, demonstrating its domestic political as well as internationalist focus.

2449. Hyatt, John, Comp., *Pacifism: A Selected Bibliography*. 52 pp. London: Housmans, 1972. (Partially annotated bibliography on historical and theoretical English–language books and pamphlets on pacifism and pacifist movements. Index.)

Studies

2450. Bussey, Gertrude, and Margaret Tims, *Pioneers for Peace: Women's International League for Peace and Freedom 1915–1965*. 255 pp. London: WILPF British Section, 1980. Originally published as *Women's International League for Peace and Freedom 1915–1965: A Record of Fifty Years' Work*. London: George Allen & Unwin, 1965. (Jubilee history of peace organization started during WWI which adopted "pacifism in practice" in the form of nonviolent resistance to war and active reconciliation. See ch. 3, 4 for activities in early inter–war years, including support for passive resistance in 1923 Ruhr struggle, pp. 44–45; ch. 11–16 for WWII and its coming; and ch. 18 for efforts to develop a response to nuclear weapons. Photos. Index.)

2451.   Buzzard, Lynn, and Paula Campbell, *Holy Disobedience: When Christians Must Resist the State*. 248 pp. Ann Arbor MI: Servant Books, 1984. (Popularized introduction to religiously motivated nonviolent action. See pp. 13–15 on war tax resistance, pp. 15–17 on anti–nuclear weapons actions, and pp. 17–18 on sanctuary. Ch. 3 is on definitions and types of "civil disobedience" broadly defined; ch. 4 contains a history of civil disobedience in the U.S.; ch. 5 is entitled "Thoreau, Gandhi, and King: The Legacy of Creative Protest"; ch. 6 gives a history of Christian nonviolent disobedience to the state; ch. 9 is on the legal aspects of civil disobedience; and pp. 215–19 are on "conscientious non–cooperation." Index.)

2452.   Childress, James F., *Moral Responsibility in Conflicts: Essays on Nonviolence, War, and Conscience*. 224 pp. Baton Rouge and London: Louisiana State Univ. Press, 1982. (Essays analyzing "tension between limits and ends in conflicts," and between means and ends, from a religious perspective. See ch. 1, "Nonviolence: Trust and Risk Taking," esp. pp. 12–28 on nonviolent resistance. See also pp. 46–57 on Reinhold Niebuhr and the question of violent and nonviolent means. Ch. 5, 6 are on conscientious objection. Index.)

2453.   Douglass, James W., *Resistance and Contemplation: The Way of Liberation*. 192 pp. New York: Dell, 1972. (Personal essays on principled nonviolence, with attention to Gandhi and Jesus and commentary on current issues.)

2454.   Friesen, Duane K., *Christian Peacemaking & International Conflict: A Realist Pacifist Perspective*. 303 pp. Scottdale PA and Kitchener, Ontario: Herald Press, 1986. (Presentation of a religious "realist pacifist" position of peacemaking. See pp. 20–28 for conflicting approaches to peacemaking and ch. 6 for a discussion of nonviolence as a normative principle of change, esp. pp. 149–157 for nonviolence as a political strategy. Consult index under *Sharp, Gene*. Indexes. Bibliography.)

2455.   Givey, David W., *The Social Thought of Thomas Merton: The Way of Nonviolence and Peace for the Future*. 135 pp. Chicago: Franciscan Herald Press, 1983. (Study of Merton's philosophy of nonviolence from a Christian perspective. See ch. 3, "The Way of Nonviolence," esp. pp. 60–66 on Gandhi, ch. 4 on Christian principles of nonviolence; and ch. 5 on nonviolent action in the civil rights movement.)

2456.   Hillegass, Robert W., *Nonviolence on Trial*. 32 pp. Wallingford PA: Pendle Hill Publications, 1987. Pendle Hill Pamphlet No. 274. (Personal reflections of a member of Ailanthus, a Boston-based religious community protesting nuclear weapons.)

2457.   Kallenburg, Arthur L., J. Donald Moon, and Daniel R. Sabia, Jr., eds., *Dissent and Affirmation: Essays in Honor of Mulford Q. Sibley*. 278 pp. Bowling Green OH: Bowling Green Univ. Popular Press, 1983. (For criticism of Mulford Sibley's views [entry 2412] on "the duty of nonviolence," see L. Earl Shaw, "Christians in Conflict: Sibley and Niebuhr on the Use of Violence," and Terence Ball, "A Critique of Pure Pacifism." Selected bibliography of Sibley's writings, pp. 272–76.)

2458.   Kumar, Krishna, ed., *Democracy and Nonviolence: A Study of Their Relationship*. 244 pp. New Delhi: Delhi Citizens' Peace Committee, sponsored by the Gandhi Peace Foundation, [1968]. (Brief essays on the relationship between principled Gandhian nonviolence and the theory of democracy. Bibliography.)

2459.   Mayer, Peter, ed., *The Pacifist Conscience*. 447 pp. New York: Holt, Rinehart & Winston; London: Rupert Hart–Davis, 1966. (Anthology of essays by advocates of pacifism, principled nonviolence, and nonviolent action. See esp. John Woolman on war tax resistance, pp. 94–99; William Lloyd Garrison on nonresistance in the Abolitionist Movement, pp. 123–28; Adin Ballou on Christian nonresistance, pp. 129–39; Thoreau on civil disobedience, pp. 140–59; Tolstoy on Christian anarchist pacifism, pp. 160–76; Gandhi on pacifism, pp. 203–19; Richard

Gregg on moral jiu–jitsu, pp. 224–34; A.A. Milne on his defection from pacifism, pp. 256–68; Martin Buber's criticism of Gandhi's advice to European Jews to adopt nonviolent resistance, pp. 269–82; Vera Brittain on her pacifist minority position, pp. 283–90. Also contains selections on conscientious objection and Christian pacifism, esp. Diderich H. Lund on pacifism under Nazi occupation, pp. 355–61, and Danilo Dolci's trial statement, pp. 391–401. Bibliography.)

2460.   Merton, Thomas, *The Nonviolent Alternative.* Ed. Gordon C. Zahn. 270 pp. New York: Farrar Straus Giroux, 1980. Revised ed. of *Thomas Merton on Peace.* (Collected brief writings on war, peace, and nonviolence. See "Peace and Protest: A Statement," pp. 67–69; a discussion of WWII resisters, pp. 134–49; and pieces in section 2, including a statement delivered to federal commission on violence, pp. 227–30.)

2461.   Seeger, Daniel A., *The Seed and the Tree: A Reflection on Nonviolence.* 51 pp. Wallingford PA: Pendle Hill Publications, 1986. Pendle Hill Pamphlet No. 269. (Personal reflections on a "nonviolent sensibility" by a conscientious objector during the Korean War.)

2462.   Shannon, Thomas A., ed., *War or Peace? The Search for New Answers.* 255 pp. Maryknoll NY: Orbis Books, 1980. (Essays on conceptual, institutional, and personal issues concerning religious pacifism and the just war theory. See esp. Michael True, "Sources of the Nonviolent Tradition in American Literature," ch. 7. See also pp. 136–44 for Catholic nonviolent resistance to the Vietnam War, and Paul Hanly Furfey, "The Civilian COs," ch. 11, describing those who oppose war in ways other than draft resistance. Index.)

2463.   Stevick, Daniel B., *Civil Disobedience and the Christian.* 211 pp. New York: Seabury Press, 1969. (Analysis of relation between Christian obedience and political civil disobedience. Author argues case for "responsible civil disobedience." See ch. 3 for pre–Christian and early Christian dissent, and ch. 7 on Christian nonviolence. Appendix one discusses ideas of Thoreau. Appendixes. Index. Bibliography.)

2464.   Teichman, Jenny, *Pacifism and the Just War: A Study in Applied Philosophy*. 138 pp. Oxford: Basil Blackwell, 1986. (Philosophical analysis of the thesis of pacifism and major objections to it, emphasizing the traditional doctrine of just war. Appendixes. Index. Bibliography.)

2465.   Unnithan, T.K.N., and Yogendra Singh, *Traditions of Non-Violence*. 317 pp. New Delhi, London: Arnold–Heinemann, 1973. (History of traditions of thought advocating non–harm and non–killing in Hindu, Chinese, Islamic, and Judeo–Christian thought. Ch. 1, 7 also contain some efforts to distinguish value–oriented from "pragmatic" approaches.)

2466.   Zahn, Franklin, *Deserter from Violence: Experiments with Gandhi's Truth*. 272 pp. New York: Philosophical Library, 1984. (Autobiography of U.S. pacifist and activist; see ch. 9–12 on imprisonment during WWII, ch. 19 on anti–nuclear testing voyage of *Everyman II*, and ch. 21 for later activities. Illustrations. Photos.)

War Resistance and Peace

The following works focus specifically on the organized pacifist tradition and the question of peace.

2467.   Cadoux, C. John, *The Early Christian Attitude to War: A Contribution to the History of Christian Ethics*. 272 pp. New York: Gordon Press, 1975 [orig. publ. 1919]. (Ethical history of early Christian beliefs about war. See chronological table, pp. xvii–xxiii; pp. 20–31 on statements of Jesus concerning "non-violence"; and part 2, "Forms of the Early Christian Disapproval of War," esp. pp. 96–160 on Christian refusal to participate in war. Index.)

2468.   Ceadel, Martin, *Thinking About Peace and War*. 222 pp. Oxford and New York: Oxford Univ. Press, 1987. (Classification and analytical examination of the major ideological positions in the "war–and–peace debate," including militarism, "crusading," "defencism," "pacific–ism," and pacifism. Ch. 7, on pacifism, includes classification of types of pacifism, pp. 141–45;

motivations, pp. 147–154; and nonviolence, pp. 154–162. Index.)

2469. Gregg, Richard B., *Pacifist Program in the Time of War, Threatened War, Or Fascism.* 61 pp. Wallingford PA: Pendle Hill, [n.d.]. Pendle Hill Pamphlet No. 5. (Practical advice for pacifists written prior to WWII, emphasizing noncooperation and the development of the "principle of silence" by avoiding militant protests and condemnation.)

2470. Moorehead, Caroline, *Troublesome People: The Warriors of Peace.* 344 pp. Bethesda MD: Adler & Adler, 1987. (Historical portraits of 20th century "pacifists" in Britain, U.S., West Germany, and Japan. Ch. 1–3 are on conscientious objection and war resistance in WWI, pp. 124–33 on the Peace Pledge Union in the 1930s, ch. 6–7 on conscientious objection and war resistance in WWII. Ch. 8 is on nonviolent action protesting nuclear weapons in the 1950s and early 1960s and ch. 9 is on similar actions in Japan. Ch. 10 is on the civil rights movement, anti–Vietnam War movement, and nonviolent action against nuclear weapons in the 1970s. Ch. 11 is on West German "pacifist" movements. See ch. 12 for current movements and discussion of the future of pacifism. Index. Bibliography.)

2471. Muste, A.J., *Non–Violence in an Aggressive World.* 3d ed. 211 pp. New York and London: Harper & Brothers, 1940. (Presents case for Christian pacifism. See ch. 5, 6 on pacifism as a revolutionary strategy focusing on complete refusal to support the "war–machine." Ch. 7 examines the relationships among democracy, state control in the form of police action, and pacifism. Ch. 8 presents a political program of pacifism. See also index under *non–violence.* Index. Bibliography.)

Conscientious Objection

The meaning of conscientious objection shifts somewhat over time as different bases may be asserted for the right of legally–recognized conscientious objection and consequent release from the legal requirement to submit to conscription. In general, conscientious objectors refuse to fight in a specific war or in all wars for reasons of overriding religious or ethical principles.

Because these principles vary, conscientious objectors may act individually or as a group. They may be assertive or not and may, if denied legal recognition, continue to reject state authority to command their participation in military service.

2472.   Seeley, Robert A., ed., *Bibliography on War, Peace, and Conscience*. 93 pp. Philadelphia: Central Committee for Conscientious Objectors, 1987. (Partially annotated bibliography designed primarily for peace activists. See esp. sections on "Conscientious Objection, War Resistance, and Pacifism," pp. 64–77; "Nonviolence," pp. 77–87; and "Biographies of Peacemakers," pp. 87–88.)

STUDIES

2473.   Axelrad, Albert S., *Call to Conscience: Jews, Judaism, and Conscientious Objection*. 207 pp. Hoboken NJ: KTAV Publishing House; Nyack NY: Jewish Peace Fellowship, 1986. (Handbook for Jewish conscientious objectors. Appendixes begin on p. 93 and contain excerpts from personal essays. Bibliography.)

2474.   Falk, Richard A., ed., *The Vietnam War and International Law: The Widening Context*. Vol. 3. 951 pp. Princeton NJ: Princeton Univ. Press, 1972. (See Section II:B on question of applicability of Nuremberg principles to war service refusal under U.S. law. Index.)

2475.   Rohr, John A., *Prophets Without Honor: Public Policy and the Selective Conscientious Objector*. 191 pp. Nashville and New York: Abingdon Press, 1971. (Concludes that there exists neither a constitutional right of selective conscientious objection nor a public policy interest in tolerating conscientious refusal to take part in a particular war, thus requiring "stoning our prophets now and building our monuments in happier times," p. 184. Index of leading cases. General Index. Bibliography.)

2476.   Schlissel, Lillian, *Conscience in America: A Documentary History of Conscientious Objection in America, 1757–1967*. 444 pp. New York: E. P. Dutton, 1968. (Selection of documents and statements on conscientious objection. Parts 1–3 mostly on religious societies before 1900, subsequent sections on the world wars and Vietnam War. Part 8, on opposition to war in Vietnam, includes selections on protest voyages of *Golden Rule* and *Phoenix* and part of a tax resistance pamphlet from 1966. Documents.)

2477. Seeley, Robert A., *Handbook for Conscientious Objectors.* Philadelphia: Central Committee For Conscientious Objectors, 1981 [orig. publ. 1952]. (Frequently revised handbook giving information and advice on conscientious objection. Index. Bibliography.)

2478. *War, Conscription, Conscience and Mormonism.* 116 pp. Santa Barbara CA: Mormon Heritage, 1971. (A collection of short articles, essays, and pamphlets written by Mormons on the question of the relation of Mormonism to war, the draft, and civil law, several maintaining that Mormons can or should be C.O.s. Documents.)

2479. Zahn, Gordon C., *War, Conscience and Dissent.* 317 pp. New York: Hawthorn Books, 1967. (Collection of articles by Catholic pacifist on conscientious objection, dissent, and disobedience. See ch. 5 on Catholic peace movement, ch. 6 on nonviolent resistance as a pacifist alternative to violence. Part 2 includes articles on Catholic conscientious objection in the U.S. during WWII, ch. 9–10, and conscientious objection in Nazi Germany, ch. 11–12. Part 3 examines Catholic Church opposition to Nazi repression. Index.)

Historic Peace Churches

The Christian churches and sects described below represent proponents of the view that authoritative religious commandments forbid participation in war or violence. Precise interpretations of these strictures and of the duties of the believer differ among them, but many such groups have defied the authority of the state where such matters are concerned and have suffered for this defiance.

2480. Barksdale, Brent E., *Pacifism and Democracy in Colonial Pennsylvania.* 65 pp. Stanford Honors Essays in Humanities,

No. 3, 1961. (Study of the dilemmas of pacifist belief and military defense during Indian wars of mid–1750s. Bibliography.)

2481.   Bowman, Rufus D., *The Church of the Brethren and War, 1708–1941*. 352 pp. Elgin IL: Brethren Publishing House, 1944. (History of Brethren's opposition to war in the U.S. from Colonial era. See index under *conscientious objectors, National Council for Religious Objectors, National Service Board for Religious Objectors, non–associators, noncombatants, nonresistance, nonresistants, Quakers,* and *war resisters*. Index. Bibliography.)

2482.   Brinton, Howard, *Friends for 300 Years: The History and Beliefs of the Society of Friends since George Fox Started the Quaker Movement*. 239 pp. New York: Harper & Brothers, 1952. (History of Quakers. See ch. 8 on Quaker political and social beliefs, esp. pp. 151–164 on "method of nonviolence," and pp. 164–70 on pacifism. Index.)

2483.   Hershberger, Guy Franklin, *War, Peace, and Nonresistance*. Rev. ed. 375 pp. Scottsdale PA: Herald Press, 1953 [orig. publ. 1944]. (Treatise on biblical and historic tradition of Christian nonresistance in the Mennonite Church. See ch. 3 on nonresistance in the New Testament, ch. 6 on Mennonite nonresistance to war in the U.S. from the French and Indian War to WWII, ch. 9 comparing Biblical nonresistance to modern pacifism. Ch. 8, 10–12 on social implications of Biblical nonresistance. Appendixes. Index.)

2484.   Hirst, Margaret E., *The Quakers in Peace and War: An Account of Their Peace Principles and Practice*. 560 pp. London: The Swarthmore Press; New York: George H. Doran, 1923. Reprint, [n.p.]: Jerome S. Ozer, 1972. (Historical study of Quaker pacifism from 17th century. See index under *alternative service in war, conscientious objectors, Doukhobors, fasts, No Conscription Fellowship, non–combatant service, non–resistance,* and *war taxes.* Index.)

2485.   Stayer, James M., *Anabaptists and the Sword*. 2d ed. 375 pp. Lawrence KS: Coronado Press, 1976 [orig. publ. 1972]. (Study of historical development of Anabaptist thought on the ethics of coercion, pacifism, and revolution in the 16th century. See esp. ch. 5 and index under *nonresistance*. Illustrations. Index. Bibliography.)

Chapter 6
Theory and Research on Conflict, Power, and Violence

Section I
Conflict and its Dynamics

One thesis that this research guide is based on is that nonviolent action is an aspect—a researchable and understandable aspect—of human conflict. Further, nonviolent action is most significantly understood in group or collective conflict, rather than interpersonal conflict and reconciliation. Each of the disciplines that undertake to study human behavior can be expected to make some significant contribution to understanding conflict and its dynamics. The majority of references that follow are drawn from social psychology, political science, and sociology, with others from economics and anthropology. Several of these works are primarily engaged in conceptual clarification and clearing the ground for a systematic approach to conflict studies. Besides these, three basic issues are most often addressed, as follows: (1) the causes and typical course of conflicts, (2) the socio–political effects of conflicts, and (3) procedures followed by participants in conflicts. This last concern includes studies of the process of contention and sanctions and the role of power in conflict outcomes. Several such works are concerned with questions of strategies in struggle and of the options open to contending parties seeking to influence the course and outcome of conflict.

2486.   Boulding, Elise, J. Robert Passmore, and Robert Scott Gassler, eds., *Bibliography on World Conflict and Peace: Second Edition.* 168 pp. Boulder CO: Westview Press, 1979. (Lists books, articles, collections and series, periodicals, and bibliographies. The main series is an alphabetical listing of books and articles and is provided with a running subject classification of each entry according to a model explained on pp. xxi–xxx.)

2487. Pondy, Louis R., Dale E. Fitzgibbons, and John A. Wayne, III, eds., *Organizational Power and Conflict: A Bibliography*. 19 pp. Monticello IL: Vance Bibliographies, 1980. (References from sociology and political science on "power and conflict in organizations.")

STUDIES

Several different manifestations or levels of conflict are discussed in the studies assembled here, including interpersonal conflicts, aggression, organizational conflicts, revolution, war, and intergroup (i.e., racial or ethnic) strife. These works also differ as to whether they take a social–psychological or structural approach and whether they are largely descriptive or largely analytical and theoretical. While the majority of these works do not make the assumption that conflict and violence are essentially the same thing, users of this guide will be careful to distinguish conflict from violence, and violence from nonviolent action.

2488. Bacharach, Samuel B., and Edward J. Lawler, *Power and Politics in Organizations: The Social Psychology of Conflict, Coalitions, and Bargaining*. 249 pp. San Francisco, Washington, and London: Jossey–Bass, 1980. (See ch. 2–3 on "form" and "content" of power in organizations; ch. 6–8 on conflict as bargaining. Index. Bibliography.)

2489. Boulding, Kenneth E., *Conflict and Defense: A General Theory*. 349 pp. New York: Harper & Row, 1963 [orig. publ. 1962]. (Systematic observations on conflict and conflict groups. Ch. 1–3 discuss conflict models, including game theory. Ch. 4 looks at power as viability in conflict, ch. 6–9 discuss group conflict, and ch. 10–13 discuss conflict in economic, industrial, and international settings. Ch. 15 reviews methods of conflict resolution and control. Index.)

2490. Bramson, Leon, and George W. Goethals, eds., *War: Studies from Psychology, Sociology, Anthropology*. 407 pp. New York and

London: Basic Books, 1964. (See especially Bronislaw Malinowski, "An Anthropological Analysis of War.")

2491.   Coser, Lewis A., *The Functions of Social Conflict*. 188 pp. New York: Free Press; London: Collier–Macmillan, 1956. (Sociological analysis of social conflict outlining sixteen propositions based primarily on work by the German sociologist Georg Simmel. Ch. 7 is on conflict as a unifying mechanism. Index.)

2492.   Coser, Lewis A., and Otto N. Larsen, eds., *The Uses of Controversy in Sociology*. 398 pp. New York: The Free Press; London: Collier Macmillan Publishers, 1976. (See Ted Robert Gurr and Raymond D. Duvall, "Introduction to a Formal Theory of Political Conflict," ch. 8 and Theda Skocpol, "Explaining Revolutions: In Quest of a Societal–Structural Approach," ch. 9. Index. Bibliography.)

2493.   Dedring, Juergen, *Recent Advances in Peace and Conflict Research: A Critical Survey*. 249 pp. Beverly Hills and London: Sage Publications, 1976. (Review of major concepts in conflict research. Ch. 1 is on "peace and conflict systems" in the international order. Ch. 3, "premises and models," contains an evaluation of research in nonviolent action on pp. 123–128, and ch. 5 discusses conflict as group interaction. Index. Bibliography.)

2494.   de Reuck, Anthony, and Julie Knight, eds., *Conflict in Society*. 467 pp. Boston: Little, Brown, 1966. (Collection of brief essays on conflict theory, including pieces on intergroup domination and aggression, conflict within organizations and communities, strategy, and conflict resolution. Index.)

2495.   Deutsch, Morton, *The Resolution of Conflict: Constructive and Destructive Processes*. 420 pp. New Haven and London: Yale Univ. Press, 1973. (Collected papers on conflict dynamics. Ch. 5 discusses intergroup conflict; ch. 7, 8 report author's research on trust and suspicion; and ch. 6, 9, 10 report on the role of sanctions [threats and promises] in conflict. Summary in ch. 13 contrasts "destructive" and "productive" process in conflicts. Index. Bibliography.)

2496.   Edelman, Murray, *Politics as Symbolic Action: Mass Arousal and Quiescence*. 188 pp. Chicago: Markham, 1971. (Study of "perception" and political "myths" in mobilization for conflict as well as promoting "quiescence." See ch. 2 on symbols and conflict process. Index.)

2497.   Edwards, P.K., *Conflict at Work: A Materialist Analysis of Workplace Relations*. 357 pp. London: Basil Blackwell, 1986. (Approach to conflict and control based on concept of relations in the workplace and production process. See ch. 1, 2 for theory and ch. 3 for "changing forms of protest," as well as ch. 6 on conflict and control. Index. Bibliography.)

2498.   Eldridge, Albert F., *Images of Conflict*. 229 pp. New York: St. Martin's Press, 1979. (Perception and communication model of conflict process. See ch. 3–5 on political violence and ch. 7, 8 on conflict resolution. Index. Bibliography.)

2499.   Fried, Morton, Marvin Harris, and Robert Murphy, eds., *War: The Anthropology of Armed Conflict and Aggression*. 262 pp. Garden City NY: The Natural History Press for the American Museum of Natural History, 1968. (Chapters and commentary on significant aspects of war in both preliterate and modern societies. Index. Bibliography.)

2500.   Gurr, Ted R., ed., *Handbook of Political Conflict: Theory and Research*. 566 pp. New York: Free Press, 1980. (In addition to papers on psychological aspects of conflict and part 3 on war and international conflict, see Edward M. Muller, "The Psychology of Political Protest and Violence," ch. 2 which assesses deprivation–frustration and relative deprivation theories as against utilitarian and normative explanations of collective action; Harry Eckstein, "Theoretical Approaches to Explaining Collective Violence," ch. 4 which endeavors to show that opposing views of the "inherency" or "contingency" of political violence ought not to be confused; Ekkart Zimmerman, "Macro–Comparative Research on Political Protest," ch. 5 which shifts the focus specifically to "protest" and admits nonviolent means into the repertoire; Ted Robert Gurr, "On the Outcome of Violent Conflict," ch. 6 which presents views on the success–failure dimension of conflict and systemic consequences of political violence; Terry Nardin, "Theory and Practice of Conflict Research," ch. 12 which offers a criticism of conflict studies from the point of view of conflict practice; and J. David Singer, "Conflict Research, Political Action, and Epistemology," ch. 13 which is a brief reflection on conflict knowledge and practice. Index. Bibliography.)

2501.   Himes, Joseph S., *Conflict and Conflict Management*. 332 pp. Athens: Univ. of Georgia Press, 1980. (Introduction to contemporary ideas of conflict that view it as "purposeful behavior" and therefore give some attention to "conflict tactics" and power. See ch. 4 on power, ch. 5 on violence, and section 2 on "conflict management," including prevention, resolution, and suppression of conflict. Index. Bibliography.)

2502.   The International Sociological Association, in collaboration with Jessie Bernard, T. H. Pear, Raymond Aron, and Robert C. Angell, *The Nature of Conflict: Studies on the Sociological Aspects of International Tensions*. 314 pp. Paris: United Nations Educational, Scientific and Cultural Organization, 1957. (Studies in conflict, including Jessie Bernard, "The Sociological Study of Conflict," pp. 33–117, and Robert C. Angell, "Discovering Paths to Peace," pp. 204–23. Volume also includes 1160 entry bibliography on intergroup conflict and international relations.)

2503.   Kriesberg, Louis, *Social Conflicts*. 2d ed. 349 pp. Englewood Cliffs NJ: Prentice–Hall, 1982 [orig. publ. 1973 as *The Sociology of Social Conflicts*]. (Comprehensive sociological study of conflicts adopting a multidimensional approach. Employs concept of the stages of conflict as an organizing principle of the discussion. See ch. 1 for stages and ch. 2–6 on the progress of conflicts through those stages. Ch. 7 discusses third party roles and mediation. Ch. 8 is on the consequences of conflict. Issues of violent and nonviolent conflict discussed throughout; consult index under *civil disobedience, coercion, conversion, nonviolence, nonviolent coercion, sanctions, satyagraha,* and *violence*. Index.)

2504.   McNeil, Elton B., ed., *The Nature of Human Conflict*. 315 pp. Englewood Cliffs NJ: Prentice–Hall, 1965. (Interdisciplinary textbook on conflict. Disciplines surveyed include psychology, ch. 3, 4; sociology, ch. 5; anthropology, ch. 6; political science, ch. 7; history, ch. 8; economics, ch. 9; and international relations, ch. 10–13. See esp. Donald F. Keys, "The American Peace Movement," ch. 14.)

2505. Pruitt, Dean G., and Jeffrey Z. Rubin, *Social Conflict: Escalation, Stalemate, and Settlement*. New York: Random House, 1986. (Analysis and model of conflict based on concept of five "strategic choices" [contending, problem solving, yielding, withdrawing, inaction]. Of interest are ch. 3 on "strategic choice," including pp. 51–56 on promises and threats, ch. 4 on "contentious tactics," ch. 5–8 on escalation of conflict, and ch. 9, 10 on conflict resolution. Index. Bibliography.)

2506. Rapoport, Anatol, *Strategy and Conscience*. 2d ed. 323 pp. New York: Schocken Books, 1969 [orig. publ. New York: Harper & Row, 1964]. (Largely a criticism of trends in strategic thought. The opening section discusses ideas of "rational decision" in noncooperative situations. Index. Bibliography.)

2507. Rapoport, Anatol, and Albert M. Chammah, with the collaboration of Carol J. Orwant, *Prisoner's Dilemma: A Study in Conflict and Cooperation*. 258 pp. Ann Arbor MI: Univ. of Michigan Press, 1965. Reprint, 1970. (Report on experimental and mathematical analysis of the Prisoner's Dilemma, a noncooperative two–player game of strategy. Introduction discusses the concept of strategic games, conflict and cooperation, and strategy. Bibliography.)

2508. Rex, John, *Social Conflict: A Conceptual and Theoretical Analysis*. 136 pp. London and New York: Longmans, 1981. (Introduction to ideas of social conflict. See pp. 14–19 on sanctions and power as relationships, and ch. 4 on groups in conflict, including pp. 78–82 on state sanctions, and ch. 5 for a proposed analytical paradigm. Index.)

2509. Ridd, Rosemary, and Helen Callaway, eds., *Women and Political Conflict: Portraits of Struggle in Times of Crisis*. 246 pp. New York: New York Univ. Press, 1987. *Caught up in Conflict: Women's Responses to Political Strife*. 246 pp. Houndmills,

Basingstoke, Hampshire, and London: Macmillan Educational, 1986. (Collection of essays on women's experience of political conflict compared to men's experience. See Rosemary Ridd, "Powers of the Powerless," ch. 1 for discussion of power, powerlessness, and power relations; Lynda Edgerton, "Public Protest, Domestic Acquiescence: Women in Northern Ireland," ch. 4 on women in civil rights movement; Moiram Ali, "The Coal War: Women's Struggle During the Miners' Strike, " ch. 5 on 1984–85 English strike; pp. 132–33 on protest activity by Palestinian women in Lebanon; and Helen Callaway, "Survival and Support: Women's Forms of Political Action," ch. 10, esp. pp. 221–25. Index.)

2510.   Schellenberg, James A., *The Science of Conflict*. 291 pp. New York and Oxford: Oxford Univ. Press, 1982. (Grounding a "new science" of conflict, the author reviews studies of war and civil strife in part 3, the concept of strategy in part 4, and means of conflict resolution in part 5; including pp. 225–34 on "force." Index. Bibliography.)

2511.   Schelling, Thomas C., *The Strategy of Conflict*. 309 pp. Cambridge: Harvard Univ. Press, 1960. Reprint, London and New York: Oxford Univ. Press, 1968. (Discussion of bargaining, decision, and threat within the context of the theory of games. See ch. 2 on bargaining, esp. pp. 22–28 on "the power to bind oneself" and pp. 35–46 on threats and promises. Ch. 5 on "strategic moves" and ch. 7, 8 also discuss threats and punishments. Index.)

2512.   Simmel, Georg, *Conflict and the Web of Group–Affiliations*. Trans. Kurt H. Wolf and Reinhard Bendix. 195 pp. Glencoe IL: Free Press; London: Collier–Macmillan, 1955. (The first essay translated here, "Conflict," is a classic sociological study on social conflict, emphasizing intergroup dynamics, ch. 1; competition, ch. 2; and intragroup effects of conflict, ch. 3.)

2513.   Swingle, Paul, ed., The *Structure of Conflict*. 305 pp. New York and London: Academic Press, 1970. (Essays on the social–psychology of conflict, negotiation, and game theory. See Bertram H. Raven and Arie W. Kruglanski, "Conflict and Power," ch. 3, in which power is conceived of largely in terms of influence in dyads, and James T. Tedeschi, "Threats and Promises," ch. 5, on the communication of willingness to sanction another party's behavior. Index.)

2514.   Tichenor, Phillip J., George A. Donohue, and Clarice N. Olien, *Community Conflict and the Press*. 240 pp. Beverly Hills CA and London: Sage Publications, 1980. (Study of the influences of media coverage and public knowledge on development and control of community conflict.)

2515.   Williams, Robin M., Jr., *The Reduction of Intergroup Conflict: A Survey of Research on Problems of Ethnic, Racial, and Religious Group Relations*. Social Science Research Council Bulletin 57. 153 pp. New York: Social Science Research Council, 1947. (An assessment of action programs designed to reduce prejudice and group conflicts and the assumptions on which such efforts are or might be based. Research projects list follows. See pp. 12–25 for the variety of approaches to the problem as then understood including "direct action," and pp. 94–96 for research suggestions on political tactics. Index. Bibliography.)

2516.   Wilkinson, David, *Cohesion and Conflict: Lessons From the Study of Three–Party Interaction*. 269 pp. New York: St. Martin's Press, 1976. (Formal and mathematical analysis, with use of game theory, of the triad in the conduct of conflicts and coalitions. Ch. 2 discusses the nature and potential roles of the third party; ch. 3 and 4 take up power in consensus and conflict; and ch. 6–8 describe the model derived from the research. Index. Bibliography.)

2517.   Ziegenhagen, Eduard A., *The Regulation of Political Conflict*. 224 pp. New York, Westport CT, and London: Praeger, 1986. (Analysis of governmental regulation of political conflict, including mass protest against the state, using cybernetic theory and a new conceptualization of the "conflict episode." See ch. 6–8 for models of governmental intervention based on assessment of coercive capacity and effectiveness of sanctions. Index.)

Section II
Political Power

Political power, like conflict, is a disputed concept. This is in part because its nature appears to shift as the contexts in which it appears change. In one setting, power appears as authority, in another as domination, and in yet another as violence and force. With these features in mind, the following references are divided among theories that focus primarily on power in established systems, those that relate power to sanctions and state hegemony, and those that stress the creation and maintenance of political obligation and social control.

These entries are primarily theoretical in nature and mostly concerned with power in structures and structured relationships such as organizations. While in general they understand power as a form of domination, several are oriented toward a social–psychological view that sees social power as influence (either in face–to–face interaction or in groups). One area in which the structurally–oriented studies differ is whether they understand power as the control of one group by another (or of decisions significant to groups) [e.g., entry 2529] or whether they see power as a capacity of a group to act together [e.g., entry 2519]. Nearly all modern studies, however, view power as interactive and contingent rather than fixed. Students of nonviolent action will be interested in these ideas to the extent that they assist in understanding the circumstances under which protest, noncooperation, and nonviolent intervention may affect structures of power; some ideas on this are found in entries 2518, 2519, 2528, 2526, 2533, and 2536.

2518. Bachrach, Peter, and Morton S. Baratz, *Power and Poverty: Theory and Practice.* 220 pp. New York, London, and Toronto: Oxford Univ. Press, 1970. (Theoretical inquiry into political power combined with a sociological study of poverty and anti–poverty action, Baltimore, 1966–68. See part 1 for theory of power and decision–making. Index.)

2519. Barnes, Barry, *The Nature of Power.* 205 pp. Cambridge, England: Polity Press, 1988. (Presents a sociological view of social power as based on the "calculative" behavior of individuals. See ch. 1, 3 on definition, containing in part the idea that "social power is the capacity for action in a society." Issues discussed include sanctions and acquiescence; esp. on pp. 39–40 and in ch. 4, 5; and "collective deviance" or disruption on pp. 42–44. The problem of collective action is the topic of ch. 5. Index. Bibliography.)

2520. de la Boétie, Etienne, *The Politics of Obedience: The Discourse of Voluntary Servitude.* Trans. Harry Kurtz. 54 pp. New York: Columbia Univ. Press, 1942. Reprint, 87 pp. New York: Free Life Editions; Montreal: Black Rose Books, 1975. (Translation with introduction of an essay by the sixteenth–century political thinker Etienne de la Boétie, proposing that voluntary obedience or consent is the essential basis of the power of government, particularly tyrannies, and including observations on why this fact is not often recognized or acted upon. Significant not so much for its influence in its own time as for the example it afforded more recent students of nonviolent action.)

2521. Cartwright, Dorwin, ed., *Studies in Social Power.* 224 pp. Ann Arbor: Univ. of Michigan, Institute for Social Research, Center for Group Dynamics, 1959. (Empirical and theoretical studies on power and power relations in social psychology, including social interactions based upon power, threat, and leadership. See esp. John R.P. French and Bertram Raven, "The Bases of Social Power," ch. 9, and Dorwin Cartwright, "A Field Theoretical Conception of Power," ch. 11. Index.)

2522. Clegg, Stewart R., *Frameworks of Power.* 297 pp. London, Newbury Park CA, and New Delhi: Sage Publications, 1989. (Selective, historically–oriented review of power concepts in modern political and social theory. Ch. 8 restates contradictory or inadequate aspects of these ideas by means of a concept of "circuits of power" that relates to power in organizations, with some attention to resistance and coercion. Index. Bibliography.)

2523. ———, *Power, Rule, and Domination: A Critical and Empirical Understanding of Power in Sociological Theory and Organizational Life.* 208 pp. London and Boston: Routledge & Kegan Paul, 1975. (Ch. 1–4 review the problems of developing a theory of power; later chapters develop a concept of rules and rationality in the power context in organizations. Index. Bibliography.)

2524.   Coleman, James S., *The Asymmetric Society*. 191 pp. Syracuse NY: Syracuse Univ. Press, 1982. (Lectures on changes in power structure attributable to increase in organizations acting as juristic persons and power asymmetry between real and artificial persons. Index. Bibliography.)

2525.   ——, *Power and the Structure of Society*. 112 pp. New York: W.W. Norton, 1974. (Four lectures on social power in light of the growth of self–contained "corporate actors" which act as legally–created "persons, such as corporations" and the "separation of power from its sources" that is implied by this growth. Index. Bibliography.)

2526.   Janeway, Elizabeth, *Powers of the Weak*. 350 pp. New York: Alfred A. Knopf, 1980. (Philosophical essay on nature of power from feminist perspective. Ch. 6 examines definitions of power [including Sharp, pp. 81–84] and ch. 8 is on issues of authority, obedience, and the relationship between those in power and the powerless. See ch. 11, 12 on powers of the weak, including dissent and organizing. Ch. 13–15 are on "extreme conditions" and resistance and rebellion. Ch. 18, 19 are on "impractical politics"; see esp. ch. 19 on action and pp. 296–303 on nonviolent action. Index. Bibliography.)

2527.   Lasswell, Harold D., and Abraham Kaplan, *Power and Society: A Framework for Political Inquiry*. 295 pp. New Haven: Yale Univ. Press; London: Geoffrey Cumberlege, Oxford Univ. Press, 1950. (Theoretical conception of power and political process. See pp. 48–49 on sanctions; ch. 4 on influence; ch. 5 on power, esp. pp. 97–102 on choice and coercion; ch. 6 on political symbols, esp. pp. 111–16 on propaganda; pp. 152–61 on leadership; and ch. 10 on power and the political process. Index.)

2528.   Lipsky, Michael, *Protest in City Politics: Rent Strikes, Housing and the Power of the Poor*. 214 pp. Chicago: Rand McNally, 1970. (Author derives theory of "protest as a political resource" from studies of low–income peoples' rent strikes in New York City. See ch. 3–5 on the rent strikes and their effects and ch. 6, 7 for theory of protest action and "the power of relatively powerless groups." Index.)

2529.   Lukes, Steven, *Power: A Radical View*. 64 pp. London and Basingstoke: Macmillan Press, 1974. (Argues that structures of power are best understood as control in the face of conflict, especially to the point of preventing expression of conflict. See esp. ch. 5 and pp. 52–56 on power exercise by collectivities. Bibliography.)

2530.   Martin, Roderick, *The Sociology of Power*. 203 pp. London, Henley, and Boston: Routledge & Kegan Paul, 1977. (See ch. 3 for perspective used, ch. 4 on "power relations and dependence," and summary in ch. 11. Index.)

2531.   Nagel, Jack H., *The Descriptive Analysis of Power*. 200 pp. New Haven and London: Yale Univ. Press, 1975. (Conceptual and methodological discussion of "power and causation by preferences." Index. Bibliography.)

2532.   Ng, Sik Hung, *The Social Psychology of Power*. 280 pp. London and New York: Published in Cooperation with European Association of Experimental Social Psychology by Academic Press, 1980. (Author attempts to form a broad perspective on power based on integrating viewpoints from social psychology, general psychology, sociology, and politics. Parts 1–3 contain a critical evaluation of traditional analyses of power. Appendix. Index. Bibliography.)

2533.   Parenti, Michael, *Power and the Powerless*. 238 pp. New York: St. Martin's Press, 1978. (Study of power in American society and relationship to social structure, political consciousness, and powerlessness. See ch. 1 for definition of power, ch. 6 for structure of power and powerlessness, ch. 9 on obedience and social control, pp. 210–13 on the cooptation of protest. Index.)

2534.   Rogowski, Ronald, *Rational Legitimacy: A Theory of Political Support*. 313 pp. Princeton: Princeton Univ. Press, 1974. (Theoretical essay examining question of how people choose to accept or not accept particular governments. Author contends that people make political decisions rationally and that ethnic and occupational divisions are the principal factors influencing this choice. Index. Bibliography.)

2535.   Salaman, Graeme, and Kenneth Thompson, eds., *People and Organizations.* 423 pp. London: Longman, 1973. (See D.J. Hickson, C.R. Hinings, C.A. Lee, R.E. Schneck, and J.M. Pennings, "A Strategic Contingencies Theory of Intraorganizational Power," ch. 11, which defines the confronting of uncertainty, substitutability, centrality, and control of contingencies as sources of power. Index.)

2536.   Sharp, Gene, *Social Power and Political Freedom.* 440 pp. Boston: Porter Sargent, 1980. (Collection of essays on social and political power. Author advocates "rethinking politics" in order to solve political problems of dictatorship, genocide, war, and social oppression. Nonviolent means rely on two principles: governmental power depends on the consent of the governed, and people have the right to withdraw consent and change the government. On power, see esp. ch. 2, "Social Power and Political Freedom," ch. 11, "The Societal Imperative," and ch. 12, "Popular Empowerment." On power and state control, see ch. 3, "The Lesson of Eichmann" and ch. 4, "Facing Dictatorships With Confidence." On civil disobedience, see ch. 5. On resistance and revolution, see ch. 6, "Freedom and Revolution" and ch. 7 on nonviolent strategic means for South African black resistance. See ch. 9–10 for civilian–based defense. See Appendix B for "Twenty Steps in Development and Evaluation of Nonviolent Sanctions" and Appendix D, "Nonviolent Sanctions and Ethics." Index.)

2537.   Tedeschi, James T., ed., *Social Influence Processes.* 432 pp. Chicago: Aldine–Atherton, 1972. (Theoretical and empirical articles on social influence and social power from the social-psychological viewpoint. James T. Tedeschi and Thomas V. Bonoma, "Power and Influence: An Introduction," ch. 1 reviews the field with particular reference to issues of compliance and resistance. H. Andrew Michener and Robert W. Suchner, "The Tactical Use of Social Power," ch. 6 studies the power to influence and the power to resist as a process of social exchange. Other papers by Tedeschi and colleagues study sources of influence and their relation to compliance. Index.)

2538. Wrong, Dennis H., *Power: Its Forms, Bases and Uses*. 326 pp. New York, Evanston, and San Francisco: Harper and Row, 1979. (Theoretical analysis of power. Ch. 2–5 discuss the "forms" of power, including pp. 24–25 on issue of nonviolence and force; ch. 6–8 discuss "bases" of power, and ch. 9 its uses. Index. Bibliography.)

Power and Sanctions

Sanctions and coercion may be absent from much day–to–day interactions but nevertheless be of great significance for the results of power relationships when there are disputes. Sanctions may be key in the international sphere but are not absent from domestic relations.

2539. Knorr, Klaus, *The Power of Nations: The Political Economy of International Relations*. 353 pp. New York: Basic Books, 1975. (See pp. 4–13 and ch. 5, 6 for a view of power and sanctions in context of a discussion of the "bases" of state power and its uses. Ch. 10 contains a brief discussion of "nonpower influence." Index.)

2540. Miller, Gerald R., and Herbert W. Simons, eds., *Perspectives on Communication in Social Conflict*. 257 pp. Englewood Cliffs NJ: Prentice–Hall, 1974. (See Herbert W. Simons, "The Carrot and the Stick as Handmaidens of Persuasion in Conflict Situations," pp. 172–205, and other articles on communication in real and simulated conflicts. Index. Bibliography.)

2541. Pennock, J. Roland, and John W. Chapman, eds., *Coercion*. 328 pp. NOMOS 14. Chicago and New York: Aldine/Atherton, 1972. (Papers on definition and meaning of coercion, moral aspects of coercion, the problem of avoidability of coercion, and the role of coercion in international relations. See Samuel DuBois Cook, "Coercion and Social Change," ch. 7, esp. pp. 130–43 on "creative coercion," and Donald McIntosh,

"Coercion and International Politics: A Theoretical Analysis," ch. 13, on coercion and sanctions. Index.)

2542. Pranger, Robert J., *Action, Symbolism, and Order: The Existential Dimensions of Politics in Modern Citizenship.* 225 pp. Nashville TN: Vanderbilt Univ. Press, 1968. Political–philosophical examination of "personal politics" of citizenship; see ch. 4 on action and ch. 5 on the nature and development of political symbolism. Index.)

2543. Rosenbaum, Alan S., *Coercion and Autonomy: Philosophical Foundations, Issues, and Practices.* 196 pp. New York, Westport CT, and London: Greenwood Press, 1986. (Inquiry into coercion as "relational and dynamic concept." Index. Bibliography.)

Power, Sanctions, and the State

These works are on the practices by which states insure their power, control, and survival. In authoritarian and despotic states, these methods often involve sanctions of various kinds. Critics of democratic states, however, also point to patterns that insure political support in ways that are marginal to democratic process.

2544. Amnesty International, *Report on Torture.* 285 pp. U.S. edition. New York: Farrar, Straus, and Giroux, 1975. (Report on cases, methods, and prevalence of political torture worldwide. See ch. 1 on personal aspects of torture, ch. 2 for case studies of legal response in Middle East, Greece, and Northern Ireland; and ch. 3 for country–by–country survey. Bibliography.)

2545. Arendt, Hannah, *The Origins of Totalitarianism.* 520 pp. 2nd edition. New York: Meridian Books, 1960 [orig. publ. New York: Harcourt, Brace, 1951]. (See part 3 on the nature of totalitarianism. Bibliography.)

2546. Buchheim, Hans, *Totalitarian Rule: Its Nature and Characteristics.* 112 pp. Middletown CT: Wesleyan Univ. Press, 1968. (Analysis of nature of totalitarian rule. See esp. ch. 7 on "The Limits of Totalitarian Power." Bibliography.)

2547. Buchner, Johannes, *The Agent Provocateur in the Labour Movement*. 55 pp. New York: Workers Library, [1940]. (Discusses anti–Communist and anti–labor "political provocation" by the state in the form of agents provocateurs. See pp. 21–24 for "chief forms and methods of political provocation and police espionage" and pp. 44–51 for suggestions for combating agents provocateurs.)

2548. Momboisse, Raymond M., *Riots, Revolts, and Insurrections*. Springfield IL: Charles C Thomas, 1967. (Manual for police, national guard, and other social control agencies confronting public protest and riots. See pp. 32–49 for view of crowd violence and sections 2–4 on procedures. Ch. 27 discusses police responses to demonstrations and civil disobedience, ch. 28 is on strikes and picketing, and ch. 29–35 review procedure in riots and civil insurrection. Illustrations. Index.)

2549. Poggi, Gianfranco, *The Development of the Modern State: A Sociological Introduction*. 175 pp. Stanford CA: Stanford Univ. Press, 1978. (Developmental study of state institutions from Carolingian times, see ch. 1 for model and ch. 6 for the modern form of the state. Index.)

2550. Vesey, Lawrence, ed., *Law and Resistance: American Attitudes toward Authority*. 345 pp. New York: Harper Torchbooks, 1970. (Collected documents and essays. See esp. LeRoy Jones, "What is Nonviolence?," ch. 9; "Emma Goldman and Ben Reitman in San Diego," ch. 11, on anti–radical vigilantism; Philip Grosser, "Uncle Sam's Devil's Island," ch. 13, for a memoir of a WWI draft resister; and Ammon Hennacy, "Tax Refusal and Life on the Land," ch. 14. Index.)

2551. Wolfe, Alan, *The Seamy Side of Democracy: Repression in America*. 306 pp. New York: David McKay, 1973. (Ch. 1 defines repression as the process by which power holders maintain power by "attempting to destroy or render harmless" challenges to their position. See also ch. 4 on violent repression, ch. 7 on exporting repression, and ch. 8 on repression in liberal states. Index.)

2552.   Wright, James D., *The Dissent of the Governed: Alienation and Democracy in America*. 329 pp. New York, San Francisco, and London: Academic Press, 1976. (On theories of the character of political alienation in the liberal state with empirical tests. Ch. 1, 2 discuss these theories and the concept of "mass moderation." Ch. 9, 10 assess the findings on adherence to "extremist" movements and effects on the state, esp. p. 268 on "consent, dissent, and assent." Index. Bibliography.)

Obligation, Persuasion, and Control

When thinking about nonviolent action and political obligation, the issue is why the subject agrees to be compliant. This question arises because nonviolent action often involves refusing in some way to recognize political obligations, declining to be persuaded, or challenging social control. Likewise, nonviolent action may attempt to persuade (through appeals), to assert an alternative obligation, or to engage in a form of control (through social boycotts). For students of nonviolent action, the question of the nature and limits of political and legal obligation is central because it involves the question of how active groups understand the limits of obligation and, therefore, of how they understand the point at which resistance or refusal of obligations may be justified.

2553.   Brown, J.A.C., *Techniques of Persuasion: From Propaganda to Brainwashing*. 325 pp. Baltimore: Penguin Books. (Theoretical conceptualization of various kinds of persuasion. See ch. 1 for introduction, ch. 5 on political propaganda, and ch. 11 on brainwashing. Index. Bibliography.)

2554.   Cobb, Roger W., and Charles D. Elder, *Participation in American Politics: The Dynamics of Agenda–Building*. 170 pp. Boston: Allyn and Bacon, 1972. (Examination of participation and government decision–making through analysis of "agenda–building" and symbol use. Index. Bibliography.)

2555.   Doob, Leonard W., *Propaganda: Its Psychology and Technique*. 424 pp. New York: Henry Holt, 1935. (Analysis of concept of propaganda. Ch. 17 is on war and peace propaganda. See part 5 on various "vehicles" or methods of propaganda, esp. ch. 21 for discussion of various methods used in nonviolent action, including pamphlets, leaflets, handouts, billboards, placards, sandwich–boards, sky writing, meetings and parades. Index.)

2556. Edelman, Murray, *The Symbolic Uses of Politics.* 221 pp. Reprint. Urbana and Chicago: Univ. of Illinois Press, 1985 [orig. publ. 1964]. (Political symbolism studied as a source of control and authority; see ch. 2, "Symbols and Political Acquiescence" and ch. 9, "Mass Responses to Political Symbols." Index.)

2557. Ellul, Jacques, *Propaganda: The Formation of Men's Attitudes.* Trans. Konrad Kellen and Jean Lerner. 329 pp. New York: Vintage Books, 1973. (Unorthodox theoretical model of propaganda, broadly defined as a sociological phenomenon inherent in modern, highly technological states. See ch. 1, section three on the categories of propaganda; esp. pp. 70–79 on propaganda of agitation versus propaganda of integration. Appendix 1 contains "Effectiveness of Propaganda." Index. Bibliography.)

2558. Flathman, Richard E., *Political Obligation.* 334 pp. New York: Atheneum, 1972. (Theoretical analysis of political obligation. Chapters focus on concepts relative to obligation, such as ideals, rules, "social rules," social change, political freedom and coercion, and consent. See esp. pp. 50–62 on the "contagious effects of disobedience," pp. 179–86 on use of sanctions, pp. 186–198 on coercion and political freedom, pp. 205–33 on the "antecedent assent" interpretation of obligation emphasizing consent, pp. 233–41 on consent and utility, and ch. 8 on the utility of obligation. Index. Bibliography.)

2559. Gibbs, Jack P., *Norms, Deviance, and Social Control: Conceptual Matters.* 190 pp. New York and Oxford: Elsevier, 1981. (Concept development and definition in areas related to social control. See part 2 for conceptualization of social control, esp. pp. 73–75 on means of social control, and ch. 6 on theories of social control and punishment. Index. Bibliography.)

2560. Gibbs, Jack P., ed., *Social Control: Views From the Social Sciences.* 288 pp. Beverly Hills, London, and New Delhi: Sage Publications, 1982. (See Austin T. Turk, "Social Control and Social Conflict," ch. 11. Index.)

2561. Gordon, George N., *Persuasion: The Theory and Practice of Manipulative Communication.* 558 pp. New York: Hastings House, 1971. (Reconstruction of concept of persuasion. See ch. 8 on political persuasion. Index. Bibliography.)

2562. Huxley, Aldous, *Brave New World and Brave New World Revisited.* 388 pp. London: Hogarth Press, 1984. (See "Brave New World Revisited," pp. 229–388 for essay examining genetic manipulation, "over–organization," propaganda, brainwashing, torture, biochemical persuasion, and subconscious persuasion as means of state control. Ch. 11, 12 discuss "education for freedom" to counter this trend.)

2563. Jowett, Garth S., and Victoria O'Donnell, *Propaganda and Persuasion.* 244 pp. Newbury Park CA, Beverly Hills, London, and New Delhi: Sage Publications, 1986. (Overview of the history of propaganda and a review of social scientific research on its effects and applications. Illustrations. Index. Bibliography.)

2564. Keijzer, Nico, *Military Obedience.* 312 pp. Alphen aan den Rijn, The Netherlands: Sijthoff & Noordhoff, 1978. (Study of the military duty to obey by former Dutch Naval officer. Contains extensive comparative analysis of the limits of this duty in six nations. Index. Bibliography.)

2565. Milgram, Stanley, *Obedience to Authority: An Experimental View.* 224 pp. New York, Hagerstown, San Francisco and London: Harper & Row, 1974. (Description of psychological experiments on obedience to authority as a psychological mechanism. Experiment consisted of ordering a subject to inflict increasing pain [by electric shock] on a protesting victim [actually an associate of the experimenter receiving no shock]. Milgram concludes that a person viewing himself or herself as an instrument or agent carrying out an authority's command ceases to feel personal responsibility for such actions. Index. Bibliography.)

2566. Milosz, Czeslaw, *The Captive Mind.* Trans. Jane Zielonko. 251 pp. New York: Octagon Books, 1981. (An essay by a former

Polish diplomat on Communist Party ideological control of intellectuals in Eastern Europe, esp. Poland.)

2567.   Rosenbaum, Max, ed., *Compliant Behavior: Beyond Obedience to Authority.* 254 pp. New York: Human Sciences Press, 1983. (Papers on the psychology of uncompelled compliance. See esp. Kurt W. Back, "Compliance and Conformity in an Age of Sincerity," ch. 2, including pp. 59–63 on the role of rhetoric and pp. 63–64 on persuasion, and Raymond Battegay, "Compliance? Between Freedom and Compulsion," ch. 3. Index.)

Section III
Political Violence

The relationship between political violence and nonviolent action has multiple dimensions. First, as mechanisms or techniques of action in conflicts, they may function as, and be viewed by participants as, alternative approaches. In this case, activists may seek a basis to compare the two approaches and make a judgement as to whether one is preferable. Second, like nonviolent action, violence can be approached as a strategy for influencing the outcome of a struggle. Third, violence by the state or by other actors may be one of the primary mechanisms for repressing or opposing nonviolent action. Therefore, both researchers and activists have a reason to assess violence as a behavior and determine its effects as a resource for opposition and repression. Beyond these points, the idea of violence has spawned its own literature that is concerned with its causes, moral status, prevention, and whether certain cultures can be characterized as essentially violent or violence prone. Because of this, the definition and justification of violence are themselves disputed as several entries demonstrate. The entries below are generally concerned with violence as an act or behavior in which deliberate physical harm is done to human beings, most usually as a means to some end. Violence as a characteristic of systems ("structural violence") is not of concern here.

These entries discuss the definition, nature, ethical status, and methods of violence. In addition, several works discuss the causes or "conditions" of violence, the relation of coercive violence to the power of the state, and the justification for using violence.

2568. Candland, Christopher, *The Spirit of Violence: An Interdisciplinary Bibliography of Religion and Violence*. 136 pp. Occasional Papers of the Harry Frank Guggenheim Foundation. No. 6. New York: Harry Frank Guggenheim Foundation, 1992. (Annotated bibliography of practices and beliefs relative to violence in various religious traditions. Index.)

THEORIES AND STUDIES

2569.   Arendt, Hannah, *On Violence*. 106 pp. New York: Harcourt, Brace and World, 1969. (Philosophical reflections on collective violence as deliberate, if uncertain, behavior. See ch. 1 for a review of ideas of violence, including those of Sorel, Fanon, and Sartre. Ch. 2 contains a view of the relationship between violence and power, maintaining that they are opposites because violence may destroy power. Index.)

2570.   Barton, Anthony, *Revolutionary Violence: The Theories*. 147 pp. London: Leo Cooper, 1977. (Brief reviews of leaders' and thinkers' concepts of violence in revolution; includes Lenin, Trotsky, Mao, Guevara, Torres, and Marighela. Photos. Index.)

2571.   Black–Michaud, Jacob, *Cohesive Force: Feud in the Mediterranean and the Middle East*. 270 pp. Oxford: Basil Blackwell, 1975. (Anthropological study of the nature and conditions of a type of collective violence, the blood feud. Index. Bibliography.)

2572.   Camus, Albert, *Neither Victims nor Executioners*. Trans. Dwight Macdonald. 55 pp. Philadelphia PA: New Society Publishers, 1986. (Essay written in 1946 rejecting the social reality of modern violence and urging personal responsibility in choosing alternatives to violence. See introduction by R. Scott Kennedy and Peter Klotz–Chamberlain, pp. 1–21.)

2573.   von Clausewitz, Carl, *On War*. 732 pp. Ed. and trans. Michael Howard and Peter Paret. Princeton NJ: Princeton Univ. Press, 1984 [orig. publ. 1976]. (Modern translation of Clausewitz's compendious theory of war, first published in 1832, with introductory material by the editors and Bernard Brodie and an appended commentary by Bernard Brodie. Of interest in the study of strategy in nonviolent struggle may be book 1, parts one and two, book 3 on strategy, and book 8 on plans. Indexes.)

2574.   Clutterbuck, Richard, *The Media and Political Violence*. 191 pp. London and Basingstoke: Macmillan Press, 1981. (Personal view, focusing on Britain, of the relationship between reportage and violence in the context of strikes, reportage and violence in the context of strikes, demonstrations, and terrorist actions. See case studies and comments on violence in strikes, pp. 22–26, 31–40, 42–46, and political demonstrations, ch. 5. Index. Bibliography.)

2575. Daniels, David N., M.D., Marshall F. Gilula, M.D., and Frank M. Ochberg, M.D., eds., [Stanford University School of Medicine, Department of Psychology, Committee on Violence], *Violence and the Struggle for Existence*. 451 pp. Boston: Little, Brown, 1970. (See Frederic W. Ilfeld, Jr., M.D. and Richard J. Metzner, M.D., "Alternatives to Violence: Strategies for Coping with Social Conflict," ch. 5, including pp. 150–58 on nonviolent action and Thomas E. Bittker, M.D., "The Choice of Collective Violence in Intergroup Conflict," ch. 6. Index.)

2576. Conner, Robert H., ed., *Urban Riots: Violence and Social Change*. Proceedings of the Academy of Political Science, Columbia University 29, 1. 190 pp. New York: The Academy of Political Science, Columbia University, 1968. (See St. Clair Drake, "Urban Violence and American Social Movements," for a view of the effects of violence by and against change–oriented groups; Bruce L.R. Smith, "The Politics of Protest: How Effective is Violence?" with cases of nonviolent and violent disruptive actions; and pieces by Fogelson, Gans, and Macchliarola. Bibliography.)

2577. Dick, James C., *Violence and Oppression*. 189 pp. Athens GA: Univ. of Georgia Press, 1979. (Moral–historical inquiry based on premise that "there is moral and social significance" in the choice of "violence to property" and "violence to persons" in conflict. Ch. 4 is concerned with "criteria of justification." Index. Bibliography.)

2578. Ellul, Jacques, *Violence: Reflections from a Christian Perspective*. Trans. Cecelia Gaul Kings. 179 pp. New York: Seabury Press, 1969. (Religious perspective on violence. See pp. 9–17 on nonviolence and ch. 3, 4 on issue of the necessity of violence. Index.)

2579. Fanon, Frantz, *The Wretched of the Earth*. Trans. Constance Farrington. 255 pp. New York: Grove Press, 1966. (See first section, "Concerning Violence," for rationale of anti–colonialist violence against colonialist violence; including pp. 52–53 on equation of nonviolent means with reformism.)

2580.   Feierabend, Ivo K., Rosalind L. Feierabend, and Ted Robert Gurr, eds., *Anger, Violence, and Politics: Theories and Research.* 423 pp. Englewood Cliffs NJ: Prentice–Hall, 1972. (Collection of pieces on political violence and aggression, including sections on revolution and civil violence and international studies. But see also ch. 19 on nonviolent action and Ann Ruth Willner, "Public Protest in Indonesia." Index.)

2581.   Giddens, Anthony, *The Nation–State and Violence: Volume Two of A Contemporary Critique of Historical Materialism.* 399 pp. Berkeley and Los Angeles: Univ. of California Press, 1985. (Social theory of nation–states and control of the means of violence. See esp. ch. 2, 11. Index. Bibliography.)

2582.   Gray, J. Glenn, *The Warriors: Reflections on Men in Battle.* 242 pp. New York: Harcourt, Brace, 1959. Reprint, New York: Harper & Row, 1967; 2d ed., 1970. (On the personal experience of warfare. Ch. 2 discusses its pleasures, ch. 5 studies views of the adversary, and ch. 6 looks at the issue of conscience in the conduct of war.)

2583.   Gross, Feliks, *Violence in Politics: Terror and Assassination in Eastern Europe and Russia.* 139 pp. The Hague and Paris: Mouton, 1972. (History and nature of political violence in Russia, Poland, and the Balkans, ca. 1850–1945. See ch. 1 for analysis of types of political violence and further thoughts in ch. 6. Documents.)

2584.   Grundy, Kenneth W., and Michael A. Weinstein, *The Ideologies of Violence.* 117 pp. Columbus OH: Charles E. Merrill, 1974. (Analysis of the rhetoric of justification, identifying legitimist, expansionist, pluralist, and intrinsic ideologies as main strategies in justifying violence.)

2585.   Gunn, John, *Violence in Human Society.* 200 pp. Newton Abbot, England: David & Charles, 1973. (Reviews research on violence. See ch. 4 on psychological factors and ch. 6 on "group violence." Glossary. Index.)

2586. Gurr, Ted, with Charles Ruttenberg, *The Conditions of Civil Violence: First Tests of A Causal Model*. Princeton University Center for International Studies, Woodrow Wilson School of Public and International Affairs, Research Monograph No. 28, 1967. 111 pp. (Early version of Gurr's predictive causal model of civil violence, based on a version of the frustration-aggression concept and relative deprivation. See ch. 1 for the theory, ch. 3 for measures of civil violence, and analysis in ch. 5–10.)

2587. Gurr, Ted Robert, *Why Men Rebel*. 421 pp. Princeton NJ: Princeton Univ. Press, 1970. (Classic study of the causes, legitimation, and use of opposition political violence and of the "coercive balance" between regime and opposition. The general "relative deprivation" causal model is discussed in ch. 2–5; see also pp. 210–23 on "utilitarian justifications for political violence." Appendix lists hypotheses. Index. Bibliography.)

2588. Hibbs, Douglas A., Jr., *Mass Political Violence: A Cross–National Causal Analysis*. 253 pp. New York, Sydney, London, and Toronto: John A. Wiley & Sons, 1973. (Mathematical–statistical analysis of factors causing "collective protest" and "internal war" [the former including at least one measure based on nonviolent action], comparing several "imbalance" theories with author's multiequation model. See part 2 and ch. 8. Pp. 180–187 discuss relations among collective protest, internal war, and repression. Appendixes. Index. Bibliography.)

2589. Hirsch, Herbert, and David C. Perry, eds., *Violence as Politics: A Series of Original Essays*. 262 pp. New York, Evanston IL, San Francisco, and London: Harper & Row, 1973. (Essays on various social–science approaches to collective violence, inspired largely by the events of the 1960s. In addition to papers on U.S. political violence, social–psychological views, and systems approaches, see Norman Frohlich and Joe A. Oppenheimer, "Governmental Violence and Tax Revenue," ch. 4; Harlan Hahn and Joe R. Feagin, "Perspectives on Collective

Violence: A Critical View," ch. 7; Ivo K. Feierabend and Rosalind L. Feierabend, "Violent Consequences of Violence," ch. 9; James A. Bill, "Political Violence and Political Change," ch. 10; and Sheldon G. Levy, "Improving the State of Research on Violence," ch. 11.)

2590. Hoefnagels, Marjo, ed., *Repression and Repressive Violence*. 194 pp. Amsterdam and Lisse: Swets & Zeitlinger, 1977. (Proceedings of the Third International Working Conference on Violence and Nonviolent Action in Industrialized Countries, Brussels, 1976. See Marjo Hoefnagels, "Political Violence and Peace Research," pp. 29–39; Abram de Swaan, "Terror as a Government Service," pp. 40–50; Christine Van den Wijngaert, "Repressive Violence: A Legal Perspective," pp. 51–67; Steve Wright, "An Assessment of the New Technologies of Repression," pp. 133–65; and Herbert M. Kritzer, "A Theory of Unconventional Political Action: The Dynamics of Confrontation," pp. 109–32.)

2591. Hudson, Michael C., *Conditions of Political Violence and Instability: A Preliminary Test of Three Hypotheses*. 294 pp. Beverly Hills CA: Sage Publications, 1970. (Working paper testing three hypotheses on causes of civil violence, effects of incomplete modernization, lack of well–institutionalized politics, and "violence–begets–violence." See pp. 278–282 for findings on last–mentioned factor. Bibliography.)

2592. Iglitzin, Lynne B., *Violent Conflict in American Society*. 164 pp. San Francisco, Scranton, London, and Toronto: Chandler, 1972. (Ch. 2 discusses "The Resolution of Conflict: From Nonviolence to Violence," and part 2 studies political violence in the U.S. context. See esp. ch. 6 on violence and the state. Index.)

2593. Laqueur, Walter, *Terrorism*. 277 pp. Boston–Toronto: Little, Brown, 1977. (Sociological analysis of terrorism with historical examples. See ch. 3, "The Sociology of Terrorism," esp. pp. 104–8 for varieties of terrorist tactics. Index. Bibliography.)

2594. Macfarlane, L.J., *Violence and the State*. 155 pp. London: 1974. (Essay on relation between the state and coercion. See ch. 4 for a definition distinguishing violence from force by the possession of legitimacy in the latter, ch. 5 on state uses of violence, and ch. 6 on violent opposition to the state. Index.)

2595. Mackenzie, W.J.M., *Power, Violence, Decision.* 272 pp. Harmondsworth, England: Penguin Books, 1975. (See ch. 7 on conflict and part 3, esp. ch. 12, on violence in context of impressionistic essay on politics. Index. Bibliography.)

2596. Maple, Terry, and Douglas W. Matheson, eds., *Aggression, Hostility, and Violence: Nature or Nurture?* 374 pp. New York: Holt, Rinehart and Winston, 1973. (Reprints essays including Irving L. Janis and Daniel Katz, "The Reduction of Intergroup Hostility: Research Problems and Hypotheses," ch. 13; William James, "The Moral Equivalent of War," ch. 16; and Arne Naess, "A Systematization of the Gandhian Ethics of Conflict Resolution," ch. 20. Index.)

2597. Marongu, Pietro, and Graeme Newman, *Vengeance: The Fight Against Injustice.* 176 pp. Totowa NJ: Rowman & Littlefield, 1987. (See ch. 6, 7 for psychological/anthropological points on the blood feud. Index.)

2598. Meckl, Peter H., ed., *Political Violence and Terror: Motifs and Motivations.* 380 pp. Berkeley, Los Angeles, and London: Univ. of California Press, 1986. (Introduced and summarized by papers by the editor, this volume contains essays on political violence in Italy, Northern Ireland, the Basque region of Spain, Federal Republic of Germany, Latin America, and the "Near East," most of which avoid reducing all political violence to terrorism. Index.)

2599. Nagler, Michael N., *America Without Violence: Why Violence Persists and How You Can Stop It.* 186 pp. Covelo CA: Island Press, 1982. (Informal and analytical policy study of the nature of violence and how to "stop it." See ch. 5 on "forgotten history" of nonviolent action, ch. 1, 2 on definition and uses of violence. Index. Bibliography.)

2600. Newman, Graeme, *Understanding Violence.* 310 pp. New York, Hagerstown MD, Philadelphia, San Francisco, and London:

J.B. Lippincott, 1979. (Pp. 1–4 discuss problems of definition and part 1, ch. 1 analyzes the forms of political violence, including pp. 30–32 which explain why "nonviolence" is not an option. See also part 3, ch. 8 on "mobs, riots, and gangs." Index.)

2601.   Nieburg, H.L., *Political Violence: The Behavioral Process.* 184 pp. New York: St. Martin's Press, 1969. (Extended essay on political violence as a form of action. Defines the subject to include nonviolent but "disruptive" behavior. See pp. 10–14 on definition, pp. 125–31 on efficacy, and ch. 2 for criticism of popular theories of violence. Index. Bibliography.)

2602.   Pinkney, Alphonso, *The American Way of Violence.* 235 pp. New York: Random House, 1972. (History of acts of violence in an "unusually violent society." See ch. 6 on "cultural supports for violence." Index. Bibliography.)

2603.   Rosenbaum, H. John, and Peter C. Sederberg, eds., *Vigilante Politics.* 292 pp. [Philadelphia]: Univ. of Pennsylvania Press, 1976. (Cross–cultural historical and sociological studies. See esp. ch. 1, 4, 7, 9–13. Index.)

2604.   Rule, James B., *Theories of Civil Violence.* 345 pp. Berkeley, Los Angeles, and London: Univ. of California Press, 1988. (A study of the history and systematics of social and political theories of collective violence, with emphasis upon sociologists' contributions. Each theorist or theoretical tradition is treated as generating specific empirically testable, here called "falsifiable," propositions about the conditions of civil violence. Theories and allied lines of reasoning discussed include the following: violence seen as the outcome of individual rational and utilitarian behavior from Hobbes to the present, the class– and stratification–based theories of Marx and Pareto, "collective behavior" theories of the essentially nonrational bases of violence by unorganized groups, contributions from both classical and contemporary sociological theories stressing moral integration and its vicissitudes, the role of the "polity" and power as explored by Charles Tilly, and social–psychological approaches such as relative deprivation. Ch. 8 discusses these various approaches as social theory *per se,* assessing the possibilities for effective theorizing in this area and the nature of conclusions. Index. Bibliography.)

2605. Sanders, David, *Patterns of Political Instability.* 244 pp. New York: St. Martin's Press, 1981. (Posits existence of both "peaceful challenge instability" and "violent challenge instability" [roughly, collective protest and political violence], testing hypotheses derived from, among others, Gurr, Hibbs, Huntington, and Snyder and Tilly. See ch. 1 for overview, ch. 3, 4 for definitions, and later chapters for findings. Index.)

2606. Schmid, Alex P., and Albert J. Jongman, *Political Terrorism: A New Guide to Actors, Authors, Concepts, Data Bases, Theories and Literature.* 2d ed. 700 pp. Amsterdam, Oxford, and New York: North–Holland Publishing; New Brunswick NJ: Transaction Books, 1988. (Comprehensive survey and review. See ch. 1, 2 on concepts and theories, including pp. 62–68 on relation to political violence theory. Ch. 3, 4 present data bases and literature review. Extensive bibliography, with author and title indexes, is in pp. 237–483. Also included is a world directory of "terrorist and other organizations associated with guerrilla warfare, political violence, and protest.")

2607. Short, James F., Jr., and Marvin E. Wolfgang, eds., *Violence: Theories and Interpretations.* 263 pp. *The Annals of the American Academy of Political and Social Science,* 391 (1970). (Several selections originate in U.S. riot commission research undertaken in the late 1960s. See Gary Marx, "Issueless Riots," pp. 21–33, which questions various assumptions about riots; Elliot Currie and Jerome H. Skolnick, "A Critical Note on Conceptions of Collective Behavior," pp. 34–45, a criticism of Neil Smelser's theory of collective behavior as representative of a "managerial or administrative perspective on collective action"; Neil Smelser, "Two Critics in Search of a Bias: A Response to Currie and Skolnick," pp. 46–55; and James L. Campbell, "The Usefulness of Commission Studies of Collective Violence," pp. 168–76. Index.)

2608. Skolnick, Jerome H., *The Politics of Protest: A Report Submitted by Jerome H. Skolnick, Director Task Force on Violent Aspects of*

Protest and Confrontation of the National Commission on the Causes and Prevention of Violence. 419 pp. New York: Simon and Schuster, 1969. (A study of anti–war protests during the Vietnam war, student protests in general, black militancy, white militancy, police involvement, and the judicial response to these problems. Selected bibliography.)

2609.   Stark, Rodney, *Police Riots: Collective Violence in Law Enforcement.* 250 pp. Belmont CA: Wadsworth, 1972. (Collective behavior model of conditions of relatively uncontrolled violence by police against demonstrations and other such gatherings. See ch. 1 for description of problem and ch. 5–7 on issues of ideology and control. Index.)

2610.   Stoll, Michael, *War and Domestic Political Violence: The American Capacity for Repression and Reaction.* 151 pp. Beverly Hills CA and London: Sage Publications, 1976. (Theoretical and empirical study of relationships among political stratification and structure, war, and internal violence. See esp. ch. 6, 7. Bibliography.)

2611.   von der Mehden, Fred R., *Comparative Political Violence.* 124 pp. Englewood Cliffs NJ: Prentice–Hall, 1973. (Introduction to concepts and research with brief case examples. See esp. part 2 on causes and contexts of political violence. Index. Bibliography.)

2612.   Welch, Claude E., Jr., *Anatomy of Rebellion.* 387 pp. Albany NY: State Univ. Press of New York, 1980. (Analysis of basic features of collective political violence in rural uprisings. Case studies of "rebellions" in China, independence–era India, Kenya, and Zaire. See ch. 2, 4, 6 on internal factors in group violence and ch. 5, 8 on government response and repression. Index. Bibliography.)

2613.   Wiener, Philip P., and John Fisher, eds., *Violence and Aggression in the History of Ideas.* 273 pp. New Brunswick NJ: Rutgers Univ. Press, 1974. (Includes Adam Roberts, "The Uses of Civil Resistance in International Relations," pp. 113–32; Hajime Nakamura, "Violence and Nonviolence in Buddhism," pp. 173–86; Lia Formigari, "The Right to Violence: From Locke to

Lenin," pp. 221–34; and Mihailo Markovic, "Violence and Human Self-Realization," pp. 234–52.)

2614. Wilber, Charles G., ed., *Contemporary Violence: A Multidisciplinary Examination*. 163 pp. Springfield IL: Charles C. Thomas Publishers, 1975. (See "The Laws of Violence," pp. 45–71, and comment on civil disobedience on pp. 142–193. Index.)

2615. Zimmerman, Ekkart, *Political Violence, Crises, and Revolutions: Theories and Research*. 791 pp. Boston: G.K. Hall; Cambridge MA: Schenkman, 1983. (Thorough review and bibliography of book and periodical literature on various forms of political violence [works up to 1979 cited], with some analysis of empirical and conceptual issues. Ch. 2 reviews concepts of violence and definitional issues and ch. 3 reviews theory and research on aggression. Ch. 5 organizes concepts, causal theories, and empirical research on political violence, while ch. 6 and 7 look at "crises" and the *coup d'etat*. Ch. 8 discusses theories and models of revolution. Summary comments in passing on the relevance of the study of nonviolent struggle to issues raised throughout, pp. 427–34. Index. Bibliography.)

Aggression and Violence

Two approaches to violence have enjoyed a degree of currency for some years. One is that violence is related to human aggression, which is, in turn, innate in human beings. The second is that psycho–social factors explain human violent aggression. On influential version of this idea is the frustration–aggression hypothesis, which argues that, when individuals will respond with aggression when expectations are blocked.

2616. Bandura, Albert, *Aggression: A Social Learning Analysis*. 390 pp. Englewood Cliffs NJ: Prentice–Hall, 1973. (Models interpersonal and intrasocietal aggression primarily, but see pp. 107–113 on warfare in preliterate societies, pp. 166–174 for frustration as an explainer of collective violence, and pp. 194–200 on suffering and empathy. Photos. Index. Bibliography.)

2617. Berkowitz, Leonard, ed., *Roots of Aggression: A Re–examination of the Frustration–Aggression Hypothesis*. 136 pp. New York:

Atherton Press, 1969. (Analytical essays and reports of experiments testing the validity of the frustration–aggression hypothesis thirty years after its genesis. Authors attempt to modify the thesis given that frustration does not always lead to aggression and occurrence of aggressive behavior does not necessarily presuppose the existence of frustration. See esp. James C. Davis, "Toward a Theory of Revolution," ch. 8, for application of theory to Marxist analysis of revolution. Index.)

2618. Frank, Jerome D., *Sanity and Survival in the Nuclear Age: Psychological Aspects of War and Peace.* 330 pp. New York: Random House, 1982. Orig. publ. as *Sanity and Survival,* 1967. (Psychiatrist's analysis of "psychological forces that keep leaders trapped in the nuclear arms race." Ch. 3 is on biological explanations for aggression, ch. 5 is on psychosocial determinants of aggression and violence, and ch. 6–9 discuss psychological factors leading to war. See esp. ch. 12, "Conflict Without Violence," on nonviolent action. Index.)

2619. Green, Russell, and Edward I. Donnerstein, eds., *Aggression: Theoretical and Empirical Reviews.* 2 vols. Vol. 1, 269 pp. Vol. 2, 209 pp. New York: Academic Press, 1983. (Theoretical and research–based essays on psychological and social-psychological aspects of aggression. See esp. James T. Tedeschi, "Social Influence Theory and Aggression," vol. 1, ch. 5 for a discussion of the "use of coercive power." Index.)

2620. Group for the Advancement of Psychiatry, *Psychiatric Aspects of the Prevention of Nuclear War.* Vol. 5. Report number 57. 94 pp. New York: Group for the Advancement of Psychiatry, 1964. (Psychiatrists examine psychological issues pertaining to war, violence, and aggression, emphasizing the prevention of nuclear war.)

2621. Larsen, Knud S., *Aggression: Myths and Models.* 317 pp. Chicago: Nelson–Hall, 1976. (Theory of aggression, based on fear of rejection and desire for approval, applied to interpersonal and international hostility, emphasizing the amelioration or resolution of aggression. Part 3 is on international hostility. Ch. 9–11 focus on conflict management and resolution. Index. Bibliography.)

2622. Lorenz, Konrad, *On Aggression*. Trans. Marjorie Kerr Wilson. 306 pp. New York: Harcourt, Brace & World, 1963. (Behavioral psychologist's theory of aggression as instinctual and essential for species preservation. Examines functional aspects of aggression in social organizations and the need to channel aggression rather than eliminate it, ch. 14. Bibliography.)

2623. Montagu, M.F. Ashley, ed., *Man and Aggression*. 2d ed. 178 pp. New York: Oxford Univ. Press, 1973 [orig. publ. 1968]. (Essays highly critical of works of Konrad Lorenz [entry 2622] and Robert Ardrey, who argue that human aggression is instinctual.)

2624. Scott, John P., *Aggression*. Rev. ed. 233 pp. Chicago and London: Univ. of Chicago Press, 1975 [orig. publ. 1958]. (Presents diverse theories about the causes and nature of aggression. Bibliography.)

2625. Siann, Gerda, *Accounting for Aggression: Perspectives on Aggression and Violence*. 294 pp. Boston, London, and Sydney: Allen & Unwin, 1985. (Survey of the study of aggression and violence, including biological, Darwinian, psychoanalytic, experimental psychological, social psychological, sociological, and phenomenological approaches. See ch. 1 for issues of definition. Index. Bibliography.)

2626. Storr, Anthony, *Human Aggression*. 127 pp. New York: Atheneum, 1968. (Examines aggression and hostility in the social context.)

2627. *UNESCO Yearbook on Peace and Conflict Studies: 1983*. 406 pp. Westport CT: Greenwood Press; Paris: Unesco, 1985. (See Hakan Wiberg, in collaboration with Felisa Tibbitts, "On the Relevance of Theories of Aggression for the Study of Macro Conflicts," pp. 187–216, which relates biological, psychological, and sociological theories of aggression to large scale conflicts. Index.)

Genocide and Mass Violence

Genocide and mass violence are among the most intransigent aspects of political violence, in part because of their relationship to more general processes such as war, inter–ethnic strife, and the state. Despite the catch-phrase "never again," mass killings occur with some regularity. From the viewpoint of nonviolent action, the significance of mass violence is at least threefold. First, mass violence may be directed against a resisting population as a method of repression, with results that may be assessed by the researcher. Second, nonviolent action may be attempted in order to reduce the severity of mass violence, to protect threatened populations, or to shelter or save some remnant of a population under genocidal attack. Third, nonviolent action may play some role in efforts to prevent genocide and mass violence. Works in this section include historical, sociological, and political analyses of genocide and mass violence as an extreme form of state or collective violence against a particular social group.

2628.   Arendt, Hannah, *Eichmann in Jerusalem: A Report on the Banality of Evil*. 275 pp. New York: Viking Press, 1963. (A discussion of the Final Solution with particular reference to the role of Otto Adolf Eichmann, cooperation with the extermination, and nonviolent resistance. Bibliography.)

2629.   Hilberg, Raul, *The Destruction of the European Jews*. 3 vols. Rev. ed. 1274 pp. New York: Holmes & Meier, 1985. (Comprehensive study of the genocide of European Jews, 1933–45. See esp. ch. 3, "The Structure of Destruction," for German genocidal strategy. Appendixes. Index.)

2630.   Horowitz, Irving Louis, *Genocide: State Power and Mass Murder*. 80 pp. New Brunswick NJ: Transaction Books, 1976. (Sociologist's theoretical essay on the institutionalization of genocide in the state. Index. Bibliography.)

2631.   Kuper, Leo, *Genocide: Its Political Use in the Twentieth Century*. 255 pp. New Haven and London: Yale Univ. Press, 1981. (Comparative study of domestic genocide. Ch. 3–5 are on theories of genocide, social supports, and ideological aspects, respectively. Ch. 6–9 give comparative descriptions of genocidal campaigns. See esp. ch. 10 on structural conditions which prevent domestic genocide. Appendixes. Index. Bibliography.)

2632.   ———, *The Pity of It All: Polarisation of Racial and Ethnic Relations*. 302 pp. Minneapolis: Univ. of Minnesota Press, 1977. (Study of social and political processes leading beyond ethnic polarization to genocidal actions, with cases from Algeria, Zanzibar, Rwanda, and Burundi. Index. Bibliography.)

2633.   ———, *The Prevention of Genocide*. 286 pp. New Haven and London: Yale Univ. Press, 1985. (Drawing on previous work cited above, this study focuses on domestic genocide based on internal divisions within a society. It includes discussion of different types of domestic genocide and the United Nations' failure to provide protection against such attempts, as well as proposals for short–term action to prevent genocide. For mention of nonviolent pressures, particularly by non-governmental organizations, see ch. 12. Appendixes. Index. Bibliography.)

2634.   Levin, Nora, *The Holocaust: The Destruction of European Jewry, 1933–1945*. 768 pp. Reprint, New York: Schocken Books, 1973. (Analysis of Nazi genocide of Jews. Traces how European anti-Semitism combined with certain German cultural traits paved the way for a Hitler, thus attempts to answer the question of how the "civilized" world could permit such an atrocity. See esp. ch. 18, "Resistance in the Forests" for accounts of resistance by Jews, largely sporadic and unorganized, which included forming guerrilla hideouts and joining Russian troops in fighting the Nazis. Illustrations. Photos. Appendix. Index.)

2635.   Walliman, Isidor, and Michael N. Dolsowski, eds., *Genocide and the Modern Age: Etiology and Case Studies of Mass Death*. 322 pp. New York, Westport CT, and London: Greenwood Press, 1987. (Part 1 contains interpretive articles and part 2 contains case studies and reflections on the conditions of genocide. See esp. Barbara Hauft, "The Etiology of Genocides," ch. 3. Index. Bibliography.)

Section IV
Collective Action

From the social scientist's point of view, while some nonviolent action may be individual, the majority is a form of "collective action," or coordinated social action oriented toward some good or benefit presumed to relate to a target population as a whole. The idea of collective action generally implies non–governmental activities but is not restricted to protest or resistance. Studies not cited here are concerned with collective action for charitable causes, organizational patterns in collective self–assertion, and the like. References here are more concerned with conflictual behavior, such as protest and resistance, as well as mechanisms for conducting and settling contentious collective action.

Theories and studies of collective action, collective behavior, and social movements are concerned with a great variety of activity, ranging from organizing mainstream social–voluntarism groups to revolutions. The works assembled in this section touch on several issues helpful for understanding nonviolent action. These include questions of where and how "unconventional" acts of protest and opposition arise, how they are organized, typical processes of rise and decline, and the dynamics of strategy and tactics. Users will notice that there are disputes among scholars about the best ways of looking at social movements. Roughly, these break down into the "collective behavior" viewpoint, which sees protest as a symbolic expression of underlying social strains, the "resource mobilization" viewpoint, which stresses the organizational aspects of the shift from normal to conventional politics, the "political opportunity" model, which stresses factors that make it possible for oppressed groups to rise up, and the "rational choice" model, which explores the economic rationality of protest.

2636.   Morrison, Denton E., and Kenneth E. Hornback, *Collective Behavior: A Bibliography*. 534 pp. New York and London: Garland, 1976. (This work contains a 5000 entry bibliography plus indexes of subjects, titles, and names of persons, places, incidents, and groups. Subject index headings of interest include those on the abolition movement, black civil rights movement, conflict, counter–movements, pacifism and related topics including nonviolent action, "programmatic protest," revolution and related topics, strategy, strikes and boycotts, and violence. Index.)

2637. Vance, Mary, "Political Participation: A Bibliography." 14 pp. Monticello IL: Vance Bibliographies, 1983. Vance bibliography P1152. (References on various forms of citizen involvement in political action.)

COLLECTIVE ACTION AND SOCIAL MOVEMENTS

2638. Anderson, William R., and Russell R. Dynes, *Social Movements, Violence, and Change: The May Movement in Curacao*. 175 pp. Columbus OH: Ohio State Univ. Press, 1975. (Study of extension of labor protest and strikes into the political sphere and of associated nonviolent and violent actions. See ch. 1, 4–6, esp. pp. 125–33 on conditions of violence. Index.)

2639. Barnes, Samuel H., and Max Kaase, *Political Action: Mass Participation in Five Western Democracies*. 607 pp. Beverly Hills and London: Sage Publications, 1979. (Comparative research on the social–psychology of political action and protest. Ch. 17 makes the case that protest is a lasting feature of democracies. Consult index under *politicalization: protest potential* and *political action: repressive potential* for findings. Index.)

2640. Cantor, Norman F., *The Age of Protest: Dissent and Rebellion in the Twentieth Century*. 368 pp. New York: Hawthorn Books, 1969. (An interpretation of protest as a basic characteristic of the twentieth century, based upon its subdivision into general intellectual dissent versus deliberate confrontation. Chapters chronicle fifteen protests of various sorts, including the women's suffrage campaign in Britain, the French army mutinies of 1917, the British general strike of 1926, Gandhian anti–colonialism in India, African–American movements in the U.S., early phases of Soviet dissent, and the French events of May 1968. Epilogue presents some observations on dissent and "guidelines for successful confrontation protest" and how to control it, pp. 335–36. Photos. Index.)

2641.   Dalton, Russell J., and Manfred Kuechler eds., *Challenging the Political Order: New Social and Political Movements in Western Democracies.* 329 pp. Cambridge and Oxford: Polity Press, 1990. (Collected articles examining "New Social Movements" in the West and analyzing their threat to political order as well as their originality in political context. Dieter Rucht, "The Strategies and Action Repertoires of New Movements," ch. 9 devotes some attention to "civil disobedience" and the question of strategy. Index. Bibliography.)

2642.   Evans, Robert R., ed., *Readings in Collective Behavior.* 660 pp. Chicago: Rand McNally, 1969. (Reader in the social-psychology of collective behavior. Part 4, "Protest: Collective Resentment," includes studies of Berkeley Free Speech Movement participants, ch. 23; farm protests, ch. 24, 25; and protests by relocated Japanese Americans, ch. 26; as well as several pieces on racial violence. Index.)

2643.   Evans, Sara M., and Harry C. Boyte, *Free Spaces: The Sources of Democratic Change in America.* 228 pp. New York: Harper & Row, 1986. (Analysis of concept of "free spaces," areas of freedom in which social movements exist and social change occurs. See pp. 17–25 for initial conceptualization of "free spaces." Ch. 2 is on black protest movements, ch. 3 is on women's movements, ch. 4 is on labor movements, and ch. 5 is on agrarian and populist movements. Ch. 6 contains a summary discussion of free spaces. Index.)

2644.   Fellman, Gordon, in association with Barbara Brandt, *The Deceived Majority: Politics and Protest in Middle America.* 244 pp. New Brunswick NJ: Transaction Books, 1973. (Study of community protest focusing on a Massachusetts anti–highway campaign in the 1960s. Ch. 3–6 discuss limited protest and its political functions in a working class and lower–middle–class constituency. Index.)

2645.   Garner, Roberta Ash, *Social Movements in America.* 2d ed. 233 pp. Chicago: Rand McNally College Publishing, 1977. (See section 1 for discussion of nature of social movements; significant episodes of collective action are described in ch. 3, 6, 9. Index. Bibliography.)

2646.   Genevie, Louis E., ed., *Collective Behavior and Social Movements*. 531 pp. Itasca IL: F.E. Peacock, 1978. (Among the articles reprinted here are James W. Vander Zanden, "Resistance and Social Movements," pp. 130–40; Norma Haan, "Hypothetical and Actual Moral Reasoning in a Situation of Civil Disobedience," pp. 182–93; Nan Lin, "The McIntire March: A Study of Recruitment and Commitment," pp. 238–45; and Frank E. Myers, "Civil Disobedience and Organizational Change: The British Committee of 100," pp. 275–83. Index. Bibliography.)

2647.   Gusfield, Joseph R., ed., *Protest, Reform, and Revolt: A Reader in Social Movements*. 576 pp. New York, London, Sydney, and Toronto: John Wiley & Sons, 1970. (Reprinted and new pieces on nature and dynamics of social movements. See David H. Bayley, "Public Protest and Political Process in India," pp. 298–308, on political violence in post–independence India; Norman R. Jackman, "Collective Protest in Relocation Centers," pp. 333–44, on Japanese–American opposition to WWII internment; and Mayer N. Zald and Roberta Ash, "Social Movement Organizations: Growth, Decay, and Change," pp. 516–37. Index.)

2648.   Hardin, Russell, *Collective Action*. 248 pp. Baltimore and London: Johns Hopkins Univ. Press, 1982. (Study of the rationality of "collective action for mutual gain" with analysis of the Prisoner's Dilemma and other perennial issues. Index. Bibliography.)

2649.   Heberle, Rudolf, *Social Movements: An Introduction to Political Sociology*. 478 pp. New York: Appleton–Century–Crofts, 1951. (General sociological theory of social and political movements. See ch. 16 on tactics and strategy, especially pp. 377–87 on tactics of "direct action." Index. Bibliography.)

2650.   Hechter, Michael, ed., *The Microfoundations of Macrosociology*. 289 pp. Philadelphia: Temple Univ. Press, 1983. (See Deborah Friedman, "Why Workers Strike: Individual Decisions and Structural Constraints," ch. 9 for a rational–choice approach to the decision to take part in collective action.)

2651.   Hirschman, Albert O., *Exit, Voice and Loyalty: Responses to Decline in Firms, Organizations, and States.* 162 pp. Cambridge MA and London: Harvard Univ. Press, 1970. (Economic and political analysis of options open to the dissatisfied, including withdrawal or "exiting" and voicing general protest in response to failings of organizations and states. See pp. 15–20 on "exit" and "voice" as economic and political mechanisms. See ch. 3 on voice, ch. 7 on loyalty and its relation to exit and voice, esp. p. 86 on boycott. Ch. 8 applies theory to American ideology and political practice. Index.)

2652.   ———, *Shifting Involvements: Private Interest and Public Action.* 138 pp. Princeton NJ: Princeton Univ. Press, 1982. (Describes and analyzes the perceived tendency of public attention to alternate between private and collective concerns. Ch. 5 discusses the attractions of collective endeavor and ch. 6, 7, its disappointments. Index.)

2653.   Hoffer, Eric, *The True Believer: Thoughts on the Nature of Mass Movements.* 176 pp. New York: Harper, 1951. (Inquiries into participants of "mass movements," such as Nazism. See part 3 for review of "factors promoting self–sacrifice" and "unifying agents.")

2654.   Knoke, David, and James R. Wood, *Organized for Action: Commitment in Voluntary Associations.* 263 pp. New Brunswick NJ: Rutgers Univ. Press, 1981. (Empirical study of mobilization factors in social movement organizations based on the study of "social influence associations" in Indianapolis. Index. Bibliography.)

2655.   Kornhauser, William, *The Politics of Mass Society.* 256 pp. New York: Free Press; London: Collier–Macmillan, 1959. (A study of the vulnerability of "mass societies" to social movements, especially those favoring Communism and fascism.)

2656.   Lancourt, Joan E., *Confront or Concede: The Alinsky Citizen Action Organizations.* 197 pp. Lexington MA: Lexington Books, 1979. (Analysis of Saul Alinsky's organizations and their methods based upon case studies. See ch. 3 on community organizations' choice of "contest" tactics and their effects. Index. Bibliography.)

2657. Landsberger, Henry A., ed., *Rural Protest: Peasant Movements and Social Change*. 430 pp. London: Macmillan, 1974. (Discusses peasant revolts in medieval Europe, the English peasant revolt of 1381, the 1873 Cantonalist revolution in Spain, the Pugachev revolt in Russia, and peasant political movements in eastern Europe, Poland, Asia, Africa, Bolivia, and Mexico.)

2658. Lawson, Kay and Peter H. Merkl, eds., *When Parties Fail: Emerging Alternative Organizations*. 596 pp. Princeton NJ and Surrey: Princeton Univ., Press, 1988. (Collected studies on major–party decline and the variety of organizations that crop up to fill the gap created. Examines a range of organizations characterized by the editors in ch. 1 as environmental, supplementary, communitarian, and antiauthoritarian; also contains studies on why parties persist despite alternatives. Pieces commenting on collective action include David E. Apter, "Sanrizuka: A Case of Violent Protest in a Multiparty State," ch. 8; Myron J. Aronoff, "The Failure of Israel's Labor Party and the Emergence of Gush Emunim," ch. 12; and Zvi Gittelman, "The Limits of Organization and the Enthusiasm: The Double Failure of Solidarity and the Polish United Workers Party," ch. 16. Index.)

2659. Marsh, Alan, *Protest and Political Consciousness*. 234 pp. Beverly Hills and London: Sage Publications, 1977. (Examines social psychological aspects of the use of demonstrations, strikes, and other nonviolent or violent methods to effect non-revolutionary social change. Bibliography.)

2660. McAdam, Doug, "Tactical Innovation and the Pace of Insurgency." *American Sociological Review* 48 (1983): 735–754. (Identifies process of *tactical interaction*, as exemplified in the U.S. civil rights movement, which is composed of *tactical innovation* by the social movement and countervailing *tactical adaptation* by the adversary. Relates these factors to the absence of institutionalized power of movement constituencies and to rates of movement activity and their rise and decline.)

2661.   Morris, Aldon D., and Carol McClurg Miller, eds., *Frontiers in Social Movement Theory*. 382 pp. New Haven and London: Yale Univ. Press, 1992. (Collection of essays on current issues that demonstrates little concern with "strategy and tactics" among theorists; but see Clarence Y. Lo, "Communities of Challengers in Social Movement Theory," ch. 10 and Frances Fox Piven and Richard A. Cloward, "Normalizing Collective Protest," ch. 13. Index.)

2662.   Olson, Mancur, *The Logic of Collective Action: Public Goods and the Theory of Groups*. 186 pp. Cambridge MA and London, England: Harvard Univ. Press, 1971. (Economist's analysis of collective action, arguing against the view that individuals will unite voluntarily to achieve collective interests out of self–interest. Argues that a group of a certain size must coerce individuals or offer incentives to maintain itself. Ch. 3 applies this logic to union organization. Index.)

2663.   Opp, Karl Dieter, *The Rationality of Political Protest: A Comparative Analysis of Rational Choice Theory*. 297 pp. Boulder CO, San Francisco, and London: Westview Press, 1989. (A careful explication of the logic of viewing collective protest from the viewpoint of a rational choice concept of individual action in social circumstances, with research designed to test propositions about protest and participation derived from this model. The theory is presented in ch. 2; research design and the hypothetical model in ch. 3, 4; and the relations among various factors such as social integration, relative deprivation, and demographic position are discussed in following chapters. Does not distinguish causally among constitutionally mandated, nonviolent, and violent means of political action insofar as nonviolent action is split between categories of legal and illegal protest. Appendix. Index. Bibliography.)

2664.   Piven, Frances Fox, and Richard A. Cloward, *Poor People's Movements: Why They Succeed, How They Fail*. 381 pp. New York: Pantheon Books, 1977. (Ch. 1, "The Structuring of Protest," presents a theory of how disruptive protest movements arise in the U.S. and the factors that restrict their lasting effects; see esp. pp. 23–36 on the limits and demise of protest. Case studies of the unemployed workers' movement of the 1930s, the twentieth century industrial labor movement, the Civil Rights Movement, and the welfare mothers movement of the 1960s and 1970s follow. Index.)

2665. Primack, Joel, and Frank von Hippel, *Advice and Dissent: Scientists in the Public Arena.* 299 pp. New York: Basic Books, 1974. (On specialized knowledge as a resource for policy making and the facilitation and suppression of debate over policy. Primarily concerned with institutionalized debate, but see chapters on scientists in the anti–ballistic missile protests, ch. 13, and the nuclear reactor safety question, ch. 15. Ch. 16, 17 are on "public interest science" as potential pressure from outside the system for policy change. Appendix. Index.)

2666. Pugh, Meredith David, ed., *Collective Behavior: A Source Book.* 293 pp. St. Paul, New York, Los Angeles, and San Francisco: West Publishing, 1980. (Collected sociological papers on theory and aspects of collective behavior and social movements. Section 3 contains pieces on causes of and participation in collective violence. Section 4 contains articles on social movements, including Mayer N. Zald and Roberta Ash, "Social Movement Organizations: Growth, Decay and Change," and Raymond J. Adamek and Jerry M. Lewis, "Social Control Violence and Radicalization: The Kent State Case.")

2667. Smith, Anthony D., *The Concept of Social Change: A Critique of the Functionalist Theory of Social Change.* 198 pp. London and Boston: Routledge and Kegan Paul, 1973. (Analysis of a school of sociological theory stressing evolutionary factors in social change and downplaying conflict. See ch. 5 for functionalist views of collective behavior and revolutions. Index. Bibliography.)

2668. Stewart, Charles J., Craig Allen Smith, and Robert E. Denton, Jr., *Persuasion and Social Movements.* 227 pp. Prospect Heights IL: Waveland Press, 1984. (Part 1 focuses on the role of persuasion in social movements and part 2 outlines theoretical frameworks. Ch. 9 is on protest music, ch. 10 is on protest slogans, and ch. 11 is on protest rhetoric. Index. Bibliography.)

2669.   Touraine, Alain, *The Voice and the Eye: An Analysis of Social Movements*. Trans. Alan Duff. 225 pp. Cambridge, London, New York, New Rochelle, Melbourne, and Sydney: Cambridge Univ. Press, 1981. (Model of social movements as class–based conflicts. Presents the derivation of a research methodology of "sociological intervention," or action research in which the investigator "enters into a relationship" with the movement. Bibliography.)

2670.   Useem, Michael, *Protest Movements in America*. 66 pp. Indianapolis IN: Bobbs–Merrill, 1975. (Discusses origins and mobilization of protest movements.)

2671.   Willner, Ann R., *Public Protest in Indonesia*. 14 pp. Athens OH: Ohio Univ., Center for International Studies, Southeast Asia Program, 1968. (Discussion of nonviolent "public protest" is on pp. 1–3. Three types of protest in Indonesia are described; withdrawal or noncompliance in pp. 3–4, demonstration in pp. 4–5, and extra–legal action in pp. 5–6. Characteristics of protests are discussed in pp. 6–14.)

2672.   Wright, Sam, *Crowds and Riots: A Study in Social Organization*. 206 pp. Beverly Hills and London: Sage Publications, 1978. (Study of the "tasks" and "forms" of crowd behavior, and therefore of the social organization of apparently unorganized activity, in violent and nonviolent confrontations. Appendixes. Index. Bibliography.)

2673.   Zald, Mayer N., and John D. McCarthy, eds., *The Dynamics of Social Movements: Resource Mobilization, Social Control, and Tactics*. 274 pp. Cambridge MA: Winthrop Publishers, 1979. (Theoretical essays and empirical studies based on resource mobilization theory of social movements, focusing on societal supports and constraints, tactical dilemmas, social control, media influence, and external supports. See Bruce Fireman and William A. Gamson, "Utilitarian Logic in the Resource Mobilization Perspective," for an application and critique of the concepts of Mancur Olsen; John Lofland, "White–Hot Mobilization: Strategies of a Millenarian Movement," and Jo Freeman, "Resource Mobilization and Strategy: A Model for Analyzing Social Movement Organization Actions," on social movement tactics. See also Charles Perrow, "The Sixties Observed," on U.S. movements of that decade, and David Snyder and William Kelly, "Strategies for Investigating Violence and Social Change: Illustrations from Analyses of Racial Disorders and Implications for Mobilization Research." Index. Bibliography.)

LEADERSHIP

Effective leadership has long been considered as a crucial element of nonviolent struggle, but precisely how it contributes and what leadership is have not been very well specified. The usual assumption is that leaders of nonviolent action movements must possess "charisma." Just what charisma might be is hard to state, while many leaders have appeared to possess rather little of the attractive qualities the word suggests. Several studies below are of leaders rather than leadership, but see especially 2677 for a framework within which political leadership can be understood.

2674. Bathory, Peter Dennis, ed., *Leadership in America: Consensus, Corruption and Charisma.* 200 pp. New York and London: Longman, 1978. (See esp. Reverend Willie K. Smith, "Dr. Martin Luther King, Jr.: The Politics of Sounds and Feelings," ch. 6 and Ed Schwartz, "Cesar Chavez: The Leader as Organizer," ch. 7. See also ch. 5 for a study of George Meany and the institutionalization of labor politics. Index.)

2675. Downton, James V., Jr., *Rebel Leadership: Commitment and Charisma in the Revolutionary Process.* 306 pp. New York: The Free Press; London: Collier–Macmillan Publishers, 1973. (Attempt to develop a theory of rebel leadership in context of general theories of leadership, commitment, and social change. Ch. 3, 4 discuss processes of commitment and leader–follower exchange. Ch. 6–8 present a critique of the concept of the charismatic leader. Index. Bibliography.)

2676. Jennings, Eugene E., *An Anatomy of Leadership: Princes, Heroes, and Supermen.* 256 pp. New York: Harper and Brothers, 1960. (Leadership in organizations discussed in terms of typology in the title, plus the "team man" and the "midwife," or leader in struggle, which discusses Marx, Plekhanov, and Lenin, ch. 10. Index. Bibliography.)

2677.   Paige, Glenn D., *The Scientific Study of Leadership*. 416 pp. New York: Free Press; London: Collier Macmillan, 1977. (Proposes multidimensional concept of leadership; see pp. 139–49 contrasting Gandhi and Hitler. Appendixes. Index. Bibliography.)

2678.   *Studies in Leadership: Leadership and Democratic Action*. 736 pp. New York: Russell & Russell, 1965 [orig. publ. New York: Harper & Brothers, 1950]. (Includes articles on labor leadership, leadership in politics and organizations, and leadership in change. Especially Oliver Cox, "Leadership among Negroes in the United States," pp. 228–71; Arnold W. Green and Elinor Melnick, "What Has Happened to the Feminist Movement?," pp. 277–302; and Seymour M. Lipset, "Leadership in New Social Movements," pp. 342–62. Index.)

CONFLICT RESOLUTION

Conflict resolution can be roughly classified under negotiation, mediation, third–party intervention, and conflict management as well as methods that contribute to the effective workings of those techniques, such as meeting facilitation. Generally, conflict resolution techniques avoid the elements of confrontation, sanctions, and pressure, and "direct action" that characterize nonviolent action. It is true that various pressure methods may be used within negotiation or mediation or as threats to go outside the conflict resolution context and into direct action, but as a rule these methods are oriented toward the settlement of conflict rather than its prosecution.

2679.   Kilpatrick, Anne Osborne, *Resolving Community Conflict: An Annotated Bibliography*. 80 pp. Athens GA: Institute of Community and Area Development, Univ. of Georgia, 1983. (Entries on conflict resolution methods; including litigation, mediation, negotiation, and meeting facilitation. Matrixes to guide the book's use are on pp. 5–5c. Annotated entries appear on pp. 6–39 and other entries on pp. 40–80.)

STUDIES

2680. Bacharach, Samuel B., and Edward J. Lawler, *Bargaining: Power, Tactics, and Outcomes*. 234 pp. San Francisco, Washington, and London: Jossey–Bass, 1981. (Theoretical analysis of bargaining as a power relationship; with study of bargaining power and tactics, ch. 2, 3; "punitive tactics" and deterrence, ch. 4, 5; and the development of a theory of power in bargaining, ch. 8. Index. Bibliography.)

2681. Bercovitch, Jacob, *Social Conflicts and Third Parties: Strategies of Conflict Resolution*. 163 pp. Boulder CO: Westview Press, 1984. (Analysis of third–party participation in resolution of conflicts. See esp. ch. 6 for points on the conflict resolution process and "interventions" by the third party. Index. Bibliography.)

2682. Curle, Adam, *Making Peace*. 301 pp. London: Tavistock, 1971. (Introduction and part 2 describe "peacemaking" interventions and conflict. See also ch. 18 on confrontations, esp. pp. 203–6 for discussion of nonviolent action under the rubric "revolutionary confrontation." Index. Bibliography.)

2683. Druchman, Daniel, ed., *Negotiations: Social–Psychological Perspectives*. 416 pp. Beverly Hills and London: Sage Publications, 1977. (Empirical and interpretive articles on the social–psychology of negotiation. See esp. James T. Tedeschi and Thomas V. Bonoma, "Measures of Last Resort: Coercion and Aggression in Bargaining," ch. 7. Index.)

2684. Folger, Joseph P., and Marshall Scott Poole, *Working Through Conflict: A Communication Perspective*. 208 pp. Glenview IL, Oakland NJ, Palo Alto CA, Tucker, South Africa, and London: Scott, Foresman, 1984. (Training text on the management of interpersonal and organizational conflicts. Ch. 2 discusses "escalation and avoidance cycles," ch. 4 is on power, and ch. 6 is on interventions. Index. Bibliography.)

2685. Isard, Walter, and Christine Smith, *Conflict Analysis and Practical Conflict Management Procedures: An Introduction to Peace Science*. 611 pp. Cambridge MA: Ballinger, 1982. (Extended effort to identify bases of procedures useful to third parties in resolving conflicts; ch. 3 sets the groundwork; ch. 4–8 use formal and game–theoretic methods to identify possible procedures, which are further discussed in ch. 9. Ch. 10–12 take up "qualitative" procedures, such as problem–solving workshops, and discuss them in combination with the prior points. Ch. 14, 15 then present a systems–theory based "definition of peace science.")

2686.   Juergensmeyer, Mark, *Fighting with Gandhi*. 182 pp. San Francisco: Harper & Row, 1984. (Evaluates Gandhi's methods of conflict and proposes their usefulness in various life situations. See ch. 6–8 on group conflicts and noncooperation and scenarios in section 2. Index.)

2687.   Kniveton, Bromley, *The Psychology of Bargaining*. 169 pp. Avebury, England, Brookfield VT, Hong Kong, Singapore, and Sydney: Avebury, 1989. (Review of research and applications on the set of broadly social–psychological factors that make for an effective approach to negotiation and persuasion, esp. in labor relations. In addition to chapters on the strategies, tactics, and skills of bargaining and on its setting, see ch. 10, "Putting on the Pressure," which considers concessions, punitive action, strikes, and related methods. Appendixes. Bibliography.)

2688.   Mitchell, C.R., *Peacemaking and the Consultant's Role*. 169 pp. Westmead, Hampshire: Gower; New York: Nichols, 1981. (Assumptions, approaches, and assessments of resolution through formal third–party mediation. See ch. 5 on sources of concept, including pp. 71–73 on nonviolent action. Index. Bibliography.)

2689.   Pruitt, Dean G., *Negotiation Behavior*. 263 pp. New York, London, Toronto, Sydney, and San Francisco: Academic Press, 1981. (Experimental and conceptual exploration of social–psychology of negotiating. Ch. 3, 4 discuss competition and coordination by bargainers and ch. 7 looks at third–party interventions. Index. Bibliography.)

2690.   Robbins, Stephen P., *Managing Organizational Conflict: A Nontraditional Approach*. 156 pp. Englewood Cliffs NJ: Prentice–Hall, 1974. (Advocates the view that intra–organizational conflict can be of use to goal–attainment. See sections 3, 4; esp. ch. 9 on "stimulation techniques." Index. Bibliography.)

2691. Roloff, Michael E., and Gerald R. Miller, eds., *Persuasion: New Directions in Theory and Research*. 311 pp. Beverly Hills and London: Sage Publications, 1980. (See James T. Tedeschi and Paul Rosenfeld, "Communications in Bargaining and Negotiation," ch. 8, esp. pp. 233–39 on modes of influence, including "coercion.")

2692. Rubin, Jeffrey Z., and Bert R. Brown, *The Social Psychology of Bargaining and Negotiation*. 359 pp. New York, San Francisco, and London: Academic Press, 1975. (Experimentally–based overview of bargaining processes. Ch. 3 discusses research paradigms such as the Prisoner's Dilemma and the major variables. Ch. 4–7 review components of bargaining, ch. 8 looks at the role of interdependence, and ch. 9 takes up influences strategies, esp. pp. 278–88 on promises and threats. Index. Bibliography.)

2693. Stanford, Barbara, ed., *Peacemaking: A Guide to Conflict Resolution for Individuals, Groups, and Nations*. 500 pp. Toronto, New York, London: Bantam Books, 1976. (Short selections and simple exercises on concepts and methods of recognizing and responding to conflict, force, and violence. Illustrations.)

2694. Swope, George S., *Dissent: The Dynamic of Democracy*. 247 pp. New York: AMACOM, A Division of the American Management Association, 1972. (Written for business managers faced with conflict in organizations, with suggestions for techniques of managing conflict in ch. 6–11, including ch. 9, "The Management of Violence." Index.)

2695. Wehr, Paul. *Conflict Regulation*. 245 pp. Boulder CO: Westview Press, 1979. (Ch. 2 describes the concept of conflict regulation and ch. 3–5 are on "self–limiting conflict" in three contexts— Gandhian actions, Norwegian national resistance to Nazism, and a 1978 demonstration in the U.S. at Rocky Flats arsenal. Appendixes. Index. Bibliography.)

2696. Zartman, William, and Maureen Berman, *The Practical Negotiator*. 250 pp. New Haven and London: Yale Univ. Press, 1982. (Generally oriented toward international negotiations. Ch. 2 discusses the "practical negotiator" and ch. 3–5 present a phased model of the process. Index. Bibliography.)

PEACE MOVEMENTS

The following studies are concerned with peace, anti–war, and anti–armaments campaigns, mostly in the twentieth century, and with traditions of peace action.

2697. Bernstein, Elizabeth, Robert Elias, Randall Forsberg, Mathew Goodman, Deborah Mapes, and Peter M. Steven, *Peace Resource Book: A Comprehensive Guide to Issues, Groups, and Literature, 1986*. 416 pp. Cambridge MA: Ballinger, 1986. (Resources include essay on peace issues and strategies, see esp. pp. 21–33 on peace movement strategy; directory of U.S. peace groups; and guide to "peace–related literature." Illustrations. Bibliography.)

2698. Josephson, Harold, ed., *Biographical Dictionary of Modern Peace Leaders*. 1133 pp. Westport CT and London: Greenwood Press, 1985. (Brief biographical sketches of international peace leaders, broadly defined, from 1800. See pp. xxi–xxvii for chronology of the peace movement. Brief bibliographies follow each entry. Index.)

STUDIES

2699. Giles, Kevin S., *Flight of the Dove: The Story of Jeannette Rankin*. 256 pp. Beaverton OR: Luchsa Experience, 1980. (Political biography of congressional opponent of U.S. entry into WWI and WWII. See ch. 8 on inter–war years, ch. 10 on influence of Gandhi, and ch. 11 on the 1968 Jeannette Rankin Brigade. Bibliography.)

2700. Laqueur, Walter, and Robert Hunter, eds., *European Peace Movements and the Future of the Western Alliance.* 450 pp. New Brunswick NJ and Oxford: Transaction Books in association with the Center for Strategic and International Studies, Georgetown Univ., 1985. (Articles on the development of peace movements in Europe and the U.S. and the future of NATO. See Pierre Hassner, "Pacifism and East–West Relations," ch. 6, for a discussion of the influence of pacifism on contemporary peace movements and on East–West relations. See also various chapters for articles on peace movements in specific nations, including the Nordic countries, ch. 7; the Netherlands, ch. 9; Britain, ch. 10, 12; France, ch. 11; West Germany, ch. 13–16; and the U.S., ch. 17. Index.)

2701. McGuiness, Elizabeth Anne, *People Waging Peace: Stories of Americans Striving for Peace and Justice in the World Today.* 388 pp. San Pedro CA: Alberti Press, 1988. (Journalist's biographical sketches of approx. 50 U.S. activists involved in "peace and justice" movements. Descriptions of nonviolent action throughout. Photographs. Appendix: "How to Get Involved in a Group." Index.)

2702. McNeal, Patricia F., *The American Catholic Peace Movement, 1928–1972.* 312 pp. New York: Arno Press, 1978. (History of U.S. Catholic peace activities, see ch. 3 on dissent in WWII, ch. 4 on Thomas Merton and the acceptance of nonviolent resistance, and ch. 6, 7 on movement in 1970s. Classified bibliography. Appendix I: bibliography of Catholic Association for International Peace publications. Appendix II: bibliography on Association of Catholic Conscientious Objectors.)

2703. Musto, Ronald G., *The Catholic Peace Tradition.* 365 pp. Maryknoll NY: Orbis Books, 1986. (History of peace and anti-military traditions from the early church to the twentieth century. See ch. 3 on resistance to military service in ancient Rome; ch. 12, esp. pp. 179–86 on Catholics opposed to Nazism; ch. 13 on Catholic–influenced pacifism and protest in the 1960s and 1970s, including Northern Ireland and Poland; ch. 14 on church involvement in Africa, Asia, and Latin America; and ch. 15 on Catholic pacifism and anti–war activities in the U.S. Illustrations. Photos. Index. Bibliography.)

2704. Overy, Bob, *How Effective are Peace Movements?* 78 pp. Rev. ed., Montreal: Harvest House, 1982 [orig. publ. 1981]. (Discussion of ideas and actions relevant to nonviolent action appears in pp. 7–9, 13–18, 21–22, 31–41. Bibliography.)

2705. Wank, Solomon, ed., *Doves and Diplomats: Foreign Offices and Peace Movements in the Twentieth Century.* 303 pp. Westport CT: Greenwood Press, 1978. (Essays on various peace movements in Germany, France, and Great Britain and on organizations. Essays include judgements on motives and the effects of action, especially in failure. See esp. Frank E. Myers, "The Failure of Protest Against Postwar British Defense Policy," ch. 12 on the Campaign for Nuclear Disarmament, and Milton S. Katz and Neil H. Katz, "Pragmatists and Visionaries in the Post–World War II American Peace Movement: SANE and CNVA," ch. 13 on the Committee for Non–Violent Action. Index.)

RESISTANCE AND REVOLUTION

As is true of many of the terms encountered in the study of mass contentious action, the idea of revolution has several meanings. These include mass action for radical change, change of government, and seizure of power, in addition to ideas stressing the character of the social changes that take place after seizure of power. The works compiled here offer perspectives on why and how revolutions occur, with many focusing particularly on the methods and procedures by which revolutionary changes of power are achieved.

2706. Blackey, Robert, *Modern Revolutions and Revolutionists: A Bibliography.* 257 pp. Santa Barbara CA and Oxford: Clio Books, 1976. (Section 1 compiles entries on theories of revolution and related topics, including violence, *coup d'etat*, and "nonviolence." Later sections have references to specific revolutions, revolts, and independence struggles from the sixteenth through twentieth centuries; including the Indian independence movement, pp. 220–23. Chronology, pp. ix–xii. Index.)

STUDIES

2707.   Archer, Jules, *Resistance*. 222 pp. Philadelphia: Macrae Smith, 1973. (Popular history of the concept and practice of resistance with discussion of nonviolent and violent means. See esp. ch. 1, 3, 4, 15, 18, 19. Index. Bibliography.)

2708.   Arendt, Hannah, *On Revolution*. 350 pp. Middlesex, New York, Victoria, Ontario, and Auckland: Penguin Books, 1977 [orig. publ. New York: Viking Press, 1963]. (Focuses on the role of popular direct democracy and dangers of violence and elitism in revolution. Index. Bibliography.)

2709.   Baechler, Jean, *Revolution*. Trans Joan Vickers. 208 pp. Oxford: Basil Blackwell, 1975. Orig. publ. as *Les Phénomenes Révolutionnaires*, Paris: Presses Univérsitaires de France, 1970. (Introduction to "revolutionary phenomena" conceived of as all challenges to the "social order." See ch. 3–4 on political revolutions and ch. 5, sections C–E, on the author's model. Bibliography.)

2710.   Bell, David V.J., *Resistance and Revolution*. 164 pp. Boston: Houghton Mifflin, 1973. (Analytical essay on theory and practice of resistance. Ch. 4, "a typology of resistance behavior" attempts to locate nonviolent and violent means in the conflict sphere. See also ch. 1 and pp. 34–35. Index. Bibliography.)

2711.   Bell, J. Bowyer, *On Revolt: Strategies of National Liberation*. 272 pp. Cambridge and London: Harvard Univ. Press, 1976. (Case studies and analysis of revolts against British rule. See ch. 1 on the idea of revolt and pp. 23–27 on the "Indian Example" and the "Irish Alternative." Part 2 contains studies of revolts in Palestine, Malaya, Kenya, Suez, Cyprus, and South Arabia. See also pp. 71–79 on the application of India's precedent as a "strategy of agitation" in the Gold Coast [Ghana]. Photos. Index.)

2712.   Calvert, Peter, *Revolution*. 174 pp. London: Macmillan, 1970. (A "key concepts" approach to the history of rebellion and revolution. See ch. 7, 8 for analysis. Index. Bibliography.)

2713.   ———, *A Study of Revolution*. 249 pp. Oxford: Oxford Univ. Press, 1970. (Model and quantitative study of the process, incidence, and nature of twentieth–century revolutions. Index. Bibliography.)

2714.   Chorley, Katherine, *Armies and the Art of Revolution*. 274 pp. Reprint, Boston: Beacon Press, 1973 [orig. publ. London: Farber and Farber, 1943]. (Analysis of the role of armies and officers in preventing or making revolution. See ch. 4–7 on existing armed forces and ch. 11 on forces created to "consolidate" revolutions, as well as pp. 75–86 on general strikes and pp. 132–34 contrasting the 1797 naval mutinies at Spithead and the Nore. Index.)

2715.   DeNardo, James, *Power in Numbers: The Political Strategy of Protest and Rebellion*. 267 pp. Princeton: Princeton Univ. Press, 1985. (Author presents an analytical model designed to explain strategic decisions in revolutionary movements by examining the literature of radical thought. The model is based on the concept of disruption, the means by which the dissident group exerts pressure against the governing regime. Disruption contains two dimensions, "the power of numbers" and the escalation of violence. Ch. 3 examines nonviolent strategies of disruption. Ch. 7 contains analysis of organization and strategy and ch. 9 examines the strategy of violent disruption. Index.)

2716.   Eisenstadt, S.N., *Revolution and the Transformation of Societies: A Comparative Study of Civilizations*. 348 pp. New York: Free Press; London: Collier Macmillan, 1978. (Analysis of conditions and historical contexts which lead to revolutions and revolutionary transformation. See ch. 2 on protest, rebellion, heterodoxy, and change in society; ch. 7 on conditions of modern revolution; and ch. 8 on variability of patterns and outcomes. Index.)

2717.   Ellis, John, *Armies in Revolution*. 278 pp. New York: Oxford Univ. Press, 1974. (Historical study of the organization and employment of armies in revolutionary war, based on studies of seven cases from the seventeenth to the twentieth centuries. Index. Bibliography.)

2718. Friedland, William H., with Amy Barton, Bruce Dancis, Michael Rotkin, and Michael Spiro, *Revolutionary Theory*. 248 pp. Totowa NJ: Allanheld, Osmun Publishers, 1982. (Theories of revolution as divided into four categories, including theories of "the driving force," organization, mobilization, and future arrangements. See pp. 137–39 on "nonviolence" and ch. 13, which briefly discusses labor's weapons including strikes and general strikes. Chronology. Index. Bibliography.)

2719. Gross, Feliks, *The Seizure of Political Power in a Century of Revolutions*. 398 pp. New York: Philosophical Library, 1958. (Analytical study of patterns of action and major types of revolution, concentrating on the Russian revolutionary movement. Part 1 is on revolution and types of power transfer. Ch. 8 is on the Russian Revolution of 1917. Ch. 13 includes the East German uprising in 1953 and the Hungarian uprising in 1956. Index.)

2720. Hagopian, Mark N., *The Phenomenon of Revolution*. 402 pp. New York: Dodd, Mead, 1974. ("Critical synthesis of research, concepts, and theories of revolution." See pp. 101–106 for several typologies of revolutions. Ch. 4 presents theories explaining the causes of revolution and ch. 7 discusses social movement actors, collective behavior, and psycho–social factors contributing to a "revolutionary personality." Index. Select bibliography.)

2721. Huntington, Samuel P., *Political Order in Changing Societies*. 488 pp. New Haven CT and London: Yale Univ. Press, 1968. (Analysis of the societal goal of "political order," depending on the relation between the development of political institutions and the mobilization of new political social forces. See ch. 5 on revolution. Index.)

2722. Joes, Anthony James, *From the Barrel of a Gun: Armies and Revolution*. 224 pp. Washington: Pergamon–Brassey's, 1986. (A study of why governments lose to insurrectionary forces. Parts 3 and 4 contain case studies of "professional rebels," guerrilla war, and coups. See also part 2 for case studies of Hungary in 1956 and Iran in 1978, based on observation that, in both cases, "heavily armed regimes . . . were swept away by crowds of unarmed civilians." Index. Bibliography.)

2723.   Johnson, Chalmers, *Revolutionary Change*. 2d ed. 217 pp. Stanford CA: Stanford Univ. Press, 1982. (Second edition omits the original chapter 6 and adds a new chapter on terrorism, plus new material in ch. 9. Author presents a theory of revolution in the "disequilibrated social system." See ch. 7 on strategy and ch. 8 on terrorism. Index.)

2724.   Jureidini, Paul A., Norman A. Charité, Bert H. Cooper, and William A. Lybrand, *Casebook on Insurgency and Revolutionary Warfare: 23 Summary Accounts*. 607 pp. Washington DC: The American University Special Operations Research Office, 1962. (Research report prepared for the Department of the Army. Brief studies of revolutionary conflict and coups, 1933–62, in Asia, Latin America, Africa, the Middle East, and Europe. Of interest are the discussions of the Guatemala change of government in 1944 following the civic resistance against Ubico, the 1960 student protests against the Syngman Rhee government in Korea, and the Hungarian Revolution of 1956.)

2725.   Kutner, Luis, *Due Process of Rebellion*. 169 pp. Chicago: Bardian House, 1974. (Focuses on international protection of participants in revolutions. Bibliography.)

2726.   Leiden, Carl, and Karl M. Schmitt, *The Politics of Violence: Revolution in the Modern World*. 244 pp. Englewood Cliffs NJ: Prentice–Hall, 1968. Reprint, Westport CT: Greenwood Press, 1980. (Review of the concepts and process of revolution with case studies of Mexico, Turkey, Egypt, and Cuba. Index. Bibliography.)

2727.   Leites, Nathan, and Charles Wolf, Jr., *Rebellion and Authority: An Analytic Essay on Insurgent Conflicts*. 174 pp. Chicago: Markham Publishing, 1970. (Development of a theoretical model for the analysis of insurgent conflicts. See ch. 4 for rebellion's viewpoint on organization and strategy and ch. 6 on fighting and the use of sanctions. Index.)

2728. Momboisse, Raymond M., *Blueprint of Revolution: The Party, the Techniques of Revolt.* 336 pp. Springfield IL: Charles C Thomas, 1970. (Presents a systematic "blueprint of revolution," violent and nonviolent, designed to expose such movements. Bibliography.)

2729. Rejai, Mostafa, *The Comparative Study of Revolutionary Strategy.* 194 pp. New York: David McKay, 1977. (Ch. 3 describes some elements of strategy, with case studies of Bolivia, Vietnam, and the events of 1968 in France in part 2. Analysis concludes [p. 160] that "terror and violence are . . . essential ingredients of revolutionary strategy." Index. Bibliography.)

2730. Salert, Barbara, *Revolutions and Revolutionaries.* 161 pp. New York, Oxford, and Amsterdam: Elsevier, 1976. (Four approaches to the causes of revolution. See esp. ch. 2 on revolutionary action as rational choice. Index. Bibliography.)

2731. Scott, James, "Resistance without Protest: A Peasant Opposition to the Zakat in Malaysia and the Tithe in France." 35 pp. Townsville, Australia: Asian Studies Association of Australia, James Cook Univ., 1986. (Monograph on cases of "everyday" resistance in which populations were effective, but did not plan or organize their protests. Discusses forms of resistance that largely come about as related to the self–interest of those resisting and whose action is indirect, avoiding confrontation. See pp. 419–22 on definition and perspective on resistance; comparative case studies follow.)

2732. ———, *Weapons of the Weak: Everyday Forms of Peasant Resistance.* 389 pp. New Haven and London: Yale Univ. Press, 1985. (Anthropological study of everyday forms of peasant resistance in a Malaysian village, 1978–80. See pp. xvi–xvii, 28–37 for discussion of nonviolent forms of everyday resistance. Also see index under specific movements and *action, boycotts, collective resistance, cultural resistance, demonstration and riots, desertion, evasion, foot dragging, insubordination, peasant resistance, resistance, "strike" behavior,* and *tax evasion.* Photos. Index. Bibliography.)

2733.   Taylor, Stan, *Social Science and Revolutions*. 176 pp. New York: St. Martin's Press, 1984. (Review of theories of revolution from each of the social sciences. Index. Bibliography.)

Seizure of Power

Whether or not justified by the mantle of revolution, the coup d'état *and illegal seizure of power have been a central political phenomenon for decades. Seizure of power may be justified by the demands of national security (see entries in earlier chapters on Argentina, Brazil, and Chile), the failure of an existing regime to meet the people's needs, revolutionary change, or on other grounds. From the viewpoint of the study of nonviolent action, the question to be raised may not be how it can be used to acquire power but how to defend against illegitimate attempts to seize ruling power by a militarized minority.*

2734.   Andrews, William G., and Uri Ra'anan, eds., *The Politics of the Coup d'Etat: Five Case Studies*. 153 pp. New York, Cincinnati, Toronto, London, and Melbourne: Van Nostrand Reinhold, 1969. (Case studies include Ecuador in 1963, Indonesia in 1965, Iraq in 1958 and 1963, Ghana in 1966, and Bulgaria in 1965.)

2735.   David, Steven R., *Defending Third World Regimes from Coups d'Etat*. 92 pp. Lanham MD, New York, and London: University Press of America; Cambridge MA: Center for International Affairs, Harvard Univ., 1985. (Monograph on *coups d'etat* in the Third World and U.S. response. Part 3 describes possible U.S. counter-coup policy in defense of existing regimes. Bibliography.)

2736.   Decalo, Samuel, *Coups and Army Rule in Africa: Studies in Military Style*. 284 pp. New Haven and London: Yale Univ. Press, 1976. (Study of military regimes in sub-Saharan Africa from 1963. See ch. 1, pp. 5–22 on coups. Index. Bibliography.)

2737.   Ferguson, Gregor, *Coup d'Etat: A Practical Manual*. 208 pp. Poole, England: Arms and Armour Press, 1987. (Advice to those who would conduct a coup. Index. Bibliography.)

2738.   Finer, S.E., *The Man on Horseback: The Role of the Military in Politics*. 305 pp. Harmondsworth, England: Penguin Books,

1976 [orig. publ. London: Pall Mall Press, 1962]. (Original text plus supplementary chapter. Analysis of "military interventions" into national politics based on view of military institutions. See esp. ch. 10 on "modes of intervention," detailing coups as one of several options. Index. Bibliography.)

2739.   First, Ruth, *The Barrel of a Gun: Political Power in Africa and the Coup d'Etat*. 513 pp. London: Penguin Press, 1970. (Interpretation and accounts of military interventions in post–colonial Africa. See ch. 3 for a presentation of the post–colonial state and ch. 4, 5 for studies of coups in The Sudan, Nigeria, and Ghana. Index.)

2740.   Fitch, John Samuel, *The Military Coup as a Political Process: Ecuador, 1948–1966*. 243 pp. Baltimore and London: Johns Hopkins Univ. Press, 1977. (Empirical study of coups and the military. See ch. 1, 3–6 for framework and history. Parts 3, 4 analyze officers' decision to support coups and part 5 presents a model of coups "as a political process." Index. Bibliography.)

2741.   Goodspeed, D.J., *The Conspirators: A Study of the Coup d'Etat*. 252 pp. Toronto: Macmillan of Canada; New York: Viking Press, 1962. (Presents case studies of six coups, both successful and failed, with a theory stressing strategy and procedure as the keys to success. See ch. 4 on 1920 Kapp Putsch. Bibliography. Index.)

2742.   Luttwak, Edward, *Coup d'Etat: A Practical Handbook*. Revised ed. 215 pp. London: Wildwood House; Sydney: Book Wise, 1979 [orig. publ. by the Penguin Press, 1968]. (Guidebook on the conditions, strategy, and method of seizing the state. See also Appendix A on "the economics of repression," or the relationship between national development and the costs of "the police and propaganda machine." Illustrations. Appendixes. Index.)

2743.   Malaparte, Curzio, *Coup d'Etat: The Technique of Revolution*. Trans. Sylvia Saunders. 251 pp. New York: E.P. Dutton, 1932. (Political examination of the *coup d'etat* as a technique of revolution, using case studies from the French Revolution to the 1930s, including 1917 Russia, ch. 1; 1920 Kapp Putsch, ch. 4; 1926 *coup d'etat* in Poland by Pilsudski which included a general strike, pp. 168–171; and the Italian civil war in 1920–21 which also included strike actions, ch. 7.)

2744. Nordlinger, Eric A., *Soldiers in Politics: Military Coups and Governments.* 224 pp. Englewood Cliffs NJ: Prentice–Hall, 1977. (Study of officers in "praetorian roles" as coup–makers and governors. See ch. 3 on coups, their antecedents, and the rules of "prudence." Index. Bibliography.)

2745. O'Kane, Rosemary H.T., *The Likelihood of Coups.* 162 pp. Aldershot, England, Brookfield VT, Hong Kong, Singapore, and Sydney: Avebury, 1987. (Ch. 1–3 discuss coups as a field of study, their definition, and underlying conditions. Appendixes present statistics on coups from 1950–1985. Index. Bibliography.)

2746. Rubin, Barry, *Modern Dictators: Third World Coup Makers, Strongmen, and Populist Tyrants.* 385 pp. New York: McGraw–Hill, 1987. (Study of "populist dictators" as successors to the traditional model, with studies of Latin America, Africa, and the Middle East. See esp. ch. 1 for model and ch. 10, 11 on techniques of rule. Index.)

2747. Woddis, Jack, *Armies and Politics.* 309 pp. London: Lawrence and Wishart, 1977. (Analysis and description of modern coups. Ch. 1–5 contain theoretical analysis and ch. 8, 10–14 contain case studies. Index.)

SUBJECT INDEX

AUTHOR INDEX

Hubbard, Amy 589
Hudson, Michael C. 66, 649
Huehnefeld, John 594
Hufbauer, Gary Clyde 538
Huggins, Nathan I. 129
Huie, William Bradford 226
Hunt, James D. 310, 319
Hunter, Charlayne A. 202
Hunter, Doris A. 586
Hunter, F. Robert 66
Hunter, Robert 571, 572, 676
Huntington, Samuel P. 680
Hurewitz, J.C. 60
Hurwitz, Ken 158
Hutchins, Frances G. 303
Hutchinson, Thomas 117
Huttenback, Robert A. 21
Huxley, Aldous 591, 603, 642
Huxley, Steven Duncan 393
Hyatt, John 612
Hyman, Richard 546
Hyslop, Jonathan 27
I-mu 269
Ibrahim, Saad E. 47
Iglitzin, Lynne B. 649
Iijima, Nobuko 341
Ilfeld, Frederic W., Jr. 646
Indian Council of Social Science
Research 305
Industrial Union Department,
AFL-CIO 222
Industrial Workers of the World
553
Ingham, Geoffrey K. 546
Interchurch World Movement 185
International Metalworkers
Federation 480
International Sociological
Association 627
Iremonger, Jack 257
Irias de Rivera, Maria Amalia 71
Irwin, Inez Haynes 141
Irwin, Leonard B. 124
Irwin, Lord 300
Isaacman, Allen 6
Isaacman, Barbara 6
Isaksson, Eva 91
Isard, Walter 672
Ishida, Takeshi 338
Israel, Ricardo 87
Isserman, Maurice 147
Itzin, Catherine 523
Iyer, Raghavan 310, 329, 557
Jabber, Fuad 61
Jack, Homer A. 319

Jackman, Norman R. 663
Jackson, J. Hampden 394
Jackson, Michael P. 547
Jacob, Philip E. 152
Jagerstatter, Franz 377
Jaksic, Ivan 90
James, C.L.R. 10
James, Henry, Sir 448
James, Louis 8
James, William 650
Jamieson, Stuart M. 98, 190
Janeway, Elizabeth 634
Janeway, Michael 560
Janis, Irving L. 650
Janouch, Frantisek 389
Jansen, Jon B. 410
Jardim, Jorge 45
Jeffery, Keith 429
Jeffreys-Jones, Rhodri 111
Jenkins, J. Craig 193
Jenkins, Mick 428
Jennings, Eugene E. 670
Jennings, Walter Wilson 119
Jensen, Merrill 117
Jensen, Richard J. 193
Jerman, William 70
Joaquin, Nick 357
Joes, Anthony James 681
Johari, J.C. 292
Johns, Sheridan, III 15
Johnson, A. Ross 480
Johnson, Amanda 467
Johnson, Bryan 358
Johnson, Chalmers 681
Johnson, Dick 259
Johnson, Donald 150
Johnson, John J. 70
Johnson, R.W. 28
Johnson, Walter 98
Johnston, Craig D. 548
Jonas, Susanne 93
Jones, Griff 7
Jones, LeRoy 639
Jones, Mary Harris 168
Jones, T. Anthony 479
Jones, Thomas 432
Jongman, Albert J. 652
Josephson, Harold 675
Joshi, P.S. 24
Josten, Josef 384, 389
Journalist M 384
Jowett, Garth S. 642
Joyner, Nelson T., Jr. 49
Juergensmeyer, Mark 673
Juliao, Francisco 80

712   *Author Index*

Potgieter, P.J.J.S. 16
Powderly, Terence V. 169
Powell, Adam Clayton 203
Powell, David E. 512
Powell, Ingeborg B. 216
Powelson, Jack 535
Power, Paul F. 312, 454, 559
Powers, Averill L. 606
Powers, Thomas 160
Prabhu, R.K. 332
Pradhan, Benudhar 312
Pradhan, R.G. 294
Pranger, Robert J. 638
Prasad, Bisheshwar 279
Prasad, K.M. 312
Prasad, Rajendra 291, 321
Prasadjha, Aditya 276
Pravda, Alex 473, 475
Precan, Vilem 388, 389
Preibisz, Joanna M. 471
Preis, Art 169
Prekerowa, Teresa 372
President's Commission on
Campus Unrest 248
Presidential Clemency Board 160
Presser, J., Dr. 464
Price, Jerome 251
Primack, Joel 667
Pritchard, Colin 440
Prittie, C.F. 49
Prosch, Harry 585
Proudfoot, Merrill 222
Prucha, Francis Paul 122
Pruitt, Dean G. 628, 673
Pryce-Jones, David 446
Pugh, Meredith David 667
Pullman, George H. 176
Puntila, L.A. 395
Puri, Rashmi-Sudha 313
Putter, Ruth 569
Pyarelal 301, 313, 321, 328, 333
Pyatt, Sherman E. 231
Pye, Lucian W. 273
Quandt, William B. 61
Quarles, Benjamin 132
Quick, Charles W. 213
Quin, Mike [Paul William Ryan] 197
Quinault, R. 428
Ra'anan, Uri 683
Radecki, Henry 99
Radhakrishnan, S. 313
Radine, Lawrence B. 160
Radosh, Ronald 159
Raeburn, Antonia 423

Raina, Peter 474, 482
Rainbolt, William R. 510
Raine, Philip 83
Raines, Howell 216
Rajagopalachari, C. 332
Ralph, Chris 528
Ram, Raja 297
Ramachandran, G. 313
Raman, T.A. 322
Ramana Murthi, V.V. 313
Ramsamy, Sam 532
Randle, Michael 385, 440, 596
Randolph, A. Philip 201
Random, Michel 610
Ranga Iyer, C.S. 302
Rani, Asha 313
Rao, M.B. 314
Rao, U.R. 332
Rapoport, Anatol 628
Raskin, A.H. 247
Rasmussen, Larry L. 412
Rasmussen, Thomas 43
Rass, Rebecca 510
Rather, Lorman 132
Rattan, Ram 314
Raven, Bertram 630, 633
Ravindran, T.K. 294
Rawlinson, Roger 398
Rawls, John 559, 560
Rawson, D.W. 257
Ray, Annada Sankar 314
Ray, Rajat Kanta 289
Ray, Sibnarayan 314
Rayback, Joseph G. 169
Rayman, Paula M. 577
Raynes, J.R. 430
Raz, Joseph 556
Rea, J. E. 102
Reccow, Louis 191
Red International of Labour
Unions 427
Reddaway, Peter 503, 505, 510
Redman, G.P. 437
Redmond, Gerald 532
Rees, Albert 548
Reeves, Ambrose 29
Regehr, Ernie 31
Reichhardt, Hans-Joachim 409
Reid, John Phillip 122
Rejai, Mostafa 682
Remer, C.F. 264
Remington, Robin A. 385
Renner, Hans 386
Renshaw, Patrick 184, 434
Reuther, Victor 187